TERRORISM

Documents of International and Local Control

VOLUME 84

TERRORISM

Documents of International and Local Control

VOLUME 84

U.S. PERSPECTIVES

Oceana®
NEW YORK

OXFORD
UNIVERSITY PRESS

Oxford University Press, Inc., publishes works that further Oxford University's objective of excellence in research, scholarship, and education.

Published by Oxford University Press, Inc.
198 Madison Avenue, New York, New York 10016

Cataloging-in-Publication information is available from the Library of Congress.

ISSN 1062-4007
Terrorism: Documents of International and Local Control

ISBN: 978-0-19-533875-1 (v. 84)

Note to Readers:

This publication is designed to provide accurate and authoritative information in regard to the subject matter covered. It is based upon sources believed to be accurate and reliable and is intended to be current as of the time it was written. It is sold with the understanding that the publisher is not engaged in rendering legal, accounting, or other professional services. If legal advice or other expert assistance is required, the services of a competent professional person should be sought. Also, to confirm that the information has not been affected or changed by recent developments, traditional legal research techniques should be used, including checking primary sources where appropriate.

(Based on the Declaration of Principles jointly adopted by a Committee of the American Bar Association and a Committee of Publishers and Associations.)

TABLE OF CONTENTS

VOLUME 84

DOCUMENTS

IRAQ

IRAQ

DOCUMENT NO. 1

OPERATION IRAQI FREEDOM AND THE GLOBAL WAR ON TERROR: SELECTED LEGISLATION FROM THE 110TH CONGRESS

CRS Report
RL34172

September 17, 2007

Kim Walker Klarman and Lisa Mages
Information Research Specialists
Knowledge Services Group
&
Pat Towell
Specialist in U.S. Defense Budget
Foreign Affairs, Defense, and Trade Division

Summary

Both the Iraq War and the Global War on Terror have been the subjects of considerable legislative activity since the opening days of the 110th Congress. After the Iraq Study Group released its recommendations on December 6, 2006, President Bush followed on January 10, 2007, with an announcement of a new strategy for the Iraq War. The President's plan proposed a surge of 28,500 U.S. troops to help improve security in Baghdad and counter Al Qaeda operatives in Anbar Province. After the President's announcement, a number of bills were introduced in the House and Senate that reflected congressional opposition to the "surge" of U.S. forces and that offered alternative plans for changing the U.S. forces' mission in Iraq.

This report consists of a series of tables that summarize the legislation concerning Operation Iraqi Freedom (OIF) considered to date during the 110th Congress, as well as a select group of amendments to H.R. 1585, the National Defense Authorization Act for Fiscal Year 2008 (currently awaiting Senate action), that relate to either OIF or the Global War on Terror (GWOT).

The tables categorize the bills and amendments into the following groups based on their principal goal: Changing U.S. Forces' Mission; Reducing the Number of U.S. Forces in Iraq; Restricting the Use of Funds; Conditioning U.S. Action on Iraqi Government Benchmarks; Adjusting Legislative Authorization for the Mission; Other Legislation Concerning Iraq War Policy; and Rules for the Treatment of Detainees.

CRS has included the bill number, date introduced, sponsor, short title, key provisions, and vote or status for each piece of legislation covered. Key provisions highlight factors that could have an impact on the policy of or the course of events in the Iraq War or the GWOT.

This report will be updated on a regular basis. For further information on Iraq War policy and options, see also CRS Report RL31339, *Iraq: Post-Saddam Governance and Security*, by Kenneth Katzman; and CRS Report RL33793, *Iraq: Regional Perspectives and U.S. Policy*, coordinated by Christopher Blanchard. For further information on the National Defense Authorization Act 2008, see also CRS Report RL33999, *Defense: FY2008 Authorization and Appropriations*, by Pat Towell, Stephen Daggett, and Amy Belasco.

Introduction

Both the Iraq War and the Global War on Terror have been the subjects of considerable legislative activity since the opening days of the 110th Congress. After the Iraq Study Group released its recommendations on December 6, 2006, President Bush followed on January 10, 2007, with an announcement of a new strategy for the Iraq War. The President's plan proposed a surge of 28,500 U.S. troops to help improve security in Baghdad and in Anbar Province. After the President's announcement, a number of bills were introduced in the House and Senate that reflected congressional opposition to the "surge" of U.S. forces and to an open-ended commitment of high level of U.S. forces in Iraq, and that offered alternative plans for changing the U.S. forces' mission in Iraq.

This report consists of a series of tables that summarize the legislation concerning Operation Iraqi Freedom (OIF) considered to date during the 110th Congress, as well as a select group of amendments to H.R. 1585, the National Defense Authorization Act for Fiscal Year 2008, that relate to either OIF or the Global War on Terror (GWOT).

The tables categorize the bills and amendments into the following groups based on their principal goal: Changing U.S. Forces' Mission; Reducing the Number of U.S. Forces in Iraq; Restricting the Use of Funds; Conditioning U.S. Action on Iraqi Government Benchmarks; Adjusting Legislative

Authorization for the Mission; Other Legislation Concerning Iraq War Policy; and Rules for the Treatment of Detainees.

CRS has included the bill number, date introduced, sponsor, short title, key provisions, and vote or status for each piece of legislation covered. Key provisions highlight factors that could have an impact on the policy of or the course of events in the Iraq War or the GWOT.

One bill, H.R. 1591, the first version of the FY2007 supplemental appropriations bill (which President Bush vetoed), is listed in two of the tables (**Tables 2** and **3**) because it includes some provisions that fall in each of two categories. Some provisions of the bill set readiness standards for U.S. forces deployed to Iraq, while other provisions condition U.S. assistance on the Iraqi government's achievement of certain benchmarks of security and political reconciliation.

Changes in the Mission of U.S. Forces in Iraq

Legislation included in this section covers those bills and amendments that address the overall strategy for the war in Iraq or that call for changes in that strategy. Several bills were introduced early in the 110th Congress that proposed comprehensive changes to the U.S. mission in Iraq, such as S. 433, S. 679, H.R. 1581, and S. 1545.[1] Most of this legislation, however, remained in committee and never reached the floor for vote.

As is evident below (**Table 1**), the earliest legislation voted on was in direct reaction to President Bush's new strategy, revealed on January 10, 2007, which called for an increase in the number of U.S. combat troops in Iraq. Most of this legislation reflected ideas presented in the Iraq Study Group's findings, which entailed a comprehensive U.S. diplomatic, political, and economic strategy for dealing with the situation in Iraq.

Table 1. Legislation Concerning Iraq Mission Changes

Bill, Date Introduced, and Sponsor	Short Title	Key Provisions	Status/Vote
S.Con.Res.2 Introduced: 01/17/07 Sen. Joseph R. Biden, Jr.	A concurrent resolution expressing the bipartisan resolution on Iraq	Sense of Congress that: It is not in U.S. national interest to increase U.S. military presence in Iraq Greater regional and international support would help Iraqis find a political solution	Motion to invoke cloture rejected: 0-97 02/01/07

Bill, Date Introduced, and Sponsor	Short Title	Key Provisions	Status/Vote
		U.S. forces' mission should transition to border security, counterterrorism activities, reduction of regional interference, and accelerated training of Iraqi forces U.S. should shift responsibility for internal security and halting sectarian violence to Iraqi forces U.S. should engage Middle Eastern nations to develop peace process	
H.Con.Res. 63 Introduced 02/12/07 Rep. Ike Skelton	Disapproving of the Decision of the President announced on January 10, 2007, to deploy more than 20,000 additional U.S. combat troops to Iraq	Resolved that: Congress and the American people continue to support the troops Congress disapproves of President Bush's "surge" strategy	Passed House: 246 -182 02/16/07
S. 470 Introduced: 01/31/07 Sen. Carl Levin	A bill to express the sense of Congress on Iraq	Sense of Congress that: The Senate disagrees with President Bush's plan to increase troop levels in Iraq The Senate believes U.S. should continue combating insurgency in Anbar province The Senate believes a failed state in Iraq would threaten long-term U.S. security interests Congress should not reduce or eliminate funding for U.S. forces in the field, as that would undermine their safety U.S. military, diplomatic, and economic strategy should not be open-ended but conditioned on benchmarks being met by Iraqi government Iraqi military should assume role of combating sectarian violence	Motion to invoke cloture rejected: 49-47 02/05/07

Bill, Date Introduced, and Sponsor	Short Title	Key Provisions	Status/Vote
S. 574 Introduced: 02/13/07 Sen. Harry Reid	A bill to express the sense of Congress on Iraq	Sense of Congress that: Congress and the American people continue to support the troops Congress disapproves of President Bush's decision to deploy more U.S. combat troops to Iraq	Motion to invoke cloture rejected: 56-34 02/17/07
S.J.Res.9 Introduced: 03/08/07 Sen. Harry Reid	U.S. Policy in Iraq Resolution of 2007	President shall commence redeployment of U.S. troops from Iraq not later than 120 days after enactment with the goal of redeploying all U.S. combat forces from Iraq by March 31, 2008 Exception for essential troops to protect U.S. personnel and infrastructure, train and equip Iraqi forces, and conduct targeted counterterrorism operations Calls for comprehensive diplomatic, political, and economic strategy that includes sustained engagement with Iraq's neighbors and international community Not later than 60 days after enactment, President shall submit report to Congress on progress made on transitioning mission and implementing redeployment; report shall be updated quarterly	Senate Rejected: 48-50 03/15/07
H.Amdt. 353, H.R. 2764 Introduced: 06/21/07 Rep. Christopher Shays	Department of State, Foreign Operations, and Related Programs Appropriations Act, 2008	Provide $1 million to the U.S. Institute of Peace to reestablish the Iraq Study Group	Agreed to in House: 355-69 06-21-07
S.Amdt.2063, H.R. 1585 Introduced: 07/10/07 Sen. Ken Salazar	National Defense Authorization Act for Fiscal Year 2008	Sense of Congress that: U.S. should implement recommendations of Iraq Study Group regarding diplomatic efforts to stabilize Iraq; policies to improve Iraq's security and	None to date

Bill, Date Introduced, and Sponsor	Short Title	Key Provisions	Status/Vote
		military forces, police and criminal justice systems, and oil sector; and efforts to strengthen U.S. military and budget process It shall be U.S. policy that continued political, military, and economic support for Iraq be conditional on the Iraqi government making substantial progress toward the following milestones: – Establishing fair process for considering amendments to Iraq's constitution that promote national reconciliation – Enacting legislation or mechanism to revise de-Baathification laws – Enacting legislation or binding mechanisms to ensure sharing of Iraqi oil revenues among all segments of Iraqi society – Holding free and fair provincial elections – Enacting legislation or other mechanism to ensure rights of women and minority communities Sense of Congress that: All U.S. combat brigades not necessary for force protection could be redeployed from Iraq by the first quarter of 2008 except those essential for protecting U.S. personnel and infrastructure; training, equipping, and advising Iraqi forces; conducting targeted counterterrorism operations; search and rescue; and rapid reaction and special operations Report on actions taken to implement policies due from President no later than 90 days after enactment and every 90 days thereafter	

Bill, Date Introduced, and Sponsor	Short Title	Key Provisions	Status/Vote
S.Amdt.2100, H.R. 1585 Introduced: 07/11/07 Sen. John Cornyn	National Defense Authorization Act for Fiscal Year 2008	Sense of the Senate that: Senate should commit to a strategy that will not leave a failed state in Iraq Senate should not pass legislation that will undermine the military's ability to prevent a failed state in Iraq	Senate passed: 94-3 07/17/07
S.Amdt.2145, H.R. 1585 Introduced: 07/12/07 Sen. E. Benjamin Nelson	National Defense Authorization Act for Fiscal Year 2008	Commencing on date of enactment, President shall immediately begin transition of U.S. mission in Iraq U.S. forces in Iraq shall be limited to: protecting U.S. personnel and infrastructure in Iraq, continuing training and equipping of Iraqi security forces, securing Iraq's borders, and conducting counterterrorism operations against Al Qaeda and other terrorist groups Goal of completing transition and redeployment of U.S. forces shall be March 31, 2008	None to date
S.Amdt.2193, H.R. 1585 Introduced: 07/13/07 Sen. Saxby Chambliss	National Defense Authorization Act for Fiscal Year 2008	[Same as Amendment 2063 (Salazar, above), with the following additional provision:] Except in event of unforeseen circumstances or developments, President's new strategy for Iraq, announced 1/10/07, shall not be significantly altered until General Petraeus and Ambassador Crocker report to Congress on the progress of that strategy in September 2007	None to date
S.Amdt.2208, H.R. 1585 Introduced: 07/13/07 Sen. John Warner	National Defense Authorization Act for Fiscal Year 2008	President, Secretaries of Defense and State, Joint Chiefs of Staff, and other senior military leaders shall consider all options, initiate planning, and present plan to Congress by October 16, 2007: – to transition U.S. combat forces from policing civil strife or sectarian violence in Iraq – redeploy forces	None to date

Bill, Date Introduced, and Sponsor	Short Title	Key Provisions	Status/Vote
		– refocus military operations on maintaining Iraq's territorial integrity, denying international terrorists a safe haven, conducting counterterrorism operations against Al Qaeda, protecting U.S. forces and facilities, and training and equipping Iraqi forces to take responsibility for their own security; – address findings of Independent Assessment of the Iraqi Security Forces Plans should be designed to be executable beginning not later than December 31, 2007 President should submit a revised version of P.L.107-243 (Authorization for Use of Military Force) Sense of Congress that U.S. Government should work with like-minded governments to establish a diplomatic forum related to Iraq that meets frequently and is open to all parties in the Middle East. In the context of a drawdown of American forces in Iraq, U.S. should attempt to secure contributions of resources or military personnel for international efforts to stabilize Iraq's borders	
S.Amdt.2241, H.R. 1585 Introduced: 07/16/07 Sen. Mitch McConnell	National Defense Authorization Act for Fiscal Year 2008	Sense of Senate that: Senate should commit to a strategy that will not leave a failed state in Iraq Senate should not pass legislation that will undermine military's ability to prevent a failed state in Iraq	Considered, but withdrawn: 07/17/07

Reducing the Number of U.S. Troops in Iraq and Afghanistan

The legislation that would reduce the number of U.S. troops falls into two groups. One set of proposals calls for withdrawal of U.S. troops from Iraq starting at a specific point in time, with some bills setting either a binding deadline or a nonbinding goal for completion of the drawdown. Most of these bills exclude from the withdrawal requirement any U.S. troops assigned to certain limited missions including the defense of U.S. facilities and the conduct of targeted anti-terrorist missions of limited duration.

A second set of proposals would indirectly compel a reduction in the number of U.S. troops in Iraq by prohibiting the deployment of units that did not meet certain standards of combat-readiness, by requiring that units be deployed for no longer than the maximum length of time allowed by the policy of their parent service, and by barring the return to Iraq of units previously deployed there unless they had a minimum period of time at their home station (or "dwell time") before the second Iraq deployment. The Army is unable to sustain its current level of deployments in Iraq unless units are deployed for longer periods and/or are redeployed after shorter dwell times than Army policy dictates. Moreover, the tempo at which units have to return to Iraq has inhibited most Army brigades from meeting some of the established readiness criteria.

The first version of the emergency supplemental appropriations bill, H.R. 1591, included both types of troop reduction requirements. It required a withdrawal to proceed according to one of two alternative timetables, depending on the extent to which the Iraqi government met certain benchmarks of security and political reconciliation. It also prohibited the deployment of units that did not meet readiness standards and the deployment of any unit for longer than was called for by its parent service (365 days in the case of Army units and 210 days for Marine Corps units). An amendment to H.R. 1591 introduced by Senator Cochran that would strike the language setting a timetable for redeployment was defeated in the Senate by a vote of 82-16. The bill narrowly passed both the House and the Senate in March, but was vetoed by President Bush on May 2, 2007.

Table 2. Legislation Regarding Reducing the Number of U.S. Forces in Iraq and Afghanistan

Bill, Date Introduced, and Sponsor	Short Title	Key Provisions	Status/Vote
H.R. 1591 Introduced: 03/20/07	U.S. Troop Readiness, Veterans' Care, Katrina	Requires the President to report by July 1, 2007 whether the Iraqi government is making "substantial progress" toward	Passed House: 218-212 03/23/07

Bill, Date Introduced, and Sponsor	Short Title	Key Provisions	Status/Vote
Rep. David R. Obey (see also **Table 3**)	Recovery, and Iraq Accountability Appropriations Act, 2007	meeting certain benchmarks of improvement in security and political reconciliation. If substantial progress is not reported, the withdrawal of U.S. troops from Iraq (except for specific, limited missions) must begin by July 1 with a goal of being completed within 180 days. If substantial progress is reported, the withdrawal must begin by Oct. 1, 2007. The withdrawal requirement exempts units remaining in Iraq for protection of U.S. diplomatic facilities and citizens, for customary diplomatic positions, for targeted operations of limited duration against terrorist organizations with global reach, and for training and equipping Iraqi security forces No funds may be used to deploy to Iraq a unit not rated "fully mission capable," to deploy any Army unit for more than 35 days, or to deploy a Marine Corps unit for more than 210 days The President may waive the readiness requirement and deployment time limits on grounds of national security	Adopted conference report: 218-208 4/25/07 Passed Senate: 51-47 03/29/07 Adopted conference report: 51-46 04/26/07 Veto Override Rejected: 222-203 05/02/07
S.Amdt.643, H.R. 1591 Introduced: 03/26/07 Sen. Thad Cochran	U.S. Troop Readiness, Veterans' Care, Katrina Recovery, and Iraq Accountability Appropriations Act, 2007	Strike language that would require withdrawal of U.S. forces from Iraq on a mandatory timetable	Senate rejected: 48-50 03/27/07

Bill, Date Introduced, and Sponsor	Short Title	Key Provisions	Status/Vote
S.Amdt.1098 to S.Amdt.1097, H.R. 1495 Introduced: 05/14/07 Sen. Russell D. Feingold	Water Resources Development Act of 2007	Redeploy U.S. troops from Iraq beginning no later than 120 days after enactment Exceptions include conducting targeted operations against Al Qaeda and other international terrorist organizations, providing security for U.S. personnel and infrastructure, and training and equipping Iraqi security forces	Motion on cloture rejected: 29-67 Amendment withdrawn 05/16/07
H.R. 2237 Introduced: 5/29/07 Rep. James P. McGovern	To provide for the redeployment of U.S. Armed Forces and defense contractors from Iraq	Redeployment to begin no later than 90 days after enactment and be completed within 180 days Funds may not be used to increase level of U.S. troops from that number in place as of January 1, 2007 Some exceptions for retaining limited U.S. armed forces in Iraq for diplomatic security, targeted terrorist actions, training Iraqi Security Forces, etc. All military facilities must be turned over to Iraq government	House rejected: 171-255 05/10/07
S.Amdt.2012, H.R. 1585 Introduced: 07/09/07 Sen. Jim Webb	National Defense Authorization Act for Fiscal Year 2008	Requires that period between deployments to Iraq (or "dwell time") for any active component unit must be as long as the duration of the unit's previous deployment Sense of Congress that the optimum dwell time between deployments for any active component unit is at least twice the duration of the previous deployment Requires that the dwell time between deployments to Iraq for any reserve component unit must be at least three years Sense of Congress that no reserve component unit should be mobilized for deployment to	Motion on cloture rejected: 56-41 Amendment withdrawn 07/11/07

Bill, Date Introduced, and Sponsor	Short Title	Key Provisions	Status/Vote
		Iraq for longer than one year at a time or within five years of its previous mobilization. Sets out optimal periods of deployment for U.S. military troops and reservists as well as periods between deployment.	
S.Amdt.2058, H.R. 1585 Introduced: 07/10/07 Sen. Chuck Hagel	National Defense Authorization Act for Fiscal Year 2008	Seek appointment of an international mediator in Iraq under auspices of the United Nations Security Council Begin phased redeployment no later than 120 days after enactment with goal of completion by March 31, 2008 Exceptions for a limited number of U.S. combat forces in Iraq for protecting U.S. diplomatic facilities and citizens, serving in diplomatic positions, training and equipping ISF, engaging in targeted actions against Al Qaeda and other global terrorist organizations, and protecting territorial integrity of Iraq Presidential waiver-President may submit written certification to Congress setting forth detailed justification Presidential report required updating diplomatic and political measures undertaken, including description of progress made in transitioning the mission	None to date
S.Amdt.2028, H.R. 1585 Introduced: 07/10/07 Sen. Robert C. Byrd	National Defense Authorization Act for Fiscal Year 2008	Not later than 60 days after enactment, President to submit comprehensive plan for rapid redeployment of U.S. forces from Iraq, and phased redeployment of U.S. forces from Iraq, with redeployment to be completed no later than 180 days after commencement	None to date

Bill, Date Introduced, and Sponsor	Short Title	Key Provisions	Status/Vote
H.R. 2956 Introduced: 07/10/07 Rep. Ike Skelton	Responsible Redeployment from Iraq Act	Begin reduction of U.S. forces serving in Iraq by no later than 120 days after enactment Complete reduction to a limited presence in Iraq by no later than April 1, 2008 President to submit comprehensive strategy for Iraq to Congress by January 1, 2008 and quarterly thereafter, including number of troops deployed to Iraq and the mission for which they were deployed	House passed: 223-201 07-12-07
S.Amdt.2032, H.R. 1585 Introduced: 7/10/07 Sen. Chuck Hagel	National Defense Authorization Act for Fiscal Year 2008	Army unit or individual may not be deployed for more than 12 consecutive months Marines may not be deployed for more than seven consecutive months President can waive these provisions	Senate rejected: 52-45 07/11/07
S.Amdt.2078, H.R. 1585 Introduced: 07/11/07 Sen. Lindsey Graham	National Defense Authorization Act for Fiscal Year 2008	Sense of Congress that: The goal for active components units should be a dwell time of no less than 12 months between deployments For members of the reserve components, the goal should be a dwell time of no less than five years between deployments	Senate rejected: 41-55 07/11/07
S.Amdt.2171, H.R. 1585 Introduced: 07/12/07 Sen. Russell D. Feingold	National Defense Authorization Act for Fiscal Year 2008	President shall commence redeployment of U.S. forces from Iraq no later than 120 days after enactment Funds may not be obligated or expended to continue the deployment after March 31, 2008 Exceptions for limited purposes: Conduct targeted operations against Al Qaeda and other international terrorist	None to date

Bill, Date Introduced, and Sponsor	Short Title	Key Provisions	Status/Vote
		organizations, provide security for U.S. personnel and infrastructure, and train and equip Iraqi security services	
S.Amdt.2263, H.R. 1585 (Earlier version S.Amdt.2027) Introduced: 07/16/07 Sen. Mark L. Pryor	National Defense Authorization Act for Fiscal Year 2008	Extend from 15 days to 20 days the maximum duration of post-deployment rest and recuperation leave for personnel deployed for more than one year	None to date
S.Amdt.2275, H.R. 1585 (similar versions of this amendment submitted by Sen. Levin include 2087 and 2274) Introduced S.Amdt.2274 and S.Amdt.2275: 07/17/07 Introduced S.Amdt.2087: 07/11/07 Sen. Carl Levin	National Defense Authorization Act for Fiscal Year 2008	Commence reduction of forces no later than 120 days after enactment Limited U.S. forces may remain in Iraq to protect U.S. personnel and infrastructure, train Iraqi Security Forces, and engage in targeted counter-terrorism activities against Al Qaeda and other international terrorist organizations Complete transition of U.S. forces to a limited presence by April 30, 2008 Reduction implemented as part of a comprehensive diplomatic, political, and economic strategy including sustained engagement with Iraq's neighbors and international community Appoint an international mediator to Iraq under auspices of the United Nations Security Council	None to date on S.Amdt. 2274 and 2275 Motion on cloture rejected for S.Amdt.2087: 52-47 07/18/07
H.R. 3159 Introduced: 07/24/07 Rep. Ellen Tauscher	Ensuring Military Readiness Through Stability and Predictability Deployment Policy Act of 2007	Prohibits any unit of the regular Armed Forces from being deployed unless the period between the most recent previous deployment and a subsequent deployment is equal to or longer than the period of the most recent previous deployment	Passed House: 229/194, 3 Present 08/02/07

Bill, Date Introduced, and Sponsor	Short Title	Key Provisions	Status/Vote
		Prohibits any unit of the reserves from being deployed unless the period between the most recent previous deployment and a subsequent deployment is at least three times longer than the period of the most recent previous deployment Provides for exceptions and presidential waivers for these deployment requirements	

Iraq War Funding

The legislation in **Table 3** concerns the use of congressionally authorized and appropriated funds for the war in Iraq. The bills range from prohibiting funding for extended deployments to restricting funds being used for operations in Iran.

Table 3. Legislation Concerning Funding of Iraq War

Bill, Date Introduced, and Sponsor	Short Title	Key Provisions	Status/Vote
S.Con.Res.20 Introduced: 03/15/07 Sen. Judd Gregg	Expressing the sense of Congress that no funds should be cut off or reduced for American troops in the field which would result in undermining their safety or their ability to complete their assigned mission	Sense of Congress that Congress should not take any action that would endanger American troops in the field, including eliminating or reducing funding	Passed Senate: 82-16 03/15/07
H.R. 1591 Introduced: 03/20/07 Rep. David R. Obey (see also **Table 2**)	U.S. Troop Readiness, Veterans' Care, Katrina Recovery, and Iraq Accountability Appropriations Act, 2007	Prohibits use of funds for deploying military units if they are not certified as fully mission capable Prohibits funds from being used for deployment after 210 days	Passed House: 218-212 03/23/07 Adopted conference report: 218-208 4/25/07 Passed Senate: 51-47 03/29/07

Bill, Date Introduced, and Sponsor	Short Title	Key Provisions	Status/Vote
		Makes funds available for immediate redeployment Allows presidential waiver for national security purposes Prohibits redeployment of Army units that have served within the past 365 days and Marines who have served within the past 210 days Specific benchmarks for Iraqi government that must be certified by President Bush	Adopted conference report: 51-46 04/26/07 Veto Override Rejected: 222-203 05/02/07
H.Amdt. 186, H.R. 1585 Introduced: 05/16/07 Rep. Robert E. Andrews	National Defense Authorization Act for Fiscal Year 2008	Prohibits the use of funds authorized for military operations in Iraq and Afghanistan from being used for operations in Iran	House rejected: 202-216 05/16/07
H.R. 3222 Introduced: 07/30/07 Rep. John Murtha	Department of Defense Appropriations Act, 2008	Funds appropriated by the act shall not be used to establish any military installation or base for the purpose of providing for the permanent stationing of United States Armed Forces in Iraq or to exercise U.S. control over Iraqi oil resources After FY2008, any request for funds for an ongoing military operation overseas, including operations in Afghanistan and Iraq, shall be included in the annual budget of the President	Passed House: 395-13 08/05/07

Establishing Benchmarks for the Iraqi Government

Legislation that specifically addressed the issue of the Iraqi government meeting benchmarks of improved security and political reconciliation is listed below. Several other pieces of legislation covered in the sections above entitled "Mission in Iraq" and "Redeployment" also had benchmarks as part of their criteria. The pieces below differ in that benchmarks are the centerpiece of these particular bills.

For additional information about the benchmarks, see CRS Report RS21968, *Iraq: Government Formation and Benchmarks*, by Kenneth Katzman.

Table 4. Legislation Concerning Establishing Benchmarks for the Iraqi Government

Bill, Date Introduced, and Sponsor	Short Title	Key Provisions	Status/Vote
H.R. 2206 Introduced: 05/08/07 Rep. David R. Obey	U.S. Troop Readiness, Veterans' Care, Katrina Recovery, and Iraq Accountability Appropriations Act of 2007	$52.8 billion for U.S. military operations is available only after the President reports, by July 13, 2007, whether Iraqi government is achieving progress toward 16 benchmarks of security and political reconciliation, and after Congress approves and the President signs a joint resolution releasing the funds No unit may be deployed not fully mission capable (President may waive this limit) No Army unit may be deployed for longer than 365 days or redeployed within 365 days of a previous deployment; nor may a Marine Corps unit be deployed for longer than 270 days or redeployed within 270 days of a previous deployment (President may waive these limits) Sense of Congress that, as Iraqi security forces achieve proficiency in independent combat operations, U.S. forces should be withdrawn. Requires monthly reports by President on capability of Iraqi security forces.	Passed House: 221-205 05/10/07

Bill, Date Introduced, and Sponsor	Short Title	Key Provisions	Status/Vote
		Requires independent, private sector assessment of Iraqi security forces No funds may be used for permanent stationing of U.S. forces in Iraq or to exercise control over Iraq's oil resources No funds may be used in contravention of U.S. laws implementing the United Nations Torture Convention	
S.Amdt.1134, H.R. 1495 Introduced: 05/15/07 Sen. John Warner	Water Resources Development Act of 2007	Requires President to withhold funding if Iraqi government fails to meet 18 benchmarks President must submit reports assessing status of each benchmark; if unsatisfactory progress has been made, then President will outline revision of strategy	Motion to invoke cloture rejected: 52-44 05/16/07

Authorization of Use of Military Forces

The Authorization for the Use of Military Force Against Iraq Resolution of 2002 (P.L. 107-243) was passed by Congress and signed by the President on October 16, 2002. The legislation requires the President to submit mandatory reports to Congress, but does not include a time limit on deployment of U.S. troops or criteria for deciding when to withdraw them. It appears that the legislation authorizes the President to use force as long as Iraq remains a threat to the United States and the U.S. presence does not conflict with relevant U.N. resolutions. The legislation discussed below would repeal the original authorization or require new authorization to maintain U.S. forces in Iraq. (For further background information, please see CRS Report RL33837, *Congressional Authority to Limit U.S. Military Operations in Iraq*, by Jennifer K. Elsea, Michael John Garcia, and Thomas J. Nicola.)

Table 5. Legislation Regarding Authorization of Use of Military Forces

Bill, Date Introduced, and Sponsor	Short Title	Specific Provisions	Vote
S.Amdt.2003, H.R. 1585 Introduced: 07/09/07 Sen. Robert C. Byrd	National Defense Authorization Act for Fiscal Year 2008	Prohibits interpretation of Act as authorizing the President to maintain U.S. forces in Iraq	None to date
S.Amdt.2146, H.R. 1585 Introduced: 07/12/07 Sen. Robert C. Byrd	National Defense Authorization Act for Fiscal Year 2008	Amends Authorization for Use of Military Force Against Iraq Resolution of 2002 by inserting expiration date of October 11, 2007 To conduct further military operations in Iraq that do not relate to withdrawal of U.S. forces from Iraq, President shall be required to request new authorization from Congress and to articulate in detail the mission, strategy, and goals of continued U.S. military presence in Iraq Any funds made available for the Department of Defense are immediately available for the planning and execution of the redeployment of U.S. Armed Forces from Iraq	None to date
S.Amdt.2351, H.R. 2669 Introduced: 07/19/07 Sen. Mitch McConnell	College Cost Reduction Act of 2007	Expressing the sense of the Senate that detainees housed at Guantanamo Bay, Cuba, including senior members of Al Qaeda, should not be released into American society, nor should they be transferred stateside into facilities in American communities and neighborhoods	Agreed to in Senate: 94-3 07/19/07

Other Legislation Concerning Iraq War Policy

This group of legislation covers a broad range of topics ranging from the medical care and equipping of U.S. troops, to relocation of endangered Iraqi citizens, to control of Iraqi oil resources and establishment of permanent U.S. bases in Iraq.

Table 6. Other Legislation Concerning Iraq War Policy

Bill, Date Introduced, and Sponsor	Short Title	Key Provisions	Status/Vote
S.Res.107 Introduced: 03/15/07 Sen. Patty Murray	Expressing the sense of the Senate that no action should be taken to undermine the safety of the Armed Forces of the United States or impact their ability to complete their assigned or future missions	Sense of Senate that: Necessary funding will be supplied for training, equipping, and supporting U.S. troops in the field President and Congress should ensure adequate medical care for troops returning from Iraq President and Congress should ensure that U.S. troops have what they need to perform successfully in Iraq and that U.S. strategy is adjusted as necessary to ensure success in Iraq	Senate passed: 96-2 03/15/07
H.Amdt. 196, H.R. 1585 Introduced: 05/16/07 Rep. Steve King	National Defense Authorization Act for Fiscal Year 2008	The provision of the bill prohibiting establishment of permanent military bases in Iraq is not to be construed to prevent the United States from entering into a basing rights agreement with Iraq for the establishment of temporary bases	Rejected in House: 201-219 05/17/07
H.Amdt. 352, H.R. 2764 Introduced: 06/21/07 Rep. Frank R. Wolf	Department of State, Foreign Operations, and Related Programs Appropriations Act, 2008	Amendment increases funding for assistance programs for Iraq by $158 million	Rejected in House: 205-219 06/21/07
S.Amdt.2097, H.R. 1585 Introduced: 07/11//07 Sen. Sherrod Brown	National Defense Authorization Act for FY 2008	Secretary of Defense shall submit to Congress a report on the cost of reestablishing the readiness status of the Armed Forces to its status before the Iraq war in 2003	None to date

Bill, Date Introduced, and Sponsor	Short Title	Key Provisions	Status/Vote
		Report shall be submitted no later than the date the President's budget is submitted to Congress for FY2009	
S.Amdt.2228, H.R. 1585 Introduced: 07/16/07 Sen. Sam Brownback	National Defense Authorization Act for Fiscal Year 2008	Authorizes the use of funds from the Commanders' Emergency Response Program to facilitate relocation of Iraqi individuals and families who are targets of violence because they are of a sect that is a minority in the region where they currently reside	None to date
S.Amdt.2242, H.R. 1585 Introduced: 07/16/07 Sen. Joseph R. Biden, Jr.	National Defense Authorization Act for Fiscal Year 2008	Sense of the Senate that: President should communicate to the Iraqi people that U.S. does not seek control of Iraq's oil resources or seek permanent U.S. military bases in Iraq Secretary of Defense shall submit report to Congress within 90 days of enactment and semi-annually thereafter until 01/01/09, on status of U.S. military installations in Iraq	None to date
S.Amdt.2311, H.R. 1585 Introduced: 07/17/07 Sen. Mary L. Landrieu	National Defense Authorization Act for Fiscal Year 2008	[Primary emphasis of bill is on strengthening troops and capabilities in Afghanistan, but calls for use of U.S. forces redeploying from Iraq] As United States begins draw down of forces in Iraq, forces should be repositioned to Afghanistan	None to date

Bill, Date Introduced, and Sponsor	Short Title	Key Provisions	Status/Vote
		Each unit of Armed Forces deployed in Operation Iraqi Freedom or Operation Enduring Freedom should be fully combat ready under established criteria before being deployed	

Global War on Terror (GWOT)

The legislation in **Table 7** directly addresses the treatment of detainees and their rights under the Geneva Convention, as well as the U.S. Constitution. One amendment also proposes closing the Department of Defense's detention center at Guantanamo Bay, Cuba.

Table 7. Legislation Concerning the Global War on Terror

Bill, Date Introduced, and Sponsor	Short Title	Key Provisions	Status/Vote
S.Amdt. 2022, H.R. 1585 Introduced: 07/09/07 Sen. Arlen Specter	To restore habeas corpus for those detained by the United States	Restores the right of habeas corpus for detainees	None to date
S.Amdt. 2064, H.R. 1585 Introduced: 7/10/07 Sen. Lindsey Graham	To strike section 1023, relating to the granting of civil rights to terror suspects	Strike section 1023 of the bill, which would establish additional procedural safeguards for detainees tried by military tribunals	None to date
S.Amdt. 2083, H.R. 1585 Introduced: 07/11/07 Sen. Christopher J. Dodd	Restoring the Constitution Act of 2007	Would establish additional procedural safeguards for detainees and would provide that the Geneva Conventions will prevail over any sections of Act that might not be consistent with obligations of United States under the Geneva Convention	None to date

Bill, Date Introduced, and Sponsor	Short Title	Key Provisions	Status/Vote
S.Amdt.2125, H.R. 1585 Introduced: 07/11/07 Sen. Dianne Feinstein	To require the President to close the Department of Defense detention facility at Guantanamo Bay, Cuba	Requires closing of Department of Defense detention facility at Guantanamo Bay, Cuba, not later than one year after date of enactment No detainee may be transferred to a facility located outside the continental United States President to submit report to Congress no later than 90 days after enactment describing plans to close facility and legal justification for continuing to detain any individual under such plan	None to date
S.Amdt.2239, H.R. 1585 Introduced 07/16/07 Sen. Arlen Specter	To prohibit the expulsion, return, or extradition of persons by the United States to countries engaging in torture	No person in the custody or control of any U.S. department, agency, officer or employee, or contractor thereof, shall be expelled, returned, or extradited to another country unless such person is being legally extradited and has recourse to a U.S. court to challenge such extradition or removal. Person has recourse to an appropriate U.S. district court in case of transfer from U.S. territory Transfer from one foreign country to another must have prior approval of the Foreign Surveillance Court If the legal basis for detaining person to be transferred no longer applies, person shall be released unless the attorney for the appropriate government agency first obtains a warrant from a U.S. district court authorizing continued detention Secretary of State shall submit to Congress on an annual basis a report listing each country where torture is known to be used	None to date

Bill, Date Introduced, and Sponsor	Short Title	Key Provisions	Status/Vote
S.Amdt.2296, H.R. 1585 Introduced: 07/17/07 Sen. Christopher S. Bond	To require that a detainee is provided an unclassified summary of the classified evidence	To require that a detainee is provided an unclassified summary of the classified evidence admitted in a tribunal against the detainee	None to date
S.Amdt.2297, H.R. 1585 Introduced: 07/17/07 Sen. Christopher S. Bond	To require that detainees are afforded a reasonable opportunity to obtain witnesses and other evidence	To require that detainees are afforded a reasonable opportunity to obtain witnesses and other evidence in a manner that is consistent with the procedures to obtain witnesses and other evidence under section 949j of title 10, United States Code	None to date
S.Amdt.2351, H.R. 2669 Introduced: 07/19/07 Sen. Mitch McConnell	College Cost Reduction Act of 2007	Expressing the sense of the Senate that detainees housed at Guantanamo Bay, Cuba, including senior members of Al Qaeda, should not be released into American society, nor should they be transferred stateside into facilities in American communities and neighborhoods	Agreed to in Senate: 94-3 07/19/07

Endnotes

[1] The full text of these bills is available online via the Legislative Information System (LIS) at [http://www.congress.gov/].

DOCUMENT NO. 2

THE EXECUTIVE BRANCH'S IRAQ BENCHMARK ASSESSMENT REPORT

Executive Branch Report

September 14, 2007

The Executive Branch

This report is submitted consistent with Section 1314 of the U.S. Troop Readiness, Veterans' Care, Katrina Recovery, and Iraq Accountability Appropriations Act, 2007 (Public Law 110-28) (the "Act"). It includes an assessment of how the sovereign Government of Iraq is performing in its efforts to achieve a series of specific benchmarks contained in the Act, as well as any adjustments to strategy that may be warranted in light of that performance. This is the second of two reports to be submitted consistent with the Act and has been prepared in consultation with the Secretaries of State and Defense; Commander, Multi-National Force-Iraq; the United States Ambassador to Iraq; and the Commander, United States Central Command, consistent with Section 1314(b)(2)(B) of the Act. This assessment complements other reports and information about Iraq provided to the Congress and is not intended as a single source of all information about the combined efforts or the future strategy of the United States, its Coalition Partners, or Iraq.

Introduction

Section 1314 of the Act states that the President is to submit to Congress two reports assessing the status of each of the 18 benchmarks contained in the Act and declaring whether, in the President's judgment, satisfactory progress is being achieved with respect to those 18 benchmarks. These benchmarks relate to Government of Iraq actions believed to be important to advance reconciliation within Iraqi society, to improve the security of the Iraqi population, to provide essential services to the population, and to promote its economic well-being. Iraqi Government efforts to achieve these benchmarks complement other U.S. and Iraqi collaborative actions as part of the New Way Forward.

Current U.S. Strategy: New Way Forward

Current U.S. strategy—the New Way Forward—recognizes that the fulfillment of commitments by both the U.S. and Iraqi Governments will be necessary to achieving our common goal: a democratic Iraq that can govern, defend, and sustain itself and be an ally in the War on Terror. The building of a strong strategic partnership with the Iraqi Government will be an important part of the effort to achieve this end state, which remains a long-term goal, and requires the application of all elements of national power, including especially diplomatic, economic, political, and military power.

Our overarching strategy continues to emphasize a transition of responsibility to the Iraqi Government and its security forces. The New Way Forward recognized that, in response to the upsurge in sectarian violence in 2006, it was necessary for Coalition Forces to temporarily play a greater role, in conjunction with the Iraqi Security Forces, in securing the Iraqi population. This is not meant to replace Iraqi efforts to provide security but to help provide the necessary time and space with which the Iraqi Government can continue to build its own capacity; can intensify efforts against the accelerants of the violence, especially al-Qaida in Iraq (AQI) and some segments of the Jaysh al-Mahdi (JAM); and can meaningfully address the all-important issue of reconciliation among the various segments of Iraqi society. The strategy recognizes that the levels of violence seen in 2006 undermined efforts to achieve political reconciliation by fueling sectarian tensions, emboldening extremists, and discrediting the Coalition and the Iraqi Government. Amid such violence, it became significantly harder for Iraqi leaders to make the difficult compromises necessary to foster reconciliation.

At the same time, we have increased our efforts to help build the capacity of the Iraqi Security Forces (ISF). Relying on lessons learned from our experience in training and equipping the ISF, we have significantly enhanced our training and mentoring commitment. We will continue this commitment through a combination of partnering Coalition units with Iraqi Army and Police organizations and embedding transition team personnel with the majority of ISF units. U.S. commanders are committed to helping the Iraqi government expand the size of the ISF to make it a more capable counter-insurgency force.

We are also increasing our efforts to build Iraqi governmental capacity not just at the national level, but at the provincial and local levels as well. Most notably, this has required an expansion of our Provincial Reconstruction Team (PRT) program with 15 new civilian PRTs paired with Brigade Combat Teams (BCTs), and giving PRT leaders and BCT commanders additional authorities, resources, and personnel. These leaders are charged with supporting moderate elements against extremists in their areas of responsibility and launching projects that have an immediate impact in areas cleared of terrorists and insurgents.

As the President explained in January, all of these efforts, together with a new diplomatic offensive in the region, are designed to set the conditions for U.S. troops to begin coming home, without risking a humanitarian catastrophe in Iraq, sanctuaries for international terrorist networks, or a broader regional conflict that would threaten U.S. national security interests for generations. (The strategy is explained in greater detail at http://www.whitehouse.gov/nsc/iraq/2007/iraq-strategy011007.pdf). While all of those conditions have not yet been met, and the new strategy is still in its early stages, there are encouraging signs that point the way to a more normalized and sustainable level of U.S. engagement in Iraq—with a decreasing number of U.S. combat forces increasingly focused on a core set of tasks, such as counterterrorism operations, and training, equipping, and supporting Iraqi forces.

The Next Phase: Building on Success

In the coming months, the United States will continue to operate along four lines of operation—security, political, economic, and diplomatic—to advance our objectives of protecting the Iraqi population while degrading terrorist and extremist networks; advancing local and national reconciliation; setting the framework for a growing economy; and expanding international support for Iraq. On the security side, General Petraeus has recommended to the President, and the President has accepted, that beginning in December 2007, we can transition to the next phase of our strategy. During this phase, U.S. forces will gradually transition from surge operations and transfer responsibility for population security to Iraqi forces—but only in a manner that preserves security and builds on success. Any adjustments in the missions of U.S. forces or transitions to Iraqi forces will vary based on local conditions. This approach stresses the need to continue the counterinsurgency strategy incorporated in the New Way Forward—but with Iraqis increasingly shouldering more of the load.

In this next phase and based on the Government of Iraq's request, we will also begin to develop the framework for an enduring relationship between Iraq and the United States—based on common principles. Iraqi leaders from all communities share the vision for a reduced American presence as soon as conditions allow and in a manner that sustains the gains seen over the course of 2007. They also understand that their success requires U.S. political, economic, diplomatic, and security engagement beyond January 2009, and they have asked to begin defining a long-term relationship between our two countries. We anticipate that the elements of this relationship will set the foundation for an enduring American commitment to Iraq—encompassing strong security, economic, and diplomatic ties—which is in the mutual interests of both the Iraqi people and the American people.

As part of the next phase in our strategy, the President has directed General Petraeus and Ambassador Crocker to update their joint operation plan for Iraq and to adjust our military and civilian resources accordingly. The President has also directed General Petraeus and Ambassador Crocker to provide a fresh assessment to the American people and to the Congress in March 2008 on the situation in Iraq and any adjustments that may be needed to our strategy based on changing conditions. This assessment will address:

- An analysis of mission progress—including security, economic, diplomatic, and political—from September 15, 2007;
- Recommended adjustments to military resources in Iraq, including further force adjustments;
- Recommended adjustments to economic assistance for Iraq, including a status report on the performance of Provincial Reconstruction Teams and governmental capacity-building programs;
- An assessment of regional and international contributions to Iraq and efforts to enhance those contributions;
- An assessment of "bottom-up" political and security initiatives, and whether the national government is supporting them;
- An assessment of "top-down" political and security initiatives, including national reconciliation initiatives; and
- An assessment of institutional adjustments within the United States Government to better support the civilian and military missions in Iraq as we transition to a longer-term posture.

The opening statements of General Petraeus and Ambassador Crocker—as delivered to the Congress on September 10 and September 11, 2007—are attached to this report as Appendices 1 and 2. These documents provide additional detail on the situation in Iraq as assessed by our experts on the ground and elements of the next phase of our strategy.

Summary of Achievements and Shortfalls

This report provides, consistent with the Act, an assessment of how the Iraqi Government is performing on 18 specified benchmarks, rather than the effects being generated. Some of the benchmarks may be leading indicators, giving some sense of future trends; but many are more accurately characterized as lagging indicators, and will only be achieved after the strategy is fully underway and generates improved conditions on the ground. Still other benchmarks do not fully measure the political accommodations that actually affect violence in Iraq and the direction that country is headed. For example, local political accommodations have dramatically improved conditions in what had been some of Iraq's most violent areas, and we are deploying our resources to help ensure that these trends continue and spread. It will take time, however, for improved conditions locally to translate into broader political accommodations at the national level; what is important is the overall trajectory, which, under our present strategy, has begun to stabilize and turn upward, compared to the deteriorating trajectory seen over the course of 2006. Thus, the assessments in this report should be viewed in a larger context: the discussion below provides a snapshot of achievements and shortfalls that can round out the picture given in the detailed assessment section of this report.

Security: Iraq faces daunting challenges: a complex security situation whose main elements include a communal struggle for power and resources between the Shi'a majority and Sunni, Kurd, and other minorities. Al-Qaida in Iraq extremists continue to act as accelerants for ethno-sectarian violence, and Iranian lethal support to Shi'a militants clearly intensifies the conflict. Foreign support to extremists in Iraq continues to exacerbate the security challenges and frustrate efforts to encourage political reconciliation.

The tempo of military actions to defeat al-Qaida increased in June as the final U.S. surge brigades arrived in Iraq. The surge effort has been complemented by carefully selected counter-terrorist targeting of key leaders of al-Qaida and other extremist groups. Tribal-based anti-terrorist initiatives have also augmented Coalition efforts to combat al-Qaida. Coalition efforts to secure the population against al-Qaida and other terrorists and extremists in Baghdad and other provinces across Iraq show signs of progress, but much hard work and tough fighting remain. Al-Qaida and Iranian-supported extremists groups have not been defeated, though we have made strong progress.

The number of attacks on Coalition forces has been on a downward trend since the middle of June. High-profile attacks (by car bombs, suicide car bombs, and suicide vests) have declined by over one-third since March of 2007. Coalition and Iraqi forces, along with Iraqi tribal elements, have pushed al-Qaida out of several former safe havens. Coalition forces have killed or captured nearly 100 key leaders and over 2,500 rank and file al-Qaida members in the past 7 months. As a result, al-Qaida's ability to coordinate its activities and conduct simultaneous attacks in multiple regions has been reduced. Nonetheless, sporadic high-profile attacks by al-Qaida continue to cause high civilian casualties, demonstrating al-Qaida's intent to use civilian casualties to provoke additional sectarian violence, shape public opinion, and destabilize the Government of Iraq.

Coalition forces report that murders and executions assessed to be ethno-sectarian in nature have declined significantly both in Baghdad and nationwide from their high in December 2006. However, the increase in ethno-sectarian deaths in July and August of 2007—largely a function of three sizable car bomb attacks in Kirkuk and Ninewa provinces—demonstrates the challenge that ethno-sectarian violence continues to pose for Iraq, particularly in rural locations that have light security force presence.

Sunni tribal groups have turned against al-Qaida in al-Anbar and Diyala provinces as well as in the Baghdad-area neighborhoods of Ameriyah, Abu Ghraib, Adhamiya, and Arab Jabour. They are cooperating with Coalition and Iraqi forces in expelling al-Qaida from their areas. Attacks in al-Anbar are now less than one-quarter the rate in January, and al-Qaida's sanctuaries have been greatly reduced. The trend of tribal engagement with the Coalition and the Government of Iraq continues to expand to other areas of Iraq. More than 40,000 concerned Iraqi citizens have volunteered to support local security initiatives since the start of the surge—and that number is growing daily. Prime Minister Maliki is personally involved in decisions to reconcile with these Sunni tribes and citizens willing to fight al-Qaida. He has directed the Government of Iraq to take steps to incorporate them into local security forces—a clear demonstration of the potential of "bottom-up" reconciliation that has occurred since January 2007. In fact, Prime Minister Maliki recently approved hiring approximately 12,000 Sunnis in al-Anbar, and 1,735 local men—including former insurgents—in Abu Ghraib. These events illustrate the growing sense among Iraqis that they need to overcome their natural trepidation and make some form of accommodation with former opponents.

Iran continues to supply Shi'a extremist groups with training, funding, and weapons, including rockets, mortars, and particularly explosively-formed projectile devices, which account for an increasing percentage of U.S. combat deaths. Coalition and Iraqi operations against these groups, combined with a growing rejection of Shi'a violence by top Government of Iraq officials, has led to some progress in reducing violent attacks from Shi'a extremists.

The Iraqi Security Forces (ISF) continue to make progress, but development of their capabilities in some areas has been slower than hoped. Progress by the Iraqi Army has exceeded that of both the national and local police. ISF performance has generally met or exceeded expectations when units are partnered with Coalition forces in combined operations or in tactical overwatch—a potential model for the future. There are still challenges in developing Iraqi institutions to sustain existing forces, delays in obtaining required equipment, persistent ethno-sectarian influences and political interference, a limited pool of trained officers and non-commissioned officers (NCOs), and attrition from combat. The Prime Minister's initiative to expand the ISF will eventually provide additional necessary forces, but the expansion will further strain the institutions that develop, train, and equip

Iraqi forces. Despite these challenges, the ISF are increasingly engaged in providing security for the Iraqi population. They are in the fight. Over the last 18 months Iraqi forces suffered combat deaths three times the number of combat deaths of Coalition forces. We have been further encouraged by the recent downturn in anti-Coalition attacks in Baghdad and southern Iraq since the early September announcement of a stand-down in Jaysh al-Mahdi (JAM) operations. Time will tell whether this has a lasting effect.

***Political Reconciliation*:** Reconciliation in a society marked by nearly four decades of dictatorship will not be linear and will take time, patience, and support from the international community. The Iraqi leadership (and the United States) has sought to set a metric for national reconciliation through a series of laws to be enacted through Iraq's Council of Representatives. Moving these laws forward depends on deal-making among major players in a society divided along sectarian, ethnic, and other lines—and navigation of a nascent democratic system with checks and balances that, while protecting minority groups, also slows legislative progress. For these reasons, most of the major political benchmarks identified in the Act may prove to be lagging indicators of whether or not the strategy is succeeding.

While key national legislation has not yet passed, the objectives of such laws are in some ways already being achieved. For example: there is no revenue sharing law, and yet significant oil revenues are being distributed by the central government to the provinces in an equitable manner. There is no provincial powers law, and yet the provincial governors and councils are making decisions on budget expenditures through engagement with the central government and ministries and are providing essential services for their constituents. There is no amnesty law, and yet immunity is being granted to many former insurgents, who in turn are being recruited to join legitimate security institutions. There is no de-Ba'athification reform law, and yet more than 45,000 former Ba'athist members of the old armed services have been granted pensions or even restored to active duty or Iraqi government service. Amnesty or de-Ba'athification laws were assumed necessary to drive a wedge between nationalist elements of the largely Sunni insurgency and al-Qaida. In fact, Sunnis in record numbers are turning against al-Qaida, reclaiming their communities, and turning towards the central government for additional resources. These are precisely the "effects" the benchmarks were intended to produce, even if the formal benchmarks themselves have not been met. In the coming months, our strategy will increasingly focus on helping the Iraqis knit together this new "bottom-up" progress with the "top-down" political process. It will still remain vital for Iraq's national government to codify what is happening in practice through formal legislation over time.

On that point, political progress at the national level has still been disappointing. The natural tension between groups has been exacerbated by political blocs threatening to withdraw support from the government. These threats were not fully carried out in most cases, but they have contributed to an environment of mistrust and gridlock. It became clear in July that the fundamental problem at the national level was not the failure to pass legislation but that the principal political groups—Sunni, Shi'a, and Kurd—could not agree on a set of decision-making processes and power sharing arrangements. Consequently, Iraq's leadership (represented by the Prime Minister, Presidency Council, and the President of the Kurdish Region) met in Baghdad in August to address these more fundamental issues of executive branch decision-making.

These leaders on August 26—following 8 days of meetings—announced a basic agreement on key benchmarks legislation on provincial powers and de-Ba'athification. They also formalized the use of the "3 plus 1 group," or the Prime Minister and the three-member Presidency Council, for collective decision-making on sensitive and strategic matters. The leaders agreed to streamline executive branch activities to facilitate swift decision-making through an "inner-cabinet" consisting of core ministers, including Oil, Electricity, Defense, and Interior. And, for the first time, they "affirmed the necessity of a long-term relationship with the United States" based on common interests for the future of Iraq. The communiqué issued by these leaders has not solved Iraq's serious problems at the national level, but it does represent an important step forward in the ongoing struggle to overcome the fear and mistrust now dividing Iraq's ethnic and religious communities. The leaders' August 26 agreement is a necessary building block to meaningful political progress—which begins with all major communities coming together for dialogue on resolving key differences.

***Diplomatic Engagement*:** Since the interim Benchmarks report in mid-July, there has been significant diplomatic activity with a focus on working with Iraq's neighbors to address problems in Iraq, especially security problems. In late July, after two trilateral meetings at the ambassador level, the United States, Iraq, and Iran formed a Security Subcommittee which met for the first time on August 6, 2007 in Baghdad. The Security Subcommittee has focused on curtailing the activities of militias and foreign terrorists in Iraq and developing ways to increase control over Iraq's borders. Despite these efforts, the Iranian government has shown no signs of curtailing their destructive activities inside Iraq—including the direct provision of lethal munitions and training to Shi'a extremist groups that are attacking Coalition forces and Iraqis. Indeed, attacks by the most dangerous roadside bombs—explosively-formed projectiles (EFPs)—have been on an upward trajectory this year, reaching a high of more than 90 attacks in July.

We have encouraged the Government of Iraq to engage in discussions with the Government of Syria to express its serious concerns about foreign terrorists, especially suicide bombers. In early August, the United States participated in a Border Security Working Group meeting in Damascus as part of the Neighbors Process. The participants discussed the issue of foreign terrorists continuing to use neighboring territories as a main transit route to Iraq and agreed to establish an experts' group to work on specific border control measures. Prime Minister Maliki followed up with a separate visit to Syria later in August, during which the Syrian Government committed to implementing border control measures. Although there has been some improvement, it remains too early to determine whether these Syrian actions have been effective in reducing foreign fighter flows into Iraq, which account for many of the high-profile terrorist attacks in Iraq aimed at instigating sectarian violence. Moreover, Syria continues to provide safe-haven to Ba'athist insurgents and financiers, and may be providing support to extremist political elements who are opposed to political reconciliation.

In addition to his visit to Syria, Prime Minister Maliki traveled to Turkey and Iran in August 2007 for discussions on security, energy, and other bilateral issues. Several other senior Iraqi government officials have traveled in the region as Iraq continues to increase its economic and diplomatic relations with neighboring states. For the first time in years, Iraq is exporting oil through Turkey. Iraq is nearing agreement on a commercial deal for Kuwait to supply critically needed diesel fuel. Jordan issued a statement welcoming the Iraqi leaders August 26 communiqué. Saudi Arabia is planning to open an Embassy in Baghdad—its first since the fall of Saddam.

The International Compact with Iraq, an initiative jointly sponsored by the United Nations and the Government of Iraq, was signed on May 3, 2007 in Sharm el-Sheikh, Egypt. The following day the Expanded Neighbors ministerial conference took place and was attended by the Permanent Five members of the U.N. Security Council, the Arab League, the Organization of Islamic Conference, and the G-8. Both events helped provide more international and regional support for Iraq. Plans are underway to create a standing secretariat for the Neighbors Process and a second ministerial-level conference is scheduled for late October in Turkey.

On August 10, the United Nations Security Council unanimously adopted UNSCR 1770, extending the mandate of the United Nations Assistance Mission for Iraq (UNAMI). The renewed UNAMI mandate provides an expanded role for the U.N. in advising, supporting, and assisting the Government of Iraq. UNAMI is also empowered to assist in the provisions for resolving disputed internal borders.

These international developments may appear independent of one another, but they are in fact part of an interrelated effort to establish a new international framework for supporting Iraq. This framework will take time to develop and mature, but its three primary components—the Expanded Neighbors Process, the International Compact, and the expanded Security Council mandate for UNAMI—provide promising new platforms for drawing the international community closer to Iraq with the full support and assistance of the Iraqi government.

***Economics and Essential Services*:** The economic picture in Iraq continues to improve, though very significant challenges remain. Key macroeconomic indicators paint a modestly improved picture—non-oil real growth is projected to be 5 percent in 2007, non-fuel inflation has further abated (year-on-year core inflation has declined to 16 percent and overall inflation to 30 percent in July 2007, while 2007 year-to-date inflation is 5 percent), and the unemployment rate appears to be easing. Government revenue remains above target due to high oil export prices.

A national investment commission head has been appointed to promote increased private sector activity and legal and regulatory reform. Idle yet viable state-owned factories have signed loan agreements to restart operations. Reopening these factories will create new private business opportunities for suppliers located near the factories. An auction of the cell phone spectrum in August netted the Government of Iraq a better-than-expected sum of $3.75 billion. However, lack of adequate security remains the largest impediment to increased private economic activity, and a major economic turnaround remains unlikely until the security picture improves.

The provision of essential services at the provincial level is generally improving. However, provincial government performance remains mixed, with those provinces experiencing continued violence and kinetic operations finding it more difficult to provide services. On average, the provinces are obligating funding for essential services and infrastructure projects at a rate faster than in 2006. The improvements are most dramatic in provinces such as al-Anbar, where security gains have, for the first time since 2003 created an environment conducive to delivery of government services. At the national level, the Ministry of Oil has finally begun the process of investment spending, but much higher rates of investment are still necessary to promote growth, fund future investment, and contribute to better quality of life.

Iraq has maintained satisfactory performance on its International Monetary Fund (IMF) Stand-by Arrangement. The IMF Executive Board completed a successful review of the program on August 1 and extended the program until December 2007. IMF Executive Board members praised the Iraqi authorities for their commitment to implementing difficult economic reforms in a dynamic political and security environment. Iraq will negotiate a new program with the IMF before the end of the year.

The Government of Iraq remains similarly committed to the International Compact with Iraq, which provides a reform framework for Iraq to become financially self-sufficient within 5 years. A semiannual review of the Compact occurred at the U.N. on July 20, during which Iraq presented a report on key developments since the Compact was signed on May 3, 2007. Of Iraq's 262 actionable benchmarks under the Compact, 169 are in progress and on track. Delegates from the international community praised the report and welcomed Iraq's efforts to implement its reform commitments. Several participants also called for greater assistance for Iraq, especially through faster progress on concluding debt relief agreements.

Congressional Benchmarks

Broad context is necessary for assessing the performance of the Iraqi government with respect to the 18 benchmarks identified in the Act. Iraqi leaders face a daunting challenge, and they and their families take great risks daily. We continue to encourage and press them to achieve established benchmarks, since we believe that those efforts will contribute over time to Iraq's stability, to its ability to provide for its own security, and to the international effort to counter violent extremism. Nonetheless, our efforts in Iraq extend far beyond these benchmarks, as the recent testimony of Ambassador Crocker and General Petraeus explained in more detail. Every day, our Embassy and military officials work with the Iraqis to establish the strategic environment in which security and meaningful reconciliation can develop and take root—in ways not easily measured by benchmarks based heavily on adopting legislation.

***Standard of Measurement*:** Section 1314(b)(2)(A) states: "The President shall submit an initial report to Congress, not later than July 15, 2007, assessing the status of each of the specific benchmarks established above, and declaring, in his judgment, **whether satisfactory progress toward meeting these benchmarks is, or is not, being achieved." Section 1314(b)(2)(D) further provides that "[t]he President shall submit a second report to the Congress, not later than September 15, 2007, following the same procedures and criteria outlined [in the paragraphs] above**."

To make this judgment (i.e., whether "satisfactory progress ... is, or is not, being achieved"), we have carefully examined all the facts and circumstances with respect to each of the 18 benchmarks and asked the following question: *As measured from a January 2007 baseline, do we assess that present trend data demonstrates a positive trajectory, which is tracking toward satisfactory accomplishment in the near term?* If the answer is yes, we have provided a "Satisfactory" assessment; if the answer is no, the assessment is "Not Satisfactory." Where benchmarks contain more than one element we have provided assessments for each element. As a result, some benchmarks show mixed progress, with some elements assessed satisfactory and other elements judged not satisfactory. Two benchmarks could not be fully assessed at this time because the preconditions for achieving them have not been reached. For benchmarks receiving a not satisfactory assessment, we have explained what, if any, strategic adjustments may be required to improve the present trajectory.

The current assessment indicates additional progress has occurred since the initial report of July 2007. In that report, the Iraq government made satisfactory progress on eight benchmarks and eight benchmarks were assessed as unsatisfactory, including two with mixed progress. Today's report is based on data available as of September 1 and reflects that the Iraqis have made satisfactory progress since January 2007 on nine benchmarks, including on de-Ba'athification reform which in July was assessed as unsatisfactory. In addition, while the current report assesses seven benchmarks as not satisfactory, this includes four benchmarks with progress on some aspects while not on others. In both the July report and today's assessment, two benchmarks are not rated because the necessary preconditions are not yet present.

It is important to note that the metric used in this report differs from that employed by the Government Accountability Office (GAO) in its August 2007 report. Legislation mandating this GAO report required a determination of **whether or not the Government of Iraq has met or not met** each benchmark and the status of achievement of these benchmarks. Additionally, the GAO report took account of information only through July 31, 2007. This report takes account of information through September 1, 2007 and evaluates whether the Iraqi government has made satisfactory progress on each benchmark.

The present analysis and assessment of the 18 benchmarks follows.

Assessment of the Benchmarks

Section 1314 (b)(2)(A) The President shall submit an initial report, in classified and unclassified format, to the Congress, not later than July 15, 2007, assessing the status of each of the specific benchmarks ... and declaring, in his judgment, whether satisfactory progress toward meeting these benchmarks is, or is not, being achieved.

Section 1314 (b)(2)(C) If the President's assessment of any of the specific benchmarks established above is unsatisfactory, the President shall include in that report a description of such revisions to the political, economic, regional, and military components of the strategy, as announced by the President on January 10, 2007. In addition, the President shall include in the report the advisability of implementing such aspects of the bipartisan Iraq Study Group, as he deems appropriate.

Section 1314 (b)(2)(D) The President shall submit a second report to the Congress, not later than September 15, 2007, following the same procedures and criteria outlined above.

Section 1314 (b)(1)(A) The United States Strategy in Iraq, hereafter, shall be conditioned on the Iraqi Government meeting benchmarks ... including:

(i) Forming a Constitutional Review Committee and then completing the constitutional review.

The Council of Representatives (COR) formed the Constitutional Review Committee (CRC) on November 15, 2006, and constitutional review is underway. The CRC, in a May 2007 interim report, offered a range of amendments for COR consideration and in addition highlighted the need to resolve outstanding issues concerning: (i) Presidential powers, (ii) the powers of the regions vs. the central government, and (iii) the status of Kirkuk (Article 140 of the Constitution).

Assessment: The Government of Iraq has made satisfactory progress toward forming a Constitutional Review Committee (CRC) and then completing the constitutional review. The Embassy has engaged the CRC Chairmen and the COR Speaker and Deputy Speakers on the need to develop a well-defined plan for the COR debate on the recommendations of the interim report. Despite the COR's August adjournment, the CRC continued to work on the three additional unresolved constitutional issues described above.

(ii) Enacting and implementing legislation on de-Ba'athification reform.

De-Ba'athification reform is potentially the most emotional issue being discussed by the Government of Iraq. Legislation necessary to reform and implement certain de-Ba'athification programs involves competing concepts of justice, accountability, reconciliation, and economic compensation. The public discussion of these issues tends to polarize Iraqis even as many of the proposed changes take place on the ground. For example, former Ba'ath party members who served in the army have been granted pensions. While the de-Ba'athification legislation is debated at the highest levels in Baghdad, more than 45,000 former army personnel have been granted pensions or reinstated to active duty.

In Recommendation 27, the Iraq Study Group emphasizes the need for United States Government support of reintegration of former Ba'athists and Arab nationalists into civic life, and the New Way Forward strategy makes de-Ba'athification reform an integral part of the United States Government's Iraq policy. The Embassy has pressed hard on all political elements to move forward.

On August 26 the leaders of Iraq's five major political groups announced an agreement had been reached on, *inter alia,* draft de-Ba'athification legislation. While the agreed-upon draft still must pass the hurdles of debate and adoption in the Council of Representatives, the work accomplished by the leaders on this legislation is a significant sign of progress.

Even in the absence of legislation, limited political accommodation remains possible, particularly when pursued through outreach by local political leaders.

Assessment: The Government of Iraq has made satisfactory progress toward enacting and implementing legislation on de-Ba'athification reform. The fact that legislation has not yet passed the COR should not diminish the significance of the agreement reached by the leaders or the re-integration of former Ba'athists taking place on the ground. The overarching goal of de-Ba'athification reform is political accommodation between the Shi'a and Sunni communities. The leaders' agreement combined with the return of former Ba'athists to civic life is a significant step in that regard. Debate on this draft law in the COR is an integral part of developing the broad political acceptance needed to promote real reconciliation.

(iii) Enacting and implementing legislation to ensure the equitable distribution of hydrocarbon resources to the people of Iraq without regard to the sect or ethnicity of recipients, and enacting and implementing legislation to ensure that the energy resources of Iraq benefit Sunni Arabs, Shi'a Arabs, Kurds, and other Iraqi citizens in an equitable manner.

The Hydrocarbon Framework Law and the companion Revenue Sharing Law are fundamentally important to defining federalism in Iraq. If adopted, they would: catalyze new sources of investment capital and technology for the oil and gas sector; facilitate substantial near term increases in government revenues which could be used for the benefit of Iraq's people; and serve as a vehicle for political reconciliation between regions and communities.

Iraq's political leaders continue to be actively engaged in developing these laws. The United States has provided technical advice, both to the Government of Iraq and to the Kurdish Regional Government (KRG), and has encouraged all parties to approve the draft laws and submit them for consideration to the full COR.

The Hydrocarbon Framework Law was approved by the Council of Ministers in February 2007 and reviewed by the Shura Council (a legal body) in the spring. Two versions of the law were submitted to the COR in July. The companion Revenue Management Law was agreed to by Kurdish and Shi'a Arab political parties in June 2007 and in July was submitted to the Shura Council for review. The Revenue Management Law must be approved by the Council of Ministers (COM) before submission to the COR. Discussions among Iraqi political leaders are ongoing, and this legislation remains a primary focus for political party leaders.

Assessment: The Government of Iraq has not made satisfactory progress toward enacting and implementing legislation to ensure the equitable distribution of hydrocarbon revenue. Passage of the national laws remains a high priority for the United States and the Government of Iraq and could be accomplished relatively quickly if a consensus in support can be constructed. Many Sunni leaders (and some Shi'a as well) continue to disagree on the appropriate balance between national and regional control of hydrocarbon exploration and production. Meanwhile, the Kurdish Regional Government has sought to reinforce its own position on the national law by passing a new hydrocarbons licensing regime through its regional parliament. Given the fluid nature of the Iraqi political process, it is difficult to predict what further progress might occur once the COR reconvenes. Despite this uncertainty, the Government of Iraq is already distributing significant oil revenue on an equitable basis to the provinces and KRG through the Iraqi budget.

(iv) Enacting and implementing legislation on procedures to form semi-autonomous regions.

In line with the Iraqi constitution, the COR enacted a "Regions Law" in October 2006 that establishes procedures for the formation of federal regions in Iraq. The legislation delayed the effective date of implementation for a period of 18 months after enactment, which means no steps can be taken to form federal regions before April 2008. The United States Government encouraged Iraqi political parties to reach a compromise on this law and believes that the 18-month delay in implementation was in the interests of Iraq and the United States, given current political conditions in Iraq.

Assessment: The Government of Iraq has made satisfactory progress toward enacting and implementing legislation on procedures to form semi-autonomous regions. The COR passed the Regions Law with a delayed effective date. Implementation of this legislation could take place after provincial elections are held and after the passage of an updated elections law.

(v) Enacting and implementing legislation establishing an Independent High Electoral Commission, provincial elections law, provincial council authorities, and a date for provincial elections.

On January 23, 2007, the COR passed the Independent High Electoral Commission (IHEC) Law, which the Presidency Council (the President and two Deputy Presidents) signed into law on February 27, 2007. On April 28, 2007, the COR appointed the nine IHEC Commissioners in a process that the U.N. deemed fair and transparent. The Commissioners have completed appropriate training and are in the process of selecting representatives to oversee elections in the provinces.

The mid-August high-level meetings produced agreement among the leaders of Iraq's five major parties on a draft law delineating provincial powers. Draft legislation is expected to be submitted to the COR shortly. This law lays out the authorities of provincial governments and their relationship to the national government in Baghdad.

In Recommendation 29, the Iraq Study Group emphasizes the need for provincial elections at the earliest possible date. Iraqi officials said in August that a provincial powers law was a prerequisite for setting a date for provincial elections, and therefore they await movement from the COR. The United States Government and the United Nations Assistance Mission for Iraq (UNAMI) are strongly encouraging the Government of Iraq to set a date for provincial elections. Additionally, the United States Government is working with Iraq Security Forces to ensure that they are adequately prepared to provide security for free and fair elections when a date is set.

Assessment: There are multiple components to this benchmark, each deserving its own assessment.

- ***Establishing the IHEC Commission*:** The Government of Iraq has made satisfactory progress toward establishing an IHEC Commission.
- ***Elections Law*:** The Government of Iraq has not made satisfactory progress toward establishing a provincial elections law.
- ***Provincial Council Authorities*:** The Government of Iraq has made satisfactory progress toward establishing provincial council authorities, which are encapsulated in the Provincial Powers law.
- ***Provincial Elections Date*:** The Government of Iraq has not made satisfactory progress toward establishing a date for provincial elections.

There remains no mechanism to address the marked under-representation of Sunnis on four provincial councils. Nevertheless, in some places, such as al-Anbar, local authorities appointed additional provincial council members in November 2006 to ease problems of a lack of representation through non-electoral means. In passing an expanded mandate for UNAMI on August 10, the United Nations Security Council reaffirmed its commitment to assist the IHEC prepare for the next round of elections. This situation does not necessitate a revision to our current plan and strategy, and positive action on this issue is one of our highest priorities.

(vi) Enacting and implementing legislation addressing amnesty.

The preconditions for a general amnesty do not yet exist. That said, the Government of Iraq established a high-level Reconciliation Committee to support and oversee efforts by groups that want to oppose al-Qaida in Iraq and other extremist elements. This committee is working with a joint U.S. Embassy/MNF-I group that is facilitating such actions in coordination with other anti-terrorist efforts on the ground. In the absence of legislation, the Government of Iraq—at the direction of the Prime Minister—has initiated a program of limited immunity for individuals who have turned away from supporting al-Qaida and have now pledged support to the government. While this program may not meet the requirement for enacting and implementing legislation, on-the-ground programs of limited immunity are accomplishing some of the desired effects of this benchmark.

Assessment: No assessment can be made until the necessary preconditions have been reached for implementing a general amnesty. However, a process of local accommodation and limited immunity has been developed and effectively implemented in al-Anbar province, Abu Ghraib, and other locations where local volunteers, including some Shi'a, have been approved for hire by the Minister of Interior or Defense while awaiting completion of the reconciliation committee's screening. Although the Government of Iraq has not enacted or implemented amnesty legislation, these local programs may be creating preconditions for future amnesty legislation. The Embassy continues to engage the Government of Iraq at the highest levels on questions of amnesty.

(vii) Enacting and implementing legislation establishing a strong militia disarmament program to ensure that such security forces are accountable only to the central government and loyal to the constitution of Iraq.

The necessary preconditions for a Disarmament, Demobilization, and Reintegration (DDR) program in any post-conflict society are steep, and key elements such as political reconciliation and security provided by the government do not yet exist, despite considerable efforts by the Government of Iraq, MNF-I, and the United States Embassy.

Although a DDR Committee has been established, there is limited momentum toward developing and implementing a comprehensive disarmament program for militia members while Iraq faces a combination of sectarian violence, terrorist attacks, and a continuing insurgency. However, there are signs that certain programs and projects designed at the local level to re-integrate certain individuals and small groups back into the population are achieving some modest success. In general, these projects include education-based programs for former detainees.

The 2007 budget of the Government of Iraq includes $150 million for DDR. However, the funds will not be released until the Government of Iraq enacts legislation and establishes a satisfactory program for implementation.

In Recommendation 38 and 39, the Iraq Study Group proposes that neutral international experts act as advisors to the Government of Iraq and that the United States Government fund and support a single office to provide assistance to these experts. The study also notes that "solving the problem of militias requires national reconciliation" and states that, as a party in the conflict, the United States Government should not be directly involved in a DDR program's implementation.

Consequently, the United Nations Security Council Resolution 1770 expanded UNAMI's mandate to include "advise, support, and assist ... the Government of Iraq at an appropriate time and in connection with progress on reconciliation efforts, on planning, funding, and implementing reintegration programs for former members of illegal armed groups."

Assessment: No assessment can be made until the necessary preconditions have been reached for implementing a strong militia disarmament program. However, the Government of Iraq has initiated a process that reintegrates former militia members into the Ministry of Defense and Ministry of Interior architecture. In effect, this may be facilitating the necessary conditions for a future DDR program.

(viii) Establishing supporting political, media, economic, and services committees in support of the Baghdad Security Plan.

Through its February 2007 establishment of the Executive Steering Committee (ESC) and related subcommittees, the Government of Iraq has established supporting political, media, economic, and services committees in support of the Baghdad Security Plan (Operation Fardh Al Qanoon). The United States Embassy and MNF-I will remain intensively engaged with the ESC to continue to improve its effectiveness and ensure that the subcommittees fulfill the purpose for which they were created.

Assessment: The Government of Iraq has made satisfactory progress toward establishing supporting political, media, economic, and services committees in support of the Baghdad Security Plan. Since the July 2007 assessment period, the ESC and related subcommittees have continued to meet weekly in their efforts to coordinate and synchronize policies, services, and other non-kinetic aspects of Operation Fardh Al Qanoon with security operations.

(ix) Providing three trained and ready Iraqi brigades to support Baghdad operations.

The Ministry of Defense has generated a total of eight Iraqi Army Brigade Headquarters and 27 Iraqi Army Battalions to support Baghdad operations. These units are actively involved in joint and independent operations throughout Baghdad and the Baghdad belts. The Government of Iraq provided the number of units required, and they were trained to the proper individual and collective baseline. As unit manning and composition issues were identified, the Government of Iraq addressed them. For example, in order to compensate for the number of soldiers absent during Operation Fardh Al Qanoon for leave or other reasons, the Government of Iraq expanded combat unit manning to 120 percent of authorization, thus achieving higher present for duty strength. Current present for duty rates are now 75 percent of authorized strength, which is within Iraqi Army standard.

Some of these units have performed exceptionally well, voluntarily extending their deployments up to 270 days and raising their operational readiness ratings. Over the past 2 months the units serving with Coalition forces in the Baghdad Area of Operations—the 6th and 9th Iraqi Army Divisions—have conducted almost 400 combined operations, 700 independent operations, and more than 7,000 independent patrols. Some units have been less impressive, suffering from a variety of issues related to a lack of leadership and equipment to support their assigned missions.

Overall, Coalition ground commanders who work side by side with these units are generally pleased with their performance and are witness to their continual development and growing confidence as they gain experience in the counterinsurgency effort. That said, Iraqi Security forces are not yet able to assume responsibility for security throughout the country. Placing that burden on the Iraqis before they are ready risks sacrificing the gains we have made. The ISF will require additional training, equipping, and logistical support.

It was an impressive achievement for the Government of Iraq to provide the equivalent of three additional trained and ready brigades to Baghdad. Programs are in place to ensure they remain capable of sustaining this level of effort through scheduled rotations and a robust training pipeline.

Assessment: The Government of Iraq has made satisfactory progress toward providing three trained and ready Iraqi brigades to support Baghdad operations.

(x) Providing Iraqi commanders with all authorities to execute this plan and to make tactical and operational decisions in consultation with U.S. Commanders, without political intervention to include the authority to pursue all extremists including Sunni insurgents and Shiite militias.

The Prime Minister has provided Iraqi commanders the necessary authority to conduct security operations and continues to reaffirm his commitment to support these authorities. ISF continue to prosecute targets across Iraq, including in operations throughout Baghdad and in provinces that have already been turned over to Provincial Iraqi Control. The Prime Minister and senior commanders increasingly recognize the threat to long-term security posed by Shi'a militia extremists and continue to support targeting such elements. In late August, the Prime Minister removed the Shi'a commander of the Karbala Operations Command, ordered the arrest of three prominent Shi'a militia extremists who were in Karbala for the 12th Imam Commemoration, ordered an Iraqi Special Forces raid on key JAM cells in Karbala, and the strong response from the Iraqi government—as well as the public outrage at the violence—appears to have led to Muqtada al-Sadr's call for his extremist militia to halt all attacks against Coalition forces.

The Iraqi Army as an institution continues to appear more nationally oriented and less susceptible to political interference than the Iraqi National Police or local forces, although some reform of the National Police has occurred. The degree of JAM influence within police forces is largely dependent upon the region or city. Within Baghdad, Iraqi Police in Sadr City and parts of Kadhamiyah are complicit with JAM activity. JAM influence is also strong in the cities of Al Amarrah, Hussaniyah, and Diwaniyah due to heavy infiltration of JAM members. Police activities in those areas that have been cleared and retained by Coalition and Iraqi forces appear to be the most even-handed.

Coalition military leaders who work closely with their Iraqi counterparts to plan and conduct security operations have seen uneven progress on efforts to reduce political interference in military decisions. Where Iraqi security forces are fighting alongside Coalition Forces or manning joint security stations, ISF tactical commanders generally act on mission orders from their established chains of command.

There are no reported instances of political interference in operations directed against Sunni insurgents. However, there is evidence of political officials attempting to limit the effectiveness of independent Iraqi operations against Shi'a extremists. Political interference typically emanates from individuals in the Government of Iraq below the level of the Prime Minister, and the Prime Minister has taken actions to limit such interference. For example, the Prime Minister was recently provided evidence of arrest lists for Sunni targets generated by an office below him that bypassed operational commanders. The Prime Minister responded by reorganizing and reducing the size of the office. As far as we can determine, any previous restrictions on targeting certain sects are no longer present.

There also is still evidence of political interference with ISF operations from both the Ministry of Interior and the Office of the Commander in Chief (OCINC). Questionable judicial warrants by the OCINC have been used to try to replace Sunni officers who demonstrated effectiveness against Jaysh al-Mahdi operations in Baghdad and in southern provinces. In Muthanna province, there is evidence that Ministry of Interior officials have used de-Ba'athification laws to replace effective Sunni police officers with Shi'a officers. JAM-associated Ministry of Interior officials continue to exert such a significant influence over the Basra Police that the new Basra Provincial Director of Police raised this issue at a meeting with the Ministerial Council on National Security.

There is strong evidence of efforts to remove sectarian commanders in the National Police. Since the start of this year, all Division Commanders, all Brigade Commanders, and 17 of 27 battalion commanders in the National Police were relieved of duty due to allegations of sectarian activity. In addition, a former Police Division Commander reassigned due to serious allegations has since been removed from his follow-on assignment as well. This is a signal that the Government of Iraq is committed to taking action with regard to sectarian bias.

While the recent interventions by the Prime Minister and other government officials to curb sectarian bias are encouraging, the fear of being replaced for political or sectarian reasons remains and continues to influence commanders' decisions on which operations to undertake. Given the importance of this issue, we will need to continue monitoring the activities of government officials for signs of interference with ISF commanders' abilities to make tactical and operational decisions.

Assessment: The Government of Iraq has made satisfactory progress toward providing Iraqi commanders with all authorities to execute this plan and to make tactical and operational decisions in consultation with U.S. Commanders, to include the authority to pursue all extremists. However, there has not been satisfactory progress towards eliminating political intervention by leaders throughout the chain of command. The historical prejudices inherent to Iraq remain a challenge that will only be fully solved by time and the experience of democratic government.

(xi) Ensuring that Iraqi Security Forces are providing even-handed enforcement of the law.

Individual Iraqi Army and National Police units that work closely with Coalition Forces generally act responsibly. The achievements of the 30 joint security stations and 31 Coalition outposts throughout Baghdad neighborhoods provide clear evidence that the Iraqi police and army are capable of fairly administering the rule of law under a partnering construct. The actions of many individual Iraqi commanders demonstrate that they independently act in a fair and professional manner. For example, operations against insurgent cells seem to be even-handed—targeting both Sunni and Shi'a elements. In the last week of August, Coalition and Iraqi Special Forces jointly killed or captured more than 100 cell members, about one third of whom were JAM members who had committed criminal actions.

Education and training have been key ingredients in improving enforcement of the law. Under the National Police Transformation plan, eight of the nine National Police brigades have completed a month-long training course on the rule of law, professionalism, and policing techniques. The latest class of 1,800 National Policemen just graduated from the Numaniyah National Police College on 20 August. Initial indications show that even seasoned units perform better after completing such a "re-bluing" program. Similar programs are also used for local police. Still, some police units operating outside of close Coalition supervision tend to gravitate to old habits of sectarianism. In late August, the Minister of Interior had to issue an arrest warrant for a police company commander and several in his command for sectarian behavior. This indicates both the persistence of the problem and a genuine desire by the leadership to clean up the image and performance of the police force.

Improvements within the Iraqi legal system are providing the Government of Iraq with new ways to handle rule of law issues. The government introduced a new military justice system, trained 16 judges and 4 prosecutors, and established a unit training program for Commanders and Disciplinary Officers that is administered by almost 100 trained legal advisors assigned across all Iraqi Army divisions. Within the past month, high-profile and high-ranking offenders within the ISF—both Sunni and Shi'a—have been arrested and are currently under investigation, pending trial for their sectarian-based crimes. Judges in the secure Rusafa Rule of Law Complex have already shown their determination to impose tough justice on both Sunni and Shi'a members of sectarian death squads. Since the start of the year they have sentenced roughly equal numbers of Sunni and Shi'a criminals to death.

Through continued mentoring and partnership, additional training of ISF units, and increased emphasis by the Government of Iraq, even-handed enforcement of the law may increasingly become the norm, even in the absence of Coalition oversight. We expect Government of Iraq actions, not Coalition oversight, to hold the ISF to a high standard in the future.

Assessment: The Government of Iraq has made satisfactory progress in ensuring that the Iraqi Army is providing even-handed enforcement of the law, though much remains to be done in this area. However the Iraqi Police has not made satisfactory progress, as some elements still act with a sectarian bias. The replacement of 28 National Police Commanders, as well as the "re-bluing" training for National Police Brigades, should produce improvements in this area over the coming months.

(xii) Ensuring that, as President Bush quoted Prime Minister Maliki as saying, "the Baghdad Security Plan will not provide a safe haven for any outlaws, regardless of [their] sectarian or political affiliation."

In accordance with the promise made by Prime Minister Maliki, the Government of Iraq has allowed Coalition forces to conduct operations in all areas of Baghdad.

Almost 3 months into surge operations, the coordinated offensive operations of ISF and Coalition forces have made significant progress against terrorist and extremist elements, particularly in Baghdad, the surrounding "belts," and Diyala. In Baghdad, the focus of operations has been along the fault lines between Sunni and Shi'a neighborhoods, where economic and social conditions make the population most susceptible to extremism. Our counterinsurgency strategy relies on establishing joint security stations in troubled neighborhoods, continuous joint ISF and Coalition Force security operations, Coalition outposts to expand the reach of Coalition forces, and reconstruction programs to restore quality of life. These actions have resulted in a steady improvement in population security, increasing trust of Baghdad residents, and a decrease in the number of areas where terrorists and extremists can operate. In late March 2007, only about 10 percent of Baghdad neighborhoods were secured by Iraqi and Coalition forces. By the end of August more than three-quarters of the city's neighborhoods had been cleared and now benefit from the continued presence of security forces.

Prior to clearing operations in Baqubah, Coalition operations were plagued by IED attacks and had difficulty locating insurgent cells and weapons caches. Once Coalition and Iraqi forces established a permanent presence in the city, weekly IED and indirect fire attacks dropped by 75 percent, and local citizens began pointing out booby-trapped houses, buried IEDs and weapons caches. Total attacks against civilians, ISF, and Coalition forces for all of Diyala province have decreased in 7 of the past 10 weeks. In the past month alone more than 140 IEDs and 61 weapons caches have been cleared, in great part due to tips from local residents.

Even in places like Sadr City, Coalition and Iraqi forces have pressured militia extremists and criminals. Since January, more than 80 operations have been conducted, spanning each sector of Sadr City and capturing or killing many insurgent and militia cell leaders. In contrast to the perception that Sadr City is a safe haven for extremists, Coalition and Iraqi patrols operate there and continue to disrupt cells that plant IEDs or launch mortar attacks in Baghdad. Reconstruction projects continue in Sadr City with hospital renovations 94 percent complete, three new water system projects completed in July and at least four ongoing medical clinic projects.

The Government of Iraq and Coalition elements are exploiting improved security by revitalizing economic and social programs, thereby preventing the reappearance of conditions that would promote a return of extremists. The Baqubah Flour Mill just received a shipment of 560 tons of grain—its first in over a year. This mill will now employ 200 local workers. In Amariyah, Ghazaliyah, Yusifiyah, Adhamiyah, and Abu Ghraib, tribal initiatives against al-Qaida are gaining momentum and have garnered the increased support of the Government of Iraq. In Adhamiyah alone, 1000 Iraqis volunteered to help the ISF and Coalition forces bring security to their neighborhood. Overall, operations in Baghdad have made an impact, but work remains to be done, especially in the Sadr City area of Baghdad and in Kadhamiyah. These neighborhoods remain some of our bigger challenges.

Assessment: The Government of Iraq has made satisfactory progress toward ensuring that the Baghdad Security Plan will not provide a safe haven for any outlaws, regardless of their sectarian or political affiliation.

(xiii) Reducing the level of sectarian violence in Iraq and eliminating militia control of local security.

Ethno-sectarian violence is incited by a variety of motivations and methods, making it difficult to measure and control. Coalition and Iraqi partners are working hard to break the vicious cycle of provocation and retaliation that was at the heart of last winter's surge in casualties and displacement from troubled neighborhoods. After considering a number of indicators developed from both host nation and Coalition reports, there are promising signs that we may be succeeding in breaking this cycle.

While there are still millions of Iraqis who have been displaced from their homes by intimidation and violence, some small groups are beginning to return to areas where violence has been reduced. By both our estimate and those of the national intelligence community, the number of ethno-sectarian attacks and deaths nationwide has fluctuated somewhat over the past several months, but they are now less than half of the December 2006 levels. Ethno-sectarian attacks in the Baghdad districts have fallen even more sharply, down to roughly one-quarter the levels of December 2006.

Total attacks on civilians across Iraq have declined in 13 of the past 18 weeks. Unfortunately, total civilian casualties did not fall as significantly over the same period, as al-Qaida launched several high-casualty vehicle IED attacks in Baghdad and the northern provinces in an attempt to provoke greater sectarian violence. However, in a sign of progress, Iraqis did not respond to these attacks with widespread sectarian-based retaliation, allowing for an underlying downward trend in civilian casualties. Overall, these trends have been achieved through increased Coalition and Iraqi presence in Baghdad, operations in the Baghdad belts, and an increase in the number of national leaders who have publicly renounced sectarian violence and called for restraint in the wake of high-profile IED attacks.

Despite these gains, progress against militia extremists is mixed. Operations conducted since May have significantly contributed to eliminating militia control of local security in areas that Coalition forces have cleared and now hold. In some cities such as Baghdad, Ramadi, Abu Ghraib, and Baqubah, local militia members are formally joining the local Iraqi security forces and providing effective community security, as well as valuable tips on caches and the location of extremist leaders. Despite the recent assassination of the elected governors in Qadisiyah and Muthanna, we believe that discrete offensive operations against militia extremist leaders in the central southern provinces offer the opportunity for larger gains against the militias. However, militias are still acting outside the law in the uncleared parts of Baghdad and the southern provinces of Karbala, Basra, Qadisiyah, and Maysan. In these areas, militia members have either infiltrated Iraqi Security Forces or brokered deals with the local ISF or civilian leadership.

The national government continues its efforts to curb militia control of Iraqi Security Forces by its selection of leaders and key arrests, but they remain one step behind the problem. It is too early to be optimistic about statements by Muqtada al-Sadr, though the increasing number of Shi'a and Sunni tribal sheikhs reaching out to become part of the solution is a promising sign. We will continue to provide guidance and support to the Government of Iraq in negotiations, reconciliation, military operations, and legal action to address this issue.

Assessment: The Government of Iraq has made satisfactory progress toward reducing sectarian violence. Where ISF and Coalition forces have conducted clear and hold operations, militia control has been significantly reduced. However, satisfactory progress has not been made toward eliminating militia control of local security, in other areas, as evidenced by continued militia influence of certain Baghdad neighborhoods and other areas across Iraq.

(xiv) Establishing all of the planned joint security stations in neighborhoods across Baghdad.

Nearly all of the planned joint security stations, Coalition outposts, and other patrol bases have been established across Baghdad and the surrounding area. As of August 31, 2007, 30 of 33 planned joint security stations were operational and 31 Coalition combat outposts had achieved operational capability. Joint security stations provide an around-the-clock security presence in most of Baghdad and are particularly effective as they merge Coalition partnering with Iraqi presence and action. There are numerous examples where Iraqi presence has facilitated a lower application of force and a more positive result. Other stations are being established in outlying areas where interaction with the local people can have a direct impact on the reduction of violence within the city. This increased interaction with the local population should continue to suppress crime and sectarian violence as well as provide valuable intelligence to support economic growth, political accommodation, and counterinsurgency operations.

Joint security stations are also being successfully employed in al-Anbar province and numerous other locations across Iraq. Coalition leaders will continue to consult with the Baghdad Operational Center and national leadership to determine additional emplacements.

Assessment: The Government of Iraq has made satisfactory progress toward establishing the planned Joint Security Stations in Baghdad neighborhoods.

(xv) Increasing the number of Iraqi Security Forces units capable of operating independently.

Iraqi Army, Air Force, and Police units[1] continue to grow in size. The Iraqi Army has expanded greatly since December 2006, when there were 149 units in operation and 9 under development. Currently, there are 152 combat units in operation and 29 under development. Since March 2007, there has been a 14 percent increase in the number of independent Iraqi Army operations, including 20 units operating independently as part of Fardh Al-Qanoon and 10 units assuming the lead role in their areas of responsibility. While only a small percentage of battalions are rated as capable of completely independent counterinsurgency operations (Operational Readiness Assessment Level One), over 75 percent are capable of planning, executing, and sustaining operations with some Coalition support and of making significant contributions to combat operations. The greatest constraints on independent operations are a shortage of trained leaders and immature logistics capability.

Iraqi Security Forces recently demonstrated their improved ability when they independently planned, rehearsed, and executed security for the annual pilgrimage in commemoration of the death of the Seventh Imam. This event, which included a march of a million Shi'a pilgrims to Baghdad's Kadhamiyah Shrine, had been marred by significant violence each of the last 3 years, including 1,000 people who were killed in a stampede in 2005 when they feared a car bomb attack. This year's event had no violence and was a great tribute to the Iraqi Security Forces and the government. The ISF planning and execution of the 12th Imam celebration in Karbala in late August 2007 was marred by JAM-instigated violence, but the Iraq security forces protected the shrines and defeated JAM attacks. Rapid reaction by the Government of Iraq—led by the Prime Minister personally—contained the violence and demonstrated another step toward eventual independent security capability.

The Iraqi Police continues to grow in size, particularly in newly cleared population centers where the increased demand for officers is often well-supported by local volunteers and the Government of Iraq. Police forces in the seven provinces under Iraqi control operate independently. Police capabilities in the remaining provinces show improvement that has been enhanced by local militias and concerned citizens joining the fight against al-Qaida. The use of additional local security forces has significantly increased the number of tips, resulting in a 50 percent increase in the number of caches found nationwide and a doubling of caches found in Baghdad. The increased number of tips has also led to the capture or killing of al-Qaida and irreconcilable militia leaders.

Although not yet capable of independent operations, three Air Force flying squadrons are progressing satisfactorily, doubling the amount of cargo and passengers flown since the start of the year. They have also conducted joint infrastructure security operations with the Iraqi Army and energy ministries and recently stood up an Iraqi Air Operations Center.

The growing size of Iraqi Security Forces and the need to increase the manning levels of existing units continues to present the Government of Iraq with force management challenges, particularly in the areas of leaders and logistics. For the present time, Coalition partnership and support remains necessary for most ISF operations. The Coalition is assisting the Government of Iraq as it develops a more mature ISF force structure that is capable of providing institutional sustainment. Again, we should be wary of placing too much strain on this force until we are comfortable it can meet the challenges posed by our determined common enemies in Iraq.

Assessment: Although there is progress in the development and operation of the Iraqi Security Forces, the Government of Iraq has not made satisfactory progress toward increasing the number of Iraqi Security Force units capable of operating independently. Many units have made considerable progress in their ability to conduct combat operations, but the number of units earning Operational Readiness Assessment Level One ratings has not increased as much as desired. However, we should not understate the marked increase in ISF capability to conduct combat operations successfully, including clearing and holding neighborhoods, planning and conducting operations, defending themselves, protecting the population, and responding to contingencies on short notice.

(xvi) Ensuring that the rights of minority political parties in the Iraqi legislature are protected.

Article 37 of the Iraqi Constitution guarantees all Iraqis freedom to form and join associations and political parties. Minorities are guaranteed equal access to and participation in elections for the COR. The COR elected in December 2005 includes representatives from the Shi'a, Sunni, Kurdish, Turkmen, Chaldo-Assyrian Christian, and Yazidi communities. The Rules of Procedure for the COR guarantee the ability of its members to express their opinions, regardless of political party or affiliation, helping to ensure the full participation of all its members, and COR leaders have followed these rules in practice. COR rules permit groups as small as 10 members out of 275 to propose legislation.

The United States Mission is fully engaged with the Iraqi parliament to ensure appreciation for the concern attached by the United States to representation of women and minorities and a role for minority parties.

Assessment: The Government of Iraq has made satisfactory progress toward ensuring that the rights of minority political parties in the Iraqi legislature are protected.

(xvii) Allocating and spending $10 billion in Iraqi revenues for reconstruction projects, including delivery of essential services, on an equitable basis.

While it is too soon to tell by how much budget execution will improve by the end of 2007, there is no doubt that the Government of Iraq is overcoming many of the problems it faced in 2006. Indeed, 2007 capital budget execution is already on par with last year's total level, and the full $10 billion capital budget has been allocated. Given the long-term nature of some capital projects, some of the 2007 capital funds will not be disbursed until later years. The Government of Iraq has also launched its 2008 budget process, which will ensure the progress in 2007 continues to move forward.

Both the central government and the provincial governments are becoming more effective at allocating and spending their capital budgets for reconstruction and the delivery of essential services.[2] The 2007 Iraqi budget represents the first time in modern Iraqi history that provincial governments have been able to formulate and implement their own capital budgets. The Government of Iraq ministries are already exceeding their 2006 levels of budget execution. The ability to allocate and spend a capital budget effectively is a necessary first step for a functioning government to meet the needs of its people. Government of Iraq and provincial officials across the country have shown by their actions that budget execution is, indeed, a focal point as they continue to improve governance and move toward self-reliance.

In 2006, the Government of Iraq spent roughly 22 percent of its $6.2 billion non-provincial capital budget. Lack of technical capacity, security issues, and, in many cases, fear of prosecution for corruption effectively paralyzed much of the Government of Iraq's spending. In 2007, an intense focus and training on budget execution at the highest levels of the Government of Iraq bolstered technical capacity and encouraged action, though capacity constraints persist. As a result, according to Ministry of Finance (MOF) data through mid-July 2007, total Government of Iraq ministries have already spent approximately 24 percent of their 2007 capital budgets.

Ministerial allocation and spending are also moving ahead, with the most successful ministries being key service providers, such as Oil, Electricity, Housing, Municipalities and Public Works, Planning, and Education. These select ministries have all spent at least 21 percent of their 2007 capital budget, with some committing as much as 57 percent. Some ministries remain challenged in the face of capacity constraints and problems associated with lack of security and will continue to be monitored appropriately.

Provincial Reconstruction Team data indicate that provincial governments have committed over 47 percent of their 2007 capital budgets. Provinces also continue to spend their remaining 2006 funds and are estimated by the MOF to have committed 100 percent of these funds, most of which were received in late December 2006.

The province of al-Anbar exemplifies the improvement in provincial budget execution. On June 4, 2007, the Anbar Provincial Council approved its province's capital budget. It then issued a call for tenders, analyzed the bids, and signed the first 17 contracts in a public ceremony on August 13, 2007. Over half of the remaining contracts to spend the rest of the provincial budget are ready for signature, bringing al-Anbar's spending commitments to $25 million as of mid-August.

Assessment: The Government of Iraq is making satisfactory progress in allocating funds to ministries and provinces. The full $10 billion capital budget is allocated, although spending units will not be able to spend all these funds by the end of 2007 given the long-term nature of some capital projects. The Ministry of Planning Development and Cooperation and the

Ministry of Finance have released 30 percent of 2007 budgeted capital funds to Iraqi government ministries, as well as 24 percent of 2007 budgeted capital funds to regions and provinces. Processing of Letters of Credit has improved, benefiting the Ministry of Electricity and other ministries that rely on international procurement. The Ministry of Planning Development and Cooperation is demonstrating leadership on procurement policy and technical assistance.

Despite these efforts and its stronger performance relative to last year, the Government of Iraq is unlikely to spend its entire $10 billion capital budget by the end of 2007. Nevertheless, it should be highlighted that both ministries and provinces are executing a greater percentage of much larger capital budgets, which significantly increases ministry and provincial expenditures on an absolute dollar basis.

(xviii) Ensuring that Iraq's political authorities are not undermining or making false accusations against members of the ISF.

Progress is clearly being made in this area, though the overall effect is difficult to accurately assess. The maturing of the inspectors general system and the continued education of commanders at all levels are positive signs. The Council of Representatives' approval of the Military Justice Law and improvements in the judicial system have helped to institutionalize the rule of law and stand in marked contrast to the legacy of former regime practices.

Sectarian bias is not limited to Shi'a officials, as some Sunni politicians have made baseless claims against ISF officials who are Shi'a. It appears from anecdotal evidence that some Iraqi authorities may not be pursuing some of these allegations. It is difficult to determine whether these accusations result from actual misconduct, inaccurate reporting, or the sectarian-bias of Iraqi political authorities. We continue to challenge the Government of Iraq to investigate each one and take action, as appropriate.

The Prime Minister and his ministerial council are trying to curb this problem. We will push for improvements, although the key to success will be our ability to institutionalize the rule of law in government practices. At the same time we will continue to press Iraqi political leaders to investigate and then confront those who make baseless accusations against ISF leaders for sectarian and political gain.

Assessment: The Government of Iraq has not made satisfactory progress in ensuring that Iraq's political authorities are not undermining or making false accusations against members of the ISF. Though there is weekly evidence of a more determined effort by the Government of Iraq to address these issues and seek resolution, there remains much work to be done in this benchmark. The historical challenge inherent in Iraq, compounded by the damage done by sectarian violence following the Samarra Mosque bombing, remains a challenge that will only be fully solved by education and time

Endnotes

[1] A unit is an Iraqi Army combat battalion or an Iraqi Army combat brigade headquarters or an Iraqi Army combat division headquarters.

[2] To aid interpretation, a terminology guide from Baghdad Cable 2541 follows:

- Government of Iraq "Spending Plan/Budget Allocation": Budgetary authority to a Government of Iraq unit, in accordance with the Budget Law, with sub-allocations defined by the Ministry of Finance (MOF.) This equates to a United States Government "commitment" or an internal reservation of funds for a particular purpose.

- Government of Iraq "Release": Equates to United States Government apportionment; release of funds from MOF (OMB has this responsibility in the United States Government) to a spending unit based on project needs or cash flow. Ministry of Planning and Development Cooperation (MOPDC) reviews and approves the spending unit's request for release, and the MOF confirms consistency with the approved budget allocation and liquidity needs of the spending unit.

- Government of Iraq "Commitment": Equates to a United States Government obligation, i.e.,the spending unit awards a contract or other binding agreement.

- Government of Iraq "Disbursed": Equates to United States Government expenditures or outlays. Two types of expenditures are often used interchangeably: 1) funds disbursed to a non-Government of Iraq entity (e.g., contractor) resulting in a net outlay; and 2) disbursements from one Government of Iraq account to another.

DOCUMENT NO. 3

MEASURING STABILITY AND SECURITY IN IRAQ: THE DEFENSE DEPARTMENT'S REPORT TO CONGRESS IN ACCORDANCE WITH THE DEPARTMENT OF DEFENSE APPROPRIATIONS ACT 2007 (SECTION 9010, PUBLIC LAW 109-289)

Defense Department Report

September 14, 2007

The Department of Defense

Executive Summary

This report to Congress, Measuring Stability and Security in Iraq, *is submitted pursuant to Section 9010 of the Department of Defense Appropriations Act 2007, Public Law 109-289. The report includes specific performance indicators and measures of progress toward political, economic, and security stability in Iraq, as directed in that legislation. This is the ninth in a series of reports on this subject. The most recent report was submitted in June 2007. The report complements other reports and information about Iraq provided to Congress and is not intended as a single source of all information about the combined efforts or the future strategy of the United States, its Coalition partners, or Iraq.*

The strategic goal of the United States in Iraq remains a unified, democratic Iraq that can govern, defend and sustain itself and is an ally in the war on terror. This report measures progress towards, and setbacks from, achieving that goal during the reporting period (June through August 2007). This period saw full implementation of the *New Way Forward* during which all U.S. "surge" brigades and combat enablers became available to operate in Baghdad and surrounding areas. Despite the decision to temporarily increase force levels in Iraq to help the Iraqi government provide security to its population, it remains the policy of the United States and its Coalition partners to transition security responsibility to the Government of Iraq over time.

The final "surge" brigade deployed to Iraq in mid-June and quickly became part of the overall effort to provide increased population security in Baghdad and surrounding areas. Another 4,000 Marines also deployed to Anbar Province. With the full complement of forces available to commanders, offensive operations such as "Operation Phantom Thunder" seized the initiative to disrupt al Qaeda and militias operating in Baghdad and the surrounding "belts." Additionally, with increased force levels, Iraqi and Coalition forces were able to clear and hold tough neighborhoods in Baghdad, with a main effort focused on the East Rashid district. Three additional Iraqi Army brigades have remained in Baghdad to conduct security operations, a marked contrast from efforts in 2006 to improve Baghdad security when a number of Ministry of Defense units proved incapable of sustained deployment. The Iraqi military and police forces also showed their improved capabilities by successfully planning and executing security for the March of the 7th Imam pilgrimage to Baghdad in early August without incident.

As a result of these efforts, there are improvements in measures of security; for example, sectarian killings and civilian casualties have decreased. Other indicators, such as the ability to carry out functions of daily life (shopping in a market, taking children to school), also show some improvement. Since July, statistically significant trends in total attacks have emerged and have been sustained, which reflects a substantial improvement in overall security. Overall, there continues to be a downward trend in total attack incidents with eight of the past 11 weeks since June 15, 2007 showing decreases down to August 2006 levels. Sunni tribal resistance to al Qaeda in Iraq (AQI) in western Iraq continues to complement Coalition efforts to force AQI out of areas it previously dominated. As a result, violence in Anbar continued to decrease markedly during the reporting period, and Iraqi citizens are increasingly providing information about insurgent operations to the Iraqi forces. In addition, the anti-AQI tribal movement has begun to spread beyond Anbar into other provinces to include the outer belts of Baghdad, Baqubah and Salah ad Din. This phenomenon has led to talks between Shi'a and Sunni tribal leaders, creating an opportunity for "bottomup reconciliation." For this reporting period, attacks against mosques such as the Samarra Mosque bombing on June 13 and the Al-Khailani Mosque bombing in Rusafa on June 19 failed to provoke widespread ethnosectarian violence. Such AQI operations are likely to continue.

Political progress is at a critical juncture. The consequences of the Iraqi government's previous indecisiveness and inaction include the loss of confidence by segments of the Iraqi public, and more importantly, the failure to invest in the emerging provincial reconciliation in Anbar and other areas by providing essential services that would secure the support of new groups as they enter the political process. The counterinsurgency operations associated with Operation Phantom Thunder have started to create the security conditions that will allow the Government of Iraq to implement reforms and pursue reconciliation initiatives. However, little political progress and reconciliation at the national level (as expressed in major legislative advances) occurred during this quarter. With the Iraqi parliament adjourning for August recess, followed closely by the Ramadan religious holiday period, key reconciliation legislation such as the Hydrocarbon Law, and progress on Article 140 (Kirkuk) will probably remain stalled in the near term. The recent Iraqi Leaders' Conference resulted in encouraging outcomes including a general agreement on a way forward on de-Ba'athification reform and Provincial Powers legislation, although work remains to be done on the details. Prospects for success in the near term hinge upon the return of key political blocs to the Maliki government. At the local and provincial levels, however, there are more indications of progress as tribal cooperation with the Coalition and the government has allowed numerous governance and economic initiatives to move forward. Provincial Reconstruction Teams (PRTs), operating alongside their military counterparts, are helping to enhance local and provincial administrative capacity.

While security concerns remain the primary obstacle to economic growth, several positive developments have recently emerged during this period. In Sharm El-Sheikh, Egypt on May 3, more than 70 countries and international organizations endorsed the International Compact with Iraq (ICI), under which Iraq committed to comprehensive economic and governance reforms. On July 20, Iraq and the UN submitted their first ICI mid-year progress report, finding that Iraq is making progress on more than two-thirds of its ICI goals. On August 1, the International Monetary Fund (IMF) completed its fifth review of Iraq's performance under the Stand-By Arrangement (SBA), in which most of the Directors praised the GoI's compliance with the SBA under such trying conditions, while at the same time voicing concerns about the lack of data provided by the Kurdish region. Additionally, the Central Bank of Iraq's tight monetary policy continued to largely mitigate the acceleration of the rate of inflation, though IMF staff recognizes that monetary tightening plays only a limited role in affecting inflation outcomes. The Department of Defense continued to help the GoI revitalize certain state-owned enterprises to increase employment and make them more attractive for privatization. Oil production, the principal economic driver in Iraq, remained at about the same levels as the last quarter due to poor infrastructure and inadequate security, though Iraq is projected to exceed its targeted revenues for the year. Additional efforts will be needed to build the capacity of Iraqi ministries and provinces to execute their capital investment budgets, particularly for the oil sector. There was some progress made in improving state-provided electricity, with Iraq's electricity plants reaching a record of 5,423 megawatts (MW) of peak power on August 21, in addition to 32 other days of power production over 5,000 MW since June 1.

As for the status of Iraqi security forces, this period saw further improvement in the maturation of the Army and, to a lesser degree, the police. The United States, its Coalition partners and the Iraqi government continued to expand the size and capability of the Iraqi forces to meet emerging requirements. As of September 3, 2007, approximately 359,600 Iraqi personnel had received U.S.-funded training and equipment against a current train-and-equip authorization of 390,000. Given the persistence of violence by insurgents, terrorists and militias, the Iraqi forces will require additional force structure, continued training, seasoning and equipment to be able to assume missions from Coalition forces. Several factors will continue to hinder the development of a unified, nonsectarian force capable of independently providing security for the nation. Some of the areas being addressed to increase Iraqi force capabilities include the creation of additional units under PM Maliki's expansion plan, reform of the Ministry of Interior (MoI) forces, development of Ministry of Defense (MoD) and MoI logistics and administrative capabilities, development of combat enablers for the military forces, and development of junior leaders. However, Shi'a militia control over significant portions of southern Iraq and Baghdad competes with legitimate Iraqi forces for popular trust, and in some cases, causes increases in sectarian behavior by these security forces.

In summary, additional forces needed to implement the *New Way Forward* arrived in Iraq during this reporting period and the surge has, since mid-June, placed greater numbers of Coalition and Iraqi Security Forces that are focused on securing the population into areas of Iraq that had been without sufficient security force presence. Through synchronized operations, Coalition and Iraqi forces have established tactical and operational momentum, and are having a significant impact on the overall security situation. In cooperation with tribal leaders, progress is being made against AQI and Shi'a militias. New initiatives, such as enhanced PRTs embedded with Brigade Combat Teams, have begun to make progress at the local level, but challenges remain at the national level. The outcomes from securing the population and advancing the legislative agenda still depend, to a great degree, on the ability of the Iraqi government to promote an environment of reconciliation and trust.

Section 1—Stability and Security

1.1 Political Stability

During this reporting period, Iraqi political leaders made little progress on critical issues such as revising the Iraqi constitution and on key legislation intended to promote national reconciliation. The *New Way Forward* that President Bush announced in January 2007 puts greater emphasis on the diplomatic, political, and economic steps to be pursued along with security operations to bring about stability and security in Iraq. The focus remains on intensified efforts to protect the population and secure turbulent areas to give Iraqis political space to implement reforms and pursue reconciliation. These efforts are not intended to substitute for increased Iraqi responsibility for managing its affairs, but to support its ability to do so. National polls show that most Iraqis continue to believe that Iraq should remain a unified state; only one third[1] of Iraqi people say that they would be better off if the country were divided into three or more regions that better reflected ethnic or sectarian populations, and those who most strongly oppose division are found in the regions of greatest sectarian mixing. Those areas with the strongest sectarian homogeneity (northern and southern Iraq) are most interested in division. Continued violence, however, reinforces sectarian tensions that undermine reconciliation. Moreover, Iraqi political leaders remain wedded to their constituencies and are increasingly uncertain about expending political capital on the necessary compromises to foster reconciliation. Iraqi political divisions were further complicated in July by the withdrawal of the Sunni Tawafuq bloc's ministers and parliamentarians from the Iraqi government. Locally generated accommodations and limited immunity are creating the most positive options for bridging sectarian lines, as national leaders are only now beginning to realize the potential these offer towards political stability on a larger scale. However, in the short term, Iraqi political leaders will likely be less concerned about reconciliation than with consolidating power and posturing for a future power struggle.

National Reconciliation

National reconciliation is an essential element for long-term stability in a representative Iraq. Despite security improvements during this reporting period, political reconciliation has shown little progress. Major impediments include a developing political system and inherent distrust due to Saddam's rule; this is a continuing challenge to political leaders as they consider reconciliation options. To advance reconciliation, the U.S. Government is working with the Government of Iraq to promote both "top-down" as well as "bottom-up" efforts. "Top-down" efforts focus on passage of key legislation intended to foster reconciliation, and establishment of the Iraqi Follow-on Committee for National Reconciliation to focus on reconciliation policy, but little progress has occurred overall on top-down reconciliation this quarter. "Bottom-up" reconciliation efforts include the expanded Provincial Reconstruction Team efforts to promote local and provincial capacity development and near-term economic initiatives. A central focus is to transcend regional, sectarian, and tribal divisions by bringing reconcilable elements into a process of accommodation and by isolating irreconcilable groups. Iraq's major sectarian groups are making some effort to overcome divisions. For example, the response to the June 13, 2007 bombing of the al-Askari Mosque in Samarra included unified statements from various leaders condemning the act and calling for calm. Despite these efforts for national reconciliation, non-Muslim minorities such as Christians and Yezidis are especially vulnerable in Iraq's current violent climate, causing some to flee to neighboring countries.

Political Commitments

The consensus nature of Iraqi politics, the checks and balances built into the system of Iraqi governance, and the zero-sum mentality of Iraqi political leaders has hindered, and at times prevented, progress on key legislation. The Council of Representatives (CoR) continues to miss Iraqi constitutional and legislative deadlines. As of this reporting period, the Presidency Council and the Prime Minister have not achieved consensus on key controversial issues, but negotiations continue. Iraq's Council of Representatives—which had previously planned a two-month recess—voted on July 8 to extend the term through July 31 and for working sessions to last six days a week from July 16 through July 31. The subsequent resignation of six Sunni ministers from the Tawafuq bloc and the Iraqi National list bloc has complicated efforts to reach consensus among Iraq's three major ethno-religious groups on key issues. The August 26, 2007 Leaders' Conference among the top Shi'a, Sunni and Kurdish leaders produced an encouraging outcome. The participants issued a communiqué that contained Prime Minister Maliki's agreement to consult more with Sunni and Kurdish leaders; a general agreement on a way forward on de-Ba'athification reform and Provincial Powers legislation; and acknowledgment of the importance of the presence of the Multinational Forces. The CoR will begin a new session in early September to attempt to work toward accommodation on important legislation, although little further progress is expected during the mid-September through mid-October Ramadan season. Key legislation includes:

A Package of Hydrocarbon Laws. This package is intended to enable all Iraqis to benefit from the nation's petroleum resources and to attract investment to the oil sector. A basic framework law and three supporting implementing laws are required to manage revenues, to re-organize the Oil Ministry, and to establish an Iraq National Oil Company. In practice, the GoI is already providing much of the hydrocarbon revenue to the citizens of Iraq through ministry and provincial programs. While the distribution of the revenues has been uneven, it nonetheless demonstrates that, absent formal legislation, the positive effects sought in the national legislation are being achieved. The Council of Ministers (CoM) approved the Hydrocarbon

Framework Law on July 2, 2007, and submitted it to the Council of Representatives, but without Tawafuq approval. The GoI and the Kurdistan Regional Government (KRG) have continued to debate the latest draft of the Framework Law; the Kurds maintain that the draft that emerged from the CoR in July has undergone substantive changes from the Shura Council document agreed to in February. The Chair of the CoR's Oil and Gas Committee said on July 8 that there would not be a first reading of the draft in the legislature until the Kurds and Shi'a agree on a draft. The Shi'a coalition in the parliament and the KRG have reached an agreement on the final text for the Revenue Management Law, which must now be approved by the CoM. The parties continue to negotiate. Meanwhile, on August 6, the KRG parliament unanimously approved an autonomous region's oil law, signaling that the Kurds are moving forward with their own petroleum policy as Iraq's federal oil plans lag.

A De-Ba'athification Law. De-Ba'athification reform remains politically sensitive as it involves competing conceptions of justice, accountability, reconciliation, and economic compensation. Although Prime Minister Maliki and President Talabani signed a cover letter in March 2007 affirming political support for a draft de-Ba'athification law, reaching consensus and compromise is proving difficult. Shi'a parties believe, for example, that the current package contains inadequate compensation for Shi'a victims of Ba'athism. The Council of Ministers recently approved a draft law incorporating the ideas of both Vice Presidents and supported by the Prime Minister. That draft is currently in the State Council for review. Passage of the new draft could take time because compromise will still be necessary, and a law that is not broadly supported would adversely affect prospects for reconciliation. The recent Iraqi Leaders' Conference included a way forward on de-Ba'athification reform although work remains to be done on the details. It is too early to tell if this agreement will lead to the speedy enactment of this important law. Despite the delay in enactment of national de-Ba'athification legislation, there is still a significant amount of outreach to Sunnis, and this outreach had led to increased volunteerism on the part of the Sunni community to fight al Qaeda in Iraq (AQI), to serve under the democratically elected central government, and to provide former government officials pensions. While these efforts would have been better executed under formal de-Ba'athification legislation, these local efforts create a similar effect.

A Constitutional Review. Iraq's Constitutional Review Committee (CRC) began work on November 15, 2006 on recommendations for amendments to the Constitution. On May 23, 2007, the CRC described the elements of a "semi-final" report to the CoR that spells out the nature of the committee's work and outstanding issues, and requested an extension for its final report, given that it missed its May 15 deadline. On June 23, 2007, the CoR voted to extend the deadline to the end of September. The outstanding issues reflect longstanding political disagreements among the CoR's political blocs on Presidential powers, the powers of the regions versus the central government, and the status of disputed territories including Kirkuk under Article 140 of the Constitution. Progress on Article 140 has not occurred as normalization—the compensation of Arabs willing to leave Kirkuk and the adjustment of provincial boundaries changed under the Saddam regime—is proceeding slowly, with the first group of Arab families resettled in June. There has been no progress on the constitutionally required census and referendum. The Kurds continue to push for reinvigoration of the stalled process but the Sunni Arabs and Turkomen continue to boycott the city council and object to unilateral Kurdish actions to control local governance and security.

Provincial Election and Powers Laws. Drafting a law that sets the date for provincial and local elections has been delayed until the September 2007 legislative session. Although Prime Minister Maliki has stated that Provincial Iraqi elections will be held in 2007, it is now unlikely that they will occur until at least March 2008. As of this reporting period, candidate lists for Governorate Electoral Officer for nine of the eighteen Governorates had been submitted to the CoR and forwarded to the Independent High Electoral Commission (IHEC). Prime Minister Maliki's office continues to work on a Provincial Election Law but has yet to release a draft. The U.S. Embassy continued engagement efforts to advance this issue. The IHEC, which was established on April 28, 2007, continues to focus on resolving logistical and security issues. The IHEC has agreed to purchase the Public Distribution System database from the Ministry of Trade used for nationwide food rationing and will convert these data to a voter registration database, a key prerequisite for provincial elections. In cooperation with the United Nations (UN), the U.S. Government is providing program support to the new IHEC in three areas: building staff capacity, particularly in public outreach and internal organization; building database capacity that will support new registration; and establishing provincial, district, and precinct-level election bodies. A Provincial Powers Law that defines the relationship between provincial governments and the central government has been read twice in the CoR. This law is not required for local or provincial elections, although the GoI reportedly intends to implement it before provincial elections are held. The recent Iraqi Leaders' Conference resulted in agreement on pressing ahead with Provincial Powers legislation but details have yet to be worked out. The lack of a budget for elections as well as the large number of internally displaced persons—about two million—complicates the holding of elections.

Government Reform

During this quarter, the U.S. Government continued to expand efforts to assist Iraqi governmental reform through development of ministerial capacity and through engagement by Provincial Reconstruction Teams (PRTs) with provincial and local governments to build capacity, energy infrastructure integrity, rule of law, and counter-corruption efforts. These efforts aim to help the GoI build strong democratic institutions that impartially serve all Iraqis, foster conditions for national reconciliation, and transcend regional, sectarian and tribal divisions.

Ministerial Capacity Development Iraqi ministries responsible for delivery of basic services require significant improvement in their ability to fund, manage and implement projects. This will require additional assistance to build ministerial capacity through efforts of advisors and trainers. These efforts are supported by the State Department's Iraq Transition Assistance Office (ITAO) and the U.S. Agency for International Development's (USAID's) National Capacity Development program, which trains Iraqi civil servants in modern management and places advisors in key ministries to provide technical assistance to improve day-to-day operations. USAID's three-year, US$165 million program supports multiple training programs in project management, leadership skills, procurement, English, and budgeting and budget process management. US$65 million has been obligated to date.

Provincial Reconstruction Teams (PRTs) PRTs are a mainstay of decentralized U.S. efforts to build the capacity of Iraq's local, municipal, and provincial governments to deliver goods and services to the Iraqi people. The establishment of ten new Embedded PRTs (ePRTs), which represents the civilian side of the "surge," is a key component of the President's *New Way Forward*. The ePRTs are now partnered with Brigade and Regimental Combat Teams and are engaging local Iraqi leaders in government, business, and civil society. As the first ePRT personnel deployed less than five months ago, it is too soon to assess their overall impact.[2] Early reports are encouraging; PRTs played a significant and positive role in the reopening of a granary in Baqubah, increasing the local employment opportunities and the availability of food.

The Ninewa PRT helped establish the Mosul branch of the Central Criminal Court of Iraq (CCCI) to adjudicate terrorism cases. Since the Court opened, 173 cases have been tried, resulting in 96 convictions and 77 acquittals. The Baghdad PRT assisted the Provincial Reconstruction Development Committee to approve 68 infrastructure projects worth US$110M. As of July 2007, 42 projects valued at US$81M have been awarded for the construction. The Anbar PRT helped reconnect broken lines of communication between the central Iraqi government in Baghdad and the Anbar provincial government. The Governor is now able to directly advocate for the needs of his province with the Prime Minister, cabinet ministers, and executive branch leaders. Multi-National Corps-Iraq (MNC-I) has requested four new ePRTs for the Baghdad area and another one for Wasit Province, indicating the importance that military commanders place on having additional interagency support to complement security operations.

Rule of Law During this reporting period, Coalition and Iraqi efforts to build the judiciary showed considerable improvement. The Law and Order Task Force (LAOTF) established by Multi-National Force-Iraq (MNF-I), drawing on support from the Department of Justice (DoJ) and the Department of State (DoS), is assisting the efforts to develop Iraqi capacity for independent, evidence-based, and transparent investigation and trial of terrorism and other major crimes in the CCCI.[3] The Rule of Law Complex (ROLC) that the GoI and MNF-I established in Baghdad earlier this year became fully operational during this reporting period and is now conducting trials. Iraqi judges have generally been professional, reliable, nonsectarian partners in the effort to return the rule of law to Iraq and are favorably viewed by most Iraqis. However, 31 of Iraq's approximately 1,100 judges have been assassinated during the last three years, contributing to low rates of prosecution of terrorist-related cases. The United States continues to support efforts to work with the Higher Juridical Council (HJC) on programs to address the growing problems associated with local intimidation of the Iraqi judiciary. Since the last report, the HJC has begun directing Judicial Review Teams (JRTs) on its own initiative, frequently without Coalition logistic or security support, to overcrowded detention facilities in and around Baghdad. In addition, Coalition advisors are assisting in the establishment of Major Crimes Courts (MCC), modeled on the CCCI concept in several provinces such as in Hillah and Basrah, to assist in prosecution of local cases with permanently assigned judges who hear cases. Another MCC in Mosul is staffed by "circuit riders" from CCCI Baghdad who visit Mosul periodically to hear cases. Since its establishment in December 2006, four panels have tried approximately 200 cases resulting in almost 100 convictions including 20 death sentences and over 30 life sentences. In July 2007, the fifth panel of judges visited Mosul. In addition, MCCs in Tikrit, Kirkuk and Kirkush are being established and should begin hearing cases this year.

Recent improvements in the security situation in Anbar Province appear to be helping to reinvigorate its criminal justice system. Since the last report, Anbar Investigative Judges have resumed reviewing criminal cases. In addition, a JRT visited Fallujah in June to review cases and ordered 259 detainees to remain in detention pending additional investigation, referring another six cases to trial. Planning continues to identify an appropriate location for a newly authorized Anbar MCC to convene trials in August.

Infrastructure Integrity The Energy Fusion Cell (EFC) is attempting to facilitate coordination among Iraqi ministries to improve the protection of Iraq's critical infrastructure, which is important to increasing the supply of essential services such as electricity. Participation by the key Iraqi ministries remains inconsistent.

Counter-Corruption Efforts U.S. advisors continued to work with the World Bank and other international institutions to support Iraq's Commission on Public Integrity (CPI), Board of Supreme Audit (BSA), and the Inspectors General (IGs) within the government ministries. On May 16, 2007 Prime Minister Maliki, representatives of the Council of Ministers, the High Court, the BSA, the CPI, and the IGs signed a charter for a new GoI council to advise the Prime Minister on ways to promote the rule of law and fight corruption. The charter is a commitment by the GoI to increase intra-Iraqi government cooperation in fighting corruption. In addition, on July 19, the Council of Ministers ratified the 2004 UN Convention Against Corruption.

Transnational Issues

During this reporting period, the United States continued to encourage support for Iraq by its neighbors, the region, and the international community. The primary concern is ensuring the territorial integrity of Iraq and eliminating negative Iranian and Syrian activity in Iraq. Efforts to build on the success of the May 3–4, 2007 meetings that Egypt hosted for the International Compact with Iraq and the Iraq Neighbors Ministerial, such as working group meetings among countries in the region on energy and refugee issues, show some progress. Iran and Syria, however, continued to support lethal and unlawful activities in Iraq during this reporting period.

Neighbors Conference Follow-up Building on the momentum established by the May Neighbors Conference, regional working groups formed at the conference have begun their activities. Turkey hosted the Energy Working Group June 28–29, 2007. Jordan hosted the Refugee Working Group on July 26, 2007 to expand assistance to the estimated two million Iraqi refugees in the region and announced that Iraqi refugee children would be admitted to Jordanian public schools regardless of the residency status of their parents. At a related conference on Iraqi Refugee Health held in Damascus July 29–30, Jordan and Syria reaffirmed their commitment to providing primary and emergency health care to Iraqi refugees in their countries. Syria hosted a Border Security Working Group in Damascus on August 8–9, 2007 and granted observer status to all P5 members (Five permanent members of the UN Security Council). Saudi Arabia's recent announcement that it will assess whether to reopen its Embassy in Baghdad could complement progress in Neighbors Conference follow-up activity.

International Compact with Iraq Since the International Compact with Iraq (ICI) was launched on May 3, 2007, a Secretariat for monitoring progress on some 400 follow-up actions under the ICI has been established. The director of the ICI Secretariat has created a database to track the status of these actions.[4] The World Bank is providing technical assistance to set up the database, and donor nations have been instructed to provide inputs about how their programs support the ICI action items. On July 20, the first progress report was presented at the UN, finding that Iraq is making progress with more than two-thirds of its ICI goals. Representatives of more than 70 countries participated in the review session; many reconfirmed their assistance or debt relief commitments.

Iranian Influence There has been no decrease in Iranian training and funding of illegal Shi'a militias in Iraq that attack Iraqi and Coalition forces and civilians. Of particular concern are the assassinations of the Governors of Qadisiyah and Muthanna Provinces during August 2007 in improvised explosive device attacks believed to have been conducted by Iranian-influenced extremist groups. Tehran's support for these groups is one of the greatest impediments to progress on reconciliation. In meetings hosted by Prime Minister Maliki, the United States and Iran have held three rounds of talks on Iraq security since May 2007. On July 24, Ambassador Crocker met with his Iranian counterpart for trilateral security talks to discuss how the United States and Iran can help Iraq to improve conditions in the country, particularly security conditions. The U.S. delegation emphasized a number of specific concerns about Iranian behavior in Iraq, including its provision of weapons, funding, training, and guidance to militias that are fighting both the Iraqi and Coalition forces and killing innocent Iraqi civilians. Most of the explosives and ammunition used by these groups are provided by the Iranian Islamic Revolutionary Guard Corps-Qods Force (IRGC-QF). The recent National Intelligence Estimate on Iraq notes that Iran has been "intensifying aspects of its lethal support for select Shi'a militants" since at least the beginning of 2006 and notes that explosively formed penetrator (EFP) attacks have risen dramatically. For the period of June through the end of August, EFP events are projected to rise by 39% over the period of March through May. Ambassador Crocker made clear that IRGC-QF's lethal activities need to cease, and that Iraq and the Coalition would be looking for results. A security subcommittee subsequently met on August 6, 2007 in Baghdad as part of an ongoing effort to change Iranian behavior. To improve diplomatic relations between Iran and Iraq, Prime Minister Maliki made his second official visit to Iran in August to meet with Iranian leadership.

Syrian Influence Terrorists and foreign fighters continue to find sanctuary, border transit opportunities, and logistical support in Syria. Syria has not made sufficient efforts to combat cross-border terrorist movements; it focuses on arresting only Iraq-bound terrorists who pose a threat to Syrian interests. Approximately 90% of suicide bombers in Iraq are foreign fighters, and most continue to use Syria as their main transit route to Iraq. This network funnels about 50 to 80 suicide bombers per month into Iraq to conduct operations. Since January, there have been nearly 280 suicide attacks, accounting for nearly 5,500 deaths, mostly of innocent Iraqi civilians. Additionally, Syria continues to serve as an organizational and coordination hub for elements of the former Iraqi regime.

Tensions on the Border with Turkey Turkey's primary concerns regarding Iraq continue to be terrorism conducted by the Kurdistan Peoples Congress (KGK, formerly Kurdistan Worker's Party (PKK)) from camps in northern Iraq, increased Kurdish autonomy from the Iraqi central government, and the final status of the oil-rich city of Kirkuk. While tension rose prior to Turkey's July 22 parliamentary election, the Iraqi-Turkish relationship is marked by continued, albeit sporadic, diplomatic efforts. In August, Prime Minister Maliki accepted an invitation from Turkish Prime Minister Erdogan to visit Turkey. During the visit, Maliki and Erdogan signed a Memorandum of Understanding (MOU) to end the presence of the KGK in Iraq and Maliki declared the KGK a terrorist organization for the first time. Turkey has also hosted the Neighbors Conference working group on energy, and participates in the border security and refugee working groups.

Conclusion

Improved security and stability is not enough to win the counterinsurgency. Political progress must also be achieved to reinforce and complement progress in securing the Iraqi population. There has been little national-level political progress in passing key legislation and implementing government reform. Efforts within Iraq's political process to seek consensus remain complicated by continued sectarian divisions and violence that exacerbates those divisions. The most promising developments are occurring at the local level through "bottom-up" reconciliation involving the development of local leaders and local governance capacity. Efforts to build regional and international support for the re-integration of Iraq into the region and world economy will require continued focus.

1.2 Economic Activity

Some positive economic developments continued during this reporting period, most notably improvements in budget execution by the central government, some provinces, and the successful review by the International Monetary Fund (IMF) of Iraq's Stand-By Arrangement (SBA). These improvements are not yet translating into broadly measurable improved living conditions. Oil production, which generates almost all of the government's budgetary revenues, remained constant at about two million barrels per day. The budget execution rates for Iraq's US$10 billion 2007 budget, mainly for capital investments in infrastructure to improve essential services, have sharply improved over 2006 and are expected to significantly surpass 2006 results by the year's end. Even if the full amount is obligated, spending units will not likely execute all of these funds by the end of 2007. Lack of oil investment and security remain the primary obstacles to economic growth. Fundamental structural problems remain to be rectified to enable sustained progress, and the GoI will have to maintain and accelerate its economic reform program, build a strong private sector, and attract greater foreign investment to achieve long-term economic stability.

Budget Execution

To support economic growth and improve delivery of essential services, the GoI will need to make significant investments in the oil sector, public works, and agriculture. The government ministries' ability to spend their investment budgets is a key determinant of whether all Iraqis receive essential services. The GoI's ability to execute its capital investment budgets remains hindered by lack of capacity in contracting, timely release of funding, and convoluted guidance in execution instructions, but the overall trend continues to be positive. Recently available data indicate that, by the inclusion of Iraqi-funded U.S. Foreign Military Sales (FMS) cases and the Accelerated Reconstruction and Development Fund, the Iraqi government executed 78% of its total budget in 2006. In 2006, although it effectively paid salaries, wages and pensions, the government executed only 22% of its non-provincial capital investment budget and only 3% of its oil sector investment budget. Most provinces are making significant progress in committing capital spending, with an average commitment rate of 47% through August, but those with security challenges still lag.

Full implementation of the Iraqi Financial Management Information System (FMIS), which is designed to provide real-time data and improve the GoI's budgetary management and transparency, had been previously projected for the end of 2008. Suspension of U.S. support for FMIS in reaction to the GoI's passive rejection of the program will delay implementation, and the GoI will return to manual bookkeeping.

In the previous quarter, the U.S. Government discussed with the GoI using Section 607 of the Foreign Assistance Act of 1961, as amended, to furnish commodities and services (such as infrastructure construction for the ministries or fuels for importation into Iraq) using GoI funds. The GoI does not, however, intend to enter into a Section 607 agreement at this time, citing the need to develop GoI capability to execute these functions without relying on USG contracting assistance.

IMF Stand-By Arrangement and Debt Relief

The IMF extended Iraq's Stand-By Arrangement (SBA) to December 2007 during a review concluded by the IMF Executive Board on August 1, 2007. The GoI continued to reform subsidies in line with its commitments under the SBA, and most of the Directors praised the GoI's compliance with the SBA under such trying conditions, while voicing concerns about the lack of data provision from the Kurdish region. On July 1, 2007, the Ministry of Oil implemented fuel price increases for regular gasoline, blended gasoline, and diesel. The regulated price of regular gasoline in Iraq increased from about 300 dinars (~US$0.23) to 400 dinars per liter, while premium gasoline increased from 400 dinars to about 450 dinars (~US$0.35) per liter. Iraq must maintain continuous coverage and satisfactory performance under this and successor SBAs with the IMF to qualify for relief from the final 20% tranche of debt relief at the end of 2008. Iraq has already earned two 30% tranches of debt relief under its agreement with the Paris Club for a total of 80% in debt reduction. Iraq's debt reduction agreements with non-Paris Club members are patterned on Paris Club terms. The previous regime incurred an estimated US$115 billion in foreign official liabilities, of which about US$43 billion and US$72 billion were owed to Paris Club and non-Paris Club countries, respectively. The only Paris Club member that has not reached a bilateral debt deal with Iraq is Russia, which holds about US$6 billion in Iraqi debt. Nine non-Paris Club members have agreed to reduce Iraq's liabilities totaling about US$4 billion. The bulk of the remaining debt is owed to Iraq's Arabian Gulf neighbors.

Indicators of Economic Activity

Economic Growth For 2007, the IMF projects that the overall economy will grow by 6.3% and that the non-oil sectors will grow by approximately 5%. If low oil production or export prices prevent Iraq from meeting its growth and revenue targets, the government will have less ability to implement its planned investment program for essential services.

Inflation Year-to-date inflation as of June 2007 is 8.5%, compared to year-to-date inflation through June 2006 of 22.5% and 5.7% in 2005. Year-to-date core inflation is 4.6%, and excluding fuel and transportation, Iraqi prices declined in June. But overall inflation increased if fuel and transport prices are included. Official fuel prices rose by 22.1% in June as part of the government's policy to reduce subsidies in compliance with the SBA. The Central Bank of Iraq remains committed to containing inflation in 2007.

Unemployment Updated unemployment and underemployment rates were not available during this reporting period. The Iraqi government's Central Organization for Statistics and Information Technology (COSIT) official estimates of unemployment and underemployment remain at 17.6% and 38.1%, respectively. The USG continues to assist the Maliki government in creating permanent, sustainable jobs. In order to help reduce poverty, promote small business development, address high rates of unemployment, and stabilize Baghdad neighborhoods, the Prime Minister approved a US$30 million Rafidain Bank loan to the Ministry of Labor and Social Affairs (MOLSA) for a pilot micro-credit program providing businesses loans up to US$8,000. Eligible recipients are college graduates, returnee families, the disabled and war-damaged business owners. The program has approved US$965,000 for 185 applications, but funds have not yet been disbursed.

The DoD Task Force to Improve Business and Stability Operations (TF-BSO) continues its work with the Government of Iraq (GoI) and U.S. Government agencies to increase re-employment of Iraqis. The TFBSO estimates that during the last quarter, at least six factories were restarted or significantly aided due to TF-BSO efforts. Additional contracting actions with Iraqi factories are in process. During this reporting period, the TF-BSO has been heavily focused on executing its US$50 million program to restart factories in close coordination with U.S. military commanders in Iraq and the GoI. Outcomes during this reporting period ranged from contracts inside Iraq for items as diverse as Iraqi-made sheep dip tanks and armored buses, to orders for export from Iraq for items ranging from hand-made carpets to clothing made for, and competitive in, the international marketplace. TF-BSO's collaboration with the Joint Contracting Command-Iraq/Afghanistan (JCC-I/A) to promote an "Iraqi First" approach to contracting continues to bear fruit and also contributed to increased employment of Iraqis. During the first three quarters of FY07, DoD contracts awarded to Iraqi firms increased from US$99.2 million as of October 2006 to US$191.3 million by the end of June 2007.

Integration into the Global Economy Integration into the global economy is important to the long-term success of Iraq and for developing a more diversified economic base. Finalizing implementation regulations for the Foreign Investment Law passed in 2006 could improve the prospects for attracting investment and reducing unemployment. The National Investment Commission, which began to form in February 2007, will focus on fully implementing the Foreign Direct Investment legislation and has responsibility for designing implementing regulations. A Chair of the National Investment Commission has been nominated, which is a positive step toward implementing the recently passed National Investment Law. The Iraqi delegation to the WTO Working Party meeting in Geneva held productive bilateral meetings on May 25, 2007, with U.S., Arab, and European delegations. Iraq's Trade Minister participated in the sessions that were considered a successful start to the WTO accession process. The next Working Party meeting could take place in early 2008.

Oil Infrastructure Integrity

Aging infrastructure, attacks on pipelines in central and northern Iraq, and poor maintenance continue to impede near-term increases in oil production and exports. Crude oil production for the May–July 2007 quarter averaged 2.06 million barrels per day (mbbl/d) compared with 2.22 mbbl/d in the same period in 2006. Crude oil exports increased to 1.58 mbbl/d, short of the GoI's goal of 1.7 mbbl/d, though higher oil prices are projected to overcome this shortfall to meet planned government budget revenue targets. Revenues will, however, be hindered by the shutdown of crude exports through Turkey for most of this year to date due to numerous interdictions.

Iraq continues to experience critically low levels of refined product because of scarce refining capacity, inadequate security for crude pipelines and for trucks that deliver refined fuels, and under-funding of imports. Refineries suffer from antiquated equipment, limited maintenance, lack of manpower, spare parts shortages, irregular electricity supplies, inadequate storage, poor distribution practices, absence of an efficient private-sector mechanism to supply imported refined fuels, and criminal infiltration and theft. Six companies have been licensed by the Ministry of Oil (MoO) under the Fuel Import Liberalization Law (FILL) to import fuel products into the Kurdistan region. This is an initial step toward the implementation of the law, which was passed in October 2006. Gray-and black-market trade in fuels continues to deny the GoI a significant portion of revenue and contributes to the shortfalls in fuel allocations that ministries rely upon to operate vehicles, generators, and other equipment. USG-funded hardening projects intended to secure both the Bayji Oil Refinery and the supporting infrastructure have begun. Iraqi and Coalition forces, through Operation Honest Hands, have recently implemented new security and loading measures at the refinery to reduce theft and corruption.

The Iraqi government intends to triple oil production by 2015, and indications that the legislature is making progress, although slowly, on the hydrocarbon legislation have prompted increased interest by foreign oil companies in Iraq's oil reserves. Russia and China have expressed interest in reviving their previous Saddam-era oil contracts, and the Czech Republic has recently signed a contract with the MoO to supply equipment for the country's oil refineries. This equipment, if delivered, would assist in the production of an additional 70,000 barrels of refined fuels daily.[5]

Essential Services

The Iraqi government's improvements in budget execution have not yet translated into improved delivery of essential services such as electricity, water, and healthcare. With the USG's Iraq Relief and Reconstruction

Fund (IRRF) now 96% obligated, Iraq must fund most reconstruction requirements.

Electricity Infrastructure Integrity Peak state-provided electricity output has not increased since the last reporting period. Production for June through August 2007 averaged 4,928 megawatts (MW), almost equal to production rates for the same period in 2006 and 55% of the estimated average peak demand of 8,881 MW. Power production continues to be hampered by the inability of the Ministry of Electricity's repair teams to repair the frequently attacked 400 kV transmission grid, continued degradation of legacy power generation stations, severe shortage of proper fuels for power generation units, inadequate security, and ineffective operations and maintenance practices across the generation and transmission infrastructure. Although the Ministry of Electricity (MoE) has produced over 5,000 MW of daily peak power for a third of the days during the past three months, overall state production of MW hours for this reporting period has remained similar to last year. During this same period, Iraqi consumers have continued to demand more electricity by purchasing increasing numbers of air conditioners, refrigerators, satellite TV's and other electrical appliances and equipment. Because state-provided electricity is not subject to market pricing, consumers have little incentive to economize use of appliances. To meet ever-increasing demand, at least 2,000 MW are provided off-grid by private owners of small generators.

Image: Oil Production, June 2006–August 2007 [Omitted]

The shortfall between state-produced electricity supply and consumer demand is aggravated by the use of suboptimal fuels, which keeps approximately 1,000 MW off the grid. As a result, government-produced electricity averaged 12.8 hours per day over the reporting period (April though June 2007) and 12.4 hours per day for the month of August, the last full month for which data is available. The quarterly average exceeded the target goal of 12 hours per day nationwide. Baghdad, however, averaged only 7.9 hours of power per day this quarter and 9.2 hours during August, with most households receiving substantially less than average amounts of power. This fell short of the goal of 12 hours, due largely to interdiction of high-voltage transmission lines, lack of rapid repair capability, and limited state-owned electrical generation capacity in the Baghdad area. In addition, the central government's failure to enforce the MoE's electricity distribution allocations on provincial authorities has resulted in multiple network black-outs, significant system degradations, and a shortchanging of power to Baghdad.

Image: Electricity Supply and Demand [Omitted]

Water and Sewer As of July 1, 2007, IRRF-funded projects have added or restored 1.7 million cubic meters per day of potable water treatment capacity, which is sufficient to serve about 5.9 million Iraqis. The end-state goal for U.S.-funded projects is to add or restore 2.37 million cubic meters per day of treatment capacity to produce potable water, which is sufficient to serve 8.4 million Iraqis. As of July 1, 2007, IRRF-funded projects have added or restored 1.2 million cubic meters per day of sewage treatment capacity, which is sufficient to serve around 5.2 million Iraqis. During this quarter, Baghdad experienced one of the worst water shortages in years because of insufficient power to pumping stations and water treatment plants and attacks on infrastructure. While Shi'a areas are often affected by water shortages, the problems this year are also cutting supplies to some Sunni neighborhoods that are normally not affected. Only one sewage project remains to be finished, the Fallujah sewer project, which will serve an additional 200,000 Iraqis. Poor security conditions have caused delays in completion of the Sadr City R3 water treatment plant, Sinjar water supply project, and Balad Ruz water supply project. The poor security environment and lack of payment by the Iraqi Government of legacy Development Fund for Iraq (DFI)-funded contracts initiated in 2003 and 2004 continue to hinder completion of the Fallujah sewage project. Poor contractor performance and cost increases of equipment for the Mosul Dam enhanced grouting program have contributed to a one-year delay in its completion. The US$270 million Nassariyah water supply project, which is substantially complete and ready for turnover to the Ministry of Municipal and Public Works (MMPW), currently lacks sufficient qualified staff to operate and maintain the treatment plant. It will likely operate on only one shift per day until the remaining 60 of 120 needed employees can be hired and trained. The USG is providing Operations and Maintenance (O&M) support for IRRF-funded essential service projects while GoI officials receive training to ensure project sustainability.

Image: Average Daily Hours of Electricity Power per Province, Aug 2007 [Omitted]

Healthcare The United States has completed construction of 69 of 142 planned Primary Healthcare Centers (PHCs), and 51 have been turned over to the Ministry of Health (MoH) with 21 currently open to the public. The PHC program is expected to be completed by January 2008 and remaining IRRF-funded hospital rehabilitation projects are scheduled for completion by February 2008. Almost all of the US$816 million in IRRF available for projects in the healthcare sector has been obligated.

Food and Agriculture On June 24, 2007, USAID officially kicked off the Iraqi National Markets and Agribusiness (INMA) program in Baghdad. INMA (meaning "growth" in Arabic) is a comprehensive three-year program (with two option years) to promote economic diversification and job creation with an emphasis on the growth of the agriculture and agri-business sectors in the provincial and sub-provincial economies. Projects will include production activities focused on technical assistance to farmers and expanding private processing in Anbar, Diyala, and Mosul. One project that had a significant impact on the Iraqi agricultural community over the past two years was the MNC-I/MNF-I-supervised ground and aerial agriculture spraying operation. This year was the first time, since the fall of Saddam, that the Iraqis were able to organize and complete this program themselves; the focus of this operation was on Iraqi date palm crop spraying in the central provinces, Baghdad and Diyala. The World Food Program continues to provide assistance through an emergency operation targeting the most vulnerable groups in Iraq. These programs serve as an alternative to the Public Distribution System (PDS) and assist an estimated 3.7 million Iraqis through provision of meals to the poorest families. Officials administering the PDS report that materials on hand are sufficient to meet current needs.

Conclusion

The Iraqi economy continues to slowly progress despite various challenges. Budget execution is improving and oil prices are increasing; however, oil production remains constant. In addition, Iraq has made efforts to re-integrate into the global economy, which is important to attracting investment. The GoI will need to continue to make further progress with economic reforms and budget execution to sustain its economic growth and diversify the economy.

1.3 Security Environment

Although some significant improvements occurred in the security environment during this quarter, multiple conflicts among communal groups for the division of power and resources continued across Iraq that challenge establishing stability and security. These conflicts involve ethno-sectarian violence, the efforts by al Qaeda in Iraq (AQI) to exacerbate these tensions with high-profile attacks, the Sunni insurgency, Shi'a militants, and the influence of foreign state actors. While AQI may not account for most of the violence in Iraq, it is responsible for the mass-casualty attacks that serve as a primary accelerant to the underlying sectarian conflict. Coalition adversaries have common objectives: build and enhance their control over the populace; drive out Coalition forces; and undermine Iraqi government institutions. Their tactics include complex ambushes on Coalition convoys, aircraft, river patrols, and fixed facilities. AQI in particular conducts calculated bombings, murders, executions, and indirect fire—targeting primarily Iraqi civilians—to intimidate them and to provoke sectarian conflict. Fragmentation within these groups resulting from disagreements over ideology and strategy is perpetuating infighting among them and weakening alliances.

Image: Sectarian Deaths and Incident, June 2006–Aug 2007 [Omitted]

The security situation in recent years has resulted in the internal displacement of nearly two million people, according to the UN High Commission on Refugees. By the end of May 2007, the number of displaced people was increasing at an average of 80,000–100,000 per month. If the GoI's February 2007 security plan for returning Internally Displaced Persons (IDPs) succeeds, the UN High Commissioner for Refugees expects this rate of displacement to decrease to 40,000–50,000 per month. The U.S., its Coalition partners, and the UN are conducting IDP working groups to assist the Iraqi Ministry of Displacement and Migration (MoDM) with IDP coordination between local government departments. A process for tracking the number of returnees is not firmly in place, with most data provided by NGOs. Return to Baghdad is hindered by continued violence, occupancy of property by squatters and destruction of houses. The security situation has also caused approximately 2.2 million Iraqis to leave the country and move to Jordan and Syria. However, in some areas of Anbar where security has improved as tribes have worked with Coalition forces to clear out AQI, some residents are beginning to return to their homes.

Iraqi and Coalition forces are conducting operations to secure the population in Baghdad and its environs to prevent and contain sectarian violence. The final complement of the increase of five U.S. Brigade Combat Teams, two Marine Infantry Battalions and a Marine Expeditionary Unit arrived during this reporting period. This enabled the launch of Operation Phantom Thunder on June 15 to target primarily AQI havens in Baghdad, Babil, Diyala and Anbar Provinces. These ongoing operations are being actively assisted by local Sunnis who have grown increasingly intolerant of AQI's intimidation and brutality, particularly its mass-casualty attacks on civilians, targeting of senior sheiks, and forcing of ordinary Iraqis to collaborate or face potential execution. Continuation of this trend of Sunni resistance to AQI is encouraging because the Sunni populace in these areas had previously assisted or tolerated AQI.

Overall Assessment of the Security Environment

During this reporting period, there has been an overall decrease in sectarian violence, high-profile attacks, murders and executions. July was the exception when ethno-sectarian attacks[6] increased slightly over June levels. Iraqi and Coalition operations and policies have limited insurgents' ability to relocate their infrastructure from one location to another, constraining their ability to operate. Combined operations in Iraq's major cities have slowly eroded insurgents' capacity to operate as freely as they did prior to FAQ, but have not degraded armed groups' capabilities or motivations to conduct attacks against Coalition and Iraqi forces, the GoI, or Baghdad residents. Iran continues to train and equip militias, including Muqtada al-Sadr's JAM. These militias continue to attack Coalition soldiers and civilians.

Image: Total Attacks by Province, May 05–July 20, 2007 [Omitted]

The level of security in Iraq varies from province to province. Decreases in violence in Baghdad, Diyala and Babil are initial signs of progress in those provinces. Similar progress in Anbar, Tamim, Irbil, Muthanna and Dhi Qar indicate the potential for improved conditions in these areas. An increase in Coalition engagement with local tribes who are renouncing the insurgency and resisting AQI, is intended to capitalize on their increasing unwillingness to tolerate such violence and their willingness to take steps to help improve security. Although some GoI statements indicate government officials are skeptical of empowering Sunni tribes, Prime Minister Maliki insists that he supports these efforts. His main concern is that the tribes do not create new militias and that the efforts are undertaken with GoI supervision and control. AQI operations are likely to continue including attacks against mosques such as the Samarra Mosque bombing on June 13 and the Al-Khailani Mosque bombing in Rusafa on June 19. Significantly, these attacks failed to provoke widespread ethno-sectarian violence in part due to the change in tribal attitudes toward AQI.

Image: Weapons Caches Found by Coalition and Iraqi Forces, July 2006–Aug 2007 [Omitted]

The mid-August assassinations of the Badr Organization-affiliated governors of Qadisiyah and Muthanna provinces were likely a JAM response to increased efforts by those provincial officials to marginalize JAM. In addition, the August 28, 2007 outbreak of fighting between JAM and the Badr Organization in Karbala highlighted growing tensions between Shia groups in southern Iraq. It is noteworthy that the central government took decisive action in restoring security to the region after the assassinations and the incident in Karbala. The Karbala incident likely sparked Sadr's August 29, 2007 announcement to restrain JAM activity, which Sadr probably intends to use to reorganize the Sadrist movement, and improve his command and control over the organization while improving its public image. This "restraint" will likely only apply to mainstream JAM elements, while specialized JAM units will probably continue violence aimed at Coalition forces and JAM rivals.

Overall Trends and Violence

As a result of the high FAQ-related operational tempo of Iraqi and Coalition forces, the total number of enemy-initiated incidents in May and June were the highest and second-highest, respectively, for any month since 2003.[7] Attacks against Coalition forces reached record levels in June, and the proportion of total attacks against Coalition forces increased to their highest levels since December 2005, accounting for 73% of all attacks. Attacks against Iraqi forces declined slightly in June, but the total is comparable to levels of the past six months. The increased operational tempo and success of Iraqi and Coalition forces have helped to slightly reduce total casualties across Iraq during this reporting period although they increased in July compared with June. Car bomb attacks in Tamim Province in July and against the two Yezidi villages in Ninewa Province in August elevate the civilian casualty numbers significantly for those two months. Since July, statistically significant downward trends in total attacks have emerged. Attacks remained concentrated in Baghdad, Salah ad Din, and Diyala. In addition, Baghdad experienced an average of 43 attacks per day from mid-June to mid-July. The other 15 provinces experienced comparatively low levels of attacks.[8]

Image: Monthly Attacks in Iraq, June 2004–August 2007 [Omitted]

By the end of August, Coalition and Iraqi forces will have already found 50% more caches than in all of 2006. Although the number of weapons caches found and cleared has decreased during this reporting period, caches continue to be discovered at a steady rate of about 110 per week and remain above pre-FAQ levels. The decrease does not necessarily reflect depletion in total caches; however, the continued high operational tempo and focused searches of Coalition and Iraqi forces are impacting the availability of safe havens, which may be reducing the ability and opportunity for insurgents and criminals to emplace caches.

Coalition forces continued to attract the majority of attacks, while the Iraqi security forces and civilians continued to suffer the majority of casualties. The GoI has reported that the number of civilians killed in Iraq, mainly due to catastrophic attacks by insurgents and terrorists, fell sharply from about 1,900 in May to 1,227 in June—the lowest level in five months—but rose again in July to 1,653. Militia activity initially decreased but rose in mid-May before falling again in June to the lowest level in a year. July's level of IED events was the lowest since November 2006, returning to pre-FAQ levels—a result of Iraqi and Coalition security operations combined with Sunni tribal engagement. It is too early to determine the sustainability of these trends.

Image: Average Daily Casualities in Iraq, June 2004–August 2007 [Omitted]

Assessment of the Security Environment—Baghdad In this reporting period, Baghdad remained the most violent area in Iraq, but levels of violence have dropped significantly since the commencement of FAQ as a result of combined Iraqi and Coalition operations. Marketplaces and high-profile places of worship are now more secure due to the implementation of physical protection measures and increased patrols by Iraqi forces. Additionally, no significant security incidents occurred on August 9 during the Commemoration of the Death of the 7th Imam, for which the Iraqi police and military planned and provided security for hundreds of thousands of Shi'a pilgrims to the Kadhamiyah Shrine in northern Baghdad. However, Coalition forces still encounter fighting in mixed sectarian areas where AQI elements continue to harass and target the local populace. Fighting between Sunni groups and Jaysh al-Mahdi (JAM) has been mostly isolated to the western districts of Baghdad, particularly West Rashid and Al Mansour. Of all the districts in Baghdad, the predominantly Shi'a Sadr City remains the most stable in terms of ethno-sectarian attacks. However, this area continues to provide support for JAM operatives who use the area for planning, logistics, and other support activities and as a base from which to launch attacks on the International Zone and neighboring areas.

Image: Total National and Regional Hotline Tips, August 2006–July 2007 [Omitted]

Assessment of the Security Environment—Western Iraq The encouraging signs of Sunni tribal resistance to AQI reported in the previous quarter have led to considerable progress in Anbar's security. Once an AQI stronghold, Anbar is no longer among the most violent provinces. Average daily attacks in the province during this period were only one-third their daily average during the November 2006–February 2007 reporting period, when Anbar had the second highest number of attacks of any province. Since January, attacks and murders against civilians and against Iraqi and Coalition security forces in Ramadi have decreased significantly, from a high of 108 in the week ending February 23 to fewer than eight per week in July. Coalition forces have worked closely with a variety of tribes and Sunni resistance groups in Anbar to expel AQI from operating in the area. In addition, cooperation from local sheikhs and tribal leaders has dramatically increased the number of new recruits for the Iraqi Army and Police in Anbar. Since December 2006, a total of 7,100 Anbar residents have received police training. The operational capabilities of the locally recruited police and Iraqi Army units are gradually increasing, and the GoI is supporting efforts to increase the number of recruits. The Minister of Interior, Anbar provincial government representatives, and Coalition forces officially opened the Anbar Iraqi Police Training Center in Habbaniyah on June 4 and can train 750 recruits in a 10-week training cycle. Iraqi citizens are increasingly providing information concerning insurgent operations to the Iraqi forces. In some parts of western Iraq, however, foreign fighters still enjoy freedom of passage from Syria.

Image: Confidence in the Iraqi Government to Improve the Situation [Omitted]

Assessment of the Security Environment—Central/Northern Iraq The security situation in Diyala, Salah ad Din and Ninewa remains fragile. Recent successes when combined Iraqi and Coalition operations targeted AQI, coupled with increasing initiatives by tribal sheiks to disavow support to terrorists, show some progress in stabilizing this difficult region. Local dissatisfaction with, and lack of confidence in, the GoI is particularly strong here, which exacerbates violence and political instability. On June 5, 2007, the GoI officially opened the Diyala Operations Command (DOC), one of several new Iraqi operations centers representing a new GoI approach to combating terrorist organizations and militia groups. The operations centers integrate command of the Iraqi Army and National Police under a single Operations Commander and expand on the role of the Provincial Joint Coordination Centers. Operation Arrowhead Ripper, which was conducted from June 19 through August 22, cleared Baqubah of AQI and reinstalled Iraqi security outposts and police stations in the city. Initial reports of an increased public sense of security, coupled with aggressive

Government of Iraq support to Phase IV reconstruction and services, are consolidating the gains of this operation. In just the past few weeks, these efforts resulted in over 2,000 new jobs in agriculture and food processing, the opening of banks across Baqubah, and the delivery of the first government wheat ration. The recent VBIED attacks in Ninewa Province demonstrate the risk of increased violence as extremists attempt to provoke greater ethnosectarian violence.

Assessment of the Security Environment—Kurdish Region Although Irbil, Dahuk and Sulaymaniyah are generally stable, AQI maintains a presence in those areas and there is some evidence that AQI is increasingly targeting the region. Attacks on infrastructure, such as roads and bridges, have increased during the reporting period, likely in an effort to hinder Iraqi and Coalition forces' mobility and undermine local confidence in the government's and Coalition forces' ability to protect them. For example, the Sarahah Highway Bridge (south of Kirkuk), which was destroyed on June 2, was a key conduit for transportation between the southern and northern provinces. Kurdish unity, to some extent, is preventing insurgent groups from establishing a presence across the provinces. The Kurdistan Regional Government (KRG) is attempting to demonstrate that security in the area will not compromise prospective investment in the region, particularly in the oil sector. Instability elsewhere in Iraq, however, always has the potential to increasingly spill over into the relatively calm Kurdish area. One destabilizing factor may be that the majority of the country's Internally Displaced Persons (IDPs) have relocated to northern provinces. The KRG and Ninewa and Tamim Provinces also could experience increased violence as various ethno-sectarian groups vie to control disputed territory prior to an Article 140 referendum on the status of Kirkuk.

Image [Omitted]

Assessment of the Security Environment—Southern Iraq The security environment in southern Iraq took a notable turn for the worse in August with the assassinations of the governors of Qadisiyah and Muthanna Provinces by Iranian-backed extremists. Both governors had been pushing back on Jaysh al-Mahdi (JAM) expansion and control. There may be retaliation and an increase in intra-Shi'a violence throughout the South, whereas before, this violence was mostly limited to Basrah. Violence in Qadisiyah, Dhi Qar and Muthanna in recent months has highlighted JAM's ability to attack Iraqi forces and cause instability in the South. After Coalition and Iraqi security operations blunted Sadrist growth in Qadisiyah, the withdrawal of these forces allowed JAM to reassert itself. An increase in its militia members has emboldened JAM to increase the frequency and intensity of attacks on

Coalition and Iraqi forces. This influx has occurred as militant elements moved out of Baghdad to avoid FAQ-related operations. Local Iraqi government security operations conducted against JAM are intended more to contain its political influence than to enforce the law.

Image [Omitted]

These operations have been able to contain much of JAM's violence but have yet to defeat JAM. High unemployment throughout Basrah and an estimated 5,000 displaced families are a potentially large recruiting pool for insurgent and militia groups.

In Basrah, various rival Shi'a militias, factions, tribes, and criminal organizations aligned with political parties are positioning themselves for greater influence over local authorities and resources. With the expected continued reduction of British forces, insurgent groups are increasingly focusing on Basrah and are posturing themselves to control the city, where violence has increased due to the presence of multiple Shi'a militias—most notably JAM and its splinter groups, the Badr Organization and the Fadilah Organization—and criminal groups. These groups all seek to exert their influence over local government and social institutions. Thus far, Basrah's oil infrastructure has not suffered serious interdiction attempts. Over 90% of Iraq's oil is exported through Basrah's oil terminals, and most Iraqi imports and exports go through Basrah's Umm Qasr port. Although various Shi'a parties and militias are locked in fierce competition over access to oil and other sources of patronage, they appear to have a common interest in ensuring the continuous flow of oil.

Public Perceptions of Security

For this reporting period, attacks against mosques incited considerable resentment among the Iraqi populace but resulted in minimal retaliatory attacks due to the GoI's rapid political and security response and widespread calls for restraint by key political and religious leaders. The Samarra Mosque bombing on June 13 and the Al-Khailani Mosque bombing in Rusafa on June 19 were attempts by AQI to undermine public confidence in the ability of the government and Coalition forces to protect them. Public perception of the Iraqi Army and police forces improved during this period due to their increased interaction with the local populace through initiatives such as the Joint Security Stations (JSSs) and Combat Outposts (COPs). An August 2007 national poll indicated that 79% of Iraqis feel safe in their own neighborhoods but only 33% feel safe traveling outside of their neighborhoods.[9] In the July poll, 71% of Iraqis surveyed were satisfied with the ability of the Iraqi Army to provide local security.[10] In addition, more than half of those surveyed had confidence in the GoI's ability to improve the situation.[11] Polling data also shows a national average of 3.5 on a scale of 0 to 10 with 0 representing violent and 10 representing peaceful/calm.[12]

Image [Omitted]

Conclusion

The increase in force levels and the growing rejection of AQI by Sunni Iraqis has changed the dynamic in Iraq's security environment. During this reporting period, there has been an overall decrease in sectarian violence, high-profile attacks, murders and executions. Most notably, violence levels continued to drop in Anbar, formerly AQI's stronghold in Iraq. Baghdad remained the most violent area in Iraq, but levels have dropped significantly since the commencement of FAQ. The level of confidence in the GoI to improve the situation has remained relatively stable since May 2006. Many of the GoI and U.S. initiatives to support the increase in security operations appear to be beginning to take hold. Whether FAQ produces sustainable, permanent improvements in the security environment will depend on the degree to which diplomatic, political and economic achievements can be realized.

1.4 Transferring Security Responsibility

A strategic objective for the USG is to transition security responsibility to the Iraqi government. A few provinces are likely to take longer than previously expected to assume responsibility for security, given the increase in violence in some parts of Iraq. So far this year, the Coalition transferred security responsibility in Maysan, Dahuk, Irbil, and Sulaymaniyah Provinces, making Iraqis responsible for security in a total of seven of 18 provinces.

Status of Provincial Iraqi Control On May 30, 2007, the Kurdish Regional Government (KRG) assumed security responsibility for the three provinces that make up the Kurdish region of Iraq: Dahuk, Irbil and Sulaymaniyah. Transfer to Iraqi control is a conditions-based process; any date-based projection is subject to change as conditions evolve. Karbala is the next province projected to assume Provincial Iraqi Control (PIC) in September 2007. The current projection is all provinces could transition to PIC as early as July 2008. If, for example, violence worsened significantly in any of the provinces yet to transition to PIC, the likely dates for transition of those provinces would be reevaluated by the Iraqi government and MNF-I. The principal impediment causing the delay in transitioning security to Iraqi control is a lack of capability in the Iraqi Police Service (IPS), which prevents them from being able to manage the provincial security situation. In addition, MNF-I and the GoI recognize that security must be addressed comprehensively before transition to provincial control can occur; this may cause some delays as political and economic environments are evaluated for their ability to support the security situation. As FAQ has resulted in an influx of terrorists, insurgents, and members of illegal militia into some provinces, the civil security forces have been unable to handle these threats alone. To assist in dealing with these threats, the GoI has created and manned joint operations commands in several provinces (Baghdad, Basrah, Karbala, Diyala, and Salah ad Din). In order to enhance the capability of the IPS, it will be necessary to increase MoI manning and equipping levels and to reduce the influence of corruption and militia over the local police forces.

Image: Provincial Security Transition Assessment, As of Aug 2007 [Omitted]

Transition to PIC is a necessary but not sufficient condition for withdrawal of Coalition forces from a given province. Once a province has transitioned to PIC, the posture of MNF-I forces changes to security overwatch. The force disposition will depend on the extent of the continued security challenges in that province. In some cases, Iraqi forces are able to deal with security incidents without Coalition assistance, and procedures are in place for the Iraqi forces to call on assistance if required. MNF-I is working with the GoI to develop ways of improving situational awareness and of assessing indications and warnings of problems that may develop in provinces that have transitioned to PIC to help prepare provincial leaders to manage security problems.

Forward Operating Base Turnover Status The turnover of Forward Operating Bases (FOBs) to the GoI has slowed due to increased force levels as part of FAQ. As the security situation permits, MNF-I will continue to reduce its presence in major cities while maintaining the ability to support PRT and Transition Team expansion. MNF-I has transitioned to the Iraqi government or closed 61 FOBs out of a total of 125; since the previous report, an additional three FOBs were established to support the increase in force levels.

Section 2—Iraqi Security Forces Training and Performance

2.1 Assessed Capabilities of the Iraqi Security Forces

Approximately 359,600 Iraqis have been trained and equipped through the primarily U.S.-funded programs for the Objective Counterinsurgency

Force and the Objective Civil Security Force against a 2007 year-end objective of approximately 389,400. This includes approximately 22,100 of a planned 32,000 expansion of personnel who have received basic training as part of the 20% manning increase for the Iraqi Army requested by Prime Minister Maliki. An additional 7,200 of a planned 24,000 military personnel increase and 5,900 of a planned 6,500 police personnel increase have been trained as part of Prime Minister Maliki's replenishment initiative.

Given the persistent violence caused by insurgents, terrorists, and illegal militias, the Ministries of Defense (MoD) and Interior (MoI) and their forces require continued advisory support, training, development, and equipping to be able to progressively assume missions from Coalition forces. The efforts of embedded advisors are focused on addressing continued shortcomings in logistics, leadership, and budget execution that hamper improvement, and in certain cases, cause regression in the readiness and capability of the Ministries and their military and police units. MoD logistics from tactical to strategic levels, and MoI logistics at the strategic level, are fragile and not capable of independent execution. The provision of tactical leadership and true institutional capacity for informed decision making continue to be a focus for the Multi-National Security Transition Command-Iraq (MNSTC-I). Tactical leadership within Iraqi units is improving, but numbers of proficient leaders, especially in the field and NCO grades, are not, as the growth in the Iraqi military and police force structure outpaces efforts to identify, recruit and develop leaders. The MoD's and MoI's underspending of their budgets is a manifestation of a developing decision-making processes. As previously reported, the GoI is making a substantial effort to address procurement and contracting problems within the MoD and MoI by very aggressively committing procurement funds to equipping and sustaining Iraqi forces through the use of U.S. Foreign Military Sales (FMS). Prime Minister Maliki is extending the US$1.72 billion in 2006 funds committed for FMS with an additional US$1.6 billion in 2007 funds, of which US$1.1 billion is for MoD and US$500 million is for MoI.

Image: Total Number of Trained Iraqi Security Forces [Omitted]

Coalition efforts to build the capacity of the Iraqi MoD and MoI and their respective forces continue to focus on four major areas: (1) developing ministerial capacity; (2) improving the proficiency of military and police forces through the assistance of embedded advisors and partnership unit relationships; (3) building the logistic, sustainment and training capacity of the MoD and MoI; and (4) supporting expansion of the Iraqi Army and the creation of a National Police (NP) Samarra (Al Askarien) brigade through the Prime Minister's Initiative. The existing Iraqi-run training centers continue to operate at full capacity to achieve these replenishment goals. Military Transition Teams (MiTTs) and National Police Transition Teams (NPTTs) consisting of over 6,000 advisors organized into more than 500 teams are embedded from division to battalion levels of Iraqi military and NP units as well as in many police stations and border enforcement units. During this reporting period, MNSTC-I's Intelligence Transition Team (I-TT) was established to assist the Government of Iraq (GoI) in developing national intelligence capabilities. The team functions in a cross-ministerial capacity advising intelligence elements in both the MoD and MoI. The team is led by an SES-level DoD civilian intelligence professional and will soon grow to 81 embedded intelligence and law enforcement advisors.

As of August 9, 2007, 105 Army battalions have been generated and are conducting operations at varying levels of capability; three of these are Special Operations Battalions. Another 25 infantry battalions are currently in the process of generation. Of the 17 planned Iraqi Army Infrastructure Battalions (IAIBs; formerly called Strategic Infrastructure Battalions (SIBs)), 12 are assessed as able to conduct operations side by side with Coalition forces or are in the lead. Of the Iraqi Army units conducting operations, 9 divisions, 33 brigades, and 103 battalions have the lead in counterinsurgency operations in their areas of responsibility (AOR) as of this reporting period. Seventy-five percent of all Iraqi Army units are rated as being able to conduct independent operations or to lead operations with Coalition assistance.[13]

Image: Iraqi Army with Lead Resposibility for Counter-Insurgency Operations in Their Areas [Omitted]

The Iraqi Army is capable of conducting counterinsurgency operations in both rural and urban environments but currently lacks the ability to conduct numerous tasks without access to Coalition enablers. The lack of those enablers also severely restricts the Iraqis' ability to defend against external threats. Although performance of Iraqi forces is adequate in limited combined operations with Coalition forces, their ability to manage the security environment independently in any part of the cities remains uncertain because of these shortcomings. In addition, the development of a unified, nonsectarian force that will be capable of securing the country in the event of a withdrawal of Coalition forces is hampered by the loyalty of soldiers within many military units to their tribal and ethno-sectarian or political affiliations and associated militias. These affiliations are often the basis for relationships between key officers and higher-level authorities who are not always in the direct chain of command. Iraqi forces continue to experience shortfalls in self-sustaining logistics and generating officer and noncommissioned officer (NCO) personnel to meet the requirements of an expanding army and high attrition rates.

The 27 authorized NP battalions are operational, with seven capable of leading operations with Coalition support, but none is assigned the lead of a specific area of responsibility. Some NP units lack personnel, individual soldier equipment, and reliable vehicles to conduct operations without Coalition support. Seven brigades are conducting security operations in Baghdad, and one brigade was moved to Samarra in order to provide security throughout the city. Another brigade is conducting retraining at the Numaniyah Training Facility as part of the National Police improvement training plan. As of August 1, 2007, seven of nine NP brigades have completed cohort training. This does not include Prime Minister Maliki's initiatives, such as the Al Askariyah NP Brigade to guard the reconstruction of Samarra's Golden Mosque. A brigade-sized operational reserve consisting of a mechanized battalion from the Army, an NP battalion, and a Special Forces company was established.

Challenge to Iraqi Army and Iraqi Police Expansion—Officer Corps Limits Further large expansions of MoD and MoI authorized end-strength—currently at 488,000 personnel with 445,500 on the payroll—will require addressing an already existing leadership shortage within the officer and noncommissioned officer (NCO) ranks.[14]

Ministry of Defense. The Iraqi Army (IA) is short of leadership in the mid-range NCO ranks as well as the mid-range officer ranks. The IA is taking several steps to mitigate the leader shortage, such as actively recruiting prior service officers and NCOs using mobile recruiting teams and exploring accelerated promotions of personnel currently in the Army. It is unclear if sufficient candidates can be recruited to offset increased requirements. The MoD is also considering other ways of generating officer candidates from within the current force.

Ministry of Interior. Because the training effort of the past four years has focused on generating policemen, and because of the time it takes to grow professional junior officers, there have been inadequate numbers of officer-rank police entering at junior levels. The resulting low officer manning has affected command and control, planning functions, street-level supervision, morale, retention, and ethical conduct. The Iraqi Police Service (IPS) and the NP use various paths to acquire officers. Both of the police services are actively seeking to increase officers through four methods: a three-year officer course; a nine-month officer course; a six-month police commissioner's course; and a three-week officer transition program (for previously trained police officers). The police services have difficulty attracting officer candidates because they compete with the Iraqi Army for the same pool. The MoI is also considering various incentive programs to attract new recruits.

2.2 Ministry of Interior

The MoI forces consist of the IPS, the NP, the Directorate of Border Enforcement (DBE), and other, smaller forces. Recently the MoI assumed responsibility for the Facilities Protection Service (FPS). This transition will take place in phases and will run into 2008. The MoI has hired a significant number of police beyond those trained by MNSTC-I, mainly as a result of pressure from provincial and local governments that want additional police in their jurisdictions. MoI data indicate that there are about 298,100 police, National Police, Border Enforcement, and Forensics personnel on the payroll and a total of 297,000 authorized positions. Approximately 36,000 ministry staff employees are also on the payroll. Previous attrition rates for MoI forces were estimated at 20%, but closer analysis indicates that current attrition is closer to 17% for the IPS, 15% for the NP, and 6% for Border Enforcement forces.

Ministry Transition Issues

Ministerial Capacity Development Coalition advisors continue to report marginal improvement in the MoI's ability to perform key ministry functions such as developing and implementing plans and policies, intelligence, personnel management, logistics, and communications. The MoI continues to have particular difficulty in budget programming and execution, processing and commitment of funds, and executing direct contracts in general. The MoI does not yet have accurate personnel accountability and reporting procedures. MNSTC-I continues to assist the MoI in developing the capability to account for how many of the more than 330,000 employees on the Ministry's payroll are present for duty on a given day. For example the MoI has trained on and is adding data to E-Ministry, an MoIfunded web-based database system that will significantly enhance quick access to accurate human resources, financial, payroll, and logistic information. The heightened sensitivity of personal information in the environment of severe intimidation and threats to which MoI employees are subject will, however, likely hamper implementation of the system. Corruption, illegal activity, and sectarian and militia influence continue to constrain progress in developing MoI forces and gaining more popular support.

The MoI continues to struggle with internal corruption, but the Ministry has made continued efforts this quarter to confront this problem. Key to these efforts is effective investigations when allegations appear to have some credibility. For example, from April 1, 2007, through June 30, 2007, MoI Internal Affairs opened 1,482 new misconduct and corruption-related investigations resulting in dismissal of 110 employees and referral of 20 to the Commission on Public Integrity for further investigation. Eighty-four are pending trial, and internal disciplinary action is pending against 90. Almost 1,500 cases are open and currently under investigation. As of June 30, 2007, 1,026 employees were dismissed since the beginning of the year due to Internal Affairs Directorate efforts. In addition, the Automated Fingerprint Identification System (AFIS) project identified 535 false applications for the reporting period of April 1, 2007 through June 30, 2007. Of these 535 cases, the most serious convictions identified by individual fingerprint comparisons to criminal court records included 48 murderers, 94 burglars, and two rapists. The MoI Inspector General initiated a program to inspect and assess the conditions of short-term detention facilities using checklists based on international standards. Along with support from Multi-National Forces-Iraq's Task Force-134, 1st Division NPTT and the Coalition Police Assistance Training Team's (CPATT) MoI Transition Team (MoI-TT), MoI inspectors assigned to the Human Rights Directorate conducted five facility inspections. The results of these inspections were formalized and forwarded to the MoI for appropriate action. Deficient areas identified during the visits include overcrowding, lack of adequate medical care, and a lack of legal due process.

Embedded Advisory Support In order to achieve its goals within the MoI, MNSTC-I has embedded the MoI-TT with deputy ministers and their subordinates throughout the Ministry to assist in building capacity. The MoI-TT is comprised of approximately 50 military and civilian contractor advisors divided into six teams, each assigned to a directorate in the MoI. These advisors work with their Iraqi partners on a daily basis, enabling them to provide monthly assessments of each directorate's progress and a formal quarterly readiness assessment. The MoI-TT, in conjunction with other Coalition partners, has conducted training both in Iraq and in other countries across a number of areas. MoI procurement staff received training in Jordan to improve procurement practices. The High Institute (based at the Baghdad Police College) has produced a detailed plan to improve facilities, teaching standards, and programs and will likely receive substantial funding in 2008. In addition, foundations have been laid for future legal education programs designed by MoI lawyers, and work is being done to prepare for the enactment of the MoI's internal disciplinary system by yearend.

Multi-National Corps-Iraq (MNC-I) also fields 238 Police Transition Teams (PTTs) that assist in the development of the IPS at the field level. Ten of these teams advise at the provincial police headquarters level, 63 at the district level, and 165 at the police station level. Each team has approximately 12 to 15 members, two to four of whom are civilian International Police Advisors (IPA) hired as contractors by the Department of State and funded by the Department of Defense's Iraq Security Forces Fund.[15] The remaining personnel are from the military, many of whom are Military Police. IPAs provide civilian law enforcement expertise in technical aspects of criminal investigation and police station management. PTTs travel to stations to mentor the Iraqi police and conduct joint patrols to promote community policing activities. On a nationwide basis, PTTs are assigned between 1 to 10 stations each and can conduct between one to four visits or patrols at stations daily. Current funding levels for the IPA program and availability of military assets do not allow for full coverage of the more than 1,100 provincial and local police headquarters and stations in Iraq. Security concerns at over half of these sites prevent safe transit and visits.

Based on feedback from the PTTs, in December 2006 the MoI-TT coached the MoI to initiate an MoI-led Iraqi Police Reform Program called "Quicklook" to review all aspects of performance and effectiveness of Baghdad police stations. The MoI successfully inspected all but three of the 47 police stations within Baghdad. Building on this program, the MoI initiated its own series of inspections. As a result of the April 2007 Provincial Directors of Police conference, the Minister of Interior directed that senior officers from the Police Affairs Agency conduct inspections throughout all of the Iraqi provinces. The Minister specified that the focus of the provincial inspections would be on personnel and equipment issues.

In the MoI-TT Operations Directorate, the Command and Control focus was further refined. Additional internal procedural documents for the Provincial Joint Coordination Centers have been completed and are being reviewed by senior MoI officials, and exercises are being planned to develop linkages to the Iraqi National Command Center (NCC). Construction of the tips call center adjacent to the NCC is proceeding on schedule.

Logistics and Sustainment MNSTC-I is focused on assisting the MoI to improve key logistic shortfalls, particularly in equipment maintenance. For example, the MoI is developing policies, plans, and processes for acquisition, distribution, and maintenance of vehicles. The MoI has begun to centrally purchase vehicles and repair parts using self-generated and FMS contracts. Shortfalls of adequate fuel continue to hinder mission performance. All life-support contracts were transferred to the MoI, except for those used by the Baghdad Police College, training centers in Numaniyah, Habbaniyah, and Camp Dublin in Baghdad, which are expected to transition to the MoI by November 1, 2007. Small-scale life-support contracts have been reestablished at the Basrah, Al Kut, and Sulaymaniyah Joint Training Centers to support the NP Replenishment Plan. Efforts to improve equipment accountability at the MoI are continuing. Transition teams in the field receive equipment from Coalition-contracted warehouses and issue the equipment directly to the IPS, at which point it becomes Government of Iraq property. This transfer is tracked using forms containing signatures and thumbprints. To obtain equipment, subordinate elements submit a standard memorandum requesting the items. Transfers are documented and tracked. After the equipment is issued to the field, MoI-TT mentors the MoI forces in conducting weekly and monthly inventories and the submission of status reports. MoI-TT continues to work with MNC-I to improve reporting procedures and mechanisms.

Force Generation The MoI and CPATT are working to replenish all NP units with personnel and key equipment items in support of FAQ. MNSTC-I is supporting the Prime Minister's initiative to build a multicomponent (Iraqi Army and National Police) division-sized force to protect the Samarra Shrine reconstruction project. Generation of additional NP by the end of 2007 is required to replace combat losses and to support the Prime Minister's Initiative. The NP replenishment goal for 2007 is approximately 14,000. MoI-TT is also assisting the MoI with consolidating the Facilities Protection Services (FPS). Phase III operations of FAQ will require an estimated 12,000 new Iraqi Police Services personnel for Baghdad over the next six months. This initiative is part of the Baghdad Security Plan and is estimated to produce a police officer to civilian ratio of 1:133. This plan brings the ratio of Iraqi police to civilians in Baghdad to that of New York, Los Angeles, and Chicago.

Iraqi Police Service

The IPS constitutes the majority of MoI forces assigned throughout Iraq's 18 provinces and is comprised of patrol, station, traffic, and forensic specialists. The IPS's mission is to enforce the law, safeguard the public, and provide local security. There are 229,300 authorized IPS positions in the MoI. Due to local hiring initiatives, police ranks have swelled in those areas where the population has turned against extremists. This has contributed to previous overhiring at the provincial level, which has resulted in a total police force of 232,000 based on payroll data. There are no reliable data on how many of these are the approximately 135,000 police who have received basic recruit and transition reintegration training from the Coalition. Estimates of the percentage of total trained by the Coalition that are still on the force range from 40% to 70%. Estimated attrition is 17% annually. For Baghdad and the nine key cities, 100% of U.S.-funded authorized vehicles and weapons have been delivered to the police.[16] Overall, the IPS has been issued approximately 93% of authorized U.S.-funded critical equipment and is expected to receive 100% by yearend. The MoI has been procuring equipment on its own for the police who have been hired in excess of the agreed Objective Civil Security Force levels.

Due to combat loss, theft, attrition, poor maintenance, and heavy use of equipment that in many cases was issued three or four years ago, a significant portion of the equipment may no longer be serviceable or in MoI inventories.

These demands, as well as growth of police authorization levels, will require continual equipment support for personal protection and other equipment items. Militia infiltration of local police remains a significant problem in select areas. Because IPS members tend to be based in their home areas, the extent of militia intimidation among the police in a particular area is often a function of general militia influence in that area. Some security forces also remain prone to intimidation by, or collusion with, criminal gangs.

National Police

The National Police (NP) is a bridging force between the local police and the Iraqi Army and, unlike the local police, is under the direct command and control of the MoI. This enables projection of national-level police capabilities across the provinces. The MoI has 24,400 NP on the payroll and 25,700 authorized positions. It is unknown how many of the 26,300 NP and Police Commandos (the NP's predecessor organization that was founded in 2004) who have received initial training and equipping from MNSTC-I are still in the force. Current attrition is estimated at 15% annually. As of July 2007, the 27 National Police Battalions have an average present-for-duty strength of 60%. The NP continue to make only minor gains in capability because their high operations tempo diverts them from training on a wide range of skills or from conducting company-level or higher training events, staff development, collective training, or unit regeneration. Moreover, the NP faces budget, logistics, maintenance, and medical care shortfalls that exacerbate officer shortages, militia influence, and disciplinary issues that hinder the overall mission.

Forty National Police Transitional Teams are embedded at the division, brigade, and battalion levels. Until October 2006, the NP were trained and served primarily in a paramilitary role and had received little traditional police training. Sunnis view the mostly Shi'a NP with distrust because of its involvement in extrajudicial abuses. Iraqi and Coalition leaders continue to work with the NP to address these problems and to improve its capabilities and public image. Since October 2006, the National Police Commander has relieved commanders of both divisions, all nine brigades and 17 of 27 battalions, comprising the majority of the NP leadership at these levels. Still, sectarianism remains a significant problem within the NP.

An adequate National Police "life cycle" rotation would significantly contribute to developing a trusted and professional organization. MNSTC-I, in coordination with the MoI, is developing such a program. National Police Cohort Training at Numaniyah NP Academy, commonly known as "re-blueing," is a four-phased NP transformation program and an opportunity for NP units to conduct limited retraining and regeneration. Phase I is complete while Phase II is ongoing; over a four-week period, policing skills training, tactical training, human rights training and limited collective training is conducted. As of mid-August 2007, seven of nine NP brigades have completed Phase II of "re-blueing" at Numaniyah. Some operational commanders indicate that re-vetted and re-trained brigades are performing better than they had previously performed. The UN-funded, NATO-approved Italian *Carabinieri* Mobile Training Team is part of Phase III of the program and is preparing to begin training the NP in October 2007. Eight NP battalions per brigade will attend courses focused on criminal investigation, crowd control, weapons handling, dignitary protection, intelligence operations and physical fitness. Phase IV, which has not yet begun, involves deployed training on contingencies such as security for pilgrimages, natural disasters and national emergencies.

Image: MoI National Police Forces: Operational Readiness [Omitted]

National Information and Investigation Agency

The National Information and Investigation Agency (NIIA) is the lead intelligence apparatus of the MoI. NIIA intelligence officers assist NP and regular police in performing their criminal investigative duties. NIIA capabilities are currently assessed as minimal in most areas such as investigations, analysis, and surveillance but continue to make modest albeit slow improvement. Since the last report, weapons and body armor issuance has remained at 95% of authorized levels while vehicle issuance has increased to 75% of authorized levels. The current security environment and the infiltration of Shi'a militia groups within the MoI continue to be the main impediment to effective, nonsectarian operations. Furthermore, lack of trust among agencies impedes the exchange of criminal intelligence and collaborative intelligence products.

Directorate of Border Enforcement and Directorate of Ports of Entry

The Directorate of Border Enforcement (DBE) and the Directorate of Ports of Entry (PoE) collectively are responsible for controlling and protecting Iraq's borders. The DBE is organized into five regions, with 12 brigades totaling 44 battalions; MNSTC-I equips 38 of the battalions. 37,700 border enforcement personnel are currently on the payroll and 38,000 positions are authorized by the MoI. The Coalition has trained and equipped about 28,000 border enforcement personnel; it is unknown how many of these are currently on the payroll. These forces staff 420 border and annex forts, of which the U.S. Government has built and equipped 258. The PoE Directorate operates 13 of 17 land PoEs into Iraq. Four land PoEs were closed as part of the increased security measures implemented in February 2007.

Currently, 29 Coalition Border Transition Teams (BTTs) support border and port operations. A new State Department contract provides 64 Border Support Advisors (BSAs) as subject matter experts on port and border operations and customs and immigration procedures to coach, mentor and train senior MoI border enforcement and PoE personnel. Each border police headquarters, from the national level to brigade level, will have a minimum of two BSAs assigned. Two BSAs will be assigned to each training academy and two to three at each PoE. These civilian contractors will enhance the operations provided by the BTTs and Department of Homeland Security Border Support Teams, intensifying current efforts to accelerate the DBE's ability to assume full operational sustainment and stability of Iraq borders and PoEs. To improve capability and establish better border control, the DBE is planning to increase the end strength of border forces.

Facilities Protection Service

The Facilities Protection Service (FPS) was originally established in 2003 by CPA Order 27 to protect infrastructure and facilities controlled by the various government ministries and independent directorates. To assert MoI authority over the FPS, the Iraqi government decided in 2006 that the FPS will be consolidated under the MoI, except for the protective forces within the Ministry of Oil, Ministry of Energy, and Supreme Judicial Council. This effort includes standardization of pay, equipment, training, and logistics of approximately 120,000 FPS personnel. Although the MoI began to take over training and vetting of FPS personnel, the Ministry of Finance has not yet centralized funding with the MoI, and the budgets for non-MoI FPS, including salaries, were not transferred to the MoI. The FPS is not part of the Coalition's programmed train-and-equip requirements. Metrics such as numbers of personnel or equipping status are not included in the overall data. Currently, the MoI FPS is developing Tables of Organization and Equipment to include the non-MoI FPS forces. The MoI FPS has begun to consolidate some of the other FPS units while awaiting the passage of the new FPS Law. The first consolidation was the Ministry of Health (MoH) FPS located in the Medical City Complex (MCC) on July 7, 2007, when responsibility for security at the MCC was transferred to the MoI FPS. The MCC was initially secured by the Iraqi Army and cleared of MoH FPS personnel suspected of insurgent and militia affiliation. With the approval of the Prime Minister and leadership of the *Fardh al-Qanoon* (FAQ) Baghdad Command, the MoI FPS then deployed a 400-person force as a part of Operation Black Crescent to begin protecting the MCC. The first 920 of 1,200 Ministry of Health FPS personnel to be retrained have graduated from the MoI's Baghdad Police College FPS training facility and have been posted at various hospitals around Baghdad. A second operation in early August 2007 successfully replaced the FPS at the Ministry of Culture with newly raised and trained FPS personnel.

2.3 Ministry of Defense

The Iraqi MoD military forces consist of the Joint Headquarters (JHQ); the Iraqi Ground Forces Command (IGFC), which commands the Army and the Iraqi Special Operations Forces (ISOF); the Air Force; and the Navy (including Marines). MoD forces currently have an authorized strength of approximately 195,200 personnel centered on an Army with 10 infantry divisions, one mechanized infantry division, one additional infantry division (being established as part of Prime Minister Maliki's Expansion Initiative), one Special Operations Brigade, and associated combat support units and infrastructure protection battalions; an Air Force consisting of six squadrons; and a Navy with two squadrons and one Marine battalion. There are approximately 151,400 military personnel on the MoD payroll. In July 2007, the Prime Minister directed the establishment of an additional division headquarters and light infantry division which, upon completion, will bring the total force structure to 13 divisions. The 12th Division Headquarters, consisting of the headquarters and Military Police and Signal Companies, was designated for generation as part of the Prime Minister's Initiatives in 2006. This divisional headquarters was to assume a portion of the 4th Division's area of operation and assume command and control of several 4th Division brigades. In July 2007, based on operational considerations, the Prime Minister directed that the 14th Division Headquarters be generated in lieu of the 12th Division Headquarters. This unit, consisting of the headquarters and Military Police and Signal Companies, would assume a portion of the 10th Division's area of operation in the southern portion of Iraq. The 14th Division (Light Infantry) would be formed by cross-leveling several 10th Division brigades. The remainder of the divisional soldiers for the 14th Division will most likely be generated during late 2007 with their training and equipping expected to be completed in 2008. The 14th Division represents the 13th division overall for the Iraqi Army; however, there will not be a 13th Division due to the cultural sensitivities regarding the number 13. Generation of the 12th Division will now be delayed to 2008 due to the increased priority of generating the 14th Division. It is unknown how many of the 165,400 Iraqi military personnel who have been trained and equipped by the Coalition are still on the payroll, or how many on the payroll have been through Coalition training.

Ministry Transition Issues

As of September 1, 2007, nine Division Headquarters, 33 Brigade Headquarters, and 103 Iraqi Army battalions had assumed the lead for counterinsurgency operations (COIN) within their assigned areas of operations. The Iraqi Ground Forces Command (IGFC) has assumed command and control of eight of the 10 fully operational Iraqi Army divisions (the 5th and 7th Divisions remain under the operational control of MNC-I).

The MoD, through the JHQ, has assumed responsibility for support and sustainment planning for these divisions as well as for forces transferring to JHQ command and control in the future. The 6th and 9th Divisions have subsequently been subordinated to the MoD's Baghdad Operations Command as part of *Fardh al-Qanoon* (FAQ). By November 2007, the IGFC is expected to gain operational control of all ten Army divisions of the Objective Counterinsurgency Force.

Ministerial Capacity Development Overall, the MoD is assessed as partially effective at managing ministry functions such as personnel management, budgeting, acquisitions and contracting, and plans and policies. Coalition assistance is required to provide fielded forces with required support. The MoD is, however, showing incremental progress in some areas such as life support contracting. Where it has already assumed the majority of responsibility, the quality and capacity of the new life support contractors servicing MoD have greatly improved this year. Moreover, the MoD's ability to perform requirements-based budgeting has also improved significantly this year, and it has produced a 2007 Capabilities Requirements Plan in support of agreed Iraqi Defense policy objectives. The plan also includes an acquisition procurement strategy for either direct Ministry purchases or use of U.S. FMS cases.

The Ministry still suffers from deficiencies, particularly in the processes for obtaining approval for commitment of funds and contracting in general. The Ministry of Planning has published a new Iraqi Procurement Law effective May 2007. The Ministry is updating its Contracts Policy and Procedures Manual including the business process flow charts and delegated approval financial thresholds. As these processes mature, the MoD will continue to pursue a substantial portion of its acquisition and sustainment requirements through U.S. FMS cases, particularly for new units being generated. The MoD remains on track to develop and deliver the 2008 Capabilities Requirements Plan to the Directorate of Programs and Budgets for preparation of the 2008 Budget in the coming months. Efforts to build MoD capacity further will be enhanced by its new Civil Service Staff Development Center, which officially opened in July 2007.

Embedded Advisory Support Transition Teams (TTs) are embedded in the MoD, the Joint Headquarters and with most battalions and brigade and division headquarters. Most of the teams at the unit level are comprised of about 10 personnel. At the national level, there are two teams that have about 50 personnel each, one for the civilian leadership of the Ministry and one for the Joint Headquarters (JHQ). The MoD-TT advises the civilian Iraqi MoD leadership and staff. The team currently consists of civilian advisors from the United States, the United Kingdom, and Australia. Since 2004, the MoD-TT has been led by an SES-level UK MoD civil servant. The MoD-TT consists of approximately 50 advisors including some

35 contractors, seven U.S. military personnel, and six UK and two Australian civil servants. An Australian general officer leads the TT that advises the JHQ. At the JHQ-TT, U.S. military personnel comprise about half of the advisors and the rest are split roughly between U.S. civilian contractors and military personnel from other Coalition countries. Both TTs report to MNSTC-I and provide mentoring support to senior officials in developing the Iraqi capacity to manage key ministerial functions. To enhance the Iraqi Army's operational unit logistic capabilities, the 316th Sustainment Command (Expeditionary) is working with Iraqi logistics units and MNSTC-I's Coalition Military Assistance Training Team (CMATT), and has teams embedded at the Taji National Depot to develop the national supply chain. Altogether, MNSTC-I has oversight of approximately 60 transition teams assigned to assist in logistics and sustainment.

Logistics and Sustainment MoD's growing but still too limited logistic and sustainment capacity remains a key hindrance to Iraqi forces' ability to permanently assume missions from the Coalition. The MoD requires significant Coalition assistance, especially in warehouse, depot, transportation, and distribution operations. Plans are underway to transition responsibility for ammunition depots and national level maintenance from contractors in JHQ logistics units. Furthermore, progress has been made in filling motor transport units, regional support units, and garrison support units—all of which continue to build the Iraqi logistics, maintenance, and support capability. Development and implementation of the MoD strategic logistics policy concept is also maturing via the combined Coalition-JHQ Logistics Concept Implementation Committee (LCIC). Chairmanship of the LCIC has shifted to the JHQ with the Coalition providing the co-chair deputy. The ability of the MoD forces to maintain accountability for U.S.-provided equipment remains a challenge. According to the latest Iraqi Army reports on the 1st through 10th Divisions, these units have an average of 75% of authorized equipment. Even though these units have previously been issued 100% of authorized equipment, battlefield attrition, normal wear and tear from a high operational tempo, theft and pilfering, and maintenance shortfalls have all resulted in equipment attrition. Without fully capable Iraqi Army, Joint Headquarters, and MoD logistics systems, accounting for this attrition is difficult. The IGFC has initiated an effort to reconcile the differences between what was issued and what is on-hand by ordering units to conduct 100% equipment inventories, and the IGFC is in the process of requiring all divisions to provide a monthly equipment report for equipment accountability purposes. The MoD, MNSTC-I and MNC-I are also focused on improving HMMWV maintenance levels. MiTT teams indicate that these Iraqi initiatives are helping to improve equipment accountability at the unit level.

MNSTC-I and the MoD continue to issue mission-critical items to the Iraqi Armed Forces, such as up-armored HMMWVs, wheeled Armored Personnel Carriers, heavy machine guns, and fuel trucks to the agreed Modified Table of Organizational Equipment (MTOE) levels. MNC-I also conducts a monthly equipment status report which tracks the issued, on-hand, and fully mission capable status of the key pacing items by the Iraqi Army divisions and Motorized Transportation Regiments. The Iraqi Army has established a Combined Logistics Operations Center (CLOC) and has been working closely with MNSTC-I on a daily basis. In coordination with the Iraqis, MNSTC-I has drafted an internal Ministry Transfer Policy that will provide accountability procedures for property transferred between different Ministries and among elements within the same Ministry. The MoD continues to receive delivery of, and train units on, U.S.-standard equipment—such as M4s, M16s, M203s, and supporting ammunition and repair parts—through FMS cases using MoD funds.

Throughout this period, DoD continued to focus on developing the MoD's logistics support capabilities in the areas of fuel supply, maintenance, budget, material management, self-sustainment, ammunition, medical equipment, supply accountability, and national warehouse operations. The FY2007 Supplemental appropriation and FY2008 funding request included additional funding for the Iraq Security Forces Fund to support this effort. A major element of the initiative is the implementation of a Logistics Management Information Technology (IT) Solution to manage more than 11,000 line items of inventory stored at more than 11 storage sites including the Taji National Depot, five Regional Support Units (RSUs), selected Garrison Support Units (GSUs), and selected Air Force and Navy support sites. A key hindrance to Iraqi self-reliance in supplying fuel to its forces is that the MoD still receives fuel allocations from the Ministry of Oil (MoO) below required levels. Although the MoO is increasing its allocation to the MoD, shortfalls still occur as the Iraqi Army fields new vehicles and as the force structure continues to grow, requiring continued provision of fuel by Coalition forces. The MoD is initiating FMS procurements to acquire military line haul fuel tanker capabilities rather than rely on commercial transportation. The MoD is assuming greater responsibility for contracting for transportation of supplies, soldiers, and equipment via a contract for line transportation. By the end of September 2007, the MoD is scheduled to provide all life support to its fighting force through contracts; the MoD's disbursements to its life support contractors have generally been on time throughout 2007—important success in MoD budget execution.

MNSTC-I is currently working with the MoD to transfer maintenance capabilities to the Iraqi Army. The MoD did not assume responsibility for the National Maintenance Contract at the end of June 2007 as planned.

MNSTC-I is now supporting the Iraqi Army Maintenance Program (IAMP) through the end of November 2007. The JHQ M4 staff has agreed to a transition plan, and the Iraqi Army will assume responsibility for maintenance at 10 sites throughout Iraq as the USG transitions out of the IAMP contract. A joint Transition Advisory Council has been established to track the transition of the maintenance capability and to make decisions on the timetable. The MoD also has two FMS contracts in place worth US$80 million for the procurement of spare parts. The total cost of maintenance support contracts to be assumed by the MoD is estimated to be US$160 million. The MoD has a number of additional FMS contracts in place and is procuring equipment to support the expansion of the Iraqi Army.

The MoD Office of the Surgeon General (OSG) fully committed the 2007 budget of US$32 million to provide much needed medical supplies and care. This did not fully fund all the MoD OSG requirements. A separate FMS case for a level III field hospital is being executed. MNSTC-I provided initial funding and one-year sustainment of medical supplies. Although the MoD's medical logistic capabilities are improving, they require continued Coalition assistance. The first of six planned mortuary facilities has been constructed and opened. Also, a medical follow-up unit has been established for administrative support to coordinate medical treatment for seriously wounded Iraqi military personnel and to coordinate death benefits for military fatalities and their survivors.

Discussions continued between the DoD and the MoD on the development of an Acquisition and Cross Servicing Agreement (ACSA) for the reciprocal provision of logistic support, supplies and services on a reimbursable basis. A draft agreement has been produced, but as of this reporting period, the Iraqi government had not determined what level of the GoI would be authorized to approve such an agreement.

Force Generation The MoD's institutional training base accounts for basic and military occupational specialty training for soldiers, noncommissioned officers, initial-entry cadets, new lieutenants, and staff officers. Embedded transition teams and partner units subordinate to MNC-I oversee and mentor operational training in counterinsurgency-oriented mission-essential tasks. The Iraqi government is funding US$950 million of the cost of increasing the Army's structure from 10 to 13 divisions. This expansion is intended to increase the MoD's ability to overmatch enemy forces, enhance its operational and tactical flexibility, and allow units to retrain and refit. MoD is procuring much of the equipment for these new units through DoD FMS cases. Iraqi staff officers in the JHQ assumed responsibility from MNSTC-I in May 2007 for force generation of Iraqi Army units and are now leading the planning for recruiting, training, manning, equipping, basing and forming of new Army units. MNSTC-I continues to mentor, partner with, and train JHQ force generation personnel.

Force Expansion MNSTC-I funded equipment for 18,000 new soldiers who were trained as replacements for losses from the last four years. Continued replenishment of battle losses and other attrition will be required. To improve present-for-duty strength, MNSTC-I also funded a 21,100 soldier increase in the manning of combat units to increase the number of personnel assigned to units to 120% of current authorizations. All of these soldiers have completed their training, and as of mid-July 2007, Iraqi Army divisions reached approximately 103% of authorized strength. This strength level is deceptively high in that the majority of the Army personnel strength is in the lowest enlisted ranks. The mid-range enlisted and officer ranks are extremely low at 38% and 69%, respectively. This shortage is a focal point of both the Coalition and Iraqi teams. There are many initiatives being explored and implemented. Currently the main focus is on mobile recruiting teams that are attempting to recruit former NCOs and officers from the old army to fill critical voids in the Army as well as the other services. With the infusion of more than 9,000 soldiers by September, the divisions will have an estimated aggregate number of assigned personnel of approximately 110% of authorized levels. This initiative will continue until the number of personnel assigned to all combat battalions is at least 120% of authorizations.

A major reason for this manning increase is that only about 65% of authorized personnel are present for duty in fielded units at any time, and this percentage varied widely among units. (For ISOF, Air Force and Navy, only 61%, 39%, and 40% of authorized personnel, respectively, were present for duty at any time.) With increased manning of divisional units, the Army's present-for-duty averages have increased to approximately 70% on any given day. Increasing assigned personnel strength to 120% of authorizations is expected to ensure a further improvement in present-for-duty averages to at least 75% of a battalion's authorized strength. The greatest contributor to the difference between authorized strength and present-for-duty strength is a policy that places about one-quarter of all soldiers on leave at any time to take pay home to their families. In addition, the Army has suffered up to 25% annual attrition due to casualties and other factors such as soldiers going absent without leave (AWOL). Iraqi Army divisions that face sustained combat operations report AWOL rates of between 5% and 8%.

The new Iraqi military justice system is being implemented by the Iraqis with the ongoing appointment, training, and posting of military judges, legal advisors, and disciplinary officers. The Iraqi Military Penal Law was enacted and became effective in July 2007, and the Military Procedures Law, establishing the military courts-martial and disciplinary system, is pending final approval by the Iraq Presidency Council and forwarding to the Ministry of Justice for publishing in the Official Gazette. Implementation of these laws, expected in September, will enable Iraqi commanders to deal fairly and effectively with absenteeism and desertion.

Army

The Army (ground forces) component currently consists of approximately 131,600 soldiers, according to MoD payroll data, organized into 12 divisions; total personnel authorized for ground forces are 171,300. Supporting elements consisting of Training and Doctrine Command, five RSUs, and 28 GSUs are currently assigned approximately 14,500 support personnel; total authorizations are 16,700. Previously, 80 GSUs were planned, but many of them have been consolidated into larger units to ensure that each possessed organic base defense capabilities. All of the RSUs and 15 of the 28 GSUs have embedded MNSTC-I transition teams.

The Prime Minister has directed that the 17 Iraqi Army Infrastructure Battalions (IAIBs) go through a two-phased re-training and reequipping process to transform them into regular Iraqi Army Battalions. These battalions will have special skills directed towards infrastructure protection and consequence management. MNSTC-I is working closely with the Iraqi Joint Headquarters to complete the planning of this phased concept to transform IAIBs into Light Infantry Battalions that are fully integrated into the regular Iraqi Army. One IAIB has already moved to a Regional Training Center and will begin training in the near future. In May 2007, all Iraqi Army divisions were assigned responsibility for infrastructure protection in their areas of responsibility with operational control of Infrastructure Battalions. Full integration is projected to occur after they are trained to the same standards as regular Army soldiers, possibly by early 2009. Efforts to improve the capability of these units are led by partnered IA units and MiTTs.

National Counter-Terror Capability

Implementation of the National Counter-Terrorism (CT) capability remains on track to achieve full operational capability by December 2007, and the CT Bureau is operating. Communications between the newly established CT Bureau (CTB) and CT Command with the Iraq Special Operations Force (ISOF) Brigade headquarters, the Ministry of Defense, and the Joint Headquarters are functioning and maintained through daily video teleconferences and across the U.S.-funded Iraqi Defense Network. The CTB completed its 2008 budget planning and is drafting a National CT Strategy. Individual and collective training is also progressing with the MiTTs working with their Iraqi counterparts. A new CT law has been drafted and is progressing through the legislature. U.S. Special Operations Forces (USSOF) and Coalition partners working as the Special Operations Iraq Transition Teams (SOITT) train the ISOF Brigade headquarters command and staff personnel. The ISOF Brigade is the operational component of the Iraqi

Counter-Terrorism Command. It has grown to an assigned strength of approximately 3,300 soldiers, which comprise the bulk of Iraq's CT strike capability, with total authorizations of about 4,500. An ISOF expansion program has begun. Currently, one commando battalion is being established with regionally based companies planned in Basrah, Mosul, Al Asad, and Diyala. Over time, these may grow to battalion strength. The Basrah Company is currently conducting operations and the Mosul Company attained initial operational capability.

Navy

The Iraqi Navy has approximately 1,100 assigned sailors and Marines organized into an operational headquarters, two afloat squadrons, and four Marine companies that are stationed for point defense of the offshore oil platforms. The Navy will grow to 2,900 personnel as acquisition of two offshore support vessels, four patrol ships, 15 patrol boats and a number of smaller vessels progresses. Contracts for the purchase of many of these ships have been definitized, but execution has been delayed due to negotiations with vendors over exchange rates and taxation. The Iraqi Navy faces significant challenges in meeting training needs for its ambitious acquisition program, including development of leadership and technical skills. The MNSTC-I Naval Transition Team and Coalition Navy, Marine, and Coast Guard Forces continue to advise the Iraqi Navy. Naval infrastructure development, funded by MNSTC-I and the MoD, remains a primary effort in preparation for the delivery of their new ships slated to arrive beginning in the fourth quarter of CY08.

Image: MoD Forces: Operational Readiness [Omitted]

Air Force

There are approximately 900 personnel assigned to the Iraqi Air Force (IqAF). A concentrated recruitment and accession effort is underway to field 1,500 airmen by the end of 2007; the MoD has authorized a total of 2,900 IqAF personnel. To develop the IqAF officer corps, the Air Force has interfaced with the Iraqi Military Academy system and recently graduated the first 19 second lieutenants. The IqAF has also implemented an officer training program at the Air Force Training School. The first graduation from this course will be in October 2007. The IqAF will also open a flight training school in October 2007 to develop professional aviators. Currently, the IqAF has 91 mission-qualified pilots for 51 on-hand aircraft and is flying missions with both its C-130 and Cessna Caravan aircraft.

The Air Force is organized and equipped for counterinsurgency operations and is advised by eight embedded teams from the Coalition Air Force

Transition Team. Intelligence, Surveillance, and Reconnaissance (ISR) aircraft are currently located at Kirkuk Air Base (3 Squadron with three Cessna 208B Caravans and 4 SAMA CH-2000s) and Basrah Air Base (70 Squadron with four SAMA CH-2000s and two Sea Bird Seeker SB7L-360s). Each unit performs daily operational missions over Baghdad and key national infrastructure locations supplying actionable intelligence to both Iraqi and Coalition ground forces. The intelligence gathered during these flights has provided timely evidence of Baghdad perimeter security breaches and detection of oil piracy. As described in previous reports, Iraq's capabilities to conduct airborne ISR are being further enhanced with additional procurements of interim and advanced platforms. The last of three Cessna Caravan interim ISR aircraft arrived in June 2007, giving the IqAF an enhanced day and night capability once initial and mission qualification training is completed.

There are currently 35 helicopters assigned to the IqAF, split among the Bell UH-1H Huey IIs, Bell 206B Jet Rangers, and Mi-17 Hips. The fielding of rotary-wing aircraft continued with the delivery of six modified UH II (Iroquois) helicopters, bringing the total delivered to 16. Aircrews are currently conducting initial qualification and tactics training. The Iroquois fleet has achieved initial operating capability and is currently conducting battlefield mobility and VIP transport missions. The first 10 MoDprocured Mi-17 helicopters are still not operationally employed due to shortfalls in defensive systems and internal/external communications. The IqAF addressed this need with a US$6 million defensive system contract with a scheduled delivery of the first system suites 90 days after payment, but this date is slipping because of problems in the acquisition and contracting process. An additional four Mi-17s arrived in May with full defensive suites installed but with significant communication problems. The initial operational capability of the Mi-17 will occur in the third quarter of 2007 after night and tactics training is complete. The MoD has ordered a total of 28 Mi-17s, with final delivery scheduled for December 2007. The Iraqi Air Force 12 Squadron continues to conduct flight training with five Bell Jet Ranger aircraft.

The 23 Squadron at New Al Muthanna Air Base has three 1960s vintage C-130E aircraft. IqAF technicians perform all routine maintenance and all-Iraqi flight crews are generally the norm. The maturity of the 23 Squadron has enabled a reduction in the number of U.S. Air Force MiTT personnel assigned to the unit. The MoD has requested an additional three Excess Defense Article C-130s from the USG to bring the squadron size to six aircraft. All IqAF aircraft are currently being integrated to assist with other ISF units in order to win the COIN fight. The ISR and helicopter assets will enhance the capabilities of the ISOF if they are able to recruit enough pilots to fly them. Advisors to both the IqAF and the MoD's CT Bureau are currently working closely to develop this capability.

Conclusion

Capable police and military forces will enable the Iraqi government to battle terrorism, neutralize the insurgency, and provide stability in Iraq. Efforts are ongoing to build the capacity of the forces and the ministries to sustain themselves without Coalition support, and to operate independently without the full range of Coalition combat enablers. This includes developing a robust FMS program assisting with GoI force expansion initiatives, continuing support for GoI efforts to procure U.S. standard equipment, and supporting efforts to improve equipment accountability.

Annex A

List of Acronyms and Abbreviations

AQI	al Qaeda in Iraq
BCT	Brigade Combat Team
BTT	Border Transition Team
CCCI	Central Criminal Court of Iraq
CoM	Council of Ministers
CoR	Council of Representatives
CPATT	Civilian Police Assistance Transition Team
CT	Counter Terrorism
DBE	Directorate of Border Enforcement
DoD	U.S. Department of Defense
EFP	Explosively Formed Projectiles
FMS	Foreign Military Sales
FAQ	Operation Fardh al-Qanoon
FPS	Facilities Protection Service
GDP	Gross Domestic Product
GoI	Government of Iraq
IED	Improvised Explosive Devices
IG	Inspector General
IGFC	Iraqi Ground Forces Command
IHEC	Independent High Electoral Commission
IMF	International Monetary Fund
IPLO	International Police Liaison Officer

IPS	Iraqi Police Forces
IqAF	Iraqi Air Force
IRRF	Iraqi Relief and Reconstruction Fund
ISF	Iraqi Security Forces
ISR	Intelligence, Surveillance, and Reconnaissance
ISOF	Iraqi Special Operations Forces
JAM	Jaysh al-Mahdi
JHQ	Joint Headquarters
KRG	Kurdistan Regional Government
mbbl/d	Million Barrels Per Day
MiTT	Military Transition Teams
MNC-I	Multi-National Corps-Iraq
MNF-I	Multi-National Force-Iraq
MNSTC-I	Multi-National Security Transition Command-Iraq
MoD	Ministry of Defense
MoE	Ministry of Electricity
MoF	Ministry of Finance
MoI	Ministry of Interior
MoO	Ministry of Oil
MW	Megawatt
NP	National Police
NPTT	National Police Transition Team
PDS	Public Distribution System
PHC	Public Healthcare Centers
PIC	Provincial Iraqi Control
POE	Directorate of Ports of Entry
PKK	Kurdistan Worker's Party
PTT	Police Transition Team
QF	Qods Force
SBA	Stand-By Arrangement
SIB	Strategic Infrastructure Battalion
TT	Transition Team
UN	United Nations
USAID	United States Agency for International Development

Endnotes

[1] Nationwide poll, August 2007: "The Iraqi people would be better off if the country were divided into 3 or more separate regions that better reflected ethnic or sectarian populations." Nationwide, 33% of Iraqis agree to this statement. Sample Size: ~12000. Margin of Error (MoE): ~1%

[2] The ePRTs differ from PRTs in that they are more closely paired with a U.S. military unit in an advisory role than existing PRTs, whose primary relationship is with a provincial government. An ePRT operates at the grass roots level in its partnered military unit's area of responsibility. The ePRTs, like the ten original PRTs, are intended to promote reconciliation, build governance capacity, support U.S. counterinsurgency strategy, encourage moderate elements, and foster local economic development.

[3] The Central Criminal Court of Iraq (CCCI) was established in 2003 pursuant to Coalition Provisional Order 13 (as revised and amended) to try terrorism, government corruption, organized crime, and other specified categories of cases.

[4] The International Compact with Iraq (ICI) provides a five-year framework for Iraq to achieve financial sustainability through economic reform commitments between Iraq and the international community. This GoI initiative, co-chaired with the United Nations (UN), commits Iraq to reforming its economy, establishing new investment laws and regulations, building the institutions needed to combat corruption, ensuring good governance, and protecting human rights. In return, members of the international community commit to supporting these efforts through financial, technical, and administrative assistance, as well as through forgiveness of Iraq's external debt. Background material can be found at www.iraqcompact.org.

[5] This quarterly report shows monthly data over a 15-month period and breaks out North and South production, whereas the last report shows weekly data for a 3-month period.

[6] "Sectarian incident" is defined as an attack by a person or a group of people of a particular ethnic/religious group directed at a different ethnic/religious person or group of people where the primary purpose/motivation is based on ethnic or religious reasons.

[7] Incidents reported in the Multi-National Corps-Iraq (MNC-I) Significant Activities Database include known attacks on Coalition and Iraqi forces, the civilian population, and infrastructure. These incidents typically involve improvised explosive devices, small arms including sniper fire, and indirect fire weapons.

[8] Beginning with this report, data on attack incidents by month will be shown in response to a Government Accountability Office (GAO) recommendation. Previously, attack incident trends were reported using weekly averages during periods of varying length. This report will also begin to report casualties by month to be consistent with incident reporting.

[9] Nationwide poll, August 2007: "Do you agree with the following statements? I feel safe and secure in my neighborhood and I feel safe traveling outside my neighborhood." Nationwide, 79% of respondents agree that they feel safe inside their neighborhoods and 33% feel safe traveling outside their neighborhoods. Sample size: ~12000. Margin of error: ~1%

[10] Nationwide poll, July 2007: "How satisfied are you with the following? The ability of the Iraqi Army to provide security in my area." Nationwide, 71% of Iraqis are either somewhat or very satisfied. Sample size: ~8000. Margin of error: ~ 1%

[11] Nationwide poll, July 2007: "In general, do you have confidence in the ability of the Iraqi government to improve the situation?" Nationwide, 57% of Iraqis answered "yes." Sample size: ~8000. Margin of error: ~ 1%

[12] Nationwide poll, August 2007: "How would you describe the situation today in the country." Nationwide, 7.3. Sample size: ~12000. Margin of error: ~1%

[13] An "independent" unit is capable of planning, executing, and sustaining counterinsurgency operations. A unit "in the lead" is capable of planning, executing and sustaining counterinsurgency operations with Coalition support. A unit fighting "side-by-side" is partially capable of conducting counterinsurgency operations in conjunction with Coalition units. A unit "forming" is at the institutional training base or is not yet capable of conducting counterinsurgency operations.

[14] Payroll numbers do not reflect present-for-duty totals. No data available on how many of those on the payroll have received initial training and equipping by the Coalition or the ministries.

[15] International Police Liaison Officers (IPLOs) and International Police Trainers (IPTs) were redesignated as International Police Advisors (IPAs) on July 5, 2007.

[16] The nine key cities are: Baqubah, Basrah, Fallujah, Kirkuk, Mosul, Najaf, N.Babil, Ramadi, and Samarra.

DOCUMENT NO. 4

ADDRESS BY PRESIDENT GEORGE W. BUSH TO THE NATION ON THE WAY FORWARD IN IRAQ

Presidential Address

September 13, 2007

THE PRESIDENT: Good evening. In the life of all free nations, there come moments that decide the direction of a country and reveal the character of its people. We are now at such a moment.

In Iraq, an ally of the United States is fighting for its survival. Terrorists and extremists who are at war with us around the world are seeking to topple Iraq's government, dominate the region, and attack us here at home. If Iraq's young democracy can turn back these enemies, it will mean a more hopeful Middle East and a more secure America. This ally has placed its trust in the United States. And tonight, our moral and strategic imperatives are one: We must help Iraq defeat those who threaten its future and also threaten ours.

Eight months ago, we adopted a new strategy to meet that objective, including a surge in U.S. forces that reached full strength in June. This week, General David Petraeus and Ambassador Ryan Crocker testified before Congress about how that strategy is progressing. In their testimony, these men made clear that our challenge in Iraq is formidable. Yet they concluded that conditions in Iraq are improving, that we are seizing the initiative from the enemy, and that the troop surge is working.

The premise of our strategy is that securing the Iraqi population is the foundation for all other progress. For Iraqis to bridge sectarian divides, they need to feel safe in their homes and neighborhoods. For lasting reconciliation to take root, Iraqis must feel confident that they do not need sectarian gangs for security. The goal of the surge is to provide that security and to help prepare Iraqi forces to maintain it. As I will explain tonight, our success in meeting these objectives now allows us to begin bringing some of our troops home.

Since the surge was announced in January, it has moved through several phases. First was the flow of additional troops into Iraq, especially Baghdad and Anbar province. Once these forces were in place, our commanders launched a series of offensive operations to drive terrorists and militias out of their strongholds. And finally, in areas that have been cleared, we are surging diplomatic and civilian resources to ensure that military progress is quickly followed up with real improvements in daily life.

Anbar province is a good example of how our strategy is working. Last year, an intelligence report concluded that Anbar had been lost to al Qaeda. Some cited this report as evidence that we had failed in Iraq and should cut our losses and pull out. Instead, we kept the pressure on the terrorists. The local people were suffering under the Taliban-like rule of al Qaeda, and they were sick of it. So they asked us for help.

To take advantage of this opportunity, I sent an additional 4,000 Marines to Anbar as part of the surge. Together, local sheiks, Iraqi forces, and coalition troops drove the terrorists from the capital of Ramadi and other population centers. Today, a city where al Qaeda once planted its flag is beginning to return to normal. Anbar citizens who once feared beheading for talking to an American or Iraqi soldier now come forward to tell us where the terrorists are hiding. Young Sunnis who once joined the insurgency are now joining the army and police. And with the help of our provincial reconstruction teams, new jobs are being created and local governments are meeting again.

These developments do not often make the headlines, but they do make a difference. During my visit to Anbar on Labor Day, local Sunni leaders thanked me for America's support. They pledged they would never allow al Qaeda to return. And they told me they now see a place for their people in a democratic Iraq. The Sunni governor of Anbar province put it this way: "Our tomorrow starts today."

The changes in Anbar show all Iraqis what becomes possible when extremists are driven out. They show al Qaeda that it cannot count on popular support, even in a province its leaders once declared their home base. And they show the world that ordinary people in the Middle East want the same things for their children that we want for ours—a decent life and a peaceful future.

In Anbar, the enemy remains active and deadly. Earlier today, one of the brave tribal sheikhs who helped lead the revolt against al Qaeda was murdered. In response, a fellow Sunni leader declared: "We are determined to strike back and continue our work." And as they do, they can count on the continued support of the United States.

Throughout Iraq, too many citizens are being killed by terrorists and death squads. And for most Iraqis, the quality of life is far from where it should be. Yet General Petraeus and Ambassador Crocker report that the success in Anbar is beginning to be replicated in other parts of the country.

One year ago, much of Baghdad was under siege. Schools were closed, markets were shuttered, and sectarian violence was spiraling out of control. Today, most of Baghdad's neighborhoods are being patrolled by coalition and Iraqi forces who live among the people they protect. Many schools and markets are reopening. Citizens are coming forward with vital intelligence. Sectarian killings are down. And ordinary life is beginning to return.

One year ago, much of Diyala province was a sanctuary for al Qaeda and other extremist groups, and its capital of Baqubah was emerging as an al Qaeda stronghold. Today, Baqubah is cleared. Diyala province is the site of a growing popular uprising against the extremists. And some local tribes are working alongside coalition and Iraqi forces to clear out the enemy and reclaim their communities.

One year ago, Shia extremists and Iranian-backed militants were gaining strength and targeting Sunnis for assassination. Today, these groups are being broken up, and many of their leaders are being captured or killed.

These gains are a tribute to our military, they are a tribute to the courage of the Iraqi security forces, and they are the tribute to an Iraqi government that has decided to take on the extremists.

Now the Iraqi government must bring the same determination to achieving reconciliation. This is an enormous undertaking after more than three decades of tyranny and division. The government has not met its own legislative benchmarks—and in my meetings with Iraqi leaders, I have made it clear that they must.

Yet Iraq's national leaders are getting some things done. For example, they have passed a budget. They're sharing oil revenues with the provinces. They're allowing former Baathists to rejoin Iraq's military or receive government pensions. Local reconciliation is taking place. The key now is to link this progress in the provinces to progress in Baghdad. As local politics change, so will national politics.

Our troops in Iraq are performing brilliantly. Along with Iraqi forces, they have captured or killed an average of more than 1,500 enemy fighters per month since January. Yet ultimately, the way forward depends on the ability of Iraqis to maintain security gains. According to General Petraeus and a panel chaired by retired General Jim Jones, the Iraqi army is becoming more capable—although there is still a great deal of work to be done to improve the national police. Iraqi forces are receiving increased cooperation from local populations. And this is improving their ability to hold areas that have been cleared.

Because of this success, General Petraeus believes we have now reached the point where we can maintain our security gains with fewer American forces. He has recommended that we not replace about 2,200 Marines scheduled to leave Anbar province later this month. In addition, he says it will soon be possible to bring home an Army combat brigade, for a total force reduction of 5,700 troops by Christmas. And he expects that by July, we will be able to reduce our troop levels in Iraq from 20 combat brigades to 15.

General Petraeus also recommends that in December we begin transitioning to the next phase of our strategy in Iraq. As terrorists are defeated, civil society takes root, and the Iraqis assume more control over their own security, our mission in Iraq will evolve. Over time, our troops will shift from leading operations, to partnering with Iraqi forces, and eventually to overwatching those forces. As this transition in our mission takes place, our troops will focus on a more limited set of tasks, including counterterrorism operations and training, equipping, and supporting Iraqi forces.

I have consulted with the Joint Chiefs of Staff, other members of my national security team, Iraqi officials, and leaders of both parties in Congress. I have benefited from their advice, and I have accepted General Petraeus's recommendations. I have directed General Petraeus and Ambassador Crocker to update their joint campaign plan for Iraq, so we can adjust our military and civilian resources accordingly. I have also directed them to deliver another report to Congress in March. At that time, they will provide a fresh assessment of the situation in Iraq and of the troop levels and resources we need to meet our national security objectives.

The principle guiding my decisions on troop levels in Iraq is "return on success." The more successful we are, the more American troops can return home. And in all we do, I will ensure that our commanders on the ground have the troops and flexibility they need to defeat the enemy.

Americans want our country to be safe and our troops to begin coming home from Iraq. Yet those of us who believe success in Iraq is essential to our security, and those who believe we should begin bringing our troops home, have been at odds. Now, because of the measure of success we are seeing in Iraq, we can begin seeing troops come home. The way forward I have described tonight makes it possible, for the first time in years, for people who have been on opposite sides of this difficult debate to come together.

This vision for a reduced American presence also has the support of Iraqi leaders from all communities. At the same time, they understand that their success will require U.S. political, economic, and security engagement that extends beyond my presidency. These Iraqi leaders have asked for an enduring relationship with America. And we are ready to begin building that relationship—in a way that protects our interests in the region and requires many fewer American troops.

The success of a free Iraq is critical to the security of the United States. A free Iraq will deny al Qaeda a safe haven. A free Iraq will counter the destructive ambitions of Iran. A free Iraq will marginalize extremists, unleash the talent of its people, and be an anchor of stability in the region. A free Iraq will set an example for people across the Middle East. A free Iraq will be our partner in the fight against terror—and that will make us safer here at home.

Realizing this vision will be difficult, but it is achievable. Our military commanders believe we can succeed. Our diplomats believe we can succeed. And for the safety of future generations of Americans, we must succeed.

If we were to be driven out of Iraq, extremists of all strains would be emboldened. Al Qaeda could gain new recruits and new sanctuaries. Iran would benefit from the chaos and would be encouraged in its efforts to gain nuclear weapons and dominate the region. Extremists could control a key part of the global energy supply. Iraq could face a humanitarian nightmare. Democracy movements would be violently reversed. We would leave our children to face a far more dangerous world. And as we saw on September the 11th, 2001, those dangers can reach our cities and kill our people.

Whatever political party you belong to, whatever your position on Iraq, we should be able to agree that America has a vital interest in preventing chaos and providing hope in the Middle East. We should be able to agree that we must defeat al Qaeda, counter Iran, help the Afghan government, work for peace in the Holy Land, and strengthen our military so we can prevail in the struggle against terrorists and extremists.

So tonight I want to speak to members of the United States Congress: Let us come together on a policy of strength in the Middle East. I thank you for providing crucial funds and resources for our military. And I ask you to join me in supporting the recommendations General Petraeus has made and the troop levels he has asked for.

To the Iraqi people: You have voted for freedom, and now you are liberating your country from terrorists and death squads. You must demand that your leaders make the tough choices needed to achieve reconciliation. As you do, have confidence that America does not abandon our friends, and we will not abandon you.

To Iraq's neighbors who seek peace: The violent extremists who target Iraq are also targeting you. The best way to secure your interests and protect your own people is to stand with the people of Iraq. That means using your economic and diplomatic leverage to strengthen the government in Baghdad. And it means the efforts by Iran and Syria to undermine that government must end.

To the international community: The success of a free Iraq matters to every civilized nation. We thank the 36 nations who have troops on the ground in Iraq and the many others who are helping that young democracy. We encourage all nations to help, by implementing the International Compact to revitalize Iraq's economy, by participating in the Neighbors Conferences to boost cooperation and overcome differences in the region, and by supporting the new and expanded mission of the United Nations in Iraq.

To our military personnel, intelligence officers, diplomats, and civilians on the front lines in Iraq: You have done everything America has asked of you. And the progress I have reported tonight is in large part because of your courage and hard effort. You are serving far from home. Our nation is grateful for your sacrifices, and the sacrifices of your families.

Earlier this year, I received an email from the family of Army Specialist Brandon Stout of Michigan. Brandon volunteered for the National Guard and was killed while serving in Baghdad. His family has suffered greatly. Yet in their sorrow, they see larger purpose. His wife, Audrey, says that Brandon felt called to serve and knew what he was fighting for. And his parents, Tracy and Jeff, wrote me this: "We believe this is a war of good and evil and we must win even if it cost the life of our own son. Freedom is not free."

This country is blessed to have Americans like Brandon Stout, who make extraordinary sacrifices to keep us safe from harm. They are doing so in a fight that is just, and right, and necessary. And now it falls to us to finish the work they have begun.

Some say the gains we are making in Iraq come too late. They are mistaken. It is never too late to deal a blow to al Qaeda. It is never too late to advance freedom. And it is never too late to support our troops in a fight they can win.

Good night, and God bless America.

DOCUMENT NO. 5

THE STATUS OF THE WAR AND POLITICAL DEVELOPMENTS IN IRAQ: THE PETRAEUS/CROCKER REPORT TO CONGRESS

Hearing Before the House Armed Services Committee

September 10, 2007

Opening Statement of Chairman Ike Skelton (D-MO)

Washington, DC—House Armed Services Committee Chairman Ike Skelton (D-MO) delivered the following opening statement during today's joint hearing with the House Foreign Affairs Committee on the status of the war and political developments in Iraq. The committees received testimony from: General David Petraeus, Commander, Multi-National Force-Iraq; and Ambassador Ryan Crocker, U.S. Ambassador to Iraq.

Today, the House Armed Services Committee and the House Foreign Affairs jointly meet for what may be the most important hearing of the year. We have today the pleasure to welcome two of America's finest, General David Petraeus and Ambassador Ryan Crocker, and I would like to thank them for appearing. It is wonderful to see you both again. Let me remind members that the testimony we will be receiving reflects the best judgment of these leaders. Later this week, the Congress will receive the Presidential report required by the 2007 supplemental appropriations bill which will reflect the reports of our two witnesses.

I also want to start this hearing by commending all of those—the troops and foreign service officers—who serve under you. Their mission is most challenging. They, and their families, have sacrificed tremendously and have served valiantly. We know that where there has been progress on the ground, it is due to their heroic efforts.

Today is a critical moment. This Congress and this nation are divided on the pace with which the United States should turn over responsibility to the Iraqis. But every member here desires that we complete our military involvement in Iraq in a way that best preserves the national security of the United States.

I think that is where we must begin, by considering the overall security of this nation. It is our responsibility under the Constitution to ensure the United States military can deter and, if needed, prevail anywhere our interests are threatened. Iraq is an important piece of that overall equation, but it is only a piece.

There are very real tradeoffs when we send one hundred and sixty thousand of our men and women in uniform to Iraq. Those troops in Iraq are not available for other missions. They are not available to go to Afghanistan to pursue Osama bin Laden and the other Al Qaeda leaders who ordered an attack on us one day short of six years ago.

These troops and their depleted equipment are also not easily available to respond to a new conflict that might emerge. It is the issue of readiness. My colleagues have heard me say this before, but in my 30 years in Congress, we have been involved in 12 military contingencies, some of them major in scope, almost all unexpected. Right now, with so many troops in Iraq, I think our response to an unexpected threat would come at a devastating cost.

Our troops have become outstanding at counter-insurgencies. But we need them prepared for the full spectrum of combat. This is a lesson we learn again and again. In 1921, in his book, "America's Duty," General Leonard Wood addressed a similar situation from his day. "The Spanish War gave little training, as did the Philippine insurrection. Campaigns of this kind are of limited value as a preparation for war with an organized prepared power."

Wars stress armies, but we should make sure that the strain on our force is undertaken consciously, and that this war is vital to our national security. We must be sure, before we talk about continuing this effort, that Iraq is the war worth the risk of breaking our army and being unable to deal with other risks to our nation.

That is the strategic context in which I consider the situation in Iraq today. Prominent for me is also how we have gotten to where we are in Iraq. We remember the discussion of weapons of mass destruction, the "Mission Accomplished" sign, and General Garner's short tenure. We recall Paul Bremer, the long debate over the summer of 2004 about whether or not there was an insurgency, and the grudging admission from the then-Secretary of Defense that fall that, yes, there was in fact a growing insurgency.

We recall the first and second battles of Fallujah, and the idea that we could quickly train the Iraqi Security Forces to replace us. We should remember this history as we evaluate the current status of our efforts in Iraq.

The surge is just the latest in a long line of operations. It frankly looks as if there has been tactical progress in the security area, but we should at this point temper any enthusiasm with the caveat that this is Iraq, and nothing has been easy there. In a poll of Iraqis released this morning sponsored by ABC News, the BBC, and the Japanese broadcaster NHK, we learned that at least 65% of Iraqis say the surge is not working and 72% say the US presence is making Iraq's security worse. This is troublesome.

I believe our valiant troops are likely improving security in the areas where they are deployed. This makes good sense. They're the best, so of course things improve when we deploy more of them. Some called for more forces to be deployed immediately after the invasion, and we just might have avoided a lot of the current troubles. One of the great ironies of this hearing today is that General Petraeus who sits here before us is almost certainly the right man for the job in Iraq, but he's the right person three years too late and 250,000 troops short. If we had your vision and approach, General, early on, we may not have gotten to the point where our troops are caught in the midst of brutal sectarian fighting without an Iraqi government bridging the political divides that drive this violence.

This surge was intended to provide "breathing space" for the Iraqis to bridge sectarian divides with real political compromises. But while our troops are holding back the opposing team to let them make a touchdown the Iraqis haven't even picking up the ball. The President's July report and the GAO report of a few days ago showed the lack of progress on individual benchmarks, and no one can make the case that the Iraqi government has made great strides. The witnesses must tell us why we should continue sending our young men and women to fight and die if the Iraqis won't make the tough sacrifices leading to reconciliation? What is the likelihood that things will change dramatically and there will be political progress in the near term? Are we merely beating a dead horse?

The Commission on the Iraqi Security Forces, chaired by retired General Jim Jones and which my committee heard from just the other day, puts it well, "At the end of the day, however, the future of Iraq ... hinges on the ability of the Iraqi people and the government to begin the process of achieving national reconciliation and to ending sectarian violence. For the time being, all progress seems to flow from this most pressing requirement."

These are powerful words, and it's a powerful truth. But the disappointing part is that the Iraqis have not stepped up to that challenge. We know there have been local political gains. In Anbar province, the Marines have done impressive work helping to turn local sheiks and tribal leaders against Al Qaeda in Iraq. It may well be that such local, tactical gains will set the stage for the political partition of Iraq. This may carry with it additional problems.

Cementing any progress requires reconciliation at the national level. Does anyone think that a national government, run by sectarian Shiite and Kurdish leaders will, in the long run, provide funds and arms to former Sunni insurgents who they suspect still wish to overthrow them? And how long will the Sunnis wait quietly to be given assurances about revenue and power sharing?

I hope, General Petraeus and Ambassador Crocker, that you can persuade us that there is substantial reason to believe that Iraq will turn around in the very near future. But you have the burden of answering these fundamental questions to those of us who have been watching Iraq for years. And every promising development has so far not turned out to be the solution we hoped.

Columnist Tom Friedman said something wise in a column not long ago. He asked, "'What will convey to you … that the surge is working and worth sustaining?'" His answer was, "If I saw … Iraq's Shiite, Kurdish and Sunni leaders stepping forward, declaring their willingness to work out their differences by a set deadline and publicly asking us to stay until they do." I think he had a point, and one we need to keep in mind while we consider where we go from here in Iraq. The Iraqi leaders have not done this, and sadly I don't think there is any likelihood they will in the near future.

"I now turn to Chairman Lantos for any comments he might wish to make."

Opening Statement by Chairman Lantos

Two of our nation's most capable public servants have come before us today to assess the situation in Iraq. General Petraeus, Ambassador Crocker, every single one of us wants you to succeed in your efforts to the maximum possible extent. We admire the heroism and sacrifice of our men and women in uniform and the dedication of our diplomatic corps in Iraq, and we fully understand the terrible burden on their families.

Our witnesses have been sent here this morning to restore credibility to a discredited policy. We and the American people already know that the situation in Iraq is grim, and a growing majority of this Congress and of the American people want our troops out.

In October of 2003 I flew in a helicopter with you, General Petraeus, over Northern Iraq around Mosul. As we passed over the countryside, you pointed out to me several ammunition dumps that had once belonged to the army of Saddam Hussein. "I don't have enough troops to guard these places," you said. "Someday, this might come back to haunt us."

Well, General Petraeus, you saw it coming. Those unguarded ammo dumps became the arsenals of insurgency. Those weapons have been turned against us. How very typical of this war.

The Administration's myopic policies in Iraq have created a fiasco. Is it any wonder that on the subject of Iraq, more and more Americans have little confidence in this Administration? We can not take ANY of this Administration's assertions on Iraq at face value anymore, and no amount of charts or statistics will improve its credibility.

This is not a knock on you, General Petraeus, or on you, Ambassador Crocker. But the fact remains, gentlemen, that the Administration has sent you here today to convince the members of these two Committees and the Congress that victory is at hand.

With all due respect to you, I must say … I don't buy it. And neither does the independent Government Accountability Office or the Commission headed by General Jones. Both recently issued deeply pessimistic reports.

The current escalation in our military presence in Iraq may have produced some tactical successes. But strategically, the escalation has failed. It was intended to buy time for Prime Minister Maliki and the other Iraqi political leaders to find ways to move toward the one thing that may end this terrible civil conflict—and that, of course, is a political settlement. As best we can see, that time has been utterly squandered.

Prime Minister Maliki has not shown the slightest inclination to move in the direction of compromise. Instead of working to build national institutions—a truly Iraqi army, a competent bureaucracy, a non-sectarian police force—Maliki has moved in the opposite direction. The so-called "Unity Accord" announced with such fanfare a couple of weeks ago, is just another in a long list of empty promises.

Instead of acting as a leader for Iraq as a whole, Maliki has functioned as the front man for Shiite partisans. And he has presided over a Shiite coalition that includes some of the most notorious militias, death squads, and sectarian thugs in Iraq.

This is not what the American people had in mind. And when Mr. Maliki states, as he recently did, that if the Americans leave, he can find, quote, "new friends," we are reminded most forcefully of his and his Party's intimate ties to Iran.

In his recent visit to Anbar Province, the President made much of our cooperation in the fight against Al Qaeda with Sunni tribal militias. This alliance may in the short run be a positive development—but it also raises some serious and profound questions.

Anbar, of course, includes just five per cent of the population of Iraq—an important five per cent, but still only five. What's more, by arming, training and funding the Sunni militias in that province, we are working against our own strategy of building national Iraqi institutions.

America should not be in the business of arming, training and funding both sides of a religious civil war in Iraq. Did the Administration learn nothing from our country's actions in Afghanistan two decades ago, when by supporting Islamist militants against the Soviet Union, we helped pave the way for the rise of the Taliban? Why are we now repeating the short-sighted patterns of the past?

In Iraq today, we are wrecking our military, forcing their families to suffer needlessly, sacrificing the lives of our brave young men and women in uniform. And the enormous financial cost of this war is limiting our ability to address our global security needs, as well as pressing domestic problems such as health care, crumbling infrastructure and public education. The cost of this war in Iraq will be passed along to our grandchildren and beyond.

In the last few days, General Petraeus, media have reported that you are prepared to support a slow drawdown of our forces in Iraq—beginning with a brigade or two, perhaps at the end of this year.

This clearly is nowhere near enough.

We need to send Maliki's government a strong message, loud and clear.

Removing a brigade is nothing but a political whisper—and it is unacceptable to the American people and to the majority of the Congress.

As long as American troops are doing the heavy lifting in Iraq, there is no reason—none at all—for the Iraqis themselves to step up. Military progress without political progress is meaningless.

It is their country—and it is their turn. Prime Minister Maliki and the Iraqi politicians need to know that the free ride is over and that American troops will not be party to their civil war.

The situation in Iraq cries out for a dramatic change of course. We need to get out of Iraq, for that country's sake and for our own. It is time to go—and to go now.

Report to Congress on the Situation in Iraq

General David H. Petraeus
Commander, Multi-National Force–Iraq
10–11 September 2007

Mr. Chairmen, Ranking Members, Members of the Committees, thank you for the opportunity to provide my assessment of the security situation in Iraq and to discuss the recommendations I recently provided to my chain of command for the way forward.

At the outset, I would like to note that this is my testimony. Although I have briefed my assessment and recommendations to my chain of command, I wrote this testimony myself. It has not been cleared by, nor shared with, anyone in the Pentagon, the White House, or Congress.

As a bottom line up front, the military objectives of the surge are, in large measure, being met. In recent months, in the face of tough enemies and the brutal summer heat of Iraq, Coalition and Iraqi Security Forces have achieved progress in the security arena. Though the improvements have been uneven across Iraq, the overall number of security incidents in Iraq has declined in 8 of the past 12 weeks, with the numbers of incidents in the last two weeks at the lowest levels seen since June 2006.

One reason for the decline in incidents is that Coalition and Iraqi forces have dealt significant blows to Al Qaeda-Iraq. Though Al Qaeda and its affiliates in Iraq remain dangerous, we have taken away a number of their sanctuaries and gained the initiative in many areas.

We have also disrupted Shia militia extremists, capturing the head and numerous other leaders of the Iranian-supported Special Groups, along with a senior Lebanese Hezbollah operative supporting Iran's activities in Iraq.

Coalition and Iraqi operations have helped reduce ethno-sectarian violence, as well, bringing down the number of ethno-sectarian deaths substantially in Baghdad and across Iraq since the height of the sectarian violence last December. The number of overall civilian deaths has also declined during this period, although the numbers in each area are still at troubling levels.

Iraqi Security Forces have also continued to grow and to shoulder more of the load, albeit slowly and amid continuing concerns about the sectarian tendencies of some elements in their ranks. In general, however, Iraqi elements have been standing and fighting and sustaining tough losses, and they have taken the lead in operations in many areas.

Additionally, in what may be the most significant development of the past 8 months, the tribal rejection of Al Qaeda that started in Anbar Province and helped produce such significant change there has now spread to a number of other locations as well.

Based on all this and on the further progress we believe we can achieve over the next few months, I believe that we will be able to reduce our forces to the pre-surge level of brigade combat teams by next summer without jeopardizing the security gains that we have fought so hard to achieve.

Beyond that, while noting that the situation in Iraq remains complex, difficult, and sometimes downright frustrating, I also believe that it is possible to achieve our objectives in Iraq over time, though doing so will be neither quick nor easy.

Having provided that summary, I would like to review the nature of the conflict in Iraq, recall the situation before the surge, describe the current situation, and explain the recommendations I have provided to my chain of command for the way ahead in Iraq.

The Nature of the Conflict

The fundamental source of the conflict in Iraq is competition among ethnic and sectarian communities for power and resources. This competition *will* take place, and its resolution is key to producing long-term stability in the new Iraq. The question is whether the competition takes place more—or less—violently. This chart shows the security challenges in Iraq. Foreign and home-grown terrorists, insurgents, militia extremists, and criminals all push the ethno-sectarian competition toward violence. Malign actions by Syria and, especially, by Iran fuel that violence. Lack of adequate governmental capacity, lingering sectarian mistrust, and various forms of corruption add to Iraq's challenges.

The Situation in December 2006 and the Surge

In our recent efforts to look to the future, we found it useful to revisit the past. In December 2006, during the height of the ethno-sectarian violence that escalated in the wake of the bombing of the Golden Dome Mosque in Samarra, the leaders in Iraq at that time—General George Casey and Ambassador Zalmay Khalilzad—concluded that the coalition was failing to achieve its objectives. Their review underscored the need to protect the population and reduce sectarian violence, especially in Baghdad. As a result, General Casey requested additional forces to enable the Coalition to accomplish these tasks, and those forces began to flow in January.

In the ensuing months, our forces and our Iraqi counterparts have focused on improving security, especially in Baghdad and the areas around it, wresting sanctuaries from Al Qaeda control, and disrupting the efforts of the Iranian-supported militia extremists. We have employed counterinsurgency practices that underscore the importance of units living among the people they are securing, and accordingly, our forces have established dozens of joint security stations and patrol bases manned by Coalition and Iraqi forces in Baghdad and in other areas across Iraq.

In mid-June, with all the surge brigades in place, we launched a series of offensive operations focused on: expanding the gains achieved in the preceding months in Anbar Province; clearing Baqubah, several key Baghdad neighborhoods, the remaining sanctuaries in Anbar Province, and important areas in the so-called "belts" around Baghdad; and pursuing Al Qaeda in the Diyala River Valley and several other areas.

Throughout this period, as well, we engaged in dialogue with insurgent groups and tribes, and this led to additional elements standing up to oppose Al Qaeda and other extremists. We also continued to emphasize the development of the Iraqi Security Forces and we employed non-kinetic means to exploit the opportunities provided by the conduct of our kinetic operations—aided in this effort by the arrival of additional Provincial Reconstruction Teams.

Current Situation and Trends

The progress our forces have achieved with our Iraqi counterparts has, as I noted at the outset, been substantial. While there have been setbacks as well as successes and tough losses along the way, overall, our tactical commanders and I see improvements in the security environment. We do not, however, just rely on gut feel or personal observations; we also conduct considerable data collection and analysis to gauge progress and determine trends. We do this by gathering and refining data from coalition *and* Iraqi operations centers, using a methodology that has been in place for well over a year and that has benefited over the past seven months from the increased presence of our forces living among the Iraqi people. We endeavor to ensure our analysis of that data is conducted with rigor and consistency, as our ability to achieve a nuanced understanding of the security environment is dependent on collecting and analyzing data in a consistent way over time. Two US intelligence agencies recently reviewed our methodology, and they concluded that the data we produce is the most accurate and authoritative in Iraq.

As I mentioned up front, and as the chart before you reflects, the level of security incidents has decreased significantly since the start of the surge of offensive operations in mid-June, declining in 8 of the past 12 weeks, with the level of incidents in the past two weeks the lowest since June 2006 and with the number of *attacks* this past week the lowest since April 2006.

Civilian deaths of *all* categories, less natural causes, have also declined considerably, by over 45% Iraq-wide since the height of the sectarian violence in December. This is shown by the top line on this chart, and the decline by some 70% in Baghdad is shown by the bottom line. Periodic mass casualty attacks by Al Qaeda have tragically added to the numbers outside Baghdad, in particular. Even without the sensational attacks, however, the level of civilian deaths is clearly still too high and continues to be of serious concern.

As the next chart shows, the number of *ethno-sectarian* deaths, an important subset of the overall civilian casualty figures, has also declined significantly since the height of the sectarian violence in December. Iraq-wide, as shown by the top line on this chart, the number of ethno-sectarian deaths has come down by over 55%, and it would have come down much further were it not for the casualties inflicted by barbaric Al Qaeda bombings attempting to reignite sectarian violence. In Baghdad, as the bottom line shows, the number of ethno-sectarian deaths has come down by some 80% since December. This chart also displays the density of sectarian incidents in various Baghdad neighborhoods and it both reflects the progress made in reducing ethno-sectarian violence in the Iraqi capital and identifies the areas that remain the most challenging.

As we have gone on the offensive in former Al Qaeda and insurgent sanctuaries, and as locals have increasingly supported our efforts, we have found a substantially increased number of arms, ammunition, and explosives caches. As this chart shows, we have, so far this year, already found and cleared over 4,400 caches, nearly 1,700 more than we discovered in all of last year. This may be a factor in the reduction in the number of overall improvised explosive device attacks in recent months, which as this chart shows, has declined sharply, by about one-third, since June.

The change in the security situation in Anbar Province has, of course, been particularly dramatic. As this chart shows, monthly attack levels in Anbar have declined from some 1,350 in October 2006 to a bit over 200 in August of this year. This dramatic decrease reflects the significance of the local rejection of Al Qaeda and the newfound willingness of local Anbaris to volunteer to serve in the Iraqi Army and Iraqi Police Service. As I noted earlier, we are seeing similar actions in other locations, as well.

To be sure, trends have not been uniformly positive across Iraq, as is shown by this chart depicting violence levels in several key Iraqi provinces. The trend in Ninevah Province, for example, has been much more up and down, until a recent decline, and the same is true in Sala ad Din Province, though recent trends there and in Baghdad have been in the right direction. In any event, the overall trajectory in Iraq—a steady decline of incidents in the past three months—*is* still quite significant.

The number of car bombings and suicide attacks has also declined in each of the past 5 months, from a high of some 175 in March, as this chart shows, to about 90 this past month. While this trend in recent months has been heartening, the number of high profile attacks is still too high, and we continue to work hard to destroy the networks that carry out these barbaric attacks.

Our operations have, in fact, produced substantial progress against Al Qaeda and its affiliates in Iraq. As this chart shows, in the past 8 months, we have considerably reduced the areas in which Al Qaeda enjoyed sanctuary. We have also neutralized 5 media cells, detained the senior Iraqi leader of Al Qaeda-Iraq, and killed or captured nearly 100 other key leaders and some 2,500 rank-and-file fighters. Al Qaeda is certainly not defeated; however, it is off balance and we are pursuing its leaders and operators aggressively. Of note, as the recent National Intelligence Estimate on Iraq explained, these gains against Al Qaeda are a result of the synergy of actions by: conventional forces to deny the terrorists sanctuary; intelligence, surveillance, and reconnaissance assets to find the enemy; and special operations elements to conduct targeted raids. A combination of these assets is necessary to prevent the creation of a terrorist safe haven in Iraq.

In the past six months we have also targeted Shia militia extremists, capturing a number of senior leaders and fighters, as well as the deputy commander of Lebanese Hezbollah Department 2800, the organization created to support the training, arming, funding, and, in some cases, direction of the militia extremists by the Iranian Republican Guard Corps' Qods Force. These elements have assassinated and kidnapped Iraqi governmental leaders, killed and wounded our soldiers with advanced explosive devices provided by Iran, and indiscriminately rocketed civilians in the International Zone and elsewhere. It is increasingly apparent to both Coalition and Iraqi leaders that Iran, through the use of the Qods Force, seeks to turn the Iraqi Special Groups into a Hezbollah-like force to serve its interests and fight a proxy war against the Iraqi state and coalition forces in Iraq.

The most significant development in the past six months likely has been the increasing emergence of tribes and local citizens rejecting Al Qaeda and other extremists. This has, of course, been most visible in Anbar Province. A year ago the province was assessed as "lost" politically. Today, it is a model of what happens when local leaders and citizens decide to oppose Al Qaeda and reject its Taliban-like ideology. While Anbar is unique and the model it provides cannot be replicated everywhere in Iraq, it does demonstrate the dramatic change in security that is possible with the support and participation of local citizens. As this chart shows, other tribes have been inspired by the actions of those in Anbar and have volunteered to fight extremists as well. We have, in coordination with the Iraqi government's National Reconciliation Committee, been engaging these tribes and groups of local citizens who want to oppose extremists and to contribute to local security. Some 20,000 such individuals are already being hired for the Iraqi Police, thousands of others are being assimilated into the Iraqi Army, and thousands more are vying for a spot in Iraq's Security Forces.

Iraqi Security Forces

As I noted earlier, Iraqi Security Forces have continued to grow, to develop their capabilities, and to shoulder more of the burden of providing security for their country. Despite concerns about sectarian influence, inadequate logistics and supporting institutions, and an insufficient number of qualified commissioned and non-commissioned officers, Iraqi units are engaged around the country.

As this chart shows, there are now nearly 140 Iraqi Army, National Police, and Special Operations Forces Battalions in the fight, with about 95 of those capable of taking the lead in operations, albeit with some coalition support. Beyond that, all of Iraq's battalions have been heavily involved in combat operations that often result in the loss of leaders, soldiers, and equipment. These losses are among the shortcomings identified by operational readiness assessments, but we should not take from these assessments the impression that Iraqi forces are not in the fight and contributing. Indeed, despite their shortages, many Iraqi units across Iraq now operate with minimal coalition assistance.

As counterinsurgency operations require substantial numbers of boots on the ground, we are helping the Iraqis expand the size of their security forces. Currently, there are some 445,000 individuals on the payrolls of Iraq's Interior and Defense Ministries. Based on recent decisions by Prime Minister Maliki, the number of Iraq's security forces will grow further by the end of this year, possibly by as much as 40,000. Given the security challenges Iraq faces, we support this decision, and we will work with the two security ministries as they continue their efforts to expand their basic training capacity, leader development programs, logistical structures and elements, and various other institutional capabilities to support the substantial growth in Iraqi forces.

Significantly, in 2007, Iraq will, as in 2006, spend more on its security forces than it will receive in security assistance from the United States. In fact, Iraq is becoming one of the United States' larger foreign military sales customers, committing some $1.6 billion to FMS already, with the possibility of up to $1.8 billion more being committed before the end of this year. And I appreciate the attention that some members of Congress have recently given to speeding up the FMS process for Iraq.

To summarize, the security situation in Iraq is improving, and Iraqis elements are slowly taking on more of the responsibility for protecting their citizens. Innumerable challenges lie ahead; however, Coalition and Iraqi Security Forces have made progress toward achieving sustainable security. As a result, the United States will be in a position to reduce its forces in Iraq in the months ahead.

Recommendations

Two weeks ago I provided recommendations for the way ahead in Iraq to the members of my chain of command and the Joint Chiefs of Staff. The essence of the approach I recommended is captured in its title: "Security While Transitioning: From Leading to Partnering to Overwatch." This approach seeks to build on the security improvements our troopers and our Iraqi counterparts have fought so hard to achieve in recent months. It reflects recognition of the importance of securing the population *and* the imperative of transitioning responsibilities to Iraqi institutions and Iraqi forces as quickly as possible, but without rushing to failure. It includes substantial support for the continuing development of Iraqi Security Forces. It also stresses the need to continue the counterinsurgency strategy that we have been employing, but with Iraqis gradually shouldering more of the load. And it highlights the importance of regional and global diplomatic approaches. Finally, in recognition of the fact that this war is not only being fought on the ground in Iraq but also in cyberspace, it also notes the need to contest the enemy's growing use of that important medium to spread extremism.

The recommendations I provided were informed by operational and strategic considerations. The *operational* considerations include recognition that:

- military aspects of the surge have achieved progress and generated momentum;
- Iraqi Security Forces have continued to grow and have slowly been shouldering more of the security burden in Iraq;
- a mission focus on either population security or transition alone will not be adequate to achieve our objectives;
- success against Al Qaeda-Iraq and Iranian-supported militia extremists requires conventional forces as well as special operations forces; and
- the security and local political situations will enable us to draw down the surge forces.

My recommendations also took into account a number of *strategic* considerations:

- political progress will take place only if sufficient security exists;
- long-term US ground force viability will benefit from force reductions as the surge runs its course;
- regional, global, and cyberspace initiatives are critical to success; and
- Iraqi leaders understandably want to assume greater sovereignty in their country, although, as they recently announced, they do desire continued presence of coalition forces in Iraq in 2008 under a new UN Security Council Resolution and, following that, they want to negotiate a long term security agreement with the United States and other nations.

Based on these considerations, and having worked the battlefield geometry with Lieutenant General Ray Odierno to ensure that we retain and build on the gains for which our troopers have fought, I have recommended a drawdown of the surge forces from Iraq. In fact, later this month, the Marine Expeditionary Unit deployed as part of the surge will depart Iraq. Beyond that, if my recommendations are approved, that unit's departure will be followed by the withdrawal of a brigade combat team without replacement in mid-December and the further redeployment without replacement of four other brigade combat teams and the two surge Marine battalions in the first 7 months of 2008, until we reach the pre-surge level of 15 brigade combat teams by mid-July 2008.

I would also like to discuss the period beyond next summer. Force reductions *will* continue beyond the pre-surge levels of brigade combat teams that we will reach by mid-July 2008; however, in my professional judgment, it would be premature to make recommendations on the pace of such reductions at this time. In fact, our experience in Iraq has repeatedly shown that projecting too far into the future is not just difficult, it can be misleading and even hazardous. The events of the past six months underscore that point. When I testified in January, for example, no one would have dared to forecast that Anbar Province would have been transformed the way it has in the past 6 months. Nor would anyone have predicted that volunteers in one-time Al Qaeda strongholds like Ghazaliyah in western Baghdad or in Adamiya in eastern Baghdad would seek to join the fight against Al Qaeda. Nor would we have anticipated that a Shia-led government would accept significant numbers of Sunni volunteers into the ranks of the local police force in Abu Ghraib. Beyond that, on a less encouraging note, none of us earlier this year appreciated the extent of Iranian involvement in Iraq, something about which we and Iraq's leaders all now have greater concern.

In view of this, I do not believe it is reasonable to have an adequate appreciation for the pace of further reductions and mission adjustments beyond the summer of 2008 until about mid-March of next year. We will, no later than that time, consider factors similar to those on which I based the current recommendations, having by then, of course, a better feel for the security situation, the improvements in the capabilities of our Iraqi counterparts, and the enemy situation. I will then, as I did in developing the recommendations I have explained here today, also take into consideration the demands on our Nation's ground forces, although I believe that that consideration should once again inform, not drive, the recommendations I make.

This chart captures the recommendations I have described, showing the recommended reduction of brigade combat teams as the surge runs its course and illustrating the concept of our units adjusting their missions and transitioning responsibilities to Iraqis, as the situation and Iraqi capabilities permit. It also reflects the no-later-than date for recommendations on force adjustments beyond next summer and provides a possible approach we have considered for the future force structure and mission set in Iraq.

One may argue that the best way to speed the process in Iraq is to change the MNF-I mission from one that emphasizes population security, counter-terrorism, and transition, to one that is strictly focused on transition and counter-terrorism. Making that change now would, in our view, be premature. We have learned before that there is a real danger in handing over tasks to the Iraqi Security Forces before their capacity and local conditions warrant. In fact, the drafters of the recently released National Intelligence Estimate on Iraq recognized this danger when they wrote, and I quote, "We assess that changing the mission of Coalition forces from a primarily counterinsurgency and stabilization role to a primary combat support role for Iraqi forces and counterterrorist operations to prevent AQI from establishing a safe haven would erode security gains achieved thus far."

In describing the recommendations I have made, I should note again that, like Ambassador Crocker, I believe Iraq's problems will require a long-term effort. There are no easy answers or quick solutions. And though we both believe this effort can succeed, it will take time. Our assessments underscore, in fact, the importance of recognizing that a premature drawdown of our forces would likely have devastating consequences.

That assessment is supported by the findings of a 16 August Defense Intelligence Agency report on the implications of a rapid withdrawal of US forces from Iraq. Summarizing it in an unclassified fashion, it concludes that a rapid withdrawal would result in the further release of the strong centrifugal forces in Iraq and produce a number of dangerous results, including a high risk of disintegration of the Iraqi Security Forces; rapid deterioration of local security initiatives; Al Qaeda-Iraq regaining lost ground and freedom of maneuver; a marked increase in violence and further ethno-sectarian displacement and refugee flows; alliances of convenience by Iraqi groups with internal and external forces to gain advantages over their rivals; and exacerbation of already challenging regional dynamics, especially with respect to Iran.

Lieutenant General Odierno and I share this assessment and believe that the best way to secure our national interests and avoid an unfavorable outcome in Iraq is to continue to focus our operations on securing the Iraqi people while targeting terrorist groups and militia extremists and, as quickly as conditions are met, transitioning security tasks to Iraqi elements.

Closing Comments

Before closing, I want to thank you and your colleagues for your support of our men and women in uniform in Iraq. The Soldiers, Sailors, Airmen, Marines, and Coast Guardsmen with whom I'm honored to serve are the best equipped and, very likely, the most professional force in our nation's history. Impressively, despite all that has been asked of them in recent years, they continue to raise their right hands and volunteer to stay in uniform. With three weeks to go in this fiscal year, in fact, the Army elements in Iraq, for example, have achieved well over 130% of the reenlistment goals in the initial term and careerist categories and nearly 115% in the mid-career category. All of us appreciate what you have done to ensure that these great troopers have had what they've needed to accomplish their mission, just as we appreciate what you have done to take care of their families, as they, too, have made significant sacrifices in recent years.

The advances you have underwritten in weapons systems and individual equipment; in munitions; in command, control, and communications systems; in intelligence, surveillance, and reconnaissance capabilities; in vehicles and counter-IED systems and programs; and in manned and unmanned aircraft have proven invaluable in Iraq. The capabilities that you have funded most recently—especially the vehicles that will provide greater protection against improvised explosive devices—are also of enormous importance. Additionally, your funding of the Commander's Emergency Response Program has given our leaders a critical tool with which to prosecute the counterinsurgency campaign. Finally, we appreciate as well your funding of our new detention programs and rule of law initiatives in Iraq.

In closing, it remains an enormous privilege to soldier again in Iraq with America's new "Greatest Generation." Our country's men and women in uniform have done a magnificent job in the most complex and challenging environment imaginable. All Americans should be very proud of their sons and daughters serving in Iraq today.

Thank you very much.

Statement of Ambassador Ryan C. Crocker
United States Ambassador to the Republic of Iraq
Before a Joint Hearing of the Committee on Foreign Affairs and the Committee on Armed Services

Introduction

Mr. Chairman,

Thank you for the opportunity to address Congress this week. I have considered it a privilege and an honor to serve in Iraq at a time when so much is at stake for our country and the people of the region—and when so many Americans of the highest caliber in our military and civilian services are doing the same. I know that a heavy responsibility weighs on my shoulders to provide the country with my best, most honest assessment of the situation in Iraq and the implications for the United States.

Americans, in this chamber and beyond, are looking for more than an update on the latest events. They want to know the answers to some key questions. Are our objectives realistic? Is it possible that Iraq will become a united, stable country with a democratic government operating under the rule of law? What is the trajectory—is Iraq, on the whole, moving in the right direction? Can we expect more and under what time frame? Are there alternative courses of action for our country which are superior?

These are sensible questions to be asked by a nation investing in and sacrificing for another country and people. In asking these questions, however, we must not lose sight of the vital interests the United States has in a successful outcome in Iraq.

My intention today is to give you an assessment of political, economic, and diplomatic developments in Iraq. In doing so, I will not minimize the enormity of the challenges faced by Iraqis, nor the complexity of the situation. Yet at the same time, I intend to demonstrate that it *is* possible for the United States to see its goals realized in Iraq and that Iraqis *are* capable of tackling and addressing the problems confronting them today. A secure, stable democratic Iraq at peace with its neighbors is attainable. In my judgment, the cumulative trajectory of political, economic, and diplomatic developments in Iraq is upwards, although the slope of that line is not steep. The process will not be quick, it will be uneven, punctuated by setbacks as well as achievements, and it will require substantial U.S. resolve and commitment. There will be no single moment at which we can claim victory; any turning point will likely only be recognized in retrospect.

This is a sober assessment, but it should not be a disheartening one. I have found it helpful, during my time in Iraq to reflect on our own history. At many points in the early years, our survival as a nation was questionable.

Our efforts to build the institutions of government were not always successful in the first instance. And tough issues—such as slavery, universal suffrage, civil rights, and state rights—were resolved only after acrimonious debate and sometimes violence.

Iraq is experiencing a revolution—not just regime change. It is only by understanding this that we can appreciate what is happening in Iraq and what Iraqis have achieved, as well as maintain a sense of realism about the challenges that remain.

Context

Evaluating where Iraqis are today only makes sense in the context of where they have been. Any Iraqi under 40 years old—and that is the overwhelming majority of the population—would have known nothing but the rule of the Ba'ath party before liberation four and a half years ago. Those 35 years were filled with crimes against humanity on every scale. Saddam Hussein ruled without any mercy, not hesitating to use lethal force and torture against even those in his inner circle. His genocidal campaign against the Kurds and savagery toward southern Shi'a are well known. But he also used violence and intimidation as tools in the complete deconstruction of Iraqi society. No organization or institution survived that was not linked in some way to regime protection. He created a pervasive climate of fear in which even family members were afraid to talk to one another.

This is the legacy that Iraqis had as their history when Saddam's statue came down on April 9, 2003. No Nelson Mandela existed to emerge on the national political scene; anyone with his leadership talents would have not survived. A new Iraq had to be built almost literally from scratch, and the builders in most cases were themselves reduced to their most basic identity, ethnic or sectarian.

Much progress has been made, particularly in building an institutional framework where there was none before. But rather than being a period in which old animosities and suspicions were overcome, the past 18 months in particular have further strained Iraqi society. The sectarian violence of 2006 and early 2007 had its seeds in Saddam's social deconstruction and it had dire consequences for the people of Iraq as well as its politics. Extensive displacement and widespread sectarian killings by al-Qa'ida and other extremist groups have gnawed away at the already frayed fabric of Iraqi society and politics. It is no exaggeration to say that Iraq is—and will remain for some time—a traumatized society.

National Politics

It is against this backdrop that developments in Iraq must be seen. Iraqis are facing some of the most profound political, economic, and security challenges imaginable. They are not simply grappling with the issue of *who* rules Iraq—but they are asking what kind of country Iraq will be, how it will be governed, and how Iraqis will share power and resources among each other. The constitution approved in a referendum in 2005 answered some of these questions in theory, but much remains uncertain in both law and practice.

Some of the more promising political developments at the national level are neither measured in benchmarks nor visible to those far from Baghdad. For instance, there is a budding debate about federalism among Iraq's leaders and, importantly, within the Sunni community. Those living in place like al-Anbar and Salahaddin are beginning to realize how localities having more of a say in daily decision making will empower their communities. No longer is an all-powerful Baghdad seen as the panacea to Iraq's problems. This thinking is nascent, but it is ultimately critical to the evolution of a common vision among all Iraqi leaders.

Similarly, there is a palpable frustration in Baghdad over the sectarian system that was used to divide the spoils of the state in the last few years. Leaders from all communities openly acknowledge that a focus on sectarian gains has led to poor governance and served Iraqis badly. And many claim to be ready to make the sacrifices that will be needed to put government performance ahead of sectarian and ethnic concerns. Such ideas are no longer controversial, although their application will be.

Finally, we are seeing Iraqis come to terms with complex issues not by first providing a national framework, but instead by tackling immediate problems. One such example is how the central government has accepted over 1700 young men from the Abu Ghurayb area west of Baghdad, including former members of insurgent groups, to be part of the Iraqi security forces. Another is how the government, without much public fanfare, has contacted thousands of members of the former Iraqi army, offering them retirement, return to the military, or public sector employment. So without the proclamation of a general amnesty, we see amnesty being granted, and de-baathification reform in advance of national legislation. In both instances, the seeds of reconciliation are being planted.

Our country, however, has come to associate progress on national reconciliation as meaning the passage of key pieces of legislation. There is logic to this, as the legislation we are urging the Iraqis to produce does—in one way or another—have to do with the question of how to share power and resources among Iraq's many communities. This legislation also has to do with the vision of the future Iraqi state. The oil and revenues sharing laws, for instance, deal with deeper issues than simply whether Iraqis in oil producing areas are willing to share their wealth with other Iraqis. What is difficult about the oil laws is that they take Iraq another step down the road toward a federal system that all Iraqis have not yet embraced. But once again, we see that even in the absence of legislation there is practical action as the central government shares oil revenues through budget allocations on an equitable basis with Iraq's provinces.

In many respects, the debates currently occurring in Iraq are akin to those surrounding our civil rights movement or struggle over states rights. With de-ba'athification, Iraqis are struggling to come to terms with a vicious past. They are trying to balance fear that the Ba'ath party would one day return to power with the recognition that many former members of the party are guilty of no crime and joined the organization not to repress others but for personal survival. With provincial powers, they are grappling with very serious questions about what the right balance between the center and the periphery is for Iraq. Some see the devolution of power to regions and provinces as being the best insurance against the rise of a future tyrannical figure in Baghdad. Others see Iraq, with its complex demographics, as in need of a strong central authority.

In short, we should not be surprised or dismayed that Iraqis have not fully resolved such issues. Rather, we should ask whether the way in which they are approaching such issues gives us a sense of their seriousness and ultimate capability to resolve Iraq's fundamental problems. Is the collective national leadership of Iraq ready to prioritize Iraq over sectarian and community interests? Can and will they come to agreement about what sort of Iraq they want?

I do believe that Iraq's leaders have the will to tackle the country's pressing problems, although it will take longer than we originally anticipated because of the environment and the gravity of the issues before them. Prime Minister al-Maliki and the other Iraqi leaders face enormous obstacles in their efforts to govern effectively. They approach the task with a deep sense of commitment and patriotism. An important part of this positive judgment was the effort made by the leaders this past summer. After weeks of preparatory work and many days of intensive meetings, Iraq's five most prominent national leaders from the three major communities issued a communiqué on August 26 that noted agreement on draft legislation dealing with de-ba'athification and provincial powers. This agreement by no means solves all of Iraq's problems. But the commitment of its leaders to work together on hard issues is encouraging.

Perhaps most significantly, these five Iraqi leaders together decided to publicly express their joint desire to develop a long term relationship with the United States. Despite their many differences in perspectives and experiences, they all agreed on language acknowledging the need for a continue presence by the multi-national forces in Iraq and expressing gratitude for the sacrifices these forces have made for Iraqis.

Provincial and Local Politics

At the provincial level, political gains have been more pronounced, particularly in the north and west of Iraq where the security improvements have been in some places dramatic. In these areas, there is abundant evidence that the security gains have opened the door for meaningful politics.

In al-Anbar, the progress on the security side has been extraordinary. Six months ago, violence was rampant, our forces were under daily attack, and Iraqis were cowering from the intimidation of al-Qa'ida. But al-Qa'ida overplayed its hand in al-Anbar and Anbaris began to reject its excesses—be they beheading school children or cutting off peoples' fingers as punishment for smoking. Recognizing the Coalition could help eject al-Qa'ida, the tribes began to fight with us, not against us, and the landscape in al-Anbar is dramatically different as a result. Tribal representatives are on the provincial council, which is now meeting regularly to find ways of restoring services, developing the economy, and executing a provincial budget. These leaders are looking for help to rebuild their cities and talking of attracting investment. Such scenes are also unfolding in parts of Diyala and Ninewa, where Iraqis have mobilized with the help of the Coalition and Iraqi security forces to evict al-Qa'ida from their communities. The world should note that when al-Qa'ida began implementing its twisted vision of the Caliphate in Iraq, Iraqis, from al-Anbar to Baghdad to Diyala', have overwhelmingly rejected it.

Shi'a extremists are also facing rejection. Recent attacks by elements of the Iranian backed Jaysh al-Mahdi on worshipers in the holy city of Karbala have provoked a backlash and triggered a call by Muqtada as-Sadr for Jaysh al-Mahdi to cease attacks against Iraqis and coalition forces.

A key challenge for Iraqis now is to link these positive developments in the provinces to the central government in Baghdad. Unlike our states, Iraqi provinces have little ability to generate funds through taxation, making them dependent on the central government for resources. The growing ability of the provinces to design and execute budgets and the readiness of the central government to resource them are success stories. On September 5, Iraq's senior federal leadership traveled to al-Anbar where they announced a 70% increase in the 2007 provincial capital budget as well as $50 million to compensate losses in the fight against al-Qa'ida. The support of the central government is also needed to maintain hard-won security in areas like al-Anbar through the rapid expansion of locally-generated police. The Government of Iraq has placed some 21,000 Anbaris on police roles.

Economics and Capacity Building

Iraq is starting to make some gains in the economy. Improving security is stimulating revival of markets, with the active participation of local communities. War damage is being cleared and buildings repaired, roads and sewers built and commerce energized.

The IMF estimates that economic growth will exceed six percent for 2007. Iraqi ministries and provincial councils have made substantial progress this year in utilizing Iraq's oil revenue for investment. The 2007 governmental budget allocated $10 billion (nearly one-third Iraq's expected oil export revenue) to capital investment. Over $3 billion was allocated to the provinces and the Kurdish Region for spending. The latest data show that spending units (national ministries and provincial councils) have proceeded to commit these funds at more than twice the rate of last year. Doing the best are the provincial authorities, in the process gaining experience with making plans and decisions, and running fair tenders. In so doing, they are stimulating local business development and providing employment. Over time we expect the experience with more responsive local authorities will change Iraqi attitudes towards their elected leaders, and of the provinces towards Baghdad.

At two conferences in Dubai in the last two weeks, hundreds of Iraqi businessmen met an equal number of foreign investors newly interested in acquiring shares of businesses in Iraq. An auction of cell phone spectrum conducted by Pricewaterhouse Coopers netted the Government a better-than-expected sum of $3.75 billion. The Minister of Finance plans to use the funds, along with all the country's oil revenue, to apply to its pressing investment and current expenditure needs.

Overall, however, the Iraqi economy is performing significantly under potential. Insecurity in the countryside raises transport costs and especially affects manufacturing and agriculture. Electricity supply has improved in many parts of the country, but is woefully inadequate in Baghdad. Many neighborhoods in the city receive two hours a day or less from the national grid, although power supplies for essential services such as water pumping stations or hospitals are much better. The Minister of Electricity said last week that it would take $25 billion through 2016 to meet demand requirements, but that by investing the $2 billion a year the Ministry is now receiving from the government's budget, as well as private investment in power generation, that goal could be met.

We are deploying our assistance funds to make a difference to ordinary Iraqis and to support our political objectives. Military units are using Commanders Emergency Response (CERP) funds to ensure that residents see a difference when neighborhood violence declines. USAID Community Stabilization Funds provide tens of thousands of jobs. With the recent apportionment of 2007 Supplemental funds, we are putting "Quick Response Funds" in the hands of our Provincial Reconstruction Team leaders to build communities and institutions in post-kinetic environments. Vocational training and microfinance programs are supporting nascent private businesses. And in Baghdad, we are increasing our engagement and capacity building efforts with ministries.

Regional and International Dynamics

There is expanding international and regional engagement with Iraq. In August, the UN Security Council, at Iraq's invitation, provided the United Nations Assistance Mission in Iraq (UNAMI) with an expanded mandate through UNSCR 1770. The work of the International Compact with Iraq moves forward, jointly chaired by Iraq and the UN. Seventy-four countries pledged support for Iraq's economic reform efforts at a Ministerial Conference in May. The UN has reported progress in 75% of the 400 areas Iraq has identified for action. Later this month, the Iraqi Prime Minister and the UN Secretary General will chair a ministerial-level meeting in New York to discuss further progress under the Compact and how UNSCR 1770 can be most effectively implemented.

Many of Iraq's neighbors recognize that they have a stake in the outcome of the current conflict in Iraq, and are engaging with Iraq in a constructive way. A neighbors' ministerial in May, also attended by the P-5 and the G-8, has been followed by meetings of working groups on security, border issues, and energy. An ambassadorial level meeting just took place in Baghdad, and another neighbors' ministerial will be held in Istanbul in October.

Against the backdrop of these new mechanisms, the business of being neighbors is quietly unfolding. For the first time in years, Iraq is exporting oil through its neighbor, Turkey, as well as through the Gulf. Iraq and Kuwait are nearing conclusion on a commercial deal for Kuwait to supply its northern neighbor with critically needed diesel. Jordan recently issued a statement welcoming the recent leaders' communiqué and supporting Iraqi efforts at reconciliation. And Saudi Arabia is planning on opening an Embassy in Baghdad—its first since the fall of Saddam.

Syria's role has been more problematic. On one hand, Syria has hosted a meeting of the border security working group and interdicted some foreign terrorists in transit to Iraq. On the other hand, suicide-bombers continue to cross the border from Syria to murder Iraqi civilians.

Iran plays a harmful role in Iraq. While claiming to support Iraq in its transition, Iran has actively undermined it by providing lethal capabilities to the enemies of the Iraqi state. In doing so, the Iranian government seems to ignore the risks that an unstable Iraq carries for its own interests.

Looking Ahead

2006 was a bad year in Iraq. The country came close to unraveling politically, economically, and in security terms. 2007 has brought improvement. Enormous challenges remain. Iraqis still struggle with fundamental questions about how to share power, accept their differences and overcome their past. The changes to our strategy last January—the surge—have helped change the dynamics in Iraq for the better. Our increased presence made besieged communities feel that they could defeat al-Qa'ida by working with us. Our population security measures have made it much harder for terrorists to conduct attacks. We have given Iraqis the time and space to reflect on what sort of country they want. Most Iraqis genuinely accept Iraq as a multi-ethnic, multi-sectarian society—it is the balance of power that has yet to be sorted out.

Whether Iraq reaches its potential is of course ultimately the product of Iraqi decisions. But the involvement and support of the United States will be hugely important in shaping a positive outcome. Our country has given a great deal in blood and treasure to stabilize the situation in Iraq and help Iraqis build institutions for a united, democratic country governed under the rule of law. Realizing this vision will take more time and patience on the part of the United States.

I cannot guarantee success in Iraq. I do believe, as I have described, that it is attainable. I am certain that abandoning or drastically curtailing our efforts will bring failure, and the consequences of such a failure must be clearly understood. An Iraq that falls into chaos or civil war will mean massive human suffering—well beyond what has already occurred within Iraq's borders. It could well invite the intervention of regional states, all of which see their future connected to Iraq's in some fundamental way. Undoubtedly, Iran would be a winner in this scenario, consolidating its influence over Iraqi resources and possibly territory. The Iranian President has already announced that Iran will fill any vacuum in Iraq. In such an environment, the gains made against al-Qa'ida and other extremists groups could easily evaporate and they could establish strongholds to be used as safehavens for regional and international operations. Our current course is hard. The alternatives are far worse.

Every strategy requires recalibration as time goes on. This is particularly true in an environment like Iraq where change is a daily or hourly occurrence. As chief of mission in Iraq, I am constantly assessing our efforts and seeking to ensure that they are coordinated with and complementary to the efforts of our military. I believe that, thanks to the support of Congress, we have an appropriate civilian posture in Iraq. Over the coming year, we will continue to increase our civilian efforts outside of Baghdad and the international zone. This presence has allowed us to focus on capacity building, especially in the provinces—units which are likely to grow in influence as more power devolves from Baghdad. The number of Provincial Reconstruction Teams has grown from ten to 25 this year. In support of these goals, we will be asking Congress for additional economic assistance including additional quick response funds for capacity building. We will also seek support for two significant proposals that hold the prospect of creating permanent jobs for thousands of Iraqis. One would be the establishment of an "Iraqi-American Enterprise Fund," modeled on our successful funds in Poland and elsewhere in Central Europe. Such a fund could make equity investments in new and revamped firms based in Iraq. The second would be a large-scale operations and maintenance facility based on our Highway Trust Fund. On a cost-sharing basis, such a fund would train Iraqis to budget for and maintain important public sector infrastructure (power plants, dams, roads). Over time, the cost-sharing would phase down and out, leaving behind well-trained professionals and instilling the habits of preventative maintenance.

We will continue our efforts to assist Iraqis in the pursuit of national reconciliation, while recognizing that progress on this front may come in many forms and must ultimately be done by Iraqis themselves. We will seek additional ways to neutralize regional interference and enhance regional and international support. And we will help Iraqis consolidate the positive developments at local levels and connect them with the national government. Finally, I expect we will invest much effort in developing the strategic partnership between the United States and Iraq, which is an investment in the future of both countries.

DOCUMENT NO. 6

THE REPORT OF THE INDEPENDENT COMMISSION ON THE SECURITY FORCES OF IRAQ

Commission Report

September 6, 2007

General James L. Jones
USMC (Ret.), Chairman

Public Law 110-28 directed the entity created by §1314 (e) (2) of that Act to make its report to the following committees of Congress:

Committee on Armed Services, United States Senate
Committee on Armed Services, United States House of Representatives
Committee on Foreign Relations, United States Senate
Committee on Foreign Affairs, United States House of Representatives
Committee on Appropriations, United States Senate
Committee on Appropriations, United States House of Representatives
Select Committee on Intelligence, United States Senate
Permanent Select Committee on Intelligence, United States House of Representatives

Dear Chairmen and Ranking Members:

As you know, Public Law 110-28, enacted on May 25, 2007, commissioned an independent private entity made up of individuals with credentials and expertise in military and law enforcement matters to conduct an independent assessment of the Iraqi Security Forces (ISF). This report is to be submitted to the House and Senate Committees on Armed Services, Appropriations, Intelligence, and Foreign Relations/Affairs within 120 days of enactment. As members of the Independent Commission on the Security Forces of Iraq we are pleased to submit, within the statutory timeline, our findings and recommendations in the attached report.

As required by the legislation, our report addresses the readiness of the Iraqi Security Forces to assume responsibility for maintaining the territorial integrity of Iraq, their ability to deny international terrorists safe haven, their ability to bring greater security to Iraq's 18 provinces in the next 12 to 18 months, and their ability to bring an end to sectarian violence to achieve national reconciliation. In addition, the Commission was tasked with an assessment of ISF capabilities in the areas of training, equipment, command, control, intelligence, and logistics.

Finally, we were asked to consider whether, after several years of training, equipping, and mentoring by Coalition forces, continued support would contribute to the readiness of the ISF to defend its territorial integrity, prevent Iraq from becoming a safe haven for terrorists, increase security throughout the nation, and end sectarian violence.

The Independent Commission on the Security Forces of Iraq is made up of 20 Commissioners whose cumulative service exceeds 500 years of military and more than 150 years of law enforcement experience. In pursuit of the facts bearing on the legislative mandate contained in Public Law 110-28, the Commission spent three weeks on the ground in Iraq and conducted extensive briefings and research. We visited more than 70 sites and interviewed more than 150 individuals. The Commission put its collective "boots on the ground" and visited troops and experts in the field. Additionally, the Commission conducted extensive meetings with senior military and civilian leaders from Iraq, the U.S. Mission, the NATO Training Mission-Iraq, and Coalition forces. We have been given the highest quality of support by the Defense Department, the State Department, and our national military and civilian representatives in Iraq.

The Commission is confident in its report to Congress and wishes to express its appreciation for having been given the opportunity to make a contribution to this important issue at this critical time. Our report and its conclusions and findings represent the unanimous opinions of the Commissioners. Finally, our report is submitted as an unclassified document. There is no classified annex.

Sincerely,

James L. Jones, General USMC (Ret.)
Chairman
Independent Commission on the Security Forces of Iraq

Acknowledgments

The Commission could not have performed this assessment without the generous assistance and support of many individuals. In particular, we are grateful for the support provided by the Office of the Secretary of Defense, especially Brigadier General Mark Kimmitt, USA (Ret.); Lieutenant Colonel Dino Pick, USA; and Mr. Chris Straub. We are also grateful for the outstanding services performed by Mr. Robert Menig and Mr. Steve Linder in the Office of the Secretary of Defense for Administration and Management, as well as Mr. Bob Batschelet at the Defense Security Service. In the Joint Staff's J-5 Directorate for Strategic Plans and Policy, we would like to thank Major General Phil Breedlove, USAF, and Colonel Joe DiSalvo, USA.

During our trips to Iraq, we were guests of the many outstanding people within the Multi-National Force–Iraq (MNF-I), the Multi-National Corps-Iraq (MNC-I), and the Multi-National Security Transition Command–Iraq (MNSTC-I). We are deeply appreciative of General David Petraeus, USA; Lieutenant General Raymond Odierno, USA; and Lieutenant General James Dubik, USA, who made themselves and their large staffs available to us prior to, during, and after our trips to Iraq. In the midst of a war, they made possible the access, mobility, billeting, and education that allowed for our assessment. Many people within these organizations were immensely helpful to us as we traveled throughout Iraq. We are especially grateful to Major General Jay Paxton, USMC; Colonel John Martin, USA; Lieutenant Colonel Barry Johnson, USA; and Mr. Walter Redman. The members of the Kentucky National Guard B/1-149th Infantry Joint Visitor's Bureau who traveled with us as our security detail were an extraordinary group of officers, NCOs, and soldiers of the utmost professionalism, and we extend to them our deepest gratitude and respect. We would also like to thank former MNSTC-I commander and current Deputy Commander of U.S. Central Command Lieutenant General Martin Dempsey, USA, who has been extremely generous to the Commission with his time and support.

We are grateful to Drs. Jon Alterman, Anthony Cordesman, and Stephen Flanagan of the Center for Strategic and International Studies for their advice and assistance. The Commission also benefited greatly from the collective insights of its Strategic Advisors: Mr. P. T. Henry, Ms. Sarah Farnsworth, the Honorable James Locher, Mr. John Raidt, and Colonel Arthur White, USMC (Ret.). In addition, we thank Dr. Kim Roberts of SAIC for her valuable assistance.

Last but not least, the Commission wishes to thank its staff at the Center for Strategic and International Studies—in particular Staff Director Ms. Christine Wormuth and staff members Mr. Samuel Brannen, Ms. Lauren Geetter, Mr. Jake Harrington, and Mr. Jeremy White. The staff helped establish the Commission quickly, traveled with the Commission to Iraq, and worked diligently to help us make this report a reality. The Commission also thanks Ms. Kaley Levitt for valuable research assistance, Alice Falk and Vinca LaFleur for their meticulous editing, and its talented interns, Mr. Nicholas Calluzzo and Midshipman Eric Gardiner, USN.

Executive Summary

Statutory Mandate. The Independent Commission on the Security Forces of Iraq was chartered by the United States Congress in Public Law 110-28, signed into law by President George W. Bush on May 25, 2007, to assess the readiness of Iraq's military and police forces to fulfill four major responsibilities: maintain the territorial integrity of Iraq, deny safe haven to international terrorists, bring greater security to the country's 18 provinces in the next 12 to 18 months, and bring an end to sectarian violence to achieve national reconciliation.

Further, the Commission was tasked to evaluate the capacity of the Iraqi Security Forces (military and police) in key functional areas, including training, equipping, command and control, intelligence, and logistics, and to consider the likelihood that continued U.S. support would contribute to the ISF's readiness. Finally, the law directed the Commission to report its full findings to Congress.

At the request of Congress, the Commission is submitting its report in advance of its statutory deadline so that policymakers can consider its findings concurrently with other progress reports on Iraqi security that will soon be submitted to the executive and legislative branches.

Organization. To carry out this important assignment, the Commission, chaired by General James L. Jones, former Commandant of the United States Marine Corps and Supreme Allied Commander, Europe, assembled a highly qualified team of 20 prominent senior retired military officers, chiefs of police, and a former deputy secretary of defense. This independent team, supported by the Center for Strategic and International Studies, brought to bear more than 600 cumulative years of military, defense, and law enforcement experience and expertise in the professional disciplines that it was chartered to examine.

To properly address the broad range of topics assigned by Congress, the Commission was organized into 10 syndicates. Each syndicate was led by a senior Commissioner and focused on either a discrete component of the ISF or a crosscutting functional area. Syndicate inputs were subject to review and integration by all Commission members (see Table 1).

Activities. During the course of its study members of the Commission traveled widely throughout Iraq on three separate occasions for a total of 20 days to gather facts and impressions firsthand. Commissioners conducted site visits to Iraqi military and ministerial headquarters and to various command centers, training facilities, and operating bases. They also visited Iraqi police stations, joint security stations, and law enforcement academies; and Commissioners traveled to border, port, and internal security installations, as well as to Coalition facilities designed to assist with Iraqi security training and transition. The Commission met with more than 100 Iraqi officials, more than 100 U.S. current and former government officials, and more than a dozen leading nongovernmental experts on the Iraqi Security Forces.

Commissioners met with the Coalition and Iraqi authorities, both military and civilian, who oversee the manning, training, equipping, and operational effectiveness of the Iraqi Security Forces, and spoke to the personnel responsible for transitioning security functions from the Multi-National Force–Iraq (MNF-I) to the Iraqi government. Commissioners spent time with trainers, transition teams, operational units, and trainees, as well as Iraqi citizens. They consulted with current and former senior U.S. government officials. Finally, the Commission examined key official data and documents with information relevant to the performance and status of the ISF, their rate of progress, and their prospects for fulfilling the responsibilities of a professional and effective security force.

ISF Defined. The Iraqi Security Forces are composed of two major components: the Iraqi military (Army, Special Forces, Navy, and Air Force), which MNF-I estimated in a June report to encompass more than 152,000 service members and which operates under the authority of the country's Ministry of Defense, and the Iraqi police (local Iraqi Police Service and National Police), along with the Department of Border Enforcement, which the command estimates to number 194,000 civilian security personnel administered by the Ministry of Interior.[1]

This study examines both components. Each is integral to the country's ability to protect its territorial integrity, deny safe haven to international terrorists, and bring security and stability to Iraq's 18 provinces. Though not specifically tasked to assess Iraqi ministerial capacity, the Commission addresses this issue because ministries are integral to the development, readiness, and capability of the country's security forces.

Context. The development of the Iraqi military and police into an effective total force capable of providing security and enforcing the rule of law has been a major focus of the Government of Iraq and the multinational Coalition.

The task of building the forces while they simultaneously engage in security operations, both in partnership with the Coalition and independently, presents the Government of Iraq with many difficulties and challenges. Senior Coalition military commanders characterize this process as "building an airplane while you're flying"—and, in this case, while getting shot at. Similarly, the challenge to Iraq's leaders of developing a loyal, professional, and cohesive military and police under battle conditions, while working to form a national government able to reconcile bitter historic tribal, ethnic, and religious differences, is a daunting one.

Security Environment. Iraq's security environment is exceedingly diverse and complex. It is characterized by a multitude of threats arising from the struggle for power among sectarian rivals, radical Islamic terrorist groups (including al Qaeda), Sunni insurgents, Shi'a militia, and criminal elements. The various factions possess a diverse range of aims, agendas, and capabilities.

These combatants, and the level of violence and instability they incite, manifest themselves differently throughout the country. Security conditions vary significantly among the provinces and localities, and they are influenced heavily by an area's geography and demographic composition, the intensity of sectarian tension, the quality of political leadership, and available resources.

In the north, Kurds, Sunni Arabs, and other groups vie for control of land and natural resources, particularly in the areas of Kirkuk and Mosul. In the south, where Iranian interference is acute, Shi'a groups fight one another for political and economic domination. In the west, Sunni insurgents continue to fight the Shi'a-dominated government and the Coalition for the purpose of restoring Sunni political power and prestige. Terrorist groups including al Qaeda are at war to achieve their goal of establishing an Islamic caliphate in Iraq. In Baghdad, the political, cultural, and economic epicenter of Iraq, the security situation is characterized by ethno-sectarian struggle and rampant criminal activity. The situation is complicated by the violence incited by terrorists, militias, and religious extremists who seek to inflame sectarian tensions, destabilize the government, and influence public opinion, particularly in the United States.

Overall, the factional tension and violence within Iraq is fed by the slow and disappointing pace of national reconciliation; intensified by the inflow of foreign fighters, terrorists, and weapons; and promoted by neighboring countries, such as Iran and Syria. These two countries and certain non-state entities are generally acknowledged to be pursuing sectarian, political, and security objectives within Iraq and providing manpower, weapons, and support to proxy fighters and militia. Their activities substantially aid and contribute to factional discord, violence, and instability within Iraq.

Particularly in the west, and in key areas surrounding Baghdad, the security environment is being positively influenced by tribal elements who have turned against al Qaeda and are seeking to reduce violence. The most recent U.S. National Intelligence Estimate on Iraq stated: "There have been measurable but uneven improvements in Iraq's security situation since our last National Intelligence Estimate on Iraq in January 2007. The steep escalation in rates of violence has been checked for now, and overall attack levels across Iraq have fallen during seven of the last nine weeks."[2]

The body of the Commission's report includes graphics provided by the Coalition depicting the trends in the security environment.

ISF Overall Assessment. The Commission finds that in general, the Iraqi Security Forces, military and police, have made uneven progress, but that there should be increasing improvement in both their readiness and their capability to provide for the internal security of Iraq. With regard to external dangers, the evidence indicates that the Iraqi Security Forces will not be able to secure Iraqi borders against conventional military threats in the near term.

While severely deficient in combat support and combat service support capabilities, the new Iraqi armed forces, especially the Army, show clear evidence of developing the baseline infrastructures that lead to the successful formation of a national defense capability. The Commission concurs with the view expressed by U.S., Coalition, and Iraqi experts that the Iraqi Army is capable of taking over an increasing amount of day-to-day combat responsibilities from Coalition forces. In any event, the ISF will be unable to fulfill their essential security responsibilities independently over the next 12–18 months.

In the aggregate, the Commission's assessment ascribes better progress to the Iraqi Army and the Ministry of Defense and less to the Ministry of Interior, whose dysfunction has hampered the police forces' ability to achieve the level of effectiveness vital to the security and stability of Iraq.

The Iraqi police are improving at the local level predominantly where the ethnic makeup of the population is relatively homogenous and the police are recruited from the local area. Police forces are hampered by corruption and dysfunction within the Ministry of Interior. In some areas, they have been vulnerable to infiltration, and they are often outmatched in leadership, training, tactics, equipment, and weapons by the terrorists, criminals, and the militias they must combat. The rate of improvement must be accelerated if the Iraqi police are to meet their essential security responsibilities.

Ministry of Defense Assessment. The Ministry of Defense is assessed as being one of the better-functioning agencies of the Iraqi government. It is building the necessary institutions and processes to fulfill its mission of overseeing and resourcing the Iraqi armed forces. The ministry can plan and budget at a basic level, but budget execution requires significant improvement. It has established basic administrative systems, and operates an adequate training system. However, bureaucratic inexperience, excessive layering, and overcentralization hamper its capacity. These flaws reduce the operational readiness, capability, and effectiveness of the Iraqi military.

Army and Special Forces Assessment. In general, the Iraqi Army and Special Forces are becoming more proficient in counterinsurgency and counterterrorism operations; they are gaining size and strength, and will increasingly be capable of assuming greater responsibility for Iraq's security. The Special Forces brigade is highly capable and extremely effective. It is trained in counterterrorism and it is assessed to be the best element of the new Iraqi military.

The Iraqi Army possesses an adequate supply of willing and able manpower, a steadily improving basic training capability, and equipment tailored to counterinsurgency operations. There is evidence to show that the emerging Iraqi soldier is willing to fight against the declared enemies of the state, with some exceptions remaining along ethnic lines. The Army is making efforts to reduce sectarian influence within its ranks and achieving some progress. The Army's operational effectiveness is increasing; yet it will continue to rely on help in areas such as command and control, equipment, fire support, logistical support, intelligence, and transportation. Despite continued progress, the Iraqi military will not be ready to independently fulfill its security role within the next 12 to 18 months. Nevertheless, the Commission believes that substantial progress can be achieved within that period of time.

The challenge for the Army is its limited operational effectiveness, caused primarily by deficiencies in leadership, lack of disciplinary standards, and logistics shortfalls. Some of these shortcomings are typical of unseasoned units and formations being supported by a newly formed government. Many of the problems can be attributed to marginal leadership at senior military and civilian positions both in the Ministry of Defense and in the operational commands. Identifying the next generation of Iraq's leaders early and placing them in key positions will be one of the major contributors to advancing the effectiveness of the Iraqi military.

Air Force Assessment. The Iraqi Air Force's relatively late establishment hampers its ability to provide much-needed air support to ground operations. It is well designed as the air component to the existing counterinsurgency effort, but not for the future needs of a fully capable air force. Though limited by the availability of properly skilled personnel, and by an inclination to value force size and acquisition over operational effectiveness, it is nonetheless progressing at a promising rate in this formative period.

Navy Assessment. The Iraqi Navy is small and its current fleet is insufficient to execute its mission. However, it is making substantive progress in this early stage of development: it has a well-thought-out growth plan, which it is successfully executing. Its maturation is hampered by the Ministry of Defense's understandable focus on ground forces and counterinsurgency operations, as well as by its bureaucratic inefficiency. The Iraqi Navy will continue to rely on Coalition naval power to achieve its mission for the foreseeable future.

Ministry of Interior Assessment. The Ministry of Interior is a ministry in name only. It is widely regarded as being dysfunctional and sectarian, and suffers from ineffective leadership. Such fundamental flaws present a serious obstacle to achieving the levels of readiness, capability, and effectiveness in police and border security forces that are essential for internal security and stability in Iraq.

Iraqi Police Service Assessment. The Iraqi Police Service is fragile. It is better trained than in past years and is establishing presence in some areas, but the force is underequipped and compromised by militia and insurgent infiltration. In general, the Iraqi Police Service is incapable today of providing security at a level sufficient to protect Iraqi neighborhoods from insurgents and sectarian violence. The police are central to the long-term establishment of security in Iraq. To be effective in combating the threats they face, including sectarian violence, the Iraqi Police Service must be better trained and equipped. The Commission believes that the Iraqi Police Service can improve rapidly should the Ministry of Interior become a more functional institution.

The National Police Assessment. The National Police have proven operationally ineffective, and sectarianism in these units may fundamentally undermine their ability to provide security. The force is not viable in its current form.

Border Security Assessment. Iraq's border security forces are generally ineffective and need more equipment, training, and infrastructure before they can play a significant role in securing Iraq's borders. The Department of Border Enforcement suffers from poor support from the Ministry of Interior. Overall border security is undermined by the division of responsibilities between the Ministry of Interior and the Ministry of Transportation. Corruption and external infiltration of the border security forces are widespread, and the borders are porous.

Overall Capacity Building. To maintain progress in the development of the ISF over the next 12 to 18 months, the national government has to establish a competent and reliable administration to provide for the full range of support required to sustain the military and police. Doing so includes establishing functional procurement, storage, and asset management systems and providing the proper weapons, vehicles, spare parts, medical supplies, ammunition, communications assets, and other vital equipment.

Additionally, the ministries of Defense and Interior must focus on meeting the needs of their manpower in terms of benefits, career development, and support. The Iraqi government will also have to assume responsibility for ensuring that adequate services are provided to security forces, especially when they are operational. Essential services include medical, transportation, maintenance, ordinance disposal, and supply. To overcome current shortfalls and deficiencies, the Iraqi government will need to rely heavily on Coalition support to develop the appropriate practices, procedures, and organizations to accomplish these tasks to an Iraqi standard that will enable the Iraqis to directly take the lead for independent security operations.

Additional Observations. The Commission's work and the main body of this report have focused on the issues assigned by Congress. Nevertheless, the opportunity for Commissioners to immerse themselves in the dynamics of this complex engagement while in Iraq, coupled with the extraordinary access the Commission was afforded, has given rise to associated observations and findings. The Commission believes that sharing them is vital.

The Commission has done so in the concluding chapter so that Congress and the nation at large can take full advantage of the total lessons learned from its work. While the Commission was not assigned to comment on such subjects as Iraqi governance or general trends associated with our ongoing national efforts, this final chapter seeks to share observations and suggest answers to questions regarding the road ahead with respect to Iraqi security and to the larger issues that arise from this study, including the important question: "What does this all mean in terms of the future in Iraq?"

To conclude, the Commission recognizes the leadership, contributions, and sacrifice of the men and women of the United States armed forces and of our allies who have created the conditions for Iraq to emerge as a free and independent nation. The nation's military and civilian professionals have without question approached a daunting task with the same level of dedicated service to our nation that continues to be the pride of the American people past and present.

Conclusions, Key Findings, and Recommendations

Overall Assessment of the Iraqi Security Forces (ISF)—Military and Police

Conclusion: The Iraqi armed forces—Army, Special Forces, Navy, and Air Force—are increasingly effective and are capable of assuming greater responsibility for the internal security of Iraq; and the Iraqi police are improving, but not at a rate sufficient to meet their essential security responsibilities. The Iraqi Security Forces will continue to rely on the Coalition to provide key enablers such as combat support (aviation support, intelligence, and communications), combat service support (logistics, supply chain management, and maintenance), and training.

The Commission assesses that in the next 12 to 18 months there will be continued improvement in their readiness and capability, but not the ability to operate independently. Evidence indicates that the ISF will not be able to progress enough in the near term to secure Iraqi borders against conventional military and external threats.

Finding 1: *Although the Iraqi Army and Special Forces have demonstrated significant progress in counterterrorism capabilities at the operational level, the Iraqi Police Service and National Police have many challenges to overcome and cannot yet meaningfully contribute to denying terrorists safe haven in Iraq. The border security forces are assessed as being ineffective.*

Finding 2: *The ability of the Iraqi Security Forces to bring greater security to Iraq's provinces varies by region and by organization within the ISF owing to many factors, including political leadership, security environment, sectarianism, and available resources.*

Finding 3: *The "clear, hold, build" strategy being implemented by Iraqi Security Forces is on the right track and shows potential, but neither the Iraqi armed forces nor the police forces can execute these types of operations independently.*

Finding 4: *The Iraqi Army and Iraqi Police Service have the potential to help reduce sectarian violence, but ultimately the ISF will reflect the society from which they are drawn. Political reconciliation is the key to ending sectarian violence in Iraq.*

The Ministry of Defense

Conclusion: The Ministry of Defense, which is responsible for policy development and implementation as well as resource allocation for the Iraqi military, is building the necessary institutions and processes to fulfill its mission. However, its capacity is hampered by bureaucratic inexperience, excessive layering, and overcentralization. These flaws reduce the operational readiness, capability, and effectiveness of the Iraqi military. As the MOD continues to mature, it should assume the ministerial-level functions that currently fall to the Coalition.

Finding 5: *Inefficiencies and overcentralization within the Ministry of Defense and its inability to fully execute its budget impede the combat readiness and capabilities of the Iraqi armed forces.*

Finding 6: *The ability to contract efficiently is important to the MOD's mission to sustain the Iraqi armed forces. The MOD currently lacks effective processes to execute contracting requirements.*

Finding 7: *The MOD consistently compensates the members of the Iraqi military, but it has difficulty accounting for personnel.*

Finding 8: *The level of information sharing and cooperation between the Iraqi intelligence community and the Iraqi Security Forces is not satisfactory—a problem exacerbated by bureaucratic competition and distrust among duplicative intelligence organizations.*

Finding 9: *Parallel lines of direct communication to military units have been established under the control of the Prime Minister. He is perceived by many as having created a second, and politically motivated chain of command, effectively communicating orders directly to field commanders. Such a practice bypasses national command lines, which should flow through the Minister of Defense and the Commanding General of Iraqi Armed Forces.*

Finding 10: *The lack of logistics experience and expertise within the Iraqi armed forces is substantial and hampers their readiness and capability. Renewed emphasis on Coalition mentoring and technical support will be required to remedy this condition.*

The Iraqi Army and Special Forces

Conclusion: The Iraqi Army and Special Forces possess an adequate supply of willing and able manpower and a steadily improving basic training capability. The Army has a baseline supply of equipment for counterinsurgency, but much of this equipment is unavailable for operations owing to maintenance and supply chain management problems. They are making efforts to reduce sectarian influence within their ranks and are achieving some progress. Their operational effectiveness, particularly that of the Special Forces, is increasing, yet they will continue to rely on Coalition forces for key enablers such as combat support (aviation support, intelligence, and communications), combat service support (logistics, supply chain management, and maintenance), and training. Despite progress, they will not be ready to independently fulfill their security role within the next 12 to 18 months. Nevertheless, the Commission believes that substantial progress can be achieved to that end.

Finding 11: *In addition to protecting the nation against external military threats, the Iraqi Army can and should also play a role in preventing unconventional threats migrating from points outside of Iraq. The Army currently does not have sufficient forces to enhance border security and conduct counterinsurgency operations simultaneously.*

> ***Recommendation:*** *The Iraqi Army's size and capability should be developed as part of an Iraqi national security strategy that defines the roles and missions of the ISF to address both internal security and border security needs. The Army as well as the nation's police forces are currently emphasizing internal security; only ineffective border security forces are focused on*

controlling the borders. The Iraqi Army must contribute to both border and internal security. A national commitment to expand the Army's mission beyond counterinsurgency to include border security must be reflected in Army and MOD plans and policies.

Finding 12: *The Iraqi Army has become more effective in supporting Coalition-led counterinsurgency operations from the start of Iraqi and Coalition surge operations in early 2007. The reliability of Iraqi Army units continues to improve, and some units now are an integral part of the Coalition team for counterinsurgency operations. The overall rate of progress of the Army is uneven. Some units perform better than others; but there is rising confidence that progress is being made at a rate that will enable Iraqi Army tactical formations and units to gradually assume a greater leadership role in counterinsurgency operations in the next 12 to 18 months. However, they will continue to rely on Coalition support, including logistics, intelligence, fire support, equipment, training, and leadership development for the foreseeable future.*

Finding 13: *Iraqi Special Operations Forces are the most capable element of the Iraqi armed forces and are well-trained in both individual and collective skills. They are currently capable of leading counterterrorism operations, but they continue to require Coalition support. They remain dependent on the Coalition for many combat enablers, especially airlift, close air support, and targeting intelligence.*

Finding 14: *The Iraqi Army is short of seasoned leadership at all levels, and a lack of experienced commissioned and noncommissioned officers hampers its readiness, capability, and effectiveness.*

Finding 15: *A noncommissioned officer corps is not part of Iraq's military tradition, but it will be invaluable to making the Army more combat-effective.*

Recommendation: *Developing leadership in the Iraqi Army will require continued support from Coalition advisors and units. Ongoing employment of a "train the trainers" approach, and continued emphasis on the development of a functioning noncommissioned officer corps, is essential, though developing leaders will take time to achieve.*

Finding 16: *The Iraqi Army is currently structured for counterinsurgency operations with a goal of manning 13 divisions by the end of 2008. The current divisions are experiencing absenteeism, both authorized and unauthorized. MOD has established a standard of 85 percent "present-for-duty" at all times. To achieve this, units will be manned at 120 percent of authorized strength, and the abundance of volunteers for service in the new Iraqi Army should make the attainment of this goal possible. This higher manning requirement will place additional strain on equipping and combat training programs.*

Finding 17: *The implementation of an Iraqi code of military discipline, professional development programs, and benefits for members of the armed forces is key* *to improving readiness. The Commission finds that inadequate implementation of these initiatives adversely affects personnel retention and leadership development. Developing future leaders must be an important objective of personnel programs.*

Finding 18: *The Iraqi Army is adequately equipped for counterinsurgency. However, equipping the Army with more armor, artillery, and mobility is tactically advantageous and communicates a powerful message to the Iraqi people and to the enemy about the growing strength and capability of the Iraqi Army.*

Finding 19: *Logistics remains the Achilles' heel of the Iraqi ground forces. Although progress is being made, achieving an adequateforcewide logistics capability is at least 24 months away.*

Finding 20: *The current shortfall in logistics is emblematic of the urgent need to solve a major issue in terms that the Iraqi government and military can adopt. U.S. strategies and solutions rely heavily on outsourcing of logistics, an approach that has met resistance from the Iraqi leaders. In many cases, the "Iraqi way," though not always optimal, is sufficient. The solutions for the Iraqi armed forces must be developed with the goal of achieving an Iraqi standard that allows for Iraqi culture, traditions, and abilities.*

> ***Recommendation:*** *To operate independently, the Iraqi Army must develop a functioning logistics and maintenance system. The Coalition should continue working with the MOD to develop a system that meets Iraqi needs.*

The Iraqi Air Force

> ***Conclusion:*** The Iraqi Air Force's relatively late establishment hampers its ability to provide much-needed air support to ground operations. It is well designed as the air component to the existing counterinsurgency effort, but not for the future needs of a fully capable air force. Though limited by the availability of properly skilled personnel, and by an inclination to value force size and acquisition over operational effectiveness, it is nonetheless progressing at a promising rate during this formative period.

Finding 21: *The long-term capability of the Iraqi Air Force will depend on its success in recruiting quality personnel, and will require greater emphasis on basic and technical training.*

> ***Recommendation:*** *Together with its Coalition partners, the Iraqi Air Force must increase the quality of its recruits and the capacity of current and planned training programs, while also increasing the manpower authorizations to compensate for chronic absenteeism. Emphasis on the value of training must be relentless.*

Finding 22: *Although aircraft procurement has been adequate to date, maintenance and sustainment systems lag well behind the procurement program and thus impede overall Iraqi Air Force capability.*

Recommendation: *Multi-National Security Transition Command–Iraq must redouble its efforts to inculcate the value of quality maintenance and support into the culture of the MOD in general, and of the Iraqi Air Force in particular.*

Finding 23: *Although the Iraqi Air Force has had a very late start compared to the Iraqi Army, the present design of the Iraqi Air Force is appropriate for its current mission and it is making significant progress.*

Recommendation: *Given its good progress to date, the new Iraqi Air Force should stay its present course of developing a counterinsurgency air force with a view toward establishing quality operations and maintenance capability for integration into the joint fight. As these skills are refined, reliance on Coalition support can diminish.*

The Iraqi Navy

> ***Conclusion:*** The Iraqi Navy is small and its current fleet is insufficient to execute its mission. However, it is making substantive progress in this early stage of development: it has a well-thought-out growth plan, which it is successfully executing. Its maturation is hampered by the Ministry of Defense's understandable focus on ground forces and counterinsurgency operations, as well as by bureaucratic inefficiency. The Iraqi Navy will continue to rely on Coalition naval power to achieve its mission for the foreseeable future.

Finding 24: *The low profile of the Iraqi Navy within the MOD, as well as the ministry's inadequate budget allocation and execution, significantly impede Iraqi naval operations and development.*

Recommendation: *Coalition advisors must assist the Iraqi Navy leadership in advocating budget priorities within the MOD. The strategic importance of the Iraqi Navy must be better articulated to the Government of Iraq, in terms both of maintaining Iraq's territorial integrity and of providing the security needed to ensure the efficient flow of exports. Larger issues of poor ministerial capacity and poor budget execution must also be addressed with Coalition support, as detailed more extensively in the discussion on MOD capacity (Chapter 4).*

Finding 25: *The Iraqi Navy area of responsibility is small, complicated, and of vital strategic importance. Relations among the nations bordering the area of responsibility and their respective navies and coast guards are fragile at best. Furthermore, the international maritime borders with Iran and Kuwait are contested and not clearly demarcated. These issues warrant greater attention from both the MOD and the Coalition.*

Recommendation: *Absent clearly defined territorial seas, the Iraqi Navy's battle space will be further complicated. Although the Commission realizes* *that resolving this issue is made more difficult by long-standing animosities between these nations and may not be feasible in the near term, it is important that the profile of this issue be raised within the Government of Iraq and the country team.*

Finding 26: *The Iraqi Navy does not have a collaborative relationship with the Iraqi Coast Guard, though the two services operate in close proximity and have complementary missions. This lack of coordination has the potential to create vulnerable seams in a critical strategic environment.*

Recommendation: *The Coalition should work with the MOD, Iraqi Navy, and Coast Guard to examine the feasibility and potential advantages of merging the Navy and Coast Guard into a single service with responsibility for coastal maritime security. If unity of command cannot be attained by combining both forces under the MOD, then better cooperation and coordination has to be developed to prevent a serious gap in security.*

Finding 27: *The new Iraqi Navy has made significant progress over a very short time period, particularly in planning, but it remains heavily reliant on the Coalition for training, logistics, and maintenance support.*

Recommendation: *An ongoing Naval Transition Team presence in Umm Qasr is essential and should be continued.*

The Ministry of Interior

Conclusion: The Ministry of Interior is a ministry in name only. It is widely regarded as being dysfunctional and sectarian, and suffers from ineffective leadership. Such fundamental flaws present a serious obstacle to achieving the levels of readiness, capability, and effectiveness in police and border security forces that are essential for internal security and stability in Iraq.

Finding 28: *Sectarianism and corruption are pervasive in the MOI and cripple the ministry's ability to accomplish its mission to provide internal security for Iraqi citizens.*

Finding 29: *The MOI lacks sufficient administrative and logistics capability to support the civil security forces it controls.*

Recommendation: *The MOI, with the support of the Civilian Police Assistance Transition Team, must reform its organizational structure, develop a five-year strategic plan, and build sufficient administrative capacity to sustain Iraq's civil security forces in the field in a manner that is free of real or perceived sectarian favoritism.*

Finding 30: *The MOI cannot execute its budget, a failure that undermines the effectiveness of the civil security forces in the field.*

Finding 31: *The Ministry of Interior and provincial authorities share responsibility for management and payment of the Iraqi Police Service. Serious deficiencies in these efforts have led to pay and morale problems and have heightened tensions between the central government and the provinces.*

Recommendation: *The MOI Transition Team should continue to work with MOI officials to establish workable mechanisms to better manage and resolve pay problems affecting police forces. This should be done in coordination with provincial authorities.*

Finding 32: *The MOI has little control of the forces that make up the Facilities Protection Service (FPS). The allegiance of many Facilities Protection Service personnel has been to individual ministries, parties, tribes, and clans rather than to the central government, and such division of loyalties undermines their ability to provide security.*

Recommendation: *The Coalition should support consolidation of the Facilities Protection Service by encouraging the establishment of national implementing orders. As consolidation proceeds, the Coalition should assist the MOI to ensure that the Facilities Protection Service personnel can be properly vetted, trained, and equipped.*

Iraqi Police Service

Conclusion: The Iraqi Police Service is incapable today of providing security at a level sufficient to protect Iraqi neighborhoods from insurgents and sectarian violence. The police are central to the long-term establishment of security in Iraq. To be effective in combating the threats that officers face, including sectarian violence, the Iraqi Police Service must be better trained and equipped. The Commission believes that the Iraqi Police Service can improve rapidly should the Ministry of Interior become a more functional institution.

Finding 33: *The emphasis on local recruiting and assignment in the Iraqi Police Service is showing promise in establishing security at the local level; strong personnel vetting processes will remain vital.*

Recommendation: *The MOI and the Civilian Police Assistance Transition Team should work closely with provincial authorities to ensure that established vetting procedures are used consistently throughout the country to combat militia, criminal, and terrorist infiltration of the Iraqi Police Service.*

Finding 34: *Police training in Iraq is improving, particularly in areas where training is led by Iraqi instructors partnered with civilian police advisors.*

Recommendation: *The Civilian Police Assistance Transition Team should continue transitioning the lead for training to the Iraqis wherever possible* *and should consider instituting a "train the trainers" program throughout the provinces to facilitate this process.*

Finding 35: *U.S. military officers rather than senior civilian law enforcement personnel lead the Coalition training effort for the Iraqi Police Service; this arrangement has inadvertently marginalized civilian police advisors and limited the overall effectiveness of the training and advisory effort.*

> ***Recommendation:*** *Leadership of the Coalition Police Assistance Training Team and the Police Training Teams should be transferred to senior civilian law enforcement professionals.*

Finding 36: *The number of civilian international police advisors is insufficient to the task of training the Iraqi Police Service.*

> ***Recommendation:*** *The Coalition—not just the United States—should fund and recruit the requisite number of international police advisors.*

Finding 37: *Training programs to date have emphasized quantity of police trained over quality of training, thereby undermining the long-term effectiveness of the force in favor of force generation efforts.*

> ***Recommendation:*** *Particularly in light of a significantly high number of personnel in the Iraqi Police Service who have not yet undergone Coalition training, the Ministry of Interior and Civilian Police Assistance Transition Team should seek higher-quality police recruits and vet them more carefully as they continue to address the training backlog.*

Finding 38: *The Iraqi Police Service lacks a formal police leadership academy, a deficiency that impedes leadership development.*

> ***Recommendation:*** *The Iraqi Police Service should work with its Coalition advisors to establish a formal Iraqi Police Academy that is focused on developing civil policing skills in senior officers and includes a separate first-line supervisor training program.*

Finding 39: *The Iraqi Police Service is underequipped to combat the threats it faces and suffers persistent shortfalls in vital equipment.*

> ***Recommendation:*** *Multi-National Security Transition Command–Iraq should work with the Iraqi government to provide adequately armored vehicles and heavier weaponry to the Iraqi Police Service, particularly to police stations in urban areas or other areas where improvised explosive device (IED) and explosively formed penetrator (EFP) attacks are prevalent.*

Finding 40: *Quality intelligence is central to the ability of the Iraqi Police Service to take the lead for security, but intelligence supporting police operations is limited and information sharing with other security agencies is weak.*

> ***Recommendation:*** *All Iraqi security agencies and the Iraqi Police Service must work together to establish information-sharing systems, practices, and*

protocols that meet their requirements. The MOI should work with the provinces to establish mechanisms to share information from the national level down.

Finding 41: *The Iraqi Police Service has extremely weak investigative and forensic capabilities that greatly limit its effectiveness.*

Recommendation: *As the Iraqi Police Service continue to develop, Multi-National Security Transition Command–Iraq should work with the MOI to increase the investigative and forensic capabilities of the police service by expanding the Major Crimes Task Force, increasing the number of crime lab facilities in major cities, increasing training courses for criminal investigators, and establishing an investigator rank within the police service.*

Finding 42: *The Iraqi Police Service is but one element of a broader justice system that is not yet well established in Iraq.*

Recommendation: *The Government of Iraq, particularly the Ministry of Interior and the Ministry of Justice, should collaborate to create and implement a framework to enable the rule of law in Iraq. The Coalition should continue to strongly support these efforts.*

Finding 43: *The police are central to the long-term establishment of security and stability in Iraq. Today, the Iraqi Police Service is incapable of providing security at a level sufficient to protect Iraqi neighborhoods from insurgents and sectarian violence.*

Recommendation: *The Civilian Police Assistance Transition Team should work closely with the Ministry of Interior and Ministry of Defense to develop a detailed strategic plan to transition primary responsibility for internal security in Iraq from the Iraqi Army to the Iraqi Police Service.*

The National Police

Conclusion: The National Police have proven operationally ineffective. Sectarianism in its units undermines its ability to provide security; the force is not viable in its current form. The National Police should be disbanded and reorganized.

Finding 44: *In its current form, the National Police is not a viable organization. Its ability to be effective is crippled by significant challenges, including public distrust, sectarianism (both real and perceived), and a lack of clarity about its identity—specifically, whether it is a military or a police force.*

Recommendation: *The National Police should be disbanded and reorganized under the MOI. It should become a much smaller organization under a different name with responsibility for highly specialized police tasks such as explosive ordnance disposal, urban search and rescue, special threat action, and other similar functions.*

The Department of Border Enforcement

> ***Conclusion:*** Iraq's borders are porous. The Department of Border Enforcement suffers from poor ministerial support from the MOI. Border forces often lack the equipment, infrastructure, and basic supplies to conduct their mission. Overall border security is further undermined by the division of responsibilities between the MOI and the Ministry of Transportation. Corruption and external influence and infiltration are widespread. Absent major improvements in all these areas, Iraq's borders will remain porous and poorly defended.

Finding 45: *The overall capacity of the Department of Border Enforcement and the Ports of Entry Directorate is undermined by weak MOI capacity. Further, border security commanders have little confidence that the MOI will address their needs and concerns.*

Finding 46: *The divided responsibility for land, sea, and air ports of entry between the Ministry of Interior and Ministry of Transportation, together with the lack of unity of effort between these ministries, undermines the effectiveness of the Department of Border Enforcement and the Ports of Entry Directorate.*

> ***Recommendation:*** *The Government of Iraq should establish clear guidelines to facilitate unity of effort between the MOI and MOT for border security and move quickly to consolidate overall responsibility for border security under the MOI.*

Finding 47: *The MOI has not created standardized concepts of operations, operating procedures, or processes for the Ports of Entry Directorate to apply at Iraq's land ports of entry; each appears to be run according to the initiative—or lack thereof—of the local commander.*

Finding 48: *Many land ports of entry have neither the quantity nor the quality of monitoring and detection systems required for border security operations to function effectively.*

> ***Recommendation:*** *The Coalition should continue to emphasize to the MOI that the territorial integrity of the country relies heavily on the Department of Border Enforcement's ability to secure the borders and that funding for detection and monitoring equipment for those forces should be accorded a very high priority to increase the effectiveness and efficiency of ports of entry security forces.*

Finding 49: *The Department of Border Enforcement lacks sufficient logistics, support systems, and infrastructure to sustain many of its forces in the field.*

> ***Recommendation:*** *Coalition forces should strongly encourage the Department of Border Enforcement to implement its national Headquarters Distribution Plan while continuing to provide logistical and maintenance support in the near term so that Department of Border Enforcement and ports of entry personnel can accomplish their mission.*

Finding 50: *Corruption is a serious problem at many land ports of entry. This fact has not yet been adequately addressed.*

> ***Recommendation:*** *Eliminating corruption will most likely be a generational undertaking in Iraq, but Multi-National Security Transition Command–Iraq, Multi-National Corps-Iraq, and civilian agencies should work together to try to increase Border Transition Team oversight of Department of Border Enforcement and Ports of Entry Directorate facilities, as well as to develop a standardized training program emphasizing leadership and professional ethics.*

Table 1. ISF Independent Assessment Commission Organization

General James L. Jones, USMC (Ret.), Chairman	
Ministry of Defense Syndicates	*Ministry of Interior Syndicates*
Iraqi Army	**Iraqi National Police and Iraqi Police Service**
General George Joulwan, USA (Ret.), Syndicate Chair	Chief Charles Ramsey, Syndicate Chair
General John Abrams, USA (Ret.)	The Honorable Terrance Gainer
General Charles Wilhelm, USMC (Ret.)	Colonel Michael Heidingsfield, USAF (Ret.)
Lieutenant General John Van Alstyne, USA (Ret.)	Assistant Chief Constable Duncan McCausland
Command Sergeant Major Dwight Brown, USA (Ret.)	Chief John Timoney
Sergeant Major Alford McMichael, USMC (Ret.)	**Other Ministry of Interior Functions**
Iraqi Special Forces	General Charles Boyd, USAF (Ret.), Syndicate Chair*
Brigadier General Richard Potter, USA (Ret.)	Admiral Gregory Johnson, USN (Ret.)*
Iraqi Air Force	Lieutenant General Martin Berndt, USMC (Ret.)
General Charles Boyd, USAF (Ret.)*	* Denotes dual Commission role
Iraqi Navy	
Admiral Gregory Johnson, USN (Ret.)*	

Cross-Cutting Issues Syndicates	
Logistics	**Resources**
Lieutenant General Gary McKissock, USMC (Ret.)	The Honorable John Hamre
Intelligence/Command and Control	**Personnel**
Lieutenant General James King, USA (Ret.)	Major General Arnold Punaro, USMC (Ret.)

Figure 1: ISF Independent Assessment Commission Site Visits (Iraq) [Omitted]

Figure 2: ISF Independent Assessment Commission Site Visits (Baghdad) [Omitted]

Chapter 1: The Security Environment in Iraq

To put the Commission's assessment of the Iraqi Security Forces in an appropriate context, it is important to understand the internal and external threats facing Iraq and its people, as well as the requirements that those threats impose on the Iraqi Security Forces. The societal forces defining the security environment in Iraq today are enormously diverse, complex, and violent, and they directly affect the stability of the broader Middle East. The conflicts in Iraq today flow from differences over religion, from historical divides, and from disputes in Iraqi society that were unleashed following the invasion of Iraq in 2003. They also reflect the broader power dynamics of the region. The Iraqi Security Forces are attempting to develop and operate in the midst of an extraordinarily complex environment—an environment that significantly challenges far more mature international security forces as well.

Iraq's modern history is the story of different groups and tribes merged into a single nation-state by European powers. After the defeat of the Ottomans in World War I, the Franco-British plan to unite Mesopotamia was executed through the imposition of rulers and drawing of maps in European capitals—without the censuses of or consultation with the local interested parties. In carving modern Iraq out of the former Ottoman provinces of Mosul, Baghdad, and Basra, a largely Kurdish north was combined with a largely Sunni Arab center and a largely Shi'a south. This consolidation papered over existing problems and created new ones.

Figure 3: Religious / Ethnic Areas in Iraq (as of April 07) [Omitted]

The Kurds in Iraq number more than 4 million, representing perhaps 20 percent of the total Iraqi population. Significant Kurdish communities in the neighboring countries of Turkey, Iran, and Syria bring the total Kurdish population of the area to more than 25 million. Surrounding states conceive the possibility of Kurdish secession in Iraq as an inspiration to their own Kurdish minority populations, and thus as a threat to their own territorial integrity. The Sunnis also represent another 20 percent of the Iraqi population. Iraq's Sunnis traditionally have lived in the center of the country, an area without substantial oil or other economic resources. With support from the Ottomans, the British, and the Ba'athists, Sunnis ruled Mesopotamia for more than 400 years—until the fall of Saddam Hussein in 2003. The Shi'a make up about 60 percent of Iraq's population, living principally in the south, the area that possesses most of Iraq's known oil reserves and has access to the Persian Gulf. Many Iraqi Shi'as feel that after years of oppression, the time has come for them to assume a leading role in Iraq, and they profess pride in being the first inhabitants of an Arab state in centuries to be Shi'a led.

Iraq is bordered by Iran, Syria, Turkey, Jordan, Saudi Arabia, and Kuwait. Syria and Iran have long played a significant role in Iraq's affairs. Iran, a large Shi'a state governed by an avowedly revolutionary theocracy, is largely Persian, not Arab. In 1980, after a series of border disputes and growing tension between Saddam's Sunni regime and the Shi'a ruling government in Iran, Iraq invaded Iran, and the two countries battled for eight years and lost more than one million lives between them. So great and widespread was the sacrifice that in many ways, the Iran-Iraq War is as much a defining element of Iran's political culture as the Islamic Revolution itself. Today, Iran's cultural and political influence is expanding significantly in Iraq, as pan-Shi'a networks help consolidate Iraqi Shi'a power. Iranians are agreed among their leadership that Iraq should never be allowed to emerge as a powerful and hostile rival. Consolidating Shi'a control with Iranian influence over the central government is one way to achieve their goals. High among Iran's goals is to undermine U.S. influence in Iraq, since a successful, secure, and pro-U.S. Iraqi government will thwart their regional ambitions.

Syria severed relations with Iraq in 1982 after siding with Iran in the Iran-Iraq War, but the two countries renewed formal diplomatic relations in 2006. Today some 1.5 million Iraqis fleeing their country have crossed the border into Syria, and the growing refugee population is becoming a difficult issue in their bilateral relationship. Syria shelters former Ba'ath Party officials, and many of the foreign Sunni insurgents in Iraq are believed to enter through Syria. Like the Iranian government, the Syrian government believes that a U.S. success in Iraq is adverse to its own interests. But whereas much of the Iranian support appears to go to Shi'a groups and militias, it is Sunni insurgent groups who draw their support from Syria.

Other Arab governments have their own reasons for protecting the interests of Iraq's Sunnis. Though they may stop short of direct support to Sunni insurgents, they are not as aggressive as they might be in cutting off such aid from private sources. Sunni tribal leaders certainly enjoy overseas support, and some of that money goes toward protecting Sunnis—protection that has sometimes manifested itself as attacks on Shi'a.

Overall, each of Iraq's neighbors is concerned about developments in that country, and each has invested in some way—often through armed proxies—to protect itself from those developments. The resultant downward spiral in security has meant that each of these countries feels threatened by the situation in Iraq, but the perils these surrounding countries face are in no way as great as the dangers currently confronting Iraqis themselves.

Against that history and set of regional dynamics, the most significant threats currently facing Iraq are generally agreed to be al Qaeda in Iraq (AQI), Sunni insurgent groups, Shi'a militias, and the largely negative involvement of neighboring countries in Iraq's internal affairs—especially Iranian support of Jaysh al-Mahdi (JAM) and the Badr Brigade.

Al Qaeda in Iraq (AQI)

Al Qaeda in Iraq was credited with only 15 percent of the insurgent attacks in Iraq at the beginning of 2007, but its attacks were typically the most destructive, sensational, and destabilizing.[3] According to the Department of Defense, al Qaeda in Iraq is responsible for approximately 90 percent of the suicide bombings in Iraq and the kidnapping of more than 250 foreign workers. Abu Hamza al-Muhajir—an Egyptian—has been al Qaeda in Iraq's leader since the death of the organization's founder, Abu Musab al-Zarqawi, in a Coalition air strike on June 7, 2006.[4] Although al Qaeda in Iraq's leadership is foreign—a reality that members have tried to hide through information operations—its makeup is likely 90-95 percent Iraqi.[5] Even so, 80 percent of al Qaeda in Iraq suicide bombings are carried out by foreigners.[6] The relationship between al Qaeda in Iraq and the greater al Qaeda leadership in the Pakistan-Afghanistan border region remains unclear, but the groups share common goals and openly support one another through the media and sworn loyalty oaths.

Figure 4: State of Al Qaeda—Iraq [Omitted]

Al Qaeda in Iraq has consistently sought to destabilize Iraq and instigate sectarian violence in an effort to oust U.S. forces from the country. Its 2003 bombing of the United Nations headquarters in Baghdad was a turning point that led many in the international community to reconsider support for Coalition operations in Iraq. Similarly, al Qaeda in Iraq's February 22, 2006, bombing of the Shi'a Askariya Mosque in Samarra was an early accelerant of sectarian violence in Iraq, catalyzing retaliatory attacks against 60 Sunni mosques and the killing of more than 400 Sunnis by Shi'a militias in the bombing's immediate aftermath.[7]

There are indicators in some parts of Iraq that popular support for, and even tolerance of, al Qaeda in Iraq's presence may be weakening significantly, in large part because the local population and its leaders resent al Qaeda in Iraq's coercion and brutality. In Anbar province, which makes up one-third of Iraq's landmass, Sunni tribal leaders have formed alliances with Coalition and Iraqi forces during the past six months to hunt members of al Qaeda in Iraq operating in the west. Strong Coalition involvement with the local sheikhs has significantly transformed the security environment in that region—once the principal stronghold of Sunni extremist activity manifested in part through al Qaeda in Iraq operations. The ongoing ISF and Coalition presence in Anbar province encourages the population to cooperate with Coalition forces and has markedly spurred police recruiting efforts. Though these new Sunni allies have yet to earn the complete trust of the Government of Iraq—and vice versa—they have dramatically improved the security situation in Anbar province, providing Coalition forces with valuable intelligence leading to the captures of top al Qaeda in Iraq leaders. There are positive indications that popular support for al Qaeda in Iraq is decreasing dramatically in other provinces as well.

The Sunni Insurgents

Hard-line Arab Sunni Ba'athists began the insurgency in Iraq after the fall of the Saddam regime. They were originally backed by small groups of foreign fighters—mostly secular Arab nationalists—who had crossed into Iraq before the beginning of the war to support the Ba'athist cause.[8] Today Sunni insurgents target Coalition forces, Iraqi forces, and government personnel or those seen as cooperating with them, as well as Shi'a Iraqis and militia members.[9] Their goal is to restore Sunni rule in Iraq. The main Sunni insurgent groups currently operating in the country are the 1920 Revolution Brigades, the Islamic Front of Iraqi Resistance, and the Mujahideen Army in Iraq. These groups are believed to be responsible for roughly 70 percent of attacks.[10] Most Sunni insurgent groups are made up of former soldiers and Sunni Arab civilians led by former Iraqi military officers. They have been concentrated in the Sunni-dominated Anbar province, as well as several majority Sunni neighborhoods in Baghdad, including Amiriya, Adhamiya, Fadhil, Jihad, Amal, and Doura.[11] The recent U.S. and Iraqi troop surge has focused on these violent areas, forcing many insurgents to retreat from their traditional home bases into outlying provinces such as Diyala, which has seen a major spike in insurgent activity since the beginning of the surge.[12] These groups are also increasingly active in the northern, majority-Kurdish provinces and around the multi-ethnic and contested cities of Mosul and Kirkuk.

Figure 5: Anbar Attacks [Omitted]

Shi'a Militias

There are approximately 80,000 Shi'a militia members in Iraq. Their roots go back to the underground resistance to the Ba'athist regime, but the militias rapidly grew in strength after the Coalition invasion, in part to fill the security vacuum left by the sudden collapse of Saddam Hussein's regime, and also to ensure that the Ba'athists would not rise again. Shi'a individuals in government and other positions of authority throughout Iraq remain deeply insecure about their place in the new Iraq, despite their majority rule of the country.[13]

Approximately 60,000 of these militia members belong to Jaysh al-Mahdi (JAM), 15,000 to the Badr Brigades, and 5,000 to smaller organizations.[14] Jaysh al-Mahdi is loyal to the young anti-Western cleric Muqtada al-Sadr. The group controls most of Sadr City, a Baghdad slum containing more than 2.5 million Iraqis, and is also increasingly active in southern Iraq. While remaining a fierce critic of the U.S.-led occupation, Muqtada al-Sadr has repeatedly called for Jaysh al-Mahdi to avoid direct confrontation with Coalition and Iraqi forces during the current surge. At the same time, there are increasing signs that Sadr is unable to exercise control over all factions within Jaysh al-Mahdi, and that Iran's influence over the militant arm of this organization is growing.

The Badr Brigade[15] is the Iranian-trained military wing of the Supreme Islamic Iraqi Council (SIIC, formerly SCIRI), which is currently the largest Shi'a political party. The Supreme Islamic Iraqi Council controls the most seats in Iraq's parliament and governing coalition.[16] The Badr Organization is led by a member of the Iraqi parliament, Hadi al-Amiri, and also operates primarily in southern Iraq.

The Badr Brigade and Jaysh al-Mahdi are both believed to have infiltrated many of Iraq's ministries and security forces. Various units within the National Police have likely been penetrated by the Badr faction, while Jaysh al-Mahdi is believed to exercise significant influence over Iraq's Facilities Protection Service, which employs more than 140,000 armed personnel.[17] Militia members who join the ISF often remain loyal to their local militia, and may take part in sectarian "extracurricular" activities. The Iraqi government is making efforts to counter the negative influence of these groups. For example, in October 2006, Iraqi Interior Minister Jawad al-Bolani fired 3,000 ministry employees, and seven of nine National Police brigade commanders have been removed in the past six months because of sectarian behavior.[18]

Iranian Influence in Iraq

Iraq's borders with Iran are long, porous, and subject to wide-scale corruption at points of entry. While the exact nature, depth, and breadth of Iranian involvement in Iraq is not fully known, there is general consensus that Iran is a rapidly increasing threat to Iraq's stability.

American intelligence and military officials have stated publicly that there is clear evidence of Iran's providing funding, weapons, ammunition, training, and other forms of support to militia in Iraq, particularly in the southeastern region of the country. For example, U.S. officials have repeatedly asserted that members of the Al Qods Force of Iran's Revolutionary Guard have been arming Iraqi Shi'a militias with weapons and explosively forced projectiles (EFPs), which defeat up-armored vehicles.[19] Multi-National Corps-Iraq has stated that EFPs were used to carry out 99 attacks in July 2007, accounting for fully one-third of Coalition combat deaths. EFPs accounted for 18 percent of combat deaths of Americans and allied troops in Iraq in the last quarter of 2006.[20]

In December 2006 and January 2007, U.S. forces detained seven Iranians suspected of being dispatched agents of the Iranian Revolutionary Guard; five remain in U.S. custody.[21] Muqtada al-Sadr's close connections with certain Iranian factions make Jaysh al-Mahdi the most likely recipient of the aid flowing from Iran, but Iran's assistance may not be limited to Shi'a militia groups. In April 2007, Coalition officials announced that they had also uncovered evidence of Iran's aiding some Sunni insurgent groups in an apparent attempt to undermine overall Coalition policy in Iraq.[22]

Iranian influence has also contributed to increased Shi'a-on-Shi'a violence in the south, as factions vie for power and control of the region's natural resources and infrastructure. Many leading Shi'a politicians currently in power in Iraq spent decades in exile in Tehran and formed links that are certain to continue to affect the direction of Iraq's internal politics.

The Role of Iraq's Other Neighbors

Among Iraq's neighbors, Jordan, Kuwait, and Turkey have played the most productive roles in assisting the Government of Iraq. Jordan has hosted ISF training, while Kuwait is an invaluable logistics hub for ISF and Coalition supplies. Jordan has accepted some 750,000 Iraqi refugees, but it recently closed its borders as it no longer feels it can manage the unending flow of refugees.

Although their numbers are relatively small, foreign fighters of different nationalities flow into Iraq mainly through networks in Syria—a problem that the Syrian government has not taken effective measures to stop.[23] Iraq's relations with Saudi Arabia have also become increasingly strained, as more than 50 percent of all foreign fighters—and especially would-be suicide bombers—appear to be coming from Saudi Arabia.[24]

Means and Methods of Violence

Thanks to the legacy of the Ba'athist regime, insurgents and militias in Iraq are extremely well-armed. During his rule, Saddam Hussein purchased an enormous arsenal of conventional weapons, including huge stockpiles of artillery, tanks, mines, mortars, explosives, and ammunition of all types.[25] As Coalition forces advanced into Iraq in spring 2003, Ba'athist security forces melted away, leaving large, unguarded depots and armories that were quickly looted. Insurgents and militia members may also be buying on a black market weapons originally intended for the Iraqi Security Forces.[26]

Figure 6: Iraq—External Influences [Omitted]

The war in Iraq features the use of improvised explosive devices (IEDs) on a sweeping scale. Throughout the conflict, IEDs have been responsible for the majority of casualties. Their main components are explosive material, an ignition device, and a trigger. Explosive materials are abundant, and ignitions and triggers can be made from almost any small electronic device or collection of spare parts. Derivatives of the common "package-size" IEDs are vehide-borne (VBIEDs), suicide vests, or even entire blocks of houses wired together (house-borne or HBIEDs).

VBIEDs have been the most effective weapon of insurgents in Iraq. VBIED attacks include the truck bomb that hit the United Nations headquarters on August 19, 2003, and killed Special Envoy Sergio Vieira de Mello. Most IEDs are planted with a wire or pressure trigger or are remotely activated. This method is a force multiplier for the enemy, and it allows placement by unskilled foot soldiers while bomb makers and leaders remain undetected and out of danger. The tactical impact of IEDs is very similar to that of antipersonnel or antivehicle land mines; however, because of Iraq's urban terrain and the ease of IED construction, IEDs are more difficult to detect.

Levels of Violence and Their Impact on Iraqi Society

Violence remains a fact of life in Iraq. Those insurgents who perpetrate this violence are elusive, operate covertly, and seek to avoid direct engagement with Coalition and Iraqi forces. While violence has recently declined sharply in the Sunni-dominated Anbar province—the former stronghold of the insurgency—attacks have risen in Diyala, Balad, Basra, and Amarah. Violence remains endemic in Baghdad, despite measurable gains made since the implementation of Fardh al-Qanoon (the Baghdad Security Plan) in February 2007 by Coalition and Iraqi forces.

Since the beginning of Fardh al-Qanoon, the average number of sectarian killings in Baghdad has decreased. The average number of daily attacks has similarly fallen.[27] While these numbers may simply reflect the decision of many of the Shi'a militias to maintain a low profile during the Coalition-led surge, there are signs of improvements in the security situation in Baghdad.

Iraq's violent environment has placed its population under extreme duress. Iraq's population at the time of the 2003 invasion was about 26.5 million. Currently, more than 40,000 Iraqis leave Iraq each month. There are at least 2 million Iraqi refugees throughout the Middle East, whose presence places increasing pressure on Iraq's neighbors, and an additional 2.2 million displaced persons within Iraq.[28] Seventy percent of Iraqi residents lack adequate water supplies, compared with 50 percent in 2003.[29] Twenty-eight percent of children are malnourished, compared to 19 percent before the 2003 invasion. Ninety-two percent of Iraqi children suffer learning problems due to the stress of the war. Sadly, international funding for humanitarian assistance in Iraq has plummeted, from $453 million in 2005 to $95 million in 2006.[30]

Figure 7: Ethno-Sectarian Violence: Baghdad Security Districts [Omitted]

Iraqi society is being convulsed by sectarianism that if not swiftly and significantly curtailed could contribute to a rapid deterioration of Iraq, with "grave humanitarian, political, and security consequences."[31] Iraq's overall security environment is very complex. Elements of terror, ethnic violence, insurgency, meddling by external actors, and criminal activity all combine to define, in varying degrees, the nature of the threats. The Commission assesses that despite all that remain to be done, the single most important event that could immediately and favorably affect Iraq's direction and security is political reconciliation focused on ending sectarian violence and hatred. Sustained progress within the Iraqi Security Forces depends on such a political agreement.

Chapter 2: Overall Assessment of the Iraqi Security Forces

This report assesses each element of the Iraqi Security Forces in terms of its military readiness to contribute to the security of Iraq. Though many of the challenges facing the ISF are common across the military and police forces, each force has unique characteristics, potential strengths, and evident weaknesses. This chapter provides the Commission's perspective on the overall ability of the Iraqi Security Forces to conduct four critical missions: maintaining the territorial sovereignty of Iraq, denying safe haven to terrorists, providing greater security in the provinces, and ending sectarianism to promote national reconciliation.

Although the ISF have made significant progress in many areas, the Commission finds that they are not yet able to execute these missions independently. Without continued combat support, combat service support, and assistance from Coalition Military Transition Teams, it is unlikely that the ISF will achieve, in the near term, the proficiency and readiness needed to provide security for Iraq.

Figure 8: Glide Path: Iraqi Security Forces [Omitted]

Overview of Iraqi Security Forces

The Iraqi Security Forces are composed of Ministry of Defense (MOD) and Ministry of Interior (MOI) forces.[32] The Iraqi Army and Special Forces, Iraqi Air Force, and the Iraqi Navy report to the Ministry of Defense. Under the Ministry of Interior are the National Police, the Iraqi Police Service, the Department of Border Enforcement, the Facilities Protection Service, and the Coast Guard.

In 2004, the Coalition established the Multi-National Security Transition Command–Iraq to focus exclusively on helping to establish and develop the Iraqi Security Forces so that the Government of Iraq would be able to provide for its own security. The command is responsible for working with the Government of Iraq to generate and train Iraqi Security Forces, and to develop administrative capacity within the ministries of Defense and Interior to support the ISF. The Multi-National Corps-Iraq (the tactical unit responsible for command and control in Iraq) has joined in helping to develop the ISF, with an emphasis on providing Military Transition Teams and Police Transition Teams that partner with Iraqi military units at the division, brigade, and battalion levels and with police forces at the provincial, district, and police station levels.

Since 2003, United States has spent $19.2 billion on the development of the ISF.[33] Iraq has spent approximately $16.6 billion for the same purpose, but in 2007 its expenditures for the first time exceeded those of the United States.[34] In 2008, the Multi-National Security Transition Command–Iraq anticipates that Iraq will spend about $11.6 billion on the ISF, and has recommended that the United States contribute $5.5 billion.

Although this chapter examines each of the four missions in turn, it is clear that the missions themselves are interrelated: many of the capabilities needed to accomplish one specific mission are needed to accomplish the others as well. In order to deny terrorists safe haven in Iraq, the ISF must ultimately be able to secure Iraq's borders, an objective that is central to maintaining Iraq's territorial security. Denying terrorists a safe haven will contribute to bringing security to the provinces. In a similar vein, to accomplish any of these four missions, the ISF and the ministries that organize, train, and equip them must have functioning administrative and budgeting systems; logistics and supply chain management systems; and combat support such as aviation support, intelligence, and communications.

Maintain Territorial Integrity

To maintain Iraq's territorial integrity, the Iraqi Security Forces need to be able to protect the country from external threats, secure the nation's borders and maritime approaches, and control its air space. To fulfill these missions, the Iraqi Security Forces must be able to recruit, train, equip, and retain sufficient officers and soldiers who are loyal to the nation. They also must be able to project and sustain forces around the country, collect and act on military intelligence, command and control forces effectively, and conduct military operations successfully.

Today, the ISF is not able to secure Iraq's borders. The Iraqi Navy and Air Force do not control Iraq's maritime approaches or airspace, and the Ministry of Defense does not have the systems in place to project and sustain its military forces independently.

Iraq has 2,268 miles of land border—compared to 1,951 miles of the U.S.-Mexican border—as well as 36 miles of coastline. The nation's borders are porous, and at least two of Iraq's neighbors are actively contributing to instability within the country. Arms, munitions, and foreign fighters regularly come across the Iranian and Syrian borders. Not only is Iran providing matériel to militia groups but there are also distinct signs of Iranian influence at the political level in Iraq. Saudi Arabia has not taken effective steps to stem the flow of Saudi foreign fighters and suicide bombers into the country. However, discussions with Coalition commanders and intelligence officials in Iraq made it clear to the Commission that Iran's activities raise the greatest concern for future stability, and are making it more difficult for the Coalition to achieve its goals in Iraq.

The Iraqi armed forces are not yet a major factor in Iraq's border security effort. Iraq's 37,000 Department of Border Enforcement personnel are just over one-third the numbers that monitored Iraq's border during Saddam Hussein's rule. Border forts and land crossings lack equipment to inspect and monitor people and cargoes coming into the country. Many border facilities are crumbling, and corruption is a serious problem at many points of entry into Iraq.

Although Iraq's armed forces are not yet able to independently defend Iraq from external threats, they are increasingly capable of managing counterinsurgency operations. More than 75 percent of the battalions in the Iraqi Army can plan, conduct, execute, and sustain counterinsurgency operations with Coalition support,[35] though the degree of that support—particularly in logistics—can be substantial at times. The improvement in the Iraqi Army was aptly captured by the comment of a senior American general who noted that "a year ago we just wanted the Army to stand and fight with us and not run away—today we don't even have to think about that."[36]

As part of Fardh al-Qanoon (the Baghdad Security Plan), the Iraqi Army has participated in a large number of high-intensity operations and demonstrated an effectiveness and level of determination far greater than what Coalition forces observed during joint operations in 2005 and 2006 (this is illustrated by casualty figures). The Iraqi Minister of Defense seemed to recognize both the progress the Iraqi Army has made and the remaining challenges when he predicted to Commissioners that the Army would be 60 percent capable of independently protecting Iraq from external threats by 2012 and entirely independent in this regard by 2018. He also insisted that the Iraqi Army will be able to accept more responsibility for direct combat against internal threats in 2008.

Figure 9: Casualties in Iraq by Month and Year [Omitted]

The Iraqi Special Forces are a success story. The most capable units within the Iraqi military, they have trained extensively with U.S. Special Forces and developed a strong set of junior officers and a noncommissioned officer corps. Special operations involving both Coalition and Iraqi Special Forces are led by Iraqi commanders; their brigade provides 70 percent of the forces for these operations. Nevertheless, the Iraqi Special Operations Forces still rely extensively on Coalition forces for fire and counterfire, dose air support, fixed-wing and rotary wing mobility, and intelligence, surveillance, and reconnaissance.

The Iraqi Air Force and Navy are still too underdeveloped to contribute significantly to maintaining Iraq's territorial sovereignty. The Iraqi Air Force is organized for counterinsurgency operations and is flying operational missions over Baghdad and key critical infrastructure sites to provide Iraqi and Coalition forces with actionable intelligence, but these contributions represent a fraction of the intelligence, surveillance, and reconnaissance capability needed to combat the threats facing Iraq. Despite plans to triple its personnel by the end of 2007, the Air Force remains very small and is unlikely to be able to control Iraqi air space without outside assistance before 2010. Its ability to conduct aerial intelligence, surveillance, and reconnaissance missions is improving, however, and with the planned acquisition of additional C-130 cargo aircraft for transport, UH-II helicopters for mobility and medical evacuation, and Russian Mi-17 helicopters for counterinsurgency operations, the Iraqi Air Force will grow more capable over time.

Like the Air Force, the Iraqi Navy is very small and faces significant challenges. Most of Iraq's oil for export is pumped through two offshore oil terminals located just off Iraq's very small coastline in Basra province, a region of Iraq plagued by Jaysh al-Mahdi presence. While the Iraqi Navy's area of responsibility is of strategic importance given the volume of oil for export that is pumped from these oil terminals, the "fleet" is extremely small; some of its vessels are not seaworthy and are useful only as a source of spare parts. The Navy is in the process of acquiring a range of newer vessels that will provide it some capability to patrol continuously, protect the offshore terminals, and sustain maritime operations, but these capabilities will not be fully operational for at least another two to three years.[37]

Deny Terrorists Safe Haven

To deny international terrorists a safe haven in Iraq, Iraqi Security Forces need to be able to project force on behalf of the central government throughout the country and must have access to sufficient and actionable intelligence to ensure strategic situational awareness, secure the nation's borders, and conduct significant counterterrorism operations. Cooperation between Iraq's armed forces and its civil security forces—that is, the National Police, Iraqi Police Service, and the Department of Border Enforcement—is critical to achieving these missions.

> ***Finding:*** *Although the Iraqi Army and Special Forces have demonstrated significant progress in counterterrorism capabilities at the operational level, the Iraqi Police Service and National Police have many challenges to overcome and cannot yet effectively contribute to denying terrorists safe haven in Iraq. The border security forces are assessed as being ineffective.*[38]

Iraq's central government in Baghdad does not have national reach in terms of security, nor does it have a monopoly on the use of force—a defining characteristic of a functioning nation-state. Militias continue to play a prominent role and are seen by American and Iraqi officials alike as posing almost as significant a threat to Iraqi stability and security as al Qaeda in Iraq. Despite the heavy concentration of forces brought to the capital as part of Fardh al-Qanoon, the central government does not yet fully control security in Baghdad or its surrounding "ring cities."

The central government also lacks a clear view of activities in the provinces, although this absence of information does not necessarily mean that terrorists are establishing safe havens within them. Seven of Iraq's 18 provinces are now under "provincial Iraqi control" (PIC), meaning that in theory the Iraqi central government and provincial authorities are largely responsible for security in those areas. Three of these seven provinces are in the Kurdish region of Iraq, which essentially has a separate regional government and its own security forces. The remaining four provinces under provincial Iraqi control are in the southern part of Iraq. Despite the transition to this status, security in the four southern provinces is deteriorating because of a rise in intra-Shi'a violence. Increasing violence is particularly notable in Basra, Diyala, and Dhi Qar.[39] Unlike Diyala and Dhi Qar, Basra has not yet been transferred to provincial Iraqi control, but this transfer is expected to occur in the near future.

Figure 10: Governor and MNC-I Assessments and Projections for Provinces (1–31 Jul 2007) [Omitted]

Although the central government cannot yet control security inside the country, Iraq's ground forces, particularly its Special Forces, have demonstrated strong counterterrorism capability. Iraqi Special Forces, which have conducted many counterterrorism operations with and without Coalition forces, have achieved significant operational success in 2007.

Concurrent with improvements to the counterterrorism capabilities of the Iraqi Army and Special Forces has been the somewhat unexpected alliance of local tribes in Anbar province with Coalition and Iraqi forces. After meeting with American and Iraqi leaders in Anbar, the Commission assesses that progress in Anbar against al Qaeda in Iraq is both real and encouraging. "Provincial security forces"—local police, vetted by the tribal sheikhs, who will eventually go through formal police training—are helping to drive terrorists out of western Iraq and ensure that it is no longer a safe haven for al Qaeda in Iraq. It is not yet clear whether these new security arrangements can be exported successfully to other parts of Iraq, though there are promising signs that other provinces are experiencing a similar rejection of al Qaeda. Whether confined to Anbar province or more widely established, these alliances will have to be managed very carefully in order for them to contribute to Iraq's long-term security.

In areas where local tribes have allied themselves with Coalition and Iraqi security forces, tips against al Qaeda in Iraq and apprehensions of suspected al Qaeda in Iraq members or militiamen have increased dramatically. Coalition and ISF personnel are finding caches of weapons and improvised explosive devices (IEDs) more frequently, and the number of murders and other violent attacks is going down. Local populations and leaders in Anbar province will no longer tolerate al Qaeda in Iraq's violent attacks or attempts to inflict religious law on their more secular societies, and this rejection of the group has been a boon to Coalition forces. It is not clear whether these tribal alliances can always be trusted or will persist once al Qaeda in Iraq is largely driven from the province.[40]

To effectively eliminate terrorist activity inside Iraq, strong cooperation between the military forces and the police forces in Iraq will need to be institutionalized. Thus far the police are at a lower level of development. Most National Police units are not yet sufficiently operationally effective, and the organization as a whole is viewed as highly sectarian, given its almost exclusively Shi'a composition and its history of involvement in sectarian activities. Although Iraqi police working closely with Coalition forces have been able to establish a degree of presence in their respective communities, in many areas of Iraq, members the of the Iraqi Police Service rarely venture outside their stations. The very limited existing intelligence, surveillance, and reconnaissance capabilities of the Iraqi Police Service police leave them unable to contribute substantially to counterterrorism operations. Perhaps of greatest concern is that in many areas the Iraqi Police Service has been infiltrated by insurgents and militias.

Many of the shortcomings that prevent the Iraqi armed forces and civil security forces from independently maintaining the territorial integrity of Iraq are also weaknesses that prevent them from independently ensuring that Iraq does not become a safe haven for international terrorists. Although the Iraqi armed forces have made progress in developing greater combat proficiency, they lack the combat support and combat support services outlined previously.[41]

Across the entire ISF, Iraqi supply chain management, maintenance, and logistics systems are substandard. Multi-National Security Transition Command–Iraq is working closely with the Ministry of Defense to develop support and sustainment systems at the strategic and operational levels, and the Military Transition Teams reporting to Multi-National Corps-Iraq are working with tactical Iraqi units in the field to improve these capabilities, but the Commission foresees that the Iraqi military will rely on Coalition forces for at least another two to three years.

In a similar vein, Multi-National Security Transition Command–Iraq is working closely with the Ministry of Interior to develop support and sustainment systems for Iraq's police and border forces; but because the MOI is not as well developed as the MOD, this process will likely take more time.

Bring Security to the Provinces

In order to bring better security to Iraq's 18 provinces in the next 12 to 18 months, the Iraqi Security Forces will need to be able to better protect Iraqi citizens from ethnic, religious, terrorist, and insurgent-based violence; protect vital public and private infrastructure and transportation arteries; and project credible, effective, and sustainable military and police power throughout the entire country.

> ***Finding:*** *The ability of the Iraqi Security Forces to bring greater security to Iraq's provinces varies by region and by organization within the ISF owing to many factors, including political leadership, security environment, sectarianism, and available resources.*

While security in some parts of Iraq appears to be increasing, the country continues to be plagued by internal violence. Security gains overall have different attributes depending on the threat in the region. Relatively homogenous areas such as Anbar and the Kurdish provinces seem to be moving rapidly toward establishing provincial security by bringing together tribal leaders, Coalition forces, and Iraqi Security Forces. These developments are encouraging, but their durability is unknown and they are viewed with extreme skepticism by the predominantly Shi'a central government.

The three Kurdish provinces under Iraqi control are relatively secure, and the Iraqi Security Forces in those provinces are quite capable. There are three Iraqi Army brigades in the Kurdish region and a range of police and civil security forces, including the Asayesh, the Peshmerga, the Zeravani, and the Iraqi Police Service.[42] The Kurdish police were by far the most capable police the Commission observed during its visits to Iraq.

While some areas in Iraq seem to be stabilizing, ethnically or religiously mixed areas such as Baghdad and its ring cities continue to experience violence and intense sectarian activity. As noted above, even some of Iraq's most homogeneous Shi'a areas in the southern part of the country are seeing rising levels of intra-Shi'a militia violence.

The shift in the past year toward a greater focus on local recruiting for the Iraqi Security Forces has contributed to the ability of some ISF organizations to provide heightened security in the provinces. The Army and the

Iraqi Police Service are most effective in areas where they reflect the ethnic and sectarian composition of the public they are responsible for protecting. Though it is important for the Iraqi Security Forces at the national level to be ethnically and religiously diverse and broadly representative of Iraq's national composition, there is value in using forces that resemble local populations. In areas like western Iraq, the police force is largely Sunni, reflecting the local makeup. The "neighborhood watches" or "provincial security forces" that local sheikhs have organized in partnership with Coalition forces are representative of this kind of successful localized provision of security. In the Kurdish provinces, security forces are largely composed of Kurds. In the Shi'a south, the Iraqi Army and police are almost exclusively Shi'a.[43] Over time, if security and stability can be more broadly established in Iraq, the goal should be to field more ethnically and religiously mixed security forces—particularly in the Iraqi Army, which is intended to deploy nationally.

The Iraqi National Police, a force that reports to the Ministry of Interior, illustrates the peril of attempting to provide security with forces that are not representative of the population. There are nine brigades of National Police, and more than 85 percent of the force is Shi'a. Its members have been implicated in sectarian activities, including death squads and covert prisoner torture. When deployed to exclusively Shi'a areas, the National Police has been accepted by local communities, and its units have helped provide security under Operation Fardh al-Qanoon. At the same time, the National Police is widely rejected by Sunni communities, and efforts to recruit more Sunnis into the force have failed. Despite efforts to transform and retrain the National Police by October 2007, the organization is mistrusted by much of Iraqi society and some fear it could become a new Republican Guard.

> ***Finding:*** *The "clear, hold, build" strategy being implemented by Iraqi Security Forces is on the right track and shows potential, but neither the Iraqi armed forces nor the police forces can execute these types of operations independently.*

Reflecting the Coalition's much stronger grasp of counterinsurgency operations, the "clear, hold, build" strategy launched in March 2006 appears to be generating results in enhancing security in the provinces. The Iraqi Army's ability to conduct "clearing" operations has improved significantly; units such as the 2nd Iraqi Army Division based in Ninewa province are conducting effective intelligence and counterinsurgency operations that seem to be noticeably reducing violence levels. New cooperative relationships with local forces in Anbar and Diyala provinces exemplify how local Iraqi forces are able to "hold" Iraqi territory after it has been cleared by Coalition and Iraqi Army troops.

The "surge" of Coalition forces has made the presence of the Coalition and ISF much more visible in cities and neighborhoods all over Iraq. The morale of ISF units paired with Coalition forces appears relatively high, and trainers all over Iraq report that the ISF, particularly the Iraqi Army, seem to have the will to fight. An ISF casualty rate three times that of Coalition forces would seem to reflect this determination, albeit also the reality that neither the Iraqi Army nor the Iraqi Police Service are adequately armed or protected against the threats that they face.[44] The Joint Security Stations established in Baghdad partner Coalition forces with the Iraqi Army, National Police, and Iraqi Police Service, and they appear to be reducing levels of violence in their immediate areas.[45] The Joint Security Stations also are increasing the level of cooperation between local Iraqis, the ISF, and Coalition forces, as well as providing opportunities for in-depth mentoring and advising by Coalition forces.[46]

End Sectarian Violence

The ability of the Iraqi Security Forces to end sectarian violence in Iraq and contribute to setting the conditions for national reconciliation is limited in the absence of a strong central government and an active political reconciliation process. From a military perspective, to help end sectarian violence, the Iraqi Security Forces should represent the diversity of Iraq's population at the national level and not be a participant—actual or perceived—in sectarian violence.

> ***Finding:*** *The Iraqi Army and Iraqi Police Service have the potential to help reduce sectarian violence, but ultimately the ISF will reflect the society from which they are drawn. Political reconciliation is the key to ending sectarian violence in Iraq.*

Sectarian militias are a fact of life in Iraq. They may pose as much danger as al Qaeda in Iraq and may be an even greater threat to Iraq's long-term stability. Particularly in Baghdad and the southern provinces of Iraq, militias terrorize the population and continue to drive Iraqis out of the country.

At the ministerial level, while the Ministry of Defense has made considerable strides in developing its ability to plan, program, and budget for the Iraqi armed forces and to recruit and retain high-quality, vetted forces, the Ministry of Interior is not administratively effective and may be fueling sectarian tensions. It leans heavily toward protecting Shi'a interests, as evidenced by its recent decision to reject a religiously balanced list of new police for the city of Tal Afar in Ninewa province in favor of assigning 300 Shi'a policemen.[47] Sectarian tensions are so high that a number of MOI officials having been assassinated on their way to and from their offices, and as a result many MOI officials live permanently in the ministry.

The Iraqi Army, while not free of sectarianism, is in fact increasingly representative of the makeup of Iraqi society. About 75–80 percent of Iraqi Army soldiers are Shi'a, and 2 of the 11 divisions are 50 percent Kurdish. Sunnis are the least represented group within the Iraqi Army. Encouragingly, the Iraqi Army's leadership is relatively balanced: of the 11 divisions currently in operation, 3 are led by Kurdish commanders, 4 by Shi'a commanders, and 4 by Sunni commanders. After extensive interaction with Iraqi Army units, Coalition forces assess the majority of Iraqi Army units as operationally reliable and free from blatant sectarianism.

As noted above, the members of the National Police—in contrast to the Iraqi Army—are widely seen as sectarian and are not trusted by most Iraqis. Despite Coalition efforts to retrain the National Police and emphasize human rights and the rule of law, it is not clear that this element of the Iraqi Security Forces, in its current form, can contribute to Iraqi security and stability in a meaningful way.

Local recruiting for the ISF, at least in the short term, is critical in many parts of Iraq where, as already mentioned, developing security forces that reflect local populations will help reduce sectarianism and bring greater security to Iraq's provinces. Ethnically and religiously mixed areas such as Baghdad, the central provinces in Iraq, and areas around Kirkuk and Mosul are more challenging, because they do not lend themselves to this relatively simple model. Coalition forces and Iraqi Security Forces are already working together, neighborhood by neighborhood, to establish security in mixed areas. As a result of the robust and intense partnerships established under the leadership of General David Petraeus, Coalition forces today are already functioning as brakes on sectarian activity by the ISF. In mixed locations, Coalition forces may be the guarantors of security until sufficient stability can be achieved, but the Coalition cannot serve indefinitely in this capacity.

If recruited in a balanced fashion, vetted appropriately, and properly trained, the Iraqi Security Forces have the potential to reduce sectarian violence. At the same time, because they are drawn from the Iraqi population, the ISF will represent the society from which they come. If Iraq's national government exhibits sectarian behavior and if sectarianism is rampant in Iraqi society at large, it is unlikely that the Iraqi Security Forces will be immune to the same dynamics, regardless of their military readiness.

Since the beginning of Fardh al-Qanoon in February 2007, the Coalition and the Iraqi Security Forces have managed to create some level of security and some breathing space for Iraqi politicians. If the Coalition continues to provide key enabling support and training to the ISF over the next few years, with the expected increases in security that such support will likely bring, a more durable security environment will continue to develop and perhaps broaden. The reverse is certainly true should the government be unable to find the required political solution.[48]

Conclusion: The Iraqi armed forces—Army, Special Forces, Navy, and Air Force—are increasingly effective and are capable of assuming greater responsibility for the internal security of Iraq; and the Iraqi police are improving, but not at a rate sufficient to meet their essential security responsibilities. The Iraqi Security Forces will continue to rely on the Coalition to provide key enablers such as combat support (aviation support, intelligence, and communications), combat service support (logistics, supply chain management, and maintenance), and training. The Commission assesses that in the next 12 to 18 months there will be continued improvement in their readiness and capability. Evidence indicates that the ISF will not be able to progress enough in the near term to secure Iraqi borders against conventional military and external threats.

Chapter 3: The Ministry of Defense

The Iraqi Ministry of Defense (MOD) is a relatively new organization, coping with the challenges of managing its own development while supporting the current combat operations of the Iraqi armed forces. The MOD is strengthening its administrative capacity in several areas—notably in budget development, strategic and operational planning, and personnel management. It has a vision and strategic plan for Iraq's armed forces and is beginning to implement that vision. It has put functioning systems in place to recruit soldiers, sailors, and airmen; has developed an adequate training base in cooperation with the Coalition; and is working to improve its ability to acquire the systems its armed forces need to accomplish their missions effectively. At the same time, the ministry still struggles to ensure that its armed forces are combat ready. Iraqi commanders today rely on sometimes substantial Coalition assistance to overcome the deficiencies caused by shortfalls in budget execution, contracting, intelligence, and logistics within the MOD.

Overview of the Ministry of Defense

Under Saddam Hussein, the Ministry of Defense was controlled directly by the regime and staffed only by trusted military commanders. The Ba'athist MOD's primary mission was to protect Saddam and his immediate circle—not the Iraqi people. At the outset of the 2003 invasion, the Coalition planned to de-Ba'athify and then reform the MOD. After discovering firsthand the MOD's deep roots in the previous regime, the Coalition Provisional Authority chose to dismantle the MOD entirely at the same time that it disbanded the Iraqi Army and other military institutions, under CPA Order Number 2.[49]

Today, the MOD is led by Minister of Defense Lieutenant General (Ret.) Abdul Qadir Mohammed Jassim Obeidi, a Sunni career military officer and political independent.[50] The ministry comprises a Joint Headquarters, the Iraqi Ground Forces Command (which commands the Army), the Iraqi Special Operations Forces, and the Iraqi Army, Navy (including Marines), and Air Force.[51] The ministry's core mission and functions are organizing, training, equipping, sustaining, and employing the Iraqi Joint Forces in accordance with the Iraqi Constitution, government direction, and the law.[52]

Coalition assistance to the Ministry of Defense is provided largely through the Coalition Military Assistance Training Team (CMATT) and the two national-level transition teams assigned to the MOD. The Coalition Military Assistance Training Team advises both the MOD and the Joint Headquarters on manning, training, equipping, basing, and sustainment for ISF units throughout Iraq as they work toward operational readiness. The Ministry of Defense Transition Team (MOD-TT) advises civilian leadership at the MOD and is composed of a team of about 50 U.S. civilian advisors, 12 civilian advisors from other Coalition countries, and six U.S. military personnel, led by a Senior Executive Service-level U.K. civil servant. Most of the U.S. civilian advisors are contractors from private companies; as of July 2007, only two were U.S. civil servants. The Joint Headquarters Transition Team is led by an Australian general officer and a staff of 50 Coalition military personnel and contractors. All three organizations—the Coalition Military Assistance Training Team, the MOD Transition Team, and the Joint Headquarters Transition Team—report to Multi-National Security Transition Command–Iraq.

The Coalition transition teams working with the Iraqi MOD have separate but related missions, each with specific challenges. The MOD Transition Team is charged both with mentoring the Iraqi MOD civilian leadership as it carries out the ministry's mission and functions and with helping the ministry build its institutional capacity. The MOD Transition Team is also working to build a professional core of civil servants within the MOD. The Joint Headquarters Transition Team supports the Iraqi Joint Headquarters in its efforts to build and implement a command and control capability to train, sustain, and develop the Iraqi Joint Force's ability to address threats as directed by the Government of Iraq. The Joint Headquarters is based on a NATO standard staffing model.

During its assessment, the Commission held numerous meetings with Coalition advisors and Iraqi MOD officials, including two with the Iraqi Minister of Defense. The Commission found that the MOD has made significant strides since 2004 and is one of the more effective ministries in the Government of Iraq. As mentioned, the MOD still faces challenges in budgeting functions, contracting, personnel, intelligence, command and control, and logistics.[53]

Multi-National Security Transition Command-Iraq Definition of Success

Success is:

If they can recruit themselves, train themselves, sustain themselves, equip themselves, pay themselves, trust each other and acquire their future force requirements, then they are truly mission ready.

Budgeting

Finding: *Inefficiencies and overcentralization within the Ministry of Defense and its inability to fully execute its budget impede the combat readiness and capabilities of the Iraqi armed forces.*

The MOD has a functioning financial management system, complete with budgets that are tied to a requirements process at broad levels. MOD officials characterized their budget as having three primary dimensions: activating the armed forces and deepening their capabilities, modernizing the ground forces, and continuing expansion in manning levels. The Joint Headquarters commander drives the process to determine budgetary priorities by soliciting inputs from the four services—Iraqi Army and Special Forces, Iraqi Air Force, and the Iraqi Navy—as well as from functional commanders such as those directing logistics and communications.

The ability to build a budget is an important first step, but it may be the least complex element of a financial management system; it is not the same as the ability to execute the budget, a task that the MOD finds far more problematic. As of November 2006, MOD had spent 76 percent of its calendar year budget for salaries, 25 percent of its budget for goods and services, 1 percent of its budget for capital goods and projects, but only 32 percent of its overall budget of $3.4 billion.[54] The MOD's ability to execute its budget may be improving; when the Commission met with ministry officials in July 2007, they stated that they had already expended 46 percent of their calendar year budget for 2007.

The Iraqis have a complex internal control system that divides the entire budgeting process between multiple ministries. The Ministry of Finance (MOF) controls all funds and there are serious bureaucratic difficulties in securing the release of moneys. MOD officials shared their frustrations over this situation with the Commission, noting that Ministry of Finance control over their funding makes it difficult, if not impossible, to increase their budget.

Even when the MOD builds a budget and secures the release of funds from the Ministry of Finance, its ability to execute that budget is hindered by insufficient delegation of authority in the MOD to disburse money. The Minister of Defense is allowed to give partial expenditure authority to some staff, but overall the Commission found that budget execution remains burdensome. The specter of corruption has added another layer of internal controls to an already cumbersome budgeting and expenditure process (and as discussed in the next section, MOD's use of the Foreign Military Sales system to thwart corruption has often compounded its difficulties).

The MOD Transition Team should remain engaged and work closely with MOD officials on the crucial issue of budget execution. Continued mentoring is of particular importance, as many of the financial and administrative systems being put in place by Coalition advisors are new to their Iraqi MOD counterparts; grasping them will require significant time and training. The new financial systems may also be an example of the Coalition tendency to focus on solutions that mirror Western methods rather than on developing approaches that are more consistent with Iraqi norms, standards, and experience. Addressing the larger issue of cultural resistance to delegation of authority is more difficult but may be more critical to ensuring that the MOD can execute its budgets consistently. Changing this aspect of the MOD's corporate culture will require institutional changes at the highest levels of ministerial leadership, together with a commitment to prioritize budget execution at the same level as budget development.

Contracting

> ***Finding:*** *The ability to contract efficiently is important to the MOD's mission to sustain the Iraqi armed forces. The MOD currently lacks effective processes to execute contracting requirements.*

In order to recruit, retain, train, operate, and sustain an authorized military force of more than 195,000,[55] the MOD must be able to contract for a wide range of goods and services. This vital capability continues to be a major problem for both organizational and cultural reasons. During the 30 years of Saddam Hussein's rule, Iraqi bureaucrats learned that mistakes were punished with a severity that curbed any impulse toward initiative. This ingrained fear, coupled with a cultural bias toward centralized control at senior levels, led to an onerous process for awarding MOD contracts. For example, a minimum of three bids are required for any contract above 25 million dinars (about $20,000). MOD officials told the Commission that if fewer than three bids are received, the MOD must reissue the request for proposal. In a similar vein, the Minister of Finance apparently insists on personally reviewing all contracts over $50,000.

Because of these extensive controls and limitations, the Iraqi procurement process was accomplishing little. It also was seriously distorted by corruption. To correct both problems, U.S. advisors persuaded the Iraqi government to utilize the U.S. Foreign Military Sales (FMS) system, an elaborate arrangement developed over the past 40 years to coordinate the sales of military hardware and services to foreign governments. The United States government acts as the integrating office for a relatively small commission.

The Foreign Military Sales system is free of corruption, but it is not speedy under even the best of circumstances—and in this specific instance, its functioning has been weak and frankly embarrassing. The Commission was told by Multi-National Security Transition Command–Iraq that of $1.7 billion in sales in 2006, only $300 million of the services and equipment had been received by the Iraqis as of July 2007. They have deposited another $600 million for the Ministry of Defense in 2007, but no orders have been placed pending delivery of 2006 orders. Moreover, it appears that the New Equipment Training (NET) bought and paid for through Foreign Military Sales did not enable the Iraqis to actually learn to maintain the equipment they had received. When confronted with this record, senior U.S. commanders in Iraq lamented that the performance of the Foreign Military Sales system is "a national embarrassment." The Coalition talked the Iraqi government into using the system to avoid corruption and ensure delivery of critical goods and services, yet the United States is not delivering on the commitments it made. This failure is hurting the United States as sorely as the Iraqis. The Coalition depends on the improved capabilities of Iraqi forces to replace Coalition troops. U.S. failure to make the foreign military system function is directly hindering plans to transfer warfighting responsibilities to the Iraqis. The U.S. Secretary of Defense should appoint a single senior official responsible for ensuring timely and efficient processing of Iraqi material and support contracts through the Foreign Military Sales system on an expedited basis.

MOD officials expressed frustrations about contracting processes at the MOD and also acknowledged that although the Foreign Military Sales system is the best option at present, the Iraqis must develop their own system.[56] The contracting issue is a long-term problem that requires more than a near-term work-around. Coalition personnel consistently noted to the Commission that Iraqis are more likely to address important issues when they are spending Iraqi government money. If this is true, the current practice of financially supplementing Iraqi operations may be enabling the Iraqis to avoid making needed changes to their administrative systems and processes: in this case, to their contracting system.

There also are indications that the Iraqi MOD may be improving its ability to contract effectively. In June 2007, the MOD Joint Contracting Command awarded $64.2 million in contracts, of which more than 70 percent—for items such as batteries, uniforms, undergarments, boots, and armored buses—were awarded to Iraqi-owned companies. This contracting effort is extremely important, as it demonstrates that there is an emerging capability within Iraq to provide material in support of ISF requirements.

Personnel

> ***Finding:*** *The MOD consistently compensates the members of the Iraqi military, but it has difficulty accounting for personnel.*

In general, the MOD is able to make payroll for its growing forces—despite relying on methods that are out of date by U.S. standards. Currently, unit commanders must certify who is on the rolls, and then compare those rolls to a master list. At that point, designated fiduciary agents in the units distribute moneys to the commanders, who pay military personnel in cash. Though highly cumbersome, this administrative system appears to work effectively.

The MOD also continues to develop a new banking facility that is already providing roughly 2,800 employees with direct deposit services. The MOD is working to add another 1,500 personnel to the bank's rolls. The new MOD bank will facilitate payment while also reducing the risks of corruption in the payroll system.[57] Although at present only a fraction of MOD personnel are part of the new direct deposit system, it is an important step in the right direction.

Another positive development in the MOD's administrative capacity is the rolling implementation of the Human Resource Information Management System (HRIMS),[58] which links personnel and pay functions into a single automated system and database. The purpose of HRIMS is to provide its customers, in a single format, a clear snapshot of information, tracking pay and personnel from initial recruitment to separation. The system should also be able to facilitate accurate reporting and analysis, enabling reliable auditing functions and minimizing opportunities for corruption. At present, the Commission was informed that HRIMS is in use at the MOD and division levels, and should be available for use at the brigade level by September 2007.[59]

Intelligence

> ***Finding:*** *The level of information sharing and cooperation between the Iraqi intelligence community and the Iraqi Security Forces is not satisfactory—a problem exacerbated by bureaucratic competition and distrust among duplicative intelligence organizations.*

There are four significant, known intelligence organizations that support the Iraqi Security Forces. The Directorate General of Intelligence and Security (DGIS) is within the MOD; the National Information and Investigation Agency (NIIA), is under the Ministry of the Interior; and the Iraqi National Intelligence System (INIS) is considered Iraq's primary intelligence agency. An independent intelligence organization has been established by the Ministry of State for National Security Affairs (MSNSA).

Most Iraqi officials that met with the Commission noted that there is relatively little information sharing between these organizations—or, in some cases, even between operational units of the same organization in the field. The reluctance to share information seems particularly apparent at the intersection point of the military and police forces. There is very little understanding in the Iraqi armed forces or in the Ministry of Interior—where many senior officials are former military officers—of how to use intelligence effectively to support operations. The Commission was concerned by the apparent lack of access by the Iraqi Army and police to the Iraqi National Intelligence System.

Information-sharing challenges between intelligence organizations and security forces are not unique to Iraq, but the active competition among Iraq's intelligence organizations is making the typical problems much more difficult. For example, the MSNSA is organized along the lines of the former regime state security apparatus and is operating in direct competition with INIS, the more established national-level intelligence agency. Commissioners believe that MSNSA was created in part as a reaction to perceptions that INIS was too closely linked to the Coalition. These internal turf battles detract from the critical task of building greater intelligence capacity. Multi-National Security Transition Command–Iraq has a new intelligence transition team function that is working closely with members of the Iraqi intelligence community to facilitate coordination among these agencies.

Iraq is principally a human intelligence (HUMINT) theater of operations and will remain so for the foreseeable future. The challenge for all of Iraq's security forces is how to share information gathered at the local level without compromising sources, and how to convince information holders to trust and communicate with one another. From a fusion center would come "actionable intelligence"—which then would have to be converted into "immediate-use" intelligence for operations. At that point, certain technologies and intelligence, surveillance, and reconnaissance (ISR) would be applied to continually monitor the target.

The Commission believes that the U.S. military intelligence model, which is heavily based on technology, is unlikely to work well in the Iraqi environment. Iraqi officials stressed repeatedly that what they need is mentoring and time to develop and adjust their own approaches rather than to adopt the complicated doctrine, structures, and technological solutions that are the hallmark of the U.S. system. Examples of low-technology techniques described to the Commission that have worked well in Iraq include the "National Tips Hotline," which enables the public to provide information to the police and military via cellular telephone, and the working relationships that are being developed through partnership arrangements such as the Joint Security Stations and brigade-level Military Transition Teams.

Command and Control

> ***Finding:*** *Parallel lines of direct communication to military units have been established under the control of the Prime Minister. He is perceived by many as having created a second, and politically motivated chain of command, effectively communicating orders directly to field commanders. Such a practice bypasses national command lines, which should flow through the Minister of Defense and the Commanding General of Iraqi Armed Forces.*

In creating the Office of the Commander in Chief, the Counter-Terrorism Bureau, and in claiming command and control over Iraq's highly capable Special Forces, the Prime Minister is perceived to have established a separate chain of command. At the very least, there now exists the appearance that a senior elected official can bypass existing military command structures for sectarian reasons. In Iraq's developing military culture, this has a potentially divisive effect reminiscent of the previous era. The two organizations most associated with this perception are the Office of the Commander in Chief and the Counter-Terrorism Bureau, both of which report directly to the Prime Minister. Any perception that elements of the ISF are influenced along sectarian and political lines is not in the best interest of Iraq's newly formed Armed Forces. The Commission believes that the Office of the Commander in Chief should be abolished and that the Prime Minister should immediately emphasize that command and control of Iraqi Special forces is to be executed through the national chain of command. The existence of any other parallel or additional structures fosters mistrust, creates confusion, impedes military effectiveness, and perpetuates sectarian tension in the Armed Forces.

Logistics

> ***Finding:*** *The lack of logistics experience and expertise within the Iraqi armed forces is substantial and hampers their readiness and capability. Renewed emphasis on Coalition mentoring and technical support will be required to remedy this condition.*

The Multi-National Security Transition Command–Iraq 2007 Campaign Action Plan for the "Year of Leaders and Logistics" called for the Iraqi Joint Headquarters to assume responsibility for providing logistical support to the Iraqi Army by November 2007. Although steps have been made in contracting and procurement strategies, information technology systems rollout, infrastructure improvement, logistics force structure design, and leadership development, the progress to date has been slow by Coalition standards, and Iraqi logistics is unlikely to be ready for this transition by the end of 2007.

The MOD has a plan to roll out an information system designed to support the command and control of the logistics enterprise. This is a vital requirement, as the MOD currently relies on an unresponsive, paper-driven process. Multi-National Security Transition Command–Iraq advisors to the MOD informed Commissioners that they are planning to field a new software system within the next 6 to 10 months, but before that can happen the software needs to be translated into Arabic, soldiers will need to gain the skills to operate it, and solutions are needed to the problems of connectivity that the regular electricity shortages will inevitably cause. In light of these challenges, fielding a workable logistics information technology system in support of the Iraqi Armed Forces is very unlikely in the near term.

There has been progress in providing the infrastructure required to logistically support the Iraqi armed forces. The comprehensive plan is centered around the Taji National Depot, which, when completed, will provide the national hub for training, supply support, and intermediate maintenance. Construction of warehouses, small arms and ammunition storage, and generator facilities are under way. Much work remains before this plan will be realized, however. The Commission was informed that the end point of the phased timeline is early 2008, but funding and construction delays will most likely push actual completion to between 2010 and 2012. Only $55 million has been funded, just one-tenth of the total required.

Another challenge for the MOD is logistics force structure design. The Iraqi Army remains heavily dependent on contracted support to satisfy day-to-day requirements, and it appears that contracted logistics support (CLS) in some form will be necessary for two to three years. The MOD has developed a detailed plan that will, when in place, adequately provide all required support. This plan is well understood by all key stakeholders, and the structure will provide not only ministerial oversight but also operating components down to the tactical level. Manning the logistics force structure will be a major undertaking, as the Iraqi Army has concentrated on its combat units and has only recently begun the process of manning and training logistics organizations. The Commission was informed that arriving at the final force structure design will likely take two to four years.

The final element needed for logistics development at the MOD level is critical: leadership. At present, there is little logistics expertise at the national level, and both uniformed and civilian leaders require one-on-one mentoring. At the operational and tactical level, transition teams are embedded with operational units. These teams provide technical support and mentoring to the battalion, brigade, and division headquarters and appear to be working very well.

> *Conclusion:* The Ministry of Defense, which is responsible for policy development and implementation as well as resource allocation for the Iraqi military, is building the necessary institutions and processes to fulfill its mission. However, its capacity is hampered by bureaucratic inexperience, excessive layering, and overcentralization. These flaws reduce the operational readiness, capability, and effectiveness of the Iraqi military. As the MOD continues to mature, it should assume the ministerial-level functions that currently fall to the Coalition.

Chapter 4: The Iraqi Army and Iraqi Special Operations Forces

The Iraqi Army (IA) is a newly forming light infantry army already fighting a difficult counterinsurgency as it comes into being. Though the Iraqi Army is enjoying increasing success at the tactical level, significant challenges remain. Most units can muster only 60–75 percent of their assigned strength on any given day, owing to the need for soldiers to travel home to give their families their pay, the lack of enforcement of the Iraqi Code of Military Discipline, the counting of wounded soldiers who remain on the personnel rolls but cannot fight, and the number of soldiers on scheduled leave.[60] Although many units in the Iraqi Army can now fight well at the small unit level and appear to have a greater will to fight than was present in 2005 and 2006, Iraqi Army units are often outgunned because they lack crew-served and indirect fire weapons, possess limited capacity to handle medical evacuation and combat casualty, and have few "soldier support" systems. Reflecting these capability gaps, the Iraqi Army is at present highly dependent on the Coalition for combat enablers such as fires and counterfires, close air support, fixed wing and rotary wing mobility, C^{4}ISR (command, control, communications, computers, intelligence, surveillance, and reconnaissance), reinforcing capability, partnered presence with Multi-National Corps-Iraq units on the battlefield, supplemental logistics, and maintenance support.

The Iraqi Special Operations Forces (ISOF) is a small, elite group that has trained very closely with Coalition Special Forces and has developed into one of the most capable special forces in the Middle East. Like the Iraqi Army, however, the Iraqi Special Operations Forces remain dependent on Coalition combat enablers. The fact that the chain of command to the Special Forces is outside the established Ministry of Defense chain of command, reporting directly to the Prime Minister's office, raises concerns about the politicization of these units.

Overview of the Iraqi Army and Special Forces

From 1980 to 1988, the Iraqi Army fought a corps-level war against Iran over a terrain larger than the entire Western front of World War II. At the end of the Iran-Iraq War in 1988, Iraq's army was the world's fourth-largest, composed of seven corps and five armored divisions and having mobilized 1.7 million Iraqis.[61] During the Gulf War in 1991, the Coalition destroyed this force-significantly weakening the armed forces of Iraq.

Prewar planning for the invasion of Iraq in the 2002–2003 time frame "called for the dismantlement of the Spedal Republican Guard, the Republican Guard, and paramilitary structures and for the creation of a core of a new force, consisting of three to five divisions and geared to self-defense."[62] As the United States advanced into thc country, thc Iraqi forces put up very little resistance—but instead of surrendering, they shed their uniforms and melted back into the civilian population.[63] Along with other top Ba'athist leadership, the 400,000 regular troops and 10,000 generals of the Iraqi Army simply went home. The rampant looting that followed destroyed what was left of the Iraqi Army facilities, including many hardware and ammunition depots.

On May 23, 2003, Order 2 of the Coalition Provisional Authority (CPA) formally disbanded the Ministry of Defense, Ministry of State for Military Affairs, National Security Bureau, Iraqi Army, Republican Guard, Special Republican Guard, Directorate of Military Intelligence, and Saddam's many irregular units.[64] CPA Order 1 concerning de-Ba'athification had already essentially liquidated and sent into hiding or resistance the top cadre of military leadership.[65] CPA Order 2 also initiated the extensive task of reconstructing Iraq's security forces and establishing the New Iraqi Corps, which became the New Iraqi Army (NIA) in August 2003. Under civilian control, the army's mission was to provide "defense of the nation, including defense of the national territory and the military protection of the security of critical installations, facilities, infrastructure, lines of communication and supply, and population."[66] The objective was to create a force that could deter regional aggressors and unwanted foreign factions without threatening the regional balance of power. This force was to be 44,000-strong, "oriented toward external threats ... with a clear focus on border security ... [to] fill the growing need for a national military force, but with a measured equipping program and without any true logistical capacity."[67]

In September 2003, the Coalition Provisional Authority increased end strength and added force structures: an air component, coastal defense, and an Iraqi counterterrorism force that became the Iraqi Special Operations Forces.[68] Also that month, CPA Order 28 recognized a need for more Iraqi forces to deal with the continued degradation of the security situation in the country, creating the internally oriented Iraqi Civil Defense Corps, later renamed the Iraqi National Guard.[69] The Iraqi National Guard worked alongside Coalition forces to address Iraq's internal security challenges, but it quickly developed a poor reputation and became a prime target of the insurgency.[70] In March 2004, the CPA redesignated the New Iraqi Army as a component of the Iraqi Armed Forces under the control of a newly constructed Ministry of Defense.[71] In April 2004, it transferred control of the Iraqi National Guard from the Ministry of Interior to the MOD.

In June 2004, Prime Minister Ayad Allawi of the Interim Iraqi Government announced the formation of another military service—the Iraqi Intervention Force, a branch of the Iraqi Army specializing in counterinsurgency warfare.[72] This was a force designed to surge to urban hot spots within the country. Because the missions of the Iraqi Intervention Force and the Iraqi Army were becoming difficult to distinguish, the CPA and MOD decided to merge the Iraqi National Guard and Iraqi Intervention Force into the Iraqi Army.

The Iraqi Army, in all its various forms, has been an all-volunteer force since the fall of the Ba'athist regime and is the core of Prime Minister Maliki's "Objective Counterinsurgency Force." It is composed of:

- Nine light infantry divisions (with one more division in development and two more planned)
- One mechanized infantry division
- Associated support/combat support units
- Nine motorized transportation regiments
- Four logistics battalions
- Two support battalions
- Five regional support units
- Eighty garrison support units[73]

Figure 11: Iraqi Army Size and Capability Growth [Omitted]

The Iraqis also formed the Strategic Infrastructure Brigade, dedicated to protecting key energy and other infrastructure. It comprises three brigade headquarters commanding 17 battalions. The Prime Minister has directed that the Strategic Infrastructure Battalions go through a retraining and equipping process to bring them to Iraqi Army battalion standards, but with additional training in infrastructure protection and consequence management.[74]

The Iraqi Army's training base is still developing. Currently there are three dedicated training battalions and six Regional Training Centers under the direction of the Iraqi Training and Doctrine Command. Also under Training and Doctrine Command are the Defense Language Institute, the Tactical Doctrine Center, and the Lessons Learned Center. Within the training base are the nascent National Defense University, the Joint Staff College, and the Defense Strategic Studies Institute. Finally, the Iraqi Army has established a noncommissioned officer school, a counterinsurgency center, and the Iraqi Military Academy at Rustamiyah.

The Iraqi Special Operations Forces is the operational component of the Iraqi Counterterrorism Command. Iraqi Special Operations Forces is a brigade-size force composed of approximately 1,500 soldiers: a counterterrorism battalion, a commando battalion, a support battalion, and a special reconnaissance unit. A key component in developing an Iraqi counterterrorism capability is the ongoing effort to double the number of soldiers in the Iraqi Special Operations Forces.[75] This expansion will include an additional commando battalion with forward-based commando companies in Basra, Mosul, and Al Asad.

Like the other elements of the Iraqi military, the Iraqi Army today receives training and mentoring from both Multi-National Security Transition Command–Iraq and Multi-National Corps-Iraq. As Iraqi Army units become capable of operating in combination with Coalition forces, their tactical control is transferred to the appropriate Multi-National Corps-Iraq unit, which embeds advisors and partners Coalition forces with Iraqi units. The Iraqi Assistance Group, which reports to the Multi-National Corps-Iraq commander, provides advisors in the form of Military Transition Teams. The Military Transition Teams are composed of 10–15 Coalition soldiers—along with marines, airmen, and sailors—ranking from staff sergeant to colonel (or equivalent service rank). There are currently 5,000 Coalition personnel serving in more than 500 Military Transition Teams throughout the country. Military Transition Teams advise, coach, teach, and mentor the Iraqi Security Forces in infantry tactics, intelligence, communications, fire support, and logistics.[76] They seek to develop and improve Iraqi leaders, support Iraqi units' continued training, and assist with logistics and battlefield enablers such as medical evacuation and close air and artillery support. Military Transition Teams are linked to brigade combat teams deployed throughout Iraq. As Iraqi Army units sustain themselves more effectively, the goal is ultimately for them to operate without the Military Transition Teams. To gauge unit progress, the Military Transition Team leader and counterpart Iraqi Army commander prepare monthly classified Operational Readiness Assessments[77] (for the readiness level definitions and the Iraqi Army's progression to ORA levels 1 and 2; for the disposition of Iraqi Army divisions and their respective ORA levels).

Figure 12: Iraqi Army Operational Readiness Assessment (ORA) Level Definitions [Omitted]

Figure 13: Iraqi Army Progression to ORA Levels 1 and 2 [Omitted]

Figure 14: Iraqi Army Division Disposition (2007) [Omitted]

Challenges for the Iraqi Army and Special Operations Forces

During its assessment, the Commission held discussions with more than 50 American officials and 50 Iraqi officials directly involved in the development of the Iraqi Army and Special Operations Forces, including meetings with a large number of Military Transition Teams and partnered

Multi-National Corps-Iraq forces. The Commission also visited more than 30 Iraqi Army and Special Operations Forces facilities throughout Iraq, including Army bases, training centers, logistics and maintenance centers, and units at the division, brigade, and battalion levels.

The Commission believes that the Iraqi ground forces have made considerable progress, particularly in the past two years. However, the Iraqi Army and Special Forces face significant challenges in several mission and functional areas, including border protection, counterinsurgency and counterterrorism operations, leadership, personnel, equipment, and logistics and maintenance.

Border Protection

> ***Finding:*** *In addition to protecting the nation against external military threats, the Iraqi Army can and should also play a role in preventing unconventional threats migrating from points outside of Iraq. The Army currently does not have sufficient forces to enhance border security and conduct counterinsurgency operations simultaneously.*

Iraqi and American officials noted to the Commission that the Iraqi insurgency is a "vehicle-borne insurgency." Controlling main routes to and from border areas and in other key regions is necessary to stop the inflow of foreign fighters and to control the spread of explosively formed penetrators (EFPs) and other deadly technologies that defeat up-armored vehicles and kill or injure Coalition and Iraqi forces in large numbers. More than 80 percent of suicide bombers in Iraq—including the drivers who deliver vehicle-borne improvised explosive devices to their targets—are foreigners.[78]

Senior officials at the Iraqi Ministry of Defense made clear to the Commission that they are aware of a serious problem with Iraq's border security. The MOI's Department of Border Enforcement forces, as the first line of defense, are failing to control the borders adequately (as discussed in Chapter 11). Coalition and Iraqi commanders who use Iraqi Army units to reinforce less capable border forces are finding success—apprehending foreign fighters and intercepting significant amounts of weapons.[79] Despite the Iraqi Army's achievements in assisting with border security in some areas, it relies deeply on the Coalition for intelligence, surveillance, and reconnaissance. In addition, although the Army needs to play a role in thickening Iraq's border defenses, given its demanding internal security responsibilities, it does not yet have adequate forces to fill the gap.

> ***Recommendation:*** *The Iraqi Army's size and capability should be developed as part of an Iraqi national security strategy that defines the roles and missions of the ISF to address both internal security and border security needs. The Army as well as the nation's police forces are currently emphasizing internal security; only ineffective border security forces are focused on controlling the borders. The Iraqi Army must contribute to both border and internal security. A national commitment to expand the Army's mission*

beyond counterinsurgency to include border security must be reflected in Army and MOD plans and policies.

Given Iraq's evident border security challenges, the Iraqi Army should assist in "thidcening" or "reinforcing" border enforcement as part of its broader mission to protect the country from external threats. In the near term, the Government of Iraq may need to consider expanding the size of the Iraqi Army to backstop less reliable border enforcement police without compromising the Iraqi Army's ability to combat internal threats. To be effective in this role in the near term, the Iraqi Army will require key enabling support from the Coalition, particularly in intelligence, surveillance, and reconnaissance.

Counterinsurgency and Counterterrorism Operations

The Iraqi Army

Finding: *The Iraqi Army has become more effective in supporting Coalition-led counterinsurgency operations from the start of Iraqi and Coalition surge operations in early 2007. The reliability of Iraqi Army units continues to improve, and some units now are an integral part of the Coalition team for counterinsurgency operations. The overall rate of progress of the Army is uneven. Some units perform better than others; but there is rising confidence that progress is being made at a rate that will enable Iraqi Army tactical formations and units to gradually assume a greater leadership role in counterinsurgency operations in the next 12 to 18 months. However, they will continue to rely on Coalition support, including logistics, intelligence, fire support, equipment, training, and leadership development for the foreseeable future.*

Changes to U.S. counterinsurgency strategy since 2006 have significantly altered the dynamic between U.S. and Iraqi forces, and have led to noticeable improvements in the Iraqi Army's ability to conduct counterinsurgency and counterterrorism operations (internal defense). The lessons learned and best practices resulting from the new approach to counterinsurgency operations are spreading to Iraqi Army units, in part because those units are working hand-in-glove with the Americans. The Iraqi Security Forces have developed their own counterinsurgency doctrine, and unit commanders are cycled through the Iraqi Counterinsurgency School at Taji.

The Commission observed Iraqi Army units operating alongside U.S. troops in joint security stations, patrol bases, and command outposts. The American and Iraqi field-grade officers indicated to the Commission that they trust one another unconditionally. Even when American units are absent, the Commission observed indications that Iraqis are taking the fight to the enemy. High-intensity operations such as Fardh al-Qanoon in Baghdad plainly demonstrate that the Iraqi units are willing to combat urban counterinsurgency with far more determination and efficacy than during the generally disorganized joint operations of 2004 to 2006.

At the same time, it is clear that the relatively large numbers of Coalition advisors and partner units are a key enabler of this improved performance, as they continually provide strong leadership and mentoring, as well as combat support during actual operations. Where American and Iraqi Army units have worked closely with local communities, established patrol bases and other forward sites, and operated extensively together, there are increasing signs that local populations enjoy a credible security alternative to the lawlessness of the past few years. These closer Coalition-Iraqi community partnerships are leading to the development of stronger human intelligence networks, which in turn lead to more combat successes.

Coalition forces advise and mentor Iraqi Army units learning to conduct operations that win hearts and minds, respect human rights, separate enemies from the civilian population, and facilitate political solutions. These are complex operations for any military force, and Coalition support for the Iraqi Army has been critical to the progress made to date. Without continued training, mentoring, and key combat enablers from the Coalition, it would be difficult for the Iraqi Army to progress to a point where it can conduct effective, independent counterinsurgency and counterterrorism operations. Further, it is likely that the hard-won progress made to date would atrophy.

Iraqi Special Operations Forces

> ***Finding:*** *Iraqi Special Operations Forces are the most capable element of the Iraqi armed forces and are well-trained in both individual and collective skills. They are currently capable of leading counterterrorism operations, but they continue to require Coalition support. They remain dependent on the Coalition for many combat enablers, especially airlift, close air support, and targeting intelligence.*

The Iraqi Special Operations Forces are a strong direct action and "snatch" force—specializing in operations to place high-value targets in custody in "nonpermissive" environments. Joint special operations involving the Iraqi Special Forces are led by Iraqi commanders; their brigade provides 70 percent of the forces. Coalition Special Operations Forces have been training their Iraqi counterparts since 2003, and many Coalition operators are in Iraq on repeated tours, bringing depth, continuity, and experience to the training effort. Coalition forces have helped develop a strong noncommissioned officer corps in the Iraqi Special Operations Forces, as well as a junior officer corps. Both display considerable promise for and confidence in the future of the Iraqi armed forces.

Despite their strong and consistent performance, the Iraqi Special Operations Forces rely heavily on Coalition combat enablers. A particularly important capability gap is the lack of independent rotary air support.

Consequently, there are a variety of special operations missions and roles that the Iraqi Special Operations Forces cannot yet perform.

The Iraqi Special Operations Forces are the most capable force in the Iraqi Security Forces, but the diverse and challenging nature of the threats in Iraq leads to an extraordinarily difficult mission set. To ensure that the requirements of this mission set can be met, Special Operations in Iraq must remain a three-legged stool—Iraqi Special Forces and MOI special tactics units, Coalition Joint Special Operations Task Force units, and other U.S. Special Operations task forces.

Army Leadership

> ***Finding:*** *The Iraqi Army is short of seasoned leadership at all levels, and a lack of experienced commissioned and noncommissioned officers hampers its readiness, capability, and effectiveness.*

De-Ba'athification initially banned almost all experienced Iraqi Army leadership from continued service. Over time, the Coalition and the Government of Iraq adjusted their policies and about 20,000 officers and noncommissioned officers have returned to the Army. The most severe leadership shortage is the lack of company-grade and junior field-grade officers. According to Coalition estimates, the Iraqi Army needs at least an additional 30,000–40,000 leaders (officers and NCOs) to command units in the field. The demand for officers and NCOs in Iraq competes with the need for competent leaders throughout government bureaucracies and in the other security forces. The virtual shutdown of many Iraqi colleges and universities, and the interruption of primary and secondary schools by the events of the past few years, will likely make recruiting educated officers and noncommissioned officers a greater challenge, as has the continued emigration of many educated Iraqis.

Multi-National Security Transition Command–Iraq has many programs under way to develop an officer corps, with an emphasis on "train the trainers" approaches. The Coalition is attempting to increase the number of one-year military academies in the country, using a standardized curriculum based on that of the Royal British Military Academy at Sandhurst. The first military academy was opened in 2004 as the Iraqi Military Academy in Rustamiyah and is run by NATO (North Atlantic Treaty Organization) Training Mission-Iraq.[80] The first class of 73 cadets graduated in June 2006. More than 2,500 Iraqi officers and civilians have received training in Iraq through NATO-led courses, and close to 1,000 Iraqi personnel have been trained outside the country through additional NATO Training Mission courses.[81] NATO also has provided the Iraqi Army with much-needed equipment and has provided additional training and educational activities outside of Iraq. The Commission wishes to underscore the immense potential that the efforts of NATO nations are unleashing in Iraq.

> ***Finding:*** *A noncommissioned officer corps is not part of Iraq's military tradition, but it will be invaluable to making the Army more combat-effective.*

The Iraqi Army needs a noncommissioned officer corps in order to become a truly cohesive fighting force capable of the type of small unit operations essential to success in combating an insurgency. However, the American concept of NCOs seems to present difficulties for many Iraqi officers, particularly when newly minted NCOs are seen to perform at levels approaching NATO standards. In addition, during the Saddam era, Iraqi officers operated in an environment that emphasized centralized power over delegation to subordinates. Coalition advisors should support and encourage NCO development and should foster in Iraqi officers an appreciation for their role. However, it may take time for the Iraqis to embrace this concept.

It appears the American concept of a noncommissioned officer is fundamentally threatening to many current Iraqi officers, particularly when newly minted noncommissioned officers are seen to perform at levels approaching NATO standards. As the Iraqi Army and Coalition forces continue to develop the noncommissioned officer corps, care should be taken at the same time to develop Iraqi officers' appreciation for their role.

> ***Recommendation:*** *Developing leadership in the Iraqi Army will require continued support from Coalition advisors and units. Ongoing employment of a "train the trainers" approach, and continued emphasis on the development of a functioning noncommissioned officer corps, is essential, though developing leaders will take time to achieve.*

Developing Iraqi Army leadership will be the work of a generation and will require long-term Coalition or NATO involvement—at least in an advisory capacity. Although it will take more than 12 to 18 months to develop a functioning noncommissioned officer corps, the strong and effective Iraqi Special Operations Forces noncommissioned officer corps is an encouraging example. The NATO experience in former Eastern bloc countries further demonstrates that long-term engagement can build a world-class noncommissioned officer corps in places it never existed before.

Personnel

> ***Finding:*** *The Iraqi Army is currently structured for counterinsurgency operations with a goal of manning 13 divisions by the end of 2008. The current divisions are experiencing absenteeism, both authorized and unauthorized. MOD has established a standard of 85 percent "present-for-duty" at all times. To achieve this, units will be manned at 120 percent of authorized strength, and the abundance of volunteers for service in the new Iraqi Army should make*

the attainment of this goal possible. This higher manning requirement will place additional strain on equipping and combat training programs.

In its most recent report to Congress, the Department of Defense estimated the Iraqi Army's strength to be around 135,000.[82] Outside analysts put the figure at closer to 100,000.[83] The Government of Iraq would like an end strength of 190,000, and it plans to add 24 battalions in 2007 for an increase of approximately 45,000 soldiers.[84] The force structure is planned to be 13 divisions.

At any given time, Iraqi units are at 60–75 percent of their manning strength, and annual attrition is 15–18 percent in the Iraqi Army.[85] Iraqi soldiers return home to bring their pay to their families and check on their safety, contributing to a lack of accountability. In addition, assassinations of Iraqi soldiers, noncommissioned officers, and officers further compound manning problems.

Not only does the Iraqi Army suffer from manning shortages, but many of the soldiers that do report for duty are at different standards of training, owing to the many different training programs in place since 2003. Standardization of the forces and of training is only a recent development. As a result, Iraqi Army divisions are uneven in ability.

The Commission visited a camp of fresh recruits going through five weeks of basic training. Beginning in spring 2007, the earlier thirteen-week basic training course was compressed into five weeks, largely to accelerate force generation efforts. The average Iraqi *jundi* (private or soldier) has a fourth-grade education. He has been familiar with "guns" his whole life but has probably not fought in the military. The minimum age for enlistment in this volunteer force is 18. In basic training, soldiers are taught everything from hand washing before meals to proficiency with an M-16 or AK-47 rifle. Discipline is maintained by corporal punishment.

Further complicating basic training efforts is the need to identify those recruits with links to militias, who must either be converted or dismissed from the Iraqi Security Forces. Despite the risks associated with service in the ISF, military pay is high enough to make enlistment attractive, and recruiters are often simply overwhelmed by the sheer numbers in need of vetting.[86] Following basic training, Iraqi soldiers' collective skills and basic unit skills are frequently developed under combat conditions.

Finding: *The implementation of an Iraqi code of military discipline, professional development programs, and benefits for members of the armed forces is key to improving readiness. The Commission finds that inadequate implementation of these initiatives adversely affects personnel retention and leadership development. Developing future leaders must be an important objective of personnel programs.*

Currently, mechanisms to prevent Iraqi soldiers from being absent without leave are not enforced. The Commission was repeatedly informed that no penalty is applied for desertion or being absent without leave in the Iraqi Army. Present-for-duty numbers are verified once a month by the Coalition Military Transition Team.[87] Despite Coalition confidence in these numbers, the military is still plagued by high rates of absenteeism, particularly in Iraqi Army units deployed for combat operations outside their usual area of operation. Such units have leave rates as high as 50 percent.[88]

Although the Iraqi Army is aware of the need to establish a personnel and professional development system that could create positive incentives for soldiers to remain in the military, problems remain. For example, there are currently few rewards for obedience and performance: promotions are slow, time-in-grade pay does not exist, and combat pay for deployments is just coming into being. Battlefield promotions do not occur. The number of captains in the Iraqi Army is very large, reflecting a preliminary rank inflation—captain is the de facto entry grade for officers on the promotion track. Lieutenants are often left without opportunity for promotion and perform the function of noncommissioned officers.

The Commission was struck by one outstanding young Iraqi captain who had been fighting in the Army for the past three years. His American counterparts at a forward operating base were a colonel, a lieutenant colonel, and a major. The Iraqi remained a captain and was frustrated by the slow promotion process. In another case, the Commission discovered that the Sergeant Major of the Iraqi Ground Forces Command is still salaried as a private, despite decades of service to his country and his important position.

Finally, there is no evidence in Iraq that any social compact has been established with the military. Formal support for wounded veterans and for the families of soldiers killed in action is almost nonexistent. As stated above, in Iraq's economy, the military's high pay is very attractive and likely remains the primary motivator for service in the all-volunteer force. Soldiers earn around $460 a month—an enormous sum compared with the $2 per month they were paid during the Saddam era as conscripts. But the risks are significant, and there is no system in place to mitigate them.[89] When injured, soldiers must endure Iraq's overcrowded, underequipped, and corrupt public hospitals.[90] They receive no compensation for long-term disabilities, though in a practice that skews unit strength numbers they are often kept on payrolls by commanders, who understand the importance of loyalty to their troops.

To develop a durable and combat-effective Army, the Government of Iraq and Ministry of Defense need to develop the legal framework to support the human capital of the military—the backbone of any armed force. Current deficiencies are presenting obstacles to the development, loyalty, and effectiveness of the military. The Coalition and Government of Iraq are investing far too much in the training and equipping of Iraqi soldiers to allow them to simply walk away. The application of the Iraqi Code of Military Discipline would address this problem, as would establishing a promotion process that recognized time-in-grade and rewards combat performance as incentives for personnel to remain in service.

To address these challenges, the MOD is considering and implementing a number of new policies and requirements. For example, it is weighing the benefits of waiving time-in-grade requirements to accelerate promotions for junior noncommissioned officers, lieutenants, and captains. The MOD is also working to overcome problems in manpower accountability.

Equipment

> ***Finding:*** *The Iraqi Army is adequately equipped for counterinsurgency. However, equipping the Army with more armor, artillery, and mobility is tactically advantageous and communicates a powerful message to the Iraqi people and to the enemy about the growing strength and capability of the Iraqi Army.*

Each Iraqi Army soldier is equipped with the standard Iraqi Army uniform, Kevlar helmet, interceptor bulletproof vest, boots, and an M-16 rifle or M-4 rifle for officers. Until May 2007, Iraqi soldiers were issued AK-47 rifles; a program now under way to replace those weapons with M-16 or M-4 rifles, tracked by serial number and biometric data recorded when they are issued, will have beneficial effects when completed.

The Iraqi Army's inventory of assets is limited in comparison to its neighbors'. In Iraq's existing forces are 77 T-72s, 250 Soviet-built BMP-Is, 6 Brazilian EE-9 Cascavels, 61 MT-LB Russian-built tracked vehicles, 69 BTR-80 Russian-built six-wheel vehicles, 353 Polish DZIK four-wheel-drive vehicles, 291 Textron T-6 Badgers, 2,647 AM General Humvees, 600 Land Rover armored jeeps, and 60 small armored vehicles. Shortages of equipment include modern armor, heavy firepower, tactical mobility, air support, and proper medical capabilities. Orders have been placed for delivery by the end of 2007 of 110 BMPs and 29 Cascavels, 29 BTR-80s, 247 DZIKs, 149 Badgers, and 952 Humvees.

Iraqi units are regularly subjected to direct and indirect fire throughout the country. In almost all cases, Coalition forces must supply the counterfire, close air and artillery support, and intelligence, surveillance, and reconnaissance needed to target the enemy. The Iraqi Army is also significantly supported by Coalition airlift to quickly transport and surge forces to the fight.

As the Commission has stated, the Iraqi Army should continue to focus on its mission of internal defense while beginning to transform itself into a force capable of dealing with the longer-term challenge of external threats. Tactically advantageous to both missions are armor, artillery, and mobility (especially rotary airlift and aircraft capable of providing close air support). Acquiring and implementing these platforms, however, should not distract from the current counterinsurgency mission.

As a first step, existing platforms such as the T-72 tanks donated by NATO to the 9th Mechanized Division should be strategically arrayed around the country to leverage their psychological effect. Entering these platforms into the fight would send a powerful message to the Iraqi people and to the enemies of the Iraqi people, including neighboring states supporting terrorism and insurgents. Outward, visible indications of strength in the form of heavy armor—displayed in the capital and elsewhere—would demonstrate that the Iraqi Army has been reborn with the strength necessary to protect the nation and its people.

Figure 15: Iraqi Army Equipment by Unit [Omitted]

Logistics

> ***Finding:*** *Logistics remains the Achilles' heel of the Iraqi ground forces. Although progress is being made, achieving an adequate forcewide logistics capability is at least 24 months away.*

Although the Multi-National Security Transition Command–Iraq's 2007 goal is to "transition equipment, sustainment and infrastructure expenditures to Iraqi responsibility," completing this transition poses a great challenge to the independent operation of the Iraqi Army. Iraqi commanders and officials are assigning priority to getting soldiers into the fight; sustaining combat power remains a secondary goal.

As many U.S. commanders and trainers noted, the Coalition's desire to keep Iraqi forces from failing sometimes has the effect of rewarding bad behavior. For example, although Iraqis ostensibly took over responsibility for fuel distribution months ago through the Ministry of Oil, the Coalition often has to intervene to ensure that Iraqis have enough diesel and benzene to operate generators and continue their daily operations. This is only one symptom of "phantom" Coalition logistics support—provision of off-the-books Coalition logistics—to prevent Iraqis from failing. Phantom logistics mask the true depths of the problems not only in fuel distribution but also in maintenance and repair, ammunition, and other basic support.

Even when Iraqi Army units have the necessary equipment, faulty maintenance of that equipment can be a critical weakness. U.S. commanders and soldiers in the field repeatedly informed the Commission that the Iraqis in general fail to maintain equipment. Iraqis are unfamiliar with many of the new systems and platforms they have purchased in the past few years.[91]

When a vehicle becomes non-operational, there are no backup or reserve vehicles to replace it. Preventive maintenance is an alien concept to Iraqis, an attitude that exacerbates the lack of spare or backup vehicles. Where maintenance teams do exist and Iraqi commanders do make upkeep of equipment a priority, they face the further hurdle of acquiring spare parts from Taji National Depot, which appears unable to keep up with requirements.

As discussed in the previous chapter on the Ministry of Defense, the Commission found that the national logistics system cannot yet address the needs of Iraqi units fighting the war. The Taji National Depot is full of new vehicles, hundreds of thousands of rounds of ammunition, boots, uniforms, and many other end items that should be made available quickly to Iraqi soldiers fighting the war. According to the Department of Defense, 100 percent of individual authorized items were distributed to the Iraqi Army by the end of 2006, though there were some admitted problems of "cross-leveling between and within units that . . . [led] to shortages in some subordinate units."[92] Despite reported distribution of all individual equipment, the Commission heard repeatedly of deployed Iraqi units encountering fundamental difficulties when trying to obtain needed war materials to remain combat-ready.

> ***Finding:*** *The current shortfall in logistics is emblematic of the urgent need to solve a major issue in terms that the Iraqi government and military can adopt. U.S. strategies and solutions rely heavily on outsourcing of logistics, an approach that has met resistance from the Iraqi leaders. In many cases, the "Iraqi way," though not always optimal, is sufficient. The solutions for the Iraqi armed forces must be developed with the goal of achieving an Iraqi standard that allows for Iraqi culture, traditions, and abilities.*

Logistics are a problem in large part because the MOD bureaucracy can be complex and cumbersome, and has very little expertise in logistics. Its weaknesses have an adverse trickle-down effect to the Iraqi armed forces. At lower levels of the logistics chain, it is also clear that the Iraqi Army's Headquarters and Service Companies are undermanned and not independently capable.

The absence of support from the MOD bureaucracy frequently leaves commanders to rely on their creativity, on their thrift, and on whatever resources are available. An Iraqi commander told the Commission of using confiscated weapons caches to make repairs and provide additional ammunition for ongoing operations. To acquire the ammunition through the existing Iraqi logistics system, this commander would have had to send an officer in person to the MOD in Baghdad with a requisition request. Upon receipt of this personally delivered request, the MOD might then take months to fill and distribute the requested ammunition—all this despite the ready availability of ammunition in the MOD system.

The Iraqi Army is not enthusiastic about a contractor-based logistics and maintenance system, which might be at least part of the solution to existing capability shortfalls. The Iraqi Army staff is unimpressed with the contracts they have seen executed, and they seek to foster independence in their operations across the board. While this is a laudable goal, it is not producing results. Every command post and headquarters the Commission visited had vehicles and equipment that were inoperable—and more often than not, the Commission found that Iraqis were waiting for the Coalition to take care of the problem for them. Coalition forces recognize this dependency but find it difficult to lessen while simultaneously maintaining the pace of current operations.

As critical as the development of a functioning logistics capability is for the Iraqi military, Coalition experts may be imposing on them a more complex and elaborate logistics system than is necessary. The logistics force structure plan developed by the Coalition for the Iraq Army appears to reflect the Coalition's preferences rather than the Iraqis' needs. Over time it is likely that the current plan will be modified and an "Iraqi solution" will emerge. The Iraqi solution is one that gets the job done to an adequate level, even if not with optimal efficiency and speed. Those innovations will come in time.

> ***Recommendation:*** *To operate independently, the Iraqi Army must develop a functioning logistics and maintenance system. The Coalition should continue working with the MOD to develop a system that meets Iraqi needs.*

Although the lack of an adequate logistics and maintenance system is a critical shortfall, it is clear that solutions that are imposed on an unwilling organization will not work. A sustainable solution will require patient and consistent efforts to work with MOD officials and Iraqi Army commanders to develop systems that are consistent with the realities of Iraqi culture and bureaucratic incentives. The Coalition should work with the MOD and Iraqi Army to simplify processes wherever possible and adjust them to an Iraqi standard, which may be more effective in the near term if not necessarily as efficient as we would like.

> ***Conclusion:*** The Iraqi Army and Special Forces possess an adequate supply of willing and able manpower and a steadily improving basic training capability. The Army has a baseline supply of equipment for counterinsurgency, but much of this equipment is unavailable for operations owing to maintenance and supply chain management problems. They are making efforts to reduce sectarian influence within their ranks and are achieving some progress. Their operational effectiveness, particularly that of the Special Forces, is increasing, yet they will continue to rely on Coalition forces for key enablers such as combat support (aviation support, intelligence, and communications), combat service support (logistics, supply chain management, and maintenance), and training. Despite progress, they will not be ready to independently fulfill their security role within the next 12 to 18 months. Nevertheless, the Commission believes that substantial progress can be achieved to that end.

Chapter 5: The Iraqi Air Force

In 2004, the Iraqi Air Force had 35 people and possessed no aircraft. This meager beginning and late start as compared to the new Iraqi Army help put in context the progress the Air Force has made since then. Its personnel now number approximately 1,100 airmen equipped with 45 aircraft that are capable of 130 to 150 sorties a week.[93] They are engaged in supporting the domestic counterinsurgency fight, and as the Iraqi Air Force's capacity improves, so too will its ability to be a force multiplier for Iraqi ground forces. However, the delayed start-up of the new Iraqi Air Force resulted in a considerable lag behind the Iraqi Army's current level of maturity. Moreover, the creation of effective operational, maintenance, and support systems for an air force, with its advanced technical requirements, demands a longer period of development. The net effect of this asymmetry is that Coalition support will likely be required for a longer period for the Iraqi Air Force than for the Army. Despite steady progress and its strong future potential, today's Iraqi Air Force is heavily reliant on Coalition forces for support and training; and though its capabilities are improving, it remains far from operational independence.

Overview of the Iraqi Air Force

The Iraqi Air Force was established in the early 1930s and originally consisted of five pilots and a supporting crew of less than three dozen. From 1931 until the arrival of Coalition forces in 2003, the Air Force took part in a number of armed conflicts, including the May 1941 war against British occupation and the 1948 and June 1967 wars against Israel. The Air Force contributed significantly at the end of the protracted Iran-Iraq War of the 1980s by quashing Iran's final offensive; during that war, it grew to roughly 950 aircraft. By the time of the first Gulf War, the Iraqi Air Force was the largest in the Middle East, though it suffered from uneven quality in both aircraft and aircrew.[94]

In general, Saddam Hussein preferred not to use his air force for combat, saving it instead as a reserve force to defend Baghdad. It proved most effective against fixed economic targets such as oil facilities, and Hussein structured his air defenses along the Soviet model.[95] During the Gulf War, U.S.-led coalition forces devastated the Iraqi Air Force, greatly degrading its overall capacity. Most of the aircraft that did survive the war are now in Iran, where they were moved before the Gulf War to save them from being destroyed. Although the Commander of the Iraqi Air Force has expressed a desire to retrieve some of those aircraft, this retrieval has not yet occurred.[96]

Lieutenant General Kamal al-Barzanji, who leads the new Iraqi Air Force, reports to the Iraqi Joint Headquarters.[97] The main objectives of the new

Iraqi Air Force are to organize, train, and equip air operations; to conduct day/night/all-weather counterinsurgency operations; and to provide homeland capabilities to the Government of Iraq.[98] The Iraqi Air Force is focused mainly on counterinsurgency missions, particularly aerial observation and surveillance and air transportation, and units perform daily operational missions that collect intelligence for Iraqi and Coalition forces.

The Iraqi Air Force operates with a small mix of platforms: intelligence, surveillance, and reconnaissance platforms; fixed wing transport; and rotary wing capabilities. The intelligence, surveillance, and reconnaissance platforms are now eight SAMA CH-2000s, two Sea Bird Seekers, and three Cessna Caravans used by two squadrons.[99] By December 2007, this capability will include one more advanced platform, the King Air 350ER. In addition, a training squadron will receive its first intelligence, surveillance, and reconnaissance platforms of four Cessna 172s and two Cessna 208Bs. The fixed wing transport capability is currently supported by three C-130 transport planes, and the Ministry of Defense has requested three more to bring the squadron size to six.[100] The three rotary wing platforms, used mostly for battlefield mobility and casualty evacuation by three Iraqi Air Force squadrons, are 10 Bell Huey II helicopters, 14 Mi-17 battlefield mobility helicopters, and 5 Jet Ranger training helicopters. By December 2007, the number of Huey IIs should reach 16 and the number of Mi-17s should be 28. The 5 Jet Rangers will provide the initial capability to another training squadron, which will also receive its own 8 Huey IIs.[101]

In short, if procurement proceeds as intended, the Iraqi Air Force platforms will increase in number from the current 45 to 80 by December 2007. By 2010, the Iraqi Air Force also has plans to bring on line a counterterrorism capability with both greater numbers of existing platforms and more sophisticated platforms. These would include 18 King Air 350s, 6 Caravans, and 8 CH2000s for the intelligence, surveillance, and reconnaissance component; 6 C-130s and 4 King Air 350s for greater fixed wing airlift capacity; 41 Mi-17s and 40 Huey IIs for increased rotary wing capability; and 32 T6/Super Tucano/L-39 class aircraft for a new light attack capability.[102]

The Iraqi Air Force currently operates out of four air bases throughout Iraq. New Al Muthana Air Base handles the Iraqi Air Force's fixed wing transport functions. Because the 23 Squadron there features all-Iraqi flight crews with Iraqi Air Force maintenance technicians performing all basic maintenance, U.S. Air Force Military Training Team personnel have been able to reduce their presence. The Taji Air Base houses an interim Air Force Academy as well as most of the Iraqi Air Force's rotary wing platforms. The Basra and Kirkuk Air Bases are focused on intelligence, surveillance, and reconnaissance capabilities in support of the counterinsurgency mission.[103] To that end, units from these air bases run daily missions throughout Iraq to provide actionable intelligence back to Coalition and Iraqi ground forces.

The current capacity of the Iraqi Air Force includes a growing number of personnel. The force totals more than 1,100 at present, and aggressive recruitment efforts are seeking to raise the number of airmen above 3,000 by the end of 2007.[104] Most early manning has derived from the pre-2003 Iraqi Air Force, consisting mainly of older men who have done little flying since 1991. The current pilots are considered sufficient for the low-end counterinsurgency fight until younger, more highly trained pilots can be fielded. All current leadership is also drawn from the pre-2003 Air Force, and in general their survival skills exceed their capacity for leadership. Over time, they will need to be replaced so that the development of true quality can be fostered in the new service.

Training the growing numbers of Iraqi Air Force personnel is an ongoing challenge. The training, generally conducted in conjunction with Iraqi Training and Doctrine Command, has been run largely by Coalition Air Force Transition Teams. Basic Iraqi Air Force training consists of pilot sustainment and conversion training and maintenance training. C-130 training has taken place in United States, while language training and flight training have been conducted in Iraq, currently at Al Muthana Air Base. Some additional crews previously received training in Jordan on UH-lHs and Seekers.[105] Advisory Support Teams provide U.S.-based training for reconnaissance missions, including courses for pilots, navigators, maintenance officers, flight engineers, and loadmasters, and courses in Iraq for maintenance and aircrew personnel.[106] The Iraqi Air Force also has two training squadrons located at Kirkuk Air Base, where a flight school is scheduled to open in the fall of 2007.[107]

Challenges Facing the Air Force

During the course of this assessment, the Commission met with virtually all of the Iraqi Air Force general officers (including the Commander and Deputy Commander), numerous field and company grade officers, officer trainees, warrant officers, and enlisted personnel. The Commission visited all the Iraqi Air Force installations save one, plus numerous training and operational facilities. One member of the Commission flew four separate missions with Iraqi Air Force crews and aircraft. On the basis of these numerous meetings and site visits, the Commission developed a number of key findings that are outlined in the sections to follow.

Woven throughout these findings, the Commission notes three particular challenges:

- Identifying, recruiting, and training personnel who are technically capable and motivated to pursue a demanding military profession.

- Molding a leadership and management approach in the emerging officer corps that is consistent with Iraqi culture yet rejects the risk aversion and obsequiousness of the Saddam era.
- Inculcating the need for and developing the skills to synchronize air capabilities with joint (special operations and army) missions.

Recruiting and Training

> ***Finding:*** *The long-term capability of the Iraqi Air Force will depend on its success in recruiting quality personnel, and will require greater emphasis on basic and technical training.*

The Commission found that although Air Force recruitment is proceeding at a numerically satisfactory rate, the quality of the available recruiting pool leaves much to be desired. Much of Iraq's middle class, from which technically inclined recruits are normally drawn, has left the country. For those Iraqis remaining in the country, military service, regardless of its personal appeal, carries with it significant risk of insurgent retaliation. The future of an effective Iraqi Air Force depends on recruiting quality candidates who can absorb high standards of training and also adapt to a new culture of responsibility and choice unknown during the Saddam era. Improved screening methods and recruiting tools that reach deeper into the available recruiting pool are required.

Filling the requirement for pilots is a twofold problem: near-term requirements can be filled only by Saddam-era pilots, most of whom had questionable original training and have not flown seriously since 1991. These men generally require significant retraining even at elementary levels, and often seem more interested in enjoying the status of being pilots than in undertaking the hard work of improving their skills. To their credit, they do seem willing, even eager, to engage in the counterinsurgency fight.

The Iraqi Air Force has developed an expansive training plan that, as mentioned, it is now being implemented. Basic enlisted and officer training began in spring 2007, and technical training is scheduled to grow incrementally to adequate capacity by the summer of 2008, when the output of undergraduate pilots should be 30 per year. According to Iraqi Air Force officials, going forward the training plan will have three main facets. First, they will run Air Force Officer training at the Iraqi Military Academy in Rustamiyah. Second, they will use an interim Air Force Academy in Taji for technical training in areas such as maintenance, intelligence, and fuels, as well as for basic enlisted and warrant officer training. Third, the air base in Kirkuk will host air wing training, with a focus on rotary wing training on Jet Rangers and Huey IIs, and fixed wing training on Cessna 172 and Cessna Caravan platforms.[108] At present, absenteeism, particularly among enlisted and warrant officers, is very high (35–40 percent), effectively lengthening the training time for new technicians.

The Iraqi Air Force has shown more enthusiasm for updating its platforms than for training qualified technicians and airmen and building the necessary infrastructure to support them. The latter are more difficult tasks, but they are critical to any successful air force.

Recommendation: *Together with its Coalition partners, the Iraqi Air Force must increase the quality of its recruits and the capacity of current and planned training programs, while also increasing the manpower authorizations to compensate for chronic absenteeism. Emphasis on the value of training must be relentless.*

Maintenance

Finding: *Although aircraft procurement has been adequate to date, maintenance and sustainment systems lag well behind the procurement program and thus impede overall Iraqi Air Force capability.*

At present, the Iraqi Air Force does not have an air force-wide maintenance or supply system, in part because of the low training output mentioned above, and in part because of its resourcing priorities. In general, the enthusiasm to buy more and better platforms far exceeds the desire to purchase spare parts or perform maintenance on existing platforms and equipment. Moreover, using contractor support as a stepping-stone to developing an organic maintenance capability is often viewed with suspicion by the Iraqi Air Force leadership, who see it as a ruse to get Iraqis to give their money to U.S. firms. In the absence of a sufficient capability within the Iraqi Air Force, much of the responsibility for maintenance currently rests with Coalition advisors.

The inherently technical nature of air force equipment makes the lack of a functioning maintenance and supply system a significant problem, in terms both of establishing operational independence for the Iraqi Air Force and of supporting its growth over time.

Recommendation: *Multi-National Security Transition Command–Iraq must redouble its efforts to inculcate the value of quality maintenance and support into the culture of the MOD in general, and of the Iraqi Air Force in particular.*

Training in proper maintenance, including preventive maintenance and the timely purchase of appropriate levels of spare parts, must become the very foundation on which a capable new Iraqi Air Force is built. Until the Iraqi Air Force can take responsibility for its own maintenance, it will continue to require significant Coalition assistance. The key, then, is determining at what point the Iraqi Air Force is ready to assume this critical responsibility. It is important to wait long enough to ensure that the capability to perform the tasks adequately is present, but not so long that the motivation to take responsibility never develops. Once the transition of responsibility for maintenance occurs and a sufficient emphasis on maintenance is embedded in the culture of the Iraqi Air Force, greater numbers of more sophisticated aircraft can be absorbed and managed effectively.

However, the Commission believes that even with success in this area, the Iraqi Air Force will likely require Coalition assistance for the next two to three years.

Overall Air Force Direction and Progress

> ***Finding:*** *Although the Iraqi Air Force has had a very late start compared to the Iraqi Army, the present design of the Iraqi Air Force is appropriate for its current mission and it is making significant progress.*

The current design of the new Iraqi Air Focus is focused on supporting the domestic counterinsurgency operations while using mainly low-tech aircraft. This design appears appropriate for its present stage of development, given its relatively limited lift capacity; intelligence, surveillance, and reconnaissance capability; and rotary wing insert and retraction capabilities. The Iraqi Air Force's overall capacity is still very small compared with the size of the ground forces that it is designed to support, and it has almost no lethal capability. The procurement process has begun to acquire low-tech, fixed wing dose air support aircraft. When that capability is added to those above, a balanced air force will emerge capable of fully supporting the military's counterinsurgency mission. At that point, Coalition air forces may begin a prudent drawdown.

Current deficiencies in the Iraqi Air Force include the lack of fixed wing close air coverage to fully support the counterinsurgency capability of ground forces, a command and control program that is still largely in its infancy, and the lack of a demonstrable ability to operate jointly with other services. The Iraqi Air Force must develop operating techniques compatible with those of the ground forces that it is intended to support. Traditional independence and cultural habits among its personnel of thinking primarily of their own family or tribe may contribute to the challenge of fostering its seamless integration into joint operations. The Commission discerned some faint progress in this area, but a considerable distance remains to be traveled.

> ***Recommendation:*** *Given its good progress to date, the new Iraqi Air Force should stay its present course of developing a counterinsurgency air force with a view toward establishing quality operations and maintenance capability for integration into the joint fight. As these skills are refined, reliance on Coalition support can diminish.*

> ***Conclusion:*** The Iraqi Air Force's relatively late establishment hampers its ability to provide much-needed air support to ground operations. It is well designed as the air component to the existing counterinsurgency effort, but not for the future needs of a fully capable air force. Though limited by the availability of properly skilled personnel, and by an inclination to value force size and acquisition over operational effectiveness, it is nonetheless progressing at a promising rate during this formative period.

Chapter 6: The Iraqi Navy

The Iraqi Navy operates in an area of responsibility with significant strategic value, bordered by countries with which Iraq has difficult political relationships. The Navy is responsible for supporting ongoing counterinsurgency operations and for the security of the key Iraqi infrastructure that enables the shipping of nearly all Iraq's oil, which constitutes the majority of national revenue. In just a few years, the Iraqi Navy has made significant progress, has embarked on an ambitious training and acquisition program, and has implemented a sophisticated planning process. It continues to develop solid leadership as it works with its Coalition partners toward independent operation in its area of responsibility. This progress notwithstanding, the Iraqi Navy remains dependent on Coalition assistance and faces significant challenges in a number of areas.

Overview of the Iraqi Navy

Founded in 1937 with just four ships, the Iraqi Navy has generally remained a small part of Iraq's overall military capacity. The Iraqi Navy played almost no part in the Iran-Iraq War, but it did pose a threat to U.S. forces during the Gulf War, primarily through its large arsenal of naval mines. By the conclusion of Operations Desert Shield and Storm, more than 100 Iraqi naval vessels had been destroyed and the Navy was largely devastated. By 2002 the Iraqi Navy was in a meager state of readiness, with remaining units barely operational and crews largely untrained.[109]

The Coalition began working with Iraqis to rebuild the Navy in 2004. Challenges at that early stage included lack of personnel and appropriate vessels, the need to establish working relationships between the Iraqi Navy and Joint Headquarters, a legacy of no central planning or budgetary continuity, and poor relations with the Coast Guard.[110] In January 2004 the Coalition established the Iraqi Coastal Defense Force, whose volunteers attended eight weeks of basic training alongside Army trainees. They then pursued special maritime training in Umm Qasr, concentrating on more advanced seamanship, sea rescue, maritime law, first aid, and visit, board, search, and seizure (VBSS) training.[111] The Iraqi Coastal Defense Force was later renamed the Iraqi Navy, and the new Iraqi Navy training pipeline began in January 2005.[112]

The Iraqi Navy area of responsibility is very small but strategically important, as it includes the al Basra and Khor al Amaya oil terminals and Iraq's only deep water port (Umm Qasr), all of which are vital to Iraq's economy. Thus despite the Iraqi Navy's small size, its mission is significant—protection of these crucial assets, Iraq's territorial seas, and its economic exclusion zone; protection of the shoreline and inland waterways from insurgent and criminal infiltration; force protection; surface surveillance; point defense of offshore oil loading facilities; and visit, board, search, and seizure interdiction operations.[113] However, the Navy's development has lagged behind that of the other services, perhaps two to three years behind that of the Iraqi Army.

The new Iraqi Navy is commanded by Rear Admiral Muhammad Jawad Kadhim at the Ministry of Defense headquarters in Baghdad and by an operational commander, Commander Ahmed Maarij, in Umm Qasr; its leadership reports to the Iraqi Joint Headquarters. Today the Iraqi Navy consists of almost 1,300 personnel, with plans to expand to 2,500.[114] It is organized into an operational headquarters, a patrol squadron, an assault squadron, and four marine battalions. As the Iraqi Navy's area of responsibility is in the country's south, the Navy's personnel are predominantly Shi'a; but most other ethnic and religious groups, including Kurds, Christians, and Sunnis, are represented. Furthermore, one of the Iraqi Navy's major successes has been in remaining nonsectarian; it has put significant emphasis on instilling a sense of overarching loyalty to the Navy and the central government—not to tribal and religious affiliations.[115]

The current naval fleet is not adequate to execute the Navy's mission. It consists of Predator class patrol boats, Italian river boats, Al Faw patrol boats, and fast assault boats. Some of these assets are of such poor quality that they can at best be cannibalized for spare parts, or perhaps used for basic ship handling and navigation training. In addition, the fleet as a whole is plagued by poor maintenance practices.[116] Accordingly, a large part of current planning is an extensive and ambitious acquisition program to build the fleet to contain 15 patrol boats, 4 patrol ships, 2 offshore vessels, and up to 50 fast assault boats. These vessels will provide security for the oil terminals; patrol the Northern Arabian Gulf, the Iraqi territorial waters and economic exclusion zone; and provide command and control and forward support.[117] The contracts for the offshore support vessels, patrol ships, and three of the patrol boats are completed—though they have been delayed over negotiations regarding exchange rates and taxes—and the purchases were made with Iraqi money.[118]

At present the Iraqi Navy is using a road map formulated in conjunction with Coalition forces. The Maritime Services Transition Team encompasses many different Coalition components, including U.S. Naval Forces Central Command, Multi-National Forces-Iraq, Multi-National Security Transition Command–Iraq, the Joint Headquarters Transition Team, Combined Task Force 158 and Combined Task Group 158.1,[119] the Coalition Military Assistance Training Team, and the Naval Transition Team. The Maritime Services Transition Team works closely with the Iraqi MOD, Joint Headquarters, the Iraqi Navy, and operational elements at Umm Qasr as it provides advice and training. It should be noted that a primary player in this process is the Royal Navy, which provides the bulk of personnel and the senior liaison officers, including the principal advisor to Rear Admiral Jawad. The commander of the Naval Transition Team in Umm Qasr, who also serves as the principal advisor to Commander Ahmed, the Iraqi operational commander, is a member of the Royal Navy as well.

Although this structure is complex, in general it functions as follows: Multi-National Force–Iraq and the Multi-National Security Transition Command–Iraq advise the MOD and Iraqi Joint Headquarters. The representative of the naval component of the Joint Headquarters Transition Team in turn advises the head of the Iraqi Navy. The commander of the Naval Transition Team at Umm Qasr provides force training and mentoring to the Iraqi operational commander at Umm Qasr, who also receives training feedback from the Combined Task Group 158.1. At the same time, the operational commander is the Iraqi force provider to the Combined Task Group 158.1.[120] Combined Task Group 158.1 and Combined Task Force 158 also provide operational assistance and on-scene training to the Iraqi Navy in protecting the oil terminals and in conducting visit, board, search, and seizure operations in the Northern Arabian Gulf.

Challenges Facing the Iraqi Navy

As a part of its assessment, the Commission interviewed five senior Coalition officials from the Maritime Services Transition Team structure, the Naval Transition Team, Combined Task Force 158, and the Combined Task Group 158.1, as well as two senior officials from the Iraqi Navy.[121] The Commission also traveled to the Umm Qasr Naval Base and, via Iraqi patrol boat, to the al Basra and Khor al Amaya oil terminals in the Iraqi Navy's area of responsibility. These meetings and site visits made clear that although the new Iraqi Navy is making progress, it faces challenges raised by its low profile within the MOD, the complexity of its mission, the highly restricted maritime battle space in its area of responsibility, poor logistics and maintenance, and poor relations with the Coast Guard.

Ministry of Defense

> ***Finding:*** *The low profile of the Iraqi Navy within the MOD, as well as the ministry's inadequate budget allocation and execution, significantly impede Iraqi naval operations and development.*

The Iraqi Navy has never enjoyed a high profile within the Ministry of Defense, although this situation is changing somewhat with increased recognition of the Navy's strategic importance, not only in the role it plays in Iraq's economic well-being but also in maintaining the country's territorial integrity by protecting Iraq's economic exclusion zone. Iraqi naval officers told the Commission that they confront two main types of challenges: external threats to the nation and a weak internal relationship with the

Ministry of Defense. The Iraqi Navy frequently has problems working with the MOD on issues related to budget execution, contracting, and planning.[122] For example, because of the long lead time required to procure naval assets, the head of the Iraqi Navy recommended budgeting on a five-year cycle, but the MOD has not embraced this idea of planning further into the out years.

Like many other components of the Iraqi Security Forces, the Iraqi Navy fails to spend much of what has been appropriated for it (and what it greatly needs) because the MOD refuses to delegate budget execution authority and insists on complex bureaucratic procedures requiring multiple signatures. Senior Iraqi Navy officers also told the Commission that the Iraqi Navy does not receive sufficient funding to conduct daily operations. At present, the Iraqi Navy operational commander in Umm Qasr has a monthly operations and management budget of only $2,000. Although this figure does not include wages and fuel costs, it is insufficient to cover priorities such as routine maintenance and the purchase of spare parts, let alone such basics as buying office supplies and running the sick bay.[123] Maintenance remains drastically underfunded, largely because of budget execution problems.[124] This lack of delegation authority extends even to basic equipment and training. For example, MOD M-7 (the Training Directorate), rather than Navy operational commanders, determines how much training ammunition to allocate. Currently MOD M-7 allocates only 10 training rounds per year, per person—an amount considered wholly inadequate by both Iraqi Navy operational commanders and Naval Transition Team advisors.[125]

Some senior Iraqi Navy leaders believe that these challenges are due in part to what they see as the MOD's inability to fully understand or value the Navy's role. The MOD, which is focused more on ground forces given the current security environment, may not understand the nature of naval operations, the maintenance they involve, or their need for spare parts. Iraqi naval leaders feel that the MOD will always prioritize other components of the ISF over the Navy when facing budgetary pressures. Absent a reasonable operations and management budget, as well as sufficient access to spare parts, ammunition, and other necessities, no amount of Coalition training or support will enable the Iraqi Navy to operate independently.

> ***Recommendation:*** *Coalition advisors must assist the Iraqi Navy leadership in advocating budget priorities within the MOD. The strategic importance of the Iraqi Navy must be better articulated to the Government of Iraq, in terms both of maintaining Iraq's territorial integrity and of providing the security needed to ensure the efficient flow of exports. Larger issues of poor ministerial capacity and poor budget execution must also be addressed with Coalition support, as detailed more extensively in the discussion on MOD capacity (Chapter 4).*

Iraqi Navy Area of Responsibility

Finding: The Iraqi Navy area of responsibility is small, complicated, and of vital strategic importance. Relations among the nations bordering the area of responsibility and their respective navies and coast guards are fragile at best. Furthermore, the international maritime borders with Iran and Kuwait are contested and not clearly demarcated. These issues warrant greater attention from both the MOD and the Coalition.

The Iraqi Navy and its Coalition partners operate in an extraordinarily small and confined maritime battle space that is bordered by both Iranian and Kuwaiti waters and that includes two oil terminals. These terminals are among the most important infrastructure assets in Iraq. The al Basra oil terminal (ABOT) alone accounts for roughly 85 percent of the Government of Iraq's revenue, with more than $12,000 worth of oil running through it for export every second. This terminal can handle four tankers at a time and pump 1.2 million barrels per day, with the potential of pumping 2.2 million barrels daily. The Khor al Amaya oil terminal (KAAOT), which sits very close to the Iranian border, has only recently returned to limited operations after a serious explosion and fire; it is in a state of serious disrepair and has a much smaller capacity. It can handle about one tanker a week, pumps about 200,000 barrels per day, and brings in about 5 percent of Iraq's revenue.[126] Since it has no metering capability, many suspect that much of the oil shipped from this terminal ends up on the black market, with revenues going to local criminal elements. Together these two terminals not only are vital to Iraq's economy but are of strategic importance to the international oil market.[127]

Although the Iraqi Navy has completed some small-scale exercises with Coalition navies, including the Kuwaiti Navy, there are several challenges to overcome in Iraqi-Kuwaiti naval relations, mostly stemming from the lack of clear demarcation of international borders and territorial waters.[128] For example, the Kuwaiti government sometimes objects to dredging and maintenance work done on the channel near Umm Qasr that is critical to maintaining oceangoing access. It also stops fishing vessels, and when it judges them to be violating Kuwaiti waters it asks them to change their flags or detains the fishermen, often confiscating their boats and fishing gear. The Iraqi naval operational commander expressed a desire to meet with the Kuwaiti side to discuss and resolve political issues, but to date such a meeting has not occurred.[129] Combined Task Force 158 is also trying to encourage engagement with Kuwait on issues of mutual interest, including dredging, normalizing water space, infrastructure investments, and consequence management.[130] Consequence management in the face of a major oil spill or other such maritime disaster is a major concern, as neither the al Basra nor Khor al Amaya oil terminals have sufficient plans or assets in place for such an eventuality. For example, because of the currents, any oil spill would quickly reach the intakes of Kuwaiti and Saudi water desalinization plants.[131] It would also threaten their oil platforms and likely cause a significant boost in maritime insurance rates.

Even more is at stake in the relationship between the Iraqi Navy and its Iranian counterpart, yet apparently no strategic policy exists with respect to their maritime interactions. The Iraqi-Iranian demarcation lines remain contested, and there is a significant Iranian Revolutionary Guard Corps Navy presence in the area.[132] Further complicating the battle space is an old sunken Iraqi barge crane, now claimed and occupied by Iran, that rests in the disputed waters about one nautical mile from the Khor al Amaya oil terminal. The Iranian Revolutionary Guard Corps Navy uses it for surveillance. From the vantage point of the crane, it is possible to closely observe Iraqi Navy and Coalition naval activities as well as Combined Task Group 158.1 Headquarters, which is located on a barge attached to the Khor al Amaya oil terminal.[133] No action has been taken to remove the Iranians from their new perch.

> ***Recommendation:*** *Absent clearly defined territorial seas, the Iraqi Navy's battle space will be further complicated. Although the Commission realizes that resolving this issue is made more difficult by long-standing animosities between these nations and may not be feasible in the near term, it is important that the profile of this issue be raised within the Government of Iraq and the country team.*

Coast Guard

> ***Finding:*** *The Iraqi Navy does not have a collaborative relationship with the Iraqi Coast Guard, though the two services operate in close proximity and have complementary missions. This lack of coordination has the potential to create vulnerable seams in a critical strategic environment.*

The Iraqi Coast Guard patrols the river waterways along the Iraqi coast and focuses on smuggling interdiction.[134] The Coast Guard operates in a region heavily infiltrated with largely pro-Iranian Shi'a militia. For example, the port of Umm Qasr itself has fallen under strong Jaysh al-Mahdi influence. The Coast Guard has been trained to tactical proficiency by the Royal Navy, and is capable of taking on smugglers during encounters. Coast guardsmen tend to focus on commercial smuggling, particularly large-scale oil smuggling, though they have taken casualties.

Iraqi Naval officers appear wary of Coast Guard operations. Coalition advisors told the Commission that the coast guardsmen appeared rarely to capture smugglers they pursued or to confiscate seized weapons. It is not clear whether the Coast Guard would engage smugglers more effectively if its personnel were better armed or if its alleged poor performance indicates infiltration or cooperation with militias in the area.[135]

Because the Iraqi Navy and Coast Guard operate in such dose proximity, they need to work well together. Today the relationship between the Iraqi

Navy and the Iraqi Coast Guard is problematic. The Iraqi Navy and Coast Guard operate under separate chains of command, with the Coast Guard reporting to the Ministry of Interior and the Navy reporting to the Ministry of Defense. To date, there has been little formal contact between the two forces, though some Coalition advisors are pushing for more such interchanges. A further complication in the relationship is that many Coast Guard personnel are former Navy officers and petty officers who failed to pass through the vetting process as the new Iraqi Navy was being formed, and old resentments obviously could create tensions between the two forces.[136]

> ***Recommendation:*** *The Coalition should work with the MOD, Iraqi Navy, and Coast Guard to examine the feasibility and potential advantages of merging the Navy and Coast Guard into a single service with responsibility for coastal maritime security. If unity of command cannot be attained by combining both forces under the MOD, then better cooperation and coordination has to be developed to prevent a serious gap in security.*

Overview of Current Status

> ***Finding:*** *The new Iraqi Navy has made significant progress over a very short time period, particularly in planning, but it remains heavily reliant on the Coalition for training, logistics, and maintenance support.*

Planning is one area of real progress in the Iraqi Navy. Not only does the Navy have a multiyear transition road map, but Rear Admiral Jawad has started inviting officers to semiannual naval planning days at which the road map is explained and discussed.[137] There is also a semiannual Navy board that convenes in August and December; the December 2007 board will likely approve the Navy plan for 2008. In addition, every four to five months—most recently in May 2007—U.S. Naval Forces Central Command and the Coalition meet to take stock of the Iraqi Navy's progress. Rear Admiral Jawad himself is taking additional small but important steps, such as codifying, printing, and distributing standardized rules of engagement.[138]

The Iraqi Navy's road map includes an ambitious acquisition plan that necessitates an equally ambitious and effective technical and leadership training program.[139] Such efforts are well under way, under the auspices of the Coalition advisory structure outlined above. The Naval Transition Team works closely with the Iraqi Navy operational commander in Umm Qasr, and in general its representatives characterized the Iraqi Navy's progress toward identified milestones, its recruitment levels, and its attitude as very good. The basic Naval Transition Team mission is to mentor the Iraqi Navy in order to make possible a successful transition, and it focuses on operational capability and sustainability. The Naval Transition Team in Umm Qasr consists of 55 people from the United Kingdom and the United States. They are divided into six functional areas: operations, logistics, training, military training, engineering, and naval base construction. The Naval Transition Team, headed by a Royal Navy captain, is taking a "leading from behind" approach so that Iraqis gain a sense of ownership of their responsibilities, decision making, and progress. This captain also stressed that because of the high level of turnover (Royal Navy tours last only six months), establishing the personal relationships necessary to move forward can be challenging—particularly since building rapport before tackling daily operational issues is critical to success.[140]

The Naval Transition Team commander identified several problem areas for the Iraqis undertaking the transition. For example, the Iraqis are having trouble with the command and control portion of the road map, which eventually calls for strategic command from the Joint Headquarters in Baghdad, operational control from the naval headquarters at Umm Qasr, and tactical command from commanders on vessels in the Northern Arabian Gulf. Naval Transition Team officials characterized leadership as variable, though they consider the operational commander in Umm Qasr to be highly competent. Training is progressing well (including a good program in visit, board, search, and seizure operations), and in general the Iraqi Navy is making progress in acquiring new ships. At the tactical level, the Naval Transition Team commander cited good spirit and morale and improved base security.

The issues of poor maintenance and a weak supply chain surfaced repeatedly as major impediments to the Iraqi Navy's development. In particular, a tendency toward fixing breakdowns rather than performing preventive maintenance is a significant problem, as is the difficulty of getting funding released that can be devoted expressly to maintenance and other support operations. In fact, the Naval Transition Team Commander informed the Commission that maintenance is one of the Iraqi Navy's pressing problems, In addition, lack of access to sufficient fuel stocks and reliance on generators are problematic.[141] These issues also strongly indicate the need for continued Coalition assistance.

> ***Recommendation:*** *An ongoing Naval Transition Team presence in Umm Qasr is essential and should be continued.*

It is vital that the Iraqi Navy retain the support of its Coalition partners, both to sustain current progress and to address new priorities. Among the Naval Transition Team's future priorities are creating an Umm Qasr naval base action plan with an operational focus (building command and control, improving communications, formalizing a planning process), developing consistent and competent leadership, and, ultimately, effecting the transition. The most difficult choice will likely be regarding the extent to which Naval Transition Team should step back and allow the Iraqis to take on greater responsibility, balancing their need to learn to take risks against the need to complete the transition. The central tension may be between attempting to achieve Coalition standards and encouraging the Iraqi Navy to find Iraqi solutions to its problems.[142] In the very near term, the focus may have to be placed more on the integration of Coalition forces with Iraqi naval forces than on transition.[143]

Conclusion: The Iraqi Navy is small and its current fleet is insufficient to execute its mission. However, it is making substantive progress in this early stage of development: it has a well-thought-out growth plan, which it is successfully executing. Its maturation is hampered by the Ministry of Defense's understandable focus on ground forces and counterinsurgency operations, as well as by bureaucratic inefficiency. The Iraqi Navy will continue to rely on Coalition naval power to achieve its mission for the foreseeable future.

Chapter 7: The Ministry of Interior

A central challenge confronting the development of effective civil security forces in Iraq is the dysfunctional and sectarian Ministry of Interior (MOI) itself. In contrast to the Ministry of Defense, the MOI is rife with political and sectarian intrigues and is struggling to be even partially effective as a government institution. In most areas of administrative function, the MOI has some nascent capability, but progress is extremely slow. There is very little sense of momentum in transitioning greater responsibilities to the MOI. The ministry's physical presence—its multiple floors reportedly controlled by different factions, its location near Sadr City, and its multiple security checks and heavily armed occupants—is in itself a symbol of its dysfunction, sectarian character, and ineffectiveness. Whether the Iraq Police Service—which over time will be critical to Iraq's ability to maintain internal stability and deny terrorists safe haven—can ultimately become effective is heavily dependent on whether the MOI can become a far more functional ministry.

Overview of the Ministry of Interior

Under Saddam Hussein, the Ministry of Interior essentially was the intelligence arm of the Ba'ath Party, acting as the country's secret police. Despite the MOI's ignominious roots, the Coalition Provisional Authority did not dissolve it as it did the Ministry of Defense; instead, it sought to retain the MOI so that it could quickly transfer responsibility for policing and internal security to an Iraqi institution.[144] The Coalition Provisional Authority invested considerable effort into restructuring the MOI, but focused largely on the physical reconstruction of the ministry building itself. Although some attempts were also made at this time to develop the MOI's administrative capabilities, progress was slow because advisory staff and their Iraqi colleagues spent most of their time managing short-term crises and could devote little energy to longer-term developmental efforts.

The current Minister of Interior is Jawad al-Bolani, a Shi'a who served in the Iraqi Air Force for more than 15 years. The ministry has five deputy ministers who are responsible for running its five primary departments, eight independent directorates reporting directly to the Minister, and several senior supporting advisors. A plan has been developed to consolidate ministry functions into a more streamlined organization, but it is not clear when that restructuring process will be complete.

Coalition assistance to the Ministry of Interior and its civil security forces is provided largely by the Civilian Police Assistance Transition Team (CPATT), which was established in 2004. Recognizing the MOI's administrative weaknesses, the Civilian Police Assistance Transition Team established a 90-person Ministry Transition Team to work in various offices within the MOI to mentor senior officials, build internal capacity, and advise on policy and technical issues. A brigadier general from the United Kingdom leads this transition team and personally visits MOI offices several times each week. The transition team's overall goal is to develop the MOI's administrative capacity so that it can sustain Iraq's civil security forces, which number more than 300,000 as of July 2007 and are composed primarily of the Iraqi Police Service, National Police, and border enforcement forces.

Figure 16: MOI Force Growth [Omitted]

Challenges for the Ministry of Interior

During its assessment of the Iraqi Security Forces (ISF), the Commission met with officials at the departments of Defense and State involved in efforts to further develop the Ministry of Interior. The Commission also met with the Honorable Samir Shakir Mahmood Sumaida'ie, Iraq's Ambassador to the United States, who had served in 2004 as Minister of Interior. While in Iraq, the Commission held discussions with numerous Iraqi and American officials working for and with the MOI. In addition to meeting with senior officials working at the MOI level, the Commission also visited many Iraqi Police Service, National Police, and Department of Border Enforcement sites to gain a field-level perspective on the ministry.

It is clear from the Commission's extensive interviews and site visits that despite painstaking work, especially during the past year, the Ministry of Interior remains a highly sectarian organization that is partially effective at best and is in danger of losing ground in some administrative areas. If it is to continue to make progress, the MOI must deal more successfully with sectarianism and corruption, administration, logistics, and budgeting, as well as the status of the Facilities Protection Service.

Sectarianism and Corruption

> ***Finding:*** *Sectarianism and corruption are pervasive in the MOI and cripple the ministry's ability to accomplish its mission to provide internal security for Iraqi citizens.*

Under the previous Interior Minister, Bayan Jabr, who is now the powerful Minister of Finance, the Ministry of Interior became politicized. Jabr was a member of the Badr Organization and a member of the Supreme Council for the Islamic Revolution in Iraq (SCIRI), the largest Shi'a political party. He gave key ministry posts to members of the Badr Brigade, and Badr Brigade militia infiltrated Iraqi police units in many areas of the country. Although current Interior Minister Jawad al-Bolani wants to reform and professionalize the ministry, this is his first senior government position; he reportedly has no political affiliation or natural political constituency, and he lacks personal experience in managing police units.

Many experts outside the U.S. government have decried the present state of the Ministry of Interior.[145] It has been described as an "11-story powder keg of factions" that is plagued by battles for influence among political parties, religious groups, the existing government, and tribes and families.[146] The security environment at the MOI is so dangerous that when Western officials visit the ministry they frequently wear body armor and move only under heavily armed escort.

Although Minister al-Bolani has attempted to address the sectarianism and corruption in the MOI—steps taken include removing the commanders of 7 of the 9 National Police brigades and 17 of the 27 National Police battalions—the fundamentally sectarian nature of the ministry endures. For example, a former National Police general continues to work at the MOI, despite his having been implicated in a covert detention center operation in 2006; the Interior Minister blocked his arrest warrant. MOI employees have been arrested for smuggling explosives into the ministry, and according to some reports may have been Sunni insurgents or followers of Muqtada al-Sadr. In the past year, three of the ministry's longest-serving Sunni generals have been killed.[147] The Commission surveyed the Coalition's senior field commanders to obtain their on-the-ground assessment of the status and progress of the Iraqi Security Forces. Asked to rate the progress made by MOI forces toward ending sectarian violence and achieving national reconciliation, all four respondents rated progress as unsatisfactory.

The Commission was struck by the refrain of negative statements it heard about the MOI when it visited civil security force facilities in the provinces. Iraqi Police Service officials in particular complained bitterly about the sectarian behavior of the ministry, noting instances when the MOI simply does not pay police because they are Sunni or Kurdish, as well as cases when the MOI allegedly rejected lists of police recruits because they were perceived as being from "the wrong sect."

The MOI Transition Team is also working closely with oversight directorates in the MOI, particularly the Internal Affairs Division, to combat the pervasive climate of corruption within the ministry; but in these areas, as in combating sectarianism more broadly, there are real limits to the progress the Coalition can make, especially in the short term.[148]

Administration and Logistics

> ***Finding:*** *The MOI lacks sufficient administrative and logistics capability to support the civil security forces it controls.*

Put simply, the Ministry of Interior lacks administrative capability and capacity in most areas. As is true of other government ministries in Iraq, this deficiency stems in part from the de-Ba'athification process, which prevented many of Iraq's experienced bureaucrats from working in the government. The MOI is highly centralized and resistant to the delegation of authority, and it has very little ability to conduct long-term planning. The planning staff in the MOI is very small. The ministry also lacks systems—particularly those for tracking equipment and personnel—to enforce accountability in its administration.

The MOI has plans to streamline its organizational structure from five deputy ministers to three, though many "direct reports" to the Minister will remain even under the proposed new structure. While this restructuring may help Minister al-Bolani manage the MOI more strictly and oversee reforms, his effectiveness is limited by his physical distance from the ministry building. Because the MOI is located in the Red Zone near Sadr City, a dangerous neighborhood in Baghdad, Minister al-Bolani for the most part runs the ministry from a palace in the Green Zone.

Like the Ministry of Defense, the MOI lacks a layered bureaucracy with systems in place to get resources (e.g., uniforms, ammunition, and fuel) to the field in a timely fashion, but the logistics challenge in the MOI is much more pronounced. Without functioning systems to sustain Iraq's civil security forces in the provinces and major cities, the Iraqi Police Service, much less the National Police and other MOI civil security forces, cannot be effective.

> ***Recommendation:*** *The MOI, with the support of the Civilian Police Assistance Transition Team, must reform its organizational structure, develop a five-year strategic plan, and build sufficient administrative capacity to sustain Iraq's civil security forces in the field in a manner that is free of real or perceived sectarian favoritism.*

There is no substitute for the slow and often frustrating work of reforming the MOI, and the MOI Transition Team is an important source of advice to guide this process. As part of the planned MOI restructuring, one of the deputy ministers should have a robust strategic planning capacity and take the lead in developing a five-year strategic plan for the ministry and its civil security forces. This plan needs to be tied to budgetary requirements and should be developed in partnership with the 18 provincial police chiefs and other provincial civil security force officials. Although the Civilian Police Assistance Transition Team can play a critical role in advising the strategic planning effort, Iraqi officials in the MOI must lead the effort so that the ministry's leadership will have a vested interest in implementing the plan when it is complete.

It will be critical for the Deputy Minister for Administration and Finance to establish functioning systems for logistics and maintenance of the civil security forces and to facilitate effective, centralized tracking and accountability of the equipment that is issued to Iraqi forces. The Government Accountability Office recently published its finding that the United States did not begin to employ a centralized distribution system for the provision of Coalition-issued ISF equipment until December 2005.[149] Given the level of sectarian infiltration within the Ministry of Interior, as well as the decentralized nature of the Iraqi Police Service, the concerted efforts of ministry officials and Coalition advisors will be required not only to develop and implement a system that is able to accurately account for issued equipment but also to foster a culture of accountability within the MOI.

Budget

> ***Finding:*** *The MOI cannot execute its budget, a failure that undermines the effectiveness of the civil security forces in the field.*

The ministry suffers from several problems in the area of budget and finance. The MOI cannot execute its annual budget because of rigid constraints in budget categories and requirements to approve all expenditures at multiple layers of the bureaucracy and because there are rigid constraints on budget categories. The MOI's budget in 2007, which exceeded $3 billion, was underspent by $1 billion.[150] In some cases this underspending is an expression of the power struggle between the central government in Baghdad and the provincial authorities. For example, a senior budget official in the MOI withheld 50 percent of the overall police budget in 2007 because of her concern about corruption in the police force and the MOI's lack of insight into how police funds are spent in the provinces.[151] A major component of the MOI Transition Team's capacity-building program is working with MOI officials to develop sufficient funding mechanisms to support the MOI's forces in the field.

> ***Finding:*** *The Ministry of Interior and provincial authorities share responsibility for management and payment of the Iraqi Police Service. Serious deficiencies in these efforts have led to pay and morale problems and have heightened tensions between the central government and the provinces.*

The MOI's bifurcated system for administration and compensation of police creates particular problems in the budgeting and finance arena. Authority to hire police personnel is vested in the provincial police departments, but the payroll for the police is centralized with the MOI. The MOI also sets overall authorizations for the number of police each provincial government can hire, but provincial authorities feel they have a better understanding of local needs and in several cases have exceeded their authorized level of hires. Serious payroll problems and delays have resulted; police in some provinces claimed they have not been paid in months.[152]

MOI's inability to directly pay *shurtas* (new police recruits) and police officers is a major part of this problem. Under the existing system in Iraq, the Ministry of Finance (not the MOI) disburses funds to the provincial police chiefs, who in turn distribute salaries to line police. This indirect pay system provides little transparency for MOI officials attempting to monitor how funds are actually spent, and it creates many opportunities for corruption and the misuse of funds. Provincial police payrolls often include "shadow police"—individuals who are just names on the payroll but who do not report for duty, or former police who have been killed or who have deserted. It is not uncommon for police leadership at the provincial, district, and local level to use the "salaries" of shadow police for other purposes or to simply pocket the funds. These practices heighten budgetary tensions with the MOI in Baghdad.

> ***Recommendation:*** *The MOI Transition Team should continue to work with MOI officials to establish workable mechanisms to better manage and resolve pay problems affecting police forces. This should be done in coordination with provincial authorities.*

As part of the MOI reform effort, the ministry should establish a process to determine provincial police requirements in coordination with provincial authorities, effectively enforce the requirements that are set, and pay police directly. Direct pay for police would give the MOI greater insight into management of the police forces at the provincial level, reduce corruption, and strengthen the identification of police throughout Iraq with the national government.

Facilities Protection Service

> ***Finding:*** *The MOI has little control of the forces that make up the Facilities Protection Service (FPS). The allegiance of many Facilities Protection Service personnel has been to individual ministries, parties, tribes, and clans rather than to the central government, and such division of loyalties undermines their ability to provide security.*

The Facilities Protection Service is designed to provide protection for the personnel and facilities of the various ministries. Many of the individuals hired into this service are associated in one way or another with their respective minister and demonstrate loyalty to that minister, a political party, a tribe, or a clan. There has been no vetting or formal training of these forces at the national level. In response to this lack of control over the hiring or training of the approximately 140,000 people serving in the Facilities Protection Service, in December 2006 the Prime Minister directed that all FPS personnel be consolidated and come under the supervision of the MOI. Despite this new policy mandating consolidation, most ministries are resisting the change. Some ministries are reluctant to relinquish control of their FPS forces, and the Ministry of Finance has not transferred funding to the MOI to administer oversight of the Facilities Protection Service.

Until FPS personnel can be vetted, trained, and equipped under a central, national set of standards, the threat of sectarian violence delivered at the hands of FPS personnel will remain.

> ***Recommendation:*** *The Coalition should support consolidation of the Facilities Protection Service by encouraging the establishment of national implementing orders. As consolidation proceeds, the Coalition should assist the MOI to ensure that the Facilities Protection Service personnel can be properly vetted, trained, and equipped.*

Conclusion: The Ministry of Interior is a ministry in name only. It is widely regarded as being dysfunctional and sectarian, and suffers from ineffective leadership. Such fundamental flaws present a serious obstacle to achieving the levels of readiness, capability, and effectiveness in police and border security forces that are essential for internal security and stability in Iraq.

Chapter 8: The Iraqi Police Service

The Iraqi Police Service (IPS), Iraq's local and provincial police force, is fragile throughout Iraq.[153] On the one hand, training for the Iraqi Police Service is improving, and in some areas the police are patrolling neighborhoods more regularly, manning security checkpoints, and working with the Iraqi Army and Coalition forces to combat insurgent groups. On the other hand, the Iraqi Police Service faces many challenges. The Ministry of Interior (MOI), which supports the Iraqi Police Service, is highly dysfunctional. Infiltration of the Iraqi Police Service by militia members, insurgents, and criminals is widespread in some parts of Iraq. The police are not sufficiently equipped to combat their enemies, nor do they have the support and sustainment systems to function effectively. The Iraqi Police Service lacks investigative capabilities and sufficient intelligence and information systems, and it operates in an environment without a strong foundation in the rule of law. The Iraqi Police Service is an important part of the long-term solution for stability in Iraq, but it will be at least a few more years before the police can contribute significantly to bringing real security to the provinces. In the interim, they will continue to rely on the Coalition to provide key enablers such as intelligence, surveillance, and reconnaissance capabilities.

Overview of the Iraqi Police Service

During the years of Saddam Hussein's rule, Iraqi police were at the bottom of the hierarchy of security forces. Although there were more than 60,000 police in the force, they were poorly trained and equipped. In addition, they were often brutal and corrupt, and as a result they were widely feared by the Iraqi public. Reflecting that public distrust, looters targeted and destroyed many police stations, vehicles, and pieces of equipment in the wake of the 2003 invasion.[154] In an effort to begin reestablishing security in Iraq, the Coalition Provisional Authority called the Iraqi police back into service; and in May 2003, the Department of Justice determined that the Iraqi Police Service needed to be significantly reorganized, retrained, and reequipped in order to be effective.

Six months later the United States began a recruiting and training program for the police, relying on 500 police advisors reporting to the Department of State. By early 2004, however, it was clear that the State Department-led police training program was not sufficiently effective, primarily because of the challenging security situation. In March 2004, President Bush assigned responsibility for the police training effort to the Department of Defense. This was unprecedented; historically, the departments of Justice and State have taken the lead in training indigenous police forces. Placing the military in charge does ensure that police trainers are more secure, but it also has resulted in greater emphasis on counterinsurgency operations than on civil policing and more traditional law enforcement activities.

Today there are more than 230,000 police in the Iraqi police force. The U.S. Civilian Police Assistance Transition Team (CPATT), the military-led organization within the Coalition with responsibility for mentoring and advising the Iraqi Police Service, has trained approximately 164,000 police, but the Department of Defense estimates that only 40 to 70 percent of these Coalition-trained recruits are still serving in the police force.[155] However, the existence of ghost payrolls makes it difficult to generate reliable estimates of the precise number of personnel available for duty. It now is clear that tens of thousands of Iraqi police have entered the force without going through the Coalition training program; rather, they have been directly hired by provincial authorities, often at the urging of local sheikhs or other tribal elders.

The Iraqi Police Service falls under the Ministry of Interior, led by Minister Jawad al-Bolani. The police force is organized into provincial police departments with district chiefs, as well as into police departments in the major cities. The provincial directors of police (PDoPs) report to the provincial governors and are typically selected at the provincial government level from a pool of candidates validated by the Ministry of Interior, a process that is more art than science. Most provincial, district, and major city police forces include patrol police, station police, traffic police, and highway patrol police. There are some specialized units for forensics and criminal evidence, but in general the forensic and investigative capabilities of the Iraqi Police Service range from quite weak to nonexistent. The provinces also have Emergency Response Units (ERUs) that are similar to SWAT (special weapons and tactics) teams in the United States.[156]

Training and equipment for the Iraqi Police Service have improved markedly in the past few years, but significant challenges remain in both areas. Today there are three police academies that train police officers (mainly front-line supervisors such as sergeants and lieutenants) and six regional training centers throughout Iraq that offer a 10-week training course for new police recruits, known as *shurtas*. This basic training for Iraqi shurtas includes courses on defensive tactics, patrolling, democratic policing, and firearms, as well as other subjects. Many classes are conducted by Iraqi instructors. Police who have not gone through the Civilian Police Assistance Transition Team training pipeline do typically receive at least 80 hours of very basic training. Recognizing the need to standardize training, the Coalition has a long-term plan to put all police on the MOI payroll through the 10-week course as soon as possible. In addition to the 10-week basic training for shurtas, newly recruited police officers attend a 9-month training course at one of Iraq's training academies. The police colleges also offer a three-year advanced course for police officers. Training for the more specialized Emergency Response Units takes place at the Camp Dublin Specialized Training Center in Baghdad.

Although on average the Iraqi Police Service has received more than 80 percent of the basic equipment deemed essential for its mission, many police stations still lack uniforms, weapons, and vehicles, as well as spare parts and ammunition.[157] Iraqi police are authorized to be equipped with two uniforms, a pistol, an AK-47, sets of flexible handcuffs, and individual body armor. Police use high-frequency radios and typically patrol in unarmored Nissan pickup trucks or midsize sport utility vehicles.

Led by a two-star U.S. general, the Civilian Police Assistance Transition Team oversees about 900 senior police advisors and works closely with Coalition Police Transition Teams (PTTs). The Coalition began using Police Transition Teams in 2006 to develop closer partnerships with the Iraqi Police Service and to provide day-to-day advising and mentoring of the Iraqi Police Service. Today more than 220 Police Transition Teams throughout Iraq are working side by side with Iraqi police at the provincial, district, and police station levels.[158] Like the Military Transition Teams, the Police Transition Teams report to Multi-National Corps-Iraq (MNC-I), led by Lieutenant General Raymond Odierno. Police Transition Teams are typically composed of 11 to 15 individuals and are led by military personnel who range in rank from staff sergeants to lieutenant colonels, depending on the level of the station that the team mentors. The deputy leaders are senior international police advisors, and the rest of the team is made up of a mix of military police and civilian police advisors. There are about 1,200 police stations in Iraq, and because the number of Police Transition Teams is not large enough to partner or monitor every station, the Coalition generally has insight into about 25–30 percent of them.[159]

Figure 17: Iraqi Police Operational Readiness Assessment Level Definitions [Omitted]

Challenges for the Iraqi Police Service

Though 2006 was to be "the Year of the Police," it is widely viewed as having been less than successful.[160] At the same time, it is clear that in the past year, the Iraqi Police Service has made some progress. The police in the Kurdish region are relatively solid and are providing basic security in the three Kurdish provinces. Not only are they policing their own neighborhoods, they also have opened the police training center in Sulaymaniyah to police recruits from across the country, and the region has accepted internally displaced persons from other parts of Iraq with relatively few ensuing security problems. In Habbaniyah in Anbar province, efforts to recruit police locally are thriving, and the training being conducted at the Habbaniyah regional training center is encouraging. Finally, while the sectarian influences on the police are far greater in ethnic and religiously mixed areas like Baghdad, even there the joint security stations have demonstrated that the police can begin to establish a more meaningful neighborhood presence if Coalition forces provide mentoring and oversight.

Figure 18: Joint Security Station Evolution [Omitted]

During its assessment, the Commission met with officials at the departments of Defense and State involved in efforts to develop the Iraqi Police Service. While in Iraq, the Commission held discussions with more than 20 American officials and 25 Iraqi officials directly involved with the Iraqi Police Service. Commissioners visited 15 police-related facilities throughout Iraq, including police stations, joint security stations, and a number of police training centers and colleges.

It is clear from the Commission's extensive interviews and site visits that the Coalition and the Government of Iraq (GOI) have invested significant effort and resources into the development of the Iraqi Police Service, but considerable challenges remain in a number of areas—notably, in recruiting, training, equipment, information sharing, investigations and forensics, and the creation of a justice system.

Recruiting

> ***Finding:*** *The emphasis on local recruiting and assignment in the Iraqi Police Service is showing promise in establishing security at the local level; strong personnel vetting processes will remain vital.*

The Commission was struck by the fact that there is no shortage of Iraqis who wish to volunteer for service.[161] Despite many bombings of police recruit queues, and a suicide bombing at the Baghdad Police College in 2005 that killed more than 27 recruits, Iraqis continue to sign up for the Iraqi Police Service. Their actions, in part, are undoubtedly driven by economic necessity, but it also seems to suggest that these Iraqis perceive a stake in bringing security to their communities.

Local recruiting for the police has emerged as a focal point in the overall development of the Iraqi Police Service, reflecting the professional law enforcement view that policing is most effective when performed at the neighborhood level by people with ties to the local community. The most visible example of this emphasis on local recruiting has been the "Anbar Awakening" movement in the western Sunni stronghold of Anbar province, but it was widespread in each province the Commission visited.

One benefit of local recruiting is that recruits know their communities and are known themselves in turn, but the need for robust vetting efforts to ensure that local police forces are not infiltrated by militia, terrorists, or criminals remains strong.[162] Though the vetting of police recruits is improving, it is still a challenge.[163] When an Iraqi seeks to join the Iraqi Police Service, as either a shurta or an officer, he now is required to provide a retinal scan and set of fingerprints. The biométrie results are then provided to the MOI for a criminal history check. Candidates who have a previous criminal history are reviewed by the MOI Internal Affairs Division. Criminal history checks are more complicated in Iraq than in many other places because of the sizable number of Iraqis who were unfairly charged with crimes by Saddam's regime. If a criminal record appears to be largely a result of political activity or perceived crimes against the state, candidates are given the opportunity to explain their backgrounds rather than being automatically barred from the police service. In addition to providing the biométrie information, police recruits also fill out a questionnaire similar to that used for a basic background check in the United States. If recruits do not have a known criminal record and if they pass the literacy and physical fitness requirements, they must pass a vetting interview before entering the training center or police academy.

> ***Recommendation:*** *The MOI and the Civilian Police Assistance Transition Team should work closely with provincial authorities to ensure that established vetting procedures are used consistently throughout the country to combat militia, criminal, and terrorist infiltration of the Iraqi Police Service.*

The MOI now has a process in place to vet police recruits, but many perceive this vetting process as selecting and rejecting candidates along sectarian lines. Infiltration of the police service by militia and other criminal elements is widespread in some areas, particularly in the south. Some but not all of this infiltration can be attributed to the relative immaturity of the Iraqi databases used for background checks and to police departments' having begun only recently to collect biométrie data. Efforts by local tribal authorities to generate recruits for the police service are encouraging, but to ensure that this cooperation is beneficial for Iraqi security it is crucial that provincial police chiefs and local commanders be required to emphasize universal and consistent application of established vetting procedures.

Establishing provincial police selection boards with appropriate representation among ethnic and sectarian groups, as well as various aspects of the Iraqi Police Service community, could help formalize this localized vetting process. In particularly difficult cases, it may be appropriate to require candidates to submit to a polygraph test. Even if rarely used, the possibility of having to take such a test may prove a powerful incentive for recruits to be more transparent about their associations and allegiances.

Training

Finding: Police training in Iraq is improving, particularly in areas where training is led by Iraqi instructors partnered with civilian police advisors.

Training for police in Iraq has improved considerably in the past two years, but the progress is fragile. The regional police training center in Habbaniyah appears to be a model for police training in Iraq, as was the training center the Commission visited in Sulaymaniyah. At the Habbaniyah center, the 10-week training class for Iraqi shurtas covered a wide range of basic policing subjects as well as specific challenges, such as the threat of suicide bombers. Iraqi instructors lead most of the training, and the students appear very eager to learn. Progress was less evident at the Baghdad Police College, where most if not all of the training courses are led by American instructors. Not surprisingly, Iraqi recruits appear more receptive and attentive in courses taught by fellow Iraqis, but it is not clear there are sufficient numbers of qualified Iraqi personnel to staff all six regional police training centers and three police academies.

The continuing instability of the security environment in many parts of Iraq creates problems for military and civilian Coalition trainers as they try to do their jobs. In some areas, trainers have difficulty getting to training sites safely, and in a few cases, they have actually come under attack while conducting training. Finally, though the basic training program for shurtas and police officers is now in place, there also is a need for police command staff training, including first-line and mid-level manager training, to develop the leadership cadre of the Iraqi Police Service over the long term.

Recommendation: The Civilian Police Assistance Transition Team should continue transitioning the lead for training to the Iraqis wherever possible and should consider instituting a "train the trainers" program throughout the provinces to facilitate this process.

Having Iraqi instructors direct police training courses is clearly the most effective and desirable way to train incoming recruits. The Civilian Police Assistance Transition Team should accelerate its efforts to put Iraqi instructors in the lead at all training centers throughout the country. Establishing a robust "train the trainers" program would facilitate this effort and potentially free up civilian police advisors—who are already in scarce supply—to serve in larger numbers on Police Transition Teams.

Finding: U.S. military officers rather than senior civilian law enforcement personnel lead the Coalition training effort for the Iraqi Police Service; this arrangement has inadvertently marginalized civilian police advisors and limited the overall effectiveness of the training and advisory effort.

Because security conditions in Iraq were becoming difficult by 2004, National Security Presidential Directive 36 placed the Department of Defense in charge of the Coalition effort to train the Iraqi police. While it was clear to the Commission that the military has not intentionally sought to minimize the role of civilian police advisors in Iraq, in practice the Coalition's efforts to help develop the Iraqi Police Service have not been fully effective. Military leaders in the Civilian Police Assistance Transition Team do not have backgrounds in civilian law enforcement. In addition, the military leadership of the Civilian Police Assistance Transition Team changes about once a year; five different generals have commanded the Civilian Police Assistance Transition Team since it was established, and none of them have been military policemen by military occupational specialty. Although the Coalition program to train the Iraqi police has been ongoing for four years, one advisor noted to the Commission that "we have not had four years to implement a training plan; we have implemented a one-year training plan four times in a row."

Civil policing is fundamentally different from military policing. In civil policing, the police depend on the "consent" of those they police; it therefore requires spending considerable time building relationships with the communities being served. Civil police are trained to use defensive techniques, and to use deadly physical force only as a last resort. In contrast, military police are focused on force protection, intelligence gathering, and support of combat soldiers and combat operations.

Civilian police advisors do not have the lead role in Civilian Police Assistance Transition Team programs. In many cases, the international police advisors working within the Civilian Police Assistance Transition Team feel marginalized and unable to make contributions commensurate with their experience. This perceived marginalization is even more frustrating for the police advisors because they are better positioned to have influence in the Iraqi culture, which favors age; while most of the international police advisors are either retired or very senior law enforcement professionals, most military officers leading Police Transition Teams are captains or majors who are too young to merit their Iraqi partners' respect.

> ***Recommendation:*** *Leadership of the Coalition Police Assistance Training Team and the Police Training Teams should be transferred to senior civilian law enforcement professionals.*

The departments of Defense, State, and Justice should move quickly to establish a revised division of labor for the Iraqi police training program that would enable a senior civilian law enforcement officer with professional experience comparable to that of a two-star general to lead the Coalition Police Assistance Training Team. The level of violence in Iraq dictates that the police training programs remain indivisible from the broader military Coalition effort in Iraq in the near term; at least initially, therefore, the civilian leader of the Civilian Police Assistance Transition

Team should continue to report to the Commanding General, Multi-National Security Transition Command–Iraq.

The key reform needed at this time is to ensure that a senior civilian law enforcement official is providing the day-to-day leadership of Civilian Police Assistance Transition Team activities. A major responsibility for the civilian head of this organization should be to work in dose partnership with the MOI on developing and approving a strategic plan for civilian policing that includes the phased transition of the police development process to full Iraqi control.

Consistent with shifting leadership of the Civilian Police Assistance Transition Team from the military to the civilian law enforcement community, Multi-National Security Transition Command–Iraq should also work with Multi-National Corps-Iraq to put international police advisors in charge of the Police Transition Teams in the field. Today the Police Transition Teams are led by military officers, with civilian international police advisors serving as deputies. In the future, Police Transition Teams should be led by civilian international police advisors, with military police officers serving as deputies. Because many areas of Iraq remain dangerous, Coalition forces should continue to provide force protection for the civilian police training effort and the Police Transition Teams.

As part of the recommendation above, and to assist the overall Coalition effort to train and mentor the Iraqi Police Service, the Commission recommends establishing an international advisory board to monitor the civilian police transition program, track its progress, and make recommendations to the Government of Iraq and the Civilian Police Assistance Transition Team. This advisory board would be composed of senior civilian law enforcement personnel with experience establishing and training indigenous police forces. Not only would this body provide an additional perspective on civil policing issues for the Iraqi government and the Coalition, it also could help ensure that lessons learned from past experiences are properly brought to bear as Iraq continues to develop its police force.

Over the longer term and if the security situation in Iraq improves sufficiently, it would be appropriate to transfer lead responsibility for police training in Iraq out of the Department of Defense entirely. The departments of State and Justice both have extensive experience with civilian policing and the training of indigenous police forces. Ideally, the lead agency with responsibility for police training in Iraq would be determined after careful study of the utility of making a single agency in the U.S. government responsible for this task. During this study, consideration must be given to the ongoing and future tasks that address the rule of law, such as upgrading Iraqi courts, strengthening the Iraqi prison system, and training an Iraqi marshals system.[164]

Finding: The number of civilian international police advisors is insufficient to the task of training the Iraqi Police Service.

When Multi-National Security Transition Command–Iraq was initially established in 2004 and envisioned training a force of about 135,000 Iraqi police, the Civilian Police Assistance Transition Team requested funding for 6,000 police advisors for that training effort. Congress provided authority and funds to hire only 1,000 personnel. Today there are more than 230,000 police in the Iraqi Police Service, and it appears likely that the force will continue to grow in the foreseeable future. To assist the Ministry of Interior with development and training of this force, the Civilian Police Assistance Transition Team relies on just over 900 international police advisers and approximately 3,500 military personnel serving in Police Transition Teams.

The number of international police advisors currently working in Iraq is simply insufficient to the task. The Civilian Police Assistance Transition Team's emphasis on placing advisors out in the field wherever possible and on partnering advisors with police at police colleges and training centers is significantly improving the quality of the Iraqi Police Service and is facilitating the transition of responsibility to Iraqi police trainers. However, there are not enough police advisors to establish these partnerships in the depth and breadth that is needed to support the development of a 230,000-person force in a country as large as Iraq.

Recommendation: The Coalition—not just the United States—should fund and recruit the requisite number of international police advisors.

Fielding more international police advisors is essential to the police training effort. The White House and the Department of State should aggressively encourage Coalition partners to fund and recruit at least another 2,000 advisors as part of a broader effort to support reconstruction efforts. To create momentum, the U.S. Congress and Department of State should work closely to fund at least 1,000 of those 2,000 additional police advisors positions, drawing more extensively than in previous years on the very large pool of law enforcement officials in the United States.

Finding: Training programs to date have emphasized quantity of police trained over quality of training, thereby undermining the long-term effectiveness of the force in favor of force generation efforts.

Since 2004, there has been considerable focus on building up the Iraqi Police Service as quickly as possible. Reporting by the Department of Defense on the Iraqi Police Service has emphasized the numbers of police trained by Coalition forces—even after it became clear that neither the Coalition nor the Ministry of Interior knew how many of those Coalition-trained police were remaining in the force. The Iraqi Police Service has grown dramatically as provincial chiefs of police have become more independent from the central government, hiring thousands of recruits directly into the force at the provincial and local levels. In discussions with Civilian Police Assistance Transition Team officials, it was clear that balancing the police force's goals for quantity and quality is a constant struggle. This balancing act is made more difficult by the significant shortage of police force leaders, a result of the passive police culture under Saddam and the more recent de-Ba'athification process. Meanwhile, there are too few international advisors to establish field training officer programs and other similar quality initiatives on a large scale.

> ***Recommendation:*** *Particularly in light of a significantly high number of personnel in the Iraqi Police Service who have not yet undergone Coalition training, the Ministry of Interior and Civilian Police Assistance Transition Team should seek higher-quality police recruits and vet them more carefully as they continue to address the training backlog.*

Emphasizing quantity over quality of police recruited and trained is likely to result in a less effective Iraqi Police Service over the long term. The Civilian Police Assistance Transition Team should work closely with the MOI and provincial authorities to establish a plan for putting the more than 65,000 direct-hire police through the 10-week shurta training course. In discussions with Civilian Police Assistance Transition Team officials, Commissioners noted several instances in the past two decades when major urban police departments in the United States responded to short-term security needs by deciding to emphasize quantity of police over quality. In each case cited, the short-term emphasis on numbers resulted in weak vetting and training of recruits, and those weaknesses in turn led directly to major police scandals years later that had lasting negative effects on those police departments and on their effectiveness in their communities. To ensure that quality is the focus in developing the Iraqi Police Service, the Coalition may want to consider a comprehensive audit of the police training program that will clearly establish its breadth, depth, and consistency.

> ***Finding:*** *The Iraqi Police Service lacks a formal police leadership academy, a deficiency that impedes leadership development.*

The Commission observed that most if not all Iraqi police leaders are former military officers and have no formal training or experience in civil policing. The absence of any leadership training for these senior officers is significantly slowing the development of a corps of strong, capable leaders in the Iraqi Police Service. This lack of senior leaders with training in civil policing is impeding the effectiveness of the service as a whole. A particular shortfall is the absence of a training program to develop first-line supervisors (generally officers at the sergeant level in the United States). First-line supervisors are invaluable to any police force and provide a vital bridge between senior police leadership and junior officers.

Recommendation: The Iraqi Police Service should work with its Coalition advisors to establish a formal Iraqi Police Academy that is focused on developing civil policing skills in senior officers and includes a separate first-line supervisor training program.

A leadership academy focused on providing training for senior Iraqi police officers would complement the existing police academies offering nine-month and three-year programs for entering police officers and would enable the more rapid development of a leadership corps across all levels of the Iraqi Police Service. A program aimed specifically at developing first-line supervisors would be an important part of the curriculum for such an academy and would ensure continuity of leadership from junior officers all the way up to senior police leaders. All such advanced courses should incorporate a clear set of standards that outline what the Iraqi people can expect from the Iraqi Police Service. This set of behaviors will become the foundation of a disciplinary code, based on a fundamental respect for human rights, and will help to promote confidence in the Iraqi Police Service overall.

Equipment

Finding: The Iraqi Police Service is underequipped to combat the threats it faces and suffers persistent shortfalls in vital equipment.

There is a stark contrast between the lightly outfitted Iraqi police and the Coalition patrols that move around cities like Baghdad in armored Humvees or Stryker vehicles manned with soldiers outfitted in 60–80 pounds of full body armor and bristling with weapons. Reflecting this contrast in equipment levels, members of the Iraqi Security Forces, including the Iraqi Police Service, are killed at three times the rate of Coalition forces in Iraq. The day the Commission met with the Baghdad chief of police, two policemen had already been killed; and the day before, police in five patrol vehicles were killed. This casualty rate, which would make national headlines in the United States, was clearly not unusual for Baghdad.

Not only are the Iraqi police ill-equipped in the face of heavily armed terrorist groups and sectarian militias—particularly in Iraq's urban areas—but in many areas they have not received all of their basic equipment and supplies and lack sufficient spare parts to keep equipment in working order. The Baghdad police chief told the Commission that more than 50 percent of his vehicles are non-operational at any given time. At the Habbaniyah police training center, the local police chief and international police advisors told the Commission that requests to the MOI for ammunition for marksmanship training had gone unanswered for months.[165] Because the Ministry of Oil routinely fails to provide required fuel to the Ministry of Interior, many police departments are not able to conduct vehicle patrols. Many of these shortfalls are linked to the lack of administrative capacity in the MOI—particularly the absence of systems to track personnel and their equipment—that was discussed in the preceding chapter. They could be resolved if the MOI established a more capable sustainment system.

> ***Recommendation:*** *Multi-National Security Transition Command–Iraq should work with the Iraqi government to provide adequately armored vehicles and heavier weaponry to the Iraqi Police Service, particularly to police stations in urban areas or other areas where improvised explosive device (IED) and explosively formed penetrator (EFP) attacks are prevalent.*

Culturally, Iraqi police are far more tied to the station house than are American police. To establish security in Iraqi neighborhoods, the shurtas will have to leave the stations and go on patrol. Iraqi police will be more inclined to conduct patrols if they feel protected, and they will be far better protected in armored vehicles than in Nissan trucks. Many mid-level Civilian Police Assistance Transition Team officials and Police Transition Team leaders told the Commission that they had recommended the provision of armored vehicles for the police and expressed uncertainty as to why these recommendations had not yet been acted on. Similarly, as long as Iraqi police are confronting rocket-propelled grenades, mortars, and other forms of indirect fire, Multi-National Security Transition Command–Iraq should move quickly to find a mechanism to get far more armored vehicles and at least some quantity of heavier weapons to the Iraqi Police Service.

Information Sharing

> ***Finding:*** *Quality intelligence is central to the ability of the Iraqi Police Service to take the lead for security, but intelligence supporting police operations is limited and information sharing with other security agencies is weak.*

The Iraqi Police Service has its own intelligence system, but it is largely confined to the tactical level. There is very little understanding in the Iraqi armed forces or in the Ministry of Interior (where many senior officials are former military officers) of how to use intelligence effectively to support policing operations. Information sharing between the Iraqi Police Service and other elements of the security forces in Iraq—primarily the Iraqi Army and the National Police—is spotty due to security concerns (fueled by deep and long-standing mistrust) and the absence of a solid information technology infrastructure to enable secure communications.

Establishing Police Transition Teams and Military Transition Teams to work with the Iraqi Army has helped the flow of information from Coalition forces to the Iraqi Police Service, but this information flow is largely internal within each province. There is very little communication between police forces in different provinces, a lack that is particularly troublesome in light of the need to conduct effective counterterrorism and counterinsurgency operations and to track organized and other criminal activity.

The joint security stations in Baghdad and the partnering of Coalition forces with security forces in the provinces have significantly strengthened intelligence operations, but in many areas the general public remain reluctant to cooperate with the Coalition or Iraqi security forces. Tips hotlines are now widely advertised throughout the country, but they are not always widely used. At one joint security station in Baghdad, police and local community leaders highlighted the distribution of tips hotline cards; however, U.S. military police noted privately that most people in the neighborhood were far too fearful of retribution from Jaysh al-Madhi (often referred to as JAM or the Madhi Army) to use the hotline.

> ***Recommendation:*** *All Iraqi security agencies and the Iraqi Police Service must work together to establish information-sharing systems, practices, and protocols that meet their requirements. The MOI should work with the provinces to establish mechanisms to share information from the national level down.*

The ministries of Interior and Defense, with assistance from the Civilian Police Assistance Transition Team and the Coalition Military Assistance Transition Team, need to work together to develop the means to share intelligence with the Iraqi police in a way that protects operational security but retains information that will be useful to local police. This is not an easy problem to solve, as the United States itself has recently been reminded—the events of September 11 have spurred a renewed focus on the best ways to share information between the military, national intelligence services, and the police. That said, information sharing in Iraq between the military, the intelligence services, the police, and Coalition forces is rudimentary at best. It needs to be significantly developed and strengthened if the Iraqi police are ever to be the main providers of internal security for Iraq.

The MOI and the Civilian Police Assistance Transition Team also need to work with the provinces to establish mechanisms to share information among the provincial police departments. Today it is almost impossible to track criminal activities from one province to another, or to verify trans-province patterns of activity. Iraq will not be able to establish a mature policing system in the absence of mechanisms to share information between provincial departments of police. Creating these mechanisms would also contribute to a sense of a national policing effort in Iraq.

Investigations and Forensics

> ***Finding:*** *The Iraqi Police Service has extremely weak investigative and forensic capabilities that greatly limit its effectiveness.*

The Commission was struck in its interviews and site visits by the weakness of the Iraqi Police Service's investigative and forensic capabilities.

The day before the Commission arrived in Iraq for its first visit, a suicide vehicle bombing in Irbil killed more than 150 people—yet it was not clear in interviews what organization within the Iraqi Security Forces had the responsibility to investigate the crime, or even whether the crime would be investigated at all.

When Iraqi police are on patrol, or are called to a crime scene, they have very little ability or legal authority to secure a crime scene; collect, secure, and analyze evidence; and question witnesses or suspects. A partial explanation for their relative powerlessness is that in the Iraqi criminal justice system, unlike the American criminal justice system, the lead role in criminal investigations is held by the judiciary rather than by the law enforcement community. Moreover, the Iraqi criminal justice system traditionally puts tremendous emphasis on securing a confession in order to convict an individual of a crime, which in turn encourages the use of torture to avoid acquittals. Because confessions are seen as all-important, there is almost no appreciation for the value of physical evidence or corroborating witness statements.

The Civilian Police Assistance Transition Team is working with the MOI to change this cultural bias, but it is a slow process and the need for enhanced investigative training is urgent. The Baghdad Crime Lab was devastated in the wake of the invasion in 2003, but it has rebuilt some of its explosive ordnance disposal (EOD), ballistics, and fingerprint database capabilities with support from the British. In addition, the Baghdad Police College now offers courses in criminal investigation that cover subjects ranging from the basics of securing a crime scene to analyzing physical evidence such as footprints. The criminal investigation training facilities that the Commission visited at the Baghdad Police College and police training center at Sulaymaniyah in the north were comparable to many facilities in the United States. The challenge for the future is clearly going to be putting sufficient numbers of police through these training courses so that the Iraqi Police Service can quickly and dramatically improve its ability to investigate and analyze crime scenes.

An impressive example of the Coalition's efforts to enhance the investigative capabilities of Iraq's civil security forces is the Major Crimes Task Force in Baghdad. Following a wave of high-profile murders in 2004 and early 2005 that essentially went uninvestigated, the U.S. Department of Justice approached the MOI and proposed a joint U.S.-Government of Iraq task force to build an indigenous capacity to investigate and prosecute these types of high-profile assassinations. The task force is composed of 12 American law enforcement agents and 11 vetted Iraqi officers, as well as five translators. One Iraqi investigative judge is assigned to the task force full-time. The Task Force has successfully investigated a number of very high profile murder cases and has broken up a number of covert, unsanctioned interrogation centers. It is highly professional, but it does not have the capacity to handle the volume of cases generated in Baghdad, much less the entire country. Moreover, the high visibility of the task force's investigations has forced all of its Iraqi personnel to live inside the International Zone, and it has become apparent that they cannot safely resettle in Baghdad when their tenure ends.

> ***Recommendation:*** *As the Iraqi Police Service continue to develop, Multi-National Security Transition Command–Iraq should work with the MOI to increase the investigative and forensic capabilities of the police service by expanding the Major Crimes Task Force, increasing the number of crime lab facilities in major cities, increasing training courses for criminal investigators, and establishing an investigator rank within the police service.*

No police force can be effective if it cannot secure and investigate crime scenes. The Ministry of Interior, with support from the Civilian Police Assistance Transition Team, needs to make development of investigative and forensic skills within the Iraqi Police Service a major area of emphasis and must give the police greater authority to conduct investigations. The Major Crimes Task Force should be expanded significantly so that it can at least begin to handle the large volume of cases in Baghdad. Ideally, each province would have its own Major Crimes Task Force, equipped with an automated database to track criminal activity and facilitate information sharing. In light of the substantial history of terrorists using criminal activity to fund acts of terror, the Major Crimes Task Force should also expand its efforts into investigating significant criminal financial activities, as well as murders and other violent crime. Finally, the Iraqi Police Service should create an investigator rank so that it can begin training police to specialize in investigative and forensics skills.

Creation of a Justice System

> ***Finding:*** *The Iraqi Police Service is but one element of a broader justice system that is not yet well established in Iraq.*

The Commission did not conduct a detailed assessment of the overall judicial system in Iraq as such an investigation was beyond the scope of its mandate, but interviews made clear that a major challenge to effective policing is the absence of a well-developed judicial system. To establish lasting security in Iraq, the police must be linked to a functioning court and prison system. Police must be able to put suspects in jail while they await trial; sufficient numbers of investigative judges need to be able to conduct investigations thoroughly and without fearing for their lives; and when the legal system succeeds in convicting a suspect, criminals need to be able to serve out their sentences in well-run prisons. Iraq currently lacks this kind of coherent judicial framework. Fundamentally, the rule of law does not yet exist in Iraq. Police and judicial officials often view each other with mutual suspicion, jails are woefully overcrowded, investigative judges and their families are often targets of intimidation and violence, and courthouses are run down and poorly secured.

> ***Recommendation:*** *The Government of Iraq, particularly the Ministry of Interior and the Ministry of Justice, should collaborate to create and implement a framework to enable the rule of law in Iraq. The Coalition should continue to strongly support these efforts.*

Like the Iraq Study Group, the Commission strongly recommends that the Government of Iraq launch a major initiative to establish a functioning judicial system in Iraq, and that the Coalition strongly support that program.[166] A new focus on developing the rule of law in Iraq could build on ongoing Coalition initiatives, such as the relatively new rule of law compound that establishes a "safe zone" for members of the judiciary and their families, as well as the European Union rule of law mission in Iraq (EUJUST LEX) that has trained almost 1,500 senior Iraqi criminal justice officials. Establishing the rule of law will require expanding the number and improving the quality of detention centers, rebuilding courthouses and improving their physical security, training many more prosecutors and judges, providing for the safety of judicial system officials and their families, and establishing mechanisms to root out corruption and political influence in the judicial system.

A Long-Term Vision for Policing in Iraq

> ***Finding:*** *The police are central to the long-term establishment of security and stability in Iraq. Today, the Iraqi Police Service is incapable of providing security at a level sufficient to protect Iraqi neighborhoods from insurgents and sectarian violence.*

Although today the Iraqi Army has a considerable role in providing internal security in Iraq, ultimately the Army will focus on external defense of the country and it will be the Iraqi police who will safeguard the country's internal security. The Iraqi police today are operating in what is essentially a battlefield environment while trying to prepare for the day when more traditional civil policing is possible. Given this challenge, the Iraqi policing strategy will likely need to follow an evolutionary process, much like the police experience in Northern Ireland.

At the height of The Troubles, the police in certain parts of Belfast were restricted to responding to calls from the public and conducting limited patrols. As many as 16 British Army soldiers were required to support just two police officers on patrol, when under normal conditions these police would patrol alone. Over time, as the security situation began to improve, police officers conducted patrols in groups of two armored vehicles with three officers in each. Later, police could patrol in armored SUVs, and today police officers are starting to patrol on bicycles in what used to be the most dangerous neighborhoods. This transformation did not happen quickly; the British Army only recently ended its support to police activities in Northern Ireland after 38 years of military operations. Reductions in the military presence supporting police activities in Northern Ireland were linked to increased security on the ground, which in turn was the result of increasing political stability over time.

> ***Recommendation:*** *The Civilian Police Assistance Transition Team should work closely with the Ministry of Interior and Ministry of Defense to develop a detailed strategic plan to transition primary responsibility for internal security in Iraq from the Iraqi Army to the Iraqi Police Service.*

Working closely with the ministries of Interior and Defense, the Civilian Police Assistance Transition Team should help the Government of Iraq develop a detailed plan to shift primacy for Iraq's internal security from the Iraqi Army to the Iraqi Police Service. This plan should outline core policing principles as well as milestones for the evolution of the policing process. One core principle should be the requirement that an Iraqi police officer is always the face of a patrol for the public, and is in charge of the patrol, regardless of the size of the military escort. Another core principle should be that the military provides a secure platform to enable police to execute their primary function of upholding the rule of law until that secure platform is no longer necessary. This kind of strategic plan would include benchmarks to assess the evolution of policing away from the Army and toward the Iraqi Police Service. Such benchmarks might include the ability to replace Army units with police personnel without loss of control over an area, or the ability to rely on military capabilities only for specialized functions such as helicopter support. Whatever the milestones, a central concept in the policing plan needs to be the establishment of civil policing as the standard. Even if for many years this civil police force can function only with substantial military support, as was the case in Northern Ireland, the concept of a civil police force responsible for public security must be instituted from the outset as a societal norm.

> ***Conclusion:*** The Iraqi Police Service is incapable today of providing security at a level sufficient to protect Iraqi neighborhoods from insurgents and sectarian violence. The police are central to the long-term establishment of security in Iraq. To be effective in combating the threats that officers face, including sectarian violence, the Iraqi Police Service must be better trained and equipped. The Commission believes that the Iraqi Police Service can improve rapidly should the Ministry of Interior become a more functional institution.

Chapter 9: The National Police

Despite efforts to reform the Iraqi National Police, the organization remains a highly sectarian element of the Iraqi Security Forces and one that for the most part is unable to contribute to security and stability in Iraq. The Iraqi National Police is almost exclusively Shi'a. Trained for counterinsurgency operations, the force is constituted largely of former soldiers. The National Police suffers from significant quality problems and a lack of clarity about whether it should be a paramilitary or a police organization.

Overview of the Iraqi National Police

In addition to the Iraqi Police Service, Iraq also has just over 25,000 National Police, organized into two divisions. Intended to serve as a bridging force between the Iraqi Police Service and the Iraqi Army, the National Police is widely viewed as highly sectarian and is mistrusted by the Iraqi Police Service, the Iraqi Army, and the Iraqi public.

The roots of the National Police are varied. As the insurgency in Iraq grew more violent toward the end of 2003, the Coalition decided to create what it called "heavy police units" using former Iraqi soldiers. These public order battalions and the Emergency Response Unit (ERU) were composed largely of Sunnis and reported to the Ministry of Interior (MOI). In September 2004, under the leadership of Interior Minister Bayan Jabr, the MOI created Special Police Commandos that were largely Shi'a units; then in January 2005, the MOI created the 1st Special Police Mechanized Brigade.[167] In April 2006, Multi-National Security Transition Command–Iraq persuaded the MOI to combine all of these different units into a single organization, the National Police. The Shi'a-dominated Special Police Commandos became the 1st National Police Division, and the public order battalions became the 2nd National Police Division.

Like the Iraqi Police Service, the National Police is part of the Ministry of Interior. The National Police Commander is Major General Hussein al-Awadi, who reports to Minister of Interior Jawad al-Bolani. The National Police today comprises eight brigades organized into two divisions, a single mechanized brigade, a quick reaction force battalion, and a national-level Emergency Response Unit containing about 600 personnel. The Coalition has trained more than 31,000 National Police, but it appears that only about 25,000 are still serving. National Police missions include counterterrorism and counterinsurgency operations, military assistance for civil disturbances, and protection of high-level dignitaries. The original concept for the National Police was to use it as a reinforcement force for the Iraqi Police Service. If an incident in a province could not be adequately addressed by local police, the MOI could deploy a National Police brigade to assist and bring the situation under control. If the National Police and the police combined still could not bring the situation under control, the

MOI could request deployment of Iraqi Army forces. In this way the National Police was conceived as being employed domestically in a fashion somewhat similar to how the National Guard can be used in the United States, but it is not clear whether the National Police in its current form can execute this kind of mission effectively.

Figure 19: MOI National Police Forces' Operational Readiness [Omitted]

The National Police achieved 100 percent of its authorized equipment levels at the end of 2006. National Police personnel are outfitted with small arms, medium machine guns, rocket-propelled grenades, and body armor. National Police units have light, medium, and heavy pickup trucks, as well as sport utility vehicles. In recognition of the need for heavier equipment, given National Police involvement in counterinsurgency operations, plans have been made to up-armor more than 1,300 of the SUVs and trucks.[168] The 1st Mechanized National Police Brigade has approximately 60 M-1117 armored security vehicles, 50 Ukrainian armored personnel carriers derived from the Soviet BTR-80, and 115 South African-made Reva armored personnel carriers. In the future, the National Police aspires to have rotary wing aircraft, cargo planes, more armored vehicles, mortars, mine detectors, and unmanned aerial vehicles, but it is not clear when or whether this equipment will be acquired.

Until late 2006, training for the National Police was not standardized, and it focused largely on counterinsurgency and paramilitary operations. In October 2006, the Coalition removed the entire 8th Brigade of the 2nd National Police Division from operations and arrested its officers, who were implicated in the kidnapping of 26 Sunnis and the death of 7 of those individuals. This incident made clear the need for standardized training and reorientation of the National Police. Multi-National Security Transition Command–Iraq launched the National Police Transformation Program, which in its initial stages included limited vetting and three weeks of traditional police training—the first police training that any members of the National Police had received.

The National Police Headquarters, in cooperation with the Civilian Police Assistance Transition Team, now operates three major training facilities. New recruits undergo six weeks of basic training at the National Police Academy in Numiniyah. Basic, officer, and noncommissioned officer training is offered at Camp Solidarity, located in northern Baghdad. Finally, more specialized training, such as SWAT (special weapons and tactics) training and Emergency Response Unit training, is offered at Camp Dublin, just south of Baghdad. The Civilian Police Assistance Transition Team started a mandatory four-week training course to address concerns about National Police activities after the 8th Brigade was taken out of operations. This process, sometimes referred to as "re-bluing," is a month-long basic training program in policing skills, such as human rights training and policing in a democracy, as well as tactical training, such as patrolling and checkpoint operation.[169] All nine National Police brigades will have completed the re-bluing training by early October 2007.

Multi-National Security Transition Command–Iraq and Multi-National Corps-Iraq provide important technical advice, training, and mentoring to the National Police. The Civilian Police Assistance Transition Team plays a key role in National Police training and capacity building within the MOI to support the National Police. Multi-National Corps-Iraq is responsible for 41 National Police Transition Teams, 38 of which are partnered with National Police battalions, as well as 2 teams that are partnered with the division headquarters, and 1 team assisting National Police Headquarters. Fourteen international police advisors work with the National Police. The National Police Transition Teams work with National Police units on a daily basis, providing mentoring and assistance in the field. A major recent focus for the Civilian Police Assistance Transition Team and the National Police Transition Teams has been implementing the first two phases of the four-phase National Police Transformation Program. Under Phase 1, the National Police Transition Teams conducted technical inspections of each of the National Police battalions to identify deficiencies in areas such as personnel accountability, uniforms, fuel supplies, spare parts, and maintenance capabilities. The teams also conducted quick-look inspections and command climate surveys to get a more qualitative assessment of the National Police units.

Challenges for the National Police

The National Police is the subject of considerable concern both inside and outside Iraq. The Commission was struck by the almost universally negative descriptions of the National Police voiced by Iraqi police, Army officers, and members of the general public. The National Police has been regularly accused of sectarian abuse and illegal activities. Reports of Iraqi security forces' involvement in death squad activities have most frequently been traced to this organization, particularly its former commando units.[170] Members of the National Police were also heavily implicated in the 2005 prisoner torture scandal, and the most recent former Commanding General of Multi-National Security Transition Command–Iraq, Lieutenant General Martin Dempsey, remarked in late 2006 that "the National Police is the biggest worry, about 20 to 25 percent of them probably need to be weeded out."[171] The Commission also observed that the Coalition's sheer need for large numbers of security forces to bring the fight to al Qaeda in Iraq (AQI) and the militias may be hindering its ability to consider, in partnership with the Government of Iraq, what makes the most sense for the future of the National Police.

> ***Finding:*** *In its current form, the National Police is not a viable organization. Its ability to be effective is crippled by significant challenges, including public distrust, sectarianism (both real and perceived), and a lack of clarity about its identity—specifically, whether it is a military or a police force.*

Sectarianism

National Police members are largely recruited from Baghdad and the largely Shi'a southern provinces of Iraq. Efforts to recruit Sunni men into the National Police have generally been unsuccessful. As a result, the National Police force is 85 percent Shi'a, 13 percent Sunni, and 2 percent other affiliations; given its composition and past activities, it is widely perceived as highly sectarian.

In an effort to curb sectarian behavior, the National Police Commander has recently replaced 8 of 9 brigade commanders and 17 of 27 battalion commanders—but serious perception problems remain. As part of the Baghdad Security Plan that began in February 2007, two National Police battalions were supposed to deploy to Baghdad, one from the northern part of Iraq and another from the Tikrit/Samarra region, but ultimately political resistance prevented their transfer.[172]

The Commission heard police chiefs and senior police officials describe the National Police as "very sectarian," "making daily mistakes with the Iraqi people," "a burden on the MOI," and "not a national force at all." Even with the re-bluing training largely completed, sectarianism in the National Police may still be more than just a perception problem. The MOI is seeking to establish an additional National Police brigade in Samarra; but while the National Police leadership has proposed that its composition be 45 percent Sunni and 55 percent Shi'a, the Office of the Commander in Chief (which reports directly to the Prime Minister) has proposed that the personnel be 1 percent Sunni and 99 percent Shi'a.[173]

Quality

The National Police faces many of the same challenges in maintaining quality forces as do the Iraqi Army and Iraqi Police Service. For example, the National Police struggles to ensure that sufficient personnel are present for duty; the existence of ghost payrolling also complicates determinations of present-for-duty numbers at any given time. And like the other forces, the National Police faces a shrinking pool of quality recruits, it lacks sufficient leaders and noncommissioned officers, and it does not have an effective logistics system.

Of the approximately 25,000 National Police authorized by the MOI, on average only about 65 percent are actually present for duty on a given day. While a handful of National Police units are assigned a full complement of personnel, only two of these units have more than 80 percent of their assigned personnel present for duty.

Meetings with Civilian Police Assistance Transition Team officials highlighted additional quality concerns regarding the National Police. The pool of sufficiently high quality recruits is shrinking; identifying literate recruits has become a big challenge. In 2007 the replenishment goal for the National Police is 14,000 recruits—more than half of the entire standing National Police force. Unless this replenishment goal is an aberration, the high percentage of new recruits annually will make it hard to maintain the quality of the National Police over time. The absence of sufficient leaders is another serious concern for the National Police, where officer strength is less than 45 percent of what is authorized by the MOI. Like the Iraqi military, the National Police does not have noncommissioned officers, who could assume some of the leadership responsibilities in the organization. Finally, like the Iraqi military and Iraqi Police Service, the National Police lacks a functioning logistics or supply chain management system. As a result, the National Police struggles to maintain and repair equipment, and its operational readiness is degraded.

Future Missions and Command and Control Arrangements

There is considerable debate within the Coalition and in the broader defense community about the future of the National Police. Should it be a light infantry, a counterinsurgency force, or a civil police force? The National Police has largely been trained as a counterinsurgency force, although the Phase 2 re-bluing training places much greater emphasis on traditional police activities and includes a focus on human rights and the rule of law. At the same time, Phase 3 training under the National Police Transformation Plan is centered on a 90-day course with an emphasis on counterinsurgency operations. Presentations from Iraqis on the future of the National Police tended to emphasize "preventing rebellions," undertaking counterterrorism operations, and preventing the movement and activities of militias.[174] The lack of clarity surrounding the National Police mission is further reflected in how the National Police is equipped. An American general noted that "we ask the National Police to fight as Iraqi Army, but they are equipped like regular police."

Command and control arrangements for the National Police are part of the broader debate about this organization's future. Some argue that the MOI needs a set of security forces under its control that can deploy nationwide, but the National Police is not well-embedded in the ministry. There are five deputy ministers in the MOI, one of whom is responsible for security, including the provincial police—but this deputy minister is not responsible for the National Police. The National Police commander reports directly to the Minister, an arrangement that may, whether fairly or unfairly, fuel perceptions of sectarianism. Others argue that the National Police is essentially composed of soldiers, not police, and should be brought under the Ministry of Defense. Senior police officials noted that under the Baghdad Security Plan, the National Police in Baghdad are already under the operational control of the Ministry of Defense.

> ***Recommendation:*** *The National Police should be disbanded and reorganized under the MOI. It should become a much smaller organization under a different name with responsibility for highly specialized police tasks such as explosive ordnance disposal, urban search and rescue, special threat action, and other similar functions.*

Although the National Police cannot be effective in their current form, there is a need for the Ministry of Interior to have a security force under its control that can augment provincial police forces when necessary. The MOI, with support from the Civilian Police Assistance Transition Team, should dissolve the National Police and draw on a portion of its former personnel to establish a network of National Emergency Support Teams (NESTs), with one team in each province. To avoid many of the problems with the current National Police, NEST units should be ethnically and religiously diverse and should reflect the population makeup of their provinces.

These NEST teams would focus on providing capabilities to the police forces in each province that are necessary but too specialized in most instances to be maintained at the local level—for example, explosive ordnance disposal; consequence management for chemical, biological, nuclear, or radiological events; urban search and rescue; air support; marine/riverine patrol; and civil disturbance response. To sustain the high level of capabilities associated with these specialized missions, NEST teams would require specialized training and equipment similar to that available to the existing national-level Emergency Response Unit.

The NEST teams, while provindally based, could be deployed nationally if an area of the country needed substantial infusions of specialized capability. If deploying to assist the Iraqi Police Service, provincial NEST teams should come under the authority of the local police commander.

The existing national-level Emergency Response Unit in the National Police contains 600 personnel. The Civilian Police Assistance Transition Team personnel spoke highly of the ERU and indicated that it was a very competent organization. If each province were to have a NEST team of about 300 people, the overall size of the NEST network would be about 6,000 personnel—only 25 percent of the existing National Police force. Former National Police personnel that did not remain as part of the NEST forces could be readily absorbed into the Iraqi Army or the Iraqi Police Service.

In light of the sectarian problems that have plagued the National Police, it would be important to ensure that all former National Police members seeking to transfer to the Iraqi Army or Iraqi Police Service are sufficiently vetted prior to being accepted into either of those organizations.

Conclusion: The National Police have proven operationally ineffective. Sectarianism in its units undermines its ability to provide security; the force is not viable in its current form. The National Police should be disbanded and reorganized.

Chapter 10: The Department of Border Enforcement

The Iraqi Department of Border Enforcement and the Ports of Entry Directorate are showing uneven but improved capabilities in some locations in Iraq. Although both entities have some effective top-level leadership and have improved Iraqi border security since 2003, considerable challenges remain. For example, the Ministry of Interior (MOI), which oversees the Department of Border Enforcement (DBE), does not have authority over the nation's sea and air ports of entry. In addition, border forts, border fort annexes, and land ports of entry have only modest levels of the basic equipment they need for their personnel and daily operations, and they lack the larger pieces of equipment necessary for inspecting and monitoring the people and cargo crossing the nation's borders. Border enforcement personnel often work in conditions lacking adequate life support services and are without sufficient logistical support to meet requirements. The importance of effective border enforcement to Iraq's overall security necessitates substantial improvements in these areas and a significantly greater sense of urgency on the part of the Iraqi central government and Ministry of Interior, as well as the continued assistance of Coalition Border Transition Teams for the foreseeable future.

Overview of the Department of Border Enforcement

Iraq has 2,268 miles of land border in addition to 36 miles of coastline. Although the Department of Border Enforcement existed during the Saddam era, border security functions at that time were performed mainly by the Iraqi military and the comprehensive network of secret police. At present, the Department of Border Enforcement has a force of only 37,710 personnel to secure the border.[175]

In the wake of the 2003 invasion, the Coalition and the Government of Iraq built the new Department of Border Enforcement from scratch.[176] The Iraqi Department of Border Enforcement, which was created under Coalition Provisional Authority Order 26 on August 24, 2003, is part of the Ministry of Interior.[177] Although the MOI is responsible for all border forts, annexes, and land ports of entry, the Ministry of Transportation (MOT) maintains control over sea and air ports of entry. On several occasions, both Coalition and Iraqi officials told the Commission that the reasons for this division of responsibilities have more to do with ministries consolidating power than with advancing the overall mission of border security. Eventually, they agreed, all ports of entry should be under the MOI's domain.[178] Accordingly, in 2008 the responsibility for air and sea ports of entry will shift to the MOI.

The Director of the Department of Border Enforcement is Major General Moshen, whom Coalition officials view as resourceful, effective, and an excellent administrator. Brigadier General Farhoud, who was acting director for the Ports of Entry Directorate when the Commission first visited, is also very highly regarded. He had been replaced by Brigadier General Ali by the time of a subsequent visit. Despite the current strength of its top-level leadership, the department has experienced a high level of turnover. For example, as of July 2007, the Ports of Entry Directorate had functioned under 10 different directors in a 15-month period.[179]

The Department of Border Enforcement is organized into five divisions, one for each of Iraq's five geographic regions (as determined by the department). Each division has two to three brigades.[180] Today, there are a total of 12 brigades and 42 battalions, 38 of which are dependent on Coalition support.[181] At present, there are 258 Coalition-constructed and supported border forts, 112 department-constructed annexes, and another 47 annexes under departmental construction. The Department of Border Enforcement and its Coalition partners have a five-year plan to bring the total number of constructed border forts and annexes to 723,[182] and to reduce the distance between forts to an average of 6 to 9 miles.

The Department of Border Enforcement generally recruits from local populations near its facilities to man land border crossings. Some current border enforcement agents are former Ba'athist-era military, and most joined the Department of Border Enforcement because its jobs are considered easier and safer than those in the Iraqi Army. The Department of Border Enforcement addressed chronic personnel shortages in 2006 by cross-leveling manpower from existing Department of Border Enforcement facilities and by increasing hires. As a result, staffing levels are now at 98 percent across the department and its facilities, though its personnel are not necessarily equally trained. The Department of Border Enforcement did not establish a comprehensive training program until August 2004, and its training capacity remains modest.[183]

While the Department of Border Enforcement has overall authority for Iraqi border security, the Ports of Entry Directorate is the component within the Department of Border Enforcement that has responsibility for the land ports of entry into the country. The Ports of Entry Directorate was only recently moved under the jurisdiction of the Department of Border Enforcement, but it was transferred without a budget—an oversight that presents a significant problem. Currently, the Department of Border Enforcement is able to provide for some but not all of the Ports of Entry Directorate's needs. There are 17 land ports of entry in Iraq, 12 of which are currently functioning; 4 were closed in February 2007 as part of the enhanced security measures then put into place in an effort to focus border resources on the Iranian and Syrian crossings where they are most urgently needed.[184] One additional crossing at Al Qa'im will open in November 2007. Although some have been closed, other land ports of entry are receiving significant investments. For example, the Ports of Entry Directorate intends to make Al Qa'im on the Syrian border a model border crossing and has invested $21 million into a construction project to make the facility state-of-the-art.[185]

Today the Department of Border Enforcement has about 87 percent of the basic equipment it requires. In some areas, such as firearms and radios, the department appears to have 100 percent of its needed equipment. At the same time, some required equipment has never been issued at all. Equipping rates for the Ports of Entry Directorate are lower—about 68 percent on average, with particular shortages in patrol vehicles, flatbed trucks, uniforms, generators, and body armor.[186] In addition, major items of equipment, including technology-based systems used to track people and cargo coming across the borders, are insufficient in both quantity and quality, as will be detailed later in this chapter.

Multi-National Security Transition Command–Iraq works with the MOI and the Department of Border Enforcement to provide training and advice, primarily through advisors from the U.S. Department of Homeland Security and Border Transition Teams working in the field. Most Border Transition Teams are composed of about 13 personnel—a mix of military personnel, contractors, and DHS employees. Multi-National Security Transition Command–Iraq has identified a total requirement for 70 Border Transition Teams amounting to more than 900 people, but the Coalition has not been able to fill this requirement.[187] Today there are just 28 Border Transition Teams distributed across the Department of Border Enforcement's five geographic regions.

Although Border Transition Teams are stationed throughout Iraq, the Coalition has chosen to focus its 28 existing teams on difficult border crossings and rely on decent relations with countries such as Turkey and Kuwait to ensure sufficient border security in more stable areas.[188] The more successful land ports of entry have Border Transition Teams (also called Ports of Entry Transition Teams) that live and work with their Iraqi counterparts. For example, the port of entry director at Trebil indicated that the Border Transition Team assigned there was critical to their mission, a sentiment echoed by Iraqi officials at the Zurbatiya Port of Entry.

Challenges for the Department of Border Enforcement

The Commission met with several officials in the Iraqi Department of Border Enforcement and the Ports of Entry Directorate, held discussions with many Coalition Border Transition Team advisors, and visited multiple land ports of entry, including Zurbatiya, Trebil, and Walid. Though it is clear that border security is better today than it was in the wake of the invasion, when people and goods flowed unchecked across borders, the Department of Border Enforcement and the Ports of Entry Directorate face significant challenges and are not yet providing adequate border security for Iraq.

Ministry of Interior

> ***Finding:*** *The overall capacity of the Department of Border Enforcement and the Ports of Entry Directorate is undermined by weak MOI capacity. Further, border security commanders have little confidence that the MOI will address their needs and concerns.*

The MOI is often not in control of the land ports of entry under the Ports of Entry Directorate's jurisdiction. The Deputy Minister of Interior for Support Forces, Major General Admed al-Khafaji, told Commissioners that the Kurds, not the MOI, administer the land ports of entry in the Kurdish autonomous region. Even more troubling, in separate meetings with the Director of the Ports of Entry Directorate and Deputy Minister al-Khafaji, it was made clear to the Commission that four land ports of entry in the south are run by militia and are not under MOI control. Furthermore, efforts to install department-assigned directors at those land ports of entry were thwarted by the militia in place. The sea port of entry at Umm Qasr as well as other, smaller sea ports of entry are also reportedly controlled by militia. None of the tariffs collected at these militia-run ports of entry end up in the national coffers, and the Department of Border Enforcement has little insight as to how these ports are administered.

Both the Deputy Director of the Department of Border Enforcement and the Ports of Entry Director also expressed immense frustration with their inability to obtain funding from the MOI for infrastructure development, fuel, ammunition, and personal equipment. Border forts and annexes often experience difficulty getting required fuel and lack reliable access to electrical power. Some border fort commanders pay for fuel out of their own pockets to enable their forces to patrol. In extreme cases, Border Transition Teams have facilitated fuel delivery from Coalition resources. It is common for requests to languish for months at the MOI without explanation, and local commanders are sometimes ignored by the MOI for secular reasons.

> ***Finding:*** *The divided responsibility for land, sea, and air ports of entry between the Ministry of Interior and Ministry of Transportation, together with the lack of unity of effort between these ministries, undermines the effectiveness of the Department of Border Enforcement and the Ports of Entry Directorate.*

The systemic weakness of the MOI is exacerbated by the lack of MOI jurisdiction over Iraq's sea and air ports of entry, which are currently controlled by the Ministry of Transportation. It is the Commission's assessment, based on numerous observations and discussions, that the Ministry of Transportation is equally as corrupt and dysfunctional as the Ministry of Interior. As a result, there are no MOI personnel present to even monitor activities at the sea and air ports of entry, which are likely the entry points for foreign fighters as well as equipment for improvised explosive devices and vehicle-borne improvised explosive devices, and are the staging grounds for smuggling operations.[189]

Even at those land ports of entry where the MOI is responsible for border security, the lack of definition regarding ministerial responsibilities continues to undermine border security. Land ports of entry, though under MOI authority, involve up to 15 other ministries with border security–related functions. When the MOI appoints a port director, for example, that individual typically has no control over the non-MOI ministries and agencies (Finance, Transportation, Customs, Justice, etc.) that also operate at the border crossing. Without unity of command, or even unity of effort between the MOI, MOT, and other ministries, the Ports of Entry Directorate personnel have no choice but to compete for authority with representatives of other ministries.

> ***Recommendation:*** *The Government of Iraq should establish clear guidelines to facilitate unity of effort between the MOI and MOT for border security and move quickly to consolidate overall responsibility for border security under the MOI.*

Bringing unity of effort and centralized authority to all Iraqi ports of entry—land, sea, and air—will likely require the direct involvement of the Deputy Minister of Interior for Support Forces, the Minister of Interior, and possibly the attention of the Prime Minister as well. Because the current division of responsibility between the MOI and the MOT regarding land, sea, and air ports of entry has more to do with politics than with a logical, functional division of labor, a solution will not come overnight. In the near term, a good start would be allowing MOI personnel to work with MOT personnel at sea and air ports of entry and to participate in some aspects of inspection and administration.

> ***Finding:*** *The MOI has not created standardized concepts of operations, operating procedures, or processes for the Ports of Entry Directorate to apply at Iraq's land ports of entry; each appears to be run according to the initiative—or lack thereof—of the local commander.*

Policies and procedures at land ports of entry often defy logic. For example, at land ports of entry with Iran and Jordan, the contents of trucks from those nations are loaded into Iraqi-licensed vehicles and driven by Iraqi drivers through the land port of entry. Since the invasion in 2003, this downloading at the Iranian border has been conducted on the Iranian side of the border behind berms and fencing that block the view of Iraqi security forces. When the Iraqi trucks subsequently arrive at the Iraqi border, the inspections are cursory at best. Commissioners witnessed officials looking at the documentation provided by the driver and occasionally opening the door of a tractor-trailer, looking inside a van, or climbing over the loaded cargo. However, there was no evidence of cranes or forklifts to offload and inspect cargo. Although the coordination now occurring between

Iraqi and Jordanian land ports of entry will likely result in some improved efficiency, steady gains in effectiveness nationwide are unlikely absent standardized procedures and processes across all land ports of entry.

Equipment

> ***Finding:*** *Many land ports of entry have neither the quantity nor the quality of monitoring and detection systems required for border security operations to function effectively.*

The distribution of major security equipment to track people and goods crossing the borders at land ports of entry throughout the five regions is uneven and inadequate. Most land ports of entry use outdated, inefficient systems to monitor cargo and track people.[190] At many border crossings, even this substandard equipment is either broken or nonexistent, as the Commission observed during visits to Zurbatiya, Trebil, and Walid. Backscatter radars, if assigned, are often inoperable, and there is a dire lack of the forklifts or cranes required to access cargo for inspection. The Commission saw no logical method for apportioning even this outdated equipment. Further, even if adequate and functioning systems were in place to screen cargo and track people, loopholes would remain. For example, there are limited mechanisms in place for the personnel working at the border crossings to share intelligence with local police, so that even a functioning watch list might prove somewhat ineffectual.

Lack of adequate security equipment has an immediate impact on the Ports of Entry Directorate's capacity to function. The Deputy Director of the Department of Border Enforcement estimated that 95 percent of all traffic entering or leaving Iraq by land passes through the land ports of entry. However, only a small amount of all traffic entering these ports of entry is inspected. Port directors do not have adequate technical or mechanical means to inspect a higher volume, and the lack of technological solutions and equipment causes huge backups at the land ports of entry—waiting lines of vehicles from neighboring countries sometimes exceed 10 miles. When commissioners visited the crossing at Walid, the backup from Iraq to Syria was estimated at 15 miles, and Border Transition Team members at Trebil on the Jordanian border estimated the wait to enter Iraq at three weeks.

> ***Recommendation:*** *The Coalition should continue to emphasize to the MOI that the territorial integrity of the country relies heavily on the Department of Border Enforcement's ability to secure the borders and that funding for detection and monitoring equipment for those forces should be accorded a very high priority to increase the effectiveness and efficiency of ports of entry security forces.*

The Ports of Entry Directorate requires facilities, infrastructure, and equipment that can better check incoming personnel and cargo at the land ports of entry; its needs include concrete ramps, tarmacs, and space to conduct inspections as well as equipment such as forklifts, cranes, backscatter radar, lighting systems, and metal detectors that will enable personnel to inspect cargo. Indeed, current backscatter systems may not be sufficiently rugged or powerful enough to make an impact at Iraqi border crossings. Gamma-ray scanners such as the VACIS machine—often used in the United States—would be more useful, but also far more costly for the MOI. A senior Ports of Entry Directorate official told the Commission that if Iraqi land ports of entry were equipped with even 10 percent of the equipment used by neighboring countries, the ports of entry would function adequately.[191] In addition to direct inspection equipment, the Department of Border Enforcement needs technical solutions such as electronic surveillance to monitor sections of the borders not covered by the department's current forts and annexes. In short, infiltration of foreign fighters, contraband, and weapons through the land ports of entry will likely continue until the necessary equipment, technology, and personnel to screen and inspect a greater percentage of incoming traffic and people are provided.

Support Systems

> ***Finding:*** *The Department of Border Enforcement lacks sufficient logistics, support systems, and infrastructure to sustain many of its forces in the field.*

Many of the logistics and support system challenges that plague the Army and other elements of the Iraqi security forces are also major problems for the Department of Border Enforcement. Maintaining equipment can be difficult, particularly because in some areas it is simply too dangerous to move vehicles and other large pieces of equipment to repair facilities. Centralization of distribution in the MOI can mean that access to appropriate quantities and types of arms and ammunition is impeded. Weapons are obtained by submitting a request memo to the director general of logistics, and units must pick up the requested goods at the MOI in Baghdad. Obtaining fuel is similarly complex, time-consuming, and bureaucratic. Logistics support exists at the local level with little assistance from the MOI. Port directors and Department of Border Enforcement commanders are generally left to their own devices to support their forces with what little money they receive from the central government.

Finally, living conditions and capacity appear problematic in some border stations. In some regions, there are significant challenges related to poor life support services and lack of area Forward Operating Bases, particularly in the southeast. There is also significant unevenness in quality among the installations at different ports of entry—ranging from adequate infrastructure and staffing at some to a lack of even basic buildings at others.[192]

> ***Recommendation:*** *Coalition forces should strongly encourage the Department of Border Enforcement to implement its national Headquarters Distribution Plan while continuing to provide logistical and maintenance*

support in the near term so that Department of Border Enforcement and ports of entry personnel can accomplish their mission.

The Department of Border Enforcement needs to establish a logistics system that is driven from the top down, satisfies the requirements of provincial and local commands, and accounts fully for all personal and unit equipment. Central to this system is a mechanism that reduces the need to travel great distances from the Department of Border Enforcement forts and annexes for vehicle maintenance. Another important element of a functioning distribution and support system would be a communications network that links Department of Border Enforcement locations with one another and with the nearest land ports of entry, providing a means to pass intelligence between port directors, Department of Border Enforcement and Ports of Entry Directorate personnel, and the MOI. This system should also be centrally linked to the Iraqi Army and police.

Corruption

Finding: *Corruption is a serious problem at many land ports of entry. This fact has not yet been adequately addressed.*

Corruption continues to erode the territorial integrity of Iraq by reducing the ability of the central government to legitimately collect import tariffs, by enabling contraband to pass undetected, and by undermining the efforts of the Department of Border Enforcement. The Commission found that even points of entry under Iraqi and Coalition control suffer from pervasive corruption. In addition, the presence of several ministries at a single land port of entry fosters corruption because multiple parties at each land port of entry can maneuver for a cut of a particular type of good (e.g., agricultural commodities). Moreover, it is likely that at least some ministries view border crossings permissively once they receive their own share of kickbacks. In addition, Iraqi and Coalition officials told the Commission that personnel at the border crossings are often discouraged from doing their jobs "too well," lest they disrupt lucrative smuggling operations that benefit senior-level officers in the MOI. To address these issues, the central government has changed leadership in some areas, taken punitive action in some instances, and at times has even sent delegations to try to address corruption at the border crossings, but these efforts have not been particularly successful.[193] Coalition forces are trying to stem existing corruption by training all border crossing personnel to a common standard and by using a "train the trainers" approach.

Two additional areas that provide ample opportunity for corruption are the taxation of people and goods entering the country and the transportation of fuel across the border.[194] Border Transition Team members told the Commission that large amounts of tax revenues never make it to the MOI, and in some cases tax revenues that arrive at the MOI are not ultimately deposited in the national treasury.[195] Transport of refined fuel into Iraq is another major source of corruption. The movement of fuel back and forth across borders for refinement and distribution provides ample opportunities for payoffs and fuel "skimming." Efforts to reduce opportunities for tampering with fuel distribution have been rejected as too expensive, but such dismissals may simply reflect an unwillingness to build new systems that reduce opportunities for corruption.

> ***Recommendation:*** *Eliminating corruption will most likely be a generational undertaking in Iraq, but Multi-National Security Transition Command–Iraq, Multi-National Corps-Iraq, and civilian agencies should work together to try to increase Border Transition Team oversight of Department of Border Enforcement and Ports of Entry Directorate facilities, as well as to develop a standardized training program emphasizing leadership and professional ethics.*

Some short-term solutions can be put in place, such as an increased Border Transition Team presence at land ports of entry and more consistent punitive actions for those involved in corrupt practices at the border. However, corruption cannot be eliminated with a single training course or the implementation of an isolated new policy. It is a pervasive problem that will require real change within the Department of Border Enforcement and increased capacity—and, more importantly, will—in the MOI to exert central government authority over Iraqi border security.

> ***Conclusion:*** Iraq's borders are porous. The Department of Border Enforcement suffers from poor ministerial support from the MOI. Border forces often lack the equipment, infrastructure, and basic supplies to conduct their mission. Overall border security is further undermined by the division of responsibilities between the MOI and the Ministry of Transportation. Corruption and external influence and infiltration are widespread. Absent major improvements in all these areas, Iraq's borders will remain porous and poorly defended.

Chapter 11: Concluding Observations

Having responded to our Congressional tasking, the Commission would like to offer some additional thoughts relative to the findings and conclusions of our work. Though we were not asked specifically to comment on such related subjects as Iraqi governance, or the general trends associated with our ongoing national efforts, the three weeks the Commission spent on the ground in Iraq, coupled with the extraordinary access it was provided, enabled Commissioners to arrive at informed opinions with regard to the overall trends on Iraq. This final chapter offers a compendium of our thinking on the subject and provides some answers to the unasked question: "What does this all mean in terms of the future in Iraq?"

Assessment Recap. Though the overwhelming conclusion of the Commission is that the Iraqi government holds the key to the most pressing problem of sectarian violence, the progress of the Iraqi Army is certainly real. It is, however, limited to an increased capability to combat the internal security threats in Iraq. While still lacking in combat support and combat service support capabilities, the new Iraqi armed forces (most especially the Army) show clear evidence of developing the baseline infrastructures that lead to the successful formation of a national defense capability.

The Ministry of Defense is assessed as being one of the better functioning agencies of the Iraqi government. There is evidence to show that the emerging Iraqi soldier is willing to fight against the declared enemies of the state, with some exceptions remaining along ethnic lines. The Commission concurs with the view expressed by U.S., Coalition, and Iraqi experts that the Iraqi Army is capable of taking over an increasing amount of day-to-day combat responsibilities from Coalition forces. While a more advanced ability to function independently remains in the future, there is currently great focus on the requirements and capabilities necessary to achieve this long-term goal.

As the pace of development continues, we wish to underscore that the standard for acceptable Iraqi military readiness should not be "mirror imaged" to the U.S. standard. "Good enough" in terms of Iraqi military capabilities will indeed be "good enough." This is particularly true with regard to the development of logistics capacities.

The difference between the new Iraqi Army's ability to meet and overcome internal threats vice being capable of defending Iraq against external aggression is significant and must be well understood. While Iraq's Army, in particular, is moving toward greater capacity to achieve the former capability, the latter remains a future goal. This is to be expected, given the relatively short timeframe and the enormous task of rebuilding the Iraqi armed forces, which were defeated in 2003 and dismantled by Coalition Provisional Authority (CPA) policy directive.

The Commission noted the adverse effects of duplicate chains of command and intelligence structures within the government and concludes that they are redundant and unnecessary. They also fuel the perceptions of mistrust and sectarianism throughout the national defense community.

Offsetting the positive direction of the armed forces and the Ministry of Defense is the less positive trend of Iraqi police development, and the distinctly negative trend found in the Ministry of Interior. Sectarian partisanship, bureaucratic inefficiency, the Ministry of Interior's reputation for corruption, a near universal rejection of the National Police as currently formed and administered, and a weak and ineffective Department of Border Enforcement continue to impede Iraq's overall progress towards security and stability.

Bureaucratic bungling and ministerial incapacity are often perceived as intentional acts of sectarian bias. Achieving competence and transparency in ministerial operations and decision-making can ease this problem. While there have been some recent efforts by the Minister of Interior to reshape his ministry, much remains to be done.

The most visible sign of police success remains at the local level, where police units are organized along ethnic lines representative of their communities. The Commission believes that it should be acceptable for local police to reflect the ethno-sectarian makeup of the communities they serve. This pragmatic accommodation may be necessary until such time that national reconciliation efforts have succeeded in making sectarian and ethnic associations secondary to a prevailing sense of Iraqi national identity. The makeup of Iraq's police forces is key to bringing stability to the neighborhoods. Unfortunately, the Commission cannot report favorably on the current situation. This is due in large part to the government's failure to achieve consensus in establishing policies and practices that promote national reconciliation.

There are still too few indications that police units, the armed forces, and their respective ministries, work well together in the aggregate. National reconciliation efforts must recognize and seek to address perceptions, whether fact or fiction, that fuel sectarian animosity by improving ministerial capacity, increasing governmental transparency, and establishing more effective lines of communication between the government and all constituencies.

The Commission wishes to underscore the problems and delays associated with the U.S. Foreign Military Sales system, as other official visitors to Iraq have recently reported. Any prolonged delays in providing equipment for which the Iraqi government has already paid directly hampers progress in developing Iraq's military capabilities. The Commission was surprised by the magnitude of the Foreign Military Sales problem in Iraq, and noted the extreme frustration it has caused our military commanders and the Iraqi government. The Department of Defense and the Department of State have been made aware of this problem. Commissioners who have significant career experience with the Foreign Military Sales system believe it is in need of major reform if it is to support our global policies. Foreign Military Sales as a national program is in need of overall reform, a fact well known to those of us who have served previously in senior positions.

The Surge. Much has been said about "the surge" in operations in the Baghdad region. Though not fully recognized, there have always been two principal participants in the implementation of this tactic; the Iraqi Security Forces and Coalition forces. The Iraqi component of the surge began in January 2007, and the U.S. surge contribution became operational in May of this year. The Commission wishes to underscore that the surge should not be viewed as the introduction of a new strategy. It is more accurate to describe it as a tactic supporting our overall national strategy in Iraq.

The surge, if successful, will play an important role in enabling the evolution of our strategy. There are signs of encouraging tactical successes in the Baghdad capital region, which remains the epicenter of enemy focus and of their competing strategy. Unable to achieve conventional military victory, the opposing forces must rely on spectacular bombing attacks on innocent Iraqi citizens, as well as ISF and Coalition forces. As the international media is mostly Baghdad-based, successful attacks receive disproportionate coverage relative to some very real progress achieved in other areas of the country, such as Anbar province. The result, unfortunately, is enemy momentum in the battle of strategic messaging despite the growing popular rejection of terrorist ideology in that region. The people's outrage at al Qaeda's savagery and their realization that it is a movement not of liberation but of occupation, has helped transform this province from being the most violent to being one of the least violent in Iraq. Coupled with the emerging capabilities of the Iraqi Security Forces and the promise of the Coalition's "clear, hold, and build" tactic, there are some encouraging indications of a positive trend in this region.

Strategic Shift. The strategic implications of such continuing successes are encouraging. Coalition forces could begin to be adjusted, realigned, and re-tasked as the Iraqi Army is able to take on more responsibility for daily combat operations. The Commission finds it reasonable to believe that such adjustments could begin in early 2008, depending on the continuing rate of progress of the Iraqi Security Forces.

The circumstances of the moment may continue to present the opportunity for considering a shift in the disposition and employment of our forces. This could be characterized as a transition to a "strategic overwatch" posture. Such a strategy would include placing increasing responsibilities for the internal security of the nation on the ISF, especially in the urban areas. Coalition forces could be re-tasked to better ensure the territorial defense of the state by increasingly concentrating on the eastern and western borders and the active defense of the critical infrastructures essential to Iraq. Existing threats from Syria, coupled with the alarming increase in Iranian presence, and their combined threats to Iraq's stability, more than justify new strategic thinking. Though Iraq's armed forces are currently incapable of countering both internal security missions and the nation's external threats simultaneously, the Commission believes that the Iraqi Army has taken an important first step in proving its increasing competence in combating the nation's internal threats. The next step will come in time.

The Commission concludes that the evidence of Iran's increasing activism in the southeastern part of the country, including Basra and Diyala provinces, is compelling. Left unaddressed, this escalating threat will most certainly have the effect of delaying efforts to resolve sectarian difficulties, provide security and stability in the nation, stimulate economic reform, enhance the rule of law, and fight corruption. The current rise of the Jaysh al-Mahdi in the region is evident, and the Iranian influence over the militant arm of this militia is increasing. It is an accepted fact that most of the sophisticated weapons being used to "defeat" our armor protection comes across the border from Iran with relative impunity.

The Syrian border is more generally associated with the flow of foreign fighters, who are entering Iraq at an estimated rate of 75–80 per month. There are allegations that training camps for these fighters exist in Syria. Any increased Coalition presence capable of bringing focus to the border regions will help reduce the external threats facing Iraq and, the Commission believes, will cause the two nations in question to reassess their current destabilizing policies and practices. The Commission believes that an "overwatch" strategy, focusing on the border regions, will more comprehensively address the most serious threats facing Iraq. A key to implementing any future plans to assist Iraqi Security Forces lies in maintaining the presence and the critical contributions of the various transition teams assigned by the Coalition to work with, train, and help develop Iraqi Security Force units; they represent indispensable links in our overall effort to transform the ISF.

Perceptions and reality are frequently at odds with each other when trying to understand Iraq's problems and progress. Nowhere is this more apparent than in the impressions drawn from seeing our massive logistics "footprint," our many installations, and the number of personnel (military and civilian), especially in and around the Baghdad region. The unintended message conveyed is one of "permanence," an occupying force, as it were. What is needed is the opposite impression, one that is lighter, less massive, and more expeditionary. The decision to occupy Saddam Hussein's former palace complex with our military headquarters, while expedient in 2003, has most likely given the wrong impression to the Iraqi population. We recommend that careful consideration of the size of our national footprint in Iraq be reconsidered with regard to its efficiency, necessity, and its cost. Significant reductions, consolidations, and realignments would appear to be possible and prudent.

The Commission believes that it would be important to establish an Iraqi-Coalition Transition Headquarters designed to shape, coordinate, and monitor all aspects of transition efforts. Such a headquarters should be composed of Iraqi and Coalition civilian and military personnel, and should be jointly led by senior civilian authorities. In this manner, momentum of transition could be carefully monitored, recorded, and future plans could be more visible than they are at present. For all of its great work, Multi-National Security Transition Command–Iraq is not designed to be such a headquarters, though it would certainly play a critical role were one to be established. Visible and consistent progress toward transition ought to be one of the most important efforts of our presence in Iraq.

Provincial Iraqi Control (PIC). To further reinforce the image that we are not "occupiers" in Iraq, the Commission recommends that consideration be given to implementing two additional efforts. The first is to reform the system by which we transfer authority to the Iraqi government. The current process seeks to apply standard criteria to each of Iraq's 18 provinces in order to determine when total responsibility should be transferred to regional authorities.

To date, 7 out of 18 provinces have been transferred under this system. Upon dose inspection however, the Commission was unable to conclude that current metrics for transfer of control were being uniformly applied to each province. Further, the Commission became convinced that the conditions in many of Iraq's 18 provinces are so diverse that a uniform standard cannot be achieved, to include those pertaining to security and stability. Disparities are most visible when conditions in northern Iraq (Kurdish region) and southern Iraq (Shi'a region) are compared. In the north, three provinces have been transferred to Provisional Iraqi Control and one finds evidence of good governance, stability, security, a functioning police force, a developing economy, and public order. In the south, where four provinces have been transferred to Provisional Iraqi Control, conditions are completely different as evidenced by the rise of the Iranian-influenced Jaysh al-Mahdi, Shi'a-on-Shi'a violence, and excessive militia influence. Recently, as if to underscore the point, two southern governors have been assassinated. Nonetheless, considerations are under way to transfer Basra to Provincial Iraqi Control. Such a decision would be enthusiastically supported by the British Regional Coalition commander (Multi-National

Force-South) who considers his forces to be an impediment to progress in the region.

The Commission believes that each of Iraq's provinces should be transferred to Iraqi control as a matter of policy. The existing PIC system is not an effective vehicle; it is difficult to understand, impossible to apply uniformly, and actually impedes momentum and progress toward goals which should be to cede to Iraqi governmental institutions at the local, regional and national levels as much authority and responsibility as possible.

Such transfer of authority should be supplemented by the necessary levels of mentoring and assistance to ensure success. The Commission has discovered that the Government of Iraq wishes to be given control and responsibility for all of its provinces. Our current policy of determining when a province may or may not be controlled by its own government reinforces the popular perception of the Coalition as an occupation force. This may contribute to increased violence and instability. Granting Iraq full control of its provinces is symbolically important and vests the Iraqi government with the responsibility it needs in order to mature and develop. The workload of the Coalition resulting from such a policy would be unchanged.

The Commission wishes to emphasize that there is a fine line between assistance and dependence. Identifying those areas in which Iraqis can do things on their own, even if in ways different from those we prefer, should be acceptable wherever possible. Additional focus and help in improving the infrastructure of the country, and an increasing capability to ensure general access to basic needs such as water, power, fuel, schools, and public sanitation, will have a large impact in gaining popular support for the central, regional, and local governments.

Status of Forces Agreement. The second recommendation the Commission wishes to offer is that consideration be given to pursuing an agreement akin to a Status of Forces Agreement (SOFA) with the Government of Iraq. Appropriately drawn, it would have the effect of codifying our relationship with the host nation, reinforcing its sovereignty and independence, and would be consistent with other such agreements we enjoy with many nations where we have a military presence. Ancillary to such an agreement, we believe that all our bases in Iraq should demonstrate evidence of Iraqi national sovereignty (Iraqi headquarters and national flag). Placing Iraqi units close to Coalition forces, when and where possible, will have a positive effect on the development of national security forces.

Goals and Benchmarks. Before closing, the Commission emphasizes the vital importance of setting strategic goals, benchmarks, and metrics designed to serve the needs of all "stakeholders," including commanders, public policymakers, and the public. Such goals must be part of all planning and implementation efforts and must be among the most visible aspects of our mission to restore Iraq to its rightful and respectable place among nations.

Concluding Thoughts. The Commission wishes to thank Congress for the opportunity to conduct an independent review of the capabilities of the security forces of Iraq. While much remains to be done before success can be confidently declared, the strategic consequences of failure, or even perceived failure, for the United States and the Coalition are enormous. We approach a truly strategic moment in this still young century. Iraq's regional geo-strategic position, the balance of power in the Middle East, the economic stability made possible by the flow of energy to many parts of the world, and the ability to defeat and contain terrorism where it is most manifest are issues that do not lend themselves to easy or quick solutions. How we respond to them, however, could well define our nation in the eyes of the world for years to come.

At the end of the day, however, the future of Iraq and the prospects for establishing a professional, effective, and loyal military and police service, hinges on the ability of the Iraqi people and the government to begin the process of achieving national reconciliation and to ending sectarian violence. For the time being, all progress seems to flow from this most pressing requirement.

Appendix A: Members of the Commission

General James L. Jones, USMC (Ret.)

General James L. Jones (Ret.) is currently president and CEO of the U.S. Chamber of Commerce's Institute for 21st Century Energy. On February 1, 2007, General Jones completed 40 years of active duty service in the Marine Corps. His most senior assignments in uniform included duties as Commandant of the Marine Corps (1999–2003), Supreme Allied Commander, Europe (2003–2006), and Commander, U.S. European Command (2003–2006). During a period of great transformation of the Alliance's expeditionary capabilities and seeking to increase better agility and mobility in the forward presence of U.S. forces in Europe and Africa, General Jones advocated for greater strategic focus and understanding of the 21st century threats to our nation and to the North Atlantic Treaty Organization.

General John Abrams, USA (Ret.)

General John Abrams, U.S. Army (Ret.), currently serves on the Board of Directors of the Virginia National Defense Industrial Authority. He retired from the U.S. Army in 2003. General Abrams commanded the Army's Training and Doctrine Command and was one of the primary architects of the "Army of the 21st Century." He began his military career as a tank crewman in 1966 and, over the next 36 years, rose from private to four-star general. He is also President of Abrams Learning and Information Systems, Inc.

Lieutenant General Martin R. Berndt, USMC (Ret.)

Lieutenant General Martin R. Berndt (Ret.) retired from the Marine Corps in October 2005, having served for 36 years. He was privileged to serve as an infantry officer in a variety of service and joint billets, completing his career as Commander, U.S. Marine Corps Forces, Atlantic, Europe, and South. He currently serves as a senior mentor to the Marine Corps and U.S. Joint Forces Command. Additionally, he serves on the North Carolina Military Foundation and as a director with several private and public businesses.

General Charles G. Boyd, USAF (Ret.)

General Charles G. Boyd, U.S. Air Force (Ret.), became president and CEO of Business Executives for National Security (BENS) in May of 2002. Before joining BENS, he served as Senior Vice President and Washington Program Director of the Council on Foreign Relations. General Boyd was commissioned through the aviation cadet program in July 1960 and retired in 1995 after 35 years of service. General Boyd was the only Vietnam POW to achieve four-star rank, and his final military assignment was as Deputy Commander of U.S. European Command. Following his retirement from active duty, he served as the director of the 21st Century International Legislators Project for the Congressional Institute, Inc., and strategy consultant to then Speaker of the House Newt Gingrich. He currently serves as a member of the Board of Directors of the Nixon Center; DRS Technologies, Inc.; Forterra Systems, Inc.; and In-Q-Tel.

Command Sergeant Major Dwight J. Brown, USA (Ret.)

Command Sergeant Major Dwight J. Brown, a native of Lexington, Kentucky, enlisted in the Army in January 1973. He is a graduate of the United States Army Sergeant Major Academy, First Sergeants Course, Army Basic Noncommissioned Officer Course, Drill Sergeant School, Operations and Intelligence (Battle Staff) Course, and the Joint Fire Power Air Ground Operations Course. His assignments have included five tours in the Federal Republic of Germany: the 11th Armor Cavalry Regiment, Fulda/Bad Hersfeld; three tours in 1st Armored Division, Katterback/Ansbach, Erlangen, and Bad Kreuznach; and the 8th Infantry Division, Mainz. His deployments include Operation Desert Shield/Desert Storm, Saudi Arabia; Operation Restore/Continue Hope, Somalia; Operation Uphold Democracy, Haiti; Hurricane Andrew Relief, Florida; Operations Joint Guard/Forge, Bosnia-Herzegovina; Operation Enduring Freedom; and Operation Iraqi Freedom. Command Sergeant Major Brown served as the Command Sergeant Major, United States Central Command, MacDill Air Force Base, Tampa, Florida, from August 4, 2000, to August 1, 2004. He retired from the military on August 1, 2004, after more than 31 years of military service and went on to found D. Brown and Associates, a small, service-disabled veteran-owned business.

The Honorable Terrance Gainer

Terrance Gainer is a decorated veteran who served in the Vietnam War and as a captain in the United States Naval Reserve until 2000. During his law enforcement career, Gainer served as Deputy Inspector General of Illinois, Deputy Director of the Illinois State Police, and in the United States Department of Transportation before he was appointed as Director of the Illinois State Police in March 1991. Chief Gainer spent 20 years as a homicide detective with the Chicago Police Department. Ultimately his superior legal skills were put to use as the department's Chief Legal Counsel. Gainer went on to serve as Executive Assistant Police Chief, second in command of the Metropolitan Police Department of the District of Columbia, beginning in March 1998, and as Chief of the United States Capitol Police from June 2, 2002, to March 3, 2006. On November 14, 2006, Gainer was appointed by Senate Majority Leader Harry Reid (D-NV) as the Sergeant-at-Arms of the U.S. Senate for the 110th United States Congress.

The Honorable John J. Hamre

John Hamre was elected CSIS president and chief executive officer in January 2000. Before joining CSIS, he served as U.S. Deputy Secretary of Defense and Under Secretary of Defense (Comptroller). As comptroller, Dr. Hamre was the principal assistant to the Secretary of Defense for the preparation, presentation, and execution of the defense budget and management improvement programs. Before serving in the Department of Defense, Dr. Hamre worked for 10 years as a professional staff member of the Senate Armed Services Committee. During that time he was primarily responsible for the oversight and evaluation of procurement, research, and development programs; defense budget issues; and relations with the Senate Appropriations Committee. From 1978 to 1984, Dr. Hamre served in the Congressional Budget Office, where he became its Deputy Assistant Director for National Security and International Affairs. In that position, he oversaw analysis and other support for committees in both the House of Representatives and the Senate.

Colonel Michael Heidingsfield, USAF (Ret.)

Colonel Michael Heidingsfield served from 1991 to 1998 as the Chief of Police and Director of Public Safety for the City of Scottsdale, Arizona. Following his first three years of law enforcement service with the University of Texas System Police, Colonel Heidingsfield served with the Arlington (TX) Police Department from 1978 to 1991, leaving there as the Senior Deputy Police Chief after having been selected through a nationwide recruitment process to lead the Scottsdale Police Department. At the time of his retirement from the City of Scottsdale, he was accorded the title of Chief of Police Emeritus. Prior to the start of his law enforcement career, Colonel Heidingsfield served as an active duty Air Force officer and retired in 2004 as a full colonel in the U.S. Air Force Reserve assigned to the Security Forces Directorate at the Pentagon. Following his retirement from the military, he served from 2004 to 2006 as the State Department's first Contingent Commander for the Police Advisory Mission in Iraq. Colonel Heidingsfield is currently the president and CEO of the Memphis Shelby Crime Commission in Memphis, Tennessee.

Admiral Gregory G. Johnson, USN (Ret.)

Admiral Gregory G. Johnson, U.S. Navy (Ret.), served as former Commander, U.S. Naval Forces, Europe and Commander in Chief, Allied Forces, Southern Europe. Since retiring in December 2004, Admiral Johnson has founded Snow Ridge Associates, which provides strategic advice and counsel. While in the U.S. Navy, he oversaw the successful implementation of NATO's Operation Active Endeavor, assumed command of the NATO Response Force at the Istanbul Summit in June 2004, and was responsible for the establishment of NATO's training support mission in Iraq. He was also assigned to several senior policy positions in Washington, most notably serving as the executive assistant to the Chairman, Joint Chief of Staff (1992 to 1993) and military assistant to the Secretary of Defense (1999 to 2000). Admiral Johnson is also chairman of Snow Ridge Associates, which provides strategic advice and counsel; is active in community and civic affairs; and serves on several for-profit and nonprofit boards.

General George Joulwan, USA (Ret.)

General George A. Joulwan, U.S. Army (Ret.), is currently President of One Team, Inc., a strategic consulting firm. He retired from the Army in 1997 after 40 years of service in war and peace, including two combat tours of Vietnam. From 1990 to 1997, he was the Commander in Chief of both U.S. Southern Command and U.S. European Command, as well as Supreme Allied Commander, Europe. In 1992 he helped facilitate a peace agreement with the FMLN insurgents and the government of El Salvador. He also developed a successful strategic counternarcotics plan linking more than 40 U.S. agencies and several Central and South American nations. In 1995, as Supreme Allied Commander, Europe, General Joulwan was the architect of NATO's Bosnian Operation, which ended the vicious atrocities in that country without one NATO hostile fatal casualty in over ten years of engagement. General Joulwan was also instrumental in developing the U.S. State Partnership Program and NATO's Partnership for Peace Program, which included former communist countries of Eastern Europe and the Soviet Union, Russia and Ukraine among them.

Lieutenant General James C. King, USA (Ret.)

Lieutenant General King is the President and CEO of Athena Innovative Solutions, Inc. During his 33 years in the U.S. Army, he was involved in foreign and national security policy formulation and implementation, intelligence operations, and leadership of large organizations. He led the National Imagery and Mapping Agency, a Department of Defense and National Intelligence Agency composed of 13,000 employees and contractors, created as a result of the merger of eight distinct organizations. He served as the principal architect for the intelligence, surveillance, and reconnaissance input for information superiority and information operations planning and implementation for the Secretary of Defense and Joint Chiefs of Staff. He was responsible for implementing one of the largest digital information management acquisition programs in government, and led the Department of Defense and intelligence community effort to establish a national collaborative environment.

Assistant Chief Constable Duncan McCausland, PSNI

Duncan McCausland joined the Northern Irish Police Service in 1983 and served as a Constable and Sergeant in Belfast and Dungannon. He was promoted to the rank of Inspector in 1991 and to Chief Inspector in 1995. He was transferred on appointment to Superintendent in 1998 and took charge of Dungannon as Sub-Divisional Commander. In 2000, he returned to Headquarters as Head of Command Secretariat. From February 2001 until April 2002 he was Staff Officer to the Chief Constable. In March 2002 he was promoted to Chief Superintendent. On October 6, 2003, he was appointed Assistant Chief Constable Urban Region, including Belfast City, based at Castlereagh. As ACC Urban, he is responsible for the provision of effective professional policing within 12 District Command Units, utilizing some 4,600 police and civilian support staff.

Lieutenant General Gary S. McKissock, USMC (Ret.)

Lieutenant General Gary S. McKissock (Ret.) is the former Deputy Commandant of the Marine Corps for Installations and Logistics. Since leaving active service, McKissock has served on the board of both the Sapient Corp. of Cambridge, Massachusetts, and Acorn Growth Companies of Midwest City, Oklahoma. Additionally, he has served as an executive fellow at the Institute for Defense and Business in Chapel Hill, North Carolina, and is founder and principal of CorpsStrategy LLC, a consulting firm specializing in organizational planning.

Sergeant Major Alford McMichael, USMC (Ret.)

Alford L. McMichael is the founder and president of the 4-DREW Foundation, a foundation that supports children at risk. He also provides counseling to young men at two Catholic high schools in Harlem and the Bronx, where he teaches the importance of pursuing excellence in all endeavors in life. He has served on three congressional task forces on sexual assault in the military services, on the military academies, and on domestic violence and sexual harassment. Sergeant Major McMichael served as the 14th Sergeant Major of the United States Marine Corps from 1999 to 2003, and from 2003 to 2006 served as the 1st Sergeant Major in the history of the North Atlantic Treaty Organization (NATO). He retired from the United States Marine Corps in October 2006 after 36 years of service.

Brigadier General Richard Potter, USA (Ret.)

Brigadier General Richard Potter, U.S. Army (Ret.), currently serves as a senior advisor to Sierra Nevada Corporation-Integrated Mission Systems. After a distinguished 35-year career in the military, Brigadier General Potter retired in 1994 from his post as Deputy Commanding General, United States Army Special Operations Command. Since 1995, he has provided independent consulting services specializing in high-tech firms and companies within the defense industry, including Raytheon, Northrop Grumman, Jacobs-Sverdrup, ACS Defense, Gray Hawk Systems, Inc., and Areté Associates. Additionally, he has served as a consultant to the Assistant Secretary of Defense, Command Control Communications Computers Intelligence ($ASDC^4I$), the United States Special Operations Command (USSOCOM), and United States Army Special Operations Command (USASOC), as well as with the Department of the Army and other government agencies on special projects both domestically and abroad.

Major General Arnold L. Punaro, USMC (Ret.)

Arnold Punaro is a retired Marine Corps Major General who served as Commanding General of the 4th Marine Division (1997-2000) and Director of Reserve Affairs at Marine Corps Headquarters during the post-9/11 peak reserve mobilization periods. Following active duty service in Vietnam, he was mobilized three times: for Operation Desert Shield in the first Gulf War, to command Joint Task Force Provide Promise (Fwd) in Bosnia and Macedonia, and for Operation Iraqi Freedom in 2003. He worked on Capitol Hill for 24 years for Senator Sam Nunn and served as his Staff Director of the Senate Armed Services Committee for 14 years. He is currently Executive Vice President of Science Applications International Corporation. He is also chairing the Independent Commission on the National Guard and Reserves established by Congress in 2005.

Chief Charles H. Ramsey

Charles H. Ramsey served as Chief of the Metropolitan Police Department from April 1998 to December 2006, making him the longest-serving chief of the MPDC since home rule was granted to the District of Columbia in 1973. He has since served as consultant to the U.S. Senate Sergeant-at-Arms. Under Chief Ramsey's leadership as Chief, the MPDC regained its reputation as a national leader in urban policing: crime rates declined by approximately 40 percent, community policing and traffic safety programs were expanded, and MPDC recruiting and hiring standards, training, equipment, facilities, and fleet were all dramatically upgraded. His notable initiatives included a September 1998 reorganization of the Department that put more police resources in the community, cut bureaucracy, and enhanced accountability by creating a system of Regional Operations Commands. The Chief also oversaw a multimillion-dollar upgrade to district stations and other Department facilities, as well as new communications and information technology, including mobile data computing and the 3-1-1 non-emergency system. Chief Ramsey redefined the Department's community policing mission to focus on crime prevention. The program he instituted, Policing for Prevention, encompassed law enforcement, neighborhood-based partnerships and problem solving, and systemic prevention efforts.

Prior to joining the Metropolitan Police Department, Chief Ramsey served for 29 years in the Chicago Police Department (1968–1998), retiring as a Deputy Superintendent of Police. While serving in this capacity he developed the Chicago Alternative Policing Strategy (CAPS) that has been internationally recognized as an innovative community policing model.

Chief John F. Timoney

John Timoney was appointed Chief of Police of the Miami Police Department on January 2, 2003, after serving one year as CEO of an international private investigation and security company in New York City. He has served four years as the Police Commissioner of the Philadelphia Police Department, where he commanded a diverse police force of approximately 7,000 officers and over 900 civilian employees in the fifth-largest metropolitan city in the United States. Prior to that Chief Timoney spent more than 29 years with the New York Police Department, eventually becoming the youngest four-star chief in the department's history.

Lieutenant General John A. Van Alstyne, USA (Ret.)

John A. Van Alstyne is a career infantry officer with 36 years of service. In his last assignment on active duty, he served as Deputy Assistant Secretary of Defense for Military Personnel Policy. He currently serves as Commandant, Corps of Cadets, Texas A&M.

General Charles Wilhelm, USMC (Ret.)

A career infantry officer and a veteran of combat operations in Vietnam, Lebanon, the Persian Gulf, and Somalia, General Wilhelm commanded Marine units at every level, from Rifle Platoon and Company Commander in Vietnam to Commander of the II Marine Expeditionary Force and all Marine forces in the Atlantic, Europe, and South America. In his final military assignment, he served as Commander of the United States Southern Command, where he was responsible for all U.S. military activities with the 32 nations of the Caribbean and Central and South America. General Wilhelm currently serves as Vice President and Director of Battelle's Office of Homeland Security.

Appendix B: Enabling Legislation

SECTION 1314(e)(2)—Page 14

ASSESSMENT OF THE CAPABILITIES OF IRAQI SECURITY FORCES.–

(A) IN GENERAL.–There is hereby authorized to be appropriated for the Department of Defense, $750,000, that the Department, in turn, will commission an independent, private sector entity, which operates as a 501(c)(3), with recognized credentials and expertise in military affairs, to prepare an independent report assessing the following:

(i) The readiness of the Iraqi Security Forces (ISF) to assume responsibility for maintaining the territorial integrity of Iraq, denying international terrorists a safe haven, and bringing greater security to Iraq's 18 provinces in the next 12 to 18 months, and bringing an end to sectarian violence to achieve national reconciliation.

(ii) The training, equipping, command, control and intelligence capabilities, and logistics capacity of the ISF.

(iii) The likelihood that, given the ISF's record of preparedness to date, following years of training and equipping by U.S. forces, the continued support of U.S. troops will contribute to the readiness of the ISF to fulfill the missions outlined in clause (i).

(B) REPORT.–Not later than 120 days after the enactment of this Act, the designated private sector entity shall provide an unclassified report, with a classified annex, containing its findings, to the House and Senate Committees on Armed Services, Appropriations, Foreign Relations/ International Relations, and Intelligence.

Appendix C: Individuals Consulted During Assessment
Current and Former United States Officials

U.S. Civilian Officials

U.S. Secretary of State Condoleezza Rice

U.S. Secretary of Defense Robert Gates

Deputy Secretary of Defense Gordon England

Ambassador R. Nicholas Burns—*Under Secretary of State for Political Affairs*

Ambassador Ryan Crocker—*U.S. Ambassador to Iraq*

Ambassador Charles Snyder—*Acting Deputy Assistant Secretary of State, Bureau for International Narcotics and Law Enforcement Affairs*

Ambassador Marcie Ries—*Political Military Counselor, U.S. Embassy, Baghdad*

Ambassador David Satterfield—*Senior Advisor to Secretary of State Rice and Coordinator of Iraq Policy*

Dr. Meghan O'Sullivan—*National Security Council*

Ms. Betsy Philips—*Head of Joint Strategy, Plans, and Assessments Office, U.S. Embassy Baghdad*

Brigadier General (Ret.) Mark Kimmitt—*Deputy Assistant Secretary of Defense for the Middle East*

U.S. Military Officials

The White House

Lieutenant General Douglas Lute—*Assistant to the President and Deputy National Security Adviser for Iraq and Afghanistan Policy and Implementation*

The Joint Staff

General Peter Pace—*Chairman of the Joint Chiefs of Staff*

Admiral Edmund Giambastiani—*Vice Chairman of the Joint Chiefs of Staff*

Plans and Policy, J-5

Lieutenant General John Sattler—*Director, Plans and Policy, Joint Staff*

Major General Philip Breedlove, USAF—*Vice Director for Strategic Plans and Policy, Joint Staff*

Colonel Joseph di Salvo—*Iraq Division Chief, J-5*

Colonel Sean MacFarland—*Iraq Division Chief, J-5*

Lieutenant Colonel Larry Reeves—*Iraq Division, J-5*

Lieutenant Colonel Andrea Begel—*Iraq Division, J-5*

Central Command

Admiral William Fallon—*Commander, U.S. Central Command*

Multi-National Force–Iraq

General David Petraeus—*Commanding General, Multi-National Force–Iraq*

Major General John Paxton—*Chief of Staff, Multi-National Force–Iraq* Major

General Mastin M. Robeson—*Multi-National Force–Iraq*

Major General Douglas Stone—*Deputy Commanding General, Detainee Operations, Multi-National Force–Iraq*

Major General Michael Barbara—*Multi-National Force–Iraq*

Brigadier General Kevin Bergner—*Spokesman, Multi-National Force–Iraq*

Colonel Lawrence Morris—*Law and Order Task Force, Multi-National Force–Iraq*

Colonel Ken Tovo—*Combined Joint Special Operations Task Force*

Colonel M. Fugues—*Multi-National Force–Iraq, G-5*

Commodore Nicholas Lambert (U.K.)—*Combined Task Force 158, Royal Navy*

Captain Robert Sanguinetti (U.K.)—*Combined Task Group 158, Royal Navy*

Lieutenant Commander Nicholas Wheeler (U.K.)—*Combined Task Force 158 Liaison Officer to Multi-National Division South East*

Command Sergeant Major Marvin Hill—*Command Sergeant Major, Multi-National Force–Iraq*

Michael F. Walther—*Law and Order Task Force, Multi-National Force–Iraq*

Multi-National Security Transition Command–Iraq

Lieutenant General James Dubik—*Commander, Multi-National Security Transition Command–Iraq and Commander, NATO Training Mission-Iraq*

Lieutenant General Martin Dempsey—*Former Commander, Multi-National Security Transition Command–Iraq*

Major General Berraghan (U.K.)—*Chief Coalition Advisor, Baghdad Operations Center*

Rear Admiral Edward Winters—*Counter Terrorism Coordinator, Commander, Multi-National Security Transition Command–Iraq*

Colonel Michael Fuller—*Training and Education, Multi-National Security Transition Command–Iraq*

Colonel Juan Arcocha—*J-4, Multi-National Security Transition Command–Iraq*

Colonel David Dornblasser—*FMS, Multi-National Security Transition Command–Iraq*

Mr. John Cochrane—*Coalition Advisor, Ministry of Defense Transition Team, Multi-National Security Transition Command–Iraq*

Mr. Dan Maguire—*Intelligence Transition Team, Multi-National Security Transition Command–Iraq*

Command Sergeant Major Tommy Williams—*Command Sergeant Major, Multi-National Security Transition Command–Iraq*

Coalition Police Assistance Training Team, MNSTC-I

Major General Ken Hunzeker—*Former Commanding General, Coalition Police Assistance Training Team*

Brigadier General Mike Jones—*Commanding General, Coalition Police Assistance Training Team*

Brigadier General Pettit—*Coalition Police Assistance Training Team*

Brigadier General Robert Weighill (U.K.)—*Deputy Commanding General for MOI Capability, Coalition Police Assistance Training Team*

Brigadier General David Phillips—*Deputy Commanding General for MOI Forces, Coalition Police Assistance Training Team*

Colonel Alexander—*Coalition Police Assistance Training Team*

Colonel Mark French—*Coalition Police Assistance Training Team*

Colonel Brown—*Coalition Police Assistance Training Team*

Colonel Buechler—*Coalition Police Assistance Training Team*

Colonel Gallouds, *Police Training Team Leader, Baghdad*

Lieutenant Colonel Tye—*Coalition Advisor, Ports of Entry Directorate*

Lieutenant Colonel Goodrich—*Coalition Advisor, Border Security*

Lieutenant Colonel Mark Winn—*Former Lead, Border Transition Team, Region 2*

Major Bain—*Ports of Entry Transition Team, Walid*

Major Yi—*Ports of Entry Transition Team, Trebil*

Major Anthony Lamb—*Border Transition Team Leader*

Major Tom Harris—*National Police Transition Team Chief*

Major Phil Stauffacher—*Former Border Transition Team Lead, Trebil Port of Entry*

Captain Padill—*Border Transition Team, Trebil*

First Lieutenant Michael Warren—*Aamel Iraqi Police, Police Transition Team Leader*

Mr. Stephen Mangino—*U.S. DHS, Attaché and DHS Country Coordinator*

Mr. Walter Redman—*Coalition Police Assistance Training Team*

Ms. Kimberly Riffe—*Coalition Police Assistance Training Team*

Mr. Rick Andy—*Coalition Police Assistance Training Team*

Mr. George Murray—*Coalition Police Assistance Training Team*

Mr. James Davis—*Legal Attaché, Major Crimes Task Force*

Coalition Military Assistance Training Team

Brigadier General Robin Swan—*Iraqi Army Coordinator, Commander, Coalition Military Assistance Training Team*

Brigadier General Dice Allardice—*Commander, Coalition Air Force Training Team*

Captain Keith Harvey (U.K.)—*Advisor to the Head of the Iraqi Navy*

Captain Tim Stockings (U.K.)—*Commander, Naval Transition Team*

Colonel Andrew Bristow—*10 Iraqi Army, Military Transition Team Chief*

Colonel Pat Matlock—*Commander, Blackjack Military Transition Team, 4-9 Cavalry*

Colonel Pollock—*Military Transition Team Commander, 6th Iraqi Army*

Colonel Diemer—*Director, COIN Academy*

Colonel Mike Smith—*Chief, 3rd Iraqi Division Military Transition Team*

Colonel Steed—*Chief, Military Transition Team with Iraqi Ground Forces Command*

Colonel Chris Mitchell—*Chief, 2nd Iraqi Division Military Transition Team*

Colonel Amato—*Chief, Iraqi Army Division Military Transition Team*

Colonel Hall—*Coalition Military Assistance Training Team*

Colonel Ferral—*Coalition Military Assistance Training Team*

Colonel Johnson—*Coalition Military Assistance Training Team*

Colonel Bryant—*Coalition Military Assistance Training Team*

Lieutenant Colonel Shell—*Deputy Chief, Military Assistance Team, 1st Brigade, 3rd Iraqi Army Division*

Lieutenant Colonel Todd Walsh—*Military Transition Team, 4th Brigade, 1st Iraqi Army Division*

Lieutenant Dildar—*Coalition Military Assistance Training Team*

Major W. Caldwell—*Team Leader, Military Transition Team*

Major Kevin Nicholas—*Iraqi Army, Military Transition Team*

Captain Ferguson—*Coalition Military Assistance Training Team*

Captain Shrewsbury—*Coalition Military Assistance Training Team*

Lieutenant Biet—*Department of Border Enforcement Military Transition Team*

Ms. King—*Ministry of Defense Transition Team*

Mr. Chessnoe—*Ministry of Defense Transition Team*

Mr. Horne—*Ministry of Defense Transition Team*

Mr. Prince—*Ministry of Defense Transition Team*

Multi-National Corps–Iraq

Lieutenant General Ray Odierno—*Commander, Multi-National Corps-Iraq*

Lieutenant General Rich Zilmer—*Former Commander, Multi-National Force-West*

Major General Robert Neller—*Former Deputy Commanding General for Operations, Multi-National Force-West*

Major General Walt Gaskin—*Commander, Multi-National Division West, U.S. II Marine Expeditionary Force*

Major General Rick Lynch—*Commander, Multi-National Division Center, U.S. 3rd Infantry Division*

Major General Randy Mixon—*Commander, Multi-National Division North, U.S. 25th Infantry Division*

Major General Graham Binns (UK)—*Multi-National Corps–Iraq*

Brigadier General Jim Huggins—*Deputy Commander, Multi-National Division Center*

Brigadier General James Yarbrough—*Commander, Iraqi Assistance Group*

Brigadier General John Allen—*Deputy Commanding General, Multi-National Force-West, II Marine Expeditionary Force*

Brigadier General Vincent Brooks—*Acting Division Commander, Multinational Division Baghdad, U.S. Army 1st Cavalry Division*

Brigadier General Charles Gurganus—*Commanding General, Ground Combat Element, Multi-National Force-West*

Colonel Charlie Flynn—*82nd Airborne, Multi-National Corps-Iraq*

Colonel John Charlton—*Commander, 1st Brigade Combat Team, 3rd Infantry Division*

Colonel Paul Funk—*Commander, 1st Brigade Combat Team, 1st Cavalry Division*

Colonel Richard Simcock—*Commander, Regimental Combat Team 6, Multi-National Forces-West*

Lieutenant Colonel Swindell—*Combined Joint Special Operations Task Force, Multi-National Division-Center*

Lieutenant Colonel Jack Marr—*Commander, Command Operations Post Cleary, 1–15 Infantry*

Lieutenant Colonel Patrick Frank—*Battalion Commander, 1–28 IN, 4th Brigade Combat Team, 1st Infantry Division*

Command Sergeant Major Clifford Dockter—*1–28 IN, 4th Brigade Combat Team, 1st Infantry Division*

Sergeant Major Rodney Lewis—*1–28 IN, 4th Brigade Combat Team, 1st Infantry Division*

Captain Sean Lyons—*COP Attack, Multi-National Corps-Iraq*

Chief Warrant Officer 5 Terry Walker—*Multi-National Forces–West*

Command Sergeant Major Citola—*Multi-National Corps Iraq*

Command Sergeant Major Burrows—*Iraqi Assistance Group*

First Sergeant Jeffrey Griffith—*COP Attack, Multi-National Corps-Iraq*

Sergeant Smith—*1–28 IN, 4th Brigade Combat Team, 1st Infantry Division*

Specialist Benner—*1–28 IN, 4th Brigade Combat Team, 1st Infantry Division*

Specialist Riahi—*1–28 IN, 4th Brigade Combat Team, 1st Infantry Division*

Private First Class Graff—*1–28 IN, 4th Brigade Combat Team, 1st Infantry Division*

NATO Training Command–Iraq

Major General Pompegnani—*Commander, NATO Training Command–Iraq*

Current and Former Iraqi Officials

Iraqi Civilian Officials

President Jalal Talabani—*State President of Iraq*

Deputy Minister Barham Salih—*Deputy Prime Minister of Iraq*

His Excellency Abdul-Qader al-Obeidi—*Minister of Defense*

Deputy Minister Maliki—*Deputy Minister of Defense*

Major General Mahmood—*Director General of Programs and Budgets, Ministry of Defense*

Dr. Mumtaz—*Director General of Personnel, Ministry of Defense*

Mr. Abid Ali Jasim—*Director General of Armaments and Supply, Ministry of Defense*

Mr. Mudhfar—*Director General of Contracts and Purchases, Ministry of Defense*

Major General Kamal—*Director, National Information and Investigation Agency*

His Excellency Samir Shakir M. Sumaida'ie—*Iraqi Ambassador to the United States*

Dr. Bassima Al Jaidri—*Advisor to Prime Minister Maliki*

Iraqi Military Officials

General Faruq—*Office of the Commander in Chief*

General Mohan—*Iraqi Commander, Basra Operations Command*

Lieutenant General Ali—*Commander, Iraqi Ground Forces Command*

Lieutenant General Aboud—*Commander, Baghdad Operations Center*

Lieutenant General Talib Kinani—*Commander, Counter Terrorism Bureau*

Lieutenant General Abdulrazzak—*Joint Headquarters, M-3*

Lieutenant General Aboud—*Commander, Baghdad Operations Center*

Lieutenant-General Kamal al-Barzanji—*Commander, Iraqi Air Force*

Major General Khorsheed—*Commander, 3rd Division Iraqi Army*

Major General Abu Ghani—*Commander, Government of Iraq Counter-Terrorism Command*

Major General Abdul Amir—*Commander, 6th Iraqi Army*

Major General Ala'a—*Deputy Head of Iraqi Air Force*

Major General Jassim—*Joint Headquarters, M-7*

Major General Kamal—*Joint Headquarters, M-2*

Major General Othman—*Joint Headquarters, M-l*

Major General Jawdat—*Joint Headquarters, M-4*

Rear Admiral Muhammad Jawad Kadhim—*Head of the Iraqi Navy*

Brigadier General Kahleel—*Iraqi Air Force*

Brigadier General Qaid—*Iraqi Air Force*

Brigadier General Kareem—*Iraqi Air Force*

Brigadier General Fadhil al Berwari—*Commanding Officer, Iraqi Special Operations Forces*

Brigadier General Alaa—*Comptroller, Joint Headquarters*

Brigadier General Muttah—*Commander, 2nd Iraqi Army Division*

Colonel Abdul Rahim—*Commanding Officer, Iraqi Counter insurgency School, Iraqi Army*

Commander Ahmed Maarij—*Operational Commander, Iraqi Navy*

Captain Nasir—*Patrol Base Whiskey 1, Iraqi Army 6th Division*

Sergeant Major Kassam—*Iraqi Ground Forces Command*

Iraqi Ministry of the Interior

Ministry of the Interior Officials

His Excellency Jawad al-Bolani—*Minister of the Interior*

Major General Admed al-Khafaji—*Deputy Minister of the Interior for Support Forces*

Deputy Minister Adnan al-Assadi—*Deputy Minister of the Interior for Administration*

Deputy Minister Hala Shakir—*Deputy Minister of the Interior for Financial Affairs*

Major General Jihan—*Director of Training and Qualification, Ministry of the Interior*

Major General Jodah—*Assistant Deputy Minister, Iraqi Police Service Affairs/Security*

Major General Jawad—*Director of Contracts, Ministry of the Interior*

Brigadier General Farhoud—*Ports of Entry Directorate, Ministry of the Interior*

Brigadier General Jasim—*Ports of Entry Directorate, Ministry of the Interior*

Iraqi Police Service and National Police

Major General Mahdi Juma'a Salma al-Salami—*Dean, Baghdad Police College*

Major General Jasim Hassam Attia—*Dean, High Institute, Baghdad Police College*

Major General Ameer—*Director of Logistics, Baghdad Police College*

Brigadier General Khalid Adulani—*Dean of Police Academy*

Major General Khadim Hamid Shi'wa al-Mohammadadawi—*Baghdad, Provincial Director of Police*

Brigadier General Baha—*Commander, 5th Division 2nd Battalion Iraqi National Police*

Deputy Minister Sinjari—*Deputy Minister of Interior, Kurdish Region*

General Jamal Ahmad Muhamad—*Provincial Police Chief, Sulaymaniyah*

Major General Hussein al Awadi—*National Police Commander*

Outside Experts

Dr. Jon Alterman—*Director, Middle East Program, Center for Strategic and International Studies*

General John Abizaid (Ret.)—*Former Commander, U.S. Central Command*

Dr. Stephen Biddle—*Senior Fellow, Council on Foreign Relations*

Dr. Anthony Cordesman—*Center for Strategic and International Studies*

Colonel Paul Hughes (Ret.)—*Senior Program Officer, Center for Post-Conflict Peace and Stability Operations, U.S. Institute of Peace*

Dr. Frederick W. Kagan—*Resident Scholar, American Enterprise Institute*

Dr. Phebe Marr—*Leading U.S. Expert on Iraq, Author of The Modern History of Iraq*

Mr. Robert Perito—*Senior Program Officer, Center for Post-Conflict Peace and Stability Operations, U.S. Institute of Peace*

Ms. Sarah Farnsworth—*Strategic Advisor*

The Honorable Patrick T. Henry—*Strategic Advisor*

Mr. John Raidt—*Strategic Advisor*

Colonel Arthur White, USMC (Ret.)—*Strategic Advisor*

Note: *The Commission has made every attempt to list all individuals consulted during the course of its work. Despite best efforts, the Commission recognizes this list does not include many of the members of the U.S. and Coalition forces and the Iraqi Security Forces who spent time with the Commissioners on the ground in Iraq.*

Appendix D: Review of Major Reports & Analyses
United States Government Sources

Office of the President of the United States

National Strategy for Victory in Iraq, November 2005

Initial Benchmark Assessment Report, July 2007

Department of Defense

Interagency Assessment of Iraq Police Training, (U.S. Department of State & U.S. Department of Defense), July 2005

Measuring Stability and Security in Iraq, Report to Congress in accordance with the Department of Defense Appropriations Act 2007 (Section 9010, Public Law 109-289):

- July 2005
- October 2005
- February 2006
- March 2007
- June 2007

Central Intelligence Agency

National Intelligence Estimate: Prospects for Iraq's Stability: A Challenging Road Ahead, January 2007

Government Accountability Office

Operation Iraqi Freedom: Preliminary Observations on Iraqi Security Forces' Logistics and Command and Control Capabilities, (GAO-07-503R), March 2007

Stabilizing Iraq: DoD Cannot Ensure that U.S. Funded Equipment Has Reached Iraqi Security Forces, (GAO-07-711), July 2007

Stabilizing Iraq: Factors Impeding the Development of Capable Iraqi Security Forces, (GAO), Statement of Joseph A. Christoff, Director International Affairs and Trade, Testimony before the House Armed Services Committee, Subcommittee on Oversight and Investigations

United States Congress

Stand Up and Be Counted: The Continuing Challenge of Building the Iraqi Security Forces, U.S. House of Representatives, Committee on Armed Services, Subcommittee on Oversight & Investigations, July 2007

Statement of Admiral William J. Fallon, United States Navy Commander, United States Central Command, House Armed Services Committee, April 2007

Testimony by Gerald F. Burke, House Armed Services Committee, April 2007

Testimony by Robert M. Perito, *Reforming the Iraqi Interior Ministry, Police and Facilities Protection Service*, House Armed Services Committee, Subcommittee on Oversight and Investigations, March 2007

Testimony by Olga Oliker, *Iraqi Security Forces: Defining Challenges and Assessing Progress*, House Armed Services Committee, March 2007

Testimony by Lieutenant General Martin Dempsey, USA, Commander Multinational Security Transitional Command Iraq, Hearing of the Oversight and Investigations Subcommittee of the House Armed Services Committee, June 2007

Congressional Research Service

Jeremy M. Sharp, *The Iraqi Security Forces: The Challenge of Sectarian and Ethnic Influences*, Congressional Research Service, January 2007

Iraq: Post-Saddam Governance and Security, Congressional Research Service, April 2007

Coalition Provisional Authority

Coalition Provisional Authority Order 1, April 2003

Coalition Provisional Authority Order 2, May 2003

Coalition Provisional Authority Order 22, August 2003

Coalition Provisional Authority Order 26, August 2003

Coalition Provisional Authority Order 28, September 2003

Coalition Provisional Authority Order 67, March 2004

Non-Governmental Sources

The Baker-Hamilton Commission, *The Iraq Study Group Report: The Way Forward—A New Approach*, December 2006

Lionel Beehner, *Iraq: Militia Groups*, Council on Foreign Relations, June 2005

Stephen Biddle

- *A Gamble at Very Long Odds*, Council on Foreign Relations, January 2007
- *Hard Bargaining: If President Bush is Committed to Fighting on in Iraq, Then He Needs a Fundamentally Different Military Strategy—One that Offers the Only Realistic Chance of Compelling a Ceasefire Between Iraq's Warring Factions,"* Boston Globe, June 2007

Anthony H. Cordesman

- *Still Losing? Measuring Stability in Iraq*, June 2007
- *Force Development and the Challenge of Civil War: The Critical Problems and Failures the US Must Address if Iraqi Forces Are to Do the Job*, March 2007
- *Iraq's Sunni Insurgents: Looking Beyond Al Qa'ida*, July 2007

Mohammed Hafez, *Suicide Bombers in Iraq: The Strategy and Ideology of Martyrdom*, USIP, 2007

Frederick W. Kagan, *Iraqi Security Forces: Status and Prospects*, Testimony before the House Armed Services Committee, Subcommittee on Oversight and Investigations, March 2007

Frederick W. Kagan and Kimberly Kagan, *The New Strategy in Iraq: General Petraeus Learns from Past U.S. Mistakes*, July 2007

Thomas A. Keaney and Eliot A. Cohen, *Gulf War Air Power Survey Summary Report*, 1993

Colonel Frederick Kienle, *Creating an Iraqi Army from Scratch: Lessons for the Future*, American Enterprise Institute, May 2007

Daniel Kimmage and Kathleen Rudolfo, *Iraqi Insurgent Media, The War of Images and Ideas*, Radio Free Europe and Radio Liberty, Special Report, July 2007

Dr. Phebe Marr

- *Iraq's Reconstruction: Where is it Going?*, Testimony before the Senate Foreign Relations Committee, September 2003
- *Iraq's New Political Map*, January 2007

Oxfam, *Rising to the Humanitarian Challenge in Iraq*, Briefing paper 105, July 2007

The RAND Corporation

- *Developing Iraq's Security Sector: The Coalition Provisional Authority's Experience*, written by Andrew Rathmell, Olga Oliker, Terrence K. Kelly, David Brannan, Keith Crane, 2005
- *Rebuilding Security Forces and Institutions in Iraq*, 2005

Endnotes

[1] Department of Defense, *Measuring Stability and Security in Iraq*, Report to Congress, June 2007, p. 30. The ISF also consists of a Coast Guard, under the Ministry of Interior, and the Facilities Protection Service. Officially under the authority of the Ministry of Interior, at present the Facilities Protection Service operates under the direction of multiple ministries.

[2] Director of National Intelligence, *National Intelligence Estimate*, August 2007, p. 1.

[3] Anthony H. Cordesman, "Iraq's Sunni Insurgents: Looking Beyond Al Qa'ida," CSIS working draft, July 16, 2007, p. 7; available at http://www.csis.org/media/csis/pubs/070716_sunni_insurgents.pdf.

[4] Kenneth Katzman, *Iraq: Post-Saddam Governance and Security*, Congressional Research Service, RL31339: April 27, 2007, pp. 29–30.

[5] *Ibid.*, p. 3.

[6] Cordesman, "Iraq's Sunni Insurgents," p. 3.

[7] Cordesman, "Iraq's Sunni Insurgents," p. 32.

[8] Mohammed Hafez, "Fresh Air: Martyrs Without Borders," interview on National Public Radio, July 23, 2007; available at http://www.npr.org/templates/story/story.php?storyId=12169774.

[9] Daniel Kimmage and Kathleen Rudolfo, "Iraqi Insurgent Media: The War of Images and Ideas," Radio Free Europe and Radio Liberty, Special Report, July 2007, p. 9.

[10] Cordesman, "Iraq's Sunni Insurgents." p. 7.

[11] Katzman, *Iraq: Post-Saddam Governance and Security*, p. 29.

[12] *Ibid., p. 37.*

[13] National Intelligence Council, "Prospects for Iraq's Stability: A Challenging Road Ahead," National Intelligence Estimate, January 2007.

[14] *Ibid., p. 31.*

[15] The Badr Brigade is also called the "Badr Organization" by some experts, as the militia claims to have demilitarized.

[16] Lionel Beehner, "Iraq: Militia Groups," *Council on Foreign Relations*, June 9, 2005.

[17] Jeremy Sharp, *The Iraqi Security Forces: The Challenge of Sectarian and Ethnic Influences*, Congressional Research Service, RS22093: January 18, 2007, p. 5.

[18] Katzman, *Iraq: Post-Saddam Governance and Security*, p. 32.

[19] See, for example, Brigadier General Kevin Bergner, July 2, 2007, Multi-National Forces-Iraq press briefing, available at http://www.mnf-iraq.com/index.php?option=com_content&task=view&id=12641&Itemid=131.

[20] Information related to EFPs, unless otherwise noted, is from Michael Gordon, "U.S. Says Iran-Supplied Bomb Kills More Troops," *New York Times*, August 8, 2007.

[21] Katzman, *Iraq: Post-Saddam Governance and Security*, p. 32.

[22] *Ibid.*, p. 34.

[23] Jim Garamone, "Abizaid Says Percentage of Foreign Fighters Increasing in Iraq," American Forces Press Service, March 27, 2005; available at http://www.defenselink.mil/news/newsarticle.aspx?id=31091.

[24] Anthony Cordesman, "Iraq and Foreign Volunteers," CSIS working draft, updated November 2005; available at http://www.csis.org/media/csis/pubs/051117_iraqforeignvol.pdf. See also Sam Dagher, "Anti-Saudi Tide Rises in Iraq," *Christian Science Monitor*, August 9, 2007; Helene Cooper et al., "U.S. Officials Voice Frustration with Saudis, Citing Role in Iraq," *New York Times*, July 27, 2007.

[25] Although a large portion of Iraq's arsenal was destroyed in the 1990–1991 Gulf War, there still remained packed depots throughout Iraq.

[26] Government Accountability Office, *DOD Cannot Ensure That U.S.-Funded Equipment Has Reached Iraqi Security Forces*, GAO-07-711, July 31, 2007.

[27] Katzman, *Iraq: Post-Saddam Governance and Security*, p. 31.

[28] "Iraqi Refugees Flee War-torn Country," *Lehrer News Hour;* available at http://www.pbs.org/newshour/bb/middle_east/july-dec07/refugees_07-26.html.

[29] Oxfam, "Rising to the Humanitarian Challenge in Iraq," Briefing Paper 105, July 2007; available at http://www.oxfam.org/en/files/bpl05_humanitarian_challenge_in_iraq_0707.pdf/download.

[30] Oxfam, "Rising to the Humanitarian Challenge in Iraq."

[31] National Intelligence Council, "Prospects for Iraq's Stability: A Challenging Road Ahead," Unclassified National Intelligence Estimate: January 2007, p. 8.

[32] Kenneth Katzman, *Iraq: Post-Saddam Governance and Security*, Congressional Research Service, RL31339: April 27, 2007, pp. 35–36.

[33] U.S. House of Representatives Committee on Armed Services, Subcommittee on Oversight and Investigations, *Stand Up and Be Counted: The Continuing Challenge of Building the Iraqi Security Forces*, 110th Cong., 1st sess., July 2007, p. 41.

[34] In 2007, the Government of Iraq spent $9 billion compared to $4.5 billion by the United States (telephone interview with Lieutenant General Dempsey, Office of the Secretary of Defense, June 1, 2007, http://www.defendamerica.mil/specials/2007/blog/docs/Dempsey_June01_07_transcript.pdf).

[35] White House, "Initial Benchmark Assessment Report," July 12, 2007, p. 21.

[36] Meeting with senior U.S. commanders in Iraq, July 2007.

[37] The Commission surveyed the Coalition's senior field commanders to obtain their on-the-ground assessment of the status and progress of the Iraqi Security Forces. Asked to rate the progress that has been made by the MOD forces toward attaining the capabilities required to protect the territorial integrity of Iraq, 6 of the 8 rated the progress "satisfactory," and 2 "unsatisfactory." None rated progress as "excellent." With regard to MOI forces, 2 rated progress as satisfactory, 2 unsatisfactory, and none excellent.

[38] The Commission's survey of the Coalition's senior field commanders regarding the ISF asked to rate the progress made by the MOD forces toward attaining the capabilities required to deny international terrorists safe haven, 7 rated the progress as satisfactory, 1 as unsatisfactory, and 1 as excellent; with regard to MOI forces, 4 rated progress as satisfactory, none unsatisfactory, and none excellent.

[39] See Anthony H. Cordesman, "Success or Failure? Iraq's Insurgency and Civil Violence and US Strategy: Developments through June 2007," CSIS working draft, updated July 9, 2007; available at http://www.csis.org/media/csis/pubs/070709_iraqinsurgupdate.pdf.

[40] Sudarsan Raghavan, "In Iraq, a Perilous Alliance with Former Enemies," *Washington Post*, August 4, 2007.

[41] Anthony Cordesman, *Iraqi Force Development and the Challenge of Civil War*, August 8, 2007, pp. 14–15, p. 335; Multi-see also National Security Transition Command–Iraq, "In Stride Assessment of the Iraqi Security Forces for the FY08 ISFF Budget Review, 30 May 2007," pp. 2,10 (hereafter cited as "In-Stride Assessment").

[42] D. J. Elliott, "Brigade Order of Battle—Iraq, 31 July 2007," *The Fourth Rail: History, Politics, and the War on Terror*, http://billroggio.com/multimedia/IraqBdeOOB4.php.

[43] The Iraqi Army as a whole is 75–80 percent Shi'a. Shi'a predominate in 6 of the existing 11 battalions, but Iraqi Army units in the northern regions are 50 percent Kurdish, and a small number of battalions are almost 90 percent Sunni.

[44] In most meetings with Americans working with the ISF and Iraqi leaders of the ISF, the Commission heard that the ISF is not adequately armed against the threat, nor do they have sufficient armor protection. See also "In-Stride Assessment," p. 11.

[45] For example, there was a 26 percent decline in the number of murders and executions in Baghdad between the month of February and March, and a 60 percent reduction during the last week of March and the first week of April. See Melinda L. Larson, "Baghdad Security Plan Seeing Many Successes," American Forces Press Service, April 8, 2007.

[46] In the Commission's survey of the Coalition's senior field commanders regarding the ISF, among those asked to rate the progress made by the MOD forces toward attaining the capabilities required to bring greater security to the provinces in the respondent's area of operations 7 rated the progress as satisfactory, none as unsatisfactory, and none as excellent. With regard to MOI forces, four rated progress as satisfactory, none as unsatisfactory and none as excellent.

[47] Meeting with Multinational Division-North officials, July 2007.

[48] In the Commission's survey of the Coalition's senior field commanders regarding the ISF, among those asked to rate the progress made by the MOD forces toward ending sectarian violence and achieving national reconciliation, 6 rated the progress as satisfactory, 2 as unsatisfactory, and none as excellent. With regard to MOI forces, four rated progress as unsatisfactory, none as satisfactory, and none as excellent.

[49] Coalition Provisional Authority Order 2, May 23, 2003.

[50] Most senior staff in the MOD are retired military officers, some of whom still wear their uniforms. The large numbers of retired military officers may be fueling resistance to greater civilian control within the MOD.

[51] Department of Defense, *Measuring Stability and Security in Iraq*, Report to Congress, June 2007, p. 37.

[52] All background information comes from MOD-TT/JHQ-TT/CMATT overview briefings received by the Commission in Iraq in July 2007.

[53] In a survey conducted of senior Coalition commanders in Iraq, the majority told the Commission that progress being made by the MOD in the essential combat functions of command and control, intelligence, mobility, logistics, and fire support is unsatisfactory. Logistics is the greatest near term priority.

[54] House Armed Services Committee Subcommittee on Oversight and Investigations, 110th Cong., 1st sess., *Stand Up and be Counted*, July 2007, p. 105.

[55] Figure from MNSTC-I overview briefing received in Baghdad, July 2007.

[56] Commissioner interviews at Camp Phoenix, Baghdad, July 10, 2007.

[57] Interview with senior Iraqi MOD officials, Baghdad, July 10, 2007.

[58] Interview with MOD Logistics and Personnel Transition Team, Baghdad, July 10, 2007

[59] *Ibid.*

[60] This figure is derived from conversations with current and former MiTT team members and MNSTC-I officials throughout Iraq and in Washington. It accords with estimates of outside sources such as Dr. Anthony Cordesman and the House Subcommittee on Oversight and Investigations.

[61] "Iraqi Army," GlobalSecurity.org, http://www.globalsecurity.org/military/world/iraq/army.htm.

[62] Andrew Rathmell, Olga Oliker, Terrence K. Kelly, David Brannan, and Keith Crane, *Developing Iraq's Security Sector: The Coalition Provisional Authority's Experience*, MG-365-OSD (Santa Monica, CA: RAND, 2005), p. 10; available at http://www.rand.org/pubs/monographs/2005/RAND_MG365.pdf.

[63] Rathmell et al., *Developing Iraq's Security Sector*, p. 13.

[64] Coalition Provisional Authority Order 2, May 23, 2003.

[65] Coalition Provisional Authority Order 1, April 16, 2003.

[66] Coalition Provisional Authority Order 22, August 7, 2003.

[67] Col. Frederick Kienle, "Creating an Iraqi Army from Scratch: Lessons for the Future," *National Security Outlook*, May 2007, p. 1; available at http://www.aei.org/publications/pubID.26249/pub_detail.asp.

[68] Rathmell et al., *Developing Iraq's Security Sector*, p. 34.

[69] Coalition Provisional Authority Order 28, September 3, 2003.

[70] "Iraq to Dissolve National Guard," BBC, December 29, 2004; available at http://news.bbc.co.uk/2/hi/middle_east/4133039.stm.

[71] Coalition Provisional Authority Order 67, March 21, 2004.

[72] "Iraqi Intervention Force," GlobalSecurity.org, http://www.globalsecurity.org/military/world/iraq/iif.htm.

[73] Department of Defense, *Measuring Stability and Security in Iraq*, March 2007, p. 37, and June 2007, pp. 40–41 (reports of this title, submitted to Congress in accordance with section 9010 of various Department of Defense appropriation acts, are cited hereafter as 9010 Report).

[74] Several other battalions with this specialty skill set may be developed in the 3rd Iraqi Army Division.

[75] 9010 Report, June 2007, pp. 41–42.

[76] U.S. House of Representatives Committee on Armed Services, Subcommittee on Oversight and Investigations, *Stand Up and Be Counted: The Continuing Challenge of Building the Iraqi Security Forces.* 110th Cong., 1st sess., July 2007, pp. 127–41.

[77] These reports were formerly known as Transitional Readiness Assessments.

[78] See Anthony H. Cordesman, "Iraq's Sunni Insurgents: Looking Beyond Al Qa'ida," CSIS working draft, july 16, 2007, p. 3; available at http://www.csis.org/media/csis/pubs/070716_sunni_insurgents.pdf. Also see Mohammed Hafez, *Suicide Bombers in Iraq: The Strategy and Ideology of Martyrdom* (Washington, DC: U.S. Institute of Peace Press, 2007).

[79] Iraqi Army and Coalition commanders in the areas of responsibility of Multi-National Forces Command-West and Multi-National Division-North noted the utility of this approach.

[80] The MNSTC-I commander is dual-hatted as the commander of NTM-I.

[81] NATO Training Mission-Iraq, "Facts and Figures," July 5, 2007; available at http://www.afsouth.nato.int/JFCN_Missions/NTM-I/NTMI_Facts.htm.

[82] 9010 Report, June 2007, p.30.

[83] E.g., see Anthony Cordesman, July 24, 2007, p. vii.

[84] Lieutenant General Martin E. Dempsey, statement before the House U.S. House of Representatives Committee on Armed Services, Subcommittee on Oversight and Investigations, 110th Cong., 1st sess., June 12, 2007, p. 3.

[85] Jeremy Sharp, *The Iraqi Security Forces: The Challenge of Sectarian and Ethnic Influences*, Congressional Research Service, RS22093: January 18, 2007, p. 4.

[86] Commissioner interviews at Camp Taji, Iraq, July 10, 2007.

[87] *Ibid.*

[88] Joseph A. Christoff, Director, International Affairs and Trade, GAO, "Stabilizing Iraq: Factors Impeding the Development of Capable Iraqi Security Forces," testimony before the U.S. House of Representatives Armed Services Committee, Subcommittee on Oversight and Investigations, 110th Cong., 1st sess., March 13, 2007, p. 11; available at http://www.gao.gov/new.items/d07612t.pdf.

[89] Chilling anecdotes abound about the personal risk to Iraqi soldiers and the lack of support for wounded veterans. See, for example, Karin Brulliard, "For Iraqi Soldiers, A Medical Morass," *Washington Post*, May 6, 2007; Ben Gilbert, "An Army Where Wounded Soldiers Are on Their Own," *San Francisco Chronicle*, June 10, 2006.

[90] Coalition forces must follow strict guidelines in offering medical support to Iraqis to ensure that their own capabilities are not overwhelmed.

[91] The Iraqi Army has, for instance, dozens of different types of light-transport trucks and lacks part and maintenance know-how for the different systems.

[92] 9010 Report, March 2007, p. 40.

[93] Briefing from Iraqi Air Force officials, July 2007.

[94] "Iraqi Air Force [IQAF]," GlobalSecurity.org, http://www.globalsecurity.org/military/world/iraq/airforce.htm.

[95] *Ibid.*

[96] Ross Colvin, "Iraq Air Force Wants Iran to Give Back Its Planes," *Washington Post*, August 5, 2007.

[97] Briefing from Iraqi Air Force Officials, July 2007.

[98] Briefing from Coalition Air Force Transition Team, July 2007.

[99] *Ibid.*

[100] Department of Defense, *Measuring Stability and Security in Iraq*, Report to Congress, June 2007, p. 43 (reports of this title, submitted to Congress in accordance with section 9010 of various Department of Defense appropriation acts, are cited hereafter as 9010 Report).

[101] Briefing from Coalition Air Force Transition Team, July 2007.

[102] Briefing from Iraqi Air Force officials, July 2007.

[103] Briefing from Coalition Air Force Transition Team, July 2007.

[104] 9010 Report, June 2007, p. 42.

[105] 9010 Report, July 2005, p. 17.

[106] 9010 Report, February 2006, p. 46.

[107] Briefing from Coalition Air Force Transition Team, July 2007.

[108] Briefing from Iraqi Air Force officials, July 2007.

[109] "Saddam's Navy," GlobalSecurity.org, http://www.globalsecurity.org/military/world/iraq/navy.htm.

[110] Interview with senior Iraqi Navy official, July 2007.

[111] The Coalition Provisional Authority, "Briefing on the Iraqi Coastal Defense Force," news release, April 19, 2004; available at http://www.cpa-iraq.org/pressreleases/20040419_coastal_defense.html.

[112] "Iraqi Navy," GlobalSecurity.org, http://www.globalsecurity.org/military/world/iraq/cdf.htm.

[113] Department of Defense, *Measuring Stability and Security in Iraq*, February 2006, p. 44 (reports of this title, submitted to Congress in accordance with section 9010 of various Department of Defense appropriation acts, are cited hereafter as 9010 Report).

[114] 9010 Report, June 2007, p. 42.

[115] Briefing with Maritime Services Transition Team official, July 2007.

[116] Meeting with Naval Transition Team official, July 2007.

[117] Iraqi Navy Information Brief, July 2007.

[118] 9010 Report, June 2007, p. 42.

[119] Combined Task Force (CTF) 158 operates in the northern Persian Gulf, also known as the northern Arabian Gulf (NAG), under a separate chain of command from that of the Naval Transition Team. Task Force 158 is the maritime contribution to Operation Iraqi Freedom (OIF) and is executed by Coalition forces of the United States, Australia, and the United Kingdom working alongside elements of the Iraqi Navy and the Iraqi Marines. Task Force 158's mission is to protect Iraq's vital oil infrastructure in the NAG, to conduct maritime security operations (MSO) in the NAG, and to contribute to the development of the operational capability of the Iraqi Navy and Marines so that Coalition forces may withdraw in due course.

[120] Iraqi Navy Information Brief, July 2007.

[121] The Commission also spoke informally with many more Iraqi Navy and Coalition officers during extensive site visits.

[122] Interview with senior Iraqi Navy officer, July 2007.

[123] *Ibid.*

[124] *Ibid.*

[125] Meeting with Naval Transition Team official, July 2007.

[126] Naval Transition Team Briefing, July 2007.

[127] ABOT has been repaired with Coalition funding and is now a world-class facility. However, some Coalition officials told the Commission that they believe Iraq's Southern Oil Company would like to turn off ABOT's metering device to obscure from the Iraqi central government the amount of output from the platform. In theory, doing so would give Southern Oil Company the opportunity to take additional profits. KAAOT remains unmetered; it also lacks a surge dampener, and that absence increases operational risk.

[128] Interview with senior Iraqi Navy officer, July 2007.

[129] Interview with senior Iraqi Navy officer, July 2007.

[130] Briefing with CTF 158, July 2007.

[131] *Ibid.*

[132] Interview with senior Iraqi Navy officer, July 2007.

[133] Briefing with CTF 158, July 2007.

[134] Interview with CTF 158 official, July 2007.

[135] *Ibid.*

[136] *Ibid.*

[137] Rear Admiral Jawad is set to attend the International Sea Power Symposium in Newport, Rhode Island, in October 2007. The event is hosted by the U.S. Chief of Naval Operations.

[138] Interview with senior Iraqi Navy officer, July 2007.

[139] 9010 Report, June 2007, p. 42.

[140] Meeting with Naval Transition Team official, July 2007.

[141] *Ibid.*

[142] *Ibid.*

143 Briefing with CTF 158, July 2007.

144 Andrew Rathmell, Olga Oliker, Terrence K. Kelly, David Brannan, and Keith Crane, *Developing Iraq's Security Sector: The Coalition Provisional Authority's Experience*, MG-365-OSD (Santa Monica, CA: RAND, 2005), p. 42.

145 Robert M. Perito of the United States Institute of Peace, Dr. Olga Oliker of RAND Corporation, and Dr. Anthony H. Cordesman of the Center for Strategic and International Studies have all written in numerous publications about capacity problems and sectarianism within the Ministry of Interior.

146 Ned Parker, "Interior Ministry Mirrors Chaos of a Fractured Iraq," *Los Angeles Times*, July 30, 2007.

147 *Ibid.*

148 Interviews with senior international police advisers in Iraq, July 2007. See also the prepared statement of Robert M. Perito before the House Armed Services Committee, Subcommittee on Oversight and Investigations, 110th Cong., 1st sess., March 28, 2007. Perito specifically notes that the transition team provided the head of the Internal Affairs Division with a fingerprinting system that the division chief used to identify and remove police with criminal records.

149 Government Accountability Office, *Stabilizing Iraq: DOD Cannot Ensure That U.S.-Funded Equipment Has Reached Iraqi Security Forces*, GAO-07-711: July 2007, p. 9.

150 Briefing from MNSTC-I CPATT in Iraq, July 2007.

151 Interviews with CPATT officials, July 2007.

152 The relatively recent creation of provincial security forces in provinces like Anbar has complicated the issue: in many cases, Iraqis are forming neighborhood watches filled with individuals who view themselves as police and expect to be paid accordingly, even though they are not actually on the provincial police payroll.

153 The most solid example of civil policing the Commission saw in Iraq was in the Kurdish province of Sulaymaniyah, but it must be noted the Kurdish provinces have benefited from years of being a virtually autonomous area in Iraq.

154 Interviews with Iraqi police officials in Baghdad, July 2007. See also Robert M. Perito, "Reforming the Iraqi Interior Ministry, Police and Facilities Protection Service," Testimony before the House Armed Services Subcommittee on Oversight and Investigations, 110th Cong., 1st sess., March 28, 2007.

155 Coalition forces have trained just over 164,000 police as of August 2007, according to information from CPATT officials in MNSTC-I. See also Department of Defense, *Measuring Stability and Security in Iraq*, March 2007, p. 31 (reports of this title, submitted to Congress in accordance with section 9010 of various Department of Defense appropriation acts, are cited hereafter as 9010 Report).

156 There is also a national-level Emergency Response Unit in the National Police, containing about 600 personnel.

157 9010 Report, March 2007, p. 31. See also CPATT, "Iraqi Police Service," briefing provided in July 2007. While the national average for basic equipment is 80 percent, some provinces in Iraq are still experiencing shortfalls in particular categories of equipment. These shortfalls vary from province to province in size and type.

158 CPATT briefing, July 2007. Currently there are 10 provincial PTTs, 65 District PTTs and 148 station PTTs; see 9010 Report, March 2007, p.32.

159 CPATT briefing, July 2007. Four hundred of the almost 1,200 police stations are in areas under Provincial Iraqi Control. Of the remaining 800 stations, 200 are too dangerous for PTTs to visit. There are sufficient PTTs to visit just over half of the remaining 600 stations in the country.

160 Perito, "Reforming the Iraqi Interior Ministry, Police and Facilities Protection Service."

161 The large numbers of willing recruits are encouraging, but the Commission also notes that this abundance can contribute to problems in quality if recruits are not sufficiently vetted and trained, as discussed in more detail later this chapter.

162 Vetting is also critical to ensure that local recruits meet physical fitness and literacy standards.

163 Interviews with CPATT officials, July 2007.

164 The Iraq Study Group and well-known international policing experts such as Robert M. Perito have recommended that the Department of Justice be made the lead agency. See Iraq Study Group (James A. Baker, III, and Lee H. Hamilton, co-chairs), *The Iraq Study Group Report: The Way Forward—A New Approach* (New York: Vintage Books, 2006), pp. 81–82.

[165] Interestingly, one day before the Commission's visit to the training center, 200,000 rounds of ammunition arrived.

[166] See Iraq study Group, *The Iraq Study Group Report*, p. 83.

[167] Some experts assert that the various units created by Minister Jabr were made up of fighters from Shi'a militia organizations. See Robert M. Perito, "Reforming the Iraqi Interior Ministry, Police, and Facilities Protection Service," testimony before the House Armed Services Committee, Subcommittee on Oversight and Investigations, 110th Cong., lst sess., March 28, 2007.

[168] Walter Pincus, "US to Armor Plate Iraqi Police Vehicles," *Washington Post*, December 16, 2006.

[169] "Department of Defense Bloggers Roundtable with Colonel Mark R. French," http://www.defenselink.mil/home/blog/docs/20070730_French_Transcript.pdf.

[170] Olga Oliker, "Iraqi Security Forces: Defining Challenges and Assessing Progress," testimony before the House Armed Services Committee, Subcommittee on Oversight and Investigations, 110th Cong., 1st sess., March 28, 2007, p. 5; available at www.rand.org/pubs/testimonies/2007/RAND_CT277.pdf.

[171] U.S. House of Representatives Committee on Armed Services, Subcommittee on Oversight and Investigations, *Stand Up and Be Counted: The Continuing Challenge of Building the Iraqi Security Forces*, 110th Cong., 1st sess., july 2007, pp. 87–88.

[172] CPATT briefing, July 2007.

[173] CPATT briefing, July 2007.

[174] Meetings with Iraqi National Police officials, July 2007.

[175] CPATT Support Forces briefing, July 2007.

[176] Department of Border Enforcement and Ports of Entry Directorate overview briefing, July 2007.

[177] CPA Order 26, "Creation of the Department of Border Enforcement"; available at http://www.cpa-iraq.org/regulations/20030824_CP AORD_26_Creation_of_the_Dept_of_Border_Enforcement.pdf.

[178] Department of Border Enforcement and Ports of Entry Directorate overview briefing, July 2007.

[179] CPATT Support Forces briefing, July 2007.

[180] Interviews with DOD officials, July 2007.

[181] Department of Defense, *Measuring Stability and Security in Iraq*, June 2007, p. 35 (reports of this title, submitted to Congress in accordance with section 9010 of various Department of Defense appropriation acts, are cited hereafter as 9010 Report).

[182] MNSTC-I Border Forces briefing, July 2007.

[183] CPATT briefing, July 2007 (staffing levels); MNSTC-I Border Forces briefing, July 2007 (training).

[184] 9010 Report, June 2007, p. 35.

[185] MNSTC-I Border Forces briefing, July 2007.

[186] *Ibid.*

[187] *Ibid.*

[188] Interview with DOD officials, July 2007.

[189] Department of Border Enforcement and Ports of Entry Directorate overview briefing, July 2007.

[190] MNSTC-I Border Forces briefing, July 2007.

[191] Meeting with senior Ports of Entry Directorate official, July 2007.

[192] Meeting with senior Ministry of the Interior official, July 2007.

[193] Corruption was so prevalent in Region 2 that the central government sent members of the Commission for Public Integrity to the port of entry; but because the investigators were Shi'a in a Sunni region, little was accomplished.

[194] Interviews with former Coalition Brigade Transition Team leads, June 2007.

[195] For example, one port of entry in May 2006 recorded collecting $2.3 million in taxes on the basis of a specific amount of traffic across the border. Seven months later, in December 2006, the same port of entry processed the same amount of traffic and collected only $300,000, with no explanation given for the discrepancy.

DOCUMENT NO. 7

IRAQ: POST-SADDAM GOVERNANCE AND SECURITY

CRS Report
RL31339

September 6, 2007

Kenneth Katzman
Specialist in Middle Eastern Affairs
Foreign Affairs, Defense, and Trade Division

Summary

Operation Iraqi Freedom overthrew Saddam Hussein's regime, but much of Iraq remains violent because of Sunni Arab resentment and a related insurgency, compounded by Sunni-Shiite sectarian violence that, in the judgment of many, constitutes a "civil war." Mounting U.S. casualties and financial costs—without dramatic improvements in levels of violence or clear movement toward national political reconciliation among Iraq's major communities—have intensified a debate within the United States over whether to reduce U.S. involvement without completely accomplishing initial U.S. goals.

President Bush announced a new strategy on January 10, 2007 ("New Way Forward") consisting of deployment of an additional 28,500 U.S. forces ("troop surge") to help stabilize Baghdad and restive Anbar Province. The strategy is intended to provide security conditions conducive to Iraqi government action on a series of key reconciliation initiatives that are viewed as "benchmarks" of political progress. The FY2007 supplemental appropriation, P.L. 110-28, linked some U.S. reconstruction aid to progress on the eighteen named benchmarks, but allows for a presidential waiver to continue the aid even if little or no progress is observed in Administration reports due July 15, 2007 and September 15, 2007. The latter will include a major assessment of the effects of the "troop surge" to date. According to the required July 15, 2007 Administration report, released on July 12, the Baghdad security plan has made progress on several military indicators and some political indicators, but progress is unsatisfactory on the most important political reconciliation indicators. The Administration report asserts that the "overall trajectory … has begun to stabilize," a finding on the security situation that is corroborated, to some extent, by an August 2007 National Intelligence Estimate A required report by the GAO released September 4, 2007, assesses less progress on security benchmarks than does the Administration and is pessimistic, as is the NIE, on the prospects for political reconciliation.

Some in Congress—as well as the Iraq Study Group—believe that the United States should begin winding down U.S. combat involvement in Iraq. Both chambers adopted a FY2007 supplemental appropriation to fund U.S. operations in Iraq and Afghanistan (H.R. 1591) that would have set an outside deadline of March 31, 2008, for U.S. combat withdrawal if the President did not certify Iraqi progress on the "benchmarks." President Bush vetoed it on May 1, 2007, and subsequent bills mandating forms of withdrawal or combat reduction have not moved forward. Some observers say such legislation might see further action after the Administration's September 15 progress report, while others say some positive assessments of the "troop surge" might forestall immediate congressional action.

This report is updated regularly. See also CRS Report RS21968, *Iraq: Government Formation and Benchmarks*, by Kenneth Katzman; CRS Report RL31833, *Iraq: Reconstruction Assistance*, by Curt Tarnoff; CRS Report RL31701, *Iraq: U.S. Military Operations*, by Steve Bowman; and CRS Report RL33793, *Iraq: Regional Perspectives and U.S. Policy*, coordinated by Christopher Blanchard.

Iraq has not previously had experience with a democratic form of government, although parliamentary elections were held during the period of British rule under a League of Nations mandate (from 1920 until Iraq's independence in 1932), and the monarchy of the Sunni Muslim Hashemite dynasty (1921–1958). The territory that is now Iraq was formed from three provinces of the Ottoman empire after British forces defeated the Ottomans in World War I and took control of the territory in 1918. Britain had tried to take Iraq from the Ottomans earlier in World War I but were defeated at Al Kut in 1916. Britain's presence in Iraq, which relied on Sunni Muslim Iraqis (as did the Ottoman administration), ran into repeated resistance, facing a major Shiite-led revolt in 1920 and a major anti-British uprising in 1941, during World War II. Iraq's first Hashemite king was Faysal bin Hussein, son of Sharif Hussein of Mecca who, advised by British officer T.E Lawrence ("Lawrence of Arabia"), led the Arab revolt against the Ottoman Empire during World War I. Faysal ruled Iraq as King Faysal I and was succeeded by his son, Ghazi, who was killed in a car accident in 1939. Ghazi was succeeded by his son, Faysal II, who was only four years old.

A major figure under the British mandate and the monarchy was Nuri As-Said, a pro-British, pro-Hashemite Sunni Muslim who served as prime minister 14 times during 1930-1958. Faysal II, with the help of his pro-British Prime Minister Nuri al-Sa'id who had also served under his predecessors, ruled until the military coup of Abd al-Karim al-Qasim on July 14, 1958. Qasim was ousted in February 1963 by a Baath Party-military alliance. Since that same year, the Baath Party has ruled in Syria, although there was rivalry between the Syrian and Iraqi Baath regimes during Saddam's rule. The Baath Party was founded in the 1940s by Lebanese Christian philosopher Michel Aflaq as a socialist, pan-Arab movement, the aim of which was to reduce religious and sectarian schisms among Arabs.

One of the Baath Party's allies in the February 1963 coup was Abd al-Salam al-Arif. In November 1963, Arif purged the Baath, including Baathist Prime Minister (and military officer) Ahmad Hasan al-Bakr, and instituted direct military rule. Arif was killed in a helicopter crash in 1966 and was replaced by his elder brother, Abd al-Rahim al-Arif, who ruled until the Baath Party coup of July 1968. Following the Baath seizure, Bakr returned to government as President of Iraq and Saddam Hussein, a civilian, became the second most powerful leader as Vice Chairman of the Revolutionary Command Council. In that position, Saddam developed overlapping security services to monitor loyalty among the population and within Iraq's institutions, including the military. On July 17, 1979, the aging al-Bakr resigned at Saddam's urging, and Saddam became President of Iraq. Under Saddam Hussein, secular Shiites held high party positions, but Sunnis, mostly from Saddam's home town of Tikrit, dominated the highest party and security positions. Saddam's regime repressed Iraq's Shiites after the February 1979 Islamic revolution in neighboring Iran partly because Iraq feared that Iraqi Shiite Islamist movements, emboldened by Iran, would try to establish an Iranian-style Islamic republic of Iraq.

Table 1. Iraq Basic Facts

Population	27.5 million
Demographics	Shiite Arab—60%; Sunni Arab—17–20%; Kurd—15 20%; Christian—3%.
Comparative Area	Slightly more than twice the size of Idaho
GDP	$87.9 billion (purchasing power parity)
GDP per capita	$3,000 per year
Unemployment Rate	25–30%
Inflation Rate	60%+

Source: CIA World Factbook, updated June 2007

Policy in the 1990s Emphasized Containment

Prior to the January 16, 1991, launch of Operation Desert Storm to reverse Iraq's August 1990 invasion of Kuwait, President George H.W. Bush called on the Iraqi people to overthrow Saddam. That Administration decided not to try to do so militarily because (1) the United Nations had approved only liberating Kuwait; (2) Arab states in the coalition opposed an advance to Baghdad; and (3) the Administration feared becoming bogged down in a high-casualty occupation.[1] Within days of the war's end (February 28, 1991), Shiite Muslims in southern Iraq and Kurds in northern Iraq, emboldened by the regime's defeat and the hope of U.S. support, rebelled. The Shiite revolt nearly reached Baghdad, but the mostly Sunni Muslim Republican Guard forces were pulled back into Iraq before engaging U.S. forces and were intact to suppress the rebellion. Many Iraqi Shiites blamed the United States for not intervening on their behalf. Iraq's Kurds, benefitting from a U.S.-led "no fly zone" set up in April 1991, drove Iraqi troops out of much of northern Iraq and remained autonomous thereafter.

Subsequent to the war, the thrust of U.S. policy was containment, consisting of U.N. Security Council-authorized weapons inspections, an international economic embargo, and U.S.-led enforcement of "no fly zones" over northern and southern Iraq.[2] However, President George H.W. Bush did pursue regime change to some extent, including reportedly sending Congress an intelligence finding that the United States would try to promote a military coup. The Administration apparently believed that a coup could produce a favorable government without fragmenting Iraq. After a reported July 1992 coup failed, there was a U.S. decision to shift to supporting the Kurdish, Shiite, and other oppositionists that were coalescing into a broad movement,[3] but the United States did not help them militarily.

The Clinton Administration and Major Anti-Saddam Factions

During the Clinton Administration, the United States built ties to and progressively increased support for several of the Shiite and Kurdish factions analyzed below. Some of these factions have provided major figures in post-Saddam politics, while also fielding militias that are allegedly conducting acts of sectarian reprisals in post-Saddam Iraq. Also discussed in the table are Sunni factions, almost all of which, to varying degrees, oppose the dominant Shiites and Kurds. They are discussed in greater depth later, in the analysis of post-Saddam security issues.

During 1997–1998, Iraq's obstructions of U.N. weapons of mass destruction (WMD) inspections led to growing congressional calls to overthrow Saddam, beginning with an FY1998 supplemental appropriations act (P.L. 105-174). The sentiment was expressed more strongly in the "Iraq Liberation Act" (ILA, P.L. 105338, October 31, 1998). Signed by President

Clinton despite doubts about opposition capabilities, it was viewed as an expression of congressional support for the concept of promoting an Iraqi insurgency with U.S. air power. That law, which states that it should be the policy of the United States to "support efforts" to remove the regime headed by Saddam Hussein, is often cited as evidence of a bipartisan consensus that Saddam should be toppled. Section 8 states that the act should not be construed as authorizing the use of U.S. military force to achieve regime change. The ILA did not specifically terminate after Saddam Hussein was removed from power. Section 7 provides for post-Saddam "transition assistance" to Iraqi groups with "democratic goals." The law also gave the President authority to provide up to $97 million worth of defense articles and services, as well as $2 million in broadcasting funds, to opposition groups designated by the Administration. In mid-November 1998, President Clinton publicly articulated that regime change was a component of U.S. policy toward Iraq.

The signing of the ILA coincided with new crises over Iraq's obstructions of U.N. weapons inspections. On December 15, 1998, U.N. inspectors were withdrawn, and a three-day U.S. and British bombing campaign against suspected Iraqi WMD facilities followed (Operation Desert Fox, December 16–19, 1998). On February 5, 1999, President Clinton made seven opposition groups eligible to receive U.S. military assistance under the ILA (P.D. 99–13): INC; INA; SICI; KDP; PUK; the Islamic Movement of Iraqi Kurdistan (IMIK);[4] and the Movement for Constitutional Monarchy (MCM). In May 1999, the Clinton Administration provided $5 million worth of training and "non-lethal" defense articles under the ILA. About 150 oppositionists underwent Defense Department-run training at Hurlburt air base in Florida on how to administer a post-Saddam Iraq. However, the Administration judged that the opposition was not sufficiently capable to merit weapons or combat training. These trainees were not brought into Operation Iraqi Freedom or into the Free Iraqi Forces that deployed to Iraq.

Secular Groups: Iraqi National Congress (INC) and Iraq National Accord (INA). In 1992, the two main Kurdish parties and several Shiite Islamist groups coalesced into the "Iraqi National Congress (INC)" on a platform of human rights, democracy, pluralism, and "federalism" (Kurdish autonomy). However, many observers doubted its commitment to democracy, because most of its groups had authoritarian leaderships. The INC's Executive Committee selected Ahmad Chalabi, a secular Shiite Muslim, to run the INC on a daily basis. (A table on U.S. appropriations for the Iraqi opposition, including the INC, is an appendix).[5]

Another secular group, the Iraq National Accord (INA), was founded after Iraq's 1990 invasion of Kuwait, was supported initially by Saudi Arabia but reportedly later earned the patronage of the Central Intelligence Agency (CIA).[6] It is led by Dr. Iyad al-Allawi. The INA enjoyed Clinton

Administration support in 1996 after squabbling among other opposition groups reduced their viability,[7] but the INA was penetrated by Iraq's intelligence services, which arrested or executed over 100 INA activists in June 1996. In August 1996, Baghdad launched a military incursion into northern Iraq, at the invitation of the KDP, to help it capture Irbil from the PUK. The incursion enabled Baghdad to rout INC and INA agents in the north.

The Kurds.[8] The Kurds, who are mostly Sunni Muslims but are not Arabs, are probably the most pro-U.S. of all major groups. Historically fearful of persecution by the Arab majority, the Kurds have carved out a high degree of autonomy and run their own three-province region run by a Kurdistan Regional Government (KRG). Through legal procedures as well as population movements, the Kurds are trying to secure the mixed city of Kirkuk, which they covet as a source of oil that would ensure their autonomy or eventual independence. The Kurds achieved insertion of language in the permanent constitution requiring a vote by December 2007 on whether Kirkuk might formally join the Kurdish administered region. (The Iraq Study Group report, released December 6, 2006, in Recommendation 30 believes that this referendum should be delayed.)[9] Both major Kurdish factions—the Patriotic Union of Kurdistan (PUK) led by Jalal Talabani, and the Kurdistan Democratic Party (KDP) led by Masud Barzani—are participating in Iraqi politics, but the PUK more so; Talabani is Iraq's president.

Shiite Islamists: Ayatollah Sistani, SICI, Da'wa Party, and Sadr. Shiite Islamist organizations have become dominant in post-Saddam politics; Shiites constitute about 60% of the population but were under-represented in all pre-2003 governments. Several Shiite Islamist factions cooperated with the U.S. regime change efforts of the 1990s, but others did not. The undisputed Shiite religious leader, Grand Ayatollah Ali al-Sistani, remained in Iraq, taking a low profile, during Saddam Hussein's regime, and he was not involved in U.S.-backed regime change efforts. As the *"marja-e-taqlid"* (source of emulation) and the most senior of the four Shiite clerics that lead the Najaf-based *"Hawza al-Ilmiyah"* (a grouping of seminaries).[10] About 85 years old, Sistani was born in Iran and studied in Qom, Iran, before relocating to Najaf at the age of 21. His mentor, was Ayatollah Abol Qasem Musavi-Khoi, was head of the *Hawza* until his death in 1992. Like Khoi, Sistani is a "quietist"—generally opposing a direct political role for clerics, but he believes in clerical supervision of political leaders. He wants Iraq to maintain its Islamic culture and favors modest dress for women, and curbs on sales of alcohol and Western music and entertainment.[11]

Islamic Supreme Council of Iraq (ISCI). ISCI (in May 2007 it changed its name from the Supreme Council of the Islamic Revolution of Iraq, SCIRI), considers itself the largest party within the "United Iraqi Alliance" (UIA) of Shiite political groupings. ISCI founders were in exile in Iran after a major crackdown in 1980 by Saddam, who accused pro-Khomeini Iraqi Shiite Islamists of trying to overthrow him. During Ayatollah Khomeini's exile in Najaf (1964–1978), he was hosted by Grand Ayatollah Muhsin al-Hakim, then head of the *Hawza*, and the father of the Hakim brothers (including current leader Abd al-Aziz) that founded ISCI. ISCI leaders say they do not seek to establish an Iranian-style Islamic republic, but ISCI reportedly receives substantial amounts of financial and other aid from Iran. Although it was a member of the INC in the early 1990s, ISCI refused to accept U.S. funds, although it did have contacts with the United States.

Da'wa Party/Prime Minister Nuri al-Maliki. The Da'wa (Islamic Call) Party, which did not directly join the U.S.-led effort to overthrow Saddam Hussein during the 1990s, is both an ally and sometime rival of SCIRI. The leader of its main faction in Iraq was Ibrahim al-Jafari, a Da'wa activist since 1966 who fled to Iran in 1980 to escape Saddam's crackdown, later going to London. He was transitional Prime Minister during April 2005–April 2006. His successor as Prime Minister, Nuri al-Maliki, was named Da'wa leader in early July 2007, prompting an attempt by Jafari to agitate against Maliki. Although there is no public evidence that Jafari or Maliki were involved in any terrorist activity, the Kuwaiti branch of the Da'wa allegedly committed a May 1985 attempted assassination of the Amir of Kuwait and the December 1983 attacks on the U.S. and French embassies in Kuwait. (It was reported in February 2007 that a UIA/Da'wa parliamentarian, Jamal al-Ibrahimi, was convicted by Kuwait for the 1983 attacks.) Lebanese Hezbollah, founded by Lebanese Da'wa Party activists, attempted to link release of the Americans they held hostage in Lebanon in the 1980s to the release of 17 Da'wa prisoners held by Kuwait for those attacks in the 1980s. In post-Saddam Iraq, another faction of Da'wa—also under the UIA umbrella—is loyal to Abd al-Karim al-Anazi.

Moqtada al-Sadr Faction. Moqtada Al Sadr is emerging as a major—some believe the most powerful—figure in Iraq. After the fall of Saddam Hussein, he was viewed as a young firebrand who lacked religious and political weight, but the more established Shiite factions have since built ties to him because of his large following among poor Shiites who identify with other "oppressed Muslims" and who oppose virtually any U.S. presence in the Middle East. He is now perceived as clever and capable—at the same time participating in the political process to avoid all-out confrontation with the United States but at the same time denouncing the "U.S. occupation." This criticism has a central feature of his activities during 2007, and his "Mahdi Army" militia forces are increasingly active against British forces in southern Iraq, against U.S. forces, and against rival Shiite factions and Iraqi security forces in the south. Pro-Sadr candidates won pluralities in some southern Iraqi provinces in the elections held in January 2005, but did not compete vigorously in other important southern provinces, such as Basra. *(In Recommendation 35, the Iraq Study Group recommended that the United States try to talk to Sadr, as well as Sistani, as well as with other parties except Al Qaeda-Iraq.)*

Table 2. Major Factions in Iraq

Major Shiite and Kurdish Factions	
Iraq National Accord (INA)/ Iyad al-Allawi	The INA leads the main secular bloc (Iraqis List) in parliament. Allawi, about 61 years old (born 1946 in Baghdad), a former Baathist who helped Saddam silence Iraqi dissidents in Europe in the mid-1970s. Subsequently fell out with Saddam, became a neurologist, and presided over the Iraqi Student Union in Europe. Survived an alleged regime assassination attempt in London in 1978. He is a secular Shiite, but many INA members are Sunni ex-Baathists and ex-military officers. Allawi was interim Prime Minister (June 2004–April 2005). Won 40 seats in January 2005 election but only 25 in December 2005. Spends most of his time outside Iraq and reportedly trying to organize a non-sectarian parliamentary governing coalition to replace Maliki. Now boycotting the cabinet.
Iraqi National Congress (INC)/ Ahmad Chalabi	Chalabi, who is about 67 years old, educated in the United States (Massachusetts Institute of Technology) as a mathematician. One of the rotating presidents of the Iraq Governing Council (IGC). U.S.-backed Iraqi police raided INC headquarters in Baghdad on May 20, 2004, seizing documents as part of an investigation of various allegations, including provision of U.S. intelligence to Iran. Case later dropped. Since 2004, has allied with and fallen out with Shiite Islamist factions; was one of three deputy prime ministers in the 2005 transition government. No INC seats in parliament, but Chalabi remains chair of the Higher National De-Baathification Commission and has resisted de-Baathification reform efforts. Serves as liaison between Baghdad neighborhood committees and the government in 2007 Baghdad security plan.
Kurds/KDP and PUK	Together, the main factions run Kurdistan Regional Government (KRG) with its own executive headed by "president" Masud Barzani, Prime Minister Nechirvan Barzani, and a 111 seat legislature (elected in January 30, 2005 national elections). PUK leader Talabani remains president, despite March 2007 health problems that required treatment in Jordan and the United States. Barzani has tried to secure his clan's base in the Kurdish north and has distanced himself from national politics. Many Kurds are more supportive of outright Kurdish independence than are these leaders. Kurds field up to 100,000 *peshmerga* militia. Their joint slate won 75 seats in January 2005 national election but only 53 in December 2005. Grudgingly supported framework draft oil law sent to parliament, but strongly oppose related draft implementing law that would place 93% of Iraq's oil fields under control of a revived Iraqi National Oil Company (INOC). Both factions intent on securing control of Kirkuk.

Major Shiite and Kurdish Factions	
Grand Ayatollah Ali al-Sistani	Undisputed leading Shiite theologian in Iraq. No formal position in government but has used his broad Shiite popularity to become instrumental in major political questions. Helped forge UIA and brokered compromise over the selection of a Prime Minister nominee in April 2006. Criticized Israel's July 2006 offensive against Lebanese Hezbollah. However, acknowledges that his influence is waning and that calls for Shiite restraint are unheeded as Shiites look to militias, such as Sadr's, for defense in sectarian warfare. Does not meet with U.S. officials. Has network of agents (*wakils*) throughout Iraq and among Shiites outside Iraq. Treated for heart trouble in Britain in August 2004. Aide stabbed to death by unknown assailant in July 2007.
Supreme Islamic Council of (ISCI)	Best-organized and most pro-Iranian Shiite Islamist party and generally allied with Da'wa Party in UIA. It was established in 1982 by Tehran to centralize Shiite Islamist movements in Iraq. First leader, Mohammad Baqr Al Hakim, killed by bomb in Najaf in August 2003. Current leader is his younger brother, Abd al-Aziz al-Hakim, a lower ranking Shiite cleric and a member of parliament (UIA slate), but he holds no government position. Hakim currently undergoing lung cancer treatment, instilling uncertainty in ISCI leadership. One of his top aides, Bayan Jabr, is now Finance Minister, and another, Adel Abd al-Mahdi, is a deputy president. Controls "Badr Brigades" militia. Son, Ammar al-Hakim, is a key ISCI figure as well and is said to be favored to take over ISCI should his father's condition become fatal. As part of UIA, ISCI has 29 members in parliament. Supports formation of Shiite "region" composed of nine southern provinces and dominates provincial councils on seven of those provinces. Supports draft oil law to develop the oil sector.
Da'wa (Islamic Call) Party	Oldest organized Shiite Islamist party (founded 1957), active against Saddam Hussein in early 1980s. Its founder, Mohammad Baqr al-Sadr, uncle of Moqtada Al Sadr, was ally of Iran's Ayatollah Khomeini and was hung by Saddam regime in 1980. Da'wa members tend to follow senior Lebanese Shiite cleric Mohammad Hossein Fadlallah rather than Iranian clerics, and Da'wa is not as close to Tehran as is ISCI. Has no organized militia and a lower proportion of clerics than does ISCI. Within UIA, its two factions control 25 seats in parliament. Supports draft oil law.
Moqtada Al-Sadr Faction	Young (about 32), the lone surviving son of the revered Ayatollah Mohammed Sadiq al-Sadr (killed, along with his other two sons, by regime security forces in 1999 after he began agitating against Saddam). Inherited father's political base in "Sadr City," a large (2 million population) Shiite district of Baghdad, but also strong and challenging ISCI for control of Diwaniyah, Nassiriyah, Basra, Amarah, and other major Shiite cities. Still clouded by allegations of involvement in the April 10, 2003, killing in Iraq of Abd al-Majid Khoi, the son of the late Grand Ayatollah Khoi and head of his London-based Khoi Foundation. Formed "Mahdi Army" militia in 2003. Now part of UIA, faction controls 30 seats in parliament (under UIA) and two more under the "Mission" bloc. Sadr faction, prior to its April 2007 pullout from the cabinet, held ministries of health, transportation, and agriculture and two ministry of state posts. Opposes Shiite "region" in the south, and generally opposes draft oil law as a "sellout."

Major Shiite and Kurdish Factions	
Fadilah Party	Loyal to Ayatollah Mohammad Yacoubi, who was a leader of the Sadr movement after the death of Moqtada's father in 1999 but was later removed by Moqtada and subsequently broke with the Sadr faction. *Fadilah* (Virtue) won 15 seats parliament as part of the UIA but publicly left that bloc on March 6, 2007 to protest lack of a Fadilah cabinet seat. Holds seats on several provincial councils in the Shiite provinces and dominates Basra provincial council, whose governor is a party member. Also controls protection force for oil installations in Basra, and is popular among oil workers and unions in Basra. Opposes draft oil law as too favorable to foreign firms.
Hezbollah Iraq	Headed by ex-guerrilla leader Abdul Karim Muhammadawi, who was on the IGC and now in parliament. Party's power base is southern marsh areas around Amara (Maysan Province), north of Basra. Has some militiamen. Supports a less formal version of Shiite region in the south than does ISCI.
Tharallah	Led by Sayyid Yusuf al-Musawi. Small Shiite faction in southern Iraq.
Islamic Amal	A relatively small faction, Islamic Amal (Action) Organization is headed by Ayatollah Mohammed Taqi Modarassi, a moderate cleric. Power base is in Karbala, and it conducted attacks there against Saddam regime in the 1980s. Modarassi's brother, Abd al-Hadi, headed the Islamic Front for the Liberation of Bahrain, which stirred Shiite unrest against Bahrain's regime in the 1980s and 1990s. One member in the cabinet (Minister of Civil Society Affairs).
Ayatollah Hassani Faction	Another Karbala-based faction, loyal to Ayatollah Mahmoud al-Hassani, who also was a Sadrist leader later removed by Moqtada. His armed followers clashed with local Iraqi security forces in Karbala in mid-August 2006. Hassani, along with *Fadilah*, are considered opponents of Iran because of Iran's support for ISCI and Da'wa Party.
Major Sunni Factions	
Iraqi Consensus Front (Tariq al-Hashimi and Adnan al-Dulaymi)	Often referred to by Arabic name "Tawafuq," Front is led by Iraqi Islamic Party (IIP), headed by Tariq al-Hashimi, now a deputy president. (Ousted) COR Speaker Mahmoud Mashadani, a hardliner, is a senior member; in July 2006, he called the U.S. invasion "the work of butchers." IIP withdrew from the January 2005 election but led the Sunni "Consensus Front" coalition in December 2005 elections, winning 44 seats in COR. Front, critical but accepting of U.S. presence, also includes Iraqi General People's Council of the hardline Adnan al-Dulaymi, and the National Dialogue Council (Mashhadani's party). Hashimi visited the United States in December 2006 and met with President Bush. Opposes draft oil law as sellout to foreign companies and distrusts Shiite pledges to equitably share oil revenues. Pulled five cabinet ministers out of government on August 1, but Hashimi still deputy president.

Major Sunni Factions	
Iraqi Front for National Dialogue	Head is Saleh al-Mutlak, an ex-Baathist, was chief negotiator for Sunnis on the new constitution, but was dissatisfied with the outcome and now advocates major revisions. Bloc holds 11 seats, generally aligned with Consensus Front. Opposes draft oil law on same grounds as Consensus Front.
Muslim Scholars Association (MSA)	Hardline Sunni Islamist group led by clerics Harith al-Dhari and Abd al-Salam al-Qubaysi, has boycotted all post Saddam elections. Believed to have ties to/influence over insurgent factions. Wants timetable for U.S. withdrawal from Iraq. Iraqi government issued a warrant for Dhari's arrest in November 2006 for suspected ties to the Sunni insurgency, causing Dhari to remain outside Iraq (in Jordan). Opposes draft oil law.
Sunni Tribes	Not an organized faction per se, but one group of about 20 tribes, the National Salvation Council formed by Shaykh Abd al-Sattar al-Rishawi, credited by U.S. commanders as a source of anti-Al Qaeda support that is helping calm Anbar Province. Some accounts in June 2007 say Council is splintering due to jealousy of Rishawi. Some large tribal confederations include Dulaym (Ramadi-based), Jabburi (mixed Sunni-Shiite tribe), Zobi (near Abu Ghraib), and Shammar (Salahuddin and Diyala regions). (See CRS Report RS22626, *Iraq: Tribal Structure, Social, and Political Activities*, by Hussein Hassan.)
Iraqi Insurgents	Numerous factions and no unified leadership. Some groups led by ex-Saddam regime leaders, others by Islamic extremists. Major Iraqi factions include Islamic Army of Iraq, New Baath Party, Muhammad's Army, and the 1920 Revolution Brigades; perceived as increasingly opposed to Al Qaeda-Iraq leadership of insurgency, a trend promoting stability in Anbar and Diyala.
Al Qaeda in Iraq (AQ-I) / Foreign Fighters	AQ-I was led by Abu Musab al-Zarqawi, a Jordanian national, until his death in U.S. airstrike June 7, 2006. Succeeded by Abu Hamza al-Muhajir (Abu Ayyub al-Masri), an Egyptian. Estimated 3,000 in Iraq (about 10-15% of total insurgents) from many nations, including Egypt and Saudi Arabia, but increasingly subordinate to Iraqi Sunni insurgents under the banner of the "Islamic State of Iraq." See CRS Report RL32217, *Iraq and Al Qaeda*.

Post-September 11, 2001: Regime Change and War

Several senior Bush Administration officials had long been advocates of a regime change policy toward Iraq, but the difficulty of that strategy led the Bush Administration initially to continue its predecessor's containment policy.[12] Some accounts say that the Administration was planning, prior to September 11, to confront Iraq militarily, but President Bush has denied this. During its first year, the Administration tried to prevent an asserted erosion of containment of Iraq by achieving U.N. Security Council adoption (Resolution 1409, May 14, 2002) of a "smart sanctions" plan. The plan relaxed U.N.-imposed restrictions on exports to Iraq of purely civilian equipment[13] in exchange for renewed international commitment to enforce the U.N. ban on exports to Iraq of militarily-useful goods.

Bush Administration policy on Iraq changed to an active regime change effort after the September 11, 2001, terrorist attacks. In President Bush's State of the Union message on January 29, 2002, given as major combat in the U.S.-led war on the Taliban and Al Qaeda in Afghanistan was winding down, he characterized Iraq as part of an "axis of evil" (with Iran and North Korea). Some U.S. officials, particularly deputy Defense Secretary Wolfowitz, asserted that the United States needed to respond to the September 11, 2001 attacks by "ending states," such as Iraq, that support terrorist groups. Vice President Cheney visited the Middle East in March 2002 reportedly to consult regional countries about the possibility of confronting Iraq militarily, although the Arab leaders visited urged greater U.S. attention to the Arab-Israeli dispute and opposed war with Iraq.

Some accounts, including the books *Plan of Attack* and *State of Denial* by Bob Woodward (published in April 2004 and September 2006, respectively), say that then Secretary of State Powell and others were concerned about the potential consequences of an invasion of Iraq, particularly the difficulties of building a democracy after major hostilities ended. Press reports in May 2007 indicate that warnings of such difficulties were issued by the CIA before the invasion. Other accounts include reported memoranda (the "Downing Street Memo") by British intelligence officials (based on conversations with U.S. officials) saying that by mid2002 the Administration had already decided to go to war against Iraq and that it sought to develop information about Iraq to support that judgment. President Bush and British Prime Minister Tony Blair deny this. (On December 20, 2001, the House passed H.J.Res. 75, by a vote of 392-12, calling Iraq's refusal to readmit U.N. weapons inspectors a "mounting threat" to the United States.)

The primary theme in the Bush Administration's public case for the need to confront Iraq was that Iraq posted a "grave and gathering" threat that should be blunted before the threat became urgent. The basis of that assertion in U.S. intelligence remains under debate.

- *WMD Threat Perception*. Senior U.S. officials, including President Bush, particularly in an October 2002 speech in Cincinnati, asserted the following about Iraq's WMD: (1) that Iraq had worked to rebuild its WMD programs in the nearly four years since U.N. weapons inspectors left Iraq and had failed to comply with 16 U.N. previous resolutions that demanded complete elimination of all of Iraq's WMD programs; (2) that Iraq had used chemical weapons against its own people (the Kurds) and against Iraq's neighbors (Iran), implying that Iraq would not necessarily be deterred from using WMD against the United States; and (3) that Iraq could transfer its WMD to terrorists, particularly Al Qaeda, for use in potentially catastrophic attacks in the United States. Critics noted that, under the U.S. threat of retaliation, Iraq did not use WMD against U.S. troops in the 1991 Gulf war. A "comprehensive" September 2004 report of the Iraq Survey Group, known as the "Duelfer report,"[14] found no WMD stockpiles or production but said that there was evidence that the regime retained the intention to reconstitute WMD programs in the future. The formal U.S.-led WMD search ended December 2004,[15] although U.S. forces have found some chemical weapons left from the Iran-Iraq war.[16] UNMOVIC's work was formally terminated by U.N. Security Council Resolution 1762 (June 29, 2007).

- *Links to Al Qaeda*. Iraq was designated a state sponsor of terrorism during 1979-1982 and was again so designated after its 1990 invasion of Kuwait. Although they did not assert that Saddam Hussein's regime had a direct connection to the September 11 attacks, senior U.S. officials asserted that Saddam's regime was linked to Al Qaeda, in part because of the presence of pro-Al Qaeda militant leader Abu Musab al-Zarqawi in northern Iraq. Although this issue is still debated, the report of the 9/11 Commission found no evidence of a "collaborative operational linkage" between Iraq and Al Qaeda.[17] For more information, see CRS Report RL32217, *Iraq and Al Qaeda*, by Kenneth Katzman.

Operation Iraqi Freedom (OIF)

As major combat in Afghanistan wound down in mid-2002, the Administration began ordering a force to Kuwait (the only Gulf country that agreed to host a major U.S. ground combat force) that, by early 2003, gave the President an option to invade Iraq. In concert, the Administration tried to build up and broaden the Iraqi opposition and, according to the *Washington Post* (June 16, 2002), authorizing stepped up covert activities by the CIA and special operations forces against Saddam Hussein. In August 2002, the State and Defense Departments jointly invited six major opposition groups to Washington, D.C., and the Administration expanded its ties to several groups composed primarily of ex-military officers. The Administration also began training about 5,000 oppositionists to assist U.S. forces,[18] although reportedly only about 70 completed training at Taszar air base in Hungary, eventually serving as translators during the war. The Administration blocked a move by the major factions to declare a provisional government, believing that doing so would prevent the emergence of secular, pro-democracy groups.

In an effort to obtain U.N. backing for confronting Iraq—support that then Secretary of State Powell reportedly argued was needed—President Bush urged the United Nations General Assembly (September 12, 2002) that the U.N. Security Council should enforce its 16 existing WMD-related resolutions on Iraq. The Administration then gave Iraq a "final opportunity" to comply with all applicable Council resolutions by supporting Security Council Resolution 1441 (November 8, 2002), which gave the U.N. inspection body UNMOVIC (U.N. Monitoring, Verification, and Inspection Commission) new powers of inspection. Iraq reluctantly accepted it. In January and February 2003, UNMOVIC Director Hans Blix and International Atomic Energy Agency (IAEA) Director Mohammad al-Baradei briefed the Security Council on WMD inspections that resumed November 27, 2002. Although they were not denied access to suspect sites, they criticized Iraq for failing to actively cooperate to clear up outstanding questions, but also noted progress and said that Iraq might not have retained any WMD.

During this period, Congress debated the costs and risks of an invasion. It adopted H.J.Res. 114, authorizing the President to use military force to "defend the national security of the United States against the continuing threat posed by Iraq" and "to enforce all relevant U.N. Security Council resolutions against Iraq." It passed the House October 11, 2002 (296-133), and the Senate the following day (77-23). It was signed October 16, 2002 (P.L. 107-243).

In Security Council debate, opponents of war, including France, Russia, China, and Germany, said the pre-war WMD inspections showed that Iraq could be disarmed peacefully or contained indefinitely, and no U.N. resolution authorizing force was adopted. At a March 16, 2003, summit meeting with the leaders of Britain, Spain, and Bulgaria at the Azores, President Bush asserted that Iraq was not complying with Resolution 1441 because it was not pro-actively revealing information, and that diplomatic options had failed. The following day, President Bush gave Saddam Hussein and his sons, Uday and Qusay, an ultimatum to leave Iraq within 48 hours to avoid war. They refused and OIF began on March 19, 2003.

In the war, Iraq's conventional military forces were overwhelmed by the approximately 380,000-person U.S. and British-led 30-country[19] "coalition of the willing" force assembled, a substantial proportion of which remained afloat or in supporting roles. Of the invasion force, Britain contributed 45,000, and U.S. troops constituted the bulk of the remaining 335,000 forces. Some Iraqi units and irregulars ("Saddam's Fedayeen") put up stiff resistance and used unconventional tactics. Some post-major combat evaluations (for example, "Cobra Two," by Michael Gordon and Bernard Trainor, published in 2006) suggest the U.S. military should have focused more on combating the irregulars rather than bypassing them to take on armored forces. No WMD was used by Iraq, although it did fire some ballistic missiles into Kuwait; it is not clear whether those missiles were of prohibited ranges (greater than 150 km). The regime vacated Baghdad on April 9, 2003, although Saddam Hussein appeared with supporters that day in Baghdad's mostly Sunni Adhamiya district. (Saddam was captured in December 2003, and on November 5, 2006, was convicted for "willful killing" of Shiite civilians in Dujail in 1982. He was hanged on December 30, 2006.)

Post-Saddam Transition and Governance

According to statements by President Bush, U.S. goals are for an Iraq that can sustain, govern, and defend itself and is a partner in the global war on terrorism. Administration officials have, for the most part, dropped an earlier stated goal that Iraq serve as a model of democratic reform in the Middle East.

Early Transition Process

The formal political transition has advanced since the fall of Saddam Hussein, but has not achieved political reconciliation among the newly dominant Shiite Arabs, Sunni Arabs that have been displaced from their former perch at the apex of Iraqi politics, and the Kurds who have felt perennially oppressed by Iraq's Arabs.

Occupation Period/Coalition Provisional Authority (CPA). After the fall of the regime, the United States set up an occupation structure, reportedly grounded in concerns that immediate sovereignty would favor major factions and not produce democracy. The Administration initially tasked Lt. Gen. Jay Garner (ret.) to direct reconstruction with a staff of U.S. government personnel to administer Iraq's ministries; they deployed in April 2003. He headed the Office of Reconstruction and Humanitarian Assistance (ORHA), within the Department of Defense, created by a January 20, 2003, executive order. The Administration largely discarded the State Department's "Future of Iraq Project," that spent at least a year before the war drawing up plans for administering Iraq after the fall of Saddam.[20] Garner and then White House envoy Zalmay Khalilzad, tried to establish a representative successor regime by organizing a meeting in Nassiriyah (April 15, 2003) of about 100 Iraqis of varying views and ethnicities. A subsequent meeting of over 250 notables was held in Baghdad (April 26, 2003), ending in agreement to hold a broader meeting one month later to name an interim administration.

In May 2003, the Administration, reportedly preferring what they perceived as stronger leadership in Iraq, named ambassador L. Paul Bremer to replace Garner by heading a "Coalition Provisional Authority" (CPA), which subsumed ORHA. The CPA was an occupying authority recognized by U.N. Security Council Resolution 1483 (May 22, 2003). Bremer discontinued Garner's political transition process and instead appointed (July 13, 2003) a non-sovereign Iraqi advisory body: the 25-member "Iraq Governing Council" (IGC). In September 2003, the IGC selected a 25-member "cabinet" to run the ministries, with roughly the same factional and ethnic balance of the IGC (a slight majority of Shiite Muslims). Although there were some Sunni figures in the CPA-led administration, many Sunnis resented the new power structure as overturning their prior dominance. Adding to Sunni resentment were some of the CPA's most controversial decisions, including to pursue "de-Baathification"—a purge from government of about 30,000 Iraqis at four top ranks of the Baath Party (CPA Order 1) and not to recall members of the armed forces to service (CPA Order 2). Bremer and others maintain that recalling the former regime armed forces would have caused mistrust among Shiites and Kurds about the prospects for democracy in post-Saddam Iraq.

Transitional Administrative Law (TAL). The Bush Administration initially made the end of U.S. occupation contingent on the completion of a new constitution and the holding of national elections for a new government, tasks expected to be completed by late 2005. However, Ayatollah Sistani and others agitated for early Iraqi sovereignty. In November 2003, the United States announced it would return sovereignty to Iraq by June 30, 2004, and that national elections would be held by the end of 2005. That decision was incorporated into an interim constitution—the Transitional Administrative Law (TAL), drafted by the major anti-Saddam factions and signed on March 8, 2004.[21] It provided a roadmap for political transition, including (1) elections by January 31, 2005, for a 275-seat transitional National Assembly; (2) drafting of a permanent constitution by August 15, 2005, and put to a national referendum by October 15, 2005; and (3) national elections for a permanent government, under the new constitution (if it passed), by December 15, 2005. Under the TAL, any three provinces could veto the constitution by a two-thirds majority. If that happened, a new draft would be written and voted on by October 15, 2006. The Kurds maintained their autonomous KRG and their *peshmerga* militia could still operate.

Sovereignty Handover/Interim (Allawi) Government. The TAL did not directly address the formation of the interim government that would assume sovereignty. Sistani's opposition torpedoed an initial U.S. plan to select a national assembly through nationwide "caucuses." After considering several other options, the United States tapped U.N. envoy Lakhdar Brahimi to select a government.[22] Dominated by senior faction leaders, it was named and began work on June 1, 2004. The formal handover ceremony occurred on June 28, 2004, two days before the advertised June 30 date, partly to confuse insurgents. There was a president (Ghazi al-Yawar), and Iyad al-Allawi was Prime Minister, with executive power, heading a cabinet of 26 ministers. Six ministers were women, and the ethnicity mix was roughly the same as in the IGC. The defense and interior ministers were Sunnis.

U.N. Involvement/Coalition Military Mandate/Status of U.S. Forces/ Permanent Basing. The Administration asserts that it has consistently sought and obtained U.N. and partner country involvement in Iraq efforts. Resolution 1483 (cited above) provided for a U.N. special representative to Iraq, and "called on" governments to contribute forces for stabilization. Resolution 1500 (August 14, 2003) established U.N. Assistance Mission for Iraq (UNAMI)[23]. The size of UNAMI in Iraq, headed by former Pakistani diplomat Ashraf Jahangir Qazi, exceeds 100 in Iraq, with at least an equal number "offshore" in Jordan. It is focused on promoting political reconciliation, election assistance, and monitoring human rights practices and humanitarian affairs. U.N. Secretary General Ban Ki Moon visited Baghdad in March 2007 and later said that UNAMI would expand its presence in Iraq and perhaps take on additional duties to promote political reconciliation. A new U.N. Security Council Resolution, 1770, adopted August 10, 2007, renewed UNAMI's mandate, and with an enhanced responsibility to be lead promoter of political reconciliation in Iraq and plan a national census. (*In Recommendations 7 and 26 and several others the Iraq Study Group calls for increased U.N. participation in promoting reconciliation in Iraq.*)

In an attempt to satisfy the requirements of several nations for greater U.N. backing of the coalition force presence, the United States achieved adoption of Resolution 1511 (October 16, 2003), authorizing a "multinational force under *unified* [meaning U.S.] command." Resolution 1546 (June 8, 2004) took U.N. involvement further by endorsing the handover of sovereignty, reaffirming the responsibilities of the interim government, spelling out the duration and legal status of U.S.-led forces in Iraq, and authorizing a coalition component force to protect U.N. personnel and facilities. Resolution 1546 also:

- It "authorize[d]" the U.S.-led coalition to secure Iraq, a provision interpreted as giving the coalition responsibility for security. Iraqi forces are "a principal partner" in the U.S.-led coalition, and the relationship between U.S. and Iraqi forces is spelled out in an annexed exchange of letters between the United States and Iraq. The U.S.-led coalition retained the ability to take prisoners.
- It stipulated that the coalition's mandate would be reviewed "at the request of the government of Iraq or twelve months from the date of this resolution" (or June 8, 2005); that the mandate would expire when a permanent government is sworn in at the end of 2005; and that the mandate would be terminated "if the Iraqi government so requests." Resolution 1637 (November 11, 2005) and Resolution 1723 (November 28, 2006) each extended the coalition military mandate for an additional year (now lasting until at least December 31, 2007), unless earlier "requested by the Iraqi government." The renewal resolutions also

required review of the mandate on June 15, 2006 and June 15, 2007, respectively. In June 2007, Iraq's parliament passed a motion, led by the Sadr faction, to require the Iraqi government to seek parliamentary approval before asking that the coalition military mandate be extended. The interim review was completed on June 14, 2007 and made no changes.

- Resolution 1546 deferred the issue of the status of foreign forces (Status of Forces Agreement, SOFA) to an elected Iraqi government. Secretary of Defense Rumsfeld said in July 2005 that U.S. military lawyers were working with the Iraqis on a SOFA, but no such agreement has been signed to date. Major facilities include Balad, Tallil, and Al Asad air bases, as well as the arms depot at Taji; all are being built up with U.S. military construction funds in various appropriations. P.L. 109-289 (FY2007 DoD appropriations) contains a provision that the Defense Department not agree to allow U.S. forces in Iraq to be subject to Iraqi law.
- On permanent basing, the Defense Appropriation for FY2007 (P.L. 109-289) and the FY2007 supplemental (P.L. 110-28) contain provisions prohibiting use of U.S. funds to establish permanent military installations or bases in Iraq. These provisions comport with Recommendation 22 of the December 2006 Iraq Study Group report, which recommends that the President should state that the United States does not seek permanent military bases in Iraq. A congressionally mandated commission on the Iraq Security Forces, led by retired General James Jones ("Jones Commission") recommends that Iraqi flags fly over all installations in Iraq used by U.S. forces. The P.L. 110-28 law also says that the United States shall not control Iraq's oil resources, a statement urged by Recommendation 23 of the Iraq Study Group report. Another bill, H.R. 2929, forbidding the use of appropriated funds to establish permanent bases in Iraq or control Iraq's oil, passed the House on July 25, 2007 by a vote of 399-24.

Post-Handover U.S. Structure in Iraq. As of the June 28, 2004, handover, the state of occupation ceased, and a U.S. Ambassador (John Negroponte) established U.S.-Iraq diplomatic relations for the first time since January 1991. A U.S. embassy formally opened on June 30, 2004; it is staffed with about 1,100 U.S. personnel.[24] Negroponte was succeeded in July 2005 by Ambassador Zalmay Khalilzad, and he was succeeded in April 2007 by Ryan Crocker, formerly Ambassador to Pakistan. The large new embassy complex, with 21 buildings on 104 acres, is under construction.[25] A reported May 2007 memo by Ambassador Crocker asking for experienced State Department personnel to be assigned to Iraq was perhaps foreshadowed by the December 2006 Iraq Study Group report. In Recommendations 73–76, the Iraq Study Group report lays out several initiatives that could be taken "to ensure that [the United States] has personnel with the right skills serving in Iraq." In conjunction with the handover:

- Iraq gained control over its oil revenues and the Development Fund for Iraq (DFI), subject to monitoring for at least one year (until June 2005) by the U.N.-mandated International Advisory and Monitoring Board (IAMB). (Resolution 1723 of November 28, 2006, extends the IAMB monitoring of the DFI until December 31, 2007, subject to review by June 15, 2007. That review made no changes.) Resolution 1546 also gave Iraq responsibility for close-out of the "oil-for-food program;"[26] Resolution 1483 ended that program as of November 21, 2003.
- Reconstruction management and advising of Iraq's ministries were taken over by a State Department component called the "Iraq Reconstruction and Management Office" (IRMO). With the expiration of that unit's authority in April 2007, it was renamed the "Iraq Transition Assistance Office," ITAO, headed since June 2007 by Mark Tokola. ITAO is is intended to promote the efficiency of Iraq's ministries and Iraq's takeover of management of the projects built with U.S. reconstruction funds, although Iraq reportedly has been unable or unwilling to take control of a large percentage of completed projects, according to press reports in July 2007. The authority has also expired for a separate DoD "Project Contracting Office (PCO)," headed by Brig. Gen. William McCoy (under the Persian Gulf division of the Army Corps of Engineers). It funded large infrastructure projects such as roads, power plants, and school renovations.

Elections in 2005

After the handover of sovereignty, the United States and Iraq focused on three national votes held in 2005. On January 30, 2005, elections were held for a transitional National Assembly, 18 provincial councils, and the Kurdish regional assembly. Sunnis, still resentful of the U.S. invasion, mostly boycotted, and no major Sunni slates were offered, enabling the UIA to win a slim majority (140 of the 275 seats) and to ally with the Kurds (75 seats) to dominate the national governments formed subsequently (as well as the provincial councils). PUK leader Jalal Talabani was named president; Ibrahim al-Jafari became Prime Minister. Although it had a Sunni Arab as Assembly speaker; deputy president; deputy prime minister; Defense Minister; and five other ministers, it did not draw Sunni popular support. (See CRS Report RS21968, *Iraq: Government Formation and Performance*, by Kenneth Katzman.)

Permanent Constitution. Over Sunni opposition, the constitution drafted by a committee appointed by the elected transition government was approved on October 15, 2005. Sunni opponents achieved a two-thirds "no" vote in two provinces, but not in the three needed to defeat the constitution. The crux of Sunni opposition was the provision for a weak central government ("federalism"): it allows groups of provinces to band together to form autonomous "regions" with their own regional governments, internal security forces, and a large role in controlling revenues from any new energy discoveries. The Sunnis oppose this concept because their region, unlike those dominated by the Kurds and the Shiites, has thus far lacks significant proven oil reserves and they depend on the central government for revenues, although some new substantial oil and gas fields have recently been reported to lie in Anbar Province. It contained an article (137) that promises a special constitutional review, within a set deadline, intended to mollify Sunnis on key contentious points.

December 15, 2005, Election. In this election, some harder line Sunnis, seeking to strengthen their position to amend the constitution, put together electoral slates—the "Consensus Front" and the Iraqi Front for National Dialogue. With the UIA alone well short of the two-thirds majority needed to unilaterally form a government, Sunnis, the Sadr faction, secular groupings, and the Kurds demanded Jafari be replaced; they subsequently accepted Nuri al-Maliki as Prime Minister (April 22, 2006). Talabani was selected to continue as president, with two deputies Adel Abd al-Mahdi of ISCI and Tariq al-Hashimi of the Consensus Front. (The former has lost one and the latter has lost three siblings to sectarian violence in 2006; Abd al-Mahdi was nearly assassinated in a March 2007 bombing.)

Amid U.S. and other congratulations, Maliki named and won approval of a 36-member cabinet (including two deputy prime ministers) on May 20, 2006. Among his permanent selections were Kurdish official Barham Salih and Consensus Front member Salam al-Zubaie as deputy prime ministers. (Zubaie was seriously wounded in an assassination attempt purportedly orchestrated by one of his aides on March 22, 2007; he has now recovered.) Four ministers (environment, human rights, housing, and women's affairs) are women. Of the 34 permanent ministerial posts named, a total of seven are Sunnis; seven are Kurds; nineteen are Shiites; and one is Christian (minister of human rights, Ms. Wijdan Mikha'il, of Allawi's bloc). Maliki did not immediately name permanent figures for the major posts of Interior, Defense, and Ministry of State for National Security because major factions could not agree on nominees. But, on June 8, 2006, he achieved COR confirmation of compromise candidates for those posts.

Prime Minister Nuri Kamal al-Maliki
Born in 1950 in Karbala, has belonged to Da'wa Party since 1968. Fled Iraq in 1980 after Saddam banned the party, initially to Iran, but then to Syria when he refused Iran's orders that he join Shiite militia groups fighting Iraq during the Iran-Iraq war. Headed Da'wa offices in Syria and Lebanon and edited Da'wa Party newspaper. Reputed advocate of aggressive purge of ex-Baathists as member of the Higher National De-Baathification Commission after Saddam's fall. Elected to National Assembly (UIA list) in January 2005 and chaired its "security committee." Publicly supported Hezbollah (which shares a background with his Da'wa Party) during July-August 2006 Israel-Hezbollah conflict, prompting congressional criticism during July 2006 visit to Washington DC. Believed sympathetic to Kurds' efforts to incorporate Kirkuk into the Kurdish region. Has tense relations with ISCI, whose activists accuse him of surrounding himself with Da'wa members. Prior to 2007, repeatedly shielded Sadr's Mahdi Army militia from U.S. military sweeps. In October 2006, said he is a U.S. ally but "not America's man in Iraq." Following Bush-Maliki meeting in Jordan (November 30, 2006), President Bush reiterated that Maliki is "the right guy for Iraq" and President Bush reportedly maintains regular direct contact with him by video-conference. In August 2007, President Bush, other senior officials, and Members of Congress increasingly criticize him for sectarianism.

Maliki Government, Political Reconciliation, and "Benchmarks"

Some observers believe that the "troop surge" announced on January 10, 2007 and discussed further below will be judged by whether or not it facilitates political reconciliation. The FY2007 Supplemental Appropriation Act (P.L. 110-28) conditions the release of some funds for Iraq operations upon achievement of eighteen stated benchmarks, and the Administration is required to report on progress by July 15 and September 15, 2007. A presidential waiver to permit the flow of funds is provided for and was exercised by the Administration following the July 15 report, which was released on July 12, 2007.

By all accounts, including those of top U.S. commander in Iraq General David Petraeus and U.S. Ambassador Ryan Crocker, and discussed in the July 12, 2007 report as well as the September 4, 2007 congressionally mandated GAO report, progress on the most significant political reconciliation efforts has been unsatisfactory to date. That view is also expressed in the unclassified key judgments of an August 2007 National Intelligence Estimate (NIE). Iraqi factions are continuing to negotiate—with only minor progress—outstanding issues, even though the COR has passed over 50 laws since it was established in early 2006, including a law adopted in July 2007 to regulate the running of Iraq's oil refineries. Senior Administration officials, including Vice President Cheney (May 9, 2007), deputy Secretary of State John Negroponte (June 13–14, 2007), Secretary of Defense Robert Gates (June 15, 2007), and President Bush (September 2, 2007) have visited

Iraq recently and expressed to Iraqi leaders U.S. disappointment at the relative lack of progress to date and to urge accelerated efforts. (*This type of high level contact is suggested by Recommendation 19 of the Iraq Study Group report.*)

The dates below indicate the benchmarks—and deadlines—to have been completed—*as pledged by the Iraqis in August 2006*—although U.S. officials say that, for the required reports, particularly the July 12, 2007 report, they were looking for concrete signs of progress and not necessarily completion. The GAO report, according to P.L. 110-28, was directed to measure whether or not a benchmark was completed or not, a criteria that the Administration has criticized as failing to account for nuances that constitute progress.

(1) *By September 2006, formation of a committee to review the constitution under the special amendment process (Article 137); approval of a law to implement formation of regions; approval of an investment law; and approval of a law establishing the Independent High Electoral Commission (IHEC).* The July 12, 2007 reports assessed progress on P.L. 110-28 benchmark # 1 (constitutional review process) as satisfactory. The constitution review committee was appointed in November 2006 and made partial recommendations in late May 2007, but it did not meet a new deadline of July 2007 (beyond the May 15 deadline) to finish its draft and no referendum on amendments is scheduled. Major decisions on presidential powers, powers of individual regions, and on the status of Kirkuk (which the Kurds want to affiliate with their region) await compromise by major factions. An investment law (not one of the P.L. 110-28 benchmarks) was adopted in October 2006. The regions law (P.L. 110-28 benchmark # 4) was adopted October 12, 2006, although, to mollify Sunni opposition, major factions agreed to delay the formation of new regions for 18 months. The IHEC law (the first of three parts of benchmark # 5) was passed on January 23, 2007, and the nine commissioners were appointed.

(2) *By October 2006, approval of a provincial election law; and approval of a new oil law.* The drafting of a provincial election law is at an early stage; it is considered key to easing Sunni resentment because the current councils, which expire in January 2009, have few Sunnis on them. (The Sunnis boycotted the January 2005 elections that formed the councils.) A draft law stipulating the powers of the provinces has received two readings in parliament, although differences remain on the powers of the provincial governors and related issues. (These are the remaining two of the three parts of benchmark # 5, and progress is assessed as unsatisfactory.)

The oil law is benchmark # 3; progress is assessed as unsatisfactory because the Iraqis did not meet their revised deadline of May 31, 2007 for all related oil laws. On February 26, 2007, Iraq's cabinet passed a draft framework oil law that would set up a Federal Oil and Gas Council with broad powers to review exploration contracts signed with foreign energy companies, including those signed by Iraq's regions. Of the three implementing laws that need to be adopted simultaneously, two have been drafted, including a law on sharing oil revenues among Iraq's communities, and a law regulating the dealings with foreign energy firms. The logjam on the draft revenue sharing law was broken in June 2007 when the Kurds reportedly agreed to a 17% share of oil revenues collected, to be deposited in a separate account at the Central Bank. Another law delineating how Iraq's energy industry will run ("INOC law"—Iraq National Oil Company) has not been drafted; the Kurds vigorously opposed an early draft INOC law because it puts 93% of Iraq's oil fields under state control. None of the oil law components are yet before the COR. Poorer Shiites and many Sunnis opposed fear foreign domination of the key sector and oppose a provision of the draft gives seats on the Federal Oil and Gas Council to foreign energy firms.

(3) *By November 2006, approval of a new de-Baathification law and approval of a flag and national anthem law.* Maliki said on September 3, 2007 that a draft De-Baathification reform law (benchmark # 2) has been presented to the COR. The draft would allow all but members of the three highest Baath Party levels to return to their jobs or obtain pensions. This announcement suggests that Maliki, in line with an agreement reached with the main Sunni and Kurdish representatives on August 26, 2007, has overcome opposition to the draft by members of the Supreme National De-Baathification Commission, claiming support from revered Shiite leader Ayatollah Ali al-Sistani. On April 7, 2007, Maliki ordered pensions be given to senior officers in the Saddam-era military and permission for return to service of lower ranking soldiers.

(4) *By December 2006, approval of laws to curb militias and to offer amnesty to insurgent supporters (benchmarks # 6 and 7).* The July 12, 2007 progress report says that the prerequisites for these laws are not in place, given the security environment. Iraq's factions, concerned about the general lack of security, are unwilling to disarm. The Shiite-led government reportedly fears that Sunnis are plotting to return to power and that offering amnesty to Sunni insurgent supporters would only accelerate that process. U.S. officials say Maliki has verbally committed to a militia demobilization program, and an executive director of the program was named on May 12, 2007, but committee members have not yet been appointed and a demobilization work plan is not drafted.

(6) *By February 2007, the formation of independent commissions to oversee governance.* (Not one of the P.L. 110-28 benchmarks.) No progress is evident to date.

(8) *By April 2007, Iraqi assumption of control of its military.* Six of the ten Iraqi Army divisions are now under Iraqi control. The P.L. 110-28 benchmarks

do not include this milestone, but instead require progress creating units capable of operating independently (benchmark # 15). Progress on that was judged unsatisfactory in the July 12 report.

(10) *By September 2007, Iraqi security control of all 18 provinces.* (Not a P.L. 110–28 benchmark.) Iraq Security Forces now have security control for the provinces of Muthanna, Dhi Qar, Najaf, Maysan, Irbil, Sulaymaniyah, and Dohuk—the latter three are Kurdish (turned over May 30, 2007). Britain apparently will turn over Basra Province soon.

(11) *By December 2007, Iraqi security self-reliance.* (Not a P.L. 110-28 benchmark.)

Several other security related benchmarks required by P.L. 110-28—and on which the July 12 report finds Iraqi performance generally satisfactory—center around assisting the Baghdad security plan/"U.S. troop surge"—for example by providing three Iraqi brigades to Baghdad (benchmark # 9); setting up joint security stations (benchmark # 14); making available over $10 billion in reconstruction funds (benchmark # 17); and on ensuring that the Baghdad security plan does not provide safe haven for any outlaw, regardless of sectarian affiliation (benchmark # 12). The GAO report finds Iraq's achievement of three of the four benchmarks as mixed, and joint security stations benchmark as achieved. The July 12, 2007, report and the GAO report give Iraq an unfavorable assessment on the politically-relevant benchmark of ensuring even handed law enforcement by the security forces (benchmark # 11). The assessment of benchmark # 13 is mixed according to the Administration, and unmet according to the GAO; Iraq has reduced sectarian violence but it has not eliminated militia control of local security. The August 2007 NIE assesses overall violence as high, but with some measurable improvement from the "troop surge."

Political Fragmentation. Amid increasing Administration and congressional criticism of Maliki and the failure to achieve significant reconciliation, splits within the power structure, both between the Shiite and other blocs, and even within the Shiite bloc, have widened to the point where some predict governmental collapse. The fragmentation began in March 2007 when the Fadilah Party left the UIA on the grounds that it is not represented in the cabinet. Subsequently, in April, five Sadr faction cabinet members (Health, Transportation, and Agriculture; as well as two ministers of state) resigned. Sadr—formerly a strong ally of Maliki—instructed his bloc to boycott parliament from the June 13, 2007 second bombing of the Grand Mosque in Samarra (the first was in February 2006) until mid-July 2007.

On August 1, 2007, the Sunni Consensus Front implemented a week-old threat to pull out its six cabinet members, who already had not attended cabinet meetings for one month, asserting that Maliki is not committed to political reconciliation. The Front did not withdraw its 44 members from parliament; they had just returned to parliament in mid-July after a month long boycott over the COR's June 12, 2007 vote to require Mashhadani's resignation as COR speaker for alleged intimidation of parliamentarians. Adding to Sunni distrust was the June 2007 arrest warrant issued for Culture Minister Asad al-Hashimi, a Sunni. Perhaps sensing Maliki's vulnerability, in August 2007, former Prime Minister Allawi directed three of the five cabinet ministers from his bloc to resign. This means that at least 15 cabinet seats are now vacant, including all affiliated Sunnis. On the other hand, Deputy President Tariq al-Hashimi is still in the government, as is unaffiliated Sunni Abd-al Qadir Jasim al-Mifraji, the Defense Minister.

In an effort to rebuild what appears to be a collapsing government, in August 2007, Maliki held meetings with other major leaders ("crisis summit") intended to reach factional compromise on major issues and presumably end cabinet boycotts. Attending the meetings are Maliki, Talabani and his two deputy presidents (Tariq al-Hashimi and Adel Abd al-Mahdi), and Masud Barzani. Hardline Consensus Front leader Adnan al-Dulaymi also attended some of the related meetings, just days after he issued a public appeal for the Sunni Arab governments to come to the aid of Iraq's Sunnis against the Shiites Dulaymi says are oppressing them. On August 26, 2007 Maliki, Talabani, Tariq al-Hashimi, deputy President Adel Abd al-Mahdi (ISCI) and Kurdish regional president Masoud Barzani unveiled a "consensus agreement"—to work to pass the de-Baathification law and the oil laws, and for the release of some detainees, mostly Sunnis.

The Kurds are fully engaged in the political structure in Baghdad. No Kurds are boycotting either the cabinet or the parliament at this time. However, potential troubles loom as the oil laws (discussed above) reach crucial decisions on final adoption and passage and many of the Kurds' objections and reservations remain unresolved. An even greater concern is the promised referendum on whether Tamim (Kirkuk) Province will affiliate formally with the Kurdistan Regional Government, a vote that, under Article 140 of the constitution, is to take place by December 31, 2007. The Kurds are insisting—to the point of threatening "civil war"—that the referendum proceed as planned but the other major communities, Shiite and Sunni Arabs, backed by the United States, are said to be trying to persuade the Kurds to accept a delay in the referendum until the broader sectarian conflicts in Iraq ease. There is speculation among observers that the Kurds might accept a delay in the referendum in exchange for favorable provisions in the oil laws under consideration. Suggesting the possibility of a postponement, the Kurds did not meet a July 31, 2007 deadline to furnish voter rolls for this planned referendum. At the same time, Kurdish participation in government might also unravel if the United States fails to persuade Turkish military leaders not to launch military incursions in the

Kurdish north in pursuit of PKK guerrillas that Turkey says have safehaven there.

To date, Administration officials have maintained that the United States continues to fully support Maliki and his government. However, as noted previously, there is increasing Administration and congressional criticism of his failure to achieve substantial reconciliation. U.S. frustration was reflected in President Bush's September 2, 2007 visit to Iraq, in which he visited only Anbar Province, not Baghdad, and requested that Maliki and other Iraqi leaders meet him there. Some observers say that U.S. backing could erode completely if his government continues to fracture or if the Baghdad security plan—in the September 15, 2007 progress report—is judged a failure.

Regional and International Diplomatic Efforts to Promote Iraq Stability. The Iraqi government has received diplomatic support, even though most of its neighbors, except Iran, resent the Shiite and Kurdish domination of the regime. There are about 50 foreign missions in Iraq, including most European and Arab countries. Jordan has appointed an ambassador and Kuwait has pledged to do so. Iran upgraded its representation to Ambassador in May 2006. On the other hand, some countries, such as Portugal in March 2007, have closed their embassies because of security concerns. There were attacks on diplomats from Bahrain, Egypt, Algeria, Morocco, and Russia in 2005 and 2006. Saudi Arabia, which considers the Shiite dominated government in Baghdad an affront to what it sees as rightful Sunni preeminence, told visiting Secretary of State Rice in August 2007 that the Kingdom will consider opening an embassy in Iraq.

Iraq continued its appeal for regional support an the Iraq-sponsored regional conference of its neighbors and major regional and outside powers (the United States, the Gulf monarchy states, Egypt, the permanent members of the United Nations Security Council) in Baghdad on March 10, 2007. Iran and Syria attended, as did the United States. A follow-on meeting in Egypt was held May 3 and 4, 2007, resulting in some additional pledges of aid for Iraq ("International Compact for Iraq," and agreement to establish regional working groups on Iraq's security, fuel supplies, and Iraqi refugees. U.S.-Iran meetings on Iraq are discussed later.

Democracy and Local Governance. The United States and its coalition partners have tried to build civil society and democracy at the local level, and U.S. Ambassador to Iraq Ryan Crocker said in July 2007 that local political reconciliation might, in some cases, be a better indicator of overall progress than the national legislative "benchmarks" discussed above. In July 2007, U.S. officials and some outside observers reported evidence of such local reconciliation in some areas of Iraq, including U.S.-brokered meetings between Sunni and Shiite tribal leaders.

The State Department's report on human rights for 2006, released March 6, 2007, appears to place the blame for much of the human suffering in Iraq on the overall security environment and not on the Maliki government's performance or intentions. It says that "widespread violence seriously compromised the government's ability to protect human rights." U.S. officials say Iraqis are freer than at any time in the past 30 years, with a free press and the ability to organize politically. A State Department report to Congress details how the FY2004 supplemental appropriation (P.L. 108-106) "Iraq Relief and Reconstruction Fund" (IRRF) is being spent ("2207 Report"):

- About $1.014 billion for "Democracy Building;"
- About $71 million for related "Rule of Law" programs;
- About $159 million to build and secure courts and train legal personnel;
- About $128 million for "Investigations of Crimes Against Humanity," primarily former regime abuses;
- $10 million for U.S. Institute of Peace democracy/civil society/ conflict resolution activities;
- $10 million for the Iraqi Property Claims Commission (which is evaluating Kurdish claims to property taken from Kurds, mainly in Kirkuk, during Saddam's regime); and
- $15 million to promote human rights and human rights education centers.

Run by the State Department Bureau of International Narcotics and Law Enforcement Affairs (State/INL), USAID, and State Department Bureau of Democracy, Human Rights, and Labor (DRL), some of the democracy and rule of law building activities conducted with these funds, aside from assistance for the various elections in Iraq in 2005, include the following:

- Several projects that attempt to increase the transparency of the justice system, computerize Iraqi legal documents, train judges and lawyers, develop various aspects of law, such as commercial laws, promote legal reform, and support the drafting of the permanent constitution.
- Activities to empower local governments, policies that are receiving increasing U.S. attention and additional funding allocations from the IRRF. These programs include (1) the "Community Action Program" (CAP) through which local reconstruction projects are voted on by village and town representatives. About 1,800 community associations have been established thus far. The conference report on an FY2006 supplemental appropriation (P.L. 109-234) designated $50 million in ESF for Iraq to be used to keep the CAP operating. That level of aid is expected in FY2007 under provisions of a continuing resolution (P.L. 109-383); (2) Provincial Reconstruction Development Committees (PRDCs) to empower local governments to decide on reconstruction priorities; and (3) Provincial

Reconstruction Teams (PRTs), local enclaves to provide secure conditions for reconstruction, as discussed in the section on security, below.

- Programs to empower women and promote their involvement in Iraqi politics, as well as programs to promote independent media.
- Some funds have been used for easing tensions in cities that have seen substantial U.S.-led anti-insurgency combat, including Fallujah, Ramadi, Sadr City district of Baghdad, and Mosul. In August 2006, another $130 million in U.S. funds (and $500 million in Iraqi funds) were allocated to assist Baghdad neighborhoods swept by U.S. and Iraqi forces in "Operation Together Forward."
- As noted above, according to Iraq's national timetable, a law on elections for provincial councils was to be drafted by the end of October 2006 and provincial elections to be held by June 2007, although it this timetable has not been met.

In addition to what is already allocated:

- The FY2006 regular foreign aid appropriations (conference report on P.L. 109-102) incorporated a Senate amendment (S.Amdt. 1299) providing $28 million each to the International Republican Institute and the National Democratic Institute for Iraq democracy promotion.
- The FY2006 supplemental appropriation (P.L. 109-234) provided another $50 million in ESF for Iraq democracy promotion, allocated to various organizations performing democracy work there (U.S. Institute of Peace, National Democratic Institute, International Republican Institute, National Endowment for Democracy, and others).
- The FY2007 supplemental appropriation (P.L. 110-28) provides $250 million in "democracy funding."

Economic Reconstruction and U.S. Assistance

The Administration asserts that economic reconstruction will contribute to stability, although some aspects of that effort appear to be faltering. As discussed in reports by the Special Inspector General for Iraq Reconstruction (SIGIR), the difficult security environment has slowed reconstruction.[27] (*In Recommendation 64, the Iraq Study Group says that U.S. economic assistance to Iraq should be increased to $5 billion per year rather than be "permitted to decline." Recommendation 67 calls on the President to appoint a Senior Advisor for Economic Reconstruction in Iraq, a recommendation that was largely fulfilled with the February 2007 appointment of Timothy Carney as Coordinator for Economic Transition in Iraq.*) For more detail, see CRS Report RL31833, *Iraq: Recent Developments in Reconstruction Assistance*, by Curt Tarnoff.

A total of about $34 billion has been appropriated for reconstruction funding (including security forces), of which $20.917 billion has been appropriated for the "Iraq Relief and Reconstruction Fund" (IRRF) in two supplemental appropriations: FY2003 supplemental, P.L. 108-11, which appropriated about $2.5 billion; and the FY2004 supplemental appropriations, P.L. 108-106, which provided about $18.42 billion. Of the IRRF funds, about $19.925 billion has been obligated, and, of that, about $18.233 billion has been disbursed. According to State Department reports, the sector allocations for the IRRF are as follows:

- $5.03 billion for Security and Law Enforcement;
- $1.315 billion for Justice, Public Safety, Infrastructure, and Civil Society;
- $1.014 billion for Democracy;
- $4.22 billion for Electricity Sector;
- $1.724 billion for Oil Infrastructure;
- $2.131 billion for Water Resources and Sanitation;
- $469 million for Transportation and Communications;
- $333.7 million for Roads, Bridges, and Construction;
- $746 million for Health Care;
- $805 million for Private Sector Development (includes $352 million for debt relief for Iraq);
- $410 million for Education, Refugees, Human Rights, Democracy, and Governance (includes $99 million for education); and
- $213 million for USAID administrative expenses.

FY2006 Supplemental/FY2007/FY2008. In reconstruction funding beyond the IRRF:

- The FY2006 supplemental appropriation (P.L. 109-234) provided $1.485 billion for Iraq reconstruction.
- The regular FY2007 appropriation (P.L. 109-383, as amended) provided approximately: $182 million in ESF for Iraq reconstruction, and $20 million for counter-narcotics. The FY2007 supplemental, P.L. 110-28 provides: $3.842 billion for the security forces; $1.574 billion in ESF; $50 million in a DoD "Iraq Freedom Fund"; $250 million in a "democracy fund;" $150 million for counter-narcotics; and $456.4 million in CERP funds (includes for Afghanistan as well). These are close to requested amounts. The July 12, 2007 progress report indicates that the President will exercise waiver authority to provide FY2007 ESF even though progress on some of the "benchmarks" was judged unsatisfactory.
- The FY2007 Defense Appropriation (P.L. 109-289) provided another $1.7 billion for the Iraqi security forces (discussed further below) and $500 million

in additional funds for the Commanders Emergency Response Program (CERP) under which U.S. military can expend funds for small construction projects intended to build good will with the Iraqi population.

- For FY2008 (regular), the Administration requested: $2 billion for the security forces; and $456 million for operations and reconstruction. The House version (H.R. 2764) of the FY2008 regular foreign aid appropriation does not provide the requested amount for operations and reconstruction. For FY2008 (supplemental), the Administration requested about $2.8 billion for operations and reconstruction. The FY2008 request asks for $1 billion in CERP funds (DOD funds).

Iraq provides some additional funds for reconstruction. In 2006 the Iraqi government allocated $2 billion in Iraqi revenues for development activities. Iraq's 2007 budget, adopted February 8, 2007, allocates $10.5 billion in unspent funds for reconstruction under President Bush's January 10, 2007 plan, discussed below.

Oil Revenues. The oil industry is the driver of Iraq's economy, and rebuilding this industry has received substantial U.S. and Iraqi attention, as encapsulated in the U.S. push for the Iraqi political structure to pass the draft oil law and annexes to be considered by the COR (see above under Maliki government).[28]

Before the war, it was widely asserted by Administration officials that Iraq's vast oil reserves, believed second only to those of Saudi Arabia, would fund much, if not all, reconstruction costs. The oil industry infrastructure suffered little damage during the U.S.-led invasion (only about nine oil wells were set on fire), but it has become a target of insurgents and smugglers. Insurgents have focused their attacks on pipelines in northern Iraq that feed the Iraq-Turkey oil pipeline that is loaded at Turkey's Mediterranean port of Ceyhan. (Iraq's total pipeline system is over 4,300 miles long.) The U.S. military reports in the June 2007 Measuring Stability report that elements of the protection forces for the oil sector (Strategic Infrastructure Battalions and Facilities Protection Service for the Oil Ministry) are suspected of complicity for smuggling as much as 70% of the output of the Baiji refinery, cost Iraq as much as $2 billion in revenue per year. The northern export route is operating, although it is only exporting about 300,000 barrels per day, about half its pre-war capacity. On the other hand, high world oil prices have, to some extent, compensated for the output shortfall. The Iraqi government needs to import refined gasoline because it lacks sufficient refining capacity. A GAO report released August 2, 2007 said that inadequate metering, re-injection, corruption, theft, and sabotage, says that Iraq's oil production might be 100,000–300,000 lower than the figures shown below, taken from State Department report. *(Steps to correct some of these deficiencies in the oil sector are suggested in Recommendations 62 of the Iraq Study Group report.)*

A related issue is long-term development of Iraq's oil industry and which foreign energy firms, if any, might receive preference for contracts to explore Iraq's vast reserves. Some are concerned that the draft oil law, when implemented, will favor U.S. firms because the draft does not give preference to development contracts signed during the Saddam era, such as those signed with Russian and Chinese firms. Even before the hydrocarbons law has been enacted, some investors began entering Iraq's energy market, primarily in the Kurdish north. South Korea and Iraq signed a preliminary agreement on April 12, 2007, to invest in Iraq's industrial reconstruction and, potentially, its energy sector as well. Poland reportedly is negotiating with Iraq for possible investments in Iraq's energy sector. Several small companies, such as Norway's DNO, Turkey's Genel; Canada's Western Zagros; Turkish-American PetPrime; and Turkey/U.S.'s A and T Energy have already contracted with the Kurdistan Regional Government to explore for oil (potential output of 100,000 barrels per day) near the northern city of Zakho. The Kurds' position is that these deals will go forward even though they were signed before a formal hydrocarbons law has been enacted. (*In Recommendation 63, the Iraq Study Group says the United States should encourage investment in Iraq's oil sector and assist in eliminating contracting corruption in that sector.*)

Table 3. Selected Key Indicators

<table>
<tr><th colspan="7">Oil</th></tr>
<tr><th>Oil Production (weekly avg.)</th><th>Oil Production (pre-war)</th><th>Oil Exports</th><th>Oil Exports (prewar)</th><th>Oil Revenue (2005)</th><th>Oil Revenue (2006)</th><th>Oil Revenue (2007 to date)</th></tr>
<tr><td>1.15 million barrels per day (mbd)</td><td>2.5 mbd</td><td>1.67 mbd</td><td>2.2 mbd</td><td>$23.5 billion</td><td>$31.3 billion</td><td>$20.8 billion</td></tr>
<tr><th colspan="7">Electricity</th></tr>
<tr><th>Pre-War Load Served (MWh)</th><th>Current Load Served</th><th>Baghdad (hrs. per day)</th><th colspan="4">National Average (hrs. per day)</th></tr>
<tr><td>102,000</td><td>110,000</td><td>6.4</td><td colspan="4">10.9</td></tr>
<tr><td colspan="7">Power shortage has caused lack of water in several Baghdad districts in early August 2007 due to lack of pumping and purification capability.</td></tr>
</table>

Other Economic Indicators		
GDP Growth Rate (2006 estimate by IMF)		10.6%
GDP	$18.9 billion (2002)	$33.1 billion (2005)
New Businesses Begun Since 2003		30,000
U.S. oil imports from Iraq		approx. 660,000 bpd

Note: Figures in the table are provided by the State Department "Iraq Weekly Status Report" dated August 29, 2007. Oil export revenue is net of a 5% deduction for reparations to the victims of the 1990 Iraqi invasion and occupation of Kuwait, as provided for in U.N. Security Council Resolution 1483 (May 22, 2003). That 5% deduction is paid into a U.N. escrow account controlled by the U.N. Compensation Commission to pay judgments awarded.

Lifting U.S. Sanctions. In an effort to encourage private U.S. investment in Iraq, the Bush Administration has lifted nearly all U.S. sanctions on Iraq, beginning with Presidential Determinations issued under authorities provided by P.L. 108-7 (appropriations for FY2003) and P.L. 108-11 (FY2003 supplemental). As a result, there are almost no restrictions on U.S. trade with and investment in Iraq.

- On July 30, 2004, President Bush issued an executive order ending a trade and investment ban imposed on Iraq by Executive Order 12722 (August 2, 1990) and 12724 (August 9, 1990), and reinforced by the Iraq Sanctions Act of 1990 (Section 586 of P.L. 101-513, November 5, 1990 (following the August 2, 1990 invasion of Kuwait.) The order did not unblock Iraqi assets frozen at that time.
- On September 8, 2004, the President designated Iraq a beneficiary of the Generalized System of Preferences (GSP), enabling Iraqi products to be imported to the United States duty-free.
- On September 24, 2004, Iraq was removed from the U.S. list of state sponsors of terrorism under Section 6(j) of the Export Administration Act (P.L. 96-72). Iraq is thus no longer barred from receiving U.S. foreign assistance, U.S. votes in favor of international loans, and sales of arms and related equipment and services. Exports of dual use items (items that can have military applications) are no longer subject to strict licensing procedures.[29]
- The FY2005 supplemental (P.L. 109-13) removed Iraq from a named list of countries for which the United States is required to withhold a proportionate share of its voluntary contributions to international organizations for programs in those countries.

Debt Relief/WTO Membership. The Administration is attempting to persuade other countries to forgive Iraq's debt, built up during Saddam's regime, with mixed success. The debt is estimated to total about $116 billion, not including reparations dating to the first Persian Gulf war. In 2004, the "Paris Club" of 19 industrialized nations agreed to cancel about 80% of the $39 billion Iraq owes them. The Persian Gulf states that supported Iraq during the Iran-Iraq war have resisted writing off Iraq's approximately $50 billion in debt to those countries (Saudi Arabia, Kuwait, United Arab Emirates, and Qatar). In mid-April 2007, Saudi Arabia agreed to write off 80% of the $15 billion Iraq owes it, but no new debt relief commitments by the UAE ($4 billion in Iraq debt) or Kuwait ($15 billion) were reported at the May 3–4, 2007, meetings on Iraq in Egypt. On December 17, 2004, the United States signed an agreement with Iraq writing off 100% of Iraq's $4.1 billion debt to the United States; that debt consisted of principal and interest from about $2 billion in defaults on Iraqi agricultural credits from the 1980s.[30] On December 13, 2004, the World Trade Organization (WTO) agreed to begin accession talks with Iraq.

Security Challenges, Responses, and Options

Since the fall of Saddam Hussein, the United States has employed a multifaceted approach to stabilizing Iraq, but the effort was clearly faltering as of the end of 2006. The Iraq Study Group said in its December 6, 2006, report that the "situation in Iraq is grave and deteriorating."[31] President Bush, in his January 10, 2007, speech on Iraq, said, "The situation in Iraq is unacceptable to the American people and it is unacceptable to me." The deterioration was, at least partly, the result of continuing sectarian violence superimposed on a tenacious Sunni-led insurgency, and prompted the revision of U.S. strategy that was announced in January 2007.

Sunni Arab-Led Insurgency

The duration and intensity of a Sunni Arab-led insurgency has defied many expectations, probably because, in the view of many experts, it is supported by a large segment of the Iraqi Sunni population who feel humiliated at being ruled by the Shiites and their Kurdish partners. Some Sunni insurgents want to return the Baath Party to power, while others would accept a larger Sunni political role without the Baath. Still others are pro-Al Qaeda fighters, either foreign or Iraqi, that want to defeat the United States and spread radical Islam throughout the region. The insurgent groups are believed to be loosely coordinated within cities and provinces.

The insurgency failed to derail the political transition,[32] but it has caused high levels of sectarian violence and debate in the United States over the continuing U.S. commitment in Iraq. Sunni insurgent groups have conducting numerous complex and coordinated attacks on police stations and other fixed positions, suicide attacks on markets frequented by Shiites, and occasional mass kidnappings, most recently of the deputy oil minister on August 14, 2007. One attack in April 2007 in Diyala Province was directed at a U.S. base and killed nine U.S. soldiers. Since January 2007, insurgent groups have, on about ten occasions, exploded chlorine trucks to cause widespread civilian injury or panic. Targets of insurgent grenades, IEDs (improvised explosive devices), mortars, and direct weapons fire are U.S. forces and Iraqi officials and security forces, as well as Iraqi civilians of rival sects, Iraqis working for U.S. authorities, foreign contractors and aid workers, oil export and gasoline distribution facilities, and water, power, and other facilities. A growing trend in 2007 has been attacks on bridges, particularly those connecting regions of differing sectarian domination, most recently destroying the rest of a major bridge at Taji on August 14, 2007. A major suicide bombing in August 2007 killed over 500 members of the Yazidi (Kurdish speaking, pre-Islamic) sect in northern Iraq—the most lethal attack of the war to date. A *New York Times* report of December 19, 2006, said that Sunni insurgents had succeeded in destroying many of the power stations that feed electricity to Baghdad, and some insurgents have been able to choke off power supplies to starve rival communities of power. An April 12, 2007, bombing of the Iraqi parliament, coming amid increasing mortar attacks on the heavily fortified International Zone, demonstrate the ability of the insurgency to operate in Baghdad.

Prior to 2007, whole Sunni-dominated neighborhoods of Baghdad, including Amiriya, Adhamiya, Fadhil, Jihad, Amal, and Dora (once a mostly Christian neighborhood) were serving as Sunni insurgent bases. Sunni insurgents also made substantial inroads into the mixed province of Diyala, pushing out Shiite inhabitants.

The U.N. Security Council has adopted the U.S. interpretation of the insurgency in Resolution 1618 (August 4, 2005), condemning the "terrorist attacks that have taken place in Iraq," including attacks on Iraqi election workers and foreign diplomats in Iraq. The FY2006 supplemental (P.L. 109-234) provides $1.3 million in Treasury Department funds to disrupt insurgent financing.

Al Qaeda in Iraq (AQ-I).[33] A numerically small but politically significant component of the insurgency is non-Iraqi, mostly in a faction called Al Qaeda-Iraq (AQ-I). Increasingly in 2007, U.S. commanders have seemed to equate AQ-I with the insurgency, even though most of the daily attacks are carried out by Iraqi Sunni insurgents. AQ-I was founded by Abu Musab al-Zarqawi, who was killed in a June 7, 2006, U.S. airstrike. AQ-I has been a U.S. focus from very early on in the war because, according to U.S. commanders in April 2007, it is responsible for about 90% of the suicide bombings against both combatant and civilian targets. AQ-I is discussed in detail in CRS Report RL32217, *Iraq and Al Qaeda*, by Kenneth Katzman.

In large parts of Anbar Province and now increasingly in parts of other Sunni provinces, Sunni tribes are trying to limit Al Qaeda's influence, which they believe is detrimental to their own interests, by cooperating with U.S. counter-insurgency efforts. In other cases, there have been clashes between AQ-I and Iraqi insurgent groups, such as in June 2007 in the Amiriyah neighborhood of Baghdad, apparently representing differences over targets and AQ-I's reported abuses of Iraqis who do not fully cooperate with AQ-I. U.S. commanders say they are trying to enlarge this wedge between Sunni insurgents and AQ-I by selectively cooperating with Sunni insurgents—a strategy that is controversial because of the potential of the Sunni Iraqis to later resume fighting U.S. forces and Iraqi Shiites. The strategy is reported to have led to increased tensions between Maliki and the lead U.S. commander in Iraq, Gen. David Petraeus.

Outside Support for Sunni Insurgents. Numerous accounts have said that Sunni insurgents are receiving help from neighboring states (money and weapons),[34] although others believe that outside support for the insurgency is not decisive. Largely because of this outside support, the first 17 recommendations of the Iraq Study Group report call for intensified regional diplomacy, including multi-lateral diplomacy with Syria and Iran, in an effort to persuade outside parties not to stoke the violence in Iraq by aiding protege factions in Iraq.

In September 2005, then-U.S. ambassador Khalilzad publicly accused Syria of allowing training camps in Syria for Iraqi insurgents to gather and train before going into Iraq. These reports led to U.S. warnings, imposition of additional U.S. sanctions against Syria, and U.S. Treasury Department's blocking of assets of some suspected insurgent financiers. Syria tried to deflect the criticism by moves such as the February 2005 turnover of Saddam Hussein's half-brother Sabawi to Iraqi authorities. The latest DOD "Measuring Stability" report says that Syria provides help to Sunni insurgents, mainly Baathist factions, and remains a foreign fighter gateway into Iraq. However, some U.S. commanders said in May 2007 that they had recently observed some Syrian tightening of the border.

Other assessments say the Sunni insurgents, both Iraqi and non-Iraqi, receive funding from wealthy donors in neighboring countries such as Saudi Arabia,[35] where a number of clerics have publicly called on Saudis to support the Iraqi insurgency. Press reports say that Saudi officials told visiting Vice President Cheney in November 2006 that the Saudis might be compelled to assist Iraq's Sunnis if the United States withdraws from Iraq. As noted above, the Saudi leadership has been notably cool to the Maliki government publicly—even to the point of refusing visits by him—which likely means that the Saudi leadership is at least tolerating aid to Sunni insurgents privately.

Table 4. Key Security/Violence Indicators

Indicator	Current Level
Number of U.S. forces in Iraq	About 160,000 includes all of "surge" of 28,500 U.S. forces (17,500 combat soldiers, 4,000 Marines, and 7,000 support personnel) in place. Almost all 10,000 extra ISF are in place in Baghdad, bringing total to about 90,000 U.S. and Iraqi forces in the city. Roughly the same U.S. level as most of 2005 during election periods.
U.S./Other Casualties	3,742 U.S. forces; 3,065 by hostile action. 3,596 since end to "major combat operations" declared May 1, 2003. About 260 coalition (including 160 British). 1,000+ contractors.
U.S. Casualties by "Explosively-Forced Projectiles"	about 200
Partner forces in Iraq	11,685 from 25 other countries. Down from 28,000 in 2005
Number of Iraqi Insurgents	25,000 U.S. estimates; Iraqi estimates run to 40,000, plus 150,000 supporters
AQ-I fighters	1,300–3,500
Number of Iranian Qods Forces in Iraq	150+
Number of all Attacks/day	About 120/day, about the level of mid-2006, but apparently decreasing from 200/day in early 2007 due to "troop surge." Of these, about 15–20 per day are sectarian murders, down from 33 per day pre-surge. Substantial debate exists over what incidents are counted or constitute "sectarian" violence; DoD does not count Shiite-Shiite violence, for example. Some sectarian murders now outside Baghdad, in Kirkuk, Mosul, Kut, and other cities.
Iraqi Police Killed since 2004	12,000 +
Number of Shiite militiamen	80,000 (60,000 Mahdi, 15,000 Badr, 5,000 other); up from 20,000 (2003)
Iraqis Leaving Iraq or Displaced since fall of Saddam	2 million left, incl. 700,000 to Jordan, 1 million to Syria; another 2 million internally displaced or relocated.
Iraq Civilian Deaths	About 60/day in August 2007, including sectarian murders, but subject to large fluctuations depending on presence or absence of large car/suicide bombings such as August 2007 bombing of Yazidi villages, killing 500. Possible reduction since troop surge began.

Indicator	Current Level
Iraqi Army and Police Battalions in operations	128; up from 104 in November 2006
Total ISF Equipped and Trained	359,700, with new reported goal of 395,000
Iraqi Army Battalions in the Lead or Fully Independent	98; up from 57 in May 2006, of which as many as 7 can operate independently.
National Police Battalions in the Lead	6; same as level in May 2006
Number of Provinces Under ISF Control	7: Muthanna, Dhi Qar, Najaf, Maysan, Irbil, Dahuk, and Sulaymaniyah (latter three in May 2007). All turned over since 2005.

Sources: Information provided by a variety of sources, including U.S. government reports on Iraq, Iraqi statements, the Iraq Study Group report, DoD Measuring Stability report, and press reports. See Tables 5 and 6 for additional figures on total numbers of Iraqi security forces, by force component.

Sectarian Violence and Shiite Militias/Civil War?

The security environment in Iraq became more complex since 2006 as Sunni-Shiite sectarian violence increased. Top U.S. officials said in late 2006 that sectarian-motivated violence—manifestations of an all-out struggle for political and economic power in Iraq—had displaced the Sunni-led insurgency as the primary security challenge. According to a January 2007 National Intelligence Estimate, "... the term 'civil war' does not adequately capture the complexity of the conflict in Iraq, [but] the term 'civil war' accurately describes key elements of the Iraqi conflict ...." *In assessing benchmark # 13, the July 12, 2007 progress report says that there has been satisfactory progress reducing sectarian violence but unsatisfactory progress towards eliminating militia control of local security, and the report generally gives the Iraqis poor reviews for reducing sectarianism. The August 2007 NIE says "sectarian groups remain unreconciled" and the September 4, 2007 GAO report is more pessimistic on the reduction of sectarian violence than was the Administration report, saying benchmark #13 was "unmet."*

U.S. officials date the escalation of sectarian violence to the February 22, 2006, Al Qaeda-Iraq bombing of the Askariya Shiite mosque in Samarra. The attack set off a wave of purported Shiite militia attacks on Sunni mosques and civilians in the first days after the mosque bombing.

Since then, Shiite militias have retaliated through attacks on Sunni insurgents and Sunni civilians, intended in part to drive Sunnis out of mixed neighborhoods. Press accounts say the attacks have largely converting mixed Sunni-Shiite districts of Baghdad, such as Hurriya, into predominantly Shiite districts and that the Sunnis have largely "lost" the "battle for Baghdad." Some accounts say that Baghdad was about 35% Sunni Arab during Saddam's rule but they have now been reduced to about 20%. Many victims of sectarian violence turn up bound and gagged, dumped in about nine reported sites around Baghdad, including in strainer devices in the Tigris River, although murdered bodies are also now turning up in cities in the north, such as Mosul and in Diyala Province. Sunnis are accusing the Shiites of using their preponderant presence in the emerging security forces, as well as their party-based militias, to commit the atrocities, but many Shiites, for their part, blame Sunni insurgents for the instigation. The Samarra mosque was bombed again on June 13, 2007 and their were reprisal attacks on Sunni mosques in Basra and elsewhere, although the attack did not spark the large wave of reprisals that the original attack did, possibly because the political elite appealed for calm after this second attack.

Iraqi Christians and their churches and church leaders have become major targets of Shiite and Sunni armed factions, viewing them as allies of the United States. Since the fall of Saddam Hussein, as many as 100,000 Christians might have left Iraq, leaving the current size of the community in Iraq at about 600,000–800,000. The two most prominent Christian sects in Iraq are the Chaldean Catholics and the Assyrian Christians. The attack on the Yazidis in August 2007, noted above, also appeared to reflect the precarious situation for Iraqi minorities.

Discussed below are the three major organized militias in Iraq: the Kurdish Peshmerga, the Badr Brigades, and the Mahdi Army.

- *Kurdish Peshmerga*. Together, the KDP and PUK may have as many as 100,000 *peshmergas* (fighters), most of which are providing security in the Kurdish regional area (Dahuk, Sulaymaniyah, and Irbil Provinces). Some are in the Iraqi Security Forces (ISF) and deployed in such cities as Mosul, Tal Affar, and Baghdad (as part of the 2007 Baghdad security plan). Peshmerga units have sometimes fought each other; in May 1994, the KDP and the PUK clashed with each other over territory, customs revenues, and control over the Kurdish regional government in Irbil. *Peshmerga* do not appear to be involved in the Sunni Arab-Shiite Arab sectarian violence gripping Iraq.
- *Badr Brigades*. This militia is led by Hadi al-Amiri (a member of parliament). The Badr Brigades were recruited, trained, and equipped by Iran's Revolutionary Guard, aligned with Iran's hardliners, during the Iran-Iraq war, during which Badr guerrillas conducted forays from Iran

into southern Iraq to attack Baath Party officials. Most Badr fighters were recruited from the ranks of Iraqi prisoners of war held in Iran. However, many Iraqi Shiites viewed ISCI as an Iranian puppet and Badr operations in southern Iraq during the 1980s and 1990s did not shake Saddam's grip on power. The Badr "Organization" is under the UIA as a separate political entity, in addition to its ISCI parent. Many Badr militiamen have now folded into the ISF, as discussed further later in this paper.

- *Mahdi Army (Jaysh al-Mahdi, JAM).* Recent "Measuring Stability" reports say this militia "has replaced Al Qaeda in Iraq as the most dangerous accelerant of potentially self-sustaining sectarian violence in Iraq." It is purportedly the main perpetrator of the killings of Sunni civilians. This U.S. assessment softened after the JAM largely ceased patrolling after the U.S. "troop surge" began in mid-February 2007.

Iranian Support. U.S. officials, most specifically in a February 11, 2007, U.S. defense briefing in Baghdad, have repeatedly accused Iran of aiding Shiite militias. More specifically, they assert that the Qods (Jerusalem) Force of Iran's Revolutionary Guard is providing armed Iraqi Shiite factions (most likely Sadr's Mahdi forces) with explosives and weapons, including the highly lethal "explosively forced projectiles" (EFPs). A new development came on April 11, 2007, when U.S. military officials said they had found evidence that Iran might also be supplying Sunni insurgent factions, presumably in an attempt to cause U.S. casualties and promote the view that U.S. policy in Iraq is failing. In July 2007, U.S. commanders asserted that Iran was using its protege, Lebanese Hezbollah, to train and arm Iraqi Shiite militias, based on information from Hezbollah operatives captured in Iraq.

Iran's support for Shiite militias contributed to a U.S. decision to conduct direct talks with Iran on the issue of stabilizing Iraq. The December 2006 Iraq Study Group (*Recommendations 9, 10, and 11*) said that the United States should engage Iran multilaterally to enlist its assistance on Iraq. The Administration initially rejected that recommendation—the President's January 10, 2007, Baghdad security initiative included announcement of an additional aircraft carrier group and additional Patriot anti-missile systems to the Gulf, moves clearly directed against Iran. He also said that U.S. forces would work to dismantle Iranian (and Syrian) networks that are aiding armed elements in Iraq, and a *Washington Post* report of January 26, 2007, said that the Administration has altered its policy to allow for U.S. forces to combat Iranian agents in Iraq directly if they are observed actively assisting Iraqi armed factions. Also in December 2006 and January 2007, U.S. forces arrested alleged Iranian Revolutionary Guard Qods Forces agents—two at a ISCI compound in Baghdad and five more at a compound in Irbil. The Iraqi government compelled the release of the first two; the others are still held and their incarceration will be reviewed in October 2007.

However, in an apparent shift, the Administration supported and participated in the March 10, 2007, regional conference in Baghdad and the follow-up regional conference held in Egypt on May 3 and 4, 2007. Subsequently, the two sides announced and then held high profile direct talks, at the Ambassador level, on May 28, 2007. The two sides said they shared similar visions for Iraq, but the U.S. side said it would judge the potential to continue the dialogue on Iran's performance "on the ground"—restraint in arming Iraqi militias. Another meetings was held on July 24, 2007, with little agreement apparent at the meeting but with a decision to form a U.S.-Iran working group to develop proposals for both sides to help ease Iraq's security difficulties. The working group met for the first time on August 6. (For more information, see CRS Report RS22323, *Iran's Influence in Iraq*, and CRS Report RL32048, *Iran: U.S. Concerns and Policy Responses*, both by Kenneth Katzman.)

Iraq's Northern Border

At the same time, security on Iraq's northern border appears to be increasingly fragile. Turkey is complaining that Iraq's Kurds are harboring the anti-Turkey PKK guerrilla group in northern Iraq, and Turkey's top military leader called on April 12, 2007, for a military operation into northern Iraq to quash the group. That call came several days after Barzani, in comments to journalists, claimed that Iraqi Kurds were capable of stirring unrest among Turkish Kurds if Turkey interferes in northern Iraq. Previously, less direct threats by Turkey had prompted the U.S. naming of an envoy to Turkey on this issue in August 2006 (Gen. Joseph Ralston (ret.), former Vice Chairman of the Joint Chiefs of Staff). On February 8, 2007, Turkish Foreign Minister warned against proceeding with the December 31, 2007, referendum on Kirkuk's affiliation with the Kurdish region, reflecting broader concerns that the referendum could set off additional sectarian violence and pave the way for Kurdish independence. The most serious crisis to date occurred on June 6, 2007 when Turkish military sources said that several thousand Turkish troops had crossed into Iraq to conduct "hot pursuit" of PKK guerrillas, although Iraqi and U.S. officials denied there had been any Turkish incursion. In July 2007, Iraq asserted that Turkey has massed 140,000 forces on the northern border amid reports that Turkish political and civilian leaders have agreed on criteria under which Turkish troops might stage incursions into Iraq.

U.S. Stabilization Strategy and "Troop Surge"

For the nearly four years since the fall of Saddam Hussein, the Administration has tried to refine its stabilization strategy, with increasing focus on curbing sectarian violence. The Administration position is that the U.S. stabilization mission requires continued combat operations. U.S. military headquarters in Baghdad (Combined Joint Task Force-7, CJTF-7) is a multi-national headquarters "Multinational Force-Iraq, MNF-I," headed by Gen. David Petraeus, who previously led U.S. troops in the Mosul area and the training and equipping program for the Iraqi Security Forces (ISF). The head of Multinational Corps-Iraq is Lt. Gen. Ray Odierno.

In prior years, a major focus of U.S. counter-insurgent combat was Anbar Province, which includes the cities of Fallujah and Ramadi (provincial capital), the latter of which was the most restive of all Iraqi cities and in which the provincial governor's office was shelled or attacked nearly daily. In the run-up to the December 15, 2005, elections, U.S. (and Iraqi) forces conducted several major operations (for example Operations Matador, Dagger, Spear, Lightning, Sword, Hunter, Steel Curtain, and Ram) to clear contingents of foreign fighters and other insurgents from Sunni cities in Anbar, along the Euphrates River. None of these operations succeeded, causing the Administration to examine other options.

"Clear, Hold, and Build" Strategy/Provincial Reconstruction Teams. In its November 2005 "National Strategy for Victory in Iraq," the Administration publicly articulated a strategy called "clear, hold, and build," intended to create and expand stable enclaves by positioning Iraqi forces and U.S. civilian reconstruction experts in areas cleared of insurgents. The strategy, based partly on an idea advanced by Andrew Krepinevich in the September/October 2005 issue of *Foreign Affairs*,[36] stipulates that the United States should devote substantial resources to preventing insurgent re-infiltration and promoting reconstruction in selected areas, cultivating these areas as a model that could eventually expand throughout Iraq. The strategy formed the basis of Operation Together Forward (I and II) as well as the President's January 10, 2007, Baghdad security plan.

In conjunction with the U.S. strategy, the Administration began forming Provincial Reconstruction Teams (PRTs), a concept used extensively in Afghanistan. Each PRT in Iraq is civilian led, to be composed of about 100 U.S. State Department and USAID officials and contract personnel, to assist local Iraqi governing institutions, such as the provincial councils, representatives of the Iraqi provincial governors, and local ministry representatives. The concept ran into some U.S. military objections to taking on expanded missions, but the debate was resolved with an agreement by DOD to provide security to the U.S.-run PRTs. Initially, ten PRTs were inaugurated, of which seven are run by the United States: Mosul, Kirkuk,

Hilla, Baghdad, Anbar Province, two in Salah ad-Din Province, and Baquba. Of the partner-run PRTs, Britain has formed a PRT in Basra, Italy has formed one in Dhi Qar province, and South Korea runs one in Irbil. In conjunction with the President's new strategy announced January 10, 2007, discussed below, another fifteen PRTs have been opened (bringing the total to 25), including six more in Baghdad and three more in Anbar. This necessitated adding 400 diplomats and contractors to staff the new PRTs, although about half of these new positions are filled with military personnel at least temporarily. Observers who have visited Iraq say that some PRTs are poorly staffed and therefore ineffective, while others, such as in Mosul, are well staffed and highly effective in generating employment and establishing reconstruction priorities.

PRT Funding. An FY2006 supplemental request asked for $400 million for operational costs for the PRTs, of which the enacted version, P.L. 109-234, provides $229 million. The requested $675 million for development grants to be distributed by the PRTs is fully funded through the ESF appropriation for Iraq in this law. The FY2007 supplemental (P.L. 110-28) provides about $700 million (ESF) for PRT security, operations, and PRT-funded reconstruction projects.

Baghdad Security Plan/"Fardh Qanoon"/"Troop Surge." Acknowledging that the initiatives above had not brought security or stability, the President's January 10, 2007, "New Way Forward"—Baghdad security initiative (referred to in Iraq as *Fardh Qanoon*, Arabic for "Imposing Law") is intended primarily to bring security to Baghdad and create conditions under which Iraq's communities and political leaders can reconcile. The plan, which in many ways reflects recommendations in a January 2007 report by the American Enterprise Institute entitled "Choosing Victory: A Plan for Success in Iraq,"[37] was announced as formally under way on February 14, 2007, and includes the following components:

- The deployment of an additional 28,500 U.S. forces to Iraq—17,500 combat troops (five brigades) to Baghdad; 4,000 Marines to Anbar Province; and the remainder are support troops and military police. The plan envisioned that these forces, along with additional Iraqi forces, would secure and hold neighborhoods and areas cleared of insurgents and thereby cause the population not to depend on militias or other armed elements for security. The plan envisions that these forces, along with additional Iraqi forces, will be able to secure and hold neighborhoods and areas cleared of insurgents and thereby cause the population not to depend on militias or other armed elements for security. The forces are being based, along with Iraqi soldiers, in 100 fixed locations (both smaller Combat Outposts and the larger "Joint Security Stations"). Only one such outpost is near Sadr City. *The July 12, 2007 progress reports says that establishment of the Joint Security Stations has been satisfactory. The GAO report concurred.*

- Cooperation from the Iraqi government, such as progress on the reconciliation steps discussed earlier, the provision of $10 billion in new capital spending on reconstruction (benchmark 17), and the commitment of the Iraqi forces discussed previously 3 brigades (about 6,000 soldiers), plus about 4,000 police commandos and regular police (benchmark 9). *The July 12, 2007 progress report indicates satisfactory Iraqi performance on these measures. The GAO report gives both benchmarks a "mixed" evaluation, saying that some of the Iraqi forces are of limited effectiveness, and saying that the $10 billion is unlikely to actually be spent.*
- Provision of at least $1.2 billion in new U.S. aid, including funds for job creation and CERP projects, in part to revive long-dormant state-owned factories.
- In an apparent attempt to demonstrate cooperation with President Bush's security plan, Maliki reportedly communicated to Sadr that Maliki would not stand in the way of operations against the Mahdi forces. *Application of the surge to all factions comprised two of the benchmarks under P.L. 110-28 (benchmarks 10 and 12). The July 12, 2007 report indicates satisfactory progress on benchmark 12 (not allowing safehaven for any outlaw of any sect), but unsatisfactory progress on benchmark 10 (refraining from political interference over ISF efforts to pursue militants of all sects.) Benchmark 11, even handed ISF enforcement of the law, another very closely related indicator, is also rated as unsatisfactory.* The GAO report says benchmark 10 is unmet, and benchmark 12 is "mixed." It is not clear why there are, in both assessments, different grades for these closely related benchmarks. In 2006, U.S. commanders expressed frustration with Maliki for forcing them to release suspected Mahdi militia commanders and to dismantle U.S. checkpoints in Sadr City, set up to try to prevent Shiite sectarian militiamen from operating. U.S. officers blamed these restrictions, in part, for the failure of "Operation Together Forward I and II," Baghdad security operations. Contributing to the previous failures were Iraq's deployment of only two out of the six Iraqi battalions committed to the operation (1,500 soldiers out of 4,000 pledged).

Perhaps suggesting new ability to operate against Shiite elements, U.S. forces arrested the deputy Health Minister on February 8, 2007, for allegedly funneling money to Mahdi Army forces engaged in sectarian killings. As the Baghdad security plan began to operate, U.S. forces began to pressure Mahdi forces and to patrol at least the outskirts of Sadr City, and the Mahdi Army largely ceased active patrolling. Sadr himself fled, or at least visited, Iran as the U.S.-Iraqi plan began, perhaps fearing that he would be a U.S. target, even though he is based in Kufa (near Najaf), not Baghdad; he returned in late May 2007.

Growing Shiite on Shiite Violence. On the other hand, as noted above, despite the troop surge, the JAM is reviving somewhat in concert with Sadr's May 2007 call for the ISF and militias to join hands to combat U.S. "occupation" forces (but not Iraqis). JAM assertiveness is evident in southern Iraq as Britain has reduced its forces during 2007. At least 50 British soldiers have died in suspected JAM attacks in southern Iraq since mid-2006; JAM forces also shelled a British base near Amarah in August 2006, contributing to a British decision to leave the base, and killed 11 British soldiers in southern Iraq in April 2007 alone. The JAM took over Amarah briefly for a few days in late October 2006, and violence there resumed in June 2007. Some fighting between the U.S., partner, and Iraqi forces and the Mahdi Army have taken place since April 2007 in Diwaniyah, Nassiriyah, Basra, Amarah and parts of Sadr City as Shiite groups struggle for pre-eminence in the south. As an outgrowth of this infighting, the governor of Qadisiyah province (Diwaniyah is the capital)—an ISCI loyalist—was killed in a roadside bombing on August 11, 2007. Similarly, the ISCI-linked governor of Muthanna Province was killed about a week later. Also, U.S. officials say that Shiite militias, presumably the JAM, are directing increasingly accurate mortar fire from areas near Sadr City in northeast Baghdad into the "Green Zone." (Sunni insurgents are firing on the zone from the south.) After major clashes between the JAM and the Badr-dominated Iraqi forces in Karbala spoiled an August 2007 Shiite celebration there and necessitated the fleeing of the Shiite celebrants, Sadr said he was suspending JAM operations for six months to "reorganize." Some experts, citing independent-minded JAM commanders such as one named Abu Deraa, believe Sadr is trying to regain full control of his armed following.

Surge Assessments. P.L. 110-28 mandated the July 15, 2007 and September 15, 2007 progress reports on the troop surge, as well as a GAO report due September 1, 2007 and an outside commission report ("Jones Commission") on the Iraqi security forces. Previously, Congress has mandated two major periodic Administration reports on progress in stabilizing Iraq. A Defense Department quarterly report, which DOD has titled "Measuring Stability and Security in Iraq," was required by an FY2005 supplemental appropriation (P.L. 109-13), and renewed by the FY2007 Defense Appropriation (P.L. 109-289). Another report ("1227 Report"), is required by Section 1227 of the Defense Authorization Act for FY2006 (P.L. 109-163).

The July 12, 2007 progress report gives preliminary assessments of the surge, although the report is primarily focused on performance against the political and security benchmarks. In briefings and comments, General Petraeus, Secretary of Defense Gates, Lt. Gen. Douglas Lute (named in May

2007 to be the new White House aide to coordinate policy toward Iraq and Afghanistan), as well as outside observers,[38] have given preliminary but mostly positive assessments of the surge, while noting that the last of the five combat brigades only arrived in June 2007. These assessments have prompted U.S. commanders to suggest that the "surge" be continued beyond the fall of 2007, and that ending the surge prematurely would squander the progress they note. On the other hand, officials and observers express disappointment (as expressed by Secretary Gates on August 2, 2007) on political reconciliation. The GAO report did not specifically require an assessment of the surge, although, as noted above, some of the benchmarks assessed are related to the surge. U.S. official and outside observer accounts of results of the surge to date include:

- An apparent reduction in the number of sectarian murders per day from about 33 per day to below 20 per day.
- Substantial progress in calming approximately half—two thirds of Baghdad, including the reopening of markets and near normal life in some districts. There has been return of some displaced families to their Baghdad homes;
- A possible Iraq-wide decrease in civilian deaths per day, from about 100 per day before the surge to about 60 per day in August 2007, although there are differences in how statistics are compiled and counted.
- Continuing setbacks to progress produced by AQ-I and other car and suicide bombs that cause mass casualties, such as the simultaneous bombings that killed the 500+ Yazidis near Sinjar on August 15.
- Substantial progress in Anbar Province that Gen. Petraeus has called "breathtaking," including a substantial reduction of violence to as few as one incident per day from a high in 2006 of nearly 100 incidents per day. Press reports note the restart of long-stalled reconstruction projects in the province.
- Decreasing concern about violence in Diyala Province and in the towns in "belts" around Baghdad where insurgents have moved to in order to regroup and try to thwart the "surge." On August 2, 2007, the commander of Multi-National Division-North, Benjamin Mixon, said Baqubah (capital of Diyala) is transitioning to the "hold" phase of "clear, hold, and build." He had deployed 3,000 additional U.S. forces to Diyala in recent months, and launched "Operation Arrowhead Ripper" on June 18, 2007, involving about 10,000 U.S. soldiers, to try to capture AQ-I fighters in Diyala. Gen. Mixon is reported to be considering the northern province of Nineveh (Mosul, capital) for transition to Iraqi security control because of progress there.

- Gen. Petraeus was quoted in early September 2007 as saying he might propose a reduction of U.S. forces in early 2008 from areas where the surge has seen the most progress, such as Anbar Province.

Building Iraqi Security Forces (ISF)[39]

A major pillar of U.S. policy had been to equip and train Iraqi security forces (ISF) that could secure Iraq by themselves, although the 2007 Baghdad security plan moves away from reliance on this strategy. President Bush stated in a June 28, 2005 speech, "Our strategy can be summed up this way: As the Iraqis stand up, we will stand down."[40] However, the Baghdad security plan relies more heavily on combat by U.S. forces than on transferring security responsibilities to the ISF, and a former senior leader of training the Iraqis (Brig. Gen. Dana Pittard) said in July 2007 that training the ISF had slowed since the "troop surge" began. The commander of the ISF training mission, the Multinational Transition Security Command-Iraq (MNSTC-I), is Lt. Gen. James Dubik, who in June 2007 replaced Gen. Martin Dempsey. There are about 5,000 U.S. forces embedded with or mentoring the ISF. The degrees to which the Iraqi government has assumed operational ISF control, and of ISF security control over territory, are shown in the security indicators table. A map showing areas under Iraqi control and ISF lead can be found in the Iraq Weekly Status Report of the State Department, available online at [http://www.state.gov/p/nea/ci/c3212.htm]. *(Recommendations 42, 43 and 44 of the Iraq Study Group report advised an increase in training the ISF, and completion of the training by early 2008, but the "troop surge" strategy appears to represent a move away from that recommendation.)*

The mandated "Jones Commission" report, released September 5, 2007, clearly says the ISF will not be ready, in 12–18 months, to take over security in Iraq, even though the total ISF goal of 395,000 trained and equipped has nearly been reached. The Jones Commission report has some praise for the Iraqi Army, while recommending that the Shiite-dominated National Police commando force be scrapped entirely and reorganized. Some observers go so far as to say that the ISF is part of the security problem in Iraq, not the solution, because of incidents of involvement in sectarian involvement or even possible anti-U.S. activity. Lt. Gen. Dubik said in July 2008 that it is still difficult to find ISF leaders free of sectarian loyalties.

The July 12, 2007 progress report assesses the ISF and political leadership of it in: the ability of the ISF to operate independently, which is assessed as unsatisfactory (benchmark # 15). Enforcing the law even-handedly, which the report says is generally unsatisfactory (benchmark # 11), although some improvement is being noted. Ensuring that the political authorities are not making false accusations against or undermining the ISF (benchmark 18), is assessed as unsatisfactory. Preventing political interference in ISF operations in conjunction with the troop surge (benchmarks 10),is assessed as unsatisfactory. Enforcing the law even-handedly (benchmark 11), is assessed as unsatisfactory. Ensuring the Baghdad security plan does not allow safehaven for outlaws of any sect (benchmark 12), is assessed as satisfactory. The GAO assessment concurs with all of these assessments except benchmark 12, which GAO assesses as "mixed."

In addition, the Jones Commission report and the most recent DOD "Measuring Stability" report reiterate previously reported criticisms of the ISF, including

- That the ISF continue to lack an effective command structure or independent initiative, and that there continues to be a culture of corruption throughout the ISF structure.
- As much as one-third of ISF members are absent-without-leave or might have deserted at any given time, significantly reducing the actual fielded forces.
- As noted above, that the ISF, particularly the police, are unbalanced ethnically and by sect, penetrated by militias or even insurgents, and involved in sectarian violence, particularly among the police forces. Widely reported is that many ISF members view themselves as loyal to their former militias or party leaders, and not to a national force. In late 2005, U.S. forces uncovered militia-run detention facilities ("Site 4") and arrested those (Badr Brigade and related Iraqi police) running them.
- Press reports in June 2007 said that some roadside bombs intended for U.S. forces were being planted near police stations, presumably by Iraqi police.
- Most of the ISF, particularly the police, are Shiites, with Kurdish units mainly deployed in the north, and many Sunnis distrust the ISF as instruments of repression and responsible for sectarian killings.
- One controversial element of the Baghdad security plan is its apparent reliance on several mostly Kurdish brigades, a deployment reportedly resented by both Shiite and Sunni Arabs in the capital.
- That the 144,000 members of the "Facilities Protection Force," (FPS), which are security guards attached to individual ministries, are involved in sectarian violence. U.S. and Iraq began trying to rein in the force in May 2006 by placing it under some Ministry of Interior guidance, including issuing badges and supervising what types of weapons it uses. *(In Recommendation 54, the Iraq Study Group says the Ministry of Interior should identify, register, and otherwise control FPS.)*

On the other hand, while reports continue to point to sectarianism in the Interior Ministery, U.S. officials have praised Interior Minister Jawad Bolani for trying to remove militiamen and death squad participants from the ISF; in October 2006, he fired 3,000 Ministry employees for alleged sectarian links, along with two commanders of National Police components. That same month, an entire brigade of National Police were taken out of duty status for retraining for alleged toleration of sectarian killings in Baghdad.

Another positive trend noted by U.S. officials, even before the troop surge, is what they say is increasing tribal cooperation in Anbar Province, particularly from the National Salvation Council of an anti-Al Qaeda tribal leader, Abd al Sattar al-Rishawi. According to press reports, his coalition has persuaded 13,000 men (almost all Sunni) to join police forces in the province, and these forces are participating in securing the border with Syria as well as helping secure Ramadi and other parts of Anbar, particularly against AQ-I. U.S. commanders are reported to be attempting a similar strategy to try to stabilize Diyala, Salahuddin, and Nineveh provinces.

The Iraq Study Group (Recommendations 50-61) contain several suggestions for reforming and improving the police. Among the recommendations are: assigning the lead role in advising and training the anti-crime portions of the police forces to the U.S. Department of Justice; and transferring those police forces that are involved in anti-insurgency operations to the Ministry of Defense from their current organizational structure under the Ministry of Interior.

Weaponry. Most observers say the ISF are severely underequipped, dependent primarily on donations of surplus equipment by coalition members. The Iraqi Army is using mostly East bloc equipment, including 77 T-72 tanks donated by Poland, but has now received about 2,500 up-armored Humvees from the United States. The October 2006 report of the SIGIR [http://www.sigir.mil/reports/quarterlyreports/default.aspx] notes problems with tracking Iraqi weapons; of the approximately 370,000 weapons turned over to Iraq by the United States since Saddam's fall, only 12,000 serial numbers were properly recorded. Some fear that some of these weapons might have fallen into the hands of insurgents or sectarian militias, although it is also possible the weapons are still in Defense and Interior Ministry stocks but are not catalogued. In August 2007, the GAO reported that the Defense Department cannot fully account for the total of $19.2 billion worth of equipment provided to the ISF by the United States and partner forces. A New York Times report in August 2007 said some of the ISF weapons might have ended up in the hands of anti-Turkish PKK guerrillas. (In Recommendation 45, the Iraq Study Group said the United States should encourage the Iraqi government to accelerate its Foreign Military Sales requests for U.S. arms and that departing U.S. combat units should leave behind some of their equipment for use by the ISF.)

ISF Funding. The accelerated training and equipping of the Iraqis is a key part of U.S. policy. The Administration has been shifting much U.S. funding into this training and equipping mission:

- According to the State Department, a total of $5.036 billion in IRRF funds has been allocated to build (train, equip, provide facilities for, and in some cases provide pay for) the ISF. Of those funds, as of June 4, 2007, about $4.975 billion has been obligated and $4.797 billion of that has been disbursed.
- An FY2005 supplemental appropriation (P.L. 109-13) provided an additional $5.7 billion to equip and train the ISF, funds to be controlled by the Department of Defense and provided to MNSTC-I. Of that amount, about $4.7 billion has been obligated.
- The FY2006 supplemental (P.L. 109-234) provided another $3 billion for the ISF.
- The FY2007 Defense appropriations law (P.L. 109-289) provides an additional $1.7 billion to train and equip the ISF.
- The FY2007 supplemental (P.L. 110-28) provides the requested $3.84 billion for this purpose. The FY2008 request is for $2 billion.

Table 5. Ministry of Defense Forces

Force	Size/Strength	IRRF Funds Allocated
Iraqi Army	157,500 total. Forces in units are in 129 battalions (about 90,000 personnel), with new goal of 132 battalions. Remainder not in formed units. Trained for eight weeks, paid $60/month.	$1.097 billion for facilities; $707 million for equipment; $656 million for training, personnel, and operations
Special Operations Forces	About 1,600 divided between Iraqi Counter-Terrorist Force (ICTF) and a Commando Battalion. Trained for 12 weeks, mostly in Jordan.	
Strategic Infrastructure Battalions	About 2,900 personnel in seven battalions to protect oil pipelines, electricity infrastructure. The goal is 11 battalions.	
Mechanized Police Brigade	About 1,500. Recently transferred from Ministry of Interior control.	
Air Force	About 900, its target size. Has 9 helicopters, 3 C-130s; 14 observation aircraft. Trained for six months. UAE and Jordan to provide other aircraft and helos.	$28 million allocated for air fields (from funds for Iraqi Army, above)

Force	Size/Strength	IRRF Funds Allocated
Navy	About 1,100, the target size. Has a Patrol Boat Squadron and a Coastal Defense Regiment. Fields about 35 patrol boats for anti-smuggling and anti-infiltration. Controls naval base at Umm Qasra, Basra port, and Khor al-Amaya oil terminals. Some training by Australian Navy.	
Totals	165,500	
U.S./Other Trainers	U.S. training, including embedding with Iraqi units (10 per battalion), involves about 4,000 U.S. forces (increasing to 10,000), run by Multinational Security Transition Command—Iraq (MNSTC-I). Training at Taji, north of Baghdad; Kirkush, near Iranian border; and Numaniya, south of Baghdad. All 26 NATO nations at NATO Training Mission—Iraq (NTM-I) at Rustamiyah (300 trainers). Others trained at NATO bases in Norway and Italy. Jordan, Germany, and Egypt also have done training.	

Table 6. Ministry of Interior Forces

Ministry of Interior	Total size unknown. 3,000 employees dismissed in October for corruption/ sectarianism.	
Iraqi Police Service (IPS)	135,000, including 1,300 person Highway Patrol. (About the target size.) Gets eight weeks of training, paid $60 per month. Not organized as battalions.	$ 1.806 billion
Dignitary Protection	About 500 personnel	
National Police	About 26,300. Comprises "Police Commandos," Public Order Police," and "Mechanized Police." Organized into 28 battalions. Overwhelmingly Shiite. Gets four weeks of counter-insurgency training. Iraq Study Group (Recommendation 50) proposes transfer to MOD control.	
Emergency Response Unit	About 300, able to lead operations. Hostage rescue.	
Border Enforcement Department	32,000. Controls 258 border forts built or under construction. Has Riverine Police component to secure water crossings. Iraq Study Group (Recommendation 51) proposes transfer to MOD control.	$437 million (incl. $3 million for stipends to 150 former WMD workers).

Force	Size/Strength	IRRF Funds Allocated
Totals (all forces)	194,200	
Training	Training by 2,000 U.S. personnel (DOD-lead) as embeds and partners. Pre-operational training mostly at Jordan International Police Training Center; Baghdad Police College and seven academies around Iraq; and in UAE. Iraq Study Group (Recommendation 57) proposes U.S. training at local police station level. Countries doing training aside from U.S.: Canada, Britain, Australia, Sweden, Poland, UAE, Denmark, Austria, Finland, Czech Republic, Germany (now suspended), Hungary, Slovenia, Slovakia, Singapore, Belgium, and Egypt.	
Facilities Protection Service (FPS)	Accounted for separately, they number about 145,000, attached to individual ministries.	$53 million allocated for this service thus far.

Coalition-Building and Maintenance[41]

Some believe that the Bush Administration did not exert sufficient efforts to enlist greater international participation in peacekeeping originally and that the U.S. mission in Iraq is being complicated by diminishing foreign military contributions. The Administration view is that partner draw-downs reflect a stabilizing security environment in the areas those forces are serving. A list of contributing countries, although not force levels, can be found in the Department of State's "Iraq Weekly Status Report" referenced earlier. Britain continues to lead a multinational division in southern Iraq, based in Basra, but, in line with plans announced by then Prime Minister Tony Blair on February 21, 2007, British forces have been reduced from 7,100 to about 5,500 currently, and will be reduced further to below 5,000 by the end of 2007. New Prime Minister Gordon Brown did not alter these plans in his meetings with President Bush in late July 2007, but he added that Basra Province is on track to be turned over to ISF control. That process began in early September 2007 with the withdrawal of about 550 British soldiers from Basra Palace to the Basra airport where the rest of the British force is based. A Poland-led force (Polish forces number 900, down from a high of 2,600 in 2005) has been based near Diwaniyah and includes forces from the following foreign countries: Armenia, Slovakia, Denmark, El Salvador, Ukraine, Romania, Lithuania, Latvia, Mongolia, and Kazakhstan. Poland said in July 2007 that it has not decided whether to extend the mission beyond the end of 2007.

The coalition shrinkage began with Spain's May 2004 withdrawal of its 1,300 troops. Spain made that decision following the March 11, 2004, Madrid bombings and subsequent defeat of the former Spanish government that had supported the war effort. Honduras, the Dominican Republic, and Nicaragua followed Spain's withdrawal (900 total personnel), and the Philippines withdrew in July 2004 after one of its citizens was taken hostage. On the other hand, many nations are replacing their contingents with trainers for the ISF or financial contributions or other assistance to Iraq. Among other changes are the following.

- Ukraine, which lost eight soldiers in a January 2005 insurgent attack, withdrew most of its 1,500 forces after the December 2005 elections.
- Bulgaria pulled out its 360-member unit after the December 2005 elections. However, in March 2006 it sent in a 150-person force to take over guard duties of Camp Ashraf, a base in eastern Iraq where Iranian oppositionists are located.
- South Korea withdrew 270 of its almost 3,600 troops in June 2005, and, in line with a November 2005 decision, withdrew another 1,000 in May 2006, bringing its troop level to about 2,200 (based in Irbil in Kurdish-controlled Iraq). The deployment has been extended until the end of 2007, and the government and parliament are discussing further extensions.
- Japan completed its withdrawal of its 600-person military reconstruction contingent in Samawah on July 12, 2006, but it continues to provide air transport (and in June 2007 its parliament voted to continue that for another two years). The Australian forces protecting the Japanese contingent (450 out of the total Australian deployment in Iraq of 1,350) moved to other areas, and security in Muthanna was handed over to ISF control.
- Italy completed its withdrawal in December 2006 after turning over Dhi Qar Province over to ISF control.
- Romanian leaders are debating whether to withdraw or reduce their 890 forces.
- In line with a February 21, 2007 announcement, Denmark is in the process of withdrawing its 460 troops from the Basra area, and Denmark reportedly is also evacuating about 200 Iraqis who helped that contingent, in regard for their safety.
- Lithuania said in early 2007 that it is "seriously considering" withdrawing its 53 troops from Iraq.
- On the other hand, Georgia is increasing its Iraq force to 2,000 (from 850) to assist the policing the Iran-Iraq border, a move that Georgian officials said was linked to its efforts to obtain NATO membership. Australian Prime Minister John Howard said in early September 2007 that he was not considering a drawdown of Australian forces in Iraq.

NATO/EU/Other Civilian Training. As noted above, all NATO countries have now agreed to train the ISF through the NTM-I, as well as to contribute funds or equipment. Several NATO countries and others are offering to also train civilian personnel. In addition to the security training offers discussed above, European Union (EU) leaders have offered to help train Iraqi police, administrators, and judges outside Iraq. At the June 22, 2005 Brussels conference discussed above, the EU pledged a $130 million package to help Iraq write its permanent constitution and reform government ministries. The FY2005 supplemental appropriations (P.L. 10913) provided $99 million to set up a regional counter-terrorism center in Jordan to train Iraqi security personnel and civil servants.

Reaction to "Troop Surge," Iraq Study Group Report, Legislative Proposals, and Other Options

In formulating the new strategy announced on January 10, 2007, President Bush said he weighed the December 6, 2006, report of the Iraq Study Group, as well as input from several other reviews, including one directed by the Joint Chiefs of Staff and another under direction of the National Security Council. In the time surrounding the speech, a number of senior personnel shifts were announced: U.S. Ambassador Khalilzad's replacement by Ambassador to Pakistan Ryan Crocker, Gen. Abizaid's replacement by CENTCOM Commander by Admiral William Fallon; Gen. Casey's replacement as head of MNF-I by General David Petraeus. Robert Gates replaced Donald Rumsfeld as Defense Secretary in December 2006. In May 2007, the White House named Lt. Gen Douglas Lute, as a new aide to focus on promoting rapid and effective inter-agency cooperation on the combat and policy in Iraq and Afghanistan. In June 2007, Joint Chiefs Chairman Gen. Pace was not put forward for another term as Joint Chiefs Chairman; he is being replaced by Admiral Michael Mullen.

Iraq Study Group Report

The President's "New Way Forward" plan appeared to deviate from many aspects of the Iraq Study Group report, although the differences have narrowed since January. The Administration has noted that the Iraq Study Group said it might support a temporary surge along the lines proposed by the President. The Iraq Study Group itself was launched in March 2006; chosen by mutual agreement among its congressional organizers to co-chair were former Secretary of State James Baker and former Chairman of the House International Relations Committee Lee Hamilton. The eight other members of the Group are from both parties and have held high positions in government. The group was funded by the conference report on P.L. 109-234, FY2006 supplemental, which provided $1 million to the U.S. Institute of Peace for operations of the group.[42] Some of the specific recommendations have been discussed throughout this paper and, among the major themes of the 79 recommendations, along with comparable or contrasting features of the President's plan, are the following.

- Foremost, transition from U.S.-led combat to Iraqi security self-reliance by early 2008 (Recommendations 40–45), with continued U.S. combat against AQ-I and force protection, in addition to training and equipping the ISF. The Administration has rejected any timetable for winding down U.S. combat.
- Heightened regional and international diplomacy, including with Iran and Syria, and including the holding of a major international conference in Baghdad (Recommendations 1–12). As noted above, the Administration, after appearing to reject this recommendation, has backed the series of regional conferences on Iraq.
- As part of an international approach, renewed commitment to Arab-Israeli peace (Recommendations 13–17). This was not a major feature of the President's plan, although he has authorized stepped up U.S. diplomacy by Secretary of State Rice on this issue.
- Additional economic, political, and military support for the stabilization of Afghanistan (Recommendation 18). This was not specified in the President's January 10 plan, although, separately, there have been increases in U.S. troops and aid for Afghanistan.
- Setting benchmarks for the Iraqi government to achieve political reconciliation, security, and governance, including possibly withholding some U.S. support if the Iraqi government refuses or fails to do so (Recommendations 19–37). The President opposes reducing support for the Iraqi government if it fails to uphold its commitments, but he signed P.L. 110-28 which does link U.S. economic aid to progress on the benchmarks, although he has waived any holdup of aid.
- Giving greater control over police and police commando units to the Iraqi Ministry of Defense, which is considered less sectarian than the Ministry of Interior that now controls some of these forces, and reforming the Ministry of Interior (Recommendations 50–58). The President's plan, according to a White House fact sheet released on January 10, requires reform of the Ministry of Interior.
- Securing and expanding Iraq's oil sector (Recommendations 62–63). The President's plan expects Iraq to pass the pending oil laws, which would, in part, encourage foreign investment in Iraq's energy sector.
- Increasing economic aid to Iraq and enlisting more international donations of assistance (Recommendations 64–67). The President's plan includes increases in aid, as discussed above.

In the 110th Congress, an amendment to H.R. 2764, the FY2008 foreign aid bill, would revive the Iraq Study Group (providing $1 million for its operations) to help assess future policy after the "troop surge." The amendment passed 355-69, but press reports say the Administration does not support reviving the Group's work. In the Senate, some Senators from both parties in June 2007 proposed legislation (S. 1545) to adopt the recommendations of the Group as U.S. policy.

Congressional Reaction to Troop Surge

Judging from legislative action, congressional reaction to the President's Baghdad security plan was somewhat negative. In House action, on February 16, 2007, the House passed (246–182) a non-binding resolution (H.Con.Res. 63) expressing opposition to the sending of additional forces to Iraq. However, on February 17, 2007, the Senate did not vote to close off debate on a version of that resolution (S. 574). Earlier, a Senate resolution opposing the troop increase (S.Con.Res. 2) was reported out of the Senate Foreign Relations Committee on January 24 (12-9 vote). A cloture motion failed on February 1, 2007.

The sections below discuss options that have been under discussion even before the report of the Iraq Study Group or the troop surge, and some of these options are being more actively debated in light of the upcoming September 15, 2007 progress report by Gen. Petraeus and Ambassador Crocker, and the failure of the Iraqi political structure to achieve political reconciliation. Some of the ideas discussed may be similar to some of the recommendations of the Study Group as well as the President's plan.

Further Options: Altering Troop Levels or Mission

Insisting that the "troop surge" is producing positive military results, President Bush continues to publicly oppose major reductions in troop levels, stating that the United States must uphold its "commitment" to the Iraqi government and maintaining that the Iraqi government would collapse upon an immediate pullout. However, during his early September 2007 visit to Iraq, possibly reflecting the views of some senior military leaders who believe the troop surge is straining U.S. military capabilities, he indicated that current security improvements might be sustainable with lower troop levels at some point soon. Consequences of a more substantial pullout, according to the Administration, would be full-scale civil war, safehaven for AQ-I and emboldening of Al Qaeda more generally, and increased involvement of regional powers in the fighting in Iraq. Supporters of the Administration position say that Al Qaeda terrorists might "follow us home"—conduct attacks in the United States—if the United States were to withdraw.

Further Troop Increase. Some argue that the "surge" was too small—limited only to Baghdad and Anbar—and that the United States should consider increasing troops levels in Iraq even further to tamp down sectarian violence and prevent Sunni insurgents from re-infiltrating areas cleared by U.S. operations. In comments in July 2007, Gen. Petraeus says he does not rule out recommending augmenting the troop surge when he has a full assessment of the results some time later in 2007. However, this option appears increasingly unlikely in light of trends in public and congressional support for the overall Iraq effort.

Immediate and Complete Withdrawal. Some Members argue that the United States should begin to withdraw immediately and nearly completely, maintaining that the decision to invade Iraq was a mistake in light of the failure to locate WMD, that the large U.S. presence in Iraq is inflaming the insurgency, and that remaining in Iraq will result in additional U.S. casualties without securing U.S. national interests. Other Members argue that U.S. forces are now policing a civil war rather than fighting an insurgency. Based on the arguments discussed above, the Administration has largely ruled out this option.

Those who support a withdrawal include most of the approximately 70 Members of the "Out of Iraq Congressional Caucus," formed in June 2005. In the 110th Congress, some have introduced legislation (H.R. 508 and H.R. 413) that would repeal the original authorization for the Iraq war. A similar measure might be considered in the Senate.

In the 109th Congress, Representative John Murtha, ranking member (now chairman) of the Defense Appropriations Subcommittee, introduced a resolution (H.J.Res. 73) calling for a U.S. withdrawal "at the earliest practicable date" and the maintenance of an "over the horizon" U.S. presence, mostly in Kuwait (some say U.S. troops could be based in the Kurdish north) from which U.S. forces could continue to battle AQ-I. A related resolution, H.Res. 571 (written by Representative Duncan Hunter, chairman of the House Armed Services Committee), expressed the sense "that the deployment of U.S. forces in Iraq be terminated immediately;" it failed 403-3 on November 18, 2005. Representative Murtha has introduced a similar bill in the 110th Congress (H.J.Res. 18); a Senate bill (S. 121) as well as a few other House bills (H.R. 663, H.R. 455, and H.R. 645) contain similar provisions.

Withdrawal Timetable. The Administration has opposed legislation mandating a withdrawal timetable on the grounds that doing so would allow insurgents to "wait out" a U.S. withdrawal. The Iraq Study Group suggests a winding down of the U.S. combat mission by early 2008 but does not recommend a firm timetable.

The House leadership inserted a binding provision of FY2007 supplemental appropriations legislation (H.R. 1591) that would require the president, as a condition of maintaining U.S. forces in Iraq, to certify (by July 1, 2007) that Iraq had made progress toward several political reconciliation benchmarks, and by October 1, 2007 that the benchmarks have been met. Even if the requirements were met, the amendment would require the start of a redeployment from Iraq by March 1, 2008, to be completed by September 1, 2008. The whole bill passed the House on March 23, 2007. In the Senate-passed version of H.R. 1591, a provision would set a nonbinding goal for U.S. withdrawal of March 1, 2008, in line with S.J.Res. 9 cited above. The conference report adopted elements of both bills, retaining the benchmark certification requirement and the same dates for the start of a withdrawal but making the completion of any withdrawal (by March 31, 2008, not September 1, 2008) a goal rather than a firm deadline. President Bush vetoed the conference report on May 1, 2007, and the veto was sustained. The revised provision in the FY2007 supplemental (H.R. 2206, P.L. 110-28) was discussed previously.

Some Members, such as Senate majority leader Harry Reid and Representative John Murtha say they will continue to try to enact such legislation in such bills as the FY2008 Defense authorization (H.R. 1585) and the FY2008 defense appropriation. One proposed amendment (S.Amdt. 2087) to H.R. 1585 would begin a withdrawal within 120 days and complete it (down to a limited presence) by April 1, 2008. A similar House bill, (H.R. 2956), was adopted on July 12, 2007 by a vote of 223-201. A Senate bill (S. 433), would set a deadline for withdrawing combat troops by March 31, 2008. Press reports in early September 2007 said that the congressional leadership might alter its proposals somewhat to require a start date, but not a completion date, for a withdrawal, as an effort to forge bi-partisan compromise.

In the 109th Congress, the timetable issue was debated extensively. In November 2005, Senator Levin, who takes the view that the United States needs to force internal compromise in Iraq by threatening to withdraw, introduced an amendment to S. 1042 (FY2006 defense authorization bill) to compel the Administration to work on a timetable for withdrawal during 2006. Reportedly, on November 10, 2005, Chairman of the Senate Armed Services Committee John Warner reworked the Levin proposal into an amendment that stopped short of setting a timetable for withdrawal but requires an Administration report on a "schedule for meeting conditions" that could permit a U.S. withdrawal. That measure, which also states in its preamble that "2006 should be a period of significant transition to full Iraqi sovereignty," achieved bipartisan support, passing 79-19. It was incorporated, with only slight modifications by House conferees, in the conference report on the bill (H.Rept. 109-360, P.L. 109163). On June 22, 2006, the

Senate debated two Iraq-related amendments to an FY2007 defense authorization bill (S. 2766). One, offered by Senator Kerry, setting a July 1, 2007, deadline for U.S. redeployment from Iraq, was defeated 86-13. Another amendment, sponsored by Senator Levin, called on the Administration to begin redeployment out of Iraq by the end of 2006, but with no deadline for full withdrawal. It was defeated 60-39.

Troop Reduction/Mission Change. Some argue for a U.S. force reduction to fulfill a scaled-back U.S. mission that would involve: (1) operations against AQ-I; (2) an end to active patrolling of Iraqi streets; (3) force protection; and (4) training the ISF. The rationale for such an option would be to maintain a U.S. presence, possibly long term, to assist the Iraqi government and protect core U.S. interests but without incurring large U.S. casualties. A press report in June 2007 (*Washington Post*, June 10, 2007) said that, if this were the new mission of U.S. forces, fulfilling the mission might require retaining about 50,000–60,000 U.S. forces. Of these forces, about 20,000 would be assigned to guaranteeing the security of the Iraqi government or assist the ISF if it is having difficulty in battle. A reduced U.S. mission similar to those described are stipulated in H.R. 2451, which might be taken up in September 2007.

In the past, U.S. commanders presented to President Bush options for a substantial drawdown of U.S. forces in Iraq, dependent on security progress, to about 120,000. The plans faded when the security situation did not calm. A change of mission similar to that described—and without a deadline for withdrawal—has been proposed by several Senators for consideration of the FY2008 defense authorization (H.R. 1585).

Planning for Withdrawal. Administration officials say they will not publicly discuss whether or not there is planning for a substantial withdrawal because doing so would undermine the ongoing troop surge and other efforts. However, Secretary Gates toured facilities in Kuwait in August 2007 in what was reported as an effort to become familiar with the capabilities of the U.S. military to carry out a redeployment, if ordered. Some Members want the Administration to plan for a substantial U.S. redeployment from Iraq and to inform Congress accordingly. A bill, introduced in July 2007 by Representative Tanner (H.R. 3087) and reported out by the House Armed Services Committee on July 31, 2007, would require the Administration to give Congress a plan for redeployment from Iraq. Senator Hillary Clinton reportedly was briefed on August 2, 2007 by Defense Department officials on the status of planning for a withdrawal, if one is decided, and she and several others introduced legislation on August 2, 2007 (S. 1950), to require contingency planning for redeployment from Iraq.

International and Regional Diplomacy

As noted above, many of the Iraq Study Group recommendations propose increased regional, multi-lateral, and international diplomacy. One idea, included in the Study Group report, is to form a "contact group" of major countries and Iraqi neighbors to prevail on Iraq's factions to compromise. The Administration has taken significant steps in this direction, including a bilateral meeting with Syria at the May 3–4, 2007 meeting on Iraq in Egypt, and the bilateral meeting with Iran in Baghdad on May 28, 2007. In the 110th Congress, a few bills (H.R. 744, H.Con.Res. 43, and H.Con.Res. 45) support the Iraq Study Group recommendation for an international conference on Iraq. In the 109th Congress, these ideas were included in several resolutions, including S.J.Res. 36, S.Res. 470, S.J.Res. 33, and S. 1993, although several of these bills also include provisions for timetables for a U.S. withdrawal.

Other ideas involve recruitment of new force donors. In July 2004, then-Secretary of State Powell said the United States would consider a Saudi proposal for a contingent of troops from Muslim countries to perform peacekeeping in Iraq, reportedly under separate command. Some Iraqi leaders believed that such peacekeepers would come from Sunni Muslim states and would inevitably favor Sunni factions within Iraq. On the other hand, several experts believe that the lack of progress in stabilizing Iraq is caused by internal Iraqi disputes and processes and that new regional or international steps would yield minimal results. For more information, see CRS Report RL33793, *Iraq: Regional Perspectives and U.S. Policy*, coordinated by Christopher Blanchard.

Another idea is to identify a high-level international mediator to negotiate with Iraq's major factions. Some Members of Congress wrote to President Bush in November 2006 asking that he name a special envoy to Iraq to follow up on some of the Administration's efforts to promote political reconciliation in Iraq.

Political Reconciliation and Reorganization

Many proposals focus on the need for a "political solution," a requirement acknowledged by Gen. Petraeus and almost all senior U.S. officials. These proposals involve differing methods for altering Iraq's power structure so that no major community feels excluded or has incentive to back violence.

Reorganize the Power Structure. Some experts believe that adjusting U.S. troop levels would not address the underlying causes of violence in Iraq.

Those who want to build a unified and strong central government, including the Bush Administration, have identified the need to assuage Sunni Arab grievances, and several of the benchmarks required of the Iraqi government are intended to achieve that objective. Others believe that more sweeping political reconciliation efforts are needed, but there is little agreement on what additional or alternative package of incentives, if any, would persuade most Sunnis leaders—and their constituents—to support the government. Some believe that Sunnis might be satisfied by a wholesale cabinet/governmental reshuffle that gives several leading positions, such as that of President, to a Sunni Arab, although many Kurds might resent such a move because a Kurd now holds that post. Others oppose major governmental change because doing so might necessitate the voiding of the 2005 elections, a move that would appear un-democratic.

Support the Dominant Factions. Another view expressed by some is that the United States should place all its political, military, and economic support on the Shiite and Kurdish factions that have supported the U.S.-led political transition process and now dominate Iraq's government. According to this view, which some refer to as the "80% solution" (Shiites and Kurds are about 80% of the population),[43] the Sunni Arabs will never accept the new order in Iraq and the United States should cease trying to pressure the Shiites and Arabs to try to satisfy them. The Sunni Arabs might begin supporting the new order if they perceive that the United States might, at some point, cease trying to accommodate their concerns. Others say that the recent U.S. outreach to Sunni insurgent groups has angered the Shiites and Kurds, and further risks all-out civil war if the United States were to draw down its forces.

Opponents of this strategy say that Iraq's Sunni neighbors will not accept a complete U.S. tilt toward the Shiites and Kurds, which would likely result in even further repression of the Sunni Arab minority. Still others say that a further U.S. shift in favor of the Shiites and Kurds would contradict the U.S. commitment to the protection of Iraq's minorities.

Decentralization and Break-Up Options. Some commentators maintain that Iraq cannot be stabilized as one country and should be broken up into three separate countries: one Kurdish, one Sunni Arab, and one Shiite Arab. Another version of this idea, propounded by Senator Biden and Council on Foreign Relations expert Leslie Gelb (May 1, 2006, *New York Times* op-ed) is to form three autonomous regions, dominated by each of the major communities. A former U.S. Ambassador and an adviser to the Kurds, Peter Galbraith, also advocates this option. According to this view, decentralizing

Iraq into autonomous zones would ensure that Iraq's territorial integrity is preserved while ensuring that these communities do not enter all-out civil war with each other. Some believe that, to alleviate Iraqi concerns about equitable distribution of oil revenues, an international organization should be tapped to distribute Iraq's oil revenues. S.Con.Res. 37, with several co-sponsors from both parties, expresses the sense of the Senate that the United States should support a political settlement in Iraq that creates a federal system of government and allows for the creation of federal regions.

Critics of both forms of this idea believe that any segregation of Iraq, legal or de-facto, would cause parts of Iraq to fall firmly under the sway of Iraq's powerful neighbors. Others believe that the act of dividing Iraq's communities in any way would cause widespread violence, particularly in areas of mixed ethnicity, as each community struggles to maximize its territory and its financial prospects. This recommendation was rejected by the Iraq Study Group as potentially too violent.

Negotiating With Insurgents. Another idea is to negotiate with insurgents. The Iraq Study Group report welcomes contact with almost all parties in Iraq, with the exception of AQ-I (*Recommendations 34–35*). The Administration—and the Iraqi government—appears to have adopted this recommendation to some extent. Gen. Odierno, in June 2007, discussed with reporters a new U.S. tactic of reaching local ceasefires with Iraqi insurgent groups and, as discussed above, some U.S. commanders have gone even further by cooperating with Sunni insurgents willing to fight against AQ-I. In an interview before leaving Iraq, outgoing Ambassador Khalilzad said in late March 2007 that he had had talks with some insurgents in Jordan who are believed open to reconciliation.

"Coup" or "Strongman" Option. As discussed above, another option began receiving discussion in October 2006 as Iraqi elites began to sense a growing rift between the Administration and Maliki. Some Iraqis believe the United States might try to use its influence among Iraqis to force Maliki to resign and replace him with a military strongman or some other figure who would crack down on sectarian militias. Some say former Prime Minister Allawi might be trying to position himself as such an alternative figure. However, experts in the United States see no concrete signs that such an option might be under consideration by the Administration, and other accounts say that Iraqi leaders are divided over who would replace Maliki, thus ensuring deadlock and his continuation in office. Using U.S. influence to force out Maliki would, in the view of many, conflict with the U.S. goal of promoting democracy and rule of law in Iraq.

Economic Measures

Some believe that the key to calming Iraq is to accelerate economic reconstruction, and they see the draft oil law as drawing in the foreign investment to Iraq's key energy sector that is needed to drive economic development. Accelerated reconstruction will drain support for insurgents by creating employment, improving public services, and creating confidence in the government. This idea, propounded by DoD reconstruction official Paul Brinkley (Deputy Undersecretary of Defense for Business Transformation in Iraq), was incorporated into the President's January 10 initiative, in part by attempting to revive state-owned factories that can employ substantial numbers of Iraqis. Prior to that, the concept of using economic reconstruction to drive political accommodation was reflected in the decision to form PRTs, as discussed above. Others doubt that economic improvement alone will produce major political results because the differences among Iraq's major communities are fundamental and resistant to economic solutions.

Another idea has been to set up an Iraqi fund, or trust, that would ensure that all Iraqis share equitably in Iraq's oil wealth. In an op-ed in the *Wall Street Journal* (December 18, 2006) Senator Hillary Rodham Clinton and Senator John Ensign supported the idea of an "Iraq Oil Trust" modeled on the Alaska Permanent Fund.

Table 7. U.S. Aid (ESF) to Iraq's Opposition (Amounts in millions of U.S. $)

	INC	War crimes	Broadcasting	Unspecified opposition activities	Total
FY1998 (P.L. 105-174)	—	2.0	5.0 (RFE/RL for "Radio Free Iraq")	3.0	10.0
FY1999 (P.L. 105-277)	3.0	3.0	—	2.0	8.0
FY2000 (P.L. 106-113)	—	2.0	—	8.0	10.0
FY2001 (P.L. 106-429)	12.0 (aid in Iraq)	2.0	6.0 (INC radio)	5.0	25.0
FY2002 (P.L. 107-115)	—	—	—	25.0	25.0
FY2003 (no earmark)	3.1	—	—	6.9	10.0

	INC	War crimes	Broadcasting	Unspecified opposition activities	Total
Total, FY1998-FY2003	18.1	9.0	11.0	49.9 (about 14.5 million of this went to INC)	88.0
FY2004 (request)	—	—	—	0	0

Notes: According to the U.S. Government Accountability Office (April 2004), the INC's Iraqi National Congress Support Foundation (INCSF) received $32.65 million in U.S. Economic Support Funds (ESF) in five agreements with the State Department during 2000-2003. Most of the funds—separate from drawdowns of U.S. military equipment and training under the "Iraq Liberation Act"—were for the INC to run its offices in Washington, London, Tehran, Damascus, Prague, and Cairo, and to operate its Al *Mutamar* (the "Conference") newspaper and its "Liberty TV," which began in August 2001, from London. The station was funded by FY2001 ESF, with start-up costs of $1 million and an estimated additional $2.7 million per year in operating costs. Liberty TV was sporadic due to funding disruptions resulting from the INC's refusal to accept some State Department decisions on how U.S. funds were to be used. In August 2002, the State Department and Defense Department agreed that the Defense Department would take over funding ($335,000 per month) for the INC's "Information Collection Program" to collect intelligence on Iraq; the State Department wanted to end its funding of that program because of questions about the INC's credibility and the propriety of its use of U.S. funds. The INC continued to receive these funds even after Saddam Hussein was overthrown, but was halted after the June 2004 return of sovereignty to Iraq. The figures above do not include covert aid provided—the amounts are not known from open sources. Much of the "war crimes" funding was used to translate and publicize documents retrieved from northern Iraq on Iraqi human rights; the translations were placed on 176 CD-Rom disks. During FY2001 and FY2002, the Administration donated $4 million to a "U.N. War Crimes Commission" fund, to be used if a war crimes tribunal is formed. Those funds were drawn from U.S. contributions to U.N. programs. See General Accounting Office Report GAO-04-559, *State Department: Issues Affecting Funding of Iraqi National Congress Support Foundation*, April 2004.

Figure 1: Map of Iraq [Omitted]

Endnotes

[1] Bush, George H.W., and Brent Scowcroft. *A World Transformed*. Alfred A. Knopf, Inc. 1998.

[2] The implementation of these policies is discussed in CRS Report RL32379, *Iraq: Former Regime Weapons Programs, Human Rights Violations, and U.S. Policy*, by Kenneth Katzman.

[3] Congress more than doubled the budget for covert support to the opposition groups to about $40 million for FY1993, from previous reported levels of about $15 million to $20 million. Sciolino, Elaine. "Greater U.S. Effort Backed To Oust Iraqi." *New York Times*, June 2, 1992.

[4] Because of its role in the eventual formation of the radical Ansar al-Islam group, the IMIK did not receive U.S. funds after 2001, although it was not formally de-listed.

[5] Chalabi's father was president of the Senate in the monarchy that was overthrown in the 1958 military coup, and the family fled to Jordan. He taught math at the American University of Beirut in 1977 and, in 1978, he founded the Petra Bank in Jordan. He later ran afoul of Jordanian authorities on charges of embezzlement and he left Jordan, possibly with some help from members of Jordan's royal family, in

1989. In April 1992, he was convicted in absentia of embezzling $70 million from the bank and sentenced to 22 years in prison. The Jordanian government subsequently repaid depositors a total of $400 million.

[6] Brinkley, Joel. "Ex-CIA Aides Say Iraq Leader Helped Agency in 90's Attacks," *New York Times*, June 9, 2004.

[7] An account of this shift in U.S. strategy is essayed in Hoagland, Jim. "How CIA's Secret War On Saddam Collapsed," *Washington Post*, June 26, 1997.

[8] For an extended discussion, see CRS Report RS22079, *The Kurds in Post-Saddam Iraq*, by Kenneth Katzman and Alfred B. Prados.

[9] The report can be obtained at [http://www.usip.org].

[10] The three other senior Hawza clerics are Ayatollah Mohammad Sa'id al-Hakim (uncle of the leader of the Supreme Council of the Islamic Revolution in Iraq, Abd al-Aziz al-Hakim); Ayatollah Mohammad Isaac Fayadh, who is of Afghan origin; and Ayatollah Bashir al-Najafi, of Pakistani origin.

[11] For information on Sistani's views, see his website at [http://www.sistani.org].

[12] One account of Bush Administration internal debates on the strategy is found in Hersh, Seymour. "The Debate Within," *The New Yorker*, March 11, 2002.

[13] For more information on this program, see CRS Report RL30472, *Iraq: Oil For Food Program, Illicit Trade, and Investigations*, by Christopher Blanchard and Kenneth Katzman.

[14] Duelfer report text is at [http://news.findlaw.com/hdocs/docs/iraq/cia93004wmdrpt.html].

[15] For analysis of the former regime's WMD and other abuses, see CRS Report RL32379, *Iraq: Former Regime Weapons Programs, Human Rights Violations, and U.S. Policy*, by Kenneth Katzman.

[16] Pincus, Walter. "Munitions Found in Iraq Renew Debate." *Washington Post*, July 1, 2006.

[17] *9/11 Commission Report*, p. 66.

[18] Deyoung, Karen, and Daniel Williams, "Training of Iraqi Exiles Authorized," *Washington Post*, October 19, 2002.

[19] Many of the thirty countries listed in the coalition did not contribute forces to the combat. A subsequent State Department list released on March 27, 2003 listed 49 countries in the coalition of the willing. See *Washington Post*, March 27, 2003, p. A19.

[20] Information on the project, including summaries of the findings of its 17 working groups, can be found at [http://usinfo.state.gov/products/pubs/archive/dutyiraq/]. The project cost $5 million and had 15 working groups on major issues.

[21] The text of the TAL can be obtained from the CPA website at [http://cpa-iraq.org/ government/TAL.html].

[22] Chandrasekaran, Rajiv. "Envoy Urges U.N.-Chosen Iraqi Government," *Washington Post*, April 15, 2004.

[23] Its mandate has been renewed each year since, most recently by Resolution 1700 (August 10, 2006).

[24] See CRS Report RS21867, *U.S. Embassy in Iraq*, by Susan B. Epstein.

[25] A FY2005 supplemental appropriations, P.L. 109-13, provided $592 million of $658 million requested to construct a new embassy in Baghdad; an FY2006 supplemental appropriation (P.L. 109-234) provided $1.327 billion for U.S. embassy operations and security.

[26] For information on that program, see CRS Report RL30472, *Iraq: Oil-for-Food Program, Illicit Trade, and Investigations*, by Christopher Blanchard and Kenneth Katzman.

[27] The defense authorization bill for FY2007 (P.L. 109-364) set October 1, 2007, for termination of oversight by the SIGIR. However, P.L. 109-440 extends that term until 10 months after 80% of the IRRF have been expended but includes FY2006 reconstruction funds for Iraq in the definition of the IRRF. The SIGIR's mandate is therefore expected to extend until some time in 2008.

[28] For further information, see CRS Report RL34064, *Iraq: Oil and Gas Legislation, Revenue Sharing, and U.S. Policy*, by Christopher Blanchard.

[29] A May 7, 2003, executive order left in place the provisions of the Iran-Iraq Arms Non-Proliferation Act (P.L. 102-484); that act imposes sanctions on persons or governments that export technology that would contribute to any Iraqi advanced conventional arms capability or weapons of mass destruction programs.

[30] For more information, see CRS Report RL33376, *Iraq's Debt Relief: Procedure and Potential Implications for International Debt Relief,* by Martin A. Weiss.

[31] See p. xiii of the Executive Summary of the Iraq Study Group Report. December 6, 2006.

[32] For further information, see Baram, Amatzia. "*Who Are the Insurgents?*" U.S. Institute of Peace, Special Report 134, April 2005; and Eisenstadt, Michael and Jeffrey White. "*Assessing Iraq's Sunni Arab Insurgency.*" Washington Institute for Near East Policy, Policy Focus No. 50, December 2005.

[33] See CRS Report RL32217, *Iraq and Al Qaeda,* by Kenneth Katzman.

[34] Blanford, Nicholas. "Sealing Syria's Desolate Border," *Christian Science Monitor,* December 21, 2004.

[35] Krane, Jim. "U.S. Officials: Iraq Insurgency Bigger." Associated Press report published in the *Philadelphia Inquirer.* July 9, 2004; Schmitt, Eric, and Thom Shanker. "Estimates By U.S. See More Rebels With More Funds," *New York Times,* October 22, 2004.

[36] Krepinevich, Andrew. "How to Win in Iraq," *Foreign Affairs,* September/October 2005.

[37] The two principal authors of the report are Frederick W. Kagan and Jack Keane (General, U.S. Army, ret.).

[38] One such assessment includes, O'Hanlon, Michael and Kenneth Pollack. "A War We Might Just Win." *New York Times* op-ed. July 30, 2007.

[39] For additional information, see CRS Report RS22093, *Iraq's New Security Forces: The Challenge of Sectarian and Ethnic Influences,* by Jeremy Sharp.

[40] Speech by President Bush can be found at [http://www.whitehouse.gov/news/releases/2005/06/20050628-7.html].

[41] For additional information on international contributions to Iraq peacekeeping and reconstruction, see CRS Report RL32105, *Post-War Iraq: Foreign Contributions to Training, Peacekeeping, and Reconstruction,* by Jeremy Sharp and Christopher Blanchard.

[42] Full text at [http://www.usip.org].

[43] Krauthammer, Charles. "The 20 Percent Solution." Washington Post op-ed, July 20, 2007.

DOCUMENT NO. 8

SECURING, STABILIZING, AND REBUILDING IRAQ: IRAQI GOVERNMENT HAS NOT MET MOST LEGISLATIVE, SECURITY, AND ECONOMIC BENCHMARKS

GAO Report
GAO-07-1195

September 4, 2007

What GAO Found

The January 2007 U.S. strategy seeks to provide the Iraqi government with the time and space needed to help Iraqi society reconcile. Our analysis of the 18 legislative, security and economic benchmarks shows that as of August 30, 2007, the Iraqi government met 3, partially met 4, and did not meet 11 of its 18 benchmarks. (See next page). Overall, key legislation has not been passed, violence remains high, and it is unclear whether the Iraqi government will spend $10 billion in reconstruction funds. These results do not diminish the courageous efforts of coalition forces.

The Iraqi government has met one of eight legislative benchmarks: the rights of minority political parties in Iraq's legislature are protected. The government also partially met one other benchmark to enact and implement legislation on the formation of regions; this law was enacted in October 2006 but will not be implemented until April 2008. Six other legislative benchmarks have not been met. Specifically, a review committee has not completed work on important revisions to Iraq's constitution. Further, the government has not enacted legislation on de-Ba'athification, oil revenue sharing, provincial elections, amnesty, or militia disarmament. The Administration's July 2007 report cited progress in achieving some of these benchmarks but provided little information on what step in the legislative process each benchmark had reached.

Two of nine security benchmarks have been met. Specifically, Iraq's government has established various committees in support of the Baghdad security plan and established almost all of the planned Joint Security

Stations in Baghdad. The government has partially met the benchmarks of providing three trained and ready brigades for Baghdad operations and eliminating safe havens for outlawed groups. Five other benchmarks have not been met. The government has not eliminated militia control of local security, eliminated political intervention in military operations, ensured even-handed enforcement of the law, increased army units capable of independent operations, or ensured that political authorities made no false accusations against security forces. It is unclear whether sectarian violence in Iraq has decreased—a key security benchmark—since it is difficult to measure the perpetrator's intent and other measures of population security show differing trends.

Finally, the Iraqi government has partially met the economic benchmark of allocating and spending $10 billion on reconstruction. Preliminary data indicates that about $1.5 billion of central ministry funds had been spent, as of July 15, 2007. As the Congress considers the way forward in Iraq, it must balance the achievement of the 18 Iraqi benchmarks with the military progress, homeland security, foreign policy, and other goals of the United States. Future administration reporting to assist the Congress would be enhanced with adoption of the recommendations we make in this report.

Benchmark	**GAO assessment**	**Status**
1. Forming a Constitutional Review Committee and completing the constitutional review.	○	Committee formed but amendments not approved by the Iraqi legislature and no referendum scheduled.
2. Enacting and implementing legislation on de-Ba'athification.	○	Laws drafted.
3. Enacting and implementing legislation to ensure the equitable distribution of hydrocarbon resources of the people of Iraq without regard to the sect or ethnicity of recipients, and enacting and implementing legislation to ensure that the energy resources of Iraq benefit Sunni Arabs, Shia Arabs, Kurds, and other Iraqi citizens in an equitable manner.	○	3 of 4 components drafted; none being considered by parliament.
4. Enacting and implementing legislation on procedures to form semi-autonomous regions.	◐	Law enacted; implementation scheduled for 2008.

Benchmark	GAO assessment	Status
5. Enacting and implementing legislation establishing an Independent High Electoral Commission, provincial elections law, provincial council authorities, and a date for provincial elections.	○	Commission law enacted and implemented; however, supporting laws not enacted.
6. Enacting and implementing legislation addressing amnesty.	○	No law drafted.
7. Enacting and implementing legislation establishing a strong militia disarmament program to ensure that such security forces are accountable only to the central government and loyal to the Constitution of Iraq.	○	No law drafted.
8. Establishing supporting political, media, economic, and services committees in support of the Baghdad security plan.	●	Committees established.
9. Providing three trained and ready brigades to support Baghdad operations.	◐	Forces provided; some of limited effectiveness.
10. Providing Iraqi commanders with all authorities to execute this plan and to make tactical and operational decisions, in consultation with U.S. commanders, without political intervention, to include the authority to pursue all extremists, including Sunni insurgents and Shiite militias.	○	Political intervention continues.
11. Ensuring that Iraqi security forces are providing even-handed enforcement of the law.	○	Iraqi security forces engaged in sectarian-based abuses.
12. Ensuring that, according to President Bush, Prime Minister Maliki said "the Baghdad security plan will not provide a safe haven for any outlaws, regardless of [their] sectarian or political affiliation."	◐	Militia infiltration of some security forces enables some safe havens.
13. Reducing the level of sectarian violence in Iraq and eliminating militia control of local security.	○	Militias control some local security; unclear whether sectarian violence has decreased.

Benchmark	GAO assessment	Status
14. Establishing all of the planned joint security stations in neighborhoods across Baghdad.	●	32 of 34 stations established.
15. Increasing the number of Iraqi security forces units capable of operating independently.	○	Number of independent units declined between March and July 2007.
16. Ensuring that the rights of minority political parties in the Iraqi legislature are protected.	●	Legislators' rights protected; minority citizens' rights unprotected.
17. Allocating and spending $10 billion in Iraqi revenues for reconstruction projects, including delivery of essential services, on an equitable basis.	◐	Funds allocated but unlikely to be fully spent.
18. Ensuring that Iraq's political authorities are not undermining or making false accusations against members of the Iraqi security forces.	○	Unsubstantiated accusations continue to be made.
● Met	◐ Partially met	○ Not met

Source: GAO analysis of UN, U.S., and Iraqi data.

United States Government Accountability Office Washington, DC 20548

September 4, 2007

Congressional Committees:

Over the last 4 years, the United States has provided thousands of troops and obligated nearly $370 billion to help achieve the strategic goal of creating a democratic Iraq that can govern and defend itself and be an ally in the War on Terror. These troops have performed courageously under dangerous and difficult circumstances. The U.S. Troop Readiness, Veterans' Care, Katrina Recovery, and Iraq Accountability Appropriations Act of 2007[1] (the Act) requires GAO to submit to Congress by September 1, 2007,[2] an independent assessment of whether or not the government of Iraq has met 18 benchmarks contained in the Act, and the status of the achievement of the benchmarks. The benchmarks cover Iraqi government actions needed to advance reconciliation within Iraqi society, improve the security of the Iraqi population, provide essential services to the population, and promote economic well-being. The benchmarks contained in the Act were derived from benchmarks and commitments articulated by the Iraqi government beginning in June 2006.

The January 2007 U.S. strategy, *The New Way Forward* in Iraq, is designed to support the Iraqi efforts to quell sectarian violence and foster conditions for national reconciliation. The U.S. strategy recognizes that the levels of violence seen in 2006 undermined efforts to achieve political reconciliation by fueling sectarian tensions, emboldening extremists, and discrediting the Coalition and Iraqi government. Amid such violence, it became increasingly difficult for Iraqi leaders to make the compromises necessary to foster reconciliation through the passage of legislation aimed at reintegrating former Ba'athists and sharing hydrocarbon revenues more equitably, among other steps. Thus, the new strategy was aimed at providing the Iraqi government with the time and space needed to help address reconciliation among the various segments of Iraqi society.

As required by the Act, this report provides 1) an assessment of whether or not the Iraqi government has met 18 key legislative, security, and economic benchmarks, and, 2) provides information on the status of the achievement of each benchmark. Among these 18 benchmarks, eight address legislative actions, nine address security actions, and one is economic-related. In comparison, the Act requires the administration to report in July and September 2007 on the status of each benchmark, and to provide an assessment on whether satisfactory progress is being made toward meeting the benchmarks, not whether the benchmarks have been met. In order to meet our statutory responsibilities in a manner consistent with GAO's core values, we decided to use "partially met" criteria for selected benchmarks. See appendices I-XVIII for information on our assessment and the status of the achievement of each benchmark, and appendix XX for a comparison of GAO's assessment with the administration's July 2007 initial benchmark assessment report. We are also issuing a separate, classified report on selected benchmarks.

To complete this work, we reviewed U.S. agency documents and interviewed officials from the Departments of Defense, State, and the Treasury; the Multi-national Force-Iraq (MNF-I) and its subordinate commands; the Defense Intelligence Agency; the Central Intelligence Agency; the National Intelligence Council; and the United Nations. These officials included Ryan Crocker, the U.S. Ambassador to Iraq, and General David H. Petraeus, Commander of Multi-National Force-Iraq (MNF-I). We also reviewed translated copies of Iraqi documents and met with officials from the government of Iraq and its legislature. As part of this work, we made multiple visits to Iraq during 2006 and 2007, most recently from July 22 to August 1, 2007. Our analyses were enhanced by approximately 100 Iraq-related reports and testimonies that we have completed since May 2003.[3] We provided drafts of the report to the relevant U.S. agencies for review and comment. We received formal written comments from State and Defense and technical comments from the Central Intelligence Agency and National Intelligence Council which we incorporated as appropriate. This letter and each appendix describe the detailed criteria we used in making our assessments of the 18 benchmarks. As required by the mandate, we made a determination of whether all 18 benchmarks had been met. For 14 of the 18 benchmarks, we developed criteria for assessing whether the benchmark was "partially met." For the remaining 4 benchmarks, we determined that they should be judged as "met" or "not met" because the nature of the individual benchmarks did not lend themselves to a "partially met" assessment.

Although we analyzed classified data, including the August 2007 National Intelligence Estimate for Iraq, this report only contains unclassified information, as of August 30, 2007. We conducted our review in accordance with generally accepted government auditing standards. Appendix XXI contains a detailed description of our scope and methodology.

Results in Brief

As of August 30, 2007, the Iraqi government met 3, partially met 4, and did not meet 11 of its 18 benchmarks. Overall we found that:

- The constitutional review process is not complete, and laws on de-Ba'athification, oil revenue sharing, provincial elections, and amnesty have not passed;

- Violence remains high, the number of Iraqi security forces capable of conducting independent operations has declined, and militias are not disarmed; and
- Funding for reconstruction has been allocated but is unlikely to be spent.

As the Congress considers the way forward in Iraq, it should balance the achievement of the 18 Iraqi government benchmarks with the military progress, homeland security, foreign policy, and other goals of the United States. In addition, future administration reports on the benchmarks would be more useful to Congress if they depicted the status of each legislative benchmark, provided data on broader measures of violence from all relevant U.S. agencies, and assessed the performance and loyalties of Iraqi security forces.

Legislative Benchmarks

Our analysis shows that the Iraqi government has met one of the eight legislative benchmarks and partially met another.[4] Specifically, the rights of minority political parties in the Iraqi legislature are protected through existing provisions in the Iraqi Constitution and Council of Representatives' by-laws; however, minorities among the Iraqi population are vulnerable and their rights are often violated. In addition, the Iraqi government partially met the benchmark to enact and implement legislation on the formation of regions; this law was enacted in October 2006 but will not be implemented until April 2008.[5]

Six other legislative benchmarks have not been met. The benchmark requiring a review of the Iraqi Constitution has not been met. Fundamental issues remain unresolved as part of the constitutional review process, such as expanded powers for the presidency, the resolution of disputed areas (such as Kirkuk), and power sharing between federal and regional governments over issues such as distribution of oil revenue. In addition, five other legislative benchmarks have not been met.

Figure 1: Enactment and Implementation Status of Six Legislative Benchmarks [Omitted]

Legislation on de-Ba'athification reform has been drafted but has yet to be enacted.[6] Hydrocarbon legislation is in the early stages of legislative action; although three key components have been drafted, none are under active consideration by the Council of Representatives.[7] Although the government of Iraq has established an independent electoral commission and appointed commissioners, the government has not implemented legislation to establish provincial council authorities, provincial elections law, or a date for provincial elections. No legislation on amnesty or militia disarmament is being considered because the conditions for a successful program, particularly the need for a secure environment, are not present, according to U.S. and Iraqi officials.

Prospects for additional progress in enacting legislative benchmarks have been complicated by the withdrawal of 15 of 37 members of the Iraqi cabinet. According to an August 2007 U.S. interagency report, this boycott ends any claim by the Shi'ite-dominated coalition to be a government of national unity and further undermines Iraq's already faltering program of national reconciliation. In late August, Iraq's senior Shi'a, and Sunni Arab and Kurdish political leaders signed a Unity Accord signaling efforts to foster greater national reconciliation. The Accord covered draft legislation on de-Ba'athification reform and provincial powers laws, as well as setting up a mechanism to release some Sunni detainees being held without charges. However, these laws need to be passed by the Council of Representatives.

The Administration's July 2007 report cited progress in achieving some of these legislative benchmarks but provided little information on what step in the legislative process each benchmark had reached. Future reporting should provide this important detail.

Security Benchmarks

Our analysis shows that the Iraqi government has met two of the nine security benchmarks. Specifically, it has established political, communications, economic, and services committees[8] in support of the Baghdad security plan and, with substantial coalition assistance, 32 of the planned 34 Joint Security Stations[9] across Baghdad. Of the remaining 7 benchmarks, the Iraqi government partially met 2 and did not meet five.

Figure 2: GAO's Assessment of Whether the Iraqi Government has Achieved Security Benchmarks [Omitted]

The Iraqi government partially met the benchmark of providing three trained and ready brigades to support Baghdad operations.[10] Since February 2007, the Iraqi government deployed nine Iraqi army battalions equaling three brigades for 90-day rotations to support the Baghdad Security Plan. The administration's July 2007 report to Congress noted problems in manning the Iraqi brigades, but stated that the three brigades were operating in support of Baghdad operations. Our classified report provides additional information on the readiness levels and performance of these units, which supports our assessment of this benchmark.

The Iraqi government also partially met the benchmark of ensuring that the Baghdad security plan will not provide a safe haven for any outlaws regardless of their sectarian or political affiliation.[11] Even though the Baghad Security Plan is aimed at eliminating safe havens, and U.S. commanders report satisfaction with the coalition's ability to target extremist groups, opportunities for creating temporary safe havens exist due to the political intervention of Iraqi government officials and the strong sectarian loyalties and militia infiltration of security forces.

The Iraqi government has not met the benchmark to reduce sectarian violence and eliminate militia control of local security.[12]As discussed in appendix XIII, militia control of local security forces remains a problem. Several U.S. and UN reports have found that militias still retain significant control or influence over local security in parts of Baghdad and other areas of Iraq.

On trends in sectarian violence, we could not determine if sectarian violence had declined since the start of the Baghdad Security Plan. The administration's July 2007 report stated that MNF-I trend data demonstrated a decrease in sectarian violence since the start of the Baghdad Security Plan in mid-February 2007. The report acknowledged that precise measurements vary, and that it was too early to determine if the decrease would be sustainable. Measuring sectarian violence is difficult since the perpetrator's intent is not always clearly known. Given this difficulty, broader measures of population security should be used in judging these trends. The number of attacks targeting civilians and population displacement resulting from sectarian violence may serve as additional indicators. For example, the average number of daily attacks against civilians remained about the same over the last six months. The decrease in total average daily attacks in July is largely due to a decrease in attacks on coalition forces rather than civilians.

Figure 3: Average Number of Daily, Enemy-Initiated Attacks Against the Coalition, Iraqi Security Forces, and Civilians (May 2003–July 2007) [Omitted]

While overall attacks declined in July compared to June, levels of violence remain high. Enemy initiated attacks have increased around major religious and political events, including Ramadan and elections.[13] For 2007, Ramadan is scheduled to begin in mid-September. Our classified report provides further information on measurement issues and trends in violence in Iraq obtained from other U.S. agencies. The unclassified

August 2007 National Intelligence Estimate (NIE) on Iraq reported that Coalition forces, working with Iraqi forces, tribal elements, and some Sunni insurgents, have reduced al Qaeda in Iraq's (AQI) capabilities and restricted its freedom of movement. However, the NIE further noted that the level of overall violence, including attacks on and casualties among civilians remains high and AQI retains the ability to conduct high-profile attacks.

For the remaining four unmet security benchmarks, we found that:

- The Iraqi government has not always allowed Iraqi commanders to make tactical and operational decisions without political intervention, resulting in some operational decisions being based on sectarian interests.[14]
- The government had not always ensured that Iraqi security forces were providing even-handed enforcement of the law, since U.S. reports have cited continuing sectarian-based abuses on the part of Iraqi security forces.[15]
- Instead of increasing, the number of Iraqi army units capable of independent operations had decreased from March 2007 to July 2007.[16]
- Iraqi political authorities continue to undermine and make false accusations against Iraqi security force personnel. According to U.S. government officials, little has changed since the administration's July 2007 report.[17]

Economic Benchmark

The Iraqi government partially met the benchmark to allocate and spend \$10 billion because it allocated \$10 billion in reconstruction funds when it passed its 2007 budget in February, 2007. *The New Way Forward in Iraq* cited Iraq's inability to spend its own resources to rebuild critical infrastructure and deliver essential services as an economic challenge to Iraq's self-reliance. Iraqi government funds represent an important source of financing for rebuilding Iraq since the United States has obligated most of the \$40 billion provided to Iraq for reconstruction and stabilization activities since 2003.

However, it is unclear whether the \$10 billion allocated by the Iraqi government will be spent by the end of Iraq's fiscal year, December 31, 2007.[18] Preliminary Ministry of Finance data reports that Iraq's central ministries spent about \$1.5 billion, or 24 percent, of the approximately \$6.5 billion in capital project funds allocated to them through July 15, 2007. The remaining funds from the \$10 billion were allocated to the provinces and the Kurdish region.

Conclusions

As of August 30, 2007, the Iraqi government met 3, partially met 4, and did not meet 11 of its 18 benchmarks. The Iraqi government has not fulfilled commitments it first made in June 2006 to advance legislative, security, and economic measures that would promote national reconciliation among Iraq's warring factions. Of particular concern is the lack of progress on the constitutional review that could promote greater Sunni participation in the national government and comprehensive hydrocarbon legislation that would distribute Iraq's vast oil wealth. Despite Iraqi leaders recently signing a unity accord, the polarization of Iraq's major sects and ethnic groups and fighting among Shi'a factions diminishes the stability of Iraq's governing coalition and its potential to enact legislation needed for sectarian reconciliation.

Reconciliation was also premised on a reduction in violence. While the Baghdad security plan was intended to reduce sectarian violence, measuring such violence may be difficult since the perpetrator's intent is not clearly known. Other measures of violence, such as the number of enemy-initiated attacks, show that violence has remained high through July 2007.

As the Congress considers the way forward in Iraq, it must balance the achievement of the 18 Iraqi benchmarks with the military progress, homeland security, foreign policy and other goals of the United States. Future administration reports on the benchmarks would be more useful to the Congress if they clearly depicted the status of each legislative benchmark, provided additional quantitative and qualitative information on violence from all relevant U.S. agencies, and specified the performance and loyalties of Iraqi security forces supporting coalition operations.

Recommendations

In preparing future reports to Congress and to help increase transparency on progress made toward achieving the benchmarks, we recommend that:

1. The Secretary of State provide information to the President that clearly specifies the status in drafting, enacting, and implementing Iraqi legislation;
2. The Secretary of Defense, and the heads of other appropriate agencies, provide information to the President on trends in sectarian violence with appropriate caveats, as well as broader quantitative and qualitative measures of population security, and
3. The Secretary of Defense, and the heads of other appropriate agencies, provides additional information on the operational readiness of Iraqi security forces supporting the Baghdad security plan, particularly information on their loyalty and willingness to help secure Baghdad.

As discussed below, State and DOD concurred with these recommendations.

Agency Comments

We provided a draft of this report to the Departments of State and Defense, the National Intelligence Council, and the Central Intelligence Agency. The National Intelligence Council and the Central Intelligence Agency provided technical comments, which we incorporated as appropriate.

The Department of State provided written comments, which are reprinted in appendix XXII. State also provided us with technical comments and suggested wording changes that we incorporated as appropriate. State agreed with our recommendation to provide the President with additional information on the specific status of key Iraqi legislation in preparing future reports to Congress. State suggested that we note the standards we used in assessing the 18 benchmarks differ from the administration's standards. The highlights page and introduction of our report discuss these differing standards. State also suggested that we take into consideration recent political developments in Iraq, such as the communiqué released by Iraqi political leaders on August 26, 2007. We added additional information to the report about this communiqué and related developments.

The Department of Defense also provided written comments, which are reprinted in appendix XXIII. DOD also provided us with technical comments and suggested wording changes that we incorporated as appropriate. Defense agreed with our recommendations to provide, in concert with other relevant agencies, information to the President on trends in sectarian violence with appropriate caveats, as well as broader quantitative and qualitative measures of security. Defense also agreed to provide the President with additional information on the operational readiness of Iraqi security forces supporting the Baghdad security plan.

DOD also provided additional oral comments. DOD disagreed with our conclusion in the draft report that trends in sectarian violence are unclear. Further information on DOD's views, and our response, are contained in our classified report. However, the additional information that DOD provided did not warrant a change in our assessment of "not met." We note that the unclassified August 2007 NIE stated that the overall violence in Iraq, including attacks on and casualties among civilians, remains high, Iraq's major sectarian groups remain unreconciled, and levels of insurgent and sectarian violence will remain high over the next six to twelve months.

DOD disagreed with our initial assessment of "not met" for the training and readiness of the Iraqi brigades supporting operations in Baghdad and provided additional information on this issue. While acknowledging that some of these Iraqi units lacked personnel, fighting equipment, and vehicles, the U.S. commander embedded with the units attested to their fighting capabilities. Based on this additional information, and our classified and unclassified information, we changed our rating from "not met" to "partially met."

DOD did not agree with our initial assessment that the benchmark related to safe havens was not met. DOD provided additional information describing MNF-I efforts to conduct targeted operations in Sadr City. For example, from January to August 2007, Coalition forces and Iraqi security forces conducted over eighty operations that span each sector of Sadr City. However, due to sectarian influence and infiltration of Iraqi security forces, and support from the local population, anti-coalition forces retain the freedom to organize and conduct operations against coalition forces. Based on this additional information, we changed this assessment to "partially met."

We are sending copies of this report to appropriate Members of Congress. This report will also be available at no charge on GAO's Web site at http://www.gao.gov.

If you or your staffs have any questions about this report, please contact me on (202) 512- 5500 or Mr. Joseph A. Christoff, Director, International Affairs and Trade, at (202) 512-8979. Contact points for our Offices of Congressional Relations and Public Affairs can be found on the last page of this report. Key contributors to this report are included in appendix XXIV.

David M. Walker
United States Comptroller General
Enclosures

List of Congressional Committees

The Honorable Carl Levin
Chairman
The Honorable John McCain
Ranking Member
Committee on Armed Services
United States Senate

The Honorable Joseph R. Biden Jr.
Chairman
The Honorable Richard G. Lugar
Ranking Member Committee on Foreign Relations
United States Senate

The Honorable Daniel Inouye
Chairman
The Honorable Ted Stevens
Ranking Member
Subcommittee on Defense
Committee on Appropriations
United States Senate

The Honorable Patrick J. Leahy
Chairman
The Honorable Judd Gregg
Ranking Member
Subcommittee on State, Foreign Operations, and Related Programs
Committee on Appropriations
United States Senate

The Honorable Ike Skelton
Chairman
The Honorable Duncan Hunter
Ranking Member
Committee on Armed Services
House of Representatives

The Honorable Tom Lantos
Chairman
The Honorable Ileana Ros-Lehtinen
Ranking Member
Committee on Foreign Affairs
House of Representatives

The Honorable John P. Murtha
Chairman
The Honorable C.W. Bill Young
Ranking Member
Subcommittee on Defense
Committee on Appropriations
House of Representatives

The Honorable Nita M. Lowey
Chairwoman
The Honorable Frank R. Wolf
Ranking Member
Subcommittee on State, Foreign Operations,
and Related Programs
Committee on Appropriations
House of Representatives

The Honorable Henry A. Waxman
Chairman
The Honorable Tom Davis
Ranking Member
Committee on Oversight and Government Reform
House of Representatives

The Honorable John F. Tierney
Chairman
The Honorable Christopher Shays
Ranking Member
Subcommittee on National Security and Foreign Affairs
Committee on Oversight and Government Reform
House of Representatives

Appendix I

Benchmark 1—Constitutional Review

Forming a constitutional review committee and completing the constitutional review.

GAO Assessment as of August 30, 2007: Not met[1]

Issue

Iraq's Constitution was approved in a national referendum in October 2005, but did not resolve several contentious issues, such as claims over disputed areas including oil-rich Kirkuk. Amending the Constitution is critical to reaching national agreement on power sharing among Iraq's political blocs and furthering national reconciliation, according to Iraqi leaders, U.S. officials, and the Iraq Study Group report.

Status

Although the Iraqi legislature formed a Constitutional Review Committee (CRC) in November 2006, the review process is not yet complete.[2] First, the review committee's work is not finished. In a May 23, 2007 report, the CRC recommended a package of constitutional amendments to the Iraq Council of Representatives. However, the package did not resolve the powers of the presidency; disputed territories, including Kirkuk; and the relative powers of the regions versus the federal government. The CRC received an extension until the end of August 2007 to help resolve the outstanding issues, but, according to the chairman of the CRC, Iraq's major political groups need to reach agreement on these issues. Second, once resolved, the Iraqi legislature must approve the package of amendments by an absolute majority vote. Finally, if a package of amendments is approved, the Iraqi people will need to vote on the amendments in a referendum within 2 months after the legislature approves them.

Completion of the Constitutional Review First Requires Political Accommondation

To complete a package of necessary amendments to the Constitution, Iraq's major political groups need to reach agreement on the following three contentious issues.

- *Power of the presidency*. The Deputy Chairman of the CRC, a member of the Sunni bloc, believes that the presidency should have greater power. The Constitution gives the presidency such powers as accrediting ambassadors. It also gives the presidency council the power to approve or disapprove legislation in the current electoral term.[3] However, the legislature can adopt any disapproved legislation by a three-fifths majority vote. In contrast, the prime minister, selected from the legislature's largest political bloc, is commander-in-chief of the armed forces, names the ministers for each ministry, and directs the Council of Ministers. The Council directs the work of all government ministries and departments, develops their plans, and prepares the government budget. The high-ranking Sunni official said that giving the presidency more power could allow for better power sharing among Iraq's political groups.

- *Disputed areas, particularly Kirkuk.* Article 140 of the Constitution addresses the issue of disputed areas. It requires a census and a referendum in Kirkuk and other disputed areas by December 31, 2007 to determine the will of its citizens. According to the Kurdistan Regional Government's (KRG) prime minister, Kirkuk represents the Kurdish region and must be returned to Kurdistan. Under the former regime's policy of Arabization—removing Kurdish families from Kirkuk and replacing them with Arab families—areas of Kirkuk were given to other governorates, according to a Kurdish committee. KRG officials want the referendum held by the date specified in the Constitution. Other Iraqi legislators believe that the Kirkuk referendum should be deferred because of the disputes over the borders of Kirkuk and continuing displacement of people in the area.
- *Power of the federal government versus regions.* The CRC proposed several amendments to the Constitution to clarify the powers of the federal government and the shared powers with the regions, but has not achieved compromise among major political factions on these amendments. In particular, the CRC proposed amending Article 111 of the Constitution to clearly state that the federal government shall collect oil revenues and distribute them equally to all Iraqis in accordance with the national budget law. According to the United Nations, this amendment would provide the federal government exclusive authority for oil revenues. In contrast, the existing constitutional framework is widely interpreted as allowing regions to define how and whether they share locally generated oil revenues.[4] For this reason, the Kurdish bloc opposes the CRC-proposed amendment.

Procedural and Logistical Challenges Confront Completion of the Review

If agreement is reached on a package of constitutional amendments, the Iraqi legislature must vote on the package. The amendments will be considered approved if an absolute majority of the legislature votes for the package. One challenge is simply holding a vote.

Despite Iraqi leaders signing a unity accord, as of August 29, 2007, several Iraqi parties were boycotting the government, including Iraq's largest

Sunni bloc. Although the other parties in the legislature could form an absolute majority to pass a package of amendments, it would defeat the purpose of trying to reach a broad political accommodation.

If the legislature approves the constitutional amendments, the government must hold a national referendum within 2 months of approval. According to the United Nations, before a referendum can occur, the Iraq Electoral Commission must develop a valid voting roster, educate the public about the proposed amendments, print referendum ballots, and locate and staff polling places. In a July 2007 report, the Iraq High Electoral Commission stated that it faced challenges to developing a valid voting roster because of the large movement of displaced persons—an estimated 800,000 since February 2006.[5]

Appendix II

Benchmark 2—De-Ba'athification Reform

Enacting and implementing legislation on de-Ba'athification reform.

GAO Assessment as of August 30, 2007: Not met[1]

Issue

Coalition Provisional Authority (CPA) Order 1 dissolved the Ba'athist party, removed Ba'athist leaders and senior party members from government, and banned them from future employment in the public sector. The CPA further provided for investigation and removal of even junior members of the party from upper-level management in government ministries, universities, and hospitals. Most of Iraqi's technocratic class was pushed out of government due to de-Ba'athification and many Sunni Arabs remain angry about policies to de-Ba'athify Iraqi society, according to the Iraq Study Group report.

Status

Although Iraqi leaders have drafted several pieces of legislation to reform de-Ba'athification, none has sufficient support among Iraq's political factions to have a first reading in the Iraqi legislature, according to U.S. officials. No consensus exists on reforming the current de-Ba'athification policy and many Iraqis are concerned by the prospects of former Ba'athist tormenters returning to power. However, according to an August 2007 U.S. interagency report, Iraq's senior Shi'a and Sunni Arab and Kurdish political leaders signed a Unity Accord, including consensus on draft legislation on de-Ba'thification reform. Such a law would need to be drafted, passed by the Council of Representatives, and implemented.

According to U.S. officials, reforms to the law would more likely promote reconciliation if the reforms target Ba'athists who had command responsibility within the party or committed human rights violations or other crimes.[2] Removing individuals based purely on party membership increases the chances that segments of the Iraqi public will see the system as unfair, according to these officials. Draft legislation on de-Ba'athification reform, dated July 2007 before the Unity Accord, provides for a special commission, a panel of judges to make decisions, and the right to appeal the panel's decisions. The draft legislation also specifies that the commission will be dissolved 6 months after the law is passed.

Appendix III

Benchmark 3—Hydrocarbon Legislation

Enacting and implementing legislation to ensure the equitable distribution of hydrocarbon resources of the people of Iraq without regard to the sect or ethnicity of recipients, and enacting and implementing legislation to ensure that the energy resources of Iraq benefit Sunni Arabs, Shi'a Arabs, Kurds, and other Iraqi citizens in an equitable manner.

GAO Assessment as of August 30, 2007: Not met[1]

Issue

The importance of oil revenues for the Iraqi economy is widely recognized, as is the need to create a new legal framework for the development and management of the country's oil sector. The oil sector accounts for over half of Iraq's gross domestic product and over 90 percent of its revenues. The timely and equitable distribution of these revenues is essential to Iraq's ability to provide for its needs, including the reconstruction of a unified Iraq.

Status

The government of Iraq has not enacted and implemented any of the four separate yet interrelated pieces of legislation needed to ensure the equitable distribution of hydrocarbon resources. As of August 2007, the Iraqi government had drafted three pieces of legislation: (1) hydrocarbon framework legislation that establishes the structure, management, and oversight for the oil sector; (2) revenue-sharing legislation; and (3) legislation restructuring the Ministry of Oil. However, none of the legislation is currently under consideration by Iraq's parliament (Council of Representatives).

A fourth piece of legislation establishing the Iraq National Oil Company (INOC) has not been drafted, according to State officials.

Hydrocarbon framework legislation was approved by the Iraqi cabinet (Council of Ministers) in February 2007, and sent to the Oil and Gas Committee of Iraq's parliament for review in July 2007. However, before the legislation was submitted to the parliament, the Iraqi government amended the draft to address substantive changes made by the Shura council. According to State, the Shura council reviews draft legislation to ensure constitutionality and to avoid contradictions with Iraq's legal system, including Islamic law. The Kurdistan Regional Government (KRG) did not agree to the council's revisions. Accordingly, the Oil and Gas Committee chairman is taking no legislative action until the Iraqi cabinet and the KRG agree on a new draft, according to State. It is not clear if this legislation will include annexes intended to allocate the control of particular oil fields and exploration areas to either the central or regional governments. According to the Iraqi government, the annexes remain under consideration.

Revenue-sharing legislation is intended to ensure the equitable distribution of Iraq's financial resources, including oil and gas revenues. The central government and the KRG agreed on draft revenue-sharing legislation[2] in June 2007. However, the Iraqi cabinet has not yet approved the legislation and submitted it to Iraq's parliament for consideration.

This draft legislation is linked to proposed amendments to the Iraqi Constitution regarding the role of the federal government and regions and the management of oil revenues. Under the existing Constitution, if there is a contradiction between regional and national law with respect to a matter outside the exclusive authority of the federal government, regional law takes priority and regional powers have the right to amend the application of the national legislation within that region. As oil revenue sharing is not a power exclusively reserved for the federal government in the existing Constitution, according to officials, regions may determine how and whether they share locally generated oil revenues with the remainder of Iraq, regardless of what is stated in the federal law.[3] In response, the Iraqi Constitutional Review Committee has proposed amendments to the Constitution that would provide for the national collection and distribution of oil revenues.

Legislation restructuring the Ministry of Oil has been drafted but has not yet been submitted to the Council of Ministers, according to State.

Legislation establishing the Iraq National Oil Company (INOC) is being drafted, according to State.

Appendix IV

Benchmark 4—Semi-Autonomous Regions

Enacting and implementing legislation on procedures to form semi-autonomous regions.

GAO Assessment as of August 30, 2007: Partially met[1]

Issue

Iraq's Constitution requires the Council of Representatives to enact a law that defines the executive procedures needed to form regions within 6 months of the date of its first session. Some Iraqi legislators believe that the right to form regions, with authority similar to the Kurdistan region, would help protect their rights.

Status

In October 2006, the Iraqi legislature passed a law establishing procedures to form regions, but the law delays implementation for 18 months.[2] According to U.S. officials, this means that no steps to form regions, such as holding provincial referendums, can be taken before April 2008. According to State, this is in the best interests of Iraq as it will allow the government to deal with some outstanding issues. The United Nations has identified two issues that may impact implementation of this law—the ongoing review of Iraq's Constitution and the capacity of new regional governments.

According to members of Iraq's Constitutional Review Committee (CRC), the law on procedures to form regions was delayed for 18 months to allow the constitutional review process to be completed. Some of the proposed amendments to the constitution would clarify the powers of the federal government versus regions and governorates For example, according to the United Nations, the CRC proposed amendments that would give federal law priority over regional law with respect to water, customs, ports, and oil and revenue sharing. Other proposed amendments would give the federal government exclusive power over electricity generation, railways, and pension funds.[3] Moreover, the constitutional review could also help resolve the status of disputed areas, which could impact regional boundaries. Until the constitutional review is completed and the constitutional referendum is held, residents in areas considering regional formation may not have all the information they need to make decisions.

The capability of the regions to govern themselves will also impact implementation of the law. Article 121 of the Constitution accords significant executive, judicial, and management authorities to the regions. The regions have responsibility for maintaining their internal security forces, administering allocations from national revenues, and maintaining representational offices in embassies and consuls. Moreover, the law on formation of regions provides that once formed, the regions must undertake to create elected provisional legislative councils. According to the United Nations, this will require a substantial investment of resources and significant management responsibility. GAO has reported on significant shortages of competent personnel in national ministries charged with delivering services to the Iraqi people; moreover, these shortages are greater at the provincial level of government, according to State and USAID officials. We have also reported that the poor security situation and high levels of violence have contributed to the continued and accelerating "brain drain" of professional Iraqis that would be needed to manage the new regional administrations.[4]

Appendix V

Benchmark 5—Electoral Legislation

Enacting and implementing legislation establishing an Independent High Electoral Commission, provincial elections law, provincial council authorities, and a date for provincial elections.

GAO Assessment as of August 30, 2007: Not met[1]

Issue

When provincial elections were first held on January 2005, many Sunnis boycotted the election, resulting in largely Shi'a and Kurd provincial councils in provinces with majority Sunni populations. To redress the underrepresentation of Sunnis in provincial councils, Iraq needs to hold new provincial elections, but must first establish an electoral commission, write provincial election laws, define provincial powers so voters know the stakes, and set a date for elections.

Status

Although the government of Iraq has enacted and implemented legislation establishing an Independent High Electoral Commission (IHEC), it has not enacted and implemented legislation establishing a provincial elections law, provincial council authorities, or a date for provincial elections.

- Although the government of Iraq has enacted and implemented legislation to establish an IHEC, certain steps still remain in establishing the commission. According to the U.S. government, the Council of Representatives (COR) passed the IHEC Law on January 23, 2007, and subsequently appointed the nine IHEC Commissioners, as required under the law, in a process the UN deemed in compliance with international standards. However, a provision in the IHEC law requires the COR to nominate and the Board of Commissioners to appoint the directors of the Governorate Electoral Offices in each province. Twelve of these positions are vacant, but, according to State, the process of appointing the directors is progressing. The law also requires the IHEC to establish and update a voter registry in collaboration with the Governorate and Regional Electoral Offices. However, before they can complete an update of the voter registry (which was last updated in mid-2005), an election law must be enacted that defines the residency and voter eligibility requirements. Finally, the IHEC still needs a budget to fund its activities.

- Iraq has not enacted and implemented legislation for provincial elections. According to the U.S. Embassy in Baghdad, the Prime Minster's office is drafting legislation governing provincial elections, including setting a date for elections to occur. However, according to the Embassy, some key political parties are hesitant to hold provincial elections due to concerns that they will lose representation, potentially to more extreme parties. Additionally, several parties are demanding that any election law ensure that eligible refugees and internally displaced persons be allowed to vote.
- Provincial powers legislation, which will define the authorities and structures of local governments, has not been enacted and implemented. According to the U.S. government, the draft legislation has been approved and submitted to the Council of Representatives, where it has had two of the three required readings. However, the U.S. government reported in July 2007 that changes were being considered, particularly related to the powers of the governor and the authority of the federal government at the local level. The U.S. Embassy cited key issues with the draft, including that it cedes most power to the provinces. The United Nations pointed out that the draft fails to clarify the role of the governorate and that the draft law does not deal adequately with the effective delivery of public goods and services in the governorates. According to the U.S. Embassy, on July 8, 2007, the relevant COR committee presented a report outlining suggested changes to the law, some of which the Embassy supported.
- The government of Iraq has not set a date for provincial elections. The Iraq Study Group emphasized the need for provincial elections at the earliest possible date. The Embassy is urging the Iraqi government to take the legislative and administrative action necessary to ensure timely and fair elections. According to the U.S. Embassy, it is intensively engaged with the Iraqi government and the COR at all levels to expedite legislation or amendments to existing legislation that will allow provincial elections to take place and secure funding for elections.

In comments on this appendix, State said that this benchmark should be partially met since the Iraq High Electoral Commission has been established and the benchmark calls only for its establishment. However, the benchmark requires more than the establishment of the IHEC, and Iraq has not enacted and implemented a provincial elections law, provincial council authorities, or a date for provincial elections, as required by the benchmark.

Appendix VI

Benchmark 6—Amnesty Legislation

Enacting and implementing legislation addressing amnesty.

GAO Assessment as of August 30, 2007: Not met[1]

Issue

Iraqi government officials believe that amnesty for insurgents and others who have not committed terrorist acts is an important tool to promote reconciliation and could help pacify insurgents. In addition, the Iraqi government and coalition forces hold thousands of detainees, some of whom could be eligible for an amnesty program when conditions are right.

Status

The Iraqi government has not drafted legislation on amnesty, according to U.S. officials, and the conditions for a successful program are not present. As the cover letter shows, many steps remain in the legislative process, including drafting the legislation and obtaining approval in the Iraqi cabinet and Council of Representatives. However, the government of Iraq is not pressing for the development of amnesty legislation.

Little Progress Made in Considering Amnesty Legislation

Although amnesty was proposed as part of the Prime Minister's national reconciliation plan in June 2006, little progress has been made. The plan called for issuing amnesty to prisoners not involved in crimes against humanity or terrorist acts. At that time, the Iraqi government announced that it would release 2,500 detainees; 2,500 prisoners were subsequently released. According to U.S. officials in Baghdad, no large-scale releases have been made since 2006, and there has been little discussion of amnesty since then. However, the Prime Minister's office and Iraq's Disarmament, Demobilization, and Reintegration Committee sponsored a workshop on amnesty in May 2007. The workshop recommended that amnesty should not proceed, but rather should result from national reconciliation and that the government's military has to be superior to armed groups as a condition for offering amnesty.

The scope of an amnesty program is also an issue. The United Nations takes the position that in considering the categories of perpetrators to be included or excluded in amnesty, international law does not allow amnesty to be granted to those who committed genocide, crimes against humanity, or other serious violations of international humanitarian law. In addition, Iraqi government officials have recommended that an amnesty program consider all detained individuals held by Iraq and by coalition forces. There are currently thousands of detainees, including over 24,000 held by coalition forces. According to multinational force officials, there could be considerably more detainees in the future as the Baghdad security plan progresses. The Coalition's Task Force 134 is building and expanding prison facilities to accommodate additional detainees.

Appendix VII

Benchmark 7—Militia Disarmament

Enacting and implementing legislation establishing a strong militia disarmament program to ensure that such security forces are accountable only to the central government and loyal to the Constitution of Iraq.

GAO Assessment as of August 30, 2007: Not met[1]

Issue

Militias contribute to the high levels of violence in Iraq, are responsible for sectarian killings, fuel ongoing corruption, and have heavily infiltrated the Iraqi army and national police. Efforts to dissolve or bring militias under control have been ongoing since 2004. In March 2007, 77 percent of Iraqis in a nationwide poll agreed that militias should be dissolved.

Status

The Iraqi government has not drafted legislation on disarming militias. CPA Order 91, issued in 2004, prohibited armed forces and militias within Iraq, except for those allowed under the Order.[2] Multiple steps are needed to enact and implement further legislation to disarm militias. More importantly, according to U.S. officials, conditions are not right for a traditional disarmament, demobilization, and reintegration program (DDR); accordingly, there is currently no momentum in the government of Iraq for such a program. Thus, militias pose a severe challenge to stability and reconciliation in Iraq.

Militias Pose a Challenge, but Little Progress Has Been Made in Demobilizing Them

Militias have contributed to the high levels of violence in Iraq. According to the Defense Intelligence Agency Director, the Jayash al-Mahdi (the militia associated with Muqtada al Sadr), often operates under the protection or approval of Iraqi police to detain and kill suspected Sunni insurgents and civilians. A June 2007 Defense Department report further notes that many Jayash al-Mahdi fighters have left Baghdad as a result of expanded coalition and Iraqi presence. They now engage in ethnic and sectarian violence in northern and central Iraq and have increased conflict with the Badr Organization in southern Iraq leading to a significant increase in attacks against the coalition in Basrah. The June 2007 report also states that Shi'a militia infiltration of the Ministry of Interior is a problem. Militia influence impacts every component of the Ministry, particularly in Baghdad and other key cities.

Despite the challenge the militias pose, little progress has been made to disarm and demobilize them. Nine parties, with militias numbering an estimated 100,000 fighters, agreed to a transition and reintegration process in 2004. The Coalition Provisional Authority estimated that 90 percent of these fighters would complete the transition and reintegration process by January 2005. However, according to the administration's July 15, 2007 report, no armed group has committed to disarm. Moreover, according to U.S. officials in Baghdad, the Iraqi DDR commission has not developed a plan for DDR and has not received funding for its work.

Conditions for Traditional DDR Do Not Exist

A May 2007 UN assessment on DDR for Iraq states that minimum requirements for a successful DDR program in Iraq include a secure environment, the inclusion of all belligerent parties, an overarching political agreement, sustainable funding, and appropriate reintegration opportunities. GAO's reports and analysis show that these conditions do not exist in Iraq. For example:

- As the cover letter shows, the overall level of attacks against Iraqi civilians, coalition personnel, and Iraqi security forces has risen since 2003, creating a poor security environment. Classified and unclassified GAO reports provide further information on security in Iraq.[3]
- In June 2006, the prime minister sought to include insurgent groups as part of his reconciliation plan. However, according to administration and DOD reports, efforts at reconciliation have stalled. In addition, Iraqi officials reject terrorist groups, such as al Qaeda in Iraq, and a report done for the U.S. Embassy comments that some groups cannot be reconciled. Also, the support of external actors is an important element of

disarmament and demobilization, but according to U.S. reports, some external groups are not helpful. For example, Iran's Islamic Revolutionary Guard provides deadly arms and funding to Iraq's militias and contributes to the ongoing instability.

The Iraqi government provided $150 million for DDR in its 2007 budget and the Congress has made available up to $156 million from the Iraq Security Forces fund, to be used to assist the government of Iraq for this purpose. However, Iraq has prepared no plan for DDR and has not made progress in enacting legislation. Thus, it is uncertain whether such funding is needed at this time.

Appendix VIII

Benchmark 8—Baghdad Security Plan Committees

Establish supporting political, media, economic, and services committees in support of the Baghdad Security Plan.

GAO Assessment as of August 30, 2007: Met[1]

Issue

The U.S. and Iraqi governments began the current Baghdad security plan[2] in mid-February 2007 to stem the violence in Baghdad and surrounding areas. During the summer of 2006, MNF-I and the Iraqi security forces implemented two other plans to secure Baghdad, but these operations failed to reduce violence for a variety of reasons. Unlike the earlier operations, the current Baghdad Security Plan encompasses political, economic, and security activities that the Iraqi government needed to coordinate at the national level.

Status

In February 2007, the Iraqi government created the Executive Steering Committee (the executive committee) and six subcommittees to coordinate political, economic and military activities and make decisions in support of the Baghdad Security Plan. According to a Department of State official, the executive committee's major objective was to increase the coordination and capacity of the Iraqi government to improve the quality of life of Baghdad's population as part of the Baghdad Security Plan. Each of the subcommittees addresses one of six issues related to the plan's implementation: economics, services, political, communication, popular mobilization, and security. The executive committee and subcommittees meet on a weekly basis.

The committees consist of Iraqi and U.S. participants. The Iraqi Prime Minister chairs the executive committee, while senior-level Iraqi ministry officials chair the various subcommittees. For example, a deputy prime minister chairs the economic subcommittee and the services subcommittee. Representatives from the relevant Iraqi ministries serve on each subcommittee. Two senior U.S. officials are observers to the executive committee and attend its weekly meetings. A senior MNF-I or U.S. embassy official is also assigned to each subcommittee. This official provides advice on the subcommittees' agendas and other support when called upon.

According to a Department of State official, the executive committee and subcommittees have worked to ensure that the Iraqi government provided sufficient Iraqi forces to assist MNF-I in implementing the Baghdad Security Plan. For example, when the Iraqi Army provided brigades that were not at full strength, the executive committee and security subcommittee identified forces from other parts of the country to move to Baghdad. The committees also found ways to house and feed the Iraqi troops supporting the security plan. In addition, the communication subcommittee has helped publicize the security plan's goals and the other subcommittees' efforts to get resources to Baghdad districts that have been cleared of insurgents.

We did not assess the effectiveness of the executive committee or subcommittees in providing overall coordination and supporting the implementation of the Baghdad Security Plan. However, the administration's July 2007 report to Congress stated that the effectiveness of each committee varied.

Appendix IX

Benchmark 9—Iraqi Brigades

Provide three trained and ready Iraqi brigades to support Baghdad operations.

GAO Assessment as of August 30, 2007: Partially met[1]

Issue

During the summer of 2006, a large number of Iraqi security forces refused to deploy to Baghdad to conduct operations in support of the previous Baghdad Security Plans. In January 2007, the President said that the Iraqi government had agreed to resolve this problem under the current plan and had committed three additional Iraqi brigades to support the new plan.

Status

Since February 2007, the Iraqi government deployed nine Iraqi army battalions equaling three brigades for 90-day rotations to support the Baghdad Security Plan. In the July 2007 report, the administration stated that the Iraqi government had difficulty deploying three additional army brigades to Baghdad at sufficient strength. In commenting on our draft report, DOD stated that current present for duty rates for deployed units is 75 percent of authorized strength. However, the July 2007 administration report stated that the government has deployed battalions from multiple Iraqi Army divisions to provide the required three brigade-equivalent forces to support the Baghdad security plan. After the initial deployment of the required brigades, the Iraqi government began the rotation plan. 19 units have currently deployed in support of the Baghdad security plan. Several of these units voluntarily extended, and others were rotated every 90 days in accordance with the plan. In addition, all of the Iraqi units had pre-deployment training to support operations in Baghdad. The administration's July 2007 report states that progress toward this benchmark has been satisfactory, and the overall effect has been satisfactory in that three brigades are operating in Baghdad.

However, in commenting on this report, DOD stated that performance of the units currently supporting Baghdad operations has been varied. Some units had performed exceptionally well, proven themselves and raised their readiness ratings. Others had marked time and slowly regressed over their 90-day deployment. Of the 19 Iraqi units that had supported operations in Baghdad, 5 units had performed well while the remaining had proven to be problematic for several reasons: lack of personnel, lack of individual fighting equipment and lack of vehicles to conduct their assigned missions. We obtained classified information that indicates other problems with these Iraqi army units. Our classified briefing report provides more information on this benchmark.

Appendix X

Benchmark 10—Commander's Authority

Providing Iraqi commanders with all authorities to execute this plan and to make tactical and operational decisions, in consultation with U.S. commanders, without political intervention, to include the authority to pursue all extremists, including Sunni insurgents and Shi'ite militias.

GAO Assessment as of August 30, 2007: Not met[1]

Issue

As stated in the President's January 10, 2007, speech on the Baghdad security plan, previous Baghdad security plans failed, in part, because Iraqi political and sectarian interference prevented forces from taking action against militias. According to the administration's initial assessment, Iraq's Prime Minister stated that political or sectarian interference in the affairs of the Iraqi security forces will not be tolerated, and actions have been taken to address political intervention.

Status

In July 2007, the administration reported that the government of Iraq has not made satisfactory progress toward providing Iraqi commanders with all authorities to execute the Baghdad security plan and to make tactical and operational decisions in consultation with U.S. commanders without political intervention. The report noted that political intervention in the conduct of some security operations continues even though new rules of engagement for the Baghdad Operational Command have come into effect and commanders have been given the authority to attack insurgents and militias.

According to U.S. officials and other experts, sectarian and political interference in the conduct of military operations continues. Tribal and ethnosectarian loyalties remain strong within many Iraqi military units, hindering efforts to take actions against militias. These loyalties are often the basis for relationships between key officers in units and higher-level authorities who are not always in the direct chain of command. For example, sectarian militias control many local police. Additionally, some army units sent to Baghdad have mixed loyalties, and some have had ties to Shi'a militias making it difficult to target Shi'a extremist networks. Further, according to DOD, evidence exists of target lists emanating from the Office of the Commander in Chief that bypassed operational commanders and directed lower-level intelligence officers and commanders to make arrests, primarily of Sunnis. In addition, sectarian bias in the appointment of senior military and police commanders continues, giving rise to suspicions that political considerations may drive Iraqi commanders' decisions about which operations to undertake or support.

In commenting on this benchmark, DOD noted that all 9 of the brigade commanders and 17 of the 27 national police battalion commanders have been replaced for failure to command or enforce non-sectarian operations.

Appendix XI

Benchmark 11—Iraqi Security Forces Enforcement of the Law

Ensuring that Iraqi Security Forces are providing even-handed enforcement of the law.

GAO Assessment as of August 30, 2007: Not met[1]

Issue

During 2006, according to a Department of State human rights report, the Iraqi security forces committed serious human rights violations in Baghdad and other areas of Iraq. These actions added to the increasing violence against the civilian population during 2006. In support of the Baghdad security plan, the Iraqi Prime Minister pledged to provide even-handed enforcement of the law.

Status

According to U.S. reports, the government of Iraq has not ensured that the Iraqi security forces are providing even-handed enforcement of the law. In May 2007, the U.S. Commission on International Religious Freedom[2] reported that Iraq's Shi'a-dominated government bears responsibility for engaging in sectarian-based human rights violations, as well as tolerating abuses committed by Shi'a militias with ties to political factions in the governing coalition. According to the commission, the Iraqi government through its security forces has committed arbitrary arrest, prolonged detention without due process, targeted executions, and torture against non-Shi'a Iraqis. In committing these abuses, the security forces target Sunnis on the basis of their religious identity, as well as terrorists and insurgents.

Furthermore, the commission reported that the Iraqi government tolerates and fails to control religiously motivated attacks and other abuses carried out by Shi'a militias, specifically Jayash al-Mahdi and Badr Organization. These militias have targeted Sunnis on the basis of their religious identity and have committed such abuses as abductions, beatings, targeted killings, intimidation, forced resettlement, murder, rape, and torture. According to the commission's report, relationships between these militias and leading Shi'a factions within Iraq's ministries and governing coalition indicate that the Jayash al-Mahdi and Badr Organization are parastate actors operating with impunity or even with governmental complicity.

In mid-August 2007, Department of State officials stated that the Iraqi government and security forces continue to engage in sectarian-based abuses. State's March 2007 human rights report[3] cited widely reported incidents of unauthorized government agent involvement in extrajudicial killings throughout the country. These incidents included Shi'a militia members wearing police uniforms and driving police cars in carrying out killings and kidnapping in the southern city of Basra. In addition, death squads affiliated with the Ministry of Interior targeted Sunnis and conducted kidnapping raids in Baghdad and its environs, largely with impunity.

The administration's July 2007 report stated that the Iraqi government and many Iraqi security force units are still applying the law on a sectarian basis when left on their own. The report attributed any progress made by the security forces in enforcing the law more even-handedly to the presence of coalition units and embedded training teams, rather than to the Iraqi government.

Appendix XII

Benchmark 12—Safe Havens

Ensuring that, according to President Bush, Prime Minister Maliki said "the Baghdad security plan will not provide a safe haven for any outlaws, regardless of [their] sectarian or political affiliation."

GAO Assessment as of August 30, 2007: Partially met[1]

Issue

As stated in the President's January 10, 2007, speech on the Baghdad security plan, previous plans to secure Baghdad have failed, in part, because political and sectarian interference and rules of engagement in place for those plans prevented Iraqi and coalition forces from entering neighborhoods that are safe havens to those fueling the sectarian violence. On January 6, 2007, the Iraqi Prime Minister stated, "The Baghdad security plan will not offer a safe shelter for outlaws regardless of their ethnic and political affiliations, and we will punish anyone who hesitates to implement orders because of his ethnic and political background."

Status

Although the Iraqi government has allowed MNF-I to conduct operations in all areas of Baghdad, temporary safe havens still exist due to strong sectarian loyalties and militia infiltration of security forces. According to State, terrorist safe havens are defined as ungoverned, under-governed, or ill-governed areas of a country and non-physical areas where terrorists that constitute a threat to U.S. national security interests are able to organize, plan, raise funds, communicate, recruit, train, and operate in relative security because of inadequate governance capacity, political will, or both.

U.S. commanders report overall satisfaction with their ability to target any and all extremist groups. In commenting on our draft report, DOD stated that coalition forces and Iraqi security forces conducted over eighty operations that span each sector of Sadr City from January to August 2007. According to DOD, the surge has resulted in significant reductions in safe havens for al Qaeda in Iraq inside Baghdad and in al Anbar and Diyala provinces. In previous Baghdad operations, the Iraqi government prevented Iraqi and coalition forces from going into Sadr City. Although MNF-I conducts operations in Sadr City, MNF-I and Iraqi security forces maintain only one Joint Security Station on the border of Sadr City, with none within the city itself. In addition to Joint Security Stations, MNF-I established about 30 coalition outposts throughout Baghdad, including one on the border of Sadr City.

Figure 4: Location of Joint Security Stations and Coalition Outposts in Baghdad [Deleted Material]

However, due to sectarian influence and infiltration of Iraqi security forces and support from the local population, anti-coalition forces retain the freedom to organize and conduct operations against coalition forces. Thus temporary safe havens still exist in Baghdad, which supports a rating of partially met. A June 2007 DOD report describes some of the conditions that allow safe havens to exist. For example, the Shi'a militia continues to function as the de facto government in Sadr City. Further, militia influence impacts every component of the Iraqi Ministry of the Interior, particularly in Baghdad and several other key cities, according to the DOD report.

Our classified briefing report provides more information on the existence of safe havens.

Appendix XIII

Benchmark 13—Sectarian Violence and Militia Control

Reducing the level of sectarian violence in Iraq and eliminating militia control of local security.

GAO Assessment as of August 30, 2007: Not met[1]

Issue

During 2006, according to State and UN reports,[2] insurgents, death squads, militias, and terrorists increased their attacks against civilians, largely on a sectarian basis. In addition, the number of internally displaced persons in Iraq sharply increased following the February 2006 bombing of the Samarra mosque, primarily as a result of sectarian intimidation and violence that forced many people from their homes. By the end of 2006, according to the

UN, many Baghdad neighborhoods had become divided along Sunni and Shi'a lines and were increasingly controlled by armed groups claiming to act as protectors and defenders of these areas.[3] In January 2007, the President announced that the United States would increase force levels in Iraq to help the Iraqis carry out their campaign to reduce sectarian violence and bring security to Baghdad.

Status

While it is not clear if sectarian violence has been reduced, militia control over security forces has not been eliminated and remains a serious problem in Baghdad and other areas of Iraq.

According to the administration's July 2007 report to Congress, MNF-I data showed a decrease in sectarian violence, particularly in Baghdad, since the start of the Baghdad security plan. MNF-I counts sectarian incidents and murders in determining trends in sectarian violence.[4] The administration's July 2007 report concluded that the Iraqi government, with substantial coalition assistance, had made satisfactory progress toward reducing sectarian violence. The report acknowledged that precise measurements vary, and it was too early to determine if the decrease would be sustainable.

GAO cannot determine whether sectarian violence in Iraq has been reduced because measuring such violence requires understanding the perpetrator's intent, which may not be known. The number of attacks targeting civilians and population displacement resulting from sectarian violence may serve as additional indicators. For example, the average number of daily attacks against civilians remained about the same over the last six months. The decrease in total average daily attacks in July is largely due to a decrease in attacks on coalition forces rather than civilians.

Figure 5: Average Number of Daily, Enemy-Initiated Attacks Against the Coalition, Iraqi Security Forces, and Civilians (May 2003–July 2007) [Deleted Material]

While overall attacks declined in July compared with June, levels of violence remain high. Enemy initiated attacks have increased around major religious and political events, including Ramadan and elections.[5] For 2007, Ramadan is scheduled to begin in mid-September.

The August 2007 National Intelligence Estimate on Iraq[6] (NIE) also reports that the level of overall violence in Iraq, including attacks on and casualties among civilians, remains high. Further, the NIE states that Iraq's security will continue to improve modestly, but that levels of insurgent and sectarian violence will remain high over the next 6 to 12 months. Similarly, recent March and June 2007 United Nations reports state that attacks against civilians persist and the continuing systematic, widespread attacks against the civilian population in Iraq are tantamount to crimes against humanity and violate the laws of war.

The violence in Iraq has resulted in a large number of Iraqis displaced from their homes. A report by the Iraqi Red Crescent Organization found that internally displaced persons increased from about 499,000 in February 2007 to about 1,128,000 in July 2007. The United Nations High Commissioner for Refugees (UNHCR) estimated that an additional 1.8 million Iraqi citizens were displaced to nearby countries, primarily to Jordan, Syria, Lebanon, Iran, and Egypt. The UNHCR predicted that 40,000 to 50,000 people will continue to be displaced each month even if the security plan succeeds in solving the displacement problem. Currently, the number of displaced persons is increasing at an average of 80,000 to 100,000 each month, according to the Red Crescent.

The August 2007 National Intelligence Estimate for Iraq stated that population displacement resulting from sectarian violence continues, imposing burdens on provincial governments and some neighboring states. As the International Organization for Migration and the UN recently reported, most of Iraq's internally displaced persons are moving from mixed areas[7] to seek refuge in homogeneous areas, largely because of direct threats or forcible displacement from their homes due to their religious and sectarian identities. Where population displacements have led to significant sectarian separation, according to the August 2007 National Intelligence Estimate, conflict levels have diminished to some extent because warring communities find it more difficult to penetrate communal enclaves.

Our classified report provides further information on trends associated with violence in Iraq.

Militia control over local security forces—the second part of the benchmark—has not been eliminated. Numerous U.S. and UN reports have stated that militias still retain significant control or influence over local security in parts of Baghdad and other areas of Iraq. For example, in July 2007, the administration reported that militia presence is still strong and will likely remain so until the security situation begins to stabilize. The report stated that the Iraqi government has made unsatisfactory progress towards eliminating militia control of local security, which continues to negatively affect the public perception of the authority and fairness of the Iraqi government. In addition, DOD's June 2007 report to Congress called militia influence of local police a significant problem and added that some security forces remain prone to intimidation by, or collusion with, criminal gangs. Further, the Department of State's human rights report characterized Iraqi police effectiveness as seriously compromised by militias and sectarianism, with rampant corruption and a culture of impunity. Finally, in March 2007, the United Nations reported cases of possible collusion between armed militia and Iraqi security forces in raids and security operations, as well as the failure of these security forces to intervene and prevent kidnapping and murder and other crimes.

Appendix XIV

Benchmark 14—Joint Security Stations

Establishing all of the planned joint security stations in neighborhoods across Baghdad.

GAO Assessment as of August 30, 2007: Met[1]

Issue

Past Baghdad security plans failed, in part, because the coalition and Iraqi forces did not hold neighborhoods after clearing them of insurgents. The current Baghdad security plan and the related increase of U.S. and Iraqi forces into Baghdad is intended to clear insurgents, militias, and organized criminal gangs from neighborhoods; maintain a security presence in those areas; and provide for follow-on assistance efforts. As part of this effort, MNF-I and Iraqi security forces are establishing Joint Security Stations across Baghdad to improve population protection by providing a continuous presence in Baghdad's neighborhoods.

Status

As of August 9, 2007, the Iraqi government, with substantial coalition assistance, had established 32 of the 34 planned Joint Security Stations in Baghdad. This figure includes Joint Security Stations that had achieved initial or full operational capability.

Figure 6: Map of Joint Security Stations in Baghdad, as of August 9, 2007 [Deleted Material]

Joint Security Stations are staffed by Iraqi local police, national police, and army personnel, as well as coalition forces. According to the administration's July 2007 report, the security stations are designed to improve population protection by providing a 24-hour security presence in Baghdad neighborhoods. They also allow greater oversight of Iraqi security forces by U.S. military personnel.

Appendix XV

Benchmark 15—Iraqi Security Forces Operating Independently

Increasing the number of Iraqi security forces' units capable of operating independently.

GAO Assessment: Not met[1]

Issue

In August 2003, the Coalition Provisional Authority dissolved the Iraqi military and began the process of rebuilding the Iraqi military and police. Since 2003, the United States has provided about $19.2 billion to train and equip about 350,000 Iraqi soldiers and police officers, in an effort to develop Iraqi security forces, transfer security responsibilities to them and the Iraqi government, and ultimately withdraw U.S. troops from Iraq. The coalition began embedding transition teams with Iraqi security forces in 2005 to help develop their ability to conduct counterinsurgency operations. These teams use the Operational Readiness Assessment process to evaluate the readiness of Iraqi security force units to conduct operations with or without coalition support.[2]

Status

While the Iraqi security forces have grown in size and are increasingly leading counterinsurgency operations, the number of Iraqi army units operating independently decreased between March 2007 and July 2007.[3] According to the administration's July 2007 report, an Iraqi unit can be considered independent if it has achieved an Operational Readiness Assessment rating of level 1, which means it is capable of planning, executing, and sustaining counterinsurgency operations.[4]

Manning shortages as well as logistics and sustainment shortfalls have contributed to the decrease in the number of Iraqi battalions capable of operating independently, according to DOD reports. Sectarian and militia influences further complicate the development of Iraqi forces. In June 2007, DOD reported that while coalition forces are the target of most enemy attacks, Iraqi security forces and civilians account for the majority of casualties, contributing to the decline in the readiness of some Iraqi units. Attrition also has affected the Iraqi security forces. Annual attrition is estimated to be between 15 and 18 percent for the Iraqi army and between 20 and 22 percent for the police. In addition, according to a June 2007 report from DOD to Congress, only about 65 percent of authorized Iraqi personnel are in the field at any given time due to a liberal leave policy and absences without leave. To increase the number of soldiers on hand for operations, the Iraqi government and MNF-I decided that they will increase manning to 120 percent of authorization levels.[5]

Due to Iraq's immature logistics systems, many Iraqi military and police units will continue to depend on MNF-I for key sustainment and logistics support until December 2008. DOD reports that the Iraqi forces' limited capacity in these areas hinders their ability to assume missions from MNF-I and requires continued development in some key areas through the end of 2008. For instance, DOD has set a December 2008 goal for the Iraqi government to provide day-to-day items such as food, water, and electricity to the Ministry of Defense's National Depot. In addition, the Ministry of Interior aims to become self sufficient in procuring and managing repair parts by the end of 2008.

MNF-I and the Iraqi government continue to struggle with sectarian and militia influences while trying to develop the Iraqi security forces. Because of the sectarian leaning of some national police units, MNF-I is providing continuing oversight of Iraqi security forces. In addition, militia influence affects every component of the Ministry of the Interior, especially in Baghdad and other key cities, according to DOD. This influence, along with corruption and illegal activity, constrains progress in the development of Ministry of Interior forces.

Appendix XVI

Benchmark 16—Minority Party Rights

Ensuring that the rights of minority political parties in the Iraqi legislature are protected.

GAO Assessment as of August 30, 2007: Met[1]

Issue

Minority parties or groups had no rights under the former Ba'athist regime. Ensuring the rights of minority parties was a key Iraqi goal to ensure broad representation and fairness in the new Iraq.

Status

The rights of minority political parties in the Iraqi legislature are protected through provisions in the Iraqi Constitution and the Council of Representatives' by-laws. However, in practice, the rights of minorities throughout Iraq remain unprotected.

Rights of Minority Political Parties in the Legislature are Protected

The Iraqi Constitution and the Council of Representatives' by-laws include provisions to ensure the full participation of minority political parties within the Iraqi Council of Representatives. These provisions include:

- Article 39 of Iraq's Constitution, which guarantees the freedom to form and join associations and political parties and also prohibits forcing any person to join in any party, society, or political entity or to continue membership in it.
- Article 3 of the Council of Representatives by-laws, which guarantees the freedom of expressions, opinions, and thoughts of all members of the Council of Representatives. This guarantee is made regardless of a representative's party or political affiliation in a way that does not contradict the provisions of the Constitution, including the freedom of objective opposition, constructive criticism, and achieving cooperation between the Council of Representatives and other constitutional institutions.

According to Iraqi legislators from minority parties, their rights in the legislature are protected and they are not physically intimidated. The legislators also said that they have the right to speak before Parliament, and to offer legislation even though they are often not consulted on legislative issues. According to the U.S. government, the electoral system—provincial proportional representation—that was used to elect the current Council was chosen in 2005 to balance a number of factors, including the ability of women and small minority parties to gain representation. The Council of Representatives elected in December 2005 includes members from the Shi'a, Sunni, Kurdish, Turkmen, Chaldo-Assyrian Christian, and Yazidi communities.

Human Rights of Iraqi Minorities Across Iraq Remain Unprotected

Although the rights of minority parties are protected in the legislature, widespread violence across Iraq has seriously compromised the government's ability to protect human rights. According to the United Nations, attacks against religious and ethnic minorities continued unabated in most areas of Iraq, prompting these communities to seek ways to leave the country.[2] The conflicts reportedly bear the mark of sectarian polarization and "cleansing" in neighborhoods formerly comprised of different religions.[3] According to a non-governmental organization, all of Iraq's minority communities have suffered violations that include destruction and defacement of religious buildings; mass murder of congregations gathered in and around them; abduction, ransoming, and murder of religious and civic leaders and individuals including children; and forced conversion to Islam using tactics such as death threats, rape, and forced marriage.[4]

In comments on this benchmark, State wrote that GAO should not refer to the general human rights problems of Iraqi minorities because to do so goes beyond the scope of the benchmark and State addresses these problems in other reports. We disagree. We assessed this benchmark as met based on our interpretation of the benchmark and our criteria. However, we believe it is important to provide some context of minority rights in Iraq. Iraqi legislators we interviewed insisted that the situation in their communities has a direct bearing on their work in the legislature, their freedom of movement to and from the legislature, and their ability to engage fully in Iraq political life.

Appendix XVII

Benchmark 17—Allocating and Spending Iraqi Revenues

Allocating and spending $10 billion in Iraqi revenues for reconstruction projects, including delivery of essential services on an equitable basis.

GAO Assessment: Partially met[1]

Issue

The President's New Way Forward in Iraq identified Iraq's inability to fully spend its own resources to rebuild its infrastructure and deliver essential services as a critical economic challenge to Iraq's self-reliance. Iraqi government funds are a necessary source of financing for Iraq's rebuilding effort, particularly since the United States has obligated most of the $40 billion it provided to Iraq for reconstruction since 2003. However, the government of Iraq has had difficulty spending its resources on capital projects. In 2006, the government spent only 22 percent of its non-provincial capital projects and reconstruction budget. Furthermore, in the critical oil sector, which provides over 90 percent of Iraq's revenues, the government spent less than 3 percent of the $3.5 billion allocated for oil reconstruction projects in 2006. In its 2007 budget, Iraq committed to spending $10 billion on capital projects and reconstruction.

Status

The government of Iraq allocated $10 billion of its revenues for capital projects and reconstruction when it passed its 2007 budget in February 2007, including capital funds for the provinces based on their populations. However, available data from the government of Iraq and analysis from U.S. and coalition officials show that, while spending has increased compared with spending in 2006, a large portion of Iraq's $10 billion capital projects and reconstruction budget in fiscal year 2007 will likely go unspent.[2] Iraq's Financial Management Law generally requires budgeted funds to be spent by the end of the fiscal year. The Ministry of Oil and the provinces (excluding the Kurdistan region) were allocated almost half of the government's 2007 capital projects and reconstruction budget; however, they are unlikely to spend a large share of their budgets in 2007, according to U.S. and coalition officials. We are conducting a review of U.S. efforts to help Iraq spend its budget and will issue a separate report at a later date.

Iraq's Ministries Have Increased Spending in 2007, but Are Unlikely to Spend a Large Share of Their 2007 Capital Projects and Reconstruction Budgets

The U.S. Embassy in Baghdad reported that Iraqi government ministries spent about $1.5 billion, or 24 percent, of the $6.25 billion allocated to their capital projects and reconstruction budgets through July 15th, just over half-way through the fiscal year.[3] This level of spending already exceeds the $1.4 billion spent in 2006. However, Iraqi ministries have less than 6 months left in the year to spend the remaining 76 percent of their budgets. In its July 2007 report, the administration cited satisfactory progress with this benchmark because the Ministry of Finance was releasing funds to ministries and provinces. The U.S. Embassy reported that the Ministry of Finance released 25 percent and 10 percent of 2007 capital project and reconstruction budget funds to ministries and provinces, respectively, in the first 5 months of the year. However, funding releases are not expenditures and may not be a reliable indicator of future spending by ministries and provinces. The administration's report noted that capacity constraints and security problems may affect Iraq's ability to accelerate its spending and procurement activities.

Ministry of Oil and Provinces Are Unlikely to Spend a Large Share of Their 2007 Capital Projects and Reconstruction Budgets

The Ministry of Oil's capital project and reconstruction budget for 2007 is $2.4 billion, almost a quarter of the government's total. The ministry has already surpassed last year's spending total; however, U.S. officials stated that the ministry is not likely to spend a large share of its capital projects and reconstruction budget due to a variety of challenges, including a difficult security environment and burdensome and complex procurement rules. According to U.S. officials, the ministry has undertaken reform efforts to eliminate bottlenecks in the budget execution process. The U.S. Embassy reported that the Ministry of Oil had spent $500 million through July 15, 2007, or 21 percent of its budget for the year. However, the Special Inspector General for Iraq Reconstruction reported statements by U.S. officials that the ministry may not have spent all of these funds, but instead shifted them to its subsidiaries, such as the State Oil Marketing Organization, which have responsibility for spending much of the Oil Ministry's capital projects and reconstruction budget.[4]

In addition, the government provided over $2 billion, or over 20 percent of the 2007 capital projects and reconstruction budget, to the provinces (not including the semi-autonomous Kurdistan region) based on their populations.[5] These funds are in addition to $2 billion 2006 provincial funds for capital projects, most of which had not been transferred to the provinces until November and December of 2006.[6] U.S. and foreign officials stated that the provinces have little experience planning and executing infrastructure projects and are likely to spend little of their 2007 capital projects and reconstruction budgets. According to information collected and reported by Provincial Reconstruction Teams, the provinces had committed 44 percent of their 2007 allocation to contracts for capital projects, as of July 15, 2007.[7] However, it is not clear whether the value of committed contracts is a reliable indicator of actual spending. Given the capacity and security challenges currently facing Iraq, many committed contracts may not be executed and, therefore, would not result in actual expenditures.[8] The Government of Iraq is undertaking a number of initiatives, including budget execution training sessions, to help provincial officials spend their capital budgets, according to U.S. officials.

Appendix XVIII

Benchmark 18—False Accusations

Ensuring that Iraq's political authorities are not undermining or making false accusations against members of the Iraqi Security Forces.

GAO Assessment as of August 30, 2007: Not met[1]

Issue

According to U.S. government reporting, qualified Iraqi officers may be discouraged from operating in a professional, non-sectarian manner if Iraq's political authorities undermine or make false accusations against members of the Iraqi Security Forces (ISF).

Status

Iraq's political authorities continue to undermine and make false accusations against members of the ISF. According to U.S. government officials, little has changed since the U.S. Administration's July 2007 Initial Benchmark Assessment. Each month the U.S. government receives reports alleging wrongdoing by ISF members considered by MNF-I to be non-sectarian in their approach to security. The U.S. assessment further stated that in most cases the U.S. government was unable to determine the validity of these allegations but believed them to be untrue. The assessment concluded that these accusations undermine the independence and non-sectarianism of the ISF and that the Iraqi government does not adequately address the accusations. According to MNF-I officials in Baghdad, some cases resulted in detention of military officers, but the cases did not provide justification or specific charges against the officers. Further information is classified.

The U.S. government further reported that anecdotal evidence suggests that Iraqi political authorities may not be pursuing allegations even-handedly. According to U.S. government reporting, the de-Ba'athification Commission fabricated charges to cleanse Sunni officers from military units, and the Office of Commander in Chief has issued questionable judicial warrants as a more recent technique to target Sunni commanders. In addition, the ISF's formal command structure is compromised by influential sectarian leaders linked to the security ministries. These actions have reportedly led to the arrest and detention of several military officials. According to U.S. officials, this tactic is primarily used against Sunni Ministry of Defense officials and does not occur at the predominantly Shi'a Ministry of Interior. The U.S. government also reported that some Sunni politicians have made unsubstantiated claims against ISF officials. Moreover, Iraqi government support for the ISF has been uneven. Some members of the Council of Ministers and Council of Representatives have publicly supported ISF leaders while behind the scenes they continue to ignore sectarian activities, according to the U.S. government.

Appendix XIX

Origin of Iraqi Benchmarks

Figure 7: Origin of Iraqi Benchmarks [Deleted Material]

Appendix XX

Comparison of GAO Assessment with Administration's July 2007 Initial Benchmark Assessment Report

Benchmark	GAO assessment	Administration's assessment report
1. Forming a Constitutional Review Committee and then completing the constitutional review.	○	■
2. Enacting and implementing legislation on de-Ba'athification.	○	□
3. Enacting and implementing legislation to ensure the equitable distribution of hydrocarbon resources of the people of Iraq without regard to the sector ethnicity of recipients, and enacting and implementing legislation to ensure that the energy resources of Iraq benefit Sunni Arabs, Shia Arabs, Kurds, and other Iraqi citizens in an equitable manner.	○	□
4. Enacting and implementing legislation on procedures to form semi-autonomous regions.	◐	■
5. Enacting and implementing legislation establishing an Independent High Electoral Commission, provincial elections law, provincial council authorities, and a date for provincial elections.	○	◧
6. Enacting and implementing legislation addressing amnesty.	○	a
7. Enacting and implementing legislation establishing a strong militia disarmament program to ensure that such security forces are accountable only to the central government and loyal to the Constitution of Iraq.	○	a
8. Establishing supporting political, media, economic, and services committees in support of the Baghdad security plan.	●	■
9. Providing three trained and ready Iraqi brigades to support Baghdad operations.	◐	■
10. Providing Iraqi commanders with all authorities to execute this plan and to make tactical and operational decisions, in consultation with U.S. commanders, without political intervention, to include the authority to pursue all extremists, including Sunni insurgents and Shiite militias.	○	□
11. Ensuring that the Iraqi Security Forces are providing even-handed enforcement of the law.	○	□
12. Ensuring that, according to President Bush, Prime Minister Maliki said "the Baghdad security plan will not provide a safe haven for any outlaws, regardless of [their] sectarian or political affiliation."	◐	■
13. Reducing the level of sectarian violence in Iraq and eliminating militia control of local security.	○	◧
14. Establishing all of the planned joint security stations in neighborhoods across Baghdad.	●	■
15. Increasing the number of Iraqi security forces' units capable of operating independently.	○	□
16. Ensuring that the rights of minority political parties in the Iraqi legislature are protected.	●	■
17. Allocating and spending $10 billion in Iraqi revenues for reconstruction projects, including delivery of essential services, on an equitable basis.	◐	■
18. Ensuring that Iraq's political authorities are not undermining or making false accusations against members of the Iraqi security forces.	○	□
Summary	3 met, 4 partial, and 11 not met	8 satisfactory, 2 mixed, and 6 unsatisfactory

● Met ◐ Partially met ○ Not met ■ Satisfactory ◧ Mixed □ Unsatisfactory

Source: GAO analysis of UN, U.S.,and Iraqi data.

[a] According to the U.S. State Department,conditions are not present for these benchmarks.

Appendix XXI

Objectives, Scope, and Methodology

The U.S. Troop Readiness, Veterans' Care, Katrina Recovery, and Iraq Accountability Appropriations Act of 2007[1] (the Act) requires GAO to submit to Congress by September 1, 2007, an independent assessment of whether or not the government of Iraq has met 18 benchmarks contained in the Act and the status of the achievement of the benchmarks. This report (1) provides an assessment of whether or not the Iraqi government has met 18 legislative, security, and economic benchmarks, and (2) provides information on the status of the achievement of each benchmark. These benchmarks address 8 legislative, 9 security and 1 economic-related action.

To complete this work, we reviewed U.S. agency documents and interviewed officials from the Departments of Defense, State, and the Treasury; the Multi-national Force-Iraq (MNF-I) and its subordinate commands; the Defense Intelligence Agency; the Central Intelligence Agency; the National Intelligence Council; and the United Nations. These officials included Ryan Crocker, the U.S. Ambassador to Iraq, and General David H. Petraeus, Commander of Multi-National Force-Iraq (MNF-I). We also reviewed translated copies of Iraqi documents and met with officials from the government of Iraq and its legislature. As part of this work, we made multiple visits to Iraq during 2006 and 2007, including a visit from July 22 to August 1, 2007. Our analyses were enhanced by approximately 100 Iraq-related audits we have completed since May 2003.[2] We provided drafts of the report to the relevant U.S. agencies for review and comment, which we incorporated as appropriate. Although we analyzed classified data, this report only contains unclassified information, as of August 30, 2007. We conducted our review in accordance with generally accepted government auditing standards.

Legislative Benchmarks

To determine if the Iraqi government is completing actions related to review of the Iraqi Constitution; enacting and implementing legislation on de-Ba'athification, the equitable distribution of hydrocarbon resources, procedures to form semi-autonomous regions, the independent high electoral commission, provincial elections, provincial council authorities, amnesty, and militia disarmament; and ensuring that the rights of minority political parties in the Iraqi legislature are protected, we took a number of actions. Specifically, we interviewed and reviewed documentation from the Iraqi government, Iraqi legislators in Baghdad, UN, U.S. Institute for Peace, IFES[3], the Independent High Electoral Commission, non-governmental organizations, and the Departments of Defense and State in Washington, D.C. and Baghdad, Iraq. The documents reviewed included the administration's July 2007 initial benchmark assessment, the Iraqi Constitution, draft laws related to each of the benchmarks, the *International Compact with Iraq 2007 Mid-Year Progress Report*, and UN analyses of the laws addressed by the benchmarks.

For our assessment of the status of the hydrocarbon legislation, we relied on prior GAO reporting[4] and updated information where appropriate. We interviewed and reviewed documentation from the Iraqi government, UN, U.S. Institute for Peace, and State Department in Washington, D.C. and Baghdad, Iraq. We compared central government draft oil laws with the Iraqi Constitution and the Kurdistan Regional Government Oil and Gas law.

Additionally, to determine if the Iraqi government is ensuring that the rights of minority political parties in the Iraqi legislature are protected, we obtained and reviewed the Administration's report on progress in Iraq, the Iraqi constitution, and the *Council of Representatives Bylaws*. We interviewed Iraqi legislators in Baghdad, Iraq, including the leader of the Iraqi Minority Council. We also reviewed human rights reports from nongovernmental organizations, the United Nations, and the U.S. government to determine whether the rights of minorities throughout Iraq are protected.

Security Benchmarks

To determine if the Iraqi government is (1) establishing supporting political, media, economic, and services committees in support of the Baghdad Security Plan; (2) providing three trained and ready Iraqi brigades to support Baghdad operations; (3) providing Iraqi commanders with all authorities to execute the Baghdad Security Plan without political intervention; (4) ensuring that the Iraqi security forces are providing even-handed law enforcement; (5) eliminating safe havens; (6) reducing the level of sectarian violence and eliminating militia control of local security; (7) establishing all planned joint security stations; (8) increasing the number of security units capable of operating independently; and (9) ensuring that Iraq's political authorities are not undermining or making false accusations against members of the Iraqi Security Forces, we took a number of actions.

Specifically, we examined U.S. Department of State cables and other documents that discussed the establishment of the supporting committees. We reviewed classified and unclassified documents and reports showing the Iraqi Army units that had deployed to Baghdad and analyzed the U.S. Department of Defense Operational Readiness Assessments (ORA) formerly known as Transitional Readiness Assessments, for these units. In addition, we reviewed classified and unclassified assessments of the authorities granted to unit commanders, the level of sectarian influence and levels of militia infiltration of army and police units, and reports of incidents where Iraqi officials interfered with the chain of command.

To understand the range of methodological issues associated with measuring levels of sectarian violence, and to collect information related to broader trends in population security, we interviewed officials from the U.S. Department of State and Department of Defense in Washington, D.C., and Baghdad, Iraq; the Central Intelligence Agency; the Defense Intelligence Agency; the National Intelligence Council; the United Nations; and the International Organization for Migration in Washington, D.C., Baghdad, Iraq, and Amman, Jordan. We also met with these officials to discuss the other benchmarks.

Economic Benchmark

To assess the extent to which the government of Iraq is allocating and spending $10 billion in Iraqi revenues for reconstruction projects, including delivery of essential services on an equitable basis, we interviewed U.S. government officials and contractors, and obtained and analyzed supporting documents. We interviewed officials in Washington D.C. and Baghdad with the Departments of Defense, State, and the Treasury; the U.S. Agency for International Development; the Embassy Iraq Transition Assistance Office; and consultants to the Ministry of Finance. To assess progress in allocating and spending Iraqi revenues we reviewed official Iraqi Ministry of Finance capital budget and expenditure data for fiscal years 2006 and 2007 provided by the U.S. Department of the Treasury, and unofficial Ministry of Planning and Development Cooperation data on capital expenditures reported by Multinational Force-Iraq.

We also reviewed unofficial unreconciled data on capital budget execution by the provinces in 2006 and 2007 collected by U.S. Provincial Reconstruction Teams. We compared 2007 capital allocations to the provinces with their populations to assess the equity of capital funding allocations. We discussed the reliability of allocation and expenditure data with U.S. Treasury officials and contractors advising the Ministry of Finance. We also reviewed relevant reports by DOD and State, the Special Inspector General for Iraq Reconstruction, World Bank, IMF, public accountants and Iraqi government budget implementation documents. We found that these data were sufficiently reliable for the purpose of showing trends in budget expenditures.

Appendix XXII

Comments from the Department of State

The following are GAO's comments on the State Department's letter dated August 30, 2007.

GAO Comments

1. We agree with State that legislation on the Iraq High Electoral Commission has been enacted and implemented. However, our assessment of "not met" on the electoral benchmark is based on the Iraqi government not enacting and implementing three of four components of this benchmark—legislation on provincial authorities, provincial elections, and an election date.
2. We have highlighted the different standards of assessment between our report and the administration's reports. We also specify our assessment criteria in the cover letter and each appendix to make our judgments fully transparent.
3. We have included information about the recent communiqué in the cover letter and appendices as appropriate.
4. We have included information about the Kurdish Regional Government's new law and the U.S. position on it in the appendix on hydrocarbon legislation.
5. Our report acknowledges the progress that the Iraqi government has made in allocating and spending $10 billion of fiscal year 2007 funds on capital projects and reconstruction. While these funds have been allocated, our report also notes that a large portion of these funds will likely go unspent. Consequently, we rated this benchmark as "partially met."
6. We disagree with State's comment. We assessed this benchmark as "met." However, Iraqi legislators we interviewed insisted that the situation in their communities has a direct bearing on their work in the legislature, their freedom of movement to and from the legislature, and their ability to engage fully in Iraq political life. Thus we included additional relevant information about minority human rights in Iraq.
7. See comment 6.
8. See comment 6.
9. We revised our text.
10. Under our criteria, we considered the benchmark as "not met" because the Constitutional Review Committee was still continuing work on devising a package of necessary amendments, the Iraqi legislature had not voted on the package, and a referendum had not been held.
11. We added information to our already existing reference to the Kurdish National Assembly legislation.
12. We revised this sentence.
13. Under our criteria, this benchmark was not met.

14. We revised the text to reflect State's comments.
15. We revised the text to reflect State's comments.
16. Our paragraph provides context for the committees' work and the text makes it clear that these actions were in the past so we retained our original language.
17. See comment 6.
18. See comment 6.
19. See comment 5.
20. We revised the text.
21. See comment 6.

Appendix XXIII

Comments from the Department of Defense

The following are GAO's comments on DOD's letter dated August 30, 2007.

GAO Comments

1. We have revised the text.
2. We have revised the text.
3. We have modified the sentence by adding not "always."
4. We have replaced this chart.
5. We have qualified the sentence by adding "parts of."
6. We disagree with DOD's comment. The Iraq benchmark calls for increasing the number of Iraqi security units capable of operating independently. A key impediment to Iraqi training and readiness, particularly of the police, is sectarian and militia influence. DOD's June 2007 report to Congress states that sectarian bias has constrained the development of MOI forces.
7. DOD commented that 71 percent of Iraqi authorized personnel are in the field at any one time, compared to 65 percent, which we report. We are retaining the 65 percent in our report because it is from a published DOD source and we do not have further documentation on the new figure.

Appendix XXIV

GAO Contacts and Staff Acknowledgements

GAO Contacts

Joseph Christoff (202) 512-8979 or christoffj@gao.gov

Staff Acknowledgements

Steve Lord, David Bruno, Howard Cott, Tim Fairbanks, Mattias Fenton, Whitney Havens, Dorian Herring, Bruce Kutnick, Judy McCloskey, Tet Miyabara, and Kathleen Monahan.

In addition, Robert Alarapon Ashley Alley, Monica Brym, Lessie M Burke-Johnson, Joe Carney, Miriam Carroll, Thomas Costa, Lynn Cothern, Debra Chung, Joyee Dasgupta, Martin de Alteriis, Etana Finkler, Muriel Forster, Patrick Hickey, Michael Jenkins, Sona Kalapura, Jeremy Latimer, Mary Moutsos, Mimi Nguyen, Sidney Schwartz, Jena Sinkfield, Audrey Solis, Cynthia Taylor, and Christina Werth provided technical assistance.

GAO's Mission

The Government Accountability Office, the audit, evaluation and investigative arm of Congress, exists to support Congress in meeting its constitutional responsibilities and to help improve the performance and accountability of the federal government for the American people. GAO examines the use of public funds; evaluates federal programs and policies; and provides analyses, recommendations, and other assistance to help Congress make informed oversight, policy, and funding decisions. GAO's commitment to good government is reflected in its core values of accountability, integrity, and reliability.

Obtaining Copies of GAO Reports and Testimony

The fastest and easiest way to obtain copies of GAO documents at no cost is through GAO's Web site (www.gao.gov). Each weekday, GAO posts newly released reports, testimony, and correspondence on its Web site. To have GAO e-mail you a list of newly posted products every afternoon, go to www.gao.gov and select "Subscribe to Updates."

Order by Mail or Phone

The first copy of each printed report is free. Additional copies are $2 each. A check or money order should be made out to the Superintendent of Documents. GAO also accepts VISA and Mastercard. Orders for 100 or more copies mailed to a single address are discounted 25 percent. Orders should be sent to:

U.S. Government Accountability Office
441 G Street NW, Room LM
Washington, D.C. 20548

To order by Phone:	Voice:	(202) 512-6000
	TDD:	(202) 512-2537
	Fax:	(202) 512-6061

To Report Fraud, Waste, and Abuse in Federal Programs

Contact:

Web site: www.gao.gov/fraudnet/fraudnet.htm E-mail: fraudnet@gao.gov Automated answering system: (800) 424-5454 or (202) 512-7470

Congressional Relations

Gloria Jarmon, Managing Director, JarmonG@gao.gov (202) 512-4400 U.S. Government Accountability Office, 441 G Street NW, Room 7125 Washington, D.C. 20548

Public Affairs

Susan Becker, Acting Manager, Beckers@GAO.gov (202) 512-4800 U.S. Government Accountability Office, 441 G Street NW, Room 7149 Washington, D.C. 20548

Endnotes

[1] Section 1314 of Public Law 110-28.

[2] GAO is providing this report to Congress on September 4th, 2007, the first business day following September 1st.

[3] For example, see GAO, *Securing, Stabilizing, and Rebuilding Iraq: Key Issues for Congressional Oversight*, GAO-07-308SP (Washington, D.C.: January 9, 2007). See GAO's website at http://www.gao.gov for a complete list of GAO's Iraq-related reports.

[4] For those legislative benchmarks requiring the enacting and implementing of legislation, we defined a benchmark as "met" if all components of the relevant law have been enacted and implemented; defined the benchmark as "partially met" if the law has been enacted but not implemented or, in instances involving multiple pieces of legislation, at least half have been enacted and implemented; and defined "not met" as having not met the requirements of "met" or "partially met." For the constitutional review, we would have considered the benchmark as met if, in accordance with Article 142 of the Iraqi Constitution, (1) the Constitutional Review Committee had been formed; (2) the Council of Representatives had voted on the recommendations of the review committee; and, if approved by the Council, (3) a national referendum had been held on the proposed amendments to the constitution. We would have considered the benchmark partially met if the first two steps of the constitutional review process were completed.

[5] Because this law will not be implemented until April 2008, publication in the Official Gazette has been deferred, according to State officials, who assert that a delay in implementation is in the best interest of Iraq.

[6] According to U.S. and other officials and documents, enacting legislation generally includes the following steps, though the process is evolving: The Presidency Council and the Council of Ministers have authority to draft laws, and the Iraqi legislature—either a committee or 10 members—has the authority to propose laws. Laws drafted by the Presidency Council or Council of Ministers are reviewed on legal soundness and subject matter by the Shura Council, an institution in the Ministry of Justice. Laws drafted by the legislature must first pass through its Legal Committee. The legislation then proceeds through three readings. The legislation is presented at the first reading. The relevant committee may amend the law and the Speaker's Office places it on the calendar. After the first reading, the legislature discusses the proposed law at a second reading. At the third reading, a final vote is taken article by article. Laws that receive an affirmative vote are sent to the Presidency Council, which can disapprove the law. The legislature can override the disapproval with a three-fifths majority. This ratification process only applies during the transition period when the Presidency Council is in existence. Final laws are published in the Official Gazette and become effective on the date of publication in the gazette unless stipulated otherwise. The Prime Minister issues an order to implement the law. Laws are implemented by the appropriate ministry, commission, or government office and implementing guidance is written.

[7] For additional information on Iraq's hydrocarbon sector, see GAO, *Rebuilding Iraq: Serious Challenges Impair Efforts to Restore Iraq's Oil Sector and Enact Hydrocarbon Legislation*, GAO-07-1107T (Washington, D.C.: July 18, 2007).

[8] In February 2007, the Iraqi government created the Executive Steering Committee and six subcommittees to coordinate political, economic, and military activities and make decisions in support of the Baghdad Security Plan. According to a State department official, the executive committee's major objective was to increase the coordination and capacity of the Iraqi government to improve the quality of life of Baghdad's population as part of the Baghdad security plan. We defined this benchmark as "met" if the committees were established in support of the Baghdad Security Plan; defined this benchmark as "partially met" if at least half of the committees were established in support of the Baghdad Security Plan; and defined this benchmark as "not met" if less than half of the committees were established in support of the Baghdad Security Plan.

[9] Joint Security Stations are staffed by Iraqi local police, national police, and army personnel, as well as coalition forces. According to the administration's July 2007 report, the security stations are designed to improve population protection by providing a 24-hour security presence in Baghdad neighborhoods. We defined this benchmark as "met" if nearly all of the planned Joint Security Stations were established. We defined this benchmark as "partially met" if half of the planned Joint Security Stations were established. We defined this benchmark as "not met" if less than half of the planned Joint Security Stations were established.

[10] We defined this benchmark as "met" if the Government of Iraq had provided three trained and ready brigades, or an equivalent number of battalions, to support Baghdad operations; as "partially met" if some of the units were trained and ready to support Baghdad security operations; and as "not met" if none of the units provided were trained and ready to support Baghdad security operations. The assessment was based on each unit's transition readiness assessments and intelligence reporting on their reliability.

[11] We defined this benchmark as "met" if Iraqi government policy did not allow safe havens and none existed; defined this benchmark as "partially met" if Iraqi government policy prohibited safe havens yet some existed; and defined this benchmark as "not met" if the Iraqi government had no stated policy on safe havens.

[12] We defined this benchmark as "met" if there was clear and reliable evidence that the level of sectarian violence was reduced and militia control of local security was eliminated; defined this benchmark as "partially met" if there was clear and reliable evidence that the level of sectarian violence was reduced or if militia control of local security was eliminated, but not both; and defined this benchmark as "not met" if there was no clear and reliable evidence that the level of sectarian violence was reduced and that militia control of local security was eliminated.

[13] Ramadan is the ninth month of the Islamic calendar. Over the past 4 years, Ramadan began about October 27, 2003; October 16, 2004; October 5, 2005; and September 24, 2006.

[14] We defined this benchmark as "met" if Iraqi commanders did not face political intervention in executing the plan and making tactical and operational decisions. We defined this benchmark as "not met" if Iraqi commanders faced political intervention in executing the plan and making tactical and operational decisions.

[15] We defined this benchmark as "met" if Iraqi security forces provided even-handed enforcement of the law. We defined this benchmark as "not met" if Iraqi security forces did not provide even-handed enforcement of the law.

[16] We defined this benchmark as "met" if the government of Iraq increased the number of Iraqi security forces' units capable of operating independently. We defined this benchmark as "not met" if the government of Iraq did not increase the number of Iraqi security forces' units capable of operating independently.

[17] We defined this benchmark as "met" if there was no evidence of undermining or false accusations against Iraqi security force personnel. We defined this benchmark as "not met" if there was evidence of undermining or false accusations against Iraqi security force personnel.

[18] We defined this benchmark as "met" if the funds had been allocated and either they had been spent or there was a high likelihood that they would be spent by the end of the fiscal year. We defined this benchmark as "partially met" if funds were allocated but it appeared questionable or unlikely that the funds would be spent by the end of the fiscal year. We defined the benchmark as "not met" if the funds had not been allocated.

Appendix I

[1] For the constitutional review, we would have considered the benchmark as met if, in accordance with Article 142 of the Iraqi Constitution, the Constitutional Review Committee had been formed; the Council of Representatives had voted on the recommendations of the review committee; and, if approved by the Council, a national referendum had been held on the proposed amendments to the constitution. We would have considered the benchmark partially met if the first two steps of the constitutional review process were completed. See benchmark 2 for a description of the criteria for meeting legislative benchmarks.

[2] The constitutional review process consists of the following: (1) the Council of Representatives forms a review committee, which presents to the Council a report on recommendations of necessary amendments that could be made to the Constitution; (2) the proposed amendments shall be presented to the Council all at once for a vote upon them and are approved with the agreement of an absolute majority of the members of the Council; and (3) the articles amended by the Council shall be presented to the people in a referendum within two months from the date of approval by the Council and the referendum will be successful if approved by the majority of voters and if not rejected by two-thirds of the voters in three or more governorates.

[3] According to the Iraqi Constitution, in the current electoral term, which is 4 years, a presidency council consisting of a president and 2 vice-presidents is in place and exercises the powers of the presidency. If these constitutional provisions are not amended, at the start of the next electoral term, power will revert to a single president and the power to approve and disapprove legislation that is explicitly granted to the presidency council will lapse. The president will then have the power to ratify and issue laws passed by the legislature, although such laws are considered ratified 15 days after the president receives them.

[4] Under the existing Constitution, if there is a contradiction between regional and national law with respect to a matter outside the exclusive authority of the federal government, regional law takes priority and regional powers have the right to amend the application of the national legislation within that region.

[5] United Nations Assistance Mission for Iraq, *Humanitarian Briefing on the Crisis in Iraq*, May 2007.

Appendix II

[1] For those legislative benchmarks requiring the enacting and implementing of legislation, we defined a benchmark as "met" if all components of the relevant law have been enacted and implemented; defined the benchmark as "partially met" if the law has been enacted but not implemented or, in instances involving multiple pieces of legislation, at least half have been enacted and implemented; and defined "not met" as having not met the requirements of "met" or "partially met."

[2] The doctrine of command responsibility holds that individuals can be liable for actions they did not actually commit if: (1) they issued orders to those who committed the human rights violations or crimes; (2) they should have known or should have been in a position to know that their subordinates were committing human rights violations or crimes; or (3) they did not take reasonable measures to prevent the human rights violations or other crimes or did not punish the perpetrators.

Appendix III

[1] For those legislative benchmarks requiring the enacting and implementing of legislation, we defined a benchmark as "met" if all components of the relevant law have been enacted and implemented; defined the benchmark as "partially met" if the law has been enacted but not implemented or, in instances involving multiple pieces of legislation, at least half have been enacted and implemented; and defined "not met" as having not met the requirements of "met" or "partially met."

[2] This legislation is also referred to as the "Law of Financial Resources" and the "Revenue Management Law."

[3] The Kurdistan National Assembly (Kurdish Regional parliament) has passed a "Kurdistan Oil and Gas Law" (also referred to as the "Petroleum Law of the Kurdistan Region - Iraq"), in August, 2007, which conditions cooperation with the federal authorities in the oil sector on a set of comprehensive conditions. According to the UN, it would likely take time for full agreement on these arrangements to be reached and for implementation of national revenue sharing to begin. It is unclear how this will affect the national debate on revenue sharing or the hydrocarbon framework legislation at this time.

According to the State Department, the United States continues to believe that Iraq's interests are better served by the adoption of a single set of national oil and gas laws, which will help foster national unity and promote reconciliation.

Appendix IV

[1] For those legislative benchmarks requiring the enacting and implementing of legislation, we defined a benchmark as "met" if all components of the relevant law have been enacted and implemented; defined the benchmark as "partially met" if the law has been enacted but not implemented or, in instances involving multiple pieces of legislation, at least half have been enacted and implemented; and defined "not met" as having not met the requirements of "met" or "partially met."

[2] Iraq has 18 governorates and the Iraqi Constitution states that one or more governorates have the right to organize into a region. Article 117 of the Constitution further recognizes the region of Kurdistan, which consists of three provinces in northern Iraq. The final version of the law on executive procedures regarding the formation of regions states that a region consists of one province or more.

[3] The lack of clarity about power sharing between federal and regional governments is highlighted by problems over power generation. As of the summer of 2007, a number of provinces have been ignoring the federal government's shared authority over power generation and distribution by failing to provide their required allocations of power to Baghdad, contributing to national blackouts. In August 2007, these provincial authorities were threatening to disconnect their local power generating sources from the national electricity grid.

[4] GAO, *Securing, Stabilizing, and Rebuilding Iraq: Key Issues for Congressional Oversight,* GAO-07-308SP (Washington, D.C.: Jan. 9. 2007); GAO, forthcoming *Stabilizing and Rebuilding Iraq: U.S. Ministry Capacity Development Efforts Need an Overall Integrated Strategy to Guide Efforts and Manage Risk,* GAO-07-903 (Washington, D.C.: Sept. 18, 2007).

Appendix V

[1] For those legislative benchmarks requiring the enacting and implementing of legislation, we defined a benchmark as "met" if all components of the relevant law have been enacted and implemented; defined the benchmark as "partially met" if the law has been enacted but not implemented or, in instances involving multiple pieces of legislation, at least half have been enacted and implemented; and defined "not met" as having not met the requirements of "met" or "partially met."

Appendix VI

[1] For those legislative benchmarks requiring the enacting and implementing of legislation, we defined a benchmark as "met" if all components of the relevant law have been enacted and implemented; defined the benchmark as "partially met" if the law has been enacted but not implemented or, in instances involving multiple pieces of legislation, at least half have been enacted and implemented; and defined "not met" as having not met the requirements of "met" or "partially met."

Appendix VII

[1] For those legislative benchmarks requiring the enacting and implementing of legislation, we defined a benchmark as "met" if all components of the relevant law have been enacted and implemented; defined the benchmark as "partially met" if the law has been enacted but not implemented or, in instances involving multiple pieces of legislation, at least half have been enacted and implemented; and defined "not met" as having not met the requirements of "met" or "partially met."

[2] *Rebuilding Iraq: Resource, Security, Governance, Essential Services, and Oversight Issues* (GAO-04-902R, Washington, D.C.: June 28, 2004).

[3] GAO, Stabilizing Iraq: Factors Impeding the Development of Capable Iraqi Security Forces, GAO-07-612T) Washington, D.C.: March 13, 2007); GAO, *Securing, Stabilizing, and Rebuilding Iraq: Key Issues for Congressional Oversight,* (GAO-07-308SP) Washington, D.C.: January 9, 2007; GAO, *Rebuilding Iraq: DOD Reports Should Link Economic, Governance, and Security Indicators to Conditions for Stabilizing Iraq,* (GAO-06-217C) Washington, D.C.: October 31, 2005.

Appendix VIII

[1] We defined this benchmark as "met" if the committees were established in support of the Baghdad Security Plan; defined this benchmark as "partially met" if at least half of the committees were established in support of the Baghdad Security Plan; and defined this benchmark as "not met" if less than half of the committees were established in support of the Baghdad Security Plan.

[2] The current Baghdad security plan is also known as Operation Fardh al-Qanoon.

Appendix IX

[1] We defined this benchmark as "met" if the government of Iraq had provided three trained and ready brigades, or an equivalent number of battalions, to support Baghdad operations; as "partially met" if some of the units were trained and ready to support Baghdad security operations; and as "not met" if none of the units provided were trained and ready to support Baghdad security operations. The assessment was based on each unit's transition readiness assessments and intelligence reporting on their reliability. Consequently, our determination of "partially met" was based largely on classified information.

Appendix X

[1] We defined this benchmark as "met" if Iraqi commanders did not face political intervention in executing the plan and making tactical and operational decisions. We defined this benchmark as "not met" if Iraqi commanders faced political intervention in executing the plan and making tactical and operational decisions.

Appendix XI

[1] We defined this benchmark as "met" if Iraqi security forces provided even-handed enforcement of the law. We defined this benchmark as "not met" if Iraqi security forces did not provide even-handed enforcement of the law.

[2] U.S. Commission on International Religious Freedom, *Annual Report of the U.S. Commission on International Religious Freedom* (Washington D.C.: May 2007). The U.S. Commission on International Religious Freedom was created by the International Religious Freedom Act of 1998 (IRFA) to monitor violations of the right to freedom of thought, conscience, and religion or belief abroad, as defined in IRFA and set forth in the Universal Declaration of Human Rights and related international instruments, and to give independent policy recommendations to the President, Secretary of State, and Congress.

[3] U.S. Department of State, *Country Reports on Human Rights* (Washington, D.C.: Mar. 6, 2007).

Appendix XII

[1] We defined this benchmark as "met" if Iraqi government policy did not allow safe havens and none existed; defined this benchmark as "partially met" if Iraqi government policy prohibited safe havens yet some existed; and defined this benchmark as "not met" if the Iraqi government had no stated policy on safe havens.

Appendix XIII

[1] We defined this benchmark as "met" if there was clear and reliable evidence that the level of sectarian violence was reduced and militia control of local security was eliminated; defined this benchmark as "partially met" if there was clear and reliable evidence that the level of sectarian violence was reduced or if militia control of local security was eliminated, but not both; and defined this benchmark as "not met" if there was no clear and reliable evidence that the level of sectarian violence was reduced and that militia control of local security was eliminated.

[2] U.S. Department of State, *Country Reports on Human Rights* (Washington, D.C.: Mar. 6, 2007); UN Assistance Mission for Iraq (UNAMI), *Human Rights Report* (Sept. 1–Oct. 31, 2006); UNAMI, *Human Rights Report* (Nov. 1–Dec. 31, 2006).

[3] According to State's human rights report, an overall campaign aimed at forcibly displacing citizens was the main reason for the increasing polarization of areas within and outside Baghdad during 2006. State noted numerous reports that indicated a Shi'a militia, the Jayash al-Mahdi, was responsible for a growing number of raids and killings of Sunni citizens in Baghdad and other parts of the country during the year.

[4] DOD, *Measuring Stability and Security in Iraq* (Washington, D.C.: June 2007).

[5] Ramadan is the ninth month of the Islamic calendar. Over the past 4 years, Ramadan began about October 27, 2003; October 16, 2004; October 5, 2005; and September 24, 2006.

[6] National Intelligence Council, *Prospects for Iraq's Stability: Some Security Progress but Political Reconciliation Elusive, Update to NIE, Prospects for Iraq's Stability: A Challenging Road Ahead* (Washington, D.C.: August 2007).

[7] According to a UN report, sectarian violence was most pronounced in areas with diverse ethnic and religious groups or where such groups were located in close proximity to each other, such as in Baghdad, Diyala, Kirkuk, and Mosul. Anbar province, where attack levels have decreased significantly over the past several months, is a predominantly Sunni Arab province.

Appendix XIV

[1] We defined this benchmark as "met" if nearly all of the planned Joint Security Stations were established. We defined this benchmark as "partially met" if half of the planned Joint Security Stations were established. We defined this benchmark as "not met" if less than half of the planned Joint Security Stations were established.

Appendix XV

[1] We defined this benchmark as "met" if the government of Iraq increased the number of Iraqi security forces' units capable of operating independently. We defined this benchmark as "not met" if the government of Iraq did not increase the number of Iraqi security forces' units capable of operating independently.

[2] The Operational Readiness Assessment was previously known as the Transitional Readiness Assessment process.

[3] As of May 2007, the Iraqi army had established over 100 battalions.

[4] In 2006, MNF-I changed the definition of a level 1 unit. Previously, in guidance provided to coalition transition teams for use in evaluating Iraqi security forces, a level 1 unit was said to be fully capable of planning, executing, and sustaining independent operations. In 2006, MNF-I removed the words "fully" and "independent" from the definition. DOD officials could not provide a rationale for the change.

[5] The administration's July 2007 interim assessment stated that the number of units assessed at level 1 had decreased, in part, due to a 20-percent increase in unit authorization levels.

Appendix XVI

[1] We considered this benchmark as "met" if the Iraqi government had laws or regulations ensuring the rights of minority parties in the legislature and minority parties received these rights; considered this benchmark as "partially met" if the Iraqi government had such laws but did not protect these rights; and considered this benchmark as "not met" if the Iraqi government had no law or regulation protecting minority party rights.

[2] UN Assistance Mission for Iraq, *Human Rights Report*, Jan. 1–Mar. 31, 2007.

[3] Congressional Research Service, *Iraqi Refugees and Internally Displaced Persons: A Deepening Humanitarian Crisis?* (Washington D.C.: Mar. 23, 2007).

[4] Preti Taneja, Minority Rights Group International, *Assimilation, Exodus, Eradication: Iraq's Minority Communities Since 2003* (United Kingdom: February 2007).

Appendix XVII

[1] We would have considered this benchmark as "met" if the funds had been allocated and either the funds had been spent or there was a high likelihood that they would be spent by the end of the fiscal year. We would have considered this benchmark as "partially met" if funds were allocated but it was not clear that the funds would be spent by the end of the fiscal year. We would have considered the benchmark as "not met" if the funds had not yet been allocated or if funds were allocated but clearly not spent.

[2] Iraq's fiscal year begins on January 1st.

[3] The expenditure data presented by the U.S. Embassy are preliminary data provided by the Ministry of Finance and do not include figures for the Kurdistan region or the other provinces. In its official May 2007 monthly report, the Ministry of Finance did not report any expenditures for capital projects and reconstruction. In the absence of official data, the information presented by the U.S. Embassy provides an indication of Iraq's ability to spend its capital projects and reconstruction budget in the first half of the year.

[4] Special Inspector General for Iraq Reconstruction, *Quarterly Report and Semiannual Report to the United States Congress* (Arlington, VA, July 30, 2007).

[5] The Kurdistan region received a separate allocation of $1.56 billion, or 16 percent of the total 2007 capital projects and reconstruction budget. U.S. officials believe the Kurdistan region is able to execute its budget successfully because of its years of experience as a semi-autonomous region.

[6] The $2 billion in 2006 capital project and reconstruction funds for the provinces did not include the Kurdistan region, which received a separate allocation. The government of Iraq permitted the provinces to carry over $1.3 billion in unspent 2006 funds. Unspent 2007 capital funds for the provinces may not be carried over, according to U.S. officials.

[7] This percentage differs from preliminary Ministry of Finance data provided by the U.S. Department of the Treasury indicating that the provinces "spent and committed" 18 percent of their 2007 allocations for capital projects and reconstruction, as of July 15, 2007.

[8] The term "commitment" in Iraq is similar to an obligation under the U.S. budget process, although the government of Iraq's official expenditure data, as reported by the Ministry of Finance, does not include commitments or obligations.

Appendix XVIII

[1] We defined this benchmark as "met" if there was no evidence of undermining or false accusations against Iraqi security force personnel. We defined this benchmark as "not met" if there was evidence of undermining or false accusations against Iraqi security force personnel.

Appendix XXI

[1] Section 1314 of Public Law 110-28.

[2] For example, see GAO, *Securing, Stabilizing, and Rebuilding Iraq: Key Issues for Congressional Oversight*, GAO-07-308SP (Washington, D.C.: January 9, 2007). See GAO's website at http://www.gao.gov for a complete list of GAO's Iraq-related reports.

[3] IFES was formally known as the International Foundation for Election Systems.

[4] GAO, *Rebuilding Iraq: Serious Challenges Impair Efforts to Restore Iraq's Oil Sector and Enact Hydrocarbon Legislation*, GAO-07-1107T (Washington, D.C.: July 18, 2007) and *Rebuilding Iraq: Integrated Strategic Plan Needed to Help Restore Iraq's Oil and Electricity Sectors*, GAO-07-677 (Washington, D.C.: May 15, 2007).

DOCUMENT NO. 9

IMPROVISED EXPLOSIVE DEVICES (IEDs) IN IRAQ AND AFGHANISTAN: EFFECTS AND COUNTERMEASURES

CRS Report
RS22330

August 28, 2007

Clay Wilson
Specialist in Technology and National Security
Foreign Affairs, Defense, and Trade Division

Summary

Since October 2001, improvised explosive devices (IEDs, roadside bombs, and suicide car bombs) have been responsible for many of the more than 3,000 combat deaths in Iraq and many of the more than 240 combat deaths in Afghanistan.[1] Vehicle-borne IEDs and car bombs are now used to strike police stations, markets, and mosques, killing local citizens as well as U.S. troops. U.S. forces counter the devices through utilizing intelligence sources and by disrupting portions of the radio spectrum that insurgents use to trigger IEDs. However, insurgents quickly adapt to countermeasures, and new, more sophisticated IEDs are increasingly being used in both Iraq and Afghanistan. Department of Defense (DOD) officials have also charged that Iran may be supplying new IED technology to insurgents in Iraq. There is growing concern that IEDs might eventually be used by other insurgents and terrorists worldwide.[2] This report will be updated as events warrant.

Background

Improvised explosive devices, also known as IEDs, roadside bombs, and suicide car bombs, have caused over 60% of all American combat casualties in Iraq and 50% of combat casualties in Afghanistan, both killed and wounded.[3] Some observers speculate that much of the munitions for constructing IEDs in Iraq may have come from large Iraqi military ordnance deposits looted by insurgents, or from stockpiles scattered in secret locations throughout that country before the war.[4] In Afghanistan, the IED munitions supply is supported by funds from an expanding opium trade.[5] Afghanistan's opium crop reportedly grew 59% in 2006, yielding 6,100 tons, or 90% of the world's supply.[6] In 2007, the opium crop grew by another 34% and is now the source of 93% of the world's supply of heroin and morphine.[7]

The largest group of suicide attackers in Iraq reportedly is Sunni Iraqis, followed by foreign fighters usually from Saudi Arabia, Syria, and Kuwait.[8] Observers have indicated that the Taliban forces in Afghanistan appear to have learned some IED techniques from the Iraqi insurgents, and some areas of Afghanistan are now reportedly becoming too dangerous for reconstruction efforts there to continue.[9] DOD has found that insurgents build and deploy IEDs by using networks that, for centuries in Afghanistan and Iraq, have formed the sinews of commerce and survival for tribes and factions.[10]

In Iraq, small, highly skilled IED cells often hire themselves out to other insurgent groups, such as al-Qaeda in Iraq or the Sunni group Ansaar al Sunna. They advertise their skills on the Internet, and are temporarily contracted on a per-job basis but otherwise remain autonomous.[11] A typical IED terrorist cell consists of six to eight people, including a financier, bomb maker, emplacer, triggerman, spotter, and often a cameraman. Videos of exploding U.S. vehicles and dead Americans are distributed via the Internet to win new supporters.

DOD officials reportedly captured four Iranian terrorists in July 2007 who are accused of smuggling explosives and personnel from Iran into Iraq.[12] Iran is suspected of supplying Iraq insurgents with IEDs, training, and new designs and technology for explosive devices, such as "passive infrared" electronic sensors that are used for triggering roadside bombs. The new sensors are more resistant to electromagnetic countermeasures now employed by U.S. forces. DOD officials also suspect that Iran is supplying Iraq insurgents with a more lethal IED bomb design called an explosively formed projectile (EFP). An EFP is made from a pipe filled with explosives and capped by a specially shaped metal disk. When the explosives detonate, they transform the disk into a jet of molten metal capable of penetrating armor. EFPs reportedly strike with enough power to cause pieces of a targeted vehicle's heavy armor to turn into shrapnel, making them much more deadly than traditional IED weapons. DOD officials report there were 69 attacks utilizing EFPs in April 2007.[13]

U.S. military officials suspect that EFPs and other weapons were smuggled into Iraq by members of the Quds Force, which is part of the Iranian Revolutionary Guard. The same type of EFP device has been used by Shiite organizations in Lebanon, where Hezbollah receives military support from Iran.

However, Iranian government officials deny involvement with any transfer of these weapons to Iraq.[14] In addition, U.S. intelligence officials have reportedly said that most IED attacks against U.S. forces in Iraq come from Sunni insurgents rather than from the Shia elements most directly backed by Iran.[15] Over time, the insurgents in Iraq have adapted to many U.S. countermeasures, and several DOD officials have stated that protective equipment sometimes seems to be less effective after being deployed for only a few months.[16]

Countermeasures

DOD has established the Joint IED Defeat Organization (JIEDDO) to investigate countermeasures along with various national laboratories, the Department of Energy, contractors, and academia. The Marine Counter Improvised Explosive Device Technology Directorate and the Army Electronic Warfare Division also work with the JIEDDO to reduce the IED threat.[17] DOD has also sent electronic warfare officers from the Navy and Air Force into Iraq and Afghanistan to work on counter-IED measures.[18] The technologies being evaluated include electronic jammers and pre-detonators, radars, X-ray equipment, robotic explosive ordnance disposal equipment, physical security equipment, and armor for vehicles and personnel.[19]

In the past year, JIEDDO has funded almost 14,000 jammers for Marine and Army units, including robots for explosive ordnance disposal teams, Cougar vehicles for route clearance teams, and Guardian, a man-portable jammer for dismounted operations. The JIEDDO also uses intelligence sources to assemble and distribute products to military units daily to support their efforts to destroy the networks that create IEDs.

Some counter-IED technologies include a stoichiometric diagnostic device, which can decipher chemical signatures of unknown substances through metal or other barriers. Known as the CarBomb Finder model 3C4, it sends out neutrons that cause any substance within a container or vehicle to emit back gamma rays that contain unique signatures from which the chemical formulas are derived.[20] Electronic jamming devices include the IED Countermeasures Equipment (ICE) and the Warlock, both of which use low-power radio frequency energy to block the signals of radio controlled explosives detonators, such as cell phones, satellite phones, and long-range cordless telephones.[21] Other countermeasures include the Joint IED Neutralizer (JIN) and the Neutralizing Improvised Explosive Devices with Radio Frequency (NIRF), which produce a high-frequency field to neutralize IED electronics at a distance.[22] A system now deployed in Iraq, codenamed PING, fits inside a Humvee and sends out electromagnetic waves to penetrate the walls of buildings to detect IEDs.[23] Other sensors, such as the Laser-Induced Breakdown Spectroscopy system (LIBS), detect traces of explosives used for IEDs from as far away as 30 meters.[24]

However, the Radio Frequency (RF) spectrum in the Iraq combat theater is largely not managed, and counter-IED radio jammers can sometimes lock onto other U.S. electronic combat systems because of a lack of coordination of spectrum usage. Also, Unmanned Aerial Vehicles (UAVs) can sometimes lose their radio control links due to ground-based radio interference caused by counter-IED jammers once they are far away from their control base. Therefore, DOD is now developing an "Electronic Warfare Coordination Cell" to help sort out problems that can impede friendly operations, or endanger Explosive Ordnance Teams as they disable IEDs on the ground.[25]

Other counter-IED research involves fusing large amounts of intelligence and surveillance data to monitor when and where bombs are planted. Using such data gathered by Unmanned Aerial Vehicles (UAVs), enemy bomb makers can be targeted before attacks can be launched. Sometimes the data can be played backward to see from where the bombers and vehicles came.[26]

Threat data about IEDs is tightly controlled by DOD to avoid giving feedback to the enemy about the effectiveness or ineffectiveness of different IED designs. Also, proprietary rights must be protected for those companies who produce IED countermeasures. However, these controls may sometimes limit access by other companies to important information about the effectiveness of anti-IED systems as they are tested or used in battle.[27] As a result, some industry officials say they are not getting access to all the information they need to help them create the most effective new solutions to counter IEDs, and suggest that relaxing some of the controls might lead to more solutions.[28] However, the JIEDDO has recognized this issue and is taking steps, including modifying content on its website, to improve access to information at the appropriate clearance levels.[29]

Acquisition and Funding of Countermeasures

Some U.S. Army units in Iraq and Afghanistan reportedly lack the latest Humvee armor kits, and the new deployment of five additional Army brigades has added to that shortage.[30] Humvees can be up-armored through a rebuilding process that adds classified technology called "Frag 5" or "Frag 6," which are armor kits that are said to offer increased protection against side-penetrating EFPs.[31] However, the weight of extra armor may sometimes hinder the payload and performance of humvees. In October 2007, the Army expects to begin taking delivery of the first wave of blast-proof trucks, called Mine Resistant Ambush Protected (MRAP) vehicles.[32] All Humvees in Iraq are to be replaced by MRAPs, which are better designed to withstand traditional IEDs. However, some DOD officials have reportedly stated that the MRAP may not be able to stop EFPs unless additional armor is added, and that this known vulnerability will cause insurgents to increase their use of EFPs.[33] The Army and Marine Corps are also planning to gradually replace the humvee fleet with the new Joint Light Tactical Vehicle (JLTV), starting in FY2012. The FY2008 budget request includes $82.3 million for JLTV research and development, $4.6 million for program management, and $77.6 million for prototype design and development.[34]

On August 5, 2007, the House passed H.R. 3222, the Department of Defense Appropriations Act of 2008, where $500,000,000 was made available to the Joint IED Defeat Fund, until September 30, 2010. The Joint IED Defeat Fund allows DOD to allocate funds where needed. However, under this legislation, funds allocated for operating and administrative expenses are limited to not more than $110,000,000, and within 60 days of enactment, the Office of the Secretary of Defense (OSD) must submit a plan to the defense committees explaining the intended management and use of the amounts provided.

For FY2006 (Title IX Bridge Fund and FY-06 Supplement), the funding enacted for the Joint IED Defeat Fund was $3.3 billion. For FY2007 (Title IX Bridge Fund and FY2007 Supplement), the amount was $4.3 billion. The FY2008 budget request from DOD (Baseline DOD and FY2008 Global War On Terror Budget Request) is $4.5 billion. The FY2008 budget request includes for programs such as Attack the Network ($926,000), Defeat the Device ($2.7 million), and Train the Force ($334,000).[35] The total funding thus far is $7.6 billion, and including the FY2008 budget request, the total is $12.1 billion.[36]

Endnotes

[1] DOD Personnel and Military Casualty Statistics, Defense Manpower Data Center, *Casualty Summary by Reason, October 7, 2001 through August 18, 2007*, available at [http://siadapp.dmdc.osd.mil/personnel/CASUALTY/gwot_reason.pdf].

[2] The suicide attacks on American hotels in Jordan in November 2005 represent the first known case where Iraqis have conducted suicide bombings against the United States outside of Iraq. Brent Sadler, *Jordan Confirms Al Qaeda Behind Hotel Blasts*, CNN, November 12, 2005.

[3] DOD Personnel and Military Casualty Statistics, Defense Manpower Data Center, *Casualty Summary by Reason, October 7, 2001 through August 18, 2007*; available at[http://siadapp.dmdc.osd.mil/personnel/CASUALTY/gwot_reason.pdf].

[4] James Glanz and Jim Dwyer, "Looting Spree Gutted Ammo Dump," *San Francisco Chronicle*, October 28, 2004. Byron York, *Remember Al Qaqaa?*, National Review Online, February 28, 2005 [http://www.nationalreview.com/york/york200502280821.asp].

[5] Peter Bergen, "The Taliban, Regrouped and Rearmed," *The Washington Post*, September 10, 2006, B1. Helen Cooper, "NATO Chief Says More Troops Are Needed in Afghanistan," *The New York Times*, September 22, 2006, p.10.

[6] Jason Straziuso, *Taliban netting millions from poppies*, Associated Press, Apr 10, 2007.

[7] Colum Lynch and Griff Witte, *Afghan Opium Trade Hits New Peak, The Washington Post*, August 28, 2007, A.3.

[8] Lionel Beehner, *Iraq: suicide Attacks*, the Council on Foreign Relations, August 1, 2005. Michael O'Hanlon and Jason Campbell, *The Iraq Index*, the Brookings Institution, July 31, 2006.

[9] Peter Bergen, "The Taliban, Regrouped and Rearmed," *The Washington Post*, September 10, 2006, B4.

[10] Gen. Montgomery Meigs, *On the Offensive: The Battle Against IEDs*, Marine Times, April 16, 2007, at [http://www.harmonieweb.org:40793/news/Pages/OnTheOffensive.aspx].

[11] Times Wire Service, "Italian Troops End Iraq Mission," *The Los Angeles Times*, September 22, 2006.

[12] Sara Carter, *Iran-Arms Importers Captured in Iraq*, Washington Times, Jul 28, 2007, p.1.

[13] Tom Brook, *Military tests new armored vehicle*, USA Today, Jun 11, 2007, p.1A.

[14] Joshua Partlow, "Military Ties Iran to Arms in Iraq," *The Washington Post*, February 12, 2007, p. A1.

[15] Serial numbers for infrared triggers have been traced to bulk device orders by Iran. Precision manufacturing techniques required to produce EFP bombs indicate that some may have been constructed in Iran. Michael Isikoff and Mark Hosenball, *Terror Watch: Tracking Iran's Role in Iraq Attacks*, Newsweek, Jan 24, 2007. Tom Brook, "U.S. blames Iran for new bombs in Iraq," *USA Today*, January 31, 2007 [http://www.usatoday.com/news/world/iraq/2007-01-30-ied-iran_ x.htm].

[16] The Army has reportedly suffered losses because of ambushes that follow IED attacks. Greg Grant, "Aerial IEDs Target U.S. Copters," *Defense News*, January 16, 2006. John Anderson, Steve Fainaru, Jonathan Finer, "Bigger, Stronger Homemade Bombs Now to Blame for Half of U.S. Deaths," *The Washington Post*, October 26, 2005, p. A1. Ann Tyson, "Thousands of Army Humvees Lack Armor Upgrade," *The Washington Post*, February 12, 2007, p. A1.

[17] Brenda Steele, "Vice Chairman Visits Troops in Afghanistan, Focuses on IED Issues," *Defense Link*, September 24, 2006 [http://www.defenselink.mil/news/NewsArticle.aspx?ID=1156].

[18] Brenda Steele, "Vice Chairman Visits Troops in Afghanistan, Focuses on IED Issues," *Defense Link*, September 24, 2006 [http://www.defenselink.mil/news/NewsArticle.aspx?ID=1156].

[19] Bruce Lieberman, "SDSU professor focuses laser research on finding killer explosives in Iraq," *SignOnSanDiego.com*, December 27, 2005; available at [http://www.signonsandiego.com/ articlelink/sdsufoundation4/sdsufoundation4.html].

[20] Steve Grossman, *Car Bomb Detector Employs a Revolutionary New Approach, RFDesign*, November 9, 2005 [http://rfdesign.com/military_defense_electronics/news/car_bomb_detector/].

[21] Sgt. Stephen D'Alessio, 2nd Marine Division, *Marines schooled in new bomb protection*, July 7, 2005, available at [http://www.marines.mil/marinelink/mcn2000.nsf/0/b89628064c45144e 85257056003871f1?OpenDocument].

[22] Brendan Rivers, *U.S. to Use Directed Energy on IEDs in Iraq*, eDefenseOnline, June 7, 2005. Christopher Castelli, "General: Ability to Prematurely Detonate Enemy Bombs Badly Needed," *Inside the Navy*, August 22, 2005, at [http://www.insidedefense.com/].

[23] Loren B. Thompson, *Iraq: Stop the Bombers, Win the War*, June 10, 2005, Lexington Institute, [http://www.lexingtoninstitute.org/defense.asp?aid=616].

[24] Sebastian Sprenger, "U.S., NATO Research Could Help Troops Detect IED Threats from Afar," *Inside the Pentagon*, May 26, 2005. Noah Shachtman, "Improvised Bombs Baffle Army,"*Wired News*, January 26, 2005, [http://www.wired.com/news/technology/0,1282,66395,00.html].

[25] David Fulghum, "Jamming Jam-Up," *Aviation Week & Space Technology*, November 7, 2005,Vol. 163, No. 18, P.32.

[26] David Fulghum, "Attacking Bombs," *Aviation Week*, July 31, 2005.

[27] Michael Moss, "Many Missteps Tied to Delay Of Armor to Protect Soldiers," *The New York Times*, March 7, 2005, online at [http://www.globalsecurity.org/org/news/2005/050307-armor-missteps.htm].

[28] Anne Plummer, "Deadly Threat of Explosive Devices in Iraq Prompts Secrecy Debate," *Inside the Pentagon*, November 18, 2004, vol. 20, no. 47.

[29] Personal communication, JIEDDO, Aug 28, 2007

[30] Ann Tyson, "Thousands of Army Humvees Lack Armor Upgrade," *The Washington Post*, February 12, 2007, A1.

[31] David Crane, *New Vehicle Armor Developed to Defeat Explosively Formed Penetrators (EFPs)*, Defense Review.com, June 27, 2007.

[32] For more information about MRAP vehicles, see CRS Report RS22707, *Mine-Resistant, Ambush-Protected (MRAP) Vehicles: Background and Issues for Congress*, August 21, 2007, by Andrew Feickert.

[33] Tom Brook, *MRAPs can't stop newest weapon*, USA Today, May 31, 2007, p.1A.

[34] Newsstand, *MRAP Sheet*, the Insider.com, Jul 12, 2007, [http://defense.iwpnewsstand.com/ insider.asp?issue=07122007].

[35] Office of the Secretary of Defense, FY 2008 Global War on Terror Request, February 2007.

[36] See CRS Report RL33110, *The Cost of Iraq, Afghanistan, and Other Global War on Terror Operations Since 9/11*, by Amy Belasco, and CRS Report RL33999, *Defense: FY2008 Authorization and Appropriations*, by Pat Towell, Stephen Daggett, and Amy Belasco.

DOCUMENT NO. 10

STABILIZING IRAQ: DOD CANNOT ENSURE THAT U.S.-FUNDED EQUIPMENT HAS REACHED IRAQI SECURITY FORCES

GAO Report
GAO-07-711

July 31, 2007

What GAO Found

As of July 2007, DOD and MNF-I had not specified which DOD accountability procedures, if any, apply to the train-and-equip program for Iraq. Congress funded the train-and-equip program for Iraq outside traditional security assistance programs, providing DOD a large degree of flexibility in managing the program, according to DOD officials. These officials stated that since the funding did not go through traditional security assistance programs, the DOD accountability requirements normally applicable to these programs did not apply. Further, MNF-I does not currently have orders that comprehensively specify accountability procedures for equipment distributed to the Iraqi forces.

DOD and MNF-I cannot fully account for Iraqi forces' receipt of U.S.-funded equipment. Two factors led to this lapse in accountability. First, MNSTC-I did not maintain a centralized record of all equipment distributed to Iraqi forces before December 2005. At that time, MNSTC-I established a property book system to track issuance of equipment to the Iraqi forces and attempted to recover past records. GAO found a discrepancy of at least 190,000 weapons between data reported by the former MNSTC-I commander and the property books. Former MNSTC-I officials stated that this lapse was due to insufficient staff and the lack of a fully operational distribution network, among other reasons. Second, since the beginning of the program, MNSTC-I has not consistently collected supporting records confirming the dates the equipment was received, the quantities of equipment delivered, or the Iraqi units receiving the items. Since June 2006, the command has placed greater emphasis on collecting the supporting documents. However, GAO's review of the January 2007 property books found continuing problems with missing and incomplete records. Further, the property books consist of extensive electronic spreadsheets, which are an inefficient management tool given the large amount of data and limited personnel to maintain the system.

Image: Efforts to Account for Equipment Distributed to the Iraqi Security Forces [Omitted]

DOCUMENT NO. 11

IRAQ AND AL QAEDA

CRS Report
RL32217

July 27, 2007

Kenneth Katzman
Specialist in Middle Eastern Affairs
Foreign Affairs, Defense, and Trade Division

Summary

In building a case for invading Iraq and ousting Saddam Hussein from power, the Administration asserted that the regime of Saddam Hussein had a working relationship with the Al Qaeda organization. The Administration stated that the relationship dated to the early 1990s, and was based on a common interest in confronting the United States. The Administration assertions were derived from U.S. intelligence showing a pattern of contacts with Al Qaeda when its founder, Osama bin Laden, was based in Sudan in the early to mid-1990s and continuing after he relocated to Afghanistan in 1996.

Critics maintain that the Administration argument did not demonstrate that the relationship, if it existed, was systematic or institutionalized, and that no hard data has come to light indicating the two entities conducted any joint terrorist attacks. Some major hallmarks of a consistent relationship were absent, and several experts outside and within the U.S. government believe that contacts between Iraq and Al Qaeda were sporadic, unclear, or subject to alternate explanations.

Another pillar of the Administration argument rested on reports of contacts between Baghdad and an Islamist Al Qaeda affiliate group, called Ansar al-Islam, based in northern Iraq in the late 1990s. Although the connections between Ansar al-Islam and Saddam Hussein's regime were subject to debate, the organization apparently did evolve into what is now known as Al Qaeda in Iraq (AQ-I). AQ-I is a key component of the Sunni Arab-led insurgency that has frustrated U.S. efforts to stabilize Iraq, but there is debate about how large and significant a component of overall violence is carried out by AQ-I. At the same time, U.S. commanders are increasingly focusing combat operations on AQ-I. The U.S. military also has sought, with some success, to exploit differences between AQ-I and Iraqi Sunni political, tribal, and insurgent leaders.

There are some indications that AQ-I is attempting to conduct activities outside Iraq in a process that some describe as "spillover" from Iraq into the broader Middle East. However, another interpretation is that the U.S.-led war in Iraq has stimulated radical activities outside Iraq that are sympathetic to Al Qaeda. Analysis of the broader implications of AQ-I might depend on the degree to which AQ-I is in contact with the remaining leadership of the Al Qaeda organization as it has evolved since the September 11, 2001 attacks on the United States. That relationship remains a subject of debate among experts.

This report will be updated as warranted by developments. See also: CRS Report RL31339: *Iraq: Post-Saddam Governance and Security*, by Kenneth Katzman.

Part of the debate over the Bush Administration decision to use military action to overthrow the regime of Saddam Hussein centers on whether or not that regime was allied with Al Qaeda. In building an argument that the United States needed to oust Saddam Hussein from power militarily, the Administration asserted that Iraq constituted a gathering threat to the United States because it continued to develop weapons of mass destruction (WMD) that it could potentially transfer to international terrorist groups, including Al Qaeda, with which Iraq was allied, in the Administration view. This combination produced the possibility of a catastrophic attack on the United States, according to the Administration.

The first pillar of the Administration argument for ousting Saddam Hussein—its continued active development of WMD—has been researched extensively. After the fall of the regime in April 2003, U.S. forces and intelligence officers in an "Iraq Survey Group" (ISG) scoured Iraq for evidence of WMD stockpiles. A "comprehensive" September 2004 report of the Survey Group, known as the "Duelfer report,"[1] said that the ISG found no WMD stockpiles or production but said that there was evidence that the regime retained the intention to reconstitute WMD programs in the future. The formal U.S.-led WMD search ended December 2004,[2] although U.S. forces have found some chemical weapons caches left over from the Iran-Iraq war.[3] The UNMOVIC work remained formally active until July 2007.

The second pillar of the Administration argument—that Saddam Hussein's regime had links to Al Qaeda—is relevant not only to assess justification for the invasion decision but also because an Al Qaeda affiliate is now, by all accounts, a key part of the ongoing Iraq insurgency. The Administration maintains that the Al Qaeda presence in Iraq, fighting alongside Iraqi insurgents from the ousted ruling Baath Party and former regime security forces, demonstrates that there were pre-war linkages. On the other hand, most experts believe that Al Qaeda and other foreign fighters entered Sunni-inhabited central Iraq after the fall of Saddam Hussein, from the Kurdish controlled north and from other Middle Eastern countries, after the fall of the regime. They are motivated by an anti-U.S. ideology and a target of opportunity provided by the presence of U.S. forces there, rather than longstanding ties to the former Iraqi regime, according to this view.

Background on Saddam—Al Qaeda Links

On March 17, 2003, in a speech announcing a 48-hour deadline for Saddam Hussein and his sons to leave Iraq in order to avoid war, President Bush said:

> ... the [Iraqi] regime has a history of reckless aggression in the Middle East. It has a deep hatred of America and our friends. And it has aided, trained, and harbored terrorists, including operatives of Al Qaeda."[4]

The Administration argument for an Iraq-Al Qaeda linkage had a few major themes: (1) that there were contacts between Iraqi intelligence and Al Qaeda in Sudan, Afghanistan, and Pakistan dating from the early 1990s, including Iraq's assistance to Al Qaeda in deployment of chemical weapons; (2) that an Islamist faction called Ansar al-Islam (The Partisans of Islam) in northern Iraq, had ties to Iraq's regime; and (3) that Iraq might have been involved in the September 11, 2001 plot itself. Of these themes, the September 11 allegations are the most widely disputed by outside experts and by some officials within the Administration itself. Some Administration officials, including President Bush, have virtually ruled out Iraqi involvement in the September 11 attacks while others, including Vice President Cheney, have maintained that issue is still open.[5]

Secretary of State Powell presented the Administration view in greater public detail than any other official when he briefed the United Nations Security Council on Iraq on February 5, 2003, although most of that presentation was devoted to Iraq's alleged violations of U.N. requirements that it dismantle its weapons of mass destruction (WMD) programs. According to the presentation:[6]

> Iraq and terrorism go back decades .... But what I want to bring to your attention today is the potentially more sinister nexus between Iraq and the Al Qaeda terrorist network, a nexus that combines classic terrorist organizations and modern methods of murder. Iraq today harbors a deadly terrorist network headed by Abu Musab Al-Zarqawi, an associate and collaborator

> of Osama bin Laden and his Al Qaeda lieutenants. Going back to the early and mid-1990s, when bin Laden was based in Sudan, an Al Qaeda source tells us that Saddam and bin Laden reached an understanding that Al Qaeda would no longer support activities against Baghdad .... We know members of both organizations met repeatedly and have met at least eight times at very senior levels since the early 1990s .... Iraqis continued to visit bin Laden in his new home in Afghanistan [after bin Laden moved there in mid-1996] .... From the late 1990s until 2001, the Iraqi embassy in Pakistan played the role of liaison to the Al Qaeda organization ... Ambition and hatred are enough to bring Iraq and Al Qaeda together, enough so Al Qaeda could learn how to build more sophisticated bombs and learn how to forge documents, and enough so that Al Qaeda could turn to Iraq for help in acquiring expertise on weapons of mass destruction.

Secretary Powell did not include in his February 5, 2003, briefing the assertion that Iraq was involved in the September 11 plot. Some analysts suggest the omission indicates a lack of consensus within the Administration on the strength of that evidence. In a January 2004 press interview, Secretary Powell said that his U.N. briefing had been meticulously prepared and reviewed, saying "Anything that we did not feel was solid and multi-sourced, we did not use in that speech."[7] Additional details of the Administration's argument, as well as criticisms, are discussed below.

Post-Saddam analysis of the issue has tended to refute the Administration argument on Saddam-Al Qaeda linkages, although this issue is still debated. The report of the 9/11 Commission found no evidence of a "collaborative operational linkage" between Iraq and Al Qaeda.[8] In his book "At the Center of the Storm" in May 2007 (Harper Collins Press, pp. 341–358), former CIA Director George Tenet indicated that the CIA view was that contacts between Saddam's regime and Al Qaeda were likely for the purpose of taking the measure of each other or take advantage of each other rather than collaborating. Others note, however, that some of Tenet's pre-war testimony before Congress was in line with the prevailing Administration view on this question, contrasting with the views in his book.

Major Themes in the Administration Argument

Any relationship between Saddam Hussein's regime and Al Qaeda would have been, by its nature, clandestine. Some of the intelligence information that the Bush Administration relied on to judge linkages between Iraq and Al Qaeda was publicized not only in Secretary of State Powell's February 5, 2003, briefing to the U.N. Security Council, but also, and in more detail, in an article in *The Weekly Standard*.[9] Vice President Cheney has been quoted as saying the article represents the "best source of [open] information" on the issue.[10] The article contains excerpts from a memorandum, dated October 27, 2003, from Undersecretary of Defense for Policy Douglas Feith to Senators Pat Roberts and Jay Rockefeller, the chairman and vice chairman of the Senate Intelligence Committee. The memorandum reportedly was based on research and analysis of intelligence and other information by the "Office of Special Plans," an Iraq policy planning unit within the Department of Defense set up in early 2002 but disbanded in the fall of 2002. The following sections analyze details of the major themes in the Administration argument on the issue.

Links in Sudan, Afghanistan, and Pakistan. The "DOD memorandum," as well as other accounts,[11] include assertions that Iraqi intelligence developed a relationship with Al Qaeda in the early 1990s, brokered by the Islamist leaders of Sudan. At the time, Osama bin Laden was in Sudan. He remained there until Sudan expelled him in mid-1996, after which he went to Afghanistan. According to the purported memo, the Iraq-Al Qaeda relationship included an agreement by Al Qaeda not to seek to undermine Saddam's regime, and for Iraq to provide Al Qaeda with conventional weapons and WMD. The Administration view is that Iraq was highly isolated in the Arab world in the early 1990s, just after its invasion of Kuwait in August 1990, and that it might have sought a relationship with Al Qaeda as a means of gaining leverage over the United States and a common enemy, the regime of Saudi Arabia. From this perspective, the relationship served the interests of both, even though Saddam was a secular leader while Al Qaeda sought to replace regional secular leaders with Islamic states.

The purported DOD memorandum includes names and approximate dates on which Iraqi intelligence officers visited bin Laden's camp outside Khartoum and discussions of cooperation in manufacturing explosive devices. It reportedly discusses subsequent meetings between Iraqi intelligence officers and bin Laden and his aides in Afghanistan and Pakistan, continuing until at least the late 1990s. The memorandum cites intelligence reports that Al Qaeda operatives were instructed to travel to Iraq to obtain training in the making and deployment of chemical weapons. Secretary of State Powell, in his February 5, 2003, U.N. briefing, citing an Al Qaeda operative captured in Afghanistan, stated that Iraq had received Al Qaeda operatives "several times between 1997 and 2000 for help in acquiring poison gases."

According to press accounts, some Administration evaluations of the available intelligence, including a reported draft national intelligence estimate (NIE) circulated in October 2002, interpreted the information as inconclusive, and as evidence of sporadic but not necessarily ongoing or high-level contacts between Iraq and Al Qaeda.[12] Some CIA experts reportedly asserted that the ideological differences between Iraq and Al Qaeda were too large to be bridged permanently.[13] For example, bin Laden reportedly sought to raise an Islamic army to fight to expel Iraqi troops from Kuwait following the Iraqi invasion in August 1990, suggesting that bin

Laden might have viewed Iraq as an enemy rather than an ally. According to some accounts, the Saudi royal family rebuffed bin Laden's idea as unworkable, deciding instead to invite in U.S. forces to combat the Iraqi invasion. The rebuff prompted an open split between bin Laden and the Saudi leadership, and bin Laden left the Kingdom for Sudan in 1991.[14] Ideological differences between Iraq and Al Qaeda were evident in a February 12, 2003, bin Laden statement referring to Saddam Hussein's regime—dominated by his secular Arab nationalist Baath Party—as "socialist and infidel," although the statement also gave some support to the Administration argument when bin Laden exhorted the Iraqi people to resist impending U.S. military action.[15]

As noted above, Iraq had an embassy in Pakistan that the Administration asserts was its link to the Taliban regime of Afghanistan. However, skeptics of a Saddam-Al Qaeda link note that Iraq did not recognize the Taliban as the legitimate government of Afghanistan when the Taliban was in power during 1996–2001. It was during the period of Taliban rule that Al Qaeda enjoyed safehaven in Afghanistan. Of the 12 Al Qaeda leaders identified by the U.S. government as either "executive leaders" or "senior planners and coordinators," none is an Iraqi national.[16] Only a very small number—possibly a few dozen—of the approximately 3,000 Al Qaeda suspects arrested since the September 11, 2001, attacks reportedly are Iraqi.[17] This could suggest that the joining of Al Qaeda by Iraqi nationals did not have the sanction of Saddam Hussein. An alternate explanation is that very few Iraqis had the opportunity to join Al Qaeda during its key formative years—the years of the anti-Soviet "jihad" in Afghanistan (1979–1989). Young Iraqis who might have been attracted to volunteer in Afghanistan were serving in Iraqi units during the 1980-88 Iran-Iraq war, and were not available to participate in regional causes. On the other hand, a political alliance between Saddam Hussein and Al Qaeda might not necessarily have included Iraqi government backing for Iraqis to join Al Qaeda.

Ansar al-Islam Presence in Northern Iraq. Another major theme in the Administration assertion of Al Qaeda-Iraq linkages has been the presence in Iraq of a group called Ansar al-Islam (Partisans of Islam). This aspect of the Administration's argument factored prominently in Secretary of State Powell's U.N. presentation, and is the most directly relevant to analysis of the Al Qaeda presence in Iraq today. Ansar al-Islam is considered the forerunner of what is now known as Al Qaeda in Iraq (AQ-I).

Ansar al-Islam formed in 1998 as a breakaway faction of Islamist Kurds, splitting off from a group, the Islamic Movement of Iraqi Kurdistan (IMIK). Both Ansar and the IMIK were initially composed purely of Kurds. U.S. concerns about Ansar grew following the U.S. defeat of the Taliban and Al Qaeda in Afghanistan in late 2001, when some Al Qaeda activists, mostly Arabs, fled to Iraq and associated there with the Ansar movement. At the peak, about 600 Arab fighters lived in the Ansar al-Islam enclave, near the town of Khurmal.[18] Ansar fighters clashed with Kurdish fighters from the Patriotic Union of Kurdistan (PUK), one of the two mainstream Iraqi Kurdish parties, around Halabja in December 2002. Ansar gunmen were allegedly responsible for an assassination attempt against PUK "prime minister" of the Kurdish region Barham Salih in April 2002.

The leader of the Arab contingent within Ansar al-Islam was Abu Musab al-Zarqawi, an Arab of Jordanian origin who reputedly fought in Afghanistan. Although more recent assessments indicate Zarqawi commanded Arab volunteers in Afghanistan separate from those recruited by bin Laden, Zarqawi was linked to purported Al Qaeda plots in the 1990s and early 2000s. He allegedly was behind foiled bombings in Jordan during the December 1999 millennium celebration, to the assassination in Jordan of U.S. diplomat Lawrence Foley (2002), and to reported attempts in 2002 to spread chemical agents in Russia, Western Europe, and the United States.[19]

In explaining why the United States needed to confront Saddam Hussein's regime militarily, U.S. officials maintained that Baghdad was connected to Ansar al-Islam. In his U.N. presentation, Secretary of State Powell said:

> Iraq today harbors a deadly terrorist network headed by Abu Musab al-Zarqawi, an associate and collaborator of Osama bin Laden and his Al Qaeda lieutenants .... Baghdad has an agent in the most senior levels of the radical organization, Ansar al-Islam, that controls this corner of Iraq .... Zarqawi's activities are not confined to this small corner of northeastern Iraq. He traveled to Baghdad in May 2002 for medical treatment, staying in the capital for two months while he recuperated to fight another day. During this stay, nearly two dozen extremists converged on Baghdad and established a base of operations there .... From his terrorist network in Iraq, Zarqawi can direct his network in the Middle East and beyond.

However, some accounts question the extent of links, if any, between Baghdad and Ansar al-Islam. Baghdad did not control northern Iraq even before Operation Iraqi Freedom, and it is questionable whether Zarqawi, were he tied closely to Saddam Hussein's regime, would have located his group in territory controlled by Saddam's Kurdish opponents.[20] The Administration view on this point is that Saddam saw Ansar as a means of pressuring Saddam Hussein's Kurdish opponents in northern Iraq. An alternate interpretation is that Saddam Hussein was indifferent to Ansar's presence in Iraqi territory so long as the group remained focused on Baghdad's Kurdish opponents.

The September 11, 2001, Plot. The reputed DOD memorandum reportedly includes allegations of contacts between lead September 11 hijacker Mohammad Atta and Iraq intelligence, including as many as four meetings between Atta and Iraq's intelligence chief in Prague, Ahmad Samir al-Ani.

The DOD memo says that al-Ani agreed to provide Atta with funds at one of the meetings. The memo asserts that the CIA confirmed two Atta visits to Prague—October 26, 1999, and April 9, 2001—but did not confirm that he met with Iraqi intelligence during those visits. The DOD memo reportedly also contains reports indicating that Iraqi intelligence officers attended or facilitated meetings with Al Qaeda operatives in southeast Asia (Kuala Lumpur) in early 2000. In the course of these meetings, the Al Qaeda activists were said to be planning the October 12, 2000, attack on the U.S.S. Cole docked in Aden, Yemen, and possibly the September 11 plot as well.

As noted above, Secretary of State Powell reportedly considered the information too uncertain to include in his February 5, 2003, briefing on Iraq to the U.N. Security Council.[21] President Bush did not mention this allegation in his January 29, 2003, State of the Union message, delivered one week before the Powell presentation to the U.N. Security Council. President Bush said on September 16, 2003, that there was no evidence Saddam Hussein's regime was involved in the September 11 plot; he made the statement in response to a journalist's question about statements a few days earlier by Vice President Cheney suggesting that the issue of Iraq's complicity in September 11 is still open.[22]

There is dispute within Czech intelligence that provided the information on the meetings, that the Iraq-Atta discussions took place at all, particularly the April 2001 meeting. In November 2001, Czech Interior Minister Stanislav Gross said that Atta and al-Ani had met, but Czech Prime Minister Milos Zeman subsequently told U.S. officials that the two had discussed an attack aimed at silencing anti-Saddam broadcasts from Prague.[23] Since 1998, Prague has been the headquarters of Radio Free Europe/Radio Liberty, a U.S.-funded radio service that was highly critical of Saddam Hussein's regime. In December 2001, Czech President Vaclav Havel said that there was a "70% chance" the meeting took place. The U.S. Federal Bureau of Investigation (FBI) and the Central Intelligence Agency (CIA) eventually concluded, based on records of Atta's movements within the United States in April 2001, that the meeting probably did not take place and that there was no hard evidence of Iraqi regime involvement in the September 11 attacks.[24] Some press reports say the FBI is more confident than is the CIA in the judgment that the April 2001 meeting did not occur.[25] Al Ani himself, captured by U.S. forces in 2003, reportedly denied to U.S. interrogators that the meeting ever happened.[26]

Al Qaeda and the Iraq Insurgency

Whether or not Al Qaeda leaders and Saddam Hussein had a relationship, a major issue facing the United States is the degree to which Al Qaeda elements are playing a role in the insurgency against U.S. and coalition forces in Iraq. The Administration, including President Bush, most notably in a

July 24, 2007, speech specifically on this issue, has consistently maintained that Al Qaeda elements are a key component of the Iraq insurgency; that Al Qaeda in Iraq is connected to the Al Qaeda leadership in Pakistan; and that this Al Qaeda role is a central reason that the United States needs to continue to conduct active combat in Iraq. Commenting on the Iraq insurgency when it was in its infancy, President Bush said in a speech on September 8, 2003, that "We have carried the fight to the enemy.... We are rolling back the terrorist threat to civilization, not on the fringes of its influence but at the heart of its power."[27] A few months later, in his January 20, 2004, State of the Union message, President Bush said, "These killers [Iraq insurgents], joined by foreign terrorists, are a serious, continuing danger."[28] Similar statements followed in subsequent years as the Administration sought to assert that Iraq had become the "central front" in the broader "war on terrorism," and that that it is preferable to combat Al Qaeda in Iraq rather than allow it to congregate elsewhere in the region and hatch plots inside the United States itself.[29] In a January 10, 2007, major speech announcing a new Iraq strategy characterized by a buildup of additional combat troops to secure Baghdad, President Bush made similar points:

> ... we will continue to pursue al Qaeda and foreign fighters. Al Qaeda is still active in Iraq. Its home base is Anbar Province. Al Qaeda has helped make Anbar the most violent area of Iraq outside the capital. A captured al Qaeda document describes the terrorists' plan to infiltrate and seize control of the province. This would bring al Qaeda closer to its goals of taking down Iraq's democracy, building a radical Islamic empire, and launching new attacks on the United States at home and abroad.

In the July 24, 2007, speech mentioned above,[30] President Bush said:

> ... Our troops are serving bravely in [Iraq]. They're opposing ruthless enemies, and no enemy is more ruthless in Iraq than al Qaeda. They send suicide bombers into crowded markets; they behead innocent captives and they murder American troops. They want to bring down Iraq's democracy so they can use that nation as a terrorist safe haven for attacks against our country ....

Critics of this view maintain that Al Qaeda or pro-Al Qaeda elements were motivated by the U.S. invasion to enter Iraq and to fight the United States there, and that the U.S. presence in Iraq has generated new Al Qaeda followers—both inside and outside Iraq—who might not have become active against the United States had the war against Iraq not occurred. This view draws some support from the released "key judgements" of a July 2007 National Intelligence Estimate (NIE) that said:

> ...we assess that [Al Qaeda central leadership's] association with AQ-I helps Al Qaeda to energize the broader Sunni extremist community, raise resources, and to recruit and indoctrinate operatives, including for homeland attacks.[31]

Other critics maintain that the Administration emphasizes an "Al Qaeda" component of the insurgency as a means of bolstering flagging U.S. public support for the war effort in Iraq.

Interpretations of Al Qaeda Involvement in the Insurgency

In analyzing the debate over Al Qaeda involvement in Iraq, a major question is the degree to which AQ-I or unassociated foreign fighters are driving the Iraq insurgency against the United States and the elected government of Iraq. Few dispute that there has been, from almost the inception of the insurgency in mid-2003, a "foreign fighter" component, but the debate over the contribution of the foreign fighters is nearly as old as the insurgency itself. In November 2003, one senior U.S. commander in Iraq (Maj. Gen. Charles Swannack, commander of the 82nd Airborne Division) said, in response to reports that foreign fighters were key to the burgeoning insurgency: "I want to underscore that most of the attacks on our forces are by former regime loyalists and other Iraqis, not foreign forces."[32]

Contrasting views were apparent again a few months later. Following the January 2004 arrest in northern Iraq of suspected bin Laden aide Hassan Ghul, then commander of U.S. forces in Iraq, Lt. Gen. Ricardo Sanchez, said the arrest "is pretty strong proof that Al Qaeda is trying to gain a foothold here to continue their murderous campaigns."[33] However, Gen. John Abizaid, then overall commander of U.S. forces in the Middle East region (U.S. Central Command) made a contrasting statement, saying "I am confident that there is no flood of foreign fighters coming in [to Iraq]."[34]

Those commanders who emphasized the foreign fighter role in the insurgency maintained that the many major suicide bombings that occurred—particularly the August 19, 2003 bombing of U.N. headquarters in Baghdad and the August 29, 2003, bombing of a major mosque complex in Najaf that killed the leader of the main Shiite faction (then called the Supreme Council of the Islamic Revolution in Iraq, renamed in June 2007 to the Supreme Islamic Council of Iraq, SICI), Mohammad Baqr Al Hakim—were carried out by the "Zarqawi network." These bombings represented, to some extent, a turning point that shook confidence in the U.S. ability to stabilize post-Saddam Iraq, and heightened the U.S. focus on the foreign component of the insurgency.

On July 12, 2007, chief spokesman for the U.S. military in Iraq, Brig. Gen. Kevin Bergner, was quoted as saying that AQ-I is responsible for 80 to 90% of the suicide bombings in Iraq, many of them carried out by foreigners. U.S. officials quoted in July 2007 press reports footnoted above say that Saudis are a "majority" of suicide bombers in Iraq. He also called AQ-I "the principal threat" to Iraqis, and the main focus of the U.S. security campaign. On the other hand, some U.S. commanders say that, while most foreign fighters going to Iraq become suicide bombers, others are contributing to the overall insurgency as snipers, logisticians, and financiers.[35] However, other U.S. commanders noted—and continue to note—that these major bombings constituted a small percentage of overall attacks in Iraq (which now number a total of about 175 per day), and that most of the U.S. combat deaths came from roadside bombs and direct or indirect munitions fire likely wielded by Iraqi Sunni insurgent fighters.

Estimated Numbers of Foreign Fighters. Although there have been differences among commanders about the contribution of the foreign fighters to the overall violence in Iraq, estimates of the numbers of foreign fighters have remained fairly consistent over time, at least as a percentage of the overall insurgency. As early as October 2003, U.S. officials estimated that as many as 3,000 might be non-Iraqi,[36] although, suggesting uncertainty in the estimate, Gen. Abizaid said on January 29, 2004, that the number of foreign fighters in Iraq was "low" and "in the hundreds."[37] A September 2005 study by the Center for Strategic and International Studies estimated that there were about 3,000 non-Iraqi fighters in Iraq—about 10% of the estimated total size of the insurgency. In testimony before Congress in January 2007, the then Director of the Defense Intelligence Agency (John Negroponte) said that foreign fighters constitute less than 10% of the insurgents in Iraq. Other U.S. commanders said in July 2007 that approximately 60-80 foreign fighters come across the border every month to participate in the Iraq insurgency.[38] The specific nationalities of the foreigners are the subject of much speculation; one press report in July 2007, quoting U.S. officials in Iraq, say that about 40% of the foreign fighters in Iraq are of Saudi origin.[39]

AQ-I Strategy

Although the United States and its Iraqi partners have, from the inception of the insurgency, conducted a broad counter-insurgency campaign, a major U.S. focus has always been on Abu Musab al-Zarqawi, his network, and his successors. On March 15, 2004, Ansar al-Islam (see above) was named as "Foreign Terrorist Organization" under the Immigration and Nationality Act. On October 15, 2004, the State Department named the "Monotheism and Jihad Group"—the successor to Ansar al-Islam—as an FTO. The designation said that the Monotheism group "was ... responsible for the U.N. headquarters bombing in Baghdad."[40] Later that month, perhaps in response to that designation, Zarqawi changed the name of his organization to "Al Qaeda Jihad Organization" in the Land of Two Rivers (Mesopotamia–Iraq)—commonly known now as Al Qaeda in Iraq, or AQ-I. The FTO designation was applied to the new name.

Along with the designations came stepped up U.S. military efforts to find and capture or kill Zarqawi. There were several reported "near misses," according to press reports.[41] However, on June 7, 2006, U.S. forces were able to track Zarqawi to a safe house near the city of Baqubah, in the mixed Sunni-Shiite province of Diyala, and an airstrike by one U.S. F-16 mortally wounded him.

Related Groups/Ansar Al Sunna. While focusing primarily on Zarqawi, U.S. officials were also attempting to analyze the evolution of the foreign component of the Iraq insurgency. Attention began to focus on a group calling itself Ansar al-Sunna, which apparently was an offshoot of the Zarqawi network and was operating in northern Iraq, including the Kurdish areas and areas of Arab Iraq around Mosul. It was named as an FTO as an alias of Ansar al-Islam when the latter group was designated in March 2004, and Ansar al-Sunna remains on the FTO list. In its most significant attack after the fall of Saddam Hussein, the group claimed responsibility for February 1, 2004, twin suicide attacks in Irbil, northern Iraq. The attacks killed over 100 Kurds, including some senior Kurdish officials.[42] Another major attack—attributed to Ansar al-Sunna by the State Department "Country Reports on Terrorism: 2006" (released April 2007 by the State Department Office of the Coordinator for Counterterrorism)—was the December 2004 suicide bombing of a U.S. military dining facility at Camp Marez in the northern city of Mosul, which killed 13 U.S. soldiers. The State Department report says that Ansar al-Sunna "continues to conduct attacks against a wide range of targets including Coalition Forces, the Iraqi government and security forces, and Kurdish and Shia figures."

Before his death, Zarqawi largely set AQ-I's strategy in Iraq—an effort to provoke all out civil war between the newly dominant Shiite Arabs and the formerly pre-eminent Sunni Arabs. Zarqawi apparently calculated that provoking civil war could, at the very least, undermine Shiite efforts to consolidate their political control of post-Saddam Iraq. Ultimately, the strategy could compel U.S. forces to leave Iraq by undermining U.S. public support for the war effort, and thereby leaving the Shiite government vulnerable to continued AQ-I and Sunni attack. The strategy might have been controversial among Al Qaeda circles, as evidenced by a purported letter (if genuine) from the number two Al Qaeda leader, Ayman al-Zawahiri, to Zarqawi, in July 2005. In that letter, Zawahiri questions the strategy by arguing that committing violence against Shiite civilians and religious establishments will undermine the support of the Iraqi people for AQ-I and the Sunni "resistance" more broadly. [43]

To implement its strategy, AQ-I under Zarqawi continued to focus primarily on spectacular suicide bombings intended to cause mass Shiite casualties or to destroy sites sacred to Shiites. Several suicide bombings were conducted in 2005 against Shiite celebrations, causing mass casualties. The most notable bombing was the February 22, 2006, bombing of the Shiite "Golden Mosque" in Sunni-inhabited Samarra, which is in Salahuddin Province. The bombing largely destroyed the golden dome of the mosque.

It touched off widespread Shiite reprisals against Sunnis nationwide and is widely considered to have started the "civil war." Many sources and analyses[44] attribute the Samarra bombing to AQ-I, although the State Department terrorism report for 2006, cited earlier, does not specifically cite AQ-I as the perpetrator of the attack. On several occasions, President Bush has said that Zarqawi largely succeeded in that strategy, although he and other senior Administration officials do not say that the security situation in Iraq can be characterized as "civil war."

Reaction to AQ-I and Evolution of AQ-I Structure

The Zarqawi strategy of attempting to provoke civil war, and some of its ideology and practices, were not universally popular among Iraq's Sunnis, even among some Sunni insurgent groups. Some Iraqi Sunni insurgents believed that attacks should be confined to "combatant"targets—Iraqi government forces, most of which are Shiite, Iraqi government representatives, and U.S. and other coalition forces. Iraqi Sunnis purportedly have concrete political goals in Iraq, and some AQ-I tactics, such as attacks on Shiite civilians, might prevent any future power sharing compromise with Iraq's Shiites. AQ-I fighters had broader goals—defeating the United States, establishing an Islamic state in Iraq that could expand throughout the region, and other ambitious objectives beyond Iraq. Other Iraqi Sunnis resented AQ-I practices in the regions where AQ-I fighters congregated, including reported enforcement of strict Islamic law—segregation by sex, forcing males to wear beards, banning all alcohol sales and consumption, and like measures. In some cases, according to a variety of press reports, AQ-I fighters killed Iraqi Sunnis found violating these strictures.

Others believe that the strains between AQ-I and Iraqi Sunni insurgent fighters were a competition for power and control over the insurgency. According to this view, Iraqi Sunni leaders no more wanted to be dominated by foreign Sunnis than they did by Iraqi Shiites or U.S. soldiers. One concrete sign of the strains ermeged in May 2005 in the form of a reported battle between AQ-I fighters and Iraqi Sunni tribal militiamen in the western town of Husaybah. Still, despite these differences, during 2003–2006 these strains were mostly muted as Iraqi Sunnis cooperated with AQ-I toward the broader goal of overturning the Shiite-dominated, U.S.-backed power structure in Iraq.

In early 2006, just before the Golden Mosque bombing referenced above, there were indications that Zarqawi was aware of and attempting to counter the strains developing between AQ-I and the Iraqi Sunni political and insurgent structures. In January 2006, AQ-I announced formation of the "Mujahidin Shura Council"—an umbrella organization of six groups including AQ-I and five Iraqi Sunni insurgent groups, mostly those with an Islamist ideology. Iraqi Sunni insurgent groups dominated by ex-Baath

Party and ex-Saddam era military members apparently did not join the Mujahidin Shura Council. Forming the Mujahidin Shura Council appeared to many to be an attempt by AQ-I to demonstrate that it was working cooperatively with its Iraqi Sunni hosts and not seeking their subordination. To further this impression, in April 2006, the Mujahidin Shura Council announced that an Iraqi, Abdullah Rashid (aka Abu Umar) al-Baghdadi, had been appointed its leader, although there were doubts as to Baghdadi's true identity. (In July 2007, a captured AQ-I operative said Baghdadi does not exist at all, but was a propaganda tool to disguise AQ-I's large role in the insurgency.[45]) AQ-I continued to operate under the Mujahidin Shura Council at least until Zarqawi's death in June 2006.

The shift to increased integration with Iraqi Sunni insurgents continued after Zarqawi's demise. After his death, Abu Ayub al-Masri (an Egyptian, also known as Abu Hamza al-Muhajir) was formally named leader of the Mujahidin Shura Council (and therefore leader of AQ-I). According to the State Department terrorism report for 2006, al-Masri has "continued [Zarqawi's] strategy of targeting Coalition forces and Shi'a civilians in an attempt to foment sectarian strife." In October 2006, al-Masri declared the "Islamic State of Iraq" (ISI) organization under which AQ-I and its allied groups now claim their attacks. ISI appeared to be a replacement for the Mujahidin Shura Council. In April 2007, the ISI named a "cabinet" consisting of a minister of war (al-Masri), the head of the cabinet (al-Baghdadi), and seven other "ministers."

The AQ-I moves toward greater cooperation with the Iraqi insurgents did not satisfy the entire Sunni community, even though that community remains highly restive and resentful of the Shiite-dominated government of Prime Minister Nuri al-Maliki. The same factors—Iraqi Sunni fear of AQ-I domination of them, and resentment of AQ-I tactics—remain prevalent and have grown, according to observers. During 2007, U.S. commanders reported increasing sentiment among the Iraqi Sunni community in Anbar Province to drive AQ-I fighters out of Anbar and to cooperate with U.S. efforts to secure the cities and towns of the province. At least 23 Sunni tribal leaders in Anbar formed an "Anbar Salvation Council" that directed about 13,000 young Sunnis to join the national police force and to help secure Ramadi, Fallujah, and other cities in the province. This movement, which observers say is related to but separate from a broader Sunni political coalescence known as the "Awakening," has led to a sharp drop in the number of daily security incidents in the province, according to U.S. commanders. U.S. military leaders say they are trying to spread this trend to other restive Sunni provinces, including Salahuddin, Nineveh, and Diyala.

At the same time, some observers are skeptical that this security trend has ended AQ-I's prospects in Iraq. Suicide bombings, widely attributed to

AQ-I, have continued despite the cooperation of Sunni tribes and insurgents against AQ-I. Many AQ-I fighters have relocated to areas outside Anbar Province, including Diyala (where U.S. forces are now pressuring them with Operation Arrowhead Ripper), Mosul, Tikrit, Kirkuk, Tal Afar, and other areas. Others maintain that, because most of the daily violence is anyway committed by Iraq Sunni insurgents, the overall effect of the turn against AQ-I might be insufficient to materially calm Iraq.

Linkages to Al Qaeda Central Leadership

As discussed briefly above, perhaps the most controversial question about AQ-I is the degree to which it is linked, if at all, to the central leadership of Al Qaeda as represented by Osama bin Laden and Ayman al-Zawahiri, both of whom are widely believed to be hiding in areas of Pakistan near the border with Afghanistan. That degree of linkage, if any, might determine to what extent the U.S. combat effort in Iraq is part of the overall post-September 11 war on the Al Qaeda organization, and whether or not AQ-I might seek to be attacking the U.S. homeland.

As discussed above, on July 24, 2007, President Bush devoted a speech almost exclusively to this issue. In making an argument that AQ-I is closely related to Al Qaeda's central leadership, the President noted the following details, including:

- In 2004, Zarqawi formally joined Al Qaeda and pledged allegiance to bin Laden. Bin Laden then publicly declared that Zarqawi was the "Prince of Al Qaeda in Iraq." President Bush stated that U.S. intelligence says Zarqawi had met both bin Laden and Zawahiri. He asserted later in the speech that, according to U.S. intelligence, AQ-I is a "full member of the Al Qaeda terrorist network."
- After Zarqawi's death, bin Laden sent an aide named Abd al-Hadi al-Iraqi to help Zarqawi's successor, al-Masri, but al-Iraqi was captured before reaching Iraq.
- That AQ-I's leaders including several foreigners, including a Syrian, a Saudi, and Egyptian, and a Tunisian, and that in June 2007, U.S. forces killed in Iraq an Al Qaeda facilitator named Mehmet Yilmaz.
- That a captured AQ-I leader, an Iraqi named Khalid al-Mashhadani, had told U.S. authorities that Baghdadi was fictitious. In July 2007, Brig. Gen. Bergner, a U.S. military spokesman, told journalists that Mashhadani is an intermediary between al-Masri and bin Laden and Zawahiri.
- In line with the increasing AQ-I efforts to cooperate with Iraqi Sunni insurgents, most of AQ-I's fighters and some of its leaders are Iraqi.
- That AQ-I is the only insurgent group in Iraq "with stated ambitions to make the country a base for attacks outside Iraq." Referring to the

> November 9, 2005, terrorist attacks on hotels in Zarqawi's native Jordan, President Bush said AQ-I "dispatched terrorists who bombed a wedding reception in Jordan." Referring to an August 2005 incident, he said AQ-I "sent operatives to Jordan where they attempted to launch a rocket attack on U.S. Navy ships" docked at the port of Aqaba.

In his speech, President Bush acknowledged but refuted some of the counter-arguments. Some experts believe that links between Al Qaeda's central leadership and AQ-I are tenuous, at best, and that the few operatives linking the two do not demonstrate an ongoing, substantial relationship. Others point to the Zawahiri admonishment of Zarqawi, discussed above, as evidence that there is not a close connection between the two. Still others maintain that there is little evidence that AQ-I seeks to attack broadly outside Iraq, and that those incidents that have taken place have been in Jordan, where Zarqawi might have wanted to try to undermine King Abdullah II, whom Zarqawi opposed as too close to the United States.

Endnotes

[1] Duelfer report text is at [http://news.findlaw.com/hdocs/docs/iraq/cia93004wmdrpt.html]. The report is named for Charles Duelfer, the last head of the WMD search as part of the Iraq Survey Group. The first such head was Dr. David Kay.

[2] For analysis of the former regime's WMD and other abuses, see CRS Report RL32379, Iraq: Former Regime Weapons Programs, Human Rights Violations, and U.S. Policy, by Kenneth Katzman.

[3] Pincus, Walter. "Munitions Found in Iraq Renew Debate." *Washington Post*, July 1, 2006.

[4] Transcript: Bush Gives Saddam Hussein and Sons 48 Hours to Leave Iraq. Department of State, Washington File. March 17, 2003.

[5] Priest, Dana and Glenn Kessler. "Iraq, 9/11 Still Linked By Cheney." *Washington Post*, September 29, 2003.

[6] Secretary of State Addresses the U.N. Security Council. Transcript, February 5, 2003.

[7] Powell Affirms Confidence in Decision to Wage Iraq War. U.S. Department of State, Washington File. January 8, 2004.

[8] 9/11 Commission Report, p. 66.

[9] Hayes, Stephen. "Case Closed." The Weekly Standard, November 24, 2003. Online at [http://www.weeklystandard.com/Content/Public/Articles/000/000/003/378fmxyz.asp]

[10] Milbank, Dana. "Bush Hails Al Qaeda Arrest in Iraq; President Defends U.S. Intelligence." *Washington Post*, January 27, 2004.

[11] Goldberg, Jeffrey. "The Unknown. The CIA and the Pentagon take Another Look at Al Qaeda and Iraq." *The New Yorker*, February 10, 2003.

[12] Pincus, Walter. "Report Cast Doubt on Iraq-Al Qaeda Connection." *Washington Post*, June 22, 2003.

[13] Goldberg, Jeffrey. "The Unknown. The CIA and the Pentagon Take Another Look at Al Qaeda and Iraq." *The New Yorker*, February 10, 2003.

[14] Gunaratna, Rohan. Inside Al Qaeda. New York, Columbia University Press, 2002. Pp.27–29.

[15] Text of an audio message purported to be from Osama bin Laden. BBC News, February 12, 2003.

[16] "Al Qaeda High Value Targets." Defense Intelligence Agency chart (unclassified). September 12, 2003.

[17] Conversations with Administration officials involved in the war on terrorism. 2002-2003.

[18] Chivers, C.J. Repulsing Attack By Islamic Militants, "Iraqi Kurds Tell of Atrocities." *New York Times*, December 6, 2002.

[19] U.S. Department of State. Patterns of Global Terrorism, 2002. April 2003. p. 79.

[20] "U.S. Uncertain About Northern Iraq Group's Link to Al Qaida." Dow Jones Newswire, March 18, 2002.

[21] Priest, Dana and Glenn Kessler. "Iraq, 9/11 Still Linked By Cheney." *Washington Post*, September 29, 2003.

[22] Hosenball, Mark, Michael Isikoff and Evan Thomas. Cheney's Long Path to War. *Newsweek*, November 17, 2003.

[23] Priest, Dana and Glenn Kessler. "Iraq, 9/11 Still Linked By Cheney." *Washington Post*, September 29, 2003.

[24] Risen, James. "Iraqi Agent Denies He Met 9/11 Hijacker in Prague Before Attacks on the U.S." *New York Times*, December 13, 2003.

[25] Gertz, Bill. "September 11 Report Alludes to Iraq-Al Qaeda Meeting." *Washington Times*, July 30, 2003.

[26] Risen, James. "Iraqi Agent Denies He Met 9/11 Hijacker in Prague Before Attacks on U.S." *New York Times*, December 13, 2003.

[27] Ibid.

[28] State of the Union Message by President Bush. January 20, 2004. Text contained in *New York Times*, January 21, 2004.

[29] Miller, Greg. Iraq-Terrorism Link Continues to Be Problematic. *Los Angeles Times*, September 9, 2003.

[30] President Bush Discusses War on Terror in South Carolina. [http://www.whitehouse.gov/news/releases/2007/07/print/20070724-3.html].

[31] "'Key Judgments' on Terrorist Threat To U.S." *New York Times*, July 18, 2007.

[32] Brinkley, Joel. Few Signs of Infiltration By Foreign Fighters in Iraq. *New York Times*, November 19, 2003.

[33] Stack, Megan. U.S. General Sees Al Qaeda Evidence in Iraq. *Los Angeles Times*, January 30, 2004.

[34] Shanker, Thom. U.S. Commanders Surveys Challenges in Iraq Region. *New York Times*, January 30, 2004.

[35] "U.S. Officials Voice Frustrations With Saudis, Citing Role in Iraq." *New York Times*, July 27, 2007.

[36] Bonner, Raymond and Joel Brinkley. Latest Attacks Underscore Differing Intelligence Estimates of Strength of Foreign Guerrillas. *New York Times*, October 28, 2003.

[37] Shanker, Thom. U.S. Commanders Surveys Challenges in Iraq Region. *New York Times*, January 30, 2004.

[38] Parker, Ned. "Saudis' Role in Iraq Insurgency Outlined." *Los Angeles Times*, July 15, 2007.

[39] "U.S. Officials Voice Frustrations With Saudis, Citing Role in Iraq." Op.cit.

[40] Zarqawi Group Formally Designated Terrorists by State Department. Usinfo.state.gov., October 15, 2004.

[41] Bazzi, Mohammad. "Another Near Miss" *Long Island Newsday*, May 20, 2005.

[42] Al Qaeda Linked Islamist Group Claims Deadly Arbil Attacks in Iraq. Agence France Presse, February 4, 2004.

[43] [http://www. weeklystandard.com/Content/Public/Articles/000/000/006 /203gpuul. asp?pg=2]

[44] One such analysis is: Beehner, Lionel. Backgrounder: Al-Qaeda in Iraq: Resurging or Splintering? Council on Foreign Relations, updated July 16, 2007.

[45] Gordon, Michael. "U.S. Says Insurgent Leader It Couldn't Find Never Was." *New York Times*, July 19, 2007.

DOCUMENT NO. 12

IRAQ: AN UPDATE FROM THE FIELD

Hearing Before the Senate Committee on Foreign Relations

July 19, 2007

Opening Statement of Senator Richard G. Lugar

I join in welcoming Ambassador Crocker. His insights are timely as the Senate continues to debate U.S. policy in Iraq.

The future of that policy increasingly appears to depend on the Administration's report due in September. Regardless of what that report says, however, we must begin now to prepare for what comes next. It is likely that there will be changes in military missions and force levels as the year proceeds. If U.S. military leaders, diplomats, and, indeed, the Congress, are not prepared for these contingencies, they may be executed poorly, especially in an atmosphere in which public demands for troop withdrawals could compel action on a political timetable. We need to lay the groundwork for alternatives, so that when the President and Congress move to a new plan, it can be implemented safely and rapidly.

I am encouraged that the President has announced that he is sending Secretary of State Rice and Defense Secretary Gates to the region to engage in concentrated diplomacy. I would observe that this diplomacy must be ambitious, sustained, and innovative. It must go well beyond conferences with allied nations. We have to consider how diplomacy can change the equation in the region in ways that enhance our prospects for success in Iraq.

Regional diplomacy is not just an accompaniment to our efforts in Iraq. It is a pre-condition for the success of any policy that follows the surge. We cannot sustain a successful policy in Iraq over the long term unless we repair alliances, recruit more international participation in Iraq, anticipate refugee flows, prevent regional aggression, generate new basing options, and otherwise prepare for future developments. If we have not made substantial diplomatic progress by the time a post-surge policy is implemented, our options will be severely constrained, and we will be guessing at a viable course in a rapidly evolving environment.

I believe the most promising diplomatic approach would be to establish a consistent forum related to Iraq that is open to all parties in the Middle East. The purpose of the forum would be to improve transparency of national interests so that neighboring states, including Syria and Iran, would avoid missteps. It would be in the self-interest of every nation in the region to attend such meetings, as well as the United States, EU representatives, or other interested parties. The existence of a predictable and regular forum in the region would be especially important for dealing with refugee problems, regulating borders, exploring development initiatives, and preventing conflict between the Kurds and Turks.

A consistent forum in the Middle East is particularly salient, because that region suffers from conspiracy theories, corruption, and the opaque policies of non-democratic governments. We should be meeting with states on a constant basis and encouraging them to meet with each other as a means of achieving transparency. We should not underestimate the degree to which the lack of transparency in the Middle East intensifies risks of conflict and impedes solutions to regional problems. A constant, predictable diplomatic forum would allow countries and groups to keep an eye on one another. Such a forum would make armed incursions more risky for an aggressor. It would provide a means of applying regional peer pressure against bad behavior. It would also complicate the plans of those who would advance destructive sectarian agendas. If nations or groups decline to attend or place conditions on their participation, their intransigence will be obvious to the other players in the region.

We know the task of initiating even a partial military redeployment from Iraq will be an extremely complicated and dangerous undertaking. I am hopeful that Ambassador Crocker will shed light not just on prevailing conditions in Iraq, but also on what is being done to prepare for a post-surge strategy. I appreciate the time he is making for us, and I look forward to our discussion.

Opening Statement of Joseph R. Biden, Jr.
United States Senator

Mr. Ambassador, thank you for joining us today from Baghdad. I'd also like to welcome Ambassador Satterfield, who is here in the Committee room.

I'd like to express my appreciation to you and the Embassy staff. We recognize the hardships you face and we are grateful for your service.

The purpose of this hearing is straightforward. Mr. Ambassador, we hope to hear from you a candid, unvarnished assessment of the situation on the ground in Iraq, especially the political situation.

The primary goal of the President's military escalation, or build up, was to buy time for the Maliki government to make compromises on political reconciliation.

Last week, the Administration delivered an interim assessment of the Iraqi government's performance on 18 specific benchmarks.

The government made the least amount of progress where it matters most: on the key political benchmarks—oil laws, provincial elections, constitutional revisions, and de-Ba'athification.

The final assessment is due in two months—and the Iraqi parliament is taking one of those months off.

Given the lack of progress since the surge began six months ago, what gives you confidence that we will see any progress between now and September? What can you tell us to give us confidence the final report will be any better than the one we just received?

Mr. Ambassador, I believe that the President's policy, which you are being asked to execute, is based on a fundamentally flawed premise. "If we just give the central government time, it will secure the support and trust of all Iraqis."

In my judgment, that will not happen. There seems to be no trust within the central government, no trust of the government by the people, and no capacity on the part of the central government to deliver basic security and services. And I see no prospect of building that trust and capacity any time soon.

I've been saying that for some time. So has the director of the CIA, General Mike Hayden. Back in November of 2006, he told the Iraq Study Group: "The inability of the central government to govern is irreversible."

The truth is Iraq cannot be governed from the center absent a dictator or an indefinite occupation. Neither of these are possibilities.

Instead, I believe we should promote a political settlement that allows the warring factions breathing room in their own regions, with control over the fabric of their daily lives—police, education, jobs, marriage, religion.

A limited central government would be in charge of truly common concerns, including protecting Iraq's borders and distributing oil revenues.

None of this is an American imposition. It is entirely consistent with the Iraqi Constitution.

We also must initiate a diplomatic offensive to bring in the U.N., major countries and Iraq's neighbors to help implement and oversee the political settlement. It is past time to make Iraq the world's problem, not just our own.

Mr. Ambassador, whether you agree with what I'm proposing or not, the bottom line is this: just about everyone now agrees there is no purely military way to bring stability to Iraq. We need a political settlement.

So I want your best assessment of the prospects for a political settlement, what it would look like, and how we can still help achieve it.

I look forward to your testimony.

Testimony of Ambassador Ryan Crocker

Thank you Mr. Chairman. It is with pleasure that I appear before the Committee for the first time since my confirmation hearing in February. Last week, the President submitted to Congress an interim assessment of the Government of Iraq's progress toward achieving a number of political, economic, and security benchmarks.

I believe it is a fair assessment which demonstrates that while the Government of Iraq is making some progress, there is still much to do and much room for improvement. As we approach September, I and other senior-level Embassy officials are—on a daily basis—personally engaging with the highest levels of the Government of Iraq to make clear that progress on the benchmarks is imperative, to suggest ways forward, and to serve as honest brokers to promote compromise. At the working level, we also maintain daily contact with members of the Iraqi Council of Representatives, from committee heads to rank-and-file members, to monitor progress and serve as advocates for agreement on, and passage of, key legislation.

We do much of our work discreetly. Those who would like to see our efforts fail in the hopes of stalling forward momentum past September 15 are quick to recast our efforts as U.S. coercion and infringements upon Iraqi sovereignty. Recently, there were public demonstrations in Iraq's number one "oil city," Basra, condemning American pressure toward passage of a hydrocarbons law. But discreet should not be confused with ineffective, and we continue to make progress.

I would like to add a general note of caution, however, about benchmarks. The benchmarks can be a useful metric; but the longer I am here, the more I am persuaded that progress in Iraq cannot be analyzed solely in terms of these discrete, precisely defined benchmarks because, in many cases, these benchmarks do not serve as reliable measures of everything that is important—Iraqi attitudes toward each other and their willingness to work toward political reconciliation.

For example, I think if the Committee examines the legislative benchmarks, it is quite possible that Iraq could achieve few of them over the coming months and yet actually be moving in the right direction. Conversely, I think it is possible that all the legislative benchmarks could be achieved without making any real progress toward reconciliation. Merely passing legislation without a broad consensus of all major Iraqi communities will not meet the goals of real or lasting reconciliation. Moreover, passing laws without the requisite consensus will undermine the political will for implementation on the ground following enactment. The benchmarks are useful tools if we remain focused on the broader context—the fundamental reconciliation issues facing Iraq that the benchmark legislation represents.

Furthermore, I would note that the framework of these benchmarks focuses on the central government's capabilities and does not capture achievements made at the Provincial level. The progress in the Provinces, if properly nurtured, could be the basis for more substantial reconciliation efforts: a grassroots effort that produces security and prosperity for the citizens of Iraq.

Our Provincial Reconstruction Teams report that local governments are taking the initiative—meeting the basic security needs of their citizens, planning and budgeting for reconstruction projects, and taking control of their futures by resisting al-Qaida. It is this kind of activity that provides a level of encouragement that potential shortcomings at the national level may be offset by the affirming activities of state and local governments. Moreover, Iraqis at the local level are seeing the results of an improved political and economic process which is critical for a broader national reconciliation.

Realizing that local government, small business, services and employment must play a vital part in the stabilization and sustainability of a self-governing Iraq, we have sharply increased the number of our PRTs, and we are strengthening their staffs. We have deployed ten new PRTs this year and four more will be coming in early September. I have to be honest and say we have not yet deployed enough people in those teams, and we are in the process of expediting staffing efforts.

I know the Committee is interested in our New Embassy Compound—a project which has benefited from your support. Overseas Buildings Operations Director Williams has assured us, as well as the Congress, that the NEC is on schedule and on budget for completion in September. We seek to move personnel into the safer NEC quarters as quickly as possible following installation of the necessary communications, logistical and other support services.

I look forward to your questions and thoughts.

DOCUMENT NO. 13

U.S. POLICY OPTIONS IN THE IRAQ CRISIS

Hearing Before the House Committee on Foreign Affairs

July 17, 2007

Statement of Chairman Lantos

If there was any question about the direction of Congress on Iraq, it has become crystal clear in the past two weeks. With respected Republican leaders like Richard Lugar and John Warner breaking ranks and firmly stating the need for a change in course, the pressure on the Administration is becoming greater by the day. Soon, the chorus of voices calling for a responsible redeployment will be impossible for the White House to quell with a veto threat.

For now, the Administration remains willfully deaf to these calls. But even if the President does veto the redeployment bill that I co-sponsored and that passed the House last week, Congress will send yet another telegram to the door of the White House—and next time, more Republicans will show up to help deliver it. And the time after that, even more will stand up and be counted.

I hope it doesn't come to that, but I fear that it might. The Administration astonishingly signaled yesterday that it is considering a further increase in troop levels in Iraq. Chairman of the Joint Chiefs of Staff Peter Pace said one of the options on the table would be to boost the number after General Petraeus' crucial report in September. This would represent an irresponsible disregard for the strong will of Congress and of the American people.

The Administration is fighting against the tide with a misinformation campaign. After each damning military report and devastating development, the White House spins a story about partial progress and the slimmest of successes.

The fact is that Iraq has spiraled into a civil war that cannot be contained. Four years and four months into the war, the level of violence is once again flaring, as demonstrated by the ghastly bombings yesterday in the city of Kirkuk.

In its interim benchmark report, the Administration again tried to sugarcoat the rapidly deteriorating situation on the ground. Using the most liberal grading standard possible, the Administration could give no more than a 50-percent grade to the Iraqis.

Among the list of the unmet benchmarks were some of the most critical of all, including the disarming of militias and the ability of the Iraqi security forces to operate independently. Let's face it: the troop escalation is a categorical failure and the American people know it.

Like most Americans, I am convinced that the war has dragged on too long and cannot be "won" any time soon by any definition of winning that includes peace and good government. The issue is no longer whether we get out. It is how we get out, how soon, and how we manage the aftermath.

So even if the Senate passes a redeployment bill this week to match ours and the Administration vetoes it, we will continue to insist on a reasonable and responsible withdrawal plan that presents the least-bad option for Iraq, the region, and our national security interests.

Many doomsayers predict the direst of consequences in the aftermath of a withdrawal from Iraq. There is concern about the prospect of regional war and possibly a genocide. There is concern about the possibility of a war between Turkey and the Iraqi Kurds. And there is considerable concern about the prospect that Iraq will fall fully under the sway of Iran once the United States withdraws.

We must grapple with and address these concerns as we craft a withdrawal plan. I look forward to working with Republican leaders on ensuring that our withdrawal is safe and responsible, both for our troops and for Iraq.

A few courageous Republican Senators have seen the writing on the wall and are boldly stating that we must change our strategy urgently. The bill introduced by my friends Senators Warner and Lugar calls for the Administration to adopt a shift in our approach to Iraq by October. While I do not think that their bill goes far enough to really change course, it does employ a tactic that might accomplish a great deal: reconsidering the 2002 war authorization legislation and reshaping it for today's more realistic mission.

I applaud Republican leaders for breaking ranks and I urge Republicans in the Senate to turn up the heat on the White House by voting for a responsible redeployment plan this week as the House has already done. Congress must bring the Administration back down to Earth on Iraq.

The Administration must come to grips with what the Congress and the American people have known for months: We have to finally get our troops out of harm's way. Over the past week, it has become apparent that Congress and the Administration do not just disagree about the war, but are in fact working in two different orbits.

The Administration has no concrete plan to bring an end to the war before the conclusion of its term. Meanwhile, Congress is becoming increasingly committed to crafting strong, substantive initiatives towards a wise redeployment. I urge the Administration finally to heed the calls of the leaders of its own party and the will of the American people.

Witness Statement of Steven N. Simon
Hasib J. Sabbagh Senior Fellow for Middle Eastern Studies Council on Foreign Relations

The Interim Report

The interim surge report underscores the chasm that separates US and Iraqi conceptions of reconciliation. For Americans, reconciliation is the product of a bargaining process through which Sunnis participate in the governance of the state and get their fair share of Iraq's resources.

Iraqis see things differently. Shi'as tend to emphasize the need for justice. The centrality of justice is rooted in the history of Shi'a thought and in their painful experience as Iraqis. For them, justice demands that their suffering under previous regimes—not only Saddam's—be compensated. This in turn necessitates the subordination of Iraq's Sunni population to the needs of the Shi'a community. For the Shi'a-run government, justice must precede reconciliation.

For many Sunnis, reconciliation means restoration. This goes beyond mere inclusion in power sharing arrangements. It means regaining control of the state. For Kurds, reconciliation means recognition of Kurdish autonomy and openness to the Kurds' prospective territorial gains.

These differences will not be reconciled soon. Dethroned elites do not easily surrender their dreams of a reversal of fortune. The process resembles the way people are said to grapple with imminent death through stages of denial, anger, bargaining, depression and acceptance. Sunnis are not yet near the bargaining stage of dealing with Saddam's overthrow.

Duration of Civil Wars

Studies of civil wars since 1945 show that most last seven to ten years and generally end with the military victory of one side or the other, rather than a negotiated settlement. Where power-sharing arrangements have been reached, they have been short-lived and often led to renewed hostilities. Moreover, civil wars tend to be harder to resolve when the rebel side is fractured, a point relevant to the current US strategy of driving wedges in the Sunni insurgency. With or without the presence of US forces, the Iraqi civil war is likely to grind on for some time.

What Purpose Do US Forces Serve?

The large presence of US ground forces has had little effect on Iraqi politics, or on the insurgency. The surge has redistributed insurgent activity but not suppressed it. Ironically, violence now touches more of the country than before, with a corresponding erosion of societal stability and government credibility.

At the same time, the presence of US forces is a godsend to jihadists. Talk of a Korea-like commitment and an elaborate base structure, alongside an unwillingness to discuss a timetable for withdrawal, has fueled suspicion and further energized the jihad.

Meanwhile, given our large presence in Iraq, we are bound to be held responsible for the awful things happening there, even though we are unable to prevent them. The US is culpable, but not capable. Against the background of regrettable but unavoidable battlefield excesses, the US seems not only ineffectual but cruel. This image of America is continuously broadcast to the world in the form of the 900 insurgent communiqués and videos generated from within Iraq every month.

Why a Near Term Decision to Withdraw is Essential

Domestic public support for the war has dwindled. Casualty tolerance is weakening and could crack at any time. A US pull-out precipitated by a sudden collapse of domestic opinion will appear confused and ill-prepared; the hasty reaction to a sudden reversal. It is vital that a withdrawal appear, to the extent possible, to be a matter of volition, not compulsion. We must therefore begin planning now for a deliberate and orderly redeployment of US forces from Iraq.

Which is Worse: The Cost of Staying or the Cost of Leaving?

The Administration contends that the hypothetical costs of withdrawal are necessarily bigger than the demonstrated costs of staying. Predictions of catastrophe, like President Bush's assertion that the results of a so-called "precipitous" withdrawal will be "horrific," have miscast uncertain speculation as unquestionable fact. In consequence, the unknowable has become the unthinkable. But question we must.

Spread of Civil War

Will the withdrawal of U.S. forces open the door to "regional chaos," as the Administration says? Armed clashes between or among the armies of Iraq's neighbors do not seem likely. Mid-to-late twentieth century civil wars in the region—in Algeria, Yemen, Afghanistan, Pakistan, even Lebanon—did not spark wider wars. In most cases, surrounding countries tried to protect their interests through proxies, while avoiding the risks and costs of military intervention. Indeed, this low profile competition is already underway in Iraq, albeit confined to its borders. Without a diplomatic process designed to stave off, or at least regulate moves by neighboring countries to protect their interests using proxies, meddling will persist.

The real threat of instability is directed at Jordan, which is host to an Iraqi refugee cohort equal to one-tenth its population. This calls for international assistance and heightened vigilance by Jordanian security forces. But there is little that a large US military presence in Iraq can do to mitigate the threat.

Genocide

In thinking about genocide, it is worth remembering that Sunni insurgents already act with impunity and that only in neighborhoods where the US presence is temporarily bulked-up have militias desisted from cleansing operations. The question is how much worse it can get.

A prudent forecast is that the lack of organizational capacity, broad communal consent and heavy weapons on either side will impede a drastic increase in the already appalling casualty rate. The largely Sunni areas are uninteresting to the Shi'a as objects of conquest. Without artillery, armor, and attack aircraft, Shi'a forces will be hard pressed to reduce Sunni majority cities to rubble in the way that Serbs dealt with Croatian or Muslim urban areas in the former Yugoslavia. Ethnic cleansing in mixed areas will continue, refugees and the internally displaced will grow, bombings and death squads will claim many lives, but the necessary conditions for nationwide genocidal violence are as yet absent.

The Credibility Cost of Leaving

The Administration believes that the withdrawal of American forces would damage American credibility. This disregards the damage that floundering in Iraq has already inflicted on America's reputation for competence, integrity and military prowess.

It is also unclear how staying the very course that exposed America to worldwide ridicule and disenchantment will somehow cause America to be admired and trusted.

Al Qaeda will no doubt revel in the sight of American troops withdrawing from Iraq. But AQ already sees Iraq as a victory. If we stay, AQ will have it both ways: vindicated by America's failure to control events and by Washington's determination, despite fierce resistance, to occupy the heartland of the Arab world.

At a strategic level, an orderly, systematic withdrawal is unlikely to affect the calculation of a future state adversary deciding whether to push its luck in a confrontation with the United States. In such a crisis, the adversary will be focused on assessing the stakes for the US and Washington's ability to defend them at that moment. The adversary is unlikely to look back to what the US did or didn't do years before in Iraq.

How Should the US Deal with an Al Qaeda Mini-State in Iraq?

There is no easy fix for this problem we created. The bleed-out specter—violence radiated from Iraq to other countries near and far—is real, as the

UK, Lebanon and Jordan have experienced. AQI has also deepened the sectarian divide in Iraq. While its numbers are small, the recruitment pool is deep and mostly indigenous to Iraq.

The cracks in the Islamic Army of Iraq and the 1920 Revolution Brigade have been greeted in Washington as a welcome development. This, however, is a misreading of events. These splits reflect a tendency for insurgents to opt for more radical solutions when the so-called moderates do not appear to be capable of delivering results. Fissures in the insurgency reflect defections to al Qaeda, rather than a growing taste for moderation. It is therefore premature to celebrate episodic, local rifts between AQ affiliates and other insurgents or see them simply as a rejection of AQ.

In helping the good "bad guys" fight the bad "bad guys," we need to remember several things:

- this is not a mission for which the US needs 165,000 troops in Iraq;
- the US troop presence helps drive the very insurgency that *ad hoc* deals between US and insurgent commanders are supposed to undermine;
- for AQI, becoming the target of good "bad guys" will likely help it to recruit new fighters by conferring on AQ the glow of integrity and even nobility;
- and lastly, the moving parts of the insurgency can reengage quickly to threaten not only US forces but the Iraqi government.

Why should the US not withdraw its forces immediately?

A rapid withdrawal is logistically feasible only if we were to leave behind the equipment that couldn't be flown out. Road distances and port and shipping capacities will limit necessarily the speed with which our materiel can be redeployed.

If we wish to give the Iraqi army our equipment, that is one thing. If not, perhaps because the Iraqi army might use it for genocidal purposes, then leaving materiel behind will cause our departure to be seen as a rout. *This perception must be avoided.* Time, then, must be taken.

We will also need time to put in place a multilateral structure to support economic recovery; care for refugees and the displaced; improve border controls; and plan for an international humanitarian effort should Iraq disintegrate.

Time will also be needed to negotiate a withdrawal with the Iraqi government that might afford a window through which to assess Iraqi forces, give Washington the clout to enforce a red line against genocidal actions by the government, and to offset some of Tehran's significant influence, thereby giving Iraqi nationalists an alternative to Iranian patronage.

Conclusion

Predictions of across-the-board post-withdrawal disasters, or fantasies about Iraqi national reconciliation must not deter us from considering all available options.

Regional chaos is unlikely, as is genocide within Iraq. While the al-Qaedization of the insurgency is underway and internecine violence will remain severe, a long term US troop commitment won't stop these trends.

US credibility is already tattered. The way to restore it is by cutting our losses in Iraq, shifting the basis of our support for the country toward diplomacy and economic development, and showing that Washington can still act creatively and effectively in the region.

Withdrawal is the strategically appropriate course of action, provided that it is systematic, orderly, and geared to a coherent diplomatic gameplan. The sooner we grasp this nettle, the better.

Testimony of James Dobbins[1]
The RAND Corporation

Whether or not one believes the invasion of Iraq to have been necessary, there is little dispute that its occupation, stabilization and reconstruction have been poorly handled. Many actions have been cited as turning points in this regard, from disbanding the Iraqi army to firing much of its civil service. Personally, I am more inclined to attribute the difficulties American efforts have encountered to two more fundamental and underlying policy choices.

The first of these choices was the low priority assigned to public security. The second was the even lower priority attached to collaboration with neighboring countries.

The first responsibility of any occupying power is the security of the civilian population in its charge. In the spring of 2003, as looters stripped every public edifice in the country to the bare wall, American troops stood passively by, responding to inquiring journalists that preserving public order was not their job. Whose job, one may ask, did they think it was? They had just conquered a foreign country. Had no one reviewed the laws of armed conflict as regard occupation before launching the invasion?

Moral and legal responsibilities aside, experience has shown that the ability of any occupying force to secure the cooperation of a civilian population depends most heavily upon its ability to afford that population protection in return. If an occupied people feel safer by reason of the occupier's presence, they will be inclined to collaborate. If not, then not. The United States failed in this single measure of success from the day Saddam's statue fell. Long before any organized resistance movement emerged the Iraqi population was exposed to the depredations of thieves, rapists, and murderers. For several years thereafter, the primary focus of American military efforts was seeking out and destroying resistance elements, rather than securing the civilian population. During these years American military authorities made no effort to tabulate or keep track of civilian casualties, which should have been the primary benchmark of their success or failure.

Neighboring states bear considerable responsibility for the current state of Iraq, but the United States bears even greater responsibility for thinking that the influence of these societies could be safely ignored. If two decades of nation building experience had taught us anything, it should have been the impossibility of holding together failing nations without the cooperation of adjoining states. Nearby societies simply have too much access and too much influence, by reason of proximity, personal relationships and cultural affinity, to be ignored. Neither can these societies be persuaded to eschew interference. After all, it is they, not more distant countries like the United States that will get the refugees, the crime, the terrorism, the endemic disease, and the economic disruption caused by having a failed state on their doorstep. These neighboring societies cannot afford to remain uninvolved, and they will not.

Unfortunately, left to their own devices, neighboring states will tend to exacerbate the disintegration they would generally prefer to avoid. In any failing state, all claimants for power seek foreign sponsors, and all neighboring states back favorites in this contest. As a result, by backing rival claimants for power, they accelerate the breakup they are usually trying to stop. This effect can be avoided only if neighboring governments can be persuaded to exert their influence along convergent, rather then divergent lines, pressing the local political leaders to coalesce rather than to fight.

American success in ending the Bosnian civil war in 1995 depended upon bringing two neighboring states that were fighting a proxy war there, Serbia and Croatia, into the negotiating process. Those states, and their leaders, were personally guilty of the genocide America was trying to stop. Yet Washington engaged these leaders, gave them a privileged status in the negotiations, and then worked with them to implement the peace agreement. President Milosevic and Tudjman both won subsequent elections, based in part on the prestige they had garnered through this connection. Had the Clinton Administration not been willing to pay that price, however, the war in Bosnia would have continued.

In the aftermath of 9/11, the United States worked with all the very states that had been fomenting civil war in Afghanistan for twenty years. With their help the United States was able to overthrow the Taliban in short order, and then even more quickly replace it with a broadly based government under Hamid Karzai. These achievements were only possible because the United States sought and gained the support of all of Afghanistan's neighbors, to include basing rights in Tajikistan and Uzbekistan, over flight rights in Pakistan and diplomatic support from Iran. In fact, Iran played a decisively positive role in the negotiations that led to the formation, installation and subsequent consolidation of the Karzai government.

Unlike its approach in Afghanistan, the United States entered Iraq on the basis of a proposition that precluded this sort of support. The United States did not invade Afghanistan with the declared objective of making that country a model of democracy, which by its very existence was intended to undermine the legitimacy of all its neighboring regimes, and ultimately lead to their replacement. Had this been its stated intention, Washington would have never achieved the regional support which brought quick success in Afghanistan.

By contrast, the United States did enter Iraq loudly proclaiming the intention to turn that country into a model democracy, the example of which would undermine neighboring regimes and ultimately lead to their replacement. Needless to say, this was not a project that other regional governments were likely to buy into. Nor have they.

In so describing its mission in Iraq, the United States effectively excluded the possibility of securing regional support for its efforts there.

The question before this Committee today is whether there is still a chance for the United States, at this late date, to rectify these two errors, to win the confidence of the Iraqi people and to secure the cooperation of Iraq's neighbors. My answer to the first question is probably not; to the second, possibly, but only if Washington makes such an effort the centerpiece of its Middle Eastern diplomacy for the rest of this Administration's term.

The Administration's latest report to Congress indicates that only very limited progress has been made by the Iraqi political leadership in reconciling their differences over the future shape and direction of their country. The American military does seem to have made some progress in bringing down levels of sectarian violence and securing cooperation of Sunni tribal forces to combat Al Qaeda. Both developments reflect local accommodations which seem quite fragile. The reduced sectarian killings seem to reflect a decision by the Mahdi Army and other Shia militia to stand down temporarily while the American "surge" runs its course. The Sunni militia who are fighting Al Qaeda today could well return to attacking American forces tomorrow.

Opinion polling indicates that the overwhelming majority of the Iraqi people want American troops to leave, if not immediately, then soon. A smaller number, but still a majority of Iraqis, actually believe that attacks upon American forces are justified. Under General Petraeus's leadership American forces are finally putting the security of the civilian population at the center of their strategy. Had we done this four years ago, Iraqi attitudes toward the American presence might have been very different today. At this late stage, however, it seems unlikely that American forces can gain the confidence and thus secure the cooperation of the Iraqi people.

Neither will it be easy to gain the confidence and secure the cooperation of Iraq's neighbors. Nevertheless, all of these governments have strong incentives to avoid a total collapse of the Iraqi state, which would be the most likely consequence of an early and complete American withdrawal. The threat of military disengagement thus could give the United States some potential leverage with these states. To employ that leverage, however, Washington will need to engage them much more intensively than we have to date.

Last December the Iraq Study Group recommended a "diplomatic surge." Two weeks ago, in the Washington Post, former Secretary of State Kissinger did the same. Last week Senators Warner and Lugar introduced legislation to the same effect. No one believes that diplomacy alone will reverse the tide in Iraq, nor can one be certain of obtaining the cooperation of states like Iran, Syria and Saudi Arabia, all of whom have been quite hostile to our efforts in Iraq for the reasons I have cited. Those who advocate a diplomatic surge simply believe that trying to engage these and other regional governments is the last, best hope of retrieving something from the impending debacle.

Such a process cannot succeed unless the United States makes stabilizing Iraq its top objective in the region. In 1995 American diplomacy succeeded in ending the civil war in Bosnia because until peace was achieved, nothing else was more important. Other issues in American relations with Russia, our European allies and the Balkan states took second place to ending that war. Competing concerns, including ethic cleansing in Kosovo and democratization in Serbia were subordinated to that priority.

Similarly, in 2001, the United States succeeded in overthrowing and replacing the Taliban in a matter of weeks because all other objectives were subordinated to that goal. The Bush Administration embraced Pakistan, despite its record of nuclear proliferation and support for terrorism, it stopped hectoring Putin about human rights in Chechnya, and it even collaborated with Iran.

The United States has a number of important and legitimate objectives throughout the Middle East, to include denuclearizing Iran, curbing Syrian support for terrorism, preventing civil war in Lebanon, promoting the emergence of a Palestinian state willing to live at peace with Israel, and supporting democratic forces throughout the region. None of these interests should be abandoned, but some may need to be postponed. There is no way we can achieve, or even advance all these objectives simultaneously. It has never been likely, for instance, that the United States could stabilize Iraq and destabilize Iran and Syria at the same time, as it has been trying to do.

Statecraft, after all, is all about choosing, prioritizing and sequencing the objectives of a nation's diplomacy. In 1995, the United States and its allies brought peace to Bosnia at the expense of ignoring ethnic cleansing in Kosovo. In 1999 the United States and its allies liberated Kosovo while leaving Milosevic in power. Then in 2000, the United States and its allies supported his overthrow. Sequencing and prioritization allowed Washington to achieve all its objectives in the Balkans, but not all at the same time. Until the Administration makes hard choices of this sort in the Middle East, it will continue to fail across the board, as it has to date.

The debate in Congress has largely been about American troop levels. The obvious question, therefore, is what sort of American troop levels might emerge from such a process of regional diplomacy, and might be required thereafter to sustain it. The answer, I think is some smaller, but not insignificant number of troops, for some extended, but not indefinite period. In other words, in my judgment, consultations with Iraq and its neighbors would likely lead to a result not dissimilar to that recommended by the Iraq Study Group a year ago.

I would prefer that decisions regarding American troop levels flow from such a diplomatic process, rather than precede it. Faced with a real prospect of American withdrawal, I believe most Iraqi leaders, and all regional governments will urge us to stay, not indefinitely and not necessarily in our current numbers, but in some strength, and for some further period. Open ended consultations about America's future role can thus help us forge a regional consensus about that role, and about the shape of a future Iraq that we currently lack. Knowledge that the United States will not remain indefinitely in Iraq in current numbers, or permanently in at any level can provide American diplomats some leverage in moving governments of the region to recognize their own interests in, and responsibilities for, stabilizing Iraq. I would therefore urge Congressional action that presses the President to move in this direction, without so circumscribing his discretion as to render such diplomacy ineffective.

Admittedly, this is much easier to say than to do. So far the Administration's regional diplomacy has consisted of a series of largely substance free photo-ops without hard bargaining or meaningful follow through. In his last meeting with his Iranian opposite number, our Ambassador to Baghdad did not even have instruction that would let him agree to a second meeting. What can the Administration possibly have believed could be achieved in a single brief encounter with Iran, lasting but a few hours, after years of non-communication?

Neither has there been any visible follow through to Secretary Rice's last meeting with the Syrian Foreign Minister. It appears the Administration is actually discouraging the Israeli government from exploring accommodation with Syria over the Golan Heights. "They know what they have to do," has been the Administration's response to criticism of this policy of non-communication.

In my view President Bush should inform the Iraqi leaders and those if its neighbors that he is rethinking US policy, but wants to hear from all the factions in Iraq, and all the neighboring governments before coming to any conclusions regarding the future American military role. In doing so, he should make clear that his decision about the future size and mission of the American military in Iraq will be heavily influenced by what he hears, and what others are willing to do to help stabilize that country. Further, in order to facilitate and perpetuate these consultations, he should propose establishment of a standing forum, including representatives of Iraq, each of its neighbors and the U.S., perhaps under United Nations auspices.

These representatives should agree to meet daily, in some neutral location, for an indefinite period probably extending several months into the future to work together on common approaches toward the crisis in Iraq. Their objective would not be to produce a communiqué, or even a treaty, but rather to develop an effective, continual working relationship among all those with a stake in Iraq's future.

The gathering I suggest should not be the exclusive forum for helping bring peace to Iraq. There should also be scope, at some point, for an internationally sponsored gathering of all the warring factions in Iraq. There should also be a wider forum bringing together the many states and organizations that could contribute to the reconstruction of Iraq once some minimal level of security was restored. Neither of these gatherings is likely to be productive, however, as long as Iraq's neighbors are operating at cross purposes there. I would therefore advise the Administration to begin with the core group consisting of Iraq, its neighbors and the United States, moving to constitute the other gatherings as the situation permits.

The American habit is to decide and then consult. In this case, I would recommend the opposite. Uncertainty about our ultimate intentions can, in this instance, provide us leverage with the Iraqis and their neighbors. Obviously, in the end, we will make our own decisions. Those decisions will be wiser and more sustainable, however, if they are informed by genuine consultation and buttressed by local and regional support.

Endnotes

[1] The opinions and conclusions expressed in this testimony are the author's alone and should not be interpreted as representing those of RAND or any of the sponsors of its research. This product is part of the RAND Corporation testimony series. RAND testimonies record testimony presented by RAND associates to federal, state, or local legislative committees; government-appointed commissions and panels; and private review and oversight bodies. The RAND Corporation is a nonprofit research organization providing objective analysis and effective solutions that address the challenges facing the public and private sectors around the world. RAND's publications do not necessarily reflect the opinions of its research clients and sponsors.

Testimony of Michael Rubin, Ph.D. Resident Scholar American Enterprise Institute for Public Policy Research

Mr. Chairman, Honorable Members. Thank you for this opportunity to testify from Camp Pendleton, California, where the 11th Marine Regiment is preparing for deployment to Iraq. The danger they face and their willingness to undertake this courageous mission adds gravity to our discussion here today.

The Initial Benchmark Assessment Report, released on July 12, 2007, painted a mixed picture: While the surge has created space to further training of the Iraqi security forces and reduced death squad activity and ethnic and sectarian cleansing, it has not, however, stopped terrorism. Nor have Iraq's political leaders met our political benchmarks. Still, there is reason for guarded optimism. It took five months after President Bush's announcement of the surge approach to deploy the five additional Army brigades and Marine elements into theater. Only on June 15, 2007, with the commencement of Operation Phantom Thunder, did Generals Petraeus and Odierno inaugurate the surge strategy in earnest. Its success after only one month is impressive.

Nevertheless, today policymakers in this room and outside debate cutting short the surge and switching course. While few favor immediate withdrawal, there is open debate about other options:

- Reducing presence and limiting troops to training missions only
- Redeployment to neighboring countries
- Redeployment to Iraqi Kurdistan.
- So-called soft partition; and
- Increasing diplomatic engagement with neighboring states

None of these strategies will solve the problems that Congress has identified. They will not better the situation in Iraq nor make the United States safer. Indeed, they may make them far worse. Each involves ceding ground to terrorists or to Iranian influence. Each also sends the message that, when faced with terrorism, America runs.

Precipitous withdrawal is ill-advised. In Lebanon and in Somalia, our quick withdrawal encouraged terrorism. Usama Bin Laden has cited both examples when rallying his followers to further terrorism. There is no way to spin defeat. Nor is wise to believe that we can contain violence within Iraq should we withdraw. Such a strategy did not work when the Taliban ruled Afghanistan. It is risky to believe that, in a global age, it will work in Iraq.

Rather than bring stability or victory; partial withdrawal will ensure chaos and defeat. It is ironic that many who once criticized Defense Secretary

Donald Rumsfeld because he deployed too few troops to stabilize Iraq would now counsel replicating his strategy. The major benefit of the surge is that it creates room to further train and to develop the Iraqi Security Forces. With fewer U.S. troops in Iraq, it will not be possible to continue training at the same level and with the same rigor. The ability to train sufficient Iraqis to guarantee to stabilize Iraq will be the chief determinant of U.S. success.

Over-the-horizon deployment will place the U.S. military's ability to conduct missions hostage to the countries in which they are stationed. The diplomatic cost will be heavy, and effectiveness minimal. When our troops or our allies are engaged in a fight and need an instant response, we should not need to depend on an application to the Saudi, Kuwaiti, or Jordanian foreign ministries to cross borders or clear airspace. Cross-border operations are seldom rapid.

Nor is redeployment into Iraqi Kurdistan wise. The Iraqi Kurdish leadership's rhetorical declarations that they are America's best regional ally are more rhetorical than real. While Iraqi Kurdish leaders host visiting American delegations for lavish dinners, they also enable az-Zawraa, the most virulent anti-American and pro-insurgent television, to broadcast from their territory. Masud Barzani, the President of Iraqi Kurdistan, has both enabled the Iranian Revolutionary Guards to increase their presence in the region and interfered with U.S. attempts to intercept those planning attacks on Americans. Barzani has provided safe-haven and arms to PKK terrorists responsible for the deaths in Turkey of more than 100 people since January alone.

It is tragic that Turkish-American relations have been so rocky since 2003. This is the result both of bungled U.S. diplomacy and the rhetoric and politics of a prime minister whose tenure may end with elections this Sunday. Regardless of our differences with Ankara, Washington should not turn a blind eye toward terrorism against such an important NATO ally nor should it lend protection to those who support such terrorism. Redeploying troops in Iraqi Kurdistan short of an end to the PKK's presence in northern Iraq would likely spark greater conflict and could conceivably lead to Turkey's withdrawal from NATO. In the short-term, Congress and the State Department should demand Barzani expel PKK terrorists, renounce any interest beyond the borders of Iraq, and stop weapons smuggling from Iraqi Kurdistan into Turkey.

Partition, hard or soft, is unwise. Any partition would require significant population transfer. But rather than resolve conflict, displaced people catalyze it. The Bosnia model does not apply well. Three years of ethnic cleansing and conflict proportionately far more intense than that currently occurring in Iraq. The Bosnia civil war killed 200,000 people and resulted in the displacement of half that countries population. This would be the proportional equivalent to more than 1.5 million Iraqis killed and twelve million refugees. To advocate for the partition of Iraq would, in effect, involve accelerating civil war and making millions of refugees. But division along ethnic or sectarian lines will not bring stability. Divisions within the United Iraqi Alliance demonstrate the fractured nature of Shi'a leadership. A leadership vacuum still plagues Sunni Arab communities. Kurdish unity is more theoretical than actual. Internal tension plagues the Kurdistan Regional Government. Corruption, resource division, and revenue sharing disputes similar to those which sparked the 1994–1997 intra-Kurdish civil war are on the rise.

Partition will divide Iraq into morsels which Iraq's neighbors will find easier to digest. This is not to condemn federalism. The age of a strongman is over; some Iraqi will advocate for a strong leader, but only so long as he happens to be their brother or cousin. Federalism can ensure Iraqi stability so long as it is administrative, based on the division of resources according to the population of each governorate. The bloodshed sparked by ethno-sectarian federalism will not be contained to Iraq.

Regional diplomacy—especially outreach to Iran and Syria—may appear attractive, but the assumption that Iraq's neighbors seek a peaceful, stable Iraq is false. The Iranian leadership fears that rival Shi'ite religious leadership could emerge in Iraq which could challenge the Iranian leadership's religious and political claims. Short of political domination, Iranian strategists believe limited instability and free rein of pro-Iranian militias to be in their best interest. While diplomats may engage, Iranian diplomats have no power over the Iranians conducting operations in Iraq. Inside the former U.S. embassy in Tehran, a Revolutionary Guards' unit publishes *Amaliyat-i Ravanshenasi* (*Psychological Operations*) a journal dedicated to discussing strategies to stymie the United States in Iraq. This past Friday, July 13, Hashemi Rafsanjani, the former Iranian president whom many in Washington describe as a pragmatist, gave a speech in which he declared, "What a superpower is the United States is when it can be easily trapped in a small country like Iraq?" He continued to predict that the United States would suffer the same lesson in Afghanistan.

Many use Iraq to call for a return to realism. It is ironic that their realism bases itself on a Utopian notion of an adversary's good will. Four days after Secretary of State Condoleezza Rice offered an olive branch to the Islamic Republic, its Supreme Leader, 'Ali Khamene'i ridiculed the offer. "Why don't you admit that you are weak and your razor is blunt?" he asked. Iran's Islamic Revolutionary Guards Corps proceeded to accelerate weapons shipments into Iraq.

When assessing U.S. policy toward Iraq today, it easy to criticize Plan A. It is a leap of logic, however, to assume that Plans B, C, or D are better alternatives. While the Iraqi government has yet to make satisfactory progress toward all benchmarks, public threats to reduce or abandon the U.S. commitment to Iraq are counterproductive. To convince Iraqi politicians to make tough compromises that will anger powerful constituencies requires that the Iraqi leadership knows Washington's commitment is firm. If Washington threatens to leave or reduce its support for the Iraqi leadership, we will force even the most pro-American politicians there to make accommodation with our adversaries. A constant theme of Iranian influence operations is that the United States lacks Iran's staying power. Willing to abandon allies only plays into Tehran's hands and will reverberate far beyond Iraq's borders.

Success in Iraq is possible. It is imperative that the Iraqis take the lead in their future. The U.S. mission should be to enable them to secure their own country. This requires that the surge continues. If the Iraqis do not have the opportunity to develop their own multi-ethnic and multi-sectarian security forces then their country and the wider region will descend into chaos and war. It will take hard work. We should not pull the carpet out from beneath them.

Michael Rubin is a resident scholar at the American Enterprise Institute.

DOCUMENT NO. 14

IRAQ: IS THE ESCALATION WORKING?

Hearing Before the House Committee on Foreign Affairs

June 27, 2007

Statement of Chairman Lantos

The recent U.S. troop escalation in Iraq simply is not working. We are now the proverbial man wandering the barren desert desperately in search of an oasis that doesn't exist.

The predicament facing our nation in Iraq became quite clear long before the surge was announced in January. But even after all outside observers pointed out this mirage, the Administration refused to stop what retired General Barry McCaffrey has called "a fool's errand."

The Administration wanted to make millions of Americans believe that we should wander further into the desert, investing more and more blood and treasure there. This belief, in turn, would reduce the mounting pressure to seek a safe and wise exit. And so it has—at least for some months.

As a long-time professor of economics, let me tell you: you don't consider sunk costs when making decisions about the future. We need a sober assessment of the troop escalation and the situation in Iraq right now, and we need to stop pretending we can attain plainly delusional goals. We need more wake-up calls like we had on Monday, when veteran Republican Senator Dick Lugar said on the Senate floor that continuing to pursue the surge strategy would actually damage our national security interests.

This troop escalation has, in fact, been a categorical and catastrophic failure. The month of May claimed the most U.S. lives in Iraq in more than two-and-a-half years—127 of our brave servicemen and women were killed. June hasn't been much better, with more than 80 U.S. deaths so far.

According to the widely respected Brookings Institution Iraq Index, the number of daily attacks has increased markedly this year, and the period from March through June has been among the deadliest for Iraqi military personnel and police. Four years into the war, these metrics should be decreasing, not increasing.

For the people of Iraq, security and stability are elusive mirages, too. Insurgents have resorted to the sickening strategy of suicide bombings—just Monday, four separate attacks killed at least 40 people. One of these bombings killed six Sunni leaders who had joined with U.S. forces in the battle for stability in Iraq.

Many prominent Republicans have already stated that unless they see substantial progress by September, they will support a drawdown of U.S. forces. But with typical obstinacy, the Administration is already feeding out the line that a little more time and a few more troops will turn things around.

Instead of hoping against hope each day that the mirage will suddenly transform into the oasis of a triumphant U.S. victory in Iraq, let's figure out how to make Iraq as stable as possible. Let's figure out how to save the lives of our courageous soldiers still there—the bullets and roadside bombs that they face every day are all too real.

As we know, there is a slew of proposals on the table right now that range from full withdrawal to partial withdrawal to regional redeployment. I would like to come away from this hearing—and I think my fellow members would appreciate this, too—more informed about the real pros and cons of these plans. I would like us to think with sobriety about the safest and most prudent way out of Iraq.

We will discuss several proposals floating around Washington, some of which are emanating from some prominent and respected public figures and military experts.

Two think tanks recently released thoughtful withdrawal proposals that will serve as fodder for today's discussion. The Center for American Progress promotes withdrawing all but 8,000 to 10,000 troops by the end of 2008, with the remaining forces positioned in northern Iraq to prevent and to contain a possible cross-border conflict between the Kurds and Turkey.

The Center for a New American Security suggests slimming down our Iraq force to 60,000 troops by the beginning of 2009. That force would remain for four more years largely to train the Iraqi army and work with Iraqi leaders to fight insurgents. Improving Iraq's own security forces and army is an absolute necessity for the long-term sustainability of Iraq—a notion that the Baker-Hamilton report described in great detail. This is now long overdue.

In fact, most rational exit strategies suggest reducing our forces in Iraq to those needed for training Iraqi security forces, fighting identified terrorist cells in hotspots, protecting our embassy and reconstruction workers, and shielding important Iraqi infrastructure facilities, such as the Baghdad airport.

Some analysts have proposed variations on regional redeployment, in which the lion's share of our troops would withdraw to bases in nearby countries, such as Kuwait. Many of these troops would remain as a quick-reaction force to strike if serious flare-ups occurred in Iraq.

Others have offered a vision that would include the replacement of our troops with an international stabilization force in Iraq, with many of the troops coming from nearby Middle Eastern and North African countries. Unfortunately, precious few nations have expressed any willingness to commit troops to such a mission so this plan appears to be a non-starter.

Given the abject failure of the escalation, we are no longer debating whether to withdraw. We are discussing how to do it, when to do it, and the number of the remaining force in Iraq.

So with our expert witnesses today, I want to discuss what makes the most sense for Iraq, for the region, and for American forces. No more illusions. We must banish the mirages and take a clear-eyed view of where we are and where we go from here.

Testimony by Maj Gen John Batiste, US Army (Ret.)

Our national strategy for the global war on terror lacks strategic focus; our Army and Marine Corps are at a breaking point with little to show for it; the current "surge" in Iraq is too little, too late; the Government of Iraq is incapable of stepping up to their responsibilities; our nation has yet to mobilize to defeat a very serious threat which has little to do with Iraq; and it is past time to refocus our national strategy and begin the deliberate withdrawal of US forces from Iraq. Indeed, it is time to place America's vital interests first. Our troops are mired in the complexity of a brutal civil war and we have lost sight of the broader objective of defeating world-wide Islamic extremism. The following testimony will address the current situation and recommend a way-ahead. Iraq and Afghanistan are the first two chapters in a very long book and we are off to a terrible start.

Iraq is embroiled in a civil war and the situation is getting further out of control with each passing day. Factions in Iraq will continue killing each other whether or not we are in their country. As many as 3,000 Iraqis are murdered every month and the violence has produced nearly 4 million refugees. The various factions of the insurgency continue to regenerate their numbers at an alarming rate despite staggering losses. The insurgency goes well beyond the influence of Al Qaeda and includes a complex mosaic of Shia and Sunni Islam, Arab and Kurd centuries old animosity, tribal infighting, and a large number of criminal mafia style gangs. To further complicate the situation, Iraq's neighbors in the region all have different objectives and agendas. The situation is most alarming because Iraq is distracting the United States from the main effort of defeating world-wide Islamic extremism while draining our national treasure in blood and dollars.

The Bush administration's strategy lacks strategic focus. General John Sheehan may have said it best when he recently said, "there is no agreed-upon strategic view of the Iraq problem or the region ... the current Washington decision-making process lacks a linkage to a broader view of the region and how the parts fit together strategically." Our current Iraqi measures of effectiveness delve deep into the details of Iraq's national reconciliation and de-Ba'athification. These measures are incredibly important for Iraq, but may matter little to US strategic interests and defeating Al Qaeda. When and how will we complete the work in Afghanistan and root out the terror networks in other parts of the world, such as northwestern Pakistan? Indeed, Iraq is a side-show that is diluting our focus. Through most of this century, we will face expanding Islamic extremism, asymmetric demographics, competition for decreasing energy resources, the effects of the "haves and have nots" driven by globalization, global climate change, and unstable population migration. What American desperately needs now is a political framework defined by an ever expanding global alliance of equals—disciplined diplomacy based on a vision that is focused on long-term objectives. The security implications are staggering and American's expect our government, both the executive branch and the Congress, to address our real enemies—Islamic extremist groups to include Al Qaeda type organizations, and the nation states that support them. This enemy is world-wide, respects no national boundaries, and is concentrated in areas well outside of Iraq. Unfortunately, the current administration's near sighted strategy remains focused on Iraq and is all but dependent on the military component of strategy. Diplomacy and the critical political and economic components of a successful strategy are dangerously lacking. Clausewitz cautioned us that war is the extension of policy by other means. In other words, America should commit our young men and women into battle only when all other means are exhausted. The administration ignored this sage advice and we are paying a heavy price.

Our Army and Marine Corps are at a breaking point at a time in history when we need a strong military the most. The cycle of deployments is staggering. American formations continue to loose a battalion's worth of dead and wounded every month with little to show for it. The current recruiting system falls drastically short of long-term requirements and our all-volunteer force can not sustain the current tempo for much longer. The military is spending over $1 billion a year in incentives in a last ditch effort to keep the force together. Young officers and noncommissioned officers are leaving the service at an alarming rate. Equipment is in dismal shape, requiring hundreds of billions of dollars to refit the force to pre-invasion conditions. Active duty companies preparing for deployment to Iraq within the next six months are at less than 50 percent strength, are commanded by young and inexperienced lieutenants, and are lacking the equipment needed for training. We are setting the conditions for the next "Task Force Smith" disaster at a time in our history when we are facing a serious world-wide threat.

The current "surge" in Iraq is too little, too late. The so-called surge really amounts to nothing more than a minor reinforcement, a number which represents all that our military could muster. Our counter insurgency doctrine requires 20 soldiers for every 1,000 in the indigent population. Assuming there are 6 or 7 million people in Baghdad, the requirement to properly secure the city as a precursor to the rule of law would be over 120,000 "combat" troops. There are less than 80,000 "combat" troops in Iraq today, even with the surge. What we are seeing is the myth of Sisyphus being played out over and over again. Today's battles in places like Baghdad and Ba'qubah are not new—we have been down this road before, but lacked the number of coalition and competent Iraqi forces to clear, hold, and build. The number of "combat" troops matter and we have always lacked the right numbers. Further, our counter insurgency doctrine recognizes that fighting an insurgency is very different from combat operations and that successful operations "require Soldiers and Marines at every echelon to possess a daunting set of traits, among them a clear, nuanced, and empathetic appreciation of the essential nature of the conflict ... an understanding of the motivation, strengths, and weaknesses of the insurgent, and a knowledge of the local culture." I could not agree with this more. Success in a counter insurgency is more about relationships, improving the people's quality of life, and the incredibly hard work to change people's attitudes to give them alternatives to the insurgency, and less about the application of lethal force. Numbers mattered in March 2003 and they matter today. The current administration drove this nation to war without the military planning and capability required to be successful in this kind of war. The administration set our great military up for failure and is putting our nation at risk.

The Government of Iraq is incapable of stepping up to their responsibilities. Our current administration's notion of freedom and democracy in the Middle East is certainly noble, but completely unrealistic. Democracy is inconsistent with the tribal and religious culture in the region. The Maliki government is dominated by Shia, is all but ineffective, and will most likely accomplish few if any of the benchmarks established by the legislation passed by the US Congress last month. These benchmarks include tough milestones dependent on reconciliation, to include completing a constitutional review, enacting and implementing legislation on de-Ba'athification, enacting and implementing legislation to ensure the equitable distribution of hydrocarbon resources of the people of Iraq without regard to the sect or ethnicity of recipients, and much, much more. The expectation of a mid-September report to the President all but empowers the insurgency with the timeline they need and at the end of the day, we all know what the results will be. With respect to the Government of Iraq's responsibility to increase the number of Iraqi security force units capable of operating independently ignores the reality that historically, armed forces in the region have been perpetually ineffective due to social factors deeply rooted in Arab culture, to include secrecy and paranoia, pride, enormous class differences, an inability to coordinate, and no individual freedom of action or initiative. Why would we think our efforts in the 21st century would be any different than other nation's efforts in past centuries? Further, the world has committed inadequate resources to build effective Iraqi security forces. The Iraqi army and police require heavy weapons, helicopters, light armored vehicles, and radar assisted counter-battery artillery to control the insurgency. The Iraqi security forces have taken horrendous casualties and do not have the tools to replace US combat formations. Whether we can trust these Iraqi formations is another question. Our experience over the past four years is that most Iraqi formations will either not show up for the fight or will not hold their ground in the face of the insurgent for a myriad of reasons. America has ignored the lessons of history.

Our nation has yet to mobilize to defeat the threat of world-wide Islamic extremism which has little to do with Iraq. Iraq is distracting America from what should be our focus of main effort. Our leaders have a responsibility to galvanize the American people for what might very well be a decade's long struggle. Americans want to be told the truth—what are we facing, what will it take to win, how long will it take, and what are the consequences for failure? Americans want to be part of the solution. We want to properly fund the war with war bonds or taxes—programs that do not mortgage our children's futures. We want to properly resource our great military, to include beginning the debate on national service. We want to mobilize industry to get behind this effort. Why is the military competing with golf club manufactures for specialty metals? Why does it take years to replace a helicopter destroyed in Iraq or Afghanistan? Why do we have the huge backlog of broken military equipment in our military depots? Why is veteran medical care still broken? Why are we not serious about immigration reform and homeland security? Why is America still dependent on foreign oil? The time for half-measures is over. It is also past time for our Congress to provide constitutionally mandated oversight over the executive branch.

It is critical that we rethink our national strategy and begin the deliberate withdrawal of US forces from Iraq. It is in America's best interest to rethink our national strategy, deliberately disengage from Iraq, refit and rearm our military, get serious about homeland security, and prepare to win the next phase of the struggle against world-wide Islamic extremism. Bottom line, we have put our strategic interests in the hands of an incompetent government in Iraq and we are "waiting to see if the Iraqis can settle their differences." This is unacceptable. Our plan for withdrawal must be exponentially better than the plan to invade Iraq. Such a deliberate withdrawal will take up to a year or more to complete. With respect to the deliberate withdrawal from Iraq, the administration must establish a timeline for a withdrawal, put the onus for success squarely on the backs of the Iraqi government, and launch into a new national strategy which must include a serious diplomatic surge with friends, allies, and enemies, to include countries in the region with a vested interest in the future of Iraq. There may or may not be a long-term mission in Iraq, but that must be driven by our strategic interests in the region. Our two vital interests are that Iraq can not become a launching pad for world-wide Islamic extremism or become a source of regional instability. Secondary interests are that our withdrawal can not create a humanitarian disaster or an Iraq dominated by another state(s) in the region. This may require a residual force of up to 30,000 US troops for decades to protect the US mission, train and advise the Iraqi security forces, provide a counter balance to unintended consequences of Iran and a greater "Kurdistan," and take direct action against residual Al Qaeda in Iraq. We cannot walk away from our strategic interests. It did not have to be this way, but due to the failures of the current administration, we are where we are.

In conclusion, America's national strategy for the global war on terror lacks strategic focus. Our Army and Marine Corps are at a breaking point with little to show for it; the current "surge" in Iraq is too little, too late; the Government of Iraq is incapable of stepping up to their responsibilities; our nation has yet to mobilize to defeat a very serious threat which has little to do with Iraq; and it is past time to refocus our national strategy and begin the deliberate withdrawal of US forces from Iraq. The way-ahead is uncertain at best, but it is time to put America's vital interests first. From this point forward, America's strategy must focus on the mission is defeat world-wide Islamic extremism.

Testimony of Anthony H. Cordesman
Arleigh A. Burke Chair in Strategy to the House Committee on Foreign Affairs

Mr. Chairman, let me begin by thanking you, the ranking member, and the Committee for the opportunity to testify today. I have prepared a formal review of the Department of Defense's latest report on the surge and overall progress in Iraq to date, and I request that it be included in the record.

More broadly, there are many elements of the current US campaign in Iraq that are impressive. The US military has steadily shifted from a force oriented towards conventional war to one that can also fight counterinsurgency campaigns. It has greatly improved its tactical, intelligence, and targeting skills to attacked dispersed networks of insurgents like the Sunni Islamist extremists that include Al Qa'ida's various affiliates. It has shown it can win tactical battles with a surprisingly low ratio of forces to opponents.

Yet, it is all too clear that the US, its Coalition allies, and the Iraqi government cannot win any form of security and stability if insurgent movements can keep large areas of Iraq unstable and constantly provoke Iraq's civil conflicts. Tactical success is an important element of victory.

Tactical Victory or Stretching Too Thin and a New Form of "Whack a Mole?"

The present campaign in Iraq may be a tactical success, but there are serious issues regarding its strategic value. One key problem was raised during the debate over the surge strategy before President Bush adopted it and announced it in January 2007. It was always clear that an operation in Baghdad would simply lead many insurgents to leave the city and operate elsewhere and that most Sunni militias might simply stand down, let the US-led forces defeat the insurgents, watch a Shi'ite dominated government gain power, and resurface once the US was gone. Baghdad was important. It never made sense to see it as a decisive battlefield or center of gravity.

This is now all too clear even in a narrow military sense. The US is having to expand its counterinsurgency operations broadly outside Baghdad in ways that can steadily disperse limited US and combat-capable Iraqi military forces. Baghdad is still only 30–40% secured, but the fighting not only is dispersing limited US forces into the Baghdad ring cities, but into a troubled zone of provinces ranging from Anbar to Diyala. The US has learned it cannot ignore growing Shi'ite tensions and Iranian pressure in the south, and still faces serious potential problems with Arab-Kurdish tensions in the north.

It is too early to judge what is happening in Baquba, and the use of far more intense combat tactics coupled to broader efforts to seal and secure urban areas after tactical victories may have a more lasting effect. There is, however, an obvious risk that the US will simply end up playing "Whack a mole" on a steadily rising scale.

So far, the claims of success have often been tenuous to meaningless. As of June 23rd, MNF-I claimed that, "at least 55 al-Qa'ida operatives have been killed, 23 have been detained, 16 weapons caches have been discovered, 28 improvised explosive devices have been destroyed and 12 booby-trapped structures have been destroyed." These figures are far too low to matter.

Limited tactical successes really doesn't matter unless such casualties include substantial cadres of leaders and experts that cannot be easily and rapidly replaced. The insurgents can simply disperse, stand down, and regroup. The domestic political realities in the US also make it clear that unless the US is successfully taking out cadres and structure, the US is now so sensitive to US casualties that tactical victories can be the same kind of political and strategic defeat that occurred in Vietnam.

This risk is all too clear from the recent statements of Lt. Gen. Raymond T. Odierno, the second-ranking American commander in Iraq. If, as the general said on June 22nd, some 80 percent of the top Qa'ida leaders in the city fled before the American-led offensive began, it is not clear that it matters if "80 percent" of the recruits who were there when the offensive remained in the western half of the city. It also is pointless to call the leaders and cadres who leave "cowards." Iraqis are not foolish and they understand that such actions are an inevitable insurgent reaction to US military superiority and a key element of asymmetric warfare.

Not only have such estimates of "stay behinds" been badly exaggerated in past fighting, along with the capacity to keep them from infiltrating out or hiding, it is all too easy to move on to the next area and city and recruit more, and exploit the hostility following urban combat operations and large-scale detainments. Moreover, no major US-led or Iraqi operation will ever take place without enough signs, leaks, and infiltration to provide leaders and cadres with advanced warning.

The Critical Importance of Political Conciliation

The tactical problem, and stretching a limited pool of US forces too thin, is also only part of the problem. As both General Petraeus and Secretary Gates have made clear, none of this matters unless the Iraqis can move towards political conciliation—or at least a relatively stable form of coexistence. So far, there is only a limited promise of potential legal action by the government.

If anything, the use of Sunni tribes in the West has created new forms of Sunni vs. Shi'ite polarization, Shi'ite on Shi'ite fighting and feuding has gotten much worse in the south and central government, and the uncertainties over oil and a regional referendum on federalism in the north are increasing Kurdish, Arab, and Turcoman tensions.

Creating an Effective Bridge between Tactical Victory and Lasting Strategic Impact

There also is the problem of creating an effective bridge between tactical victory and lasting strategic impact even if political conciliation does move forward, and so far the Coalition has been virtually silent on progress in Baghdad, much less how such progress can be made in the new fighting outside it. Giving tactical victories lasting meaning requires the following additional elements:

1. ***Iraqi Army forces must begin to take over meaning operations without US embeds and US partner units, and dependence on US reinforcement and support.*** There does seem to be increasing Iraqi Army capability here, but Coalition reporting does not provide a meaningful picture of progress—merely grossly inflated figures on areas of responsibility and total numbers of battalions in the lead.

2. ***Iraqi police and local security forces must establishing a lasting security presence in the areas where tactical victories are won, and do so credibly in ways that give ordinary Iraqis security.*** There can be no "win" without "hold." So far, the US has made claim after claim to have secured cities after winning tactical battles to control them, and has never actually established lasting security in even one of them. The most critical problem has been the lack of active, combat-capable police, without corruption and sectarian and ethnic ties. Falluja and Samara are only the most obvious cases of such failures.

   Coalition reporting so far talks about the number of police posts established or with US embeds. It has not said a word about the ability provide lasting security using Iraqi police in parts of Baghdad or anywhere else. It also has not talked about the ability to support police efforts with an effective local criminal justice and court system or to screen detainees in ways that do not breed local hostility.

   The Coalition also needs to start talking about who actually does provide local security, and stop treating militias, local security forces, and police hired locally without Coalition training, as if it was always hostile or did not exist. In the real world, these forces and not the "trained and equipped" police are the real local security force in most of Iraq. There has to be a credible plan to use, absorb, or contain them.

3. ***The Iraqi government must follow-up security with a meaningful presence and by providing steady improvements in services.*** "Winning hearts and minds" doesn't come from public information campaigns and propaganda. It comes from providing real security for ordinary Iraqis, and showing the government cares, is present, and can steadily improve services. Once again, promise after promise has been made in past campaigns, and the central government has not yet shown it can follow up in even a single case. If this is happening even in the "secured" areas of Baghdad, no one has yet said so. How it can happen in Diyala or other high threat areas is even unclear.

4. ***There must also be effective local government.*** The liberation of various areas often has seen the emergence of local leaders willing to work with the Coalition—although often with little faith in, or ties to, the central government. In most cases, however, they have become targets, and the effort has broken down in local faction disputes or because of a lack of effective government support and problems in Coalition civil affairs efforts. Once again, if there is progress in creating stable, survivable, effective local government; none of the details are clear.

5. ***There has to be economic aid and progress.*** Iraqis have to give priority to physical security and key services, but unemployment, underemployment, and shut or failed businesses affect some 60% or more of Iraqis nationally and the figures are even higher in high threat and combat areas. The strategy President Bush advanced in January 2007 advanced proposals for accomplishing such an effort in Baghdad. Once again, there has been no meaningful Coalition reporting on broad progress in such efforts in the secured areas of Baghdad, and past promises such aid would be provided in "liberated" cities like Samara and Falluja were not kept.

6. ***There must be an end to sectarian and ethnic cleansing and displacement.*** There is no near and perhaps midterm answer to suicide bombings and atrocities, to attacks on sacred shrines and critical facilities. No mix of security forces can stop even small cadres of extremists from occasional successes. No tactical victory has meaning, however, unless Iraqis can be secure in neighborhoods and areas where they are in the minority, and can reach across ethnic and sectarian lines and barriers in ordinary life.

   One of the greatest single failures of the current approach to fighting in Iraq is that it does not track sectarian and ethnic separation and displacement and make ending this on a local and national level at least as important as halting major attacks and killings. It may take years to make Iraqis secure from Islamist extremists and the worst elements of Shi'ite gangs and militias. There can be no meaningful tactical success, however, unless Iraqis can be safe from their own neighbors and begin to lead ordinary lives in their own neighborhoods.

Metrics, Benchmarks, and Real Victory

The late Colonel Harry Sommers summed up the US defeat in Vietnam in a brief exchange he had with a North Vietnamese officer after the war. Sommers pointed out that the US had won virtually every tactical encounter with both the Viet Cong and North Vietnamese forces. The Vietnamese officer replied, "Yes, but this was irrelevant."

The new US Army manual on counterinsurgency, which is the result of an effort led by General Petraeus recognizes this reality, and virtually all of the points made above. It also may well be unfair to judge progress in Baghdad even in September, much less now. Historically, any campaign that has had to begin with as weak a foundation as the surge strategy began with took at least a year to seriously take hold and often several years. An Iraq in political turmoil, in local economic collapse, and without security even for senior officials and members of parliament, will not move quickly—especially in a Baghdad summer.

The fact remains, however, that tactical success will remain largely meaningless in Baghdad, Baquba, the other areas cover by Operation Ripper, and in Iraq as a whole unless it can be linked to political conciliation and progress in the other six critical elements of victory listed above. The US team in Iraq and Bush Administration need to show the American people and the Congress that they understand this, are acting on the basis of these realities, have sound plans, and are making real progress. "Spinning" the importance of tactical success does not do this.

At the same time, both the media and outside analysts need to focus far more on the full range of actions it takes to win, and do so with patience and objectivity. ***No strategy or campaign could possibly achieve significant success in all of these elements by this fall, or even ensure a successful start.*** It is reasonable to demand credible plans and transparent and meaningful reporting—something that the Administration has not yet provided in a single critical area.

It is not reasonable to demand instant progress or focus solely on the level of US troops in Iraq or casualties in the fighting. It should also be clear from the above list that US military tactical victories are almost certain to be meaningless if the US political system cannot adapt to the reality that broad success—albeit with what may be much lower US troop levels—will require an effort that extends at least several years in to the next Administration and which cannot take place without bipartisan support. The odds are bad enough given the problems in Iraq; they are hopeless if the political environment in the US offers no hope of the necessary time and bipartisanship.

Frederick W. Kagan
Resident Scholar
American Enterprise Institute

American military forces in Iraq are now entering the second phase of their kinetic operations even as political efforts continue on a separate but linked track. Ambassador Ryan Crocker and General David Petraeus are in the midst of a multi-faceted program that will not proceed in a linear way and will not generate clear and consistent metrics in all of its phases. The early signs are positive in a number of respects, although difficulties and challenges clearly remain. But it is too soon to evaluate the outcome of an operation that is just moving into the first of several phases intended to produce significant positive change in the situation overall.

It is now beyond question that the Bush Administration pursued a flawed approach to the war in Iraq from 2003 to 2007. That approach relied on keeping the American troop presence in Iraq as small as possible, pushing unprepared Iraqi Security Forces into the lead too rapidly, and using political progress as the principal means of bringing the violence under control. In other words, it is an approach similar to the one proposed by the ISG and by some who are now pushing for political benchmarks and the rapid drawdown of American forces as the keys to success in the war. It is no more likely to work now than it was then. Political progress is something that follows the establishment of security, not something that causes it. The sorts of political compromises that Iraq's parties must make are extraordinarily difficult—one might even say impossible—in the context of uncontrolled terrorism and sectarian violence. And the Iraqi Security Forces, although significantly better than they were this time last year, are still too small and insufficiently capable to *establish* security on their own or even to maintain it in difficult and contested areas without significant continuing coalition support.

For all of these reasons, the president changed his strategy profoundly in January 2007, and appointed a new commander in General Petraeus and a new Ambassador in Ryan Crocker to oversee the new approach. This new approach focuses on establishing security in Baghdad and its immediate environs as the prerequisite for political progress. It recognizes that American forces must be in the lead in many (but not all) areas, and that they will have to remain in areas that have been cleared for some time in order to ensure that security becomes permanent. The aim of the security strategy is to buy space and time for the political process in Iraq to work, and for the Iraqi Security Forces to mature and grow to the point where they can maintain the dramatically improved security situation our forces will have helped them to establish.

The scale of the problem required an increase in American forces in Iraq, which the president ordered in January, of around 40% (from the equivalent of 15 brigade combat teams to more than 21). It also required a multi-phased approach on both the military and the political side of the equation, which has been begun.

The first phase began on January 10th with the announcement of the new strategy and the beginning of the movement of the 5 additional Army brigades and Marine elements into the theater. That deployment process was only completed at the beginning of this month—in fact, critical enablers for those combat forces are still arriving in theater. As the new units entered Iraq, the U.S. military commanders began pushing those that were already in the theater forward from their operating bases into Joint Security Stations and Combat Outposts in key neighborhoods in Baghdad and elsewhere. The purpose of these movements was not to clear-and-hold—the units present in theater were not sufficient in numbers to conduct such operations. The purpose was instead to establish positions within those key areas and to develop both intelligence about the enemy and trust relationships with the local communities that would make possible decisive clear-and-hold operations subsequently. During this phase of the operation, additional Iraqi Security Forces deployed to Baghdad in accord with a plan developed jointly by the U.S. and Iraqi military commands. All of the requested units appeared in the first Iraqi Army rotation, and the Iraqi military has just completed its second rotation of units into Baghdad—again, all designated units arrived, and their fill levels were generally higher than in the first rotation.

Generals Petraeus and Odierno did not allocate the majority of the new combat power they received to Baghdad. Only 2 of the additional Army brigades went into the city. The other 3 Army brigades and the equivalent of a Marine regiment were deployed into the areas around Baghdad that our generals call the "Baghdad belts," including Baqubah in Diyala province. The purpose of this deployment was not to clear-and-hold those areas, but to make possible the second phase of the operation that began on June 15. The purpose of this operation—Phantom Thunder—is to disrupt terrorist and militia networks and bases outside of Baghdad that have been feeding the violence within the city. Most of the car bomb and suicide bomb networks that have been supporting the al Qaeda surge since January are based in these belt areas, and American commanders have rightly recognized that they cannot establish stable security in the capital without disrupting these networks and their bases.

But even this operation—the largest coordinated combat operation the U.S. has undertaken since the invasion in 2003—is not the decisive phase of the current strategy. It is an operation designed to set the preconditions for a successful clear-and-hold operation that will probably begin in late

July or early August within Baghdad itself. That is the operation that is designed to bring security to Iraq's capital in a lasting way that will create the space for political progress that we all desire.

The U.S. has not undertaken a multi-phased operation on such a large scale since 2003, and it is not surprising therefore that many commentators have become confused about how to evaluate what is going on and how to report it. Sectarian deaths in Baghdad dropped significantly as soon as the new strategy was announced in January, and remain at less than half their former levels. Spectacular attacks rose as al Qaeda conducted a counter-surge of its own, but have recently begun falling again. Violence is down tremendously in Anbar province, where the Sunni tribes have turned against al Qaeda and are actively cooperating with U.S. forces for the first time. This process has spread from Anbar into Babil, Salah-ad-Din, and even Diyala provinces, and echoes of it have even spread into one of the worst neighborhoods in Baghdad—Ameriyah, formerly an al Qaeda stronghold. Violence has risen naturally in areas that the enemy had long controlled but in which U.S. forces are now actively fighting for the first time in many years, and the downward spiral in Diyala that began in mid-2006 continued (which is not surprising, since the Baghdad Security Plan does not aim to establish security in Diyala).

All of these trends are positive. The growing skill and determination of the Iraqi Army units fighting alongside Americans is also positive. Some Iraqi Police units have also fought well. Others have displayed sectarian tendencies and participated in sectarian actions. Political progress has been very slow—something that has clearly disappointed many who hoped for an immediate turnaround, but that is not surprising for those who always believed that it would follow, not precede or accompany, the establishment of security at least in Baghdad. And negative sectarian actors within the Iraqi Government continue to resist making necessary compromises with former foes. Overall, the basic trends are rather better than could have been expected of the operation so far, primarily because of the unanticipated stunning success in Anbar and its spread. But it remains far too early to offer any meaningful evaluation of the progress of an operation whose decisive phases are only just beginning.

To say that the current plan has failed is simply incorrect. It might fail, of course, as any military/political plan might fail. Indications on the military side strongly suggest that success—in the form of dramatically reduced violence by the end of this year—is quite likely. Indications on the political side are more mixed, but are also less meaningful at this early stage before security has been established.

Great commanders in history have understood two critical truths: the situation in war is constantly changing, and decisions must take that change into account—and, therefore, that it is best to delay decisions until the last possible moment to ensure that they are made on the basis of the most recent and accurate understanding of the situation, rather than on preconceptions formed in different circumstances. The situation in Iraq is very different today from what it was in January 2007, to say nothing of November 2006. It will be very different in September, and still more different in December of this year. It would be a great error to attempt to decide now upon the strategy to pursue when the current plan has actually been implemented, because we cannot now predict what the situation will be then with any confidence or accuracy. And it would be a very grave error indeed to rush now to abandon the first strategy that offers some real prospect for success in favor of a return to an approach that has already failed repeatedly.

DOCUMENT NO. 15

RETHINKING INSURGENCY

Article

June 2007

Steven Metz
The Statergic Studies Institute

Foreword

The U.S. military and national security community lost interest in insurgency after the end of the Cold War. Other defense issues such as multinational peacekeeping and transformation seemed more pressing and thus attracted the most attention. But with the onset of the Global War on Terror in 2001 and the ensuing involvement of the U.S. military in counterinsurgency support in Iraq and Afghanistan, insurgency experienced renewed concern in both the defense and intelligence communities.

In this monograph, Dr. Steven Metz, who has been writing on insurgency and counterinsurgency for more than 2 decades, argues that this relearning process, while exceptionally important, emphasized the wrong thing, focusing on Cold War era nationalistic insurgencies rather than the complex conflicts which characterized the post-Cold War security environment. To be successful at counterinsurgency, he contends, the U.S. military and defense community must rethink insurgency. This has profound implications for American strategy and military doctrine.

The Strategic Studies Institute is pleased to offer this monograph as part of its efforts to help military and defense leaders understand the difficult security challenges faced by the United States.

DOUGLAS C. LOVELACE, JR.
Director
Strategic Studies Institute

Biographical Sketch of the Author

STEVEN METZ is Chairman of the Regional Strategy and Planning Department and Research Professor of National Security Affairs at the Strategic Studies Institute (SSI). He has been with SSI since 1993, previously serving as Henry L. Stimson Professor of Military Studies and SSI's Director of Research. Dr. Metz has also been on the faculty of the Air War College, the U.S. Army Command and General Staff College, and several universities. He has been an advisor to political campaigns and elements of the intelligence community; served on security policy task forces; testified in both houses of Congress; and spoken on military and security issues around the world. He is the author of more than 100 publications on national security, military strategy, and world politics. His most recent study from the Strategic Studies Institute was *Learning from Iraq: Counterinsurgency in American Strategy*. He serves on the RAND Corporation Insurgency Board and is working on two books: *Iraq and the Evolution of American Strategy* and *Insurgency and Counterinsurgency in the 21st Century*. Dr. Metz holds a B.A. in Philosophy and an M.A. in International Studies from the University of South Carolina, and a Ph.D. in Political Science from the Johns Hopkins University.

Summary

The September 11, 2001, attacks and Operations ENDURING FREEDOM and IRAQI FREEDOM revived the idea that insurgency is a significant threat to the United States. In response, the American military and defense communities began to rethink insurgency. Much of this valuable work, though, viewed contemporary insurgency as more closely related to Cold War era insurgencies than to the complex conflicts which characterized the post-Cold War period. This suggests that the most basic way that the military and defense communities think about insurgency must be rethought.

Contemporary insurgency has a different strategic context, structure, and dynamics than its forebears. Insurgencies tend to be nested in complex conflicts which involve what can be called third forces (armed groups which affect the outcome, such as militias) and fourth forces (unarmed groups which affect the outcome, such as international media), as well as the insurgents and the regime. Because of globalization, the decline of overt state sponsorship of insurgency, the continuing importance of informal outside sponsorship, and the nesting of insurgency within complex conflicts associated with state weakness or failure, the dynamics of contemporary insurgency are more like a violent and competitive market than war in the traditional sense where clear and discrete combatants seek strategic victory.

This suggests a very different way of thinking about (and undertaking) *counter*insurgency. At the strategic level, the risk to the United States is not that insurgents will "win" in the traditional sense, take over their country, and shift it from a partner to an enemy. It is that complex internal conflicts, especially ones involving insurgency, will generate other adverse effects: the destabilization of regions, resource flows, and markets; the blossoming of transnational crime; humanitarian disasters; transnational terrorism; and so forth. Given this, the U.S. goal should not automatically be the defeat of the insurgents by the regime (which may be impossible and which the regime may not even want), but the most rapid conflict resolution possible. In other words, a quick and sustainable resolution which integrates insurgents into the national power structure is less damaging to U.S. national interests than a protracted conflict which leads to the complete destruction of the insurgents. Protracted conflict, not insurgent victory, is the threat.

If, in fact, insurgency is not simply a variant of war, if the real threat is the deleterious effects of sustained conflict, and if it is part of systemic failure and pathology in which key elites and organizations develop a vested interest in sustaining the conflict, the objective of counterinsurgency support should *not* be simply strengthening the government so that it can impose its will more effectively on the insurgents, but systemic reengineering. This, in turn, implies that the most effective posture for outsiders is not to be an ally of the government and thus a sustainer of the flawed socio-political-economic system, but to be neutral mediators and peacekeepers (even when the outsiders have much more ideological affinity for the regime than for the insurgents). If this is true, the United States should only undertake counterinsurgency support in the most pressing instances and as part of an equitable, legitimate, and broad-based multinational coalition.

American strategy for counterinsurgency should recognize three distinct insurgency settings each demanding a different response:

- A functioning government with at least some degree of legitimacy is suffering from an erosion of effectiveness but can be "redeemed" through assistance provided according to the Foreign Internal Defense doctrine.
- There is no functioning and legitimate government, but a broad international and regional consensus supports the creation of a neo-trusteeship. In such instances, the United States should provide military, economic, and political support as part of a multinational consensus operating under the authority of the United Nations.
- There is no functioning and legitimate government and no international or regional consensus for the formation of a neo-trusteeship. In these

cases, the United States should pursue containment of the conflict by support to regional states and, in conjunction with partners, help create humanitarian "safe zones" within the conflictive state.

Rethinking Insurgency

... everything old is new again ...

Peter Allen

Introduction

Military thinkers often say that the *essence* of war does not change.[1] War is and always will be the use of violence for political purposes. It is always characterized by what Clausewitz described as "fog" (factors which complicate decisionmaking and force strategists to rely on assumptions), "friction" (the tendency of everything to operate less efficiently than in peacetime), and the "trinity" of rationality, passion, and chance. But, military theorists note, war's *nature* or *character* does change. Linear formations gave way to loose ones, columns and rows to swarming by battalions and brigades; human and animal power were replaced by mechanization; handwritten and personal communications by email; limited, seasonal operations gave way to global power projection.

Insurgency also combines continuity and change, an enduring essence and a shifting nature. Its essence is protracted, asymmetric violence; political, legal, and ethical ambiguity; and the use of complex terrain, psychological warfare, and political mobilization. It arises when a group decides that the gap between their political expectations and the opportunities afforded them is unacceptable and can only be remedied by force. Insurgents avoid battlespaces where they are at a disadvantage—often the conventional military sphere—and focus on those where they can attain parity, particularly the psychological and the political.[2]

They seek to postpone decisive action, avoid defeat, sustain themselves, expand their support, and alter the power balance in their favor. And because insurgency involves a layered psychological complexity, multiple audiences, and a range of participants with different methods and objectives, it is imbued with what Edward Luttwak called a "paradoxical logic"—what initially appears best may not be, and every positive action has negative implications as well.[3]

But while insurgency's essence persists, its nature changes. That we know. The precise direction, extent, and implications of the evolution, though, are not yet clear. We cannot yet tell which changes will have only limited significance and which will prove profound, which changes are case-specific and which universal. But we need to. From the end of the Cold War in the early 1990s until 2001, the U.S. military and defense community paid scant attention to insurgency and counterinsurgency. It faded from the curricula of professional military education. There was little interest in developing new doctrine, operational concepts, or organizations. The general sense seemed to be that American involvement in counterinsurgency was a Cold War phenomenon, irrelevant with the demise of the Soviet Union and the mellowing of China. But the September 11, 2001, attacks and Operations ENDURING FREEDOM and IRAQI FREEDOM changed that. Once again, insurgency was seen as a significant threat and counterinsurgency a strategic imperative. In response, the American military and defense community began to rethink insurgency. Or, more accurately, it revived the old idea with a few added twists.

During the 1970s, American national security strategy was shaped by what became known as the "Vietnam syndrome." The disastrous outcome of the war in Southeast Asia made Americans reluctant to intervene in Third World conflicts. Americans, it seemed, were ill-suited for participation in morally ambiguous, complex, and protracted armed struggles, particularly outside the nation's traditional geographic area of concern. Better to eschew them than to become embroiled in "another Vietnam." Ironically, even though the United States eventually overcame this variant of the Vietnam syndrome, a new one emerged. When insurgency and counterinsurgency again became important elements of the global security system and American strategy after 2001, many American policymakers, political leaders, and defense strategists used Vietnam as a model. The Viet Cong were treated as the archetypical insurgency. Insurgents who did not use the Maoist strategy stood little chance of success (defined as seizing the state and becoming the new regime).[4] The tendency was to seek new ideas from old conflicts, preparing, as so often happens, to fight the last war. But contemporary insurgencies are, in many ways, more like the complex internal conflicts of the 1990s than the insurgencies of the mid-20th century. This suggests that the military and the defense analytical community must rethink the insurgency problem once again.

The Old Conceptualization

American thinking about insurgency was forged in the Cold War. Washington's concern was that insurgents linked to the Soviet Union or China would overthrow friendly regimes, then become communist allies or proxies. The key idea was the "death by a thousand small cuts"—while any given insurgency might not pose a mortal danger, a series of them would. As the Commission on Integrated Long-Term Strategy wrote in 1988, insurgencies and other Third World conflicts "have an adverse cumulative effect on U.S. access to critical regions, on American credibility among allies and friends, and on American self-confidence. If this cumulative effect cannot be checked or reversed in the future, it will gradually undermine America's ability to defend its interests in the most vital regions..."[5] The threat from insurgency, then, was indirect and symbolic.

As communist-backed insurgencies flared throughout Asia, Africa, and South America, President John Kennedy directed the U.S. military to augment its counterinsurgency capabilities. By emphasizing the military dimension, Kennedy institutionalized the notion that insurgency is a form of war. This relatively simple idea had profound implications. If insurgency was, in fact, war, then the way that Americans thought about war more generally could be extrapolated to counterinsurgency. Insurgency, like conventional war, was seen as a struggle in which two antagonists sought to impose their will on each other. Insurgency, like war, was abnormal and episodic, with a clear beginning and end. The defeat of the enemy and a return to peace was the objective. As in conventional war, diplomatic, political, economic, psychological, and intelligence activities supported military efforts. Counterinsurgency thus became the primary responsibility of the military.

As Americans better understood insurgency, they concluded that most insurgents had valid political and economic grievances. This suggested a dual track approach to counterinsurgency, simultaneously seeking to defeat or eradicate the insurgents themselves while altering the factors which cause grievance. According to 1990 U.S. Army and Air Force doctrine, insurgents assume "that appropriate change within the existing system is not possible or likely."[6] While it was seldom stated bluntly in strategy or doctrine, only deeply flawed states—those with serious inequities, repression, or corruption—gave rise to major insurgencies. To address these flaws, most insurgents (or at least those of the greatest concern to the United States) sought to overthrow the existing state, rule the nation themselves, and launch a revolutionary transformation. Even though scholars such as Bard O'Neill reminded Americans that not all insurgencies were revolutionary, revolutionary ones posed the greatest threat to U.S. national interests and thus dominated American thinking.[7] Hence Joint Doctrine defined insurgency as "An organized movement aimed at the overthrow of a constituted government through the use of subversion and armed conflict."[8] More recent Army/Marine Corps doctrine described it more broadly as "an organized, protracted struggle designed to weaken the control and legitimacy of an established government, occupying power, or other political authority while increasing insurgent control."[9]

Based on the Cold War experience, U.S. military doctrine viewed insurgency as a "stand alone" struggle. It had "specific causes and beginnings" and "arises when the government is unable or unwilling to redress the demands of important social groups and these opponents band together and begin to use violence to change the government's position."[10]

Insurgency, like conventional war, involved two antagonists (the regime and the insurgents). Insurgents and counterinsurgents engaged in direct action against each other while simultaneously attempting to win the support of "undecideds"—the public within their state or potential external supporters. Insurgents needed "the active support of a plurality of the politically active people and the passive acquiescence of the majority."[11] If the government obtained the support of most of "the people," it attained "legitimacy" and thus "won." Failure to do this could lead to an insurgent victory. "Political power is the central issue in insurgencies and counterinsurgencies," Army/Marine Corps doctrine states, so "each side aims to get the people to accept its governance or authority as legitimate."[12]

The most successful insurgencies were ones which became more and more "state like," controlling ever larger swaths of territory and expanding their military capability to the point that they could undertake larger operations. They developed organizational specialization and complexity with separate leaders, combatants, political cadre, auxiliaries, and a mass base. U.S. thinking tended to gravitate to the Maoist insurgent strategy of "people's war" which held that the rebels sought the internal formality and differentiation of a state. Insurgency, in other words, began as an asymmetric conflict but became less so as it progressed.

The American notion of *counter*insurgency rejected the brutal "mailed fist" approach used throughout history in favor of methods more amenable to a democracy.[13] Derived from British, French, and American experience in "small wars," this stressed simultaneous actions to neutralize or destroy insurgent armed formations, separate the insurgents from "the people," and undertake political-economic reform. The American approach was to support a partner government, strengthening it and encouraging it to reform. This was done through a program called "foreign internal defense" (FID) which "promotes regional stability by supporting a host-nation program of internal defense and development (IDAD). These national programs free and protect a nation from lawlessness, subversion, and insurgency by emphasizing the building of viable institutions that respond to the needs of society."[14] Strengthening or restrengthening national governments was the key. Strategically, U.S. involvement began at a low level, escalated until the partner state could stand on its own and had institutionalized political and economic reform, then receded once the insurgents were defeated and the government controlled its territory.

Rethinking the Context

This is where we were. But where should we be? How should we understand insurgency in the first decade of the 21st century? A broad rethinking of the problem must begin with the strategic context. In the old conceptualization, insurgencies mattered to the United States when they augmented Soviet or Soviet bloc influence. But there was also an element of symbolism. American policymakers believe that the strategic *zeitgeist*—the spirit of an era—matters. Successful insurgencies, they thought, would make insurgency attractive to others, creating a climate where the violent overthrow of the existing order was acceptable, even laudable; hence the "myth of the insurgent" that gave them prestige within their own societies and even in the West.

Insurgency matters today because it is linked to the phenomenon of transnational terrorism. Insurgents have long used terrorism in the operational sense, deterring those who supported the government and creating an environment of violence and insecurity to erode public trust in the regime. But now terrorism plays a strategic role as well. Insurgents can use terrorism as a form of long-range power projection against outsiders who support the government they are fighting. This could deter or even end outside assistance. It is easy to imagine, for instance, that the already fragile backing for American involvement in Iraq would erode even further if the Iraqi insurgents launched attacks in the United States. Even more important, an insurgent movement able to seize control of a state could support transnational terrorists. The idea is that insurgents have demonstrated an affinity for violence and extremism which would flavor their policies if they came to power.

Of course, not all insurgencies are directly linked to broader transnational movements. For the United States, though, association with (or at least a similarity to) violent Islamic extremism (or narcotrafficking) determines the strategic significance of an insurgency. While not itself an insurgent movement in the purest sense, al Qaeda cultivates ties to and supports insurgencies which share its ideology and world view.[15] Even insurgencies not directly linked to Islamic extremism strengthen it by spawning underground networks and economies which transnational terrorists can then tap. Hezbollah and al Qaeda, for instance, have been linked to the conflicts in Sierra Leone and Liberia via the diamond trade.[16] In 2005 Rady Zaiter, a Lebanese citizen, was arrested in connection with a cocaine smuggling operation that sent most of its profits to Hezbollah.[17]

Still, this idea that association with Islamic extremism determines the strategic significance of an insurgency needs refinement. Does the assumption that a regime that came to power via insurgency will support transnational terrorism make sense? Perhaps, particularly if transnational terrorists directly contributed to the insurgent cause (as in Iraq). In such cases, the new regime might feel a moral obligation to support its former allies. But it is even more likely that a regime born out of insurgency would be focused inward, concentrating on consolidating power. In this era of globalization and interconnectedness, new regimes are particularly vulnerable to outside economic and military pressure and thus unlikely to undertake actions which would give the United States or some other state a justification for intervention. Even if the Iraqi or Afghan insurgents won, for instance, they would probably have learned the lessons of 2001—serving as a host to transnational terrorists is a dangerous business. While radicals can question America's ability to sustain counterinsurgency, there is no doubt that the United States can (and will) overturn regimes which overtly support transnational terrorism.

It is less the chance of an insurgent *victory* which creates a friendly environment for transnational terrorism than persistent internal conflict shattering control and restraint in a state. During an insurgency, both the insurgents and the government focus on each other, necessarily leaving parts of the country with minimal security and control. Transnational terrorists exploit this. And protracted insurgency creates a general disregard for law and order. Organized crime and corruption blossom. Much of the population loses its natural aversion to violence. Thus a society brutalized and wounded by a protracted insurgency is more likely to spawn a variety of evils, spewing violent individuals into the world long after the conflict ends.

The strategic context for 20th century insurgency was the political mobilization of excluded groups, rising nationalism, and proxy conflict between the superpowers. The strategic context of contemporary insurgency is the collapse of old methods of order and identity leading to systemic weakness and pathology. This creates failure or shortfalls in the security domain. One of the dominant characteristics of the contemporary global security environment is that it continues to give nation states responsibility for systemic maintenance and stability at the very time that they are increasingly incapable of providing acceptable levels of security, prosperity, and political identity. A variety of sub- and supra-state organizations are filling the vacuum.

There are several reasons that states—particularly in Latin America, Africa, and Asia—cannot meet the demands of their citizens. In part, it flows from the artificiality of many of today's national borders. Many do not reflect political, economic, or social distinctions on the ground. Artificial and increasingly fragile states are pummeled by globalization, interconnectedness, and the profusion of information. Globalization and information profusion make it difficult for states to manage the distribution of goods and power within their borders and expectations. To give a simple example, access to the Internet and satellite television raises awareness in poor regions, but the globalization of capital and markets makes it difficult for states to improve economic conditions rapidly enough to match demands. Expectations rise more quickly than the ability to meet them. This alone does not lead to armed conflict, but can if energized by ideology. Metaphorically, globalization is like chronic stress to a human body—stress alone does not kill, but it can make the body less able to stave off pathogens which can, in fact, kill. The effect is amplified in bodies that are already weakened by something else. Globalization makes weak states more vulnerable to ideologies of violence.

Another unintended side effect of globalization arises from the pressure on autocratic regimes to undertake political reform (or at least give the impression of undertaking political reform). Regimes must do this because the global capital market "punishes" autocrats—unless an autocratic regime controls one of the handful of extremely valuable resources such as petroleum, the global capital market assumes that investment is a high risk. Thomas Friedman calls this the "golden straitjacket"—regimes are forced to undertake actions which weaken them in order to gain access to global capital flows.[18] But "hybrid" states— part autocracy, part democracy—are more prone to political conflict than either strong autocracies or strong democracies.[19] So autocratic regimes which undertake limited reforms to attract investment inadvertently make themselves more prone to political conflict.

Most of today's armed conflicts—including those involving insurgency—grow from attempts to exert influence in or derive benefits from the "space" vacated by the weakening of the state (or never adequately filled by states in the first place). In addition, there is competition and sometimes conflict over a weakly controlled but increasingly important "space"—the infosphere. Twentieth century insurgency sought to eject the state from space it controlled (usually physical territory). Contemporary insurgency is a competition for uncontrolled spaces. Historically, it is more akin to the wars which took place at the peripheries of declining empires, be they the Roman, Ottoman, Chinese, or some other. Contemporary insurgency, then, is simply one of many manifestations of declining state control and systemic weakness. It co-exists with many others, most importantly the rise of militias, powerful criminal gangs and syndicates, informal economies, the collapse of state services, humanitarian crises or disasters, crises of identity, and transnational terrorism.

This means insurgency is no longer a "stand alone" conflict; it is "nested" within deeper and broader struggles. It is still about power (as it was during the Cold War), but it is also about economics, services, and social identity. The other dimensions of the conflict and the other participants both effect the insurgency and are affected by it. Simply asking states to exert or re-exert control over increasingly uncontrolled spaces is inadequate.

Rethinking the Structure

The most common evolutionary path for 21st century organizations—be they corporations, political organizations, or something else—is to become less rigidly hierarchical, taking the form of decentralized networks or webs of nodes (which may themselves be hierarchical). Such organizations are most effective in a rapidly changing, information saturated environment.[20] Insurgent movements organized as "flat" networks or semi-networks are more flexible and adaptable than rigidly hierarchical ones. Resources, information, and decisionmaking authority are diffused. Such organizations are effective in environments where rapid adaptation is an advantage. In the contemporary era, polyglot organizations which combine a centralized, hierarchical dimension (which gives them task effectiveness) and a decentralized, networked dimension (which gives them flexibility and adaptability) can maximize mission effectiveness.

Decentralized, networked organizations also tend to be more survivable. No single node is vital. They may not have a "center of gravity." In the past, survivability and effectiveness tended to be inverse characteristics. The most survivable were the smallest and best hidden, while the most effective were the largest and most powerful. The profusion and diffusion of information alters this (at least to some degree) by amplifying the effects of psychological operations, whether violent or nonviolent, and in part by changing the power asymmetry between insurgencies and the state. When power was strictly a factor of tangible resources like money and troops, the state held a distinct advantage. But as information becomes power (or generates power), the asymmetry between states and other organizations declines. A decentralized, networked structure allows even small insurgencies to accumulate and use information-based power (such as terrorism) and thus remain viable. And with the decline of state sponsorship, violent groups like insurgencies must be self-financing. Globalization and the information revolution provide the means to do so. As Karen Ballentine and Jake Sherman phrase it, "rapid economic globalization and the replacement of state-led economic development by market-driven free trade have created new and abundant opportunities for more systematic forms of combatant self-financing."[21] A decentralized network is better able to capitalize on shifting economic opportunities than a hierarchical one (although less able to harness the funds accumulated for the attainment of overarching objectives).

The need to generate their own resources and the absence of overt state sponsors forces insurgencies to develop a wide array of linkages, partnerships, and alliances.[22] Interconnectedness—both virtual and tangible—allows this. Insurgents can use the Internet to find partners, whether ideological supporters who share a political perspective or business partners to provide information and armaments.[23] A complex web of links means less need for a mass base. Like their forebears, contemporary insurgents still seek acquiescence from the populace—an unwillingness to provide information to the regime. But they rely less on the general population for information, money, and labor. This allows them to devote fewer resources to "carrots" designed to develop a mass base—social programs, administration, patronage, and so forth—and more to "sticks" which generate passivity (but not active support). Twentieth century insurgencies, particularly those based on the Maoist model, sought to balance carrots and sticks. Contemporary insurgencies (like contemporary organized crime) are more focused on violence, on coercion rather than patronage.

Decentralized, networked insurgencies without an overt state sponsor have a limited ability to undertake conventional military operations (or other complex activities which require extensive coordination). This is one more factor leading to a greater reliance on terrorism. It is both necessary and effective. Information profusion and the availability of diverse means of communication amplify the psychological effects of terrorism. In terrorism, it matters less how many people were killed than how many people know of and are influenced by the deaths. The terrorism of contemporary insurgents is thus designed to influence both a proximate audience and a distant one.

Because contemporary insurgencies are nested within broader crises or conflicts reflecting the diffusion of power and information, a diverse array of participants influence the outcome. During the Cold War, insurgencies involved what could be called "first" forces (the insurgents and counterinsurgents themselves) and often "second" forces—other states which supported either the insurgents or the counterinsurgents. Today, "third" and "fourth" forces are increasingly important. Third forces are armed elements other than the insurgents or counterinsurgents. Fourth forces are unarmed elements which affect and shape the conflict.

Third Forces.

Like insurgents, third forces form and survive when states are weak and unable to provide security. They play many roles in an insurgency: distracting the government from the counterinsurgency campaign, serving as a partner of the insurgents, performing functions the government cannot, or changing the basic dynamic and structure of the conflict. Three forms of third forces are particularly important for contemporary insurgencies: militias, criminal organizations, and private military companies.

Militias. Militias arise from a combination of need and opportunity. The state cannot address the basic needs of a specific group, particularly security, economic opportunity, and a basis for political identity. Colombia is a classic example, with a range of populist militias emerging as public order in the cities disintegrated.[24] Some were organized and financed directly by drug traffickers, others by local landowners, still others by military officers acting officially or unofficially.[25] Opportunity is the flip side of this: the state is too weak to prevent the emergence of militias. In Africa, for instance, militias are often the personal armed forces of powerful warlords whom the state cannot control. As William DeMars describes it:

> Warlord politics and state collapse are two sides of the same coin. State collapse means that the government no longer provides basic security and

> economic infrastructure as public goods. Behind this is a warlord political economy in which rival politicians fund patronage networks through access to international commercial ventures and provide their own security either by fielding their own militias or hiring international mercenaries.[26]

In a sense, then, militias may arise from *defensive* motives when a group faces a real threat, or they may arise *offensively* when a group or individual seeks to capitalize on the weakness of the state.

Militias have a subnational constituency and focus. They address the needs of a specific group that is something less than the entire citizenry of a country. They are "quasi-state" organizations, assuming some functions which the state would normally perform such as the provision of security, administration, and a range of activities designed to facilitate economic activity. Finally, militias have a coercive capability. They are, in other words, not simply subnational quasi-state organizations, but *armed* subnational quasi-state organizations. The coercive element may be only a small part of the militia's function, or it may be its core. But all militias have an armed component.

There are a number of variations within this basic construct. Some militias are based on personal patronage. In Congo-Brazzaville, for instance, the three major militia groups—the Ninja, Cobra, and Cocoye—are the private armies of powerful politicians (Denis Sassou Nguesso, Pascal Lissouba, and Bernard Kolelas).[27] Similarly, in the Democratic Republic of the Congo, the Union of Congolese Patriots (UPC) is the personal militia of Thomas Lubanga and Floribert Kisembo, and the Party for Unity and Safeguarding of the Integrity of Congo is the private army of Chief Kahwa Mandro Kisembo.[28] Alternatively, militias can be based on group identity such as clan, ethnicity, or sect. These can range from relatively informal, part-time self defense organizations to highly formal, hierarchical, almost state-like entities with full-time members, extensive specialization, standing military units, an organic intelligence and counterintelligence capability, a system for strategic planning, and a chain of command. Militias may raise funds in a variety of ways, from legal contributions to illegal means (extortion, protection rackets, robbery, counterfeiting, product piracy, narcotrafficking, vice, smuggling, and kidnapping).

The line between militias and large-scale organized crime is often fuzzy (and sometimes irrelevant) but, in general, militias have some political objectives other than self-aggrandizement. They are both parasites and providers of a resource (security, patronage) whereas criminal organizations are purely parasitic. It is possible, though, for a given organization to straddle or cross the boundary between the two. Pablo Escobar, one of Colombia's leading narcotraffickers, provided social services and concocted a rudimentary populist political ideology. He donated funds for roads, electric lines, and soccer fields for the poor and built a housing project.[29]

The inverse—a militia funding itself by crime—is even more common. Many of the communal militias in Iraq are involved in organized crime.[30] There are reports linking Hezbollah to an American crime syndicate and to diamond smuggling.[31]

Some militias do not behave strategically (identifying and prioritizing objectives; applying elements of power toward the attainment of the objectives; and balancing costs, risks, and expected gains). Others may have formal processes of strategy development and adjustment, perhaps even full-time strategists. The more strategic a militia, the more effective it will be at attaining political objectives. A strategic militia is also likely to exhibit more "rational" behavior, opening itself to influence by other organizations which understand its objectives and strategy. Astrategic militias are more susceptible to fracturing (which may not necessarily destroy them since they may persist as small, autonomous militias).

Militias vary greatly in organizational complexity. Some, like Hezbollah, may be highly complex, with great internal specialization and formal methods for recruitment, training, indoctrination, and even professional development. They may have suborganizations for planning, intelligence and counterintelligence, financial activities, social services, and so forth. They are likely to offer "career" progression within the organization. Others, like some of the African militias, are closer to a gang in structure, with little organizational complexity other than a hierarchy of power and informal methods for recruitment, indoctrination, and training. Complex militias are likely to be more effective at attaining objectives. Simple ones are likely to be more resilient.

Some militias, like successful insurgencies, develop a coherent ideology based on a persuasive "narrative" which explains why they were formed, what they seek to do, who opposes them, the methods they will use, and why they consider this endeavor justified and legitimate. This narrative and the ideology it reflects normally form a part of the information operations used by the militia. Other militias are more primal, seeing no need to develop a coherent ideology (or having no capacity to do so). Ideological militias have a better chance of developing active public support. Nonideological ones often rely on passive public support or patronage.

While all militias have an identified constituency, their relationship with it can range from the heavily parasitic—the militia draws resources from its constituency by relying on force and fear—to symbiotic ties where the militia, rather than the national government, is seen as the legitimate representative of the constituency. Parasitic militias are common in Africa, particularly in very weak states like the Democratic Republic of the Congo.[32] Hezbollah, by contrast, falls on the more legitimate end of the continuum.

Militias may be proxies or subordinates of a more powerful group, political party, or even the state. Others are autonomous. Some militias are extensively linked to other organizations, whether inside or outside the country. Both the quantity and depth of links matter. Other militias have few connections. Finally, militias vary greatly in the emphasis they place on violence. Some are violence-centric; others use it only as required. Generally, the more parasitic a militia, the more it relies on violence. The more legitimate a militia, the more it relies on its other elements of power.

Hezbollah is an example of a "high end" militia characterized by complexity, a strategic approach, legitimacy, deep and extensive linkages, and autonomy.[33] Some militias are created by states, some are born more "organically." Hezbollah was not only created by a state but by a foreign state. In 1982, a 1,500 member contingent of Iran's Revolutionary Guards arrived in Lebanon's Bekka Valley with the permission of the Syrian government.[34] Their objective was to spread Ayatollah Khomeini's version of Islamic revolution in the Arab world, using the affinity of Lebanon's Shi'ite community. This group had long been peripheralized in Lebanese politics and, in 1982, was suffering the effects of Israel's invasion of Lebanon (intended to break the strength of the Palestinian movement operating from there.) The "raw material" for Hezbollah was "loosely organized bands of Shi'ite gunmen."[35] Iran poured money in, paying for military training centers and community services such as schools, clinics, hospitals, and cash subsidies to the poor.[36] This was particularly important since the national government provided little to the southern Shi'ites, including those displaced to the slums of Beirut by conflict in the south.

Khomeini and the other architects of the Iranian revolution had a powerful effect on the initial ideology and narrative of Hezbollah. As Sami Hajjar noted,

> Hizballah adheres to a Manichean notion of the world as being divided between oppressors (*mustakbirun*) and oppressed (*mustad'fin*). The relationship between the two groups is inherently antagonistic—a conflict between good and evil, right and wrong.[37]

The group's justifying narrative—which Adam Shatz described as "a fiery mixture of revolutionary Khomeinism, Shi'ite nationalism, celebration of martyrdom, and militant anti-Zionism, occasionally accompanied by crude, neo-fascist anti-Semitism"[38]—is almost archetypical, linking local grievances and a transnational ideology, stressing the defensive nature of its activities. This was best spelled out in a 1985 letter attributed to Sheikh Muhammed Hussein Fadlallah, Hezbollah's spiritual guide, and published in *al-Safir* (Beirut).[39] Hezbollah, according to the letter, does not "constitute an organized and closed party in Lebanon" but "an umma linked to the

Muslims of the world by the solid doctrinal and religious connection of Islam." Each member was "a fighting soldier." The letter stated:

> We declare openly and loudly that we are an umma which fears God only and is by no means ready to tolerate injustice, aggression, and humiliation. America, its Atlantic Pact allies, and the Zionist entity in the holy land of Palestine, attacked us and continue to do so without respite.... We have no alternative but to confront aggression by sacrifice.

Although beginning as a loose umbrella of groups, Hezbollah has followed the pattern of many successful militias (and insurgencies), becoming more formally organized as it matured. As Hajjar put it, the organization was a "sophisticated movement deeply rooted in its environment... born of insurgency, reared in violent circumstances, and matured with a seemingly greater sense of realism and pragmatism."[40] Its political, military, and social services wings all became more effective. It operated hospitals, schools, discount pharmacies, groceries, and orphanages. It became Lebanon's second largest employer.[41] In southern Lebanon and the Shi'ite slums of Beirut, it performed the classic function of parallel government, developing infrastructure, and providing loans and reconstruction aid where the Lebanese government could not or would not.[42] This was particularly effective after the Israeli attacks on that part of the country in the summer of 2006. Hezbollah was at the forefront of relief and reconstruction efforts, propelling it to new heights of popularity not only among its own constituency, but among other Lebanese and Arabs as well. Hezbollah, as journalist Robert Fisk wrote, "won the war for 'hearts and minds'."[43]

Politically, Hezbollah has benefited from the skilful leadership of Hassan Nasrallah, secretary general of the organization since the assassination of Abbas al-Musawi in 1992. Nasrallah is an astute and charismatic strategist who has attained a tremendous following and status not only in Lebanon, but across the Arab world. He has adjusted Hezbollah's programs to focus on unifying issues such as opposition to Israel rather than divisive ones such as the transformation of Lebanon into an Iranian-style Islamic state. He integrated his organization into the Lebanese political process. By 2006 it held 14 seats in parliament plus several ministries. While Hezbollah continued to benefit from extensive Iranian and Syrian support, it also developed its own funding sources, in part from involvement in organized crime but, more importantly, via contributions from the extensive Lebanese diaspora.[44] Simultaneously, Hezbollah became skillful at psychological warfare, using a variety of communications techniques based on the Internet and on its own media, particularly al-Manar television.[45]

Militarily, Hezbollah has been called the "best guerrilla force in the world."[46] While using suicide bombers, it developed a significant capability for larger irregular operations, waging "an efficient, disciplined, and popular guerrilla war against the Israeli military" in southern Lebanon until Israel's withdrawal in 2000.[47] Hezbollah was connected to a number of terrorist attacks outside Lebanon, including two bombings in Buenos Aires and the 1996 attack on a U.S. military barracks at Khobar Towers in Saudi Arabia. The 2006 conflict with Israel further demonstrated Hezbollah's military prowess. As Andrew Exum notes, in comparison to other Arab forces which have faced the Israeli Defense Forces, Hezbollah is skilled at tactical maneuver, the use of its weapons systems, and flexible small unit leadership.[48] While the Israelis inflicted serious damage on Hezbollah forces and their military infrastructure, the organization began rebuilding its armed capability immediately after the end of the conflict.[49]

Hezbollah thus constitutes one end of the spectrum of militias. But is it an archetype? There is little doubt that others, particularly in the Middle East, will attempt to emulate it. But Hezbollah could not have become what it is today without the significant external support it receives from Syria and particularly Iran. The question, then, is whether sponsorship of proxy or allied militias will remain an element of statecraft. An argument can be made that it will. Iran's Quds Force trains a variety of groups, most of which would like to replicate Hezbollah's success.[50] And other states also use foreign militias as proxies. Many of the militias in the Democratic Republic of the Congo, for instance, are sponsored by bordering states.[51] But an equally strong case can be made that only Iran has made sponsorship of co-communal militias a central part of its national security strategy. Most of the militia sponsors in Central Africa (and elsewhere) would probably drop this activity in the face of even modest pressure. Ultimately some militias might attempt to copy Hezbollah, but few, if any, will succeed.

The Kamajors of Sierra Leone illustrate the other end of the spectrum. Like Hezbollah, they were formed when individuals already skilled in the use of violence were organized for a political purpose, and when public order collapsed in the face of government ineptitude and weakness.[52] The Kamajors were hunters from the south and east of Sierra Leone employed by local chiefs. Tribal hunting societies in West Africa traditionally protected their villages. Beginning as early as 1992, such groups began to confront the brutal Revolutionary United Front (RUF) insurgents.[53] In 1994 Kamajors defeated the RUF around the city of Bo. Prior to this, the RUF had convinced many of the people of Sierra Leone that they were protected by magic. The Kamajors were able to "demystify" them.[54] In 1996 President Ahmed Tejan Kabbah decided to use the Kamajors to replace foreign security contractors in government counterinsurgency operations. The group undertook autonomous actions and operated in conjunction with the foreign security corporations, government military forces, and, later, with international peacekeepers from the Economic Community of West African

States (ECOWAS) and the United Nations (UN). Within 2 years they had supplanted government forces and militarily defeated the RUF. Because of their distrust of the government, they refused to integrate with its armed forces or disarm even after a settlement was reached with the RUF in 2002. As Comfort Ero notes:

> While their original involvement in the war was essentially to defend their communities, one of the most bitter observations is that they were successfully mobilised by government forces to use extreme coercion in the fight against rebel forces. In the end, they are part of the political problem confronting Sierra Leone. The heavy reliance of the Kabbah administration during the war inevitably challenges and undermines programmes aimed at restructuring Sierra Leone's armed forces in the post-war climate.[55]

A government engaged in counterinsurgency can approach militias in several ways. It can treat them the same as insurgents, using a combination of carrots and sticks. This must include some sort of demobilization and reintegration program, providing skills and opportunities for former militia members. It must be more beneficial for militia leaders and members to become part of the legitimate economy and state power system than to maintain their own alternative ones. This holds some prospect if the conditions that led to the formation of the militia in the first place can be addressed. The government—if considered legitimate and competent by the militias—must be able to provide security to the militia's constituency. That was what was attempted (unsuccessfully) in Iraq as Ambassador J. Paul Bremer and the Coalition Provisional Authority worked out a deal with the militias which would shift their members to either the Iraqi state military or civilian society.[56] Unfortunately, the plan failed when the government could not protect the Kurdish and Shi'ite communities. If a militia was formed to advance the interests of its leaders or it mutated into this, it may be very expensive or even impossible for the government to convince it to disband.

Cooptation is another approach. Governments can leave militias intact, buying them off with concessions or even simple cash. Governments sometimes use militias as proxies, finding them useful for dirty work that attracts pressure or disapproval if performed by state forces. Sudan's use of *janjaweed* militias against rebels or potential rebel supporters in Darfur and other ethnic militias to undermine and fight the insurgency centered on the Sudanese People's Liberation Movement (SPLM), Shi'ite militias linked to the regime in Iraq, and right wing United Self-Defense Forces of Colombia (AUC) are examples.[57] This can be risky since the government has little or no control over the militias. Again the paradoxical logic is at play: militias, being less constrained, may be more effective at actually destroying insurgents, but in so doing they may undercut public support for the counterinsurgency effort, making long-term success more difficult.

The inability of governments to control militias means that it is easy for them to become involved in criminal enterprises—a fairly common pattern. The AUC in Colombia, for instance, moved into narcotics production and trafficking. In 2000 its leader admitted that 70 percent of the group's funding came from the drug trade.[58] In addition, militias may have less developed procedures than the government for vetting members or performing counterintelligence, increasing the chances of penetration by the insurgents. In Afghanistan the government has trained thousands of men affiliated with local militias to boost the security forces even though there are criminals and Taliban sympathizers among them. "We know," said Ross Davies, a Canadian police officer involved in the program, "that we are probably training some of the bad guys."[59] Militias trained and armed by the government as part of a counterinsurgency campaign may use their new prowess for other purposes, whether in conflict with each other or against the government. Again Afghanistan is instructive, with critics warning that plans to rearm the militias, even though intended to hinder the Taliban, will fuel tribal rivalries.[60] There is also the risk that militias integrated into government security forces may hijack them for their own ends, using the contacts, training, and equipment they have received to benefit their own constituency.

Even when it does not directly use militias, a government can form a loose working relationship with them. In Iraq, for instance, Sabrina Tavernise notes that most Shi'ite neighborhoods in Baghdad are run by "a complex network of relationships among the local militias, the police, and a powerful local council."[61] This too is dangerous. Members of *Jaish al Mahdi*, the Shi'ite militia led by Moqtada al Sadr, are known to infiltrate the police and military to obtain training and equipment.[62] If (or when) it faces the government in open conflict, this will make it a more challenging opponent. Similarly Iraq's Kurdish leaders have inserted more than 10,000 fighters from their Peshmerga militias into the Iraqi army, possibly to help with the development of an independent Kurdistan in the future.[63] In Iraq's south, Iranian backed militias increase the influence of Teheran at the expense of the government in Baghdad.[64]

The appropriate approach, of course, depends on the nature of the militia itself, including its relationship to the insurgents, its objectives, and its power. If the insurgents pose a major threat to the government, the wisest policy may be to tolerate or placate powerful militias, perhaps waiting until later to deal with them. If the insurgency is under control, the government might be able to deal with other security problems, including militias. And the appropriate approach to a militia or multiple militias depends on the ultimate objective of the government. If its goals are extensive—a nation where the state itself holds a monopoly on coercion—then militias must be neutralized or eradicated. If the goals are more modest, such as an acceptable level of stability and state control or simply the defeat of the insurgents, then militias might be tolerated.

Tolerating militias, though, condemns a state to perpetual weakness, increasing the likelihood of future conflict. Militias can even hinder counterinsurgency. In Iraq, for instance, the profusion of Shi'ite militias—however justified—increases the insecurity of the Sunni community and thus makes political resolution of the insurgency more difficult.[65] But beleaguered states are often forced to tolerate militias even when they do not want to, simply because of an inability to do anything about them. Few outside states—even those committed to counterinsurgency—will provide significant assistance for a countermilitia campaign. It is hard to imagine, for instance, the deployment of American troops and advisers in such a role. Since militias do not seek to take over a nation and rule it, ignoring them simply leaves the state weak but, in some sense, intact. They are like a parasite that renders its host vulnerable to other diseases but does not actually kill it. For this reason, they do not pose enough of a strategic threat that the United States or other states will become involved. So again, the paradoxical logic appears: an alliance with militias or even the creation of proxy militias might initially seem to be the best option for a state facing a serious insurgency, but may not be for long-term stabilization. It is a dangerous expedient.

One other type of militia merits consideration. Some analysts contend that the Internet has made "virtual" militias (and insurgencies) possible and potentially dangerous.[66] That runs counter to the definition of militias used here since "virtual" militias do not control territory or assume state functions. Perhaps, though, virtual militias and insurgents should be considered a separate category. Interestingly, just as the emergence of "real" insurgents sometimes spawn the creation of counterinsurgent militias, the emergence of "virtual" insurgents has led to the formation of virtual counterinsurgent vigilantes. One example is the "Internet Haganah," part of a network of private anti-terrorist web monitoring services, which collects information on extremist websites, passes this on to state intelligence services, and attempts to convince Internet service providers not to host radical sites.[67] The logic is that it takes a network to counter a network. As insurgents and terrorists become more networked and more "virtual," states, with their inherently bureaucratic procedures and hierarchical organizations, will be ineffective. Vigilantes, without such constraints, may be.

Criminal Organizations. In any society where insurgency takes root, organized crime will be pervasive. This is more than coincidence. Both sprout from common roots: ineffective governance, systemic weakness and pathology, and a culture or tradition of clandestine activity. Criminal organizations, though, tend to have different objectives and characteristics than militias and insurgencies. They have little or no sense of serving a constituency other than their members. Their relationship with society is purely parasitic; they seek public passivity rather than active support. They do provide economic opportunity and, in some cases, a sense of social identity, but only to their members. Criminal organizations may control territory or "turf," but they seldom, if ever, perform public administrative functions.[68]

Insurgents may be customers, partners, or enemies of organized crime. As customers, they purchase or trade for arms, information, other resources such as the kidnapping victims captured by Iraqi criminal gangs, or services such as smuggling and money laundering. As partners, they protect and profit from illicit activity. This is particularly common in narcotics-producing regions. According to the UN, insurgents were linked to drug trafficking in seven of the world's nine key drug producing areas.[69] "Today, the bulk of the global cultivation of opium and coca," Svante E. Cornell wrote, "is taking place in conflict zones, while the trafficking of their derivatives has come to heavily involve insurgent and terrorist groups operating between the source and destination areas of illicit drugs."[70] Crime diminishes the need to raise money from the public or external sponsors. It gives the insurgent leaders the funds to buy weapons and exercise patronage and corruption. This connection between insurgency and crime comes both from *need*—insurgents must finance and supply themselves—and *opportunity*. As Chris Dishman argues, pressure from security forces leads terrorist organizations (and, one would assume, insurgencies as well) to decentralize. Lower and mid-level components of the organization, operating with little oversight from top leadership, are free to form closer bonds with criminal organizations.[71] And they see benefits in doing so since having their own sources of income makes them even more autonomous from the upper echelons of their organization.

Insurgencies can evolve into criminal organizations. "Particularly in protracted conflicts," Cornell notes, "entire groups or parts of groups come to shift their focus increasingly toward the objective of profit."[72] The best example is the Revolutionary Armed Forces of Colombia (FARC).[73] Cornell again is instructive:

> Over time, insurgent groups tend to become increasingly involved in the drug trade. Beginning with tolerating and taxing the trade, insurgents tend to gradually shift to more lucrative self-involvement. Self-involvement, in turn, generates a risk of affecting insurgent motivational structures, tending to weaken ideological motivations and strengthen economic ones.[74]

This happens across the globe. For instance, most armed combatants in Africa's internal wars have either supplanted existing organized criminal networks or merged with them.[75]

Iraq is a classic case of preexisting organized crime initially developing a partnership with insurgents followed by a melding where the insurgents themselves became criminal organizations or, at least, barely distinguishable from organized crime.[76] The corrupt nature of Saddam Hussein's regime created a fertile environment for this. After the implementation of UN sanctions in the 1990s, the regime itself ran many rackets with Uday Hussein at the pinnacle. The Ba'ath party, Robert Looney notes, "became more an organized crime syndicate than a political organization."[77] Saddam Hussein allowed this as a form of patronage. Since former regime members played a major role in the early days of the insurgency, it was easy for the insurgents to capitalize on the criminal connections and procedures already in place. Iranian based criminal gangs added to the problem. A good portion of the looting that took place in March and April 2003 was engineered or funded by these gangs.[78]

Initially the Iraqi insurgents did not need to use criminal activity to raise funds. Former regime officials had plenty of money left from their days in power and augmented this with foreign contributions. At this point, the insurgents were primarily customers for organized crime, buying weapons and kidnapping victims from the gangs. Eventually, though, the insurgents themselves turned to crime when their prewar resources were depleted. The petroleum black market was especially lucrative, but kidnapping, money laundering, and the drug trade also generated funds.[79] By 2006, according U.S. assessments, the insurgents were raising tens of millions of dollars from smuggling, kidnapping, counterfeiting, and robbery.[80] Simultaneously, Iraq's militias merged with or became criminal organizations. This greatly complicated counterinsurgency efforts. As a report from Oxford Analytica noted, "Rampant serious and violent crime in Iraq seriously reduces the government's ability to fight terrorism and insurgency, preventing community intelligence-gathering and providing militants with a community of traffickers and 'paid-for' attackers to support militancy."[81]

Counterinsurgents can approach criminal organizations in a number of ways. They may ignore them, particularly if the criminals are not closely tied to the insurgency. Or the regime may take a more active stance, coopting criminal organizations by giving them something they want (control of a market niche, amnesty) in exchange for severing ties to the insurgents or active participation in the counterinsurgency campaign. After the 2001 American invasion of Afghanistan, for instance, U.S. officials apparently worked out a deal with Afghan drug lord Haji Bashir Noorzai to obtain information about the Taliban.[82] As with militias, such an approach simply postpones dealing with the criminal problem. This may be necessary, but it is never desirable. Again like militias, the government knows that external support may diminish or dry up after the defeat of the insurgency, leaving it to undertake an anticrime campaign on its own (unless the state hosts major narcotic producers or traffickers). Alternatively, the government may seek to neutralize or crush criminal organizations, particularly if the criminals are closely linked to the insurgents or if the insurgency itself is at a low enough level to allow the diversion of security resources to other tasks. As with militias, the appropriate response is shaped both by the nature of the insurgency and by the specific role that criminal organizations play in it.

Private Military Companies. Private military companies (PMCs) have existed for millennia. States used them to augment their own capabilities, particularly in specialized skills that their own forces lacked. A state could hire mercenaries when necessary without having to bear the cost and risk of a standing military.[83] All that was required was demand and supply—warriors with skills not needed or wanted by their own states.

Today PMCs provide the same benefits: specialized capabilities, surge capacity, and controllability. These are all important in counterinsurgency. As Herbert Howe noted, private armed organizations can deploy faster than multinational and perhaps even national forces (with fewer political restrictions). They can be less financially taxing than state forces in a multinational coalition, and the states hiring them can handpick from a pool of combat veterans.[84] There are three types of PMCs (or three types of PMC services since individual companies can provide two or even three of the services): military *provider* firms which undertake actual combat; military *consultant* firms which provide advice and training; and military *support* firms which offer functions such as logistics, intelligence, and medical care.[85] The 1990s, the breakup of the Soviet Union, the advent of majority rule in South Africa, and eventually the end of the Balkan wars produced many people with military and intelligence experience but limited prospects for using them in their own nations.[86] In the United States, the desire to rationalize defense and the demands of protracted peace operations in the Balkans and elsewhere led to an increased reliance on contractors for a wide range of services. The American military, with its very competitive career system, always retired a large number of relatively young officers and noncommissioned officers. For many, the idea of staying involved in defense issues as consultants and contractors is appealing.

Military providers are the most controversial type of PMCs. They gained worldwide attention in the 1990s through the actions of Executive Outcomes, a firm composed of former members of the South African Defence Force (SADF), most with a background in special forces. In the 1990s, the beleaguered govern- ments of Sierra Leone and Angola hired Executive Outcomes for counterinsurgency.[87] While the arrangements were eventually terminated because of the financial burden they placed on the African governments, the company had impressive tactical success, particularly in Sierra Leone.[88] Ironically, the formation of ethnically-based militias in that country—the Kamajors, Tamboro, and Kapras—led the regime to conclude it could protect itself without Executive Outcomes.[89] At about the same time, the government of Papua New Guinea hired Sandline International, another PMC initially spun off from Executive Outcomes, and Sri Lanka contracted counterinsurgency assistance from Saladin Security.[90] The primary function of PMCs in these conflicts was not pacification per se, but protecting the resources which funded the government.[91]

The Balkans conflict of the 1990s illustrated the importance of military consultant firms. Military Professional Resources International (MPRI), a firm founded by retired U.S. Army senior officers and jokingly referred to as "generals without borders," played a legendary role in professionalizing the Croatian military.[92] To some in the United States, the idea of using retired officers as trainers and advisers was very attractive. But it is not new. In 1990 Rod Paschall argued that the U.S. military itself was not well-suited for what was then called "low intensity conflict" (which included counterinsurgency) and hence should rely on contractors, especially retired Special Forces soldiers.[93]

The war on terror revived the idea of contractors as "force multipliers." Since 2003, for instance, Iraq has seen a greater reliance on PMCs than any counterinsurgency campaign in history. Military providers like Blackwater U.S.A., a company founded in 1998 by former Navy SEALs, have provided security details for American and Iraqi officials, private contractors, nongovernmental organizations, and journalists.[94] They also guarded oil fields, convoys, banks, residential compounds, and office buildings. And Blackwater is only one of many PMCs which have played a role in Iraq. A year into the insurgency, there were an estimated 20,000 foreign soldiers from a dizzying array of backgrounds.[95] By 2007, there were 48,000.[96] Much of the logistics for the U.S. military has been handled by the giant firms Halliburton and KBR (formerly Kellogg, Brown, and Root). Nearly every PMC in the United States and the United Kingdom has had a contract of some sort in Iraq, and many more were created expressly for that conflict.

For outside providers of counterinsurgency support, particularly the United States, PMCs are appealing. Like contracting in general, PMCs free uniformed service members for other tasks. The complexity of counterinsurgency makes the experience of older, retired, or former service members particularly valuable. In his February 2007 congressional testimony, for instance, Lieutenant General David Petraeus, the commander of American forces in Iraq, said he considered the thousands of contract security forces an important addition to the American military and Iraqi forces.[97] While contractors are paid more than soldiers, they are cheaper in the long run since the U.S. Government has no obligation to provide benefits or career advancement. They help retention by cutting down on the time that soldiers are deployed. PMCs also increase the chances of sustaining support for U.S. involvement in a counterinsurgency campaign. For some reason, the public seems to have greater tolerance for casualties among American contractors (and certainly among non-American contractors) than American servicemen.[98]

But there are problems. Sandline provides a good illustration. The company, led by British Lieutenant Colonel (Ret.) Tim Spicer, undertook both combat operations and training. It was closely linked to mineral and oil extraction companies, protecting them in the midst of internal conflicts and the inability of the state to provide security. In Sierra Leone, Sandline continued where Executive Outcomes left off. However, its involvement in a plan to import weapons into Sierra Leone despite an international ban discredited the company and its supporters in the British government. Then Spicer was jailed in Papua New Guinea when the government changed. According to the Sandline website, the company disbanded in 2004 because of a

> ... general lack of governmental support for Private Military Companies willing to help end armed conflicts in places like Africa, in the absence of effective international intervention ... Without such support the ability of Sandline to make a positive difference in countries where there is widespread brutality and genocidal behaviour is materially diminished.[99]

The short and tumultuous life of this company illustrates some of the problems associated with using PMCs in counterinsurgency.

Like any contractor, PMCs are more focused on fulfillment of their contract than on larger strategic objectives. For instance, former Marine Colonel T. X. Hammes has described the adverse effects of PMC personal security detachments in Iraq. They were so determined to protect their VIP that they sometimes abused or frightened Iraqi bystanders—precisely the people the counterinsurgency campaign sought to win over. As Hammes put it, "The contractor was hired to protect the principal. He had no stake in pacifying the country... and generally treated locals as expendable."[100] The same charge has been leveled against Dyncorp security contractors in Afghanistan.[101] Lines of authority can be confused when PMCs are present since contractors report to the agency that hired them rather than the military authority in a given area. PMCs are not under the same discipline as government troops. They may not follow official rules of engagement.[102] And they can abandon a conflict zone if conditions become difficult, potentially leaving government forces in the lurch.[103] With PMCs—as with most things—those who hire them get what they pay for. Quality is expensive. If a government runs out of money, PMCs leave regardless of whether the state can function without them. Ultimately, then, using PMCs for counterinsurgency may be a necessary short-term expedient, but *relying* on them is dangerous. The key is whether the government takes advantage of the breathing space given by PMCs to develop its own capability.

Fourth Forces.

Fourth forces are unarmed groups or organizations which affect an insurgency. The most common types are foreign or multinational corporations (excluding PMCs); international and nongovernmental organizations; and international media and other information organizations. As with third forces, they have proliferated. In many cases, they pursue a titular neutrality, not explicitly seeking the victory of either side. In effect, though, their actions often benefit one of the participants more than the others.

International Corporations. The involvement of international corporations in a complex conflict is a dual-edged sword. They can strengthen and fund a beleaguered government by buying its products or paying for market concessions. They may sell weapons or other goods and services needed for the counterinsurgency campaign. But they also may place conditions on sales, loans, or other deals. These are difficult enough for a weak state during peacetime, but can be even more dangerous during armed conflict. Corporations can inadvertently erode the legitimacy of governments by making them appear as the puppets or proxies of foreigners. Although it is rarer, international corporations can help insurgents when the rebels control some valuable resource such as diamonds or coltan.[104]

International Media. International news coverage can affect insurgencies even when not seeking to do so. By publicizing a conflict—particularly its humanitarian costs—the international media brings pressure to cease hostilities or arrive at a speedy settlement. But this seldom falls equally on both insurgents and counterinsurgents. There is more pressure on the government to make concessions than on insurgents to cease operations. Governments are more susceptible to international pressure than insurgencies. Most insurgencies, especially those involved in crime, can survive with little or no outside support. No government can. The world has more leverage over states than over insurgents. Media coverage leads outsiders to use this influence, holding states to higher ethical standards.

In addition, most members of the media have an inherent anti-authoritarian bias. While they may not state it openly, they often assume that there is some justification for an insurgency. The tendency is to accord insurgents "victim" status. And the public loves a victim. Hence extensive international media coverage of an insurgency tends to promote the perception of moral parity. Seldom are insurgents portrayed as illegitimate aggressors. This tendency is amplified when the United States is involved. There is a growing hostility toward the United States among the global media which leads to negative coverage of any cause that Washington supports.

International media and other sources for the transmission of information level the psychological playing field. In the 20th century, insurgents struggled to reach external audiences. Only bold and intrepid reporters would venture to the difficult, dangerous areas where insurgents operated. It was the paradoxical logic again: insurgents protected themselves by remaining in remote regions, but this made it difficult to publicize their cause. Now the global media, satellite communications, cell phones, the Internet, and other information technology gives insurgents instant access to national and world audiences. Once the communications channels opened, the flexibility of insurgents and their lack of ethical and legal constraints gave them advantages in the psychological battlespace. This did not assure success—many insurgents transmitted ineffective messages or put themselves in danger by publicity—but it did offer an opportunity to make a connection with supporters they might not otherwise have found. Like spam email, the greater the bulk of the transmission, the greater the likelihood that *someone* will be receptive (while nonreceptive audiences simply ignore unwanted messages).

In Iraq, for instance, Al Zawaraa television, which is owned by a Sunni member of Iraq's Parliament living in Damascus and distributed by Nilesat, an Egyptian-government-owned company, is considered the semi official voice of the Sunni insurgents, broadcasting propaganda videos they produce, including those showing bloody attacks.[105] It has signed a distribution deal with several European companies to broadcast it there and in the United States. The wildly popular Qatar-based news network Al Jazeera, while less overtly linked to the insurgents than Al Zawaraa, contributed to the rebel information campaign through a steady barrage of criticism of the United States and the Iraqi government (at least until expelled in 2004). Whether one believes that Al Jazeera offered a "balanced" perspective (as it claimed) or supported the insurgents, it complicated counterinsurgent information operations and provided the insurgents publicity (and hence legitimacy) they would not otherwise have had. This also helped them adjust and refine their operations. As Tony Cordesman puts it in his study of the Iraq conflict:

> Iraqi terrorist and insurgent organizations have learned that media reporting on the results of their attacks provides a powerful indicator of their success and what kind of attack to strike at in the future (sic). While many attacks are planned long in advance or use "targeting" based on infiltration or simple observation, others are linked to media reporting on events, movements, etc. The end result is that insurgents can "swarm" around given types of targets, striking at vulnerable points where the target and method of attack is known to have success.[106]

Nonmedia information sources, particularly the Internet, are an even more powerful tool for insurgents. Websites are used for recruitment and building linkages with other groups both in Iraq and externally.[107] The Internet is used to disseminate videos, pictures, and accounts of attacks as part of the insurgency's psychological operations and as a training aid. Cordesman notes that "Terrorist and insurgent organizations from all over the world have established the equivalent of an informal tactical net in which they exchange techniques for carrying out attacks, technical data on weapons, etc."[108] There may be more than 800 insurgent websites. And this does not even count the thousands of others which link to them. The Internet, even more than the media, is beyond the control of counterinsurgents. Techniques such as pressuring companies or states which host insurgent websites is futile.

International and Nongovernmental Organizations. International and nongovernmental organizations also level the playing field between insurgents and counterinsurgents. To gain access to insurgent controlled regions, international and nongovernment organizations often treat the rebels as the co-equals of the government, thus helping to legitimize them.[109] Insurgents are well aware of this and use it in their psychological campaign. Humanitarian organizations are almost always critical of military operations, whether by rebels or the government. The British relief group, Oxfam, for instance, often demands that the government of Uganda cease military operations against the brutal "Lord's Resistance Army."[110] Some observers even claim that humanitarian assistance organizations prolong conflicts once such groups develop a vested organizational interest in them.[111] Without humanitarian crises, humanitarian relief organizations would have no *raison d'etre*. Equally, the provision of humanitarian assistance relieves insurgents from the burden of caring for the population in areas they control and provides lootable or taxable income flows.[112]

External humanitarian efforts, while exceptionally valuable to alleviate suffering, may leave a state unprepared to take over the provision of services when the conflict ends or subsides. Hence the widespread involvement of international and nongovernmental organizations in an insurgency increases the chances that conflict will reemerge once the shortcomings and weaknesses of the state provide political space for insurgents or other violent actors. The paradoxical logic emerges once more: What seems best—the alleviation of suffering—may increase the chances of renewed suffering at a later date. Even so, it is impractical and counterproductive to deliberately limit the involvement of international and nongovernmental organizations in a conflict. Again, this reflects the political asymmetry of insurgency: governments who limit or control humanitarian efforts face intense pressure, while insurgents can do so with impunity.

Rethinking the Dynamics

Beginning in the 1990s, the scholarly and policy communities developed an extensive analytical literature on the internal conflicts that wracked the post-Cold War world. But when the U.S. military and other elements of the government began reassessing insurgency after 2001, they largely ignored this literature and instead drew on earlier analyses of the British experience in Malaya in the 1940s and 1950s, the French experience in Algeria in the 1950s, and the American experience in Vietnam in the 1960s and 1970s. As the U.S. Army sought to understand the conflict in Iraq, for instance, the most recommended books for its officers were John Nagl's *Learning to Eat Soup With a Knife* (which dealt with the British involvement in Malaya and the American experience in Vietnam) and David Galula's *Counterinsurgency Warfare* (which was drawn from the French campaigns in Indochina and Algeria).[113] Both are excellent. But both deal with wars of imperial maintenance or nationalistic transition, not with complex communal conflicts where armed militias and organized crime play a powerful role. This tendency to look too far back in the quest to understand contemporary insurgency is a serious flaw. More recent analysis of internal wars can tell us much about the insurgencies that the United States currently faces and may face in the future.

Because of globalization, the decline of overt state sponsorship of insurgency, the continuing importance of informal outside sponsorship, and the nesting of insurgency within complex conflicts associated with state weakness or failure, the dynamics of contemporary insurgency are more like a violent and competitive market than war in the traditional sense where clear and discrete combatants seek strategic victory. Thinking of insurgency in this way not only offers valuable insights into how it works, but also suggests a very different approach to counterinsurgency.

In economic markets, participants might dream of strategic "victory"—outright control of the market such as that exercised by Standard Oil prior to 1911—but many factors, especially competition and regulation, prevent it. The best they can hope for is to attain and sustain some degree of market *domination*. Most have even more limited objectives—survival and profitability. This also describes many insurgencies, particularly 21st century ones. Competition and other factors, such as the absence of state sponsors, mitigate against outright conquest of the state in the mode of Castro or Ho Chi Minh.[114] It is nearly impossible for a single entity, whether the state or a nonstate participant, to exercise a monopoly of power. Market domination and share constantly shift.

In contemporary complex conflicts, profitability often is literal rather than metaphorical. An extensive (and growing) analytical literature chronicles the evolution of violent movements like insurgencies from "grievance" to "greed."[115] The idea is that political grievances may instigate an insurgency but, as a conflict progresses, economic motives play a larger role, eventually even dominating. While combatants, "have continued to mobilize around political, communal, and security objectives," Karen Ballentine and Jake Sherman write, "increasingly these objectives have become obscured and sometimes contradicted by their more businesslike activities."[116] Conflict gives insurgents access to money and resources out of proportion to what they would have in peacetime. As Paul Collier, one of the pioneers of this idea, explains:

> Conflicts are far more likely to be caused by economic opportunities than by grievance. If economic agendas are driving conflict, then it is likely that some groups are benefiting from the conflict and these groups, therefore, have some interest in initiating and sustaining it.[117]

The counterinsurgents—the regime—also develop vested political and economic interests in sustaining a controllable conflict. A regime facing an armed insurgency is normally under somewhat less outside pressure for economic and political reform. It can justifiably demand more of its citizens and, conversely, postpone meeting their demands. Insurgency sometimes brings outside financial support and provides opportunities for corrupt regime members to tap black markets. Even though internal conflict may diminish overall economic activity, it increases profit margins by constraining competition. This, too, can work to the advantage of elites, including those in the government or security services. Collier continues:

> ... various identifiable groups will "do well out of the war." They are opportunistic businessmen, criminals, traders, and the rebel organizations themselves. The rebels will do well through predation on primary commodity exports, traders do well through the widened margins on the goods they sell to consumers, criminals will do well through theft, and opportunistic businessmen will do well at the expense of those businesses that are constrained to honest conduct.[118]

Internal wars "frequently involve the emergence of another alternative system of profit, power, and protection in which conflict serves the political and economic interests of a variety of groups."[119] Hence the insurgents, criminals, militias, or even the regime have a greater interest in sustaining a controlled conflict than in attaining victory.

The merging of armed violence and economics amplifies the degree to which complex conflicts emulate the characteristics and dynamics of volatile, hypercompetitive markets. For instance, like all markets, complex conflicts operate according to rules (albeit informal, unwritten ones). In the most basic sense, the rules dictate what is and is not acceptable as participants compete for market domination or share. Participants may violate the rules but doing so entails risk and cost. The more risk averse a participant—and governments are normally more risk averse than the nongovernment participants, and participants satisfied with their market position and with a positive expectation about the future are more risk averse than those which are unsatisfied and pessimistic about the future—the less likely it is to challenge the rules. And these rules are conflict- and time-specific; they periodically evolve and shift. This year's rule "road map" might not be next year's.

As in a commercial market, participants in a complex conflict may enter as small, personalistic companies. Some may even be like family businesses built on kinship or ethnicity. But, as in a commercial market, the more successful participants evolve into more complex, variegated corporate structures. Insurgencies then undertake many of the same practices as corporations:

- Acquisitions and mergers (insurgent factions may join in partnerships, or a powerful one may integrate a less powerful one);
- Shedding or closing unproductive divisions (insurgencies may pull out of geographic regions or jettison a faction of the movement);
- Forming strategic partnerships (insurgencies may arrange relationships with internal or external groups—political, criminal, etc.—which share their objectives. The profusion of information and information technology, of course, facilitates this. Just as information technology allows commercial businesses to form strategic partnerships which previously would have been impossible or ineffective, so too with insurgencies);
- Reorganizing for greater effectiveness and efficiency;
- Developing, refining, and at times abandoning products or product lines; (insurgencies develop political, psychological, economic, and military techniques, operational methods, or themes. They refine these over time, sometimes dropping those which prove ineffective or too costly);
- Advertising and creating brand identity (insurgent psychological activities are akin to advertising. Their "brands" include political and psychological themes, and particular methods and techniques);
- Accumulating and expending capital (insurgents accumulate both financial and political capital, using it as required);
- Subcontracting or contracting out functions (contemporary insurgents may contract out tasks they are ineffective at or which they wish to disassociate themselves from);
- Bringing in outside consultants (this can be done by physical presence of outside advisers or, in the contemporary environment, by "virtual" consultation);

- Entering and leaving market niches;
- Creating new markets and market niches;
- Creating and altering organizational culture; and,
- Professional development and establishing patterns of career progression.

Insurgencies, like militias, can be more or less complex, more or less formal. The more complex and formal they are, the more their behavioral dynamics emulate those of a corporation. Finally, as in commercial markets, a conflict market is affected by what happens in other markets as well—just as the automobile market is affected by the petroleum market, or the American national market by the European market, the Iraq conflict market is affected by the Afghan conflict market or by the market of political ideas in the United States and other parts of the Arab world.

That contemporary insurgents emulate corporations in a hyper competitive (and violent) market shapes their operational methods. Specifically, insurgents gravitate toward operational methods which maximize desired effects while minimizing the costs and risks. This, in conjunction with the profusion of information, the absence of state sponsors providing conventional military material, and the transparency of the operating environment, has increased the role terrorism plays for insurgents. Insurgents have always used terrorism. But one of the characteristics of this quintessentially psychological method of violence is that its effect is limited to those who know of it. When, for instance, the Viet Cong killed a local political leader, it might have had the desired psychological effect on people in the region, but did little to shape the beliefs, perceptions, or morale of those living far away. Today, information technology amplifies the psychological effects of a terrorist incident by publicizing it to a much wider audience. This includes both satellite, 24-hour media coverage, and, more importantly, the Internet which, Gordon McCormick and Frank Giordano note, "has made symbolic violence a more powerful instrument of insurgent mobilisation than at any time in the past."[120]

So terrorism is effective. It is easier and cheaper to undertake than conventional military operations. It is less costly and risky to the insurgent organization as a whole (since terrorist operations require only a very small number of personnel and a limited investment in training and materiel). It is efficient when psychological effects are compared to the resource investment. It allows insurgents to conjure an illusion of strength even when they are weak. Terrorism is less likely to lead to outright victory, but for an insurgency that does not seek that, but only market domination or survival, terrorism is the tool of choice.

As we approach the second decade of the 21st century, there are a few old-fashioned insurgencies trying to militarily defeat the government, triumphantly enter the capital city, and form their own regime. The more common pattern, though, are insurgencies which satisfy themselves with domination of all or part of the power market in their state. The insurgents in Iraq, Colombia, India, Sri Lanka, Uganda, and even Afghanistan have little hope of or even interest in becoming a regime—whether of their entire country or some break-away segment of it. To continue conceptualizing contemporary insurgency as a variant of traditional, Clausewitzean war, where two antagonists each seek to impose their will on and vanquish the opponent in pursuit of political objectives, does not capture today's reality. Clausewitz may have been right that war is always fought for political purposes, but not all armed conflict is war.

Rethinking Counterinsurgency

The rethinking of insurgency described in this monograph—the consideration of third and fourth forces, the nesting of insurgency in complex conflicts, the market approach to understanding the dynamics of insurgency, and so forth—suggests a very different way of thinking about (and undertaking) *counter*insurgency. At the strategic level, the risk to the United States is not that insurgents will "win" in the traditional sense, take over their country, and shift it from a partner to an enemy. It is that complex internal conflicts, especially ones involving insurgency, will generate other adverse effects: the destabilization of regions, resource flows, and markets; the blossoming of transnational crime; humanitarian disasters; transnational terrorism; and so forth. Given this, the U.S. goal should not automatically be the defeat of the insurgents by the regime (which may be impossible, particularly when the partner regime is only half-heartedly committed to it), but the rapid resolution of the conflict. In other words, a quick and sustainable outcome which integrates most of the insurgents into the national power structure is less damaging to U.S. national interests than a protracted conflict which leads to the complete destruction of the insurgents. Protracted conflict, not insurgent victory, is the threat.

The traditional American solution to insurgency is to strengthen the regime and encourage it to reform. Today, that may no longer be adequate. All trends are toward less effective central governments, not more so, particularly in the type of nations prone to insurgency. The norm is some sort of power-sharing arrangement between the state and other organizations and forces. And, as noted earlier, regimes themselves often develop a vested interest in sustainment of controlled conflict. Thus the state-centric approach to counterinsurgency codified in American strategy and doctrine swims against the tide of history.

Because Americans consider insurgency a form of war, U.S. strategy and doctrine are based on the same notion as the more general approach to war: it is a pathological action which evil people impose on an otherwise peace-loving society. It is a disease which sometimes infects an otherwise healthy body politic. This metaphor is a useful one. Today, Americans consider a human body without parasites and pathogens "normal." When parasites or pathogens invade, medical treatment eradicates them and restores the body to its "normal" condition. But throughout most of human history, persistent parasites and pathogens were, in fact, normal. Most people simply toler ated them. Today this characterizes conflict in many parts of the world. Rather than an abnormal and episodic condition which should be eradicated, it is normal and tolerable.

Because Americans see insurgency as a form of war and, following Clausewitz, view war as quintessentially political, they focus on the political causes and dimensions of insurgency. Certainly insurgency does have an important political component. But that is only part of the picture. Insurgency also fulfills the economic and psychological needs of the insurgents. It provides a source of income out of proportion to what the insurgents could otherwise earn, particularly for the lower ranks. And, it provides a source of identity and empowerment for those with few other sources of these things. Without a gun, most insurgent foot soldiers are simply poor, uneducated, disempowered youth with no prospects. Insurgency changes that. It makes insurgents important and powerful. And it provides them a livelihood. Again, the market metaphor is useful: so long as demand exists, supply and a market to link supply and demand will appear. So long as there are unmet human needs which can be addressed by irregular violence, markets of violence will be created.

The tendency of insurgencies to evolve into criminal organizations suggests that counterinsurgency strategy itself must undergo significant shifts during the course of a conflict. If an insurgency has reached the point that it is motivated more by greed than grievance, addressing the political causes of the conflict will not be effective. The counterinsurgency campaign must become more like a counterorganized crime or countergang program. Law enforcement should replace the military as the primary manager of a mature counterinsurgency campaign. This evolving life cycle of insurgency also implies that there is a window of opportunity early in an insurgency before its psychological, political, and economic dynamics are set. For outsiders undertaking counterinsurgency, a rapid, large-scale security, political, law enforcement, intelligence, and economic effort in the nascent stages of an insurgency will bring greater results than an incremental increase in assistance after the conflict has set. Timing matters.

In cases where a serious insurgency cannot be managed, the state and its supporters might consider an approach designed to deliberately encourage the insurgency to mutate into something less dangerous such as an organized criminal organization. This is never desirable, but there may be rare instances where organized crime is less of a threat than sustained insurgency. Call this strategic methadone.

Because Americans view insurgency as political, American counterinsurgency strategy and doctrine stress the need for political reform in societies which suffer from it. This is necessary but not sufficient. A comprehensive counterinsurgency strategy must simultaneously raise the economic and psychological costs and risks of participation in an insurgency (or other forms of conflict) and provide alternatives. David Keen has written:

> In order to move toward more lasting solution to the problem of mass violence, we need to understand and acknowledge that for significant groups this violence represents not a problem but a solution. We need to think of modifying the structure of incentives that are encouraging people to orchestrate, fund, or perpetuate acts of violence.[121]

Hence economic assistance and job training are as important to counterinsurgency as political reform. Businesses started and jobs created as are as much "indicators of success" as insurgents killed or intelligence provided. Because the margins for economic activity tend to widen during conflict, counterinsurgency should attempt to make markets as competitive as pos-sible.[122] Because economies dependent on exports of a single commodity or a few commodities are particularly prone to protracted conflict, counterinsurgency must include a plan for economic diversification.[123] A comprehensive counterinsurgency strategy must offer alternative sources of identity and empowerment for bored, disillusioned, and disempowered young males. Simply providing low paying, low status jobs or the opportunity to attend school is not enough. To develop more effective programs for this, counterinsurgent planners should consult inner city community leaders with relevant experience.

Women's empowerment—an inevitable brake on the aggression of disillusioned young males—also should be a central part of a comprehensive counterinsurgency strategy. But this illustrates one of the enduring problems and paradoxes of counterinsurgency: What are outside counterinsurgency supporters to do when some element of a nation's *culture* contributes to the conflict? Evidence suggest that cultures based on female repression, a warrior ethos, and some other social structures and factors are more prone to violence. Should counterinsurgency support attempt to alter the culture, or simply accept the fact that even when insurgency is quelled, it is likely to reappear?

The core dilemma, then, is that truly resolving insurgency requires extensive social reengineering. Yet this is extremely difficult (and expensive). This problem has many manifestations. In some cases, it may be impossible to provide forms of employment and sources of identity more lucrative than insurgency. Regimes and national elites—the very partners the

United States seeks to empower in counterinsur-gency—often see actions necessary to stem the insurgency as a threat to their hold on power. The conflict itself may be the lesser evil. For many regimes, insurgents pose less of a threat than a unified and effective security force. More regimes have been overthrown by coups than by insurgencies. Hence they deliberately keep their security forces weak and divided. Alas, those with the greatest personal interest in resolving the conflict—the people—have the least ability to create peace.[124] Yet American strategy and doctrine are based on the assumption that our partners seek the same thing we do: the quickest possible resolution of the conflict. We assume our partners will pursue political reform and security force improvement. We thus are left perplexed when insurgencies like the ongoing one in Colombia fester for decades, unable to grasp the dissonance between our objectives and those of our erstwhile allies.

The implications of this are profound. If, in fact, insurgency is not simply a variant of war, if the real threat is the deleterious effects of sustained conflict, and if it is part of systemic failure and pathology in which key elites and organizations develop a vested interest in sustaining the conflict, the objective of counterinsurgency support should *not* be simply strengthening the government so that it can impose its will more effectively on the insurgents, but systemic reengineering. The most effective posture for outsiders is not to be an ally of the government and thus a sustainer of the flawed socio-political-economic system, but to be a neutral mediator and peacekeeper (even when the outsiders have much more ideological affinity for the regime than for the insurgents).[125] If this is true, the United States should only undertake counterinsurgency support in the most pressing instances.

Outside of the historic American geographic area of concern (the Caribbean basin), the United States should only undertake counterinsurgency as part of an equitable, legitimate, and broad-based multinational coalition. Unless the world community is willing to form a neo-trusteeship such as in Bosnia, Eastern Slavonia, Kosovo, and East Timor in order to reconstruct the administration, security system, and civil society of a state in conflict, the best that can be done is ameliorating, as much as possible, the human suffering associated with the violence by creating internationally-protected "safe areas."[126] In most cases, American strategic resources are better spent attempting to prevent insurgency or containing it when it does occur. Clearly systemic reengineering is not a task for the United States acting alone. Nor is it a task for the U.S. military. When the United States is part of a stabilization coalition, the primary role for the U.S. military should be protecting civilians until other security forces, preferably local ones but possibly coalition units, can assume that task.

To summarize, then, American strategy for counterinsurgency should recognize three distinct insurgency settings, each demanding a different response:

- A functioning government with at least some degree of legitimacy can be rescued by Foreign Internal Defense.
- There is no functioning and legitimate government but a broad international and regional consensus supports the creation of a neo-trusteeship until systemic reengineering is completed. In such instances, the United States should provide military, economic, and political support as part of a multinational force operating under the authority of the UN.
- There is no functioning and legitimate government and no international or regional consensus for the formation of a neo-trusteeship. In these cases, the United States should pursue containment of the conflict by support to regional states and, in conjunction with partners, help create humanitarian "safe zones" within the conflictive state.

This is a radically different way of thinking about counterinsurgency than is currently found in U.S. strategy and doctrine. But if the American defense community fails to rethink insurgency, the United States is unlikely to be successful at counterinsurgency should future political leaders again deem it in the national interest.

Recommendations

- With the Army and the Marine Corps playing a major role, the U.S. Government should begin an interagency and multinational effort to develop new strategic concepts, strategies, doctrine, and capabilities for dealing with complex conflicts and systemic failures and pathologies which include imbedded insurgencies. The primary role for the U.S. military should be temporarily protecting civilians
- Army leader development, professional education, doctrine, training, and wargaming should be revised to reflect the results of this process.

Endnotes

1 For instance, Colin S. Gray, *Another Bloody Century: Future War*, London: Weidenfeld and Nicolson, 2005, pp. 30–34.

2 On the activities of insurgents during the initial coalescence of their movement (particularly the role of violence), see Gordon H. McCormick and Frank Giordano, "Things Come Together: Symbolic Violence and Guerrilla Mobilisation," *Third World Quarterly*, Vol. 28, No. 2, 2007, pp. 295–320; and Daniel Byman, *Understanding Proto-Insurgencies*, Santa Monica, CA: RAND Corporation, 2007.

3 Edward N. Luttwak, *Strategy: The Logic of War and Peace*, Cambridge, MA: Belknap, 1987.

4 For instance, see Gary Anderson, "The Baathists' Blundering Guerrilla War," *Washington Post*, June 26, 2003, p. A29.

5 *Discriminate Deterrence*, Report of the Commission on Integrated Long-Term Strategy, January 1988, p. 13.

[6] Field Manual (FM) 100–20/Air Force Pamphlet (AFP) 32, *Military Operations in Low Intensity Conflict*, Washington, DC: Headquarters, Department of the Army and Department of the Air Force, 1990, p. X.

[7] Bard E. O'Neill, *Insurgency and Terrorism: From Revolution to Apocalypse*, 2d Ed., revised, Washington, DC: Potomac, 2005. In this update of his 2001 book, O'Neill categorized insurgencies as anarchist, egalitarian, traditionalist, apocalyptic-utopian, pluralist, secessionist, reformist, preservationist, or commercialist.

[8] Joint Publication 1-02, *Department of Defense Dictionary of Military and Associated Terms*, April 2001, as amended through January 2007, p. 263.

[9] FM 3-24/Marine Corps Warfighting Publication (MCWP) 3-33.5, *Counterinsurgency*, Washington, DC: Headquarters, Department of the Army, and Headquarters, U.S. Marine Corps, December 2006, p. 1-1.

[10] FM 100–20/AFP 3-2, *Military Operations in Low Intensity Conflict*, p. X.

[11] *Ibid*.

[12] FM 3-24/MCWP 3-33.5, *Counterinsurgency*, p. 1–1.

[13] Some influential strategic thinkers continue to advocate a *more* aggressive, warlike approach to counterinsurgency. See, for instance, Edward N. Luttwak, "Dead End: Counterinsurgency Warfare as Military Malpractice," *Harpers*, February 2007, pp. 33–42; and Ralph Peters, *Never Quit the Fight*, Mechanicsburg, PA: Stackpole, 2006.

[14] FM 3-07, *Stability Operations and Support Operations*, Washington, DC: Headquarters, Department of the Army, February 2003, p. 3-0.

[15] Daniel L. Byman, "Friends Like These: Counterinsurgency and the War on Terrorism," *International Security*, Vol. 31, No. 2, Fall 2006, pp. 85–87. David Kilcullen argues that al Qaeda's grand strategy is, in fact, an insurgent one, and thus the war on terrorism is most accurately thought of as global counterinsurgency ("Countering Global Insurgency," *Journal of Strategic Studies*, Vol. 28, No. 4, August 2005, pp. 597–617).

[16] Douglas Farah, "Al Qaeda Cash Tied to Diamond Trade," *Washington Post*, November 2, 2001, p. A1; Douglas Farah, "Liberian Is Accused of Harboring al Qaeda," *Washington Post*, May 15, 2003, p. A18; Douglas Farah and Richard Shultz, "Al Qaeda's Growing Sanctuary," *Washington Post*, July 14, 2004, p. A19.

[17] Nathan Vardy, "Outfront: Hezbolla's Hoard," *Forbes*, August 14, 2006, p. 46.

[18] Thomas L. Friedman, *The Lexus and the Olive Tree: Understanding Globalization*, New York: Farrar, Straus, and Giroux, 2000.

[19] Jack A. Goldstone *et al.*, "A Global Forecasting Model of Political Instability," paper prepared for presentation at the Annual Meeting of the American Political Science Association, Washington, DC, September 1–4, 2005.

[20] This is not to suggest that decentralized networks will invariably be successful, but simply that they have some advantages over other types of organizations in the environment described.

[21] Karen Ballentine and Jake Sherman, "Introduction," in Karen Ballentine and Jake Sherman, eds., *The Political Economy of Armed Conflict: Beyond Greed and Grievance*, Boulder, CO: Lynne Rienner, 2003, p. 2.

[22.] See Daniel Byman *et al.*, *Trends in Outside Support for Insurgent Movements*, Santa Monica, CA: RAND Corporation, 2001.

[23] The Saudis claim that 80 percent of jihadists are recruited via the Internet (*Terrorism Focus*, Vol. IV, No, 13, May 8, 2007). While it deals with terrorist movements rather than insurgents per se, much of the analysis in Gabriel Weimann, *Terror on the Internet: The New Arena, New Challenges*, Washington, DC: United States Institute of Peace, 2006, also applies to insurgency.

[24] Francisco Guierrea Sanin and Ana Maria Jaramillo, "Crime, (Counter-)insurgency and the Privatization of Security—the Case of Medellin, Colombia," *Environment and Urbanization*, Vol. 16, No 2, October 2004, p. 29. See also Francisco Guierrea Sanin and Mauricio Baron, "Re-Stating the State: Paramilitary Territorial Control and Political Order in Colombia (1978–2004)," *Working Paper* No. 66, London: Crisis States Programme, 2005.

[25] William M. LeoGrande and Kenneth E. Sharpe, "Two Wars or One? Drugs Guerrillas, and Colombia's New *Violencia*," *World Policy Journal*, Vol. XVII, No. 3, Fall 2000, p. 8.

[26] William DeMars, "War and Mercy in Africa," *World Policy Journal*, Vol. 17, No. 2, Summer 2000, p. 5. See also Kimberly Marten, "Warlordism in Comparative Perspective," *International Security*, Vol. 31, No. 3, Winter 2006/07, pp. 41–73.

[27] Comfort Ero, "Vigilantes, Civil Defence Forces and Militia Groups: The Other Side of the Privatisation of Security in Africa," *Conflict Trends*, June 2000, p. 28.

[28] Henry Boshoff and Thierry Vircoulon, "Democratic Republic of the Congo: Update on Ituri," *African Security Review*, Vol. 13, No. 2, November 2004, pp. 66–67.

[29] Mark Bowden, *Killing Pablo: The Hunt For the World's Greatest Outlaw*, New York: Penguin, 2001, p. 29.

[30] Richard A. Oppel, Jr., "In Basra, Militia Controls by Fear," *New York Times*, October 9, 2005, p. 1.

[31] Statement of Senator Orrin G. Hatch before the U.S. Senate on the Introduction of Prevent All Cigarette Trafficking (PACT) Act of 2003; "Islamist Militants and Organized Crime," *Stratfor. com*, June 15, 2004; Angel Rabasa *et al.*, *Beyond al-Qaeda Part 2: The Outer Rings of the Terrorist Universe*, Santa Monica, CA: RAND Corporation Project Air Force, 2006, pp. 137–152; "Islamic Militants and Organized Crime," *Stratfor.com*, June 15, 2004; Mark Galeotti, "Transnational Organized Crime: Law Enforcement as a Global Battlespace," in Robert J. Bunker, ed., *Non-State Threats and Future Wars*, London: Frank Cass, 2003, p. 35; Thomas M. Sanderson, "Transnational Terror and Organized Crime: Blurring the Lines," *SAIS Review*, Vol. 24, No. 1, Winter 2004, p. 50; and David E. Kaplan, "Paying For Terror," *U.S. News and World Report*, December 5, 2005.

[32] Emily Wax, "Powerless in Congo's Lawless East," *Washington Post*, August 30, 2002, p. A12.

[33] See Judith Palmer Harik, *Hezbollah: The Changing Face of Terrorism*, London: I. B. Tauris, 2007; and Augustus Richard Norton, *Hezbollah: A Short History*, Princeton, NJ: Princeton University Press, 2007.

[34] Adam Shatz, "In Search of Hezbollah," *New York Review of Books*, Vol. 51, No. 7, April 29, 2004.

[35] Andrew Exum, "Comparing and Contrasting Hizballah and Iraq's Militias," *Policy Watch* No. 1197, Washington, DC: Washington Institute for Near East Policy, February 14, 2007; and Ely Karmon, "'Fight on All Fronts': Hizballah, the War on Terror, and the War in Iraq," *Research Memorandum* No. 45, Washington, DC: Washington Institute for Near East Policy, December 2003, p. 1.

[36] Sami G. Hajjar, *Hizballah: Terrorism, National Liberation or Menace?* Carlisle Barracks, PA: U.S. Army War College, Strategic Studies Institute, 2002, p. 6.

[37] *Ibid.*, pp. 10–11.

[38] Shatz, "In Search of Hezbollah."

[39] The letter was reprinted in *Jerusalem Quarterly*, No. 48, Fall 1998.

[40] Hajjar, *Hizballah*, pp. 15, 17.

[41] Robin Wright, "Inside the Mind of Hezbollah," *Washington Post*, July 16, 2006, p. B1.

[42] Susan Sachs, "Helping Hand of Hezbollah Emerging in South Lebanon," *New York Times*, May 30, 2000.

[43] Robert Fisk, "Hizbollah's Reconstruction of Lebanon Is Winning the Loyalty of Disaffected Shia," *The Independent* (London), August 24, 2006.

[44] Blanca Madani, "Hezbollah's Global Finance Network: The Triple Frontier," *Middle East Intelligence Bulletin*, Vol. 4, No. 1, January 2002. See also Michael P. Arena, "Hizballah's Global Criminal Operations," *Global Crime*, Vol. 7, Issues 3–4, August-November 2006, pp. 454–470.

[45] See Avi Jorisch, *Beacon of Hatred: Inside Hizballah's al-Manar Television*, Washington, DC: Washington Institute for Near East Policy, 2007. In March 2006, the U.S. Government named al-Manar and the Lebanese Media Group, which is also owned by Hezbollah, global terrorist entities.

[46] Edward Cody and Molly Moore, "The Best Guerrilla Force in the World," *Washington Post*, August 14, 2006, p. A1.

[47] Shatz, "In Search of Hezbollah."

[48] Andrew Exum, "Hizballah at War: A Military Assessment," *Policy Focus*, No. 63, Washington, DC: Washington Institute for Near East Policy, December 2006.

[49] Michael Hirt, "Hizbollah Rebuilds Its Military Force Under the Nose of the UN," *Daily Telegraph* (London), October 31, 2006, p. 21.

[50] Scott Shane, "Iranian Force, Focus of U.S., Still a Mystery," *New York Times*, February 17, 2007.

[51] Filip Reyntjens, "The Second Congo War: More Than a Remake," *African Affairs*, Vol. 98, Issue 391, April 1999, pp. 241–250; and Henri Boshoff and Thierry Vircoulon, "Democratic Republic of the Congo: Update on Itiri" *African Security Review*, Vol. 13, No. 2, 2004, p. 68.

[52] Alfred B. Zack-Williams, "Sierra Leone: The Political Economy of Civil War, 1991–1998," *Third World Quarterly*, Vol. 20, No. 1, February 1999, pp. 143–145; Ero, "Vigilantes, Civil Defence Forces and Militia

Groups," p. 26; and Yusuf Bangura, "Strategic Policy Failure and Governance in Sierra Leone," *Journal of Modern African Studies*, Vol. 38. No. 4, December 2000, pp. 551–577.

[53] Lansana Gberie, *A Dirty War in West Africa: The RUF and the Destruction of Sierra Leone*, Bloomington: Indiana University Press, 2005, pp. 83–86; and Krijn Peters and Paul Richards, "'Why We Fight': Voices of Youth Combatants in Sierra Leone," *Africa*, Vol. 68, No. 2, 1998, p. 185.

[54] Zack-Williams, "Sierra Leone," p. 150.

[55] Ero, "Vigilantes, Civil Defence Forces and Militia Groups,"p. 28.

[56] Thomas S. Mowle, "Iraq's Militia Problem," *Survival*, Vol. 48, No. 3, Autumn 2006, pp. 41–58. Mowle argues that demobilization of militias requires a neutral arbitrator, and the United States could not play that role. The absence of the UN in the settlement process was thus debilitating.

[57] Brian Brivati, "Africa's Inferno," *New Statesman*, January 15, 2007, pp. 30–32; Karanja Mbugua, "Armed Militias and Second Tier Conflicts: An Impediment to the Sudan Peace Process?" *Conflict Trends*, Issue 2, 2005, p. 32; Angel Rabasa and Peter Chalk, *Colombian Labyrinth: The Synergy of Drugs and Insurgency and Its Implications for Regional Stability*, Santa Monica, CA: RAND Corporation, 2001, pp. 53–60; Constanza Vieira, "Paramilitaries Extend Their Financial Networks," Global Information Network, October 14, 2004; "Bandits or Politicians? Colombia's Paramilitaries," *The Economist*, May 22, 2004, p. 55; and Scott Straus, "Darfur and the Genocide Debate," *Foreign Affairs*, Vol. 84, No. 1, January/ February 2005, p. 123–133.

[58] Svante E. Cornell, "Narcotics and Armed Conflict: Interaction and Implications," *Studies in Conflict and Terrorism*, Vol. 30, No. 3, 2007, p. 220.

[59] Quoted in Fisnik Abrashi, "Afghanistan Resorts to Militias to Fight the Insurgency," Associated Press, November 26, 2006.

[60] Kim Barker, "Move to Arm Afghan Tribes Raises Protests," *Chicago Tribune*, June 25, 2006; "Afghan Paper Warns Militias May Overthrow Government," BBC Monitoring South Asia, June 28, 2006.

[61] Sabrina Tavernise, "It Has Unraveled So Quickly," *New York Times*, January 28, 2007.

[62] Tom Lasseter, "Sadr's Army Feeding Off U.S. Help," *Miami Herald*, February 2, 2007, p. 1.

[63] Tom Lasseter, "Kurds Quietly Ready For Civil War," *Seattle Times*, December 29, 2005.

[64] Tom Lasseter, "Iranian-Backed Militia Groups Take Control of Much of Southern Iraq," Knight-Ridder News Service, May 26, 2006.

[65] Farah Stockman and Bryan Bender, "Militias on Rise in Iraq," *Boston Globe*, January 31, 2007, p. 1.

[66] Col (Ret) T. X. Hammes, USMC, presentation to the U.S. Army Training and Doctrine Command/U.S. Joint Forces Command seminar on the Joint Operating Environment and discussions with the author, Portsmouth, VA, January 31, 2007.

[67] See *haganah.org.il/haganah/*.

[68] There is some overlap between militias and criminal organizations, sometimes called "third generation" gangs, which have some political aims. See John P. Sullivan and Robert J. Bunker, "Drug Cartels, Street Gangs, and Warlords," in Bunker, ed., *Non-State Threats and Future Wars*; John P. Sullivan, "Maras Morphing: Revisiting Third Generation Gangs," *Global Crime*, Vol. 7, Issue 3–4, August-November 2006, pp. 487–504; and Max G. Manwaring, *Street Gangs: The New Urban Insurgency*, Carlisle Barracks, PA: U.S. Army War College, Strategic Studies Institute, 2005.

[69] "Criminal Involvement by Transnational, Non-State Actors Poses Major Threat to International Security, Third Committee Told," United Nations press release, October 5, 2006. See also Antonio Maria Costa, Executive Director, United Nations Office of Drugs and Crime, statement before the U.S. House of Representatives Committee on International Relations, September 20, 2006.

[70] Cornell, "Narcotics and Armed Conflict," p. 208.

[71] Chris Dishman, "The Leaderless Nexus: When Crime and Terror Converge," *Studies in Conflict and Terrorism*, Vol. 28, No. 3, 2005, p. 237.

[72] Cornell, "Narcotics and Armed Conflict," p. 212.

[73] On FARC involvement in narcotrafficking, see Mark S. Steinitz, "The Terrorism and Drug Connection in Latin America's Andean Region," *Policy Papers on the Americas*, Vol. XIII, Study 5, Washington, DC: Center for Strategic and International Studies, July 2002, pp. 11–14; LeoGrande and Sharpe, "Two Wars or One?" pp. 1–11.

[74] Cornell, "Narcotics and Armed Conflict," p. 208.

[75] Gail Wannenburg, "Organised Crime in West Africa," *African Security Review*, Vol. 14, No. 4, 2005, p. 8.

[76] "The Rise of Organized Crime in Iraq: Interview With Steve Castell, Senior Vice President of Vance International," *Journal of Counterterrorism and Homeland Security International*, Vol. 12, No. 3, Summer 2006.

[77] Robert E. Looney, "The Business of Insurgency: The Expansion of Iraq's Shadow Economy," *The National Interest*, Vol. 81, Fall 2005, p. 67.

[78] Interview by the author with Colonel Martin Stanton, Coalition Forces Land Component Command C9 (Civil-Military Affairs Staff Section), Baghdad, May 14, 2003.

[79] Looney, "The Business of Insurgency," p. 67.

[80] John F. Burns and Kirk Semple, "Iraq Insurgency Has Funds to Sustain Itself, U.S. Finds," *New York Times*, November 26, 2006, p. 1.

[81] "Iraq: Organised Crime Undermines Government Authority," OxResearch, Northwestern University, August 7, 2006, p. 1.

[82] Reports are that U.S. actions to counter the resurgent Taliban insurgency were not synchronized with counternarcotrafficking efforts by the U.S. Drug Enforcement Agency. As a result, Noorzai was arrested in New York in 2005 and, as of this writing, remains in an American jail. James Risen, "An Afghan's Path From Ally of U.S. to Drug Suspect," *New York Times*, February 2, 2007, p. 1.

[83] Or so they thought. There are many instances throughout history of mercenaries turning on their employers.

[84] Herbert M. Howe, "Private Security Forces and African Stability: The Case of Executive Outcomes," *Journal of Modern African Studies*, Vol. 36, No. 2, June 1998, pp. 308–309.

[85] P. W. Singer, *Corporate Warriors: The Rise of the Privatized Military Industry*, Ithaca, NY: Cornell University Press, 2003, pp. 88–100. See also David Shearer, "Private Armies and Military Intervention," *Adelphi Paper*, No. 316, London: International Institute for Strategic Studies, 1998.

[86] The adverse effects of complex internal conflicts continue for years or decades after they formally end, mostly through the production of individuals with military skills which can be marketed elsewhere, and through the institutionalization of organized crime networks. The world is still paying the price for the Balkan, Southern African, and first Afghan wars, and will pay for the Iraq conflict for many decades.

[87] On Angola, see Singer, *Corporate Warriors*, pp. 107–110; and Gerry Cleaver, "Subcontracting Military Power: The Privatisation of Security in Contemporary Sub-Saharan Africa," *Crime, Law, and Social Change*, Vol. 33, Nos. 1-2, March 2000, pp. 139–141. On Sierra Leone, see Singer, *Corporate Warriors*, pp. 110–115; and Deborah D. Avant, *The Market for Force: The Consequence of Privatizing Security*, Cambridge, UK: Cambridge University Press, 2005, pp. 82–98.

[88] David J. Francis, "Mercenary Intervention in Sierra Leone: Providing National Security or International Exploitation?" *Third World Quarterly*, Vol 20, No. 2, April 1999, pp. 319–338; and Howe, "Private Security Forces and African Stability," pp. 307–331.

[89] Mariane C. Ferme and Danny Hoffman, "Hunter Militias and the International Human Rights Discourse in Sierra Leone and Beyond," *Africa Today*, Volume 50, Number 4, Summer 2004, pp. 74–78; Ero, "Vigilantes, Civil Defence Forces and Militia Groups," pp. 27–28.

[90] Thomas K. Adams, "Private Military Companies: Mercenaries for the 21st Century," in Bunker, ed., *Non-State Threats and Future Wars*, p. 57. As with the Executive Outcomes activities in Africa, Sandline experienced problems as well, hitting political turmoil soon after arriving in Papua New Guinea. Mark Hemingway, "Warriors For Hire," *The Weekly Standard*, December 18, 2006, p. 27; and Singer, *Corporate Warriors*, pp. 191–196.

[91] Francis, "Mercenary Intervention in Sierra Leone," p. 322.

[92] See Avant, *The Market for Force*, pp. 98–113; and Steven Brayton, "Outsourcing War: Mercenaries and the Privatization of Peacekeeping," *Journal of International Affairs*, Vol. 55, No. 2, Spring 2002, p. 310.

[93] Rod Paschall, *LIC 2010: Special Operations and Unconventional Warfare in the Next Century*, Washington, DC: Brassey's, 1990.

[94] James Dao, "Private Guards Take Big Risks For Right Price," *New York Times*, April 2, 2004, p. A1.

[95] During a trip to Baghdad in April and May 2003, I noticed Gurkhas, South Africans, and many other nationalities I could not identify among the private security contractors in the "Green Zone."

[96] Jeremy Scahill, "Bush's Rent-an-Army," *Los Angeles Times*, January 25, 2007, p. A23. Where there's a market, there's a way: In February 2007, the author received an unsolicited email with the bold headline, "The leading opportunities for private security firms operating in Iraq now lie in Western-funded services on behalf of the Iraqi government."

[97] Walter Pincus, "Security Contracts to Continue in Iraq," *Washington Post*, February 4, 2007, p. 19.

[98] There are exceptions. In February 2007, the U.S. House of Representatives Oversight and Reform Committee took testimony from the family members of four Blackwater contractors killed in Fallujah in March 2004. The family members were highly critical of the U.S. military for, in their words, failing to provide adequate intelligence and equipment for the contractors. Paul Richter, "Subcontractor for Pentagon Criticized," *Los Angeles Times*, February 8, 2007, p. 14.

[99] See *www.sandline.com/*.

[100] Quoted in Thomas E. Ricks, *Fiasco: The American Military Adventure in Iraq*, New York: Penguin, 2006, p. 371. Hammes confirmed this account in a conversation with the author.

[101] LTC Raymond Millen, email correspondence with the author, May 8, 2007.

[102] General Peter Schoomaker, quoted in Nathan Hodge, "Army Chief Notes 'Problematic' Potential of Armed Contractors on the Battlefield," *Defense Daily International*, September 9, 2005, p. 1.

[103] In Renaissance Italy when mercenary armies fought each other, battles were often nearly bloodless since mercenaries sought to get paid but not to die doing so. They often reneged on a contract when it appeared that they might take significant casualties.

[104] Assis Malaquias calls diamonds the "African guerrillas' best friends." See "Diamonds Are a Guerrilla's Best Friend: The Impact of Illicit Wealth on Insurgency Strategy," *Third World Quarterly*, Vol. 22, No. 3, 2001, p. 311. Coltan is the African colloquial name for columbite-tantalite, a metallic ore used to produce tantalum for cell-phones, DVD players, personal computers, and games consoles. Coltan smuggling has fueled the conflict in the Democratic Republic of the Congo.

[105] Karen DeYoung, "Sunni-Shiite Fight Flares in Broadcasts," *Washington Post*, January 21, 2007, p. A18; Lawrence Pintak, "War of Ideas: Insurgent Channel Coming to a Satellite Near You," Los Angeles: University of Southern California Center for Public Diplomacy, January 10, 2007; Marc Santora and Damien Cave, "On the Air, the Voice of Sunni Rebels in Iraq," *New York Times*, January 21, 2007; and Sarah Gauch, "Why Is Egypt Airing Insurgent TV From Iraq?" *Christian Science Monitor*, January 17, 2007.

[106] Anthony H. Cordesman, *Iraq's Evolving Insurgency and the Risk of Civil War*, Washington, DC: Center for Strategic and International Studies, working draft, April 26, 2006, p. 104.

[107] The Search for International Terrorist Entities (SITE) Institute monitors many such sites (*www.siteinstitute.org/websites. html*).

[108] Cordesman, *Iraq's Evolving Insurgency and the Risk of Civil War*, p. 103.

[109] DeMars, "War and Mercy in Africa," p. 6.

[110] For instance, "Ugandan Government Must Fulfill Its Responsibility to Protect Civilians in War-Torn North," Oxfam press release, October 27, 2005.

[111] This point was made to the author by a senior military officer from Uganda in a March 2007 conversation, Carlisle Barracks, PA. David Shearer concludes that while there is anecdotal evidence that humanitarian assistance distorts or helps sustain internal wars, empirical evidence does not support the claim. David Shearer, "Aiding or Abetting? Humanitarian Aid and Its Economic Role in Civil War," in Mats Berdal and David M. Malone, eds., *Greed and Grievance: Economic Agendas in Civil Wars*, Boulder, CO: Lynne Rienner, 2000.

[112] Ben Barber, "Feeding Refugees, or War? The Dilemma of Humanitarian Aid," *Foreign Affairs*, Vol. 76, No. 4, July / August 1997, pp. 8–14.

[113] John A. Nagl, *Learning to Eat Soup With a Knife: Counterinsurgency Lessons From Malaya and Vietnam*, Westport, CT: Praeger, 2002, reprinted in paperback by the University of Chicago Press, 2005; and David Galula, *Counterinsurgency Warfare: Theory and Practice*, Westport, CT: Praeger, 1964, reprinted 2006. Also popular is Galula's *Pacification in Algeria 1956–1958*, Santa Monica, CA: RAND Corporation, 1963, reprinted 2006. Nagl is a U.S. Army officer who served multiple tours in Iraq after writing the book (which was derived from his Ph.D. dissertation). Galula was a French Army officer who based on his analysis on his own experience in Indochina, especially Algeria.

[114] Jeffrey Record provides a powerful analysis of the role of outside sponsors in insurgency in *Beating Goliath: Why Insurgencies Win*, Washington, DC: Potomac, 2007. His analysis, though, deals with cases where another outside force is playing a significant role in the counterinsurgency effort—proxy conflict insurgency.

[115] Paul Collier and Anke Hoeffler, "Greed and Grievance in Civil War," *Policy Research Working Paper* No. 2355, Washington, DC: The World Bank, 2000.

[116] Ballentine and Sherman, "Introduction," in Ballentine and Sherman, eds., *The Political Economy of Armed Conflict*, p. 3.

[117] Paul Collier, "Doing Well Out of War: An Economic Perspective," in Berdal and Malone, eds., *Greed and Grievance*, p. 91.

[118] *Ibid.*, pp. 103–104.

[119] Mats Berdal and David Keen, "Violence and Economic Agendas in Civil Wars: Some Policy Implications," *Millennium*, Vol. 26, No. 3, 1997, p. 797.

[120] McCormick and Giordano, "Things Come Together," p. 312.

[121] David Keen, "Incentives and Disincentives for Violence," in Berdal and Malone, eds., *Greed and Grievance*, p. 25.

[122] Collier, "Doing Well Out of War," p. 107.

[123] Ballentine and Sherman, "Introduction," in Ballentine and Sherman, eds., *The Political Economy of Armed Conflict*, p. 3.

[124] Collier, "Doing Well Out of War," p. 105.

[125] James Fearon described and advocated such an approach in "Iraq's Civil War," *Foreign Affairs*, Vol. 86, No. 2, March/April 2007, pp. 2–15.

[126] On "neo-trusteeships," see James D. Fearon and David D. Laitin, "Neotrusteeship and the Problem of Weak States," *International Security*, Vol. 28, No. 4, Spring 2004, pp. 4-43; and Richard Caplan, "From Collapsing States to Neo-Trusteeships: The Limits of Solving the Problem of 'Precarious Statehood' in the 21st Century," *Third World Quarterly*, Vol. 28, No. 2, 2007, pp. 231–244

SUBJECT INDEX

Doc/Pg

Iraq

Legislation – Federal

Presidential Documents

Senate Foreign Relations Committee

Terrorist Organizations

Printed and bound in the UK by
CPI Antony Rowe, Eastbourne